Back to Earth

A Backpacker's Journey into Self and Soul

KERRY TEMPLE

ROWMAN & LITTLEFIELD PUBLISHERS, INC.

Lanham • Boulder • New York • Toronto • Oxford

ROWMAN & LITTLEFIELD PUBLISHERS, INC.

Published in the United States of America
by Rowman & Littlefield Publishers, Inc.
A wholly owned subsidiary of The Rowman & Littlefield Publishing Group, Inc.
4501 Forbes Boulevard, Suite 200, Lanham, Maryland 20706
www.rowmanlittlefield.com

PO Box 317
Oxford
OX2 9RU, UK

Distributed by National Book Network

British Library Cataloguing in Publication Information Available

Library of Congress Cataloging-in-Publication Data

Temple, Kerry.
  Back to earth : a backpacker's journey into self and soul / Kerry Temple.
    p. cm.
  ISBN 0-7425-4394-3 (pbk. : alk. paper)
    1. Temple, Kerry. 2. Nature—Religious aspects. 3. Spiritual biography—
United States. I. Title.
BL73.T43A3 2005
204'.092—dc22   2004026667

Printed in the United States of America

♾™ The paper used in this publication meets the minimum requirements of American National Standard for Information Sciences—Permanence of Paper for Printed Library Materials, ANSI/NISO Z39.48-1992.

Civilized, crying how to be human: this will tell you how.
Turn outward, love things, not men, turn right away from humanity.
Let that doll lie. Consider if you like how the lilies grow,
Lean on the silent rock until you feel its divinity
Make your veins cold, look at the silent stars, let your eyes
Climb the great ladder out of the pit of yourself and man.
Things are so beautiful, your love will follow your eyes;
Things are the God, you will love God, and not in vain,
For what we love, we grow to it, we share its nature. At length
You will look back along the stars' rays and see that even
The poor doll humanity has a place under heaven.
Its qualities repair their mosaic around you, the chips of strength
And sickness; but now you are free, even to become human,
But born of the rock and the air, not of a woman

— *Robinson Jeffers,* Signpost

CONTENTS

PROLOGUE

*All being itself is derived from God and the presence of the
Creator is in each created thing.*

—*Rabbi Menachem Nahum of Chernobyl*

It was on the sixth day that I pulled out the box, a heavy cardboard
carton full of stuff—pieces of a past, a grab bag of things left over. I
had retrieved the box from a house I had lived in for 13 years. Actually the box and a pile of things (a bike, some books, a suitcase full of
clothes) had been set out on the curb for me to come and pick up. I
had gone backpacking in the West and, when I returned to Indiana, I
did not go home. I moved in with a friend and lived out of my backpack for awhile. I lived with Ed, who was also heading toward divorce, and we went to work and sometimes talked about how it felt to
be losing a wife and sons and the lives that we had known. Mostly we
didn't; we just went through the motions day to day. I had not really
intended to leave for good. But that's what happened.

After about a year of camping out at Ed's, I found my solitary way
to a small cabin sitting alone on 265 acres of land in northern Indiana, overlooking a pond and a cold running stream of water. By then
the separation from my wife felt permanent and, when she learned I
had settled in here, she put some of my stuff out on the curb, including this box of rocks and things, things I had picked up along the
way, and bundles of papers, stuff I had written when I was younger.
That was about all I got from there. It was nice of her to give it to me,
I guess. This box helped bring me home.

It was on the sixth day alone in this cabin, disengaged from one
life and in retreat from all the rest, that I sat down with the box,

unfolded the flaps, and started digging around in my past. I started with the cache of rocks. I had been gathering stones since I was young, and each rock had stories to tell. Of course, some I have forgotten; others are as clear as the moment they happened.

I remember sitting across the table from Little Soldier, in the shadows of his cabin on the South Dakota plains. There was no running water, no electricity, no plumbing. He had tied a red bandanna around his head "to think right thoughts" as he spoke to me. I was younger then. I had come looking for truth. "Understand this," Little Soldier had said, "and you will understand it all. You do not understand it now. It is too simple. Pray for understanding." He placed his fist on the table between us and unrolled his fingers to reveal a small stone. He handed me the stone, which I looked at and held and studied, then slipped into the pocket of my jeans. A few minutes later Sam Moves Camp, who was there to help Little Soldier prepare for a vision quest, handed me feathers from a spotted eagle, still bloody where they were joined at the quills. "Prayer feathers," he said, before giving them to me.

In that box, too, were other things I had gathered from here and there—other stones and feathers, wind-shorn bones and pieces of ancient pottery, elegant swirls of driftwood, an old guitar string (though I never played guitar), a cow skull sun-bleached white, and the tooth of a polar bear I had picked up on Ellesmere Island in the High Canadian Arctic. There was a sheaf of poetry I had written as a teenager, a stash of other writings, and slips and scraps and patches of paper preserving favorite quotations, passages, and excerpts I had saved and collected through the years. Random nuggets of truth. There was a short stack of baseball cards held together by rubber band, some little toy soldiers I had played with as a kid. Some things came by way of gift. They told stories of people and times and memories. Unlike photographs, they are real, tactile; they put weight into my hand. Not images but the very thing itself. I was given a horseshoe, a few square nails, and some metal buckles from saddlebags and belts, all gathered along the Bozeman Trail by a friend who had walked the length of that passage through old Indian country.

I have always stuffed things into my pocket: a military compass found here, a pocketknife found there. Most often it was rock I wanted—quartz crystal from the Black Hills, blue granite from the stony apron of Lake Superior, sandstone lifted from the desert floor of New Mexico. Stones—hard and smooth as bone—have a heft to them, a feel, that only a baseball may rival for rightness. These became souvenirs, mementoes, amulets. Talismans. They formed the medicine bundle of my life. They became vessels from which I sipped the holy, drew the breath out of my past. There were times—years ago now—when I would go to the attic, put some old records on the stereo, pull out that box, and revisit my younger self, trace the lines of meaning and continuity, remember where I'd been, bring parts of me forward to keep the older me in touch with who I am. I would hold Little Soldier's stone and try to understand. I would finger the grain of wood, the skin of rock, the whisper of feathers, and I would remember to keep my feet to the earth. And so I walked. I backpacked when I could, and some trips I wrote about, learning to see them as parables, journeys of illumination recorded, tethered to rocks and things picked up along the way.

But time passed and I got carried away and I forgot a lot. Life has a way of delivering detours, demands, and distractions, and those currents and whirlpools bore me away. There were sons to raise and jobs to do, houses to fix, yards to mow, the television a bad influence. I stopped going to the attic, stopped visiting the box, forgot about the meanings there. Then, in the midst of my middle years, I found myself alone again. I had gone backpacking with a mentor and friend and, when I returned, I did not get back home. The separation led to divorce and the rupture took away not only my wife but also my sons, most all of my friends, my house, virtually all of my possessions, and my life—as I had been living it. In return came some anger and resentment, the hollow of loneliness, the inescapable honesty that comes from being alone for long hours at a time . . . and this crate waiting there by the curb, the one full of rocks and feathers and pieces of a past. So here I am now, having lived alone for years in a cabin in the woods, sitting in the twilight, sifting again and again through this once-forgotten medicine bundle, reading, putting pieces back together, back on my way again, trying to understand the instructions given me years ago by an old Lakota holy man. "Understand this," he had said, "and you will understand it all. Pray for understanding."

1

🍂

I was a hidden treasure and I wanted to be known.
Therefore I created the world so that I would be known.

—*God, speaking in an ancient Islamic parable.*

I am a visitor here, a guest, a sojourner. I am a traveler passing through, having come to this place in the woods knowing it to be a temporary existence, knowing the moment would come when I would have to move on from here. But for now this tiny cabin by the pond provides refuge and anchor since my life broke in two, cut loose in the waters of my middle years. A mean divorce had taken my wife and my sons, my house, my life, and most all of my friends. So on a cold and clear Thanksgiving day I moved in, worldly possessions packed into a car, colleagues at work offering pots and pans and mattress, two forks, some knives, and a plate—housewarming gifts to go along with the armful of stuff I brought from before. Now comes "after," and the intersection of the two is this retreat to the woods, a withdrawal from the commotion of life, so that I can step back and be alone with myself for awhile.

The place is a hermit's paradise. The house is cozy, tidy, and snug, tucked into a hillside in the northern Indiana woods. It is surrounded by 265 acres of rolling hills, some marshy lowlands, some flat spots, some ravines and hills, some open fields. Mainly there are old-growth stands of deciduous trees—towering oak, expansive maples, vast and leafy sycamores, majestic cottonwoods. They form a canopy that makes me feel sheltered and hugged—like a child playing under the dining room table.

A coldwater creek traverses the property, running clear to its sandy bottom—a slender creek but one traveled by slippery trout and wayfaring salmon. Occasional fishermen, trespassing in their plaid flannel shirts and hip-high waders, ply these spring-fed waters, which swell in the spring and after heavy rains. I was told by the person who first showed me around to shoo away any fishermen, but I do not, even though the landlords want no trespassers here. I can see the creek from the house as it cuts a diagonal from here to there. Thick grasses and cattails grow along its banks as well as periodic tangles of brush and logs, stumps and trees—trees whose fingery limbs stretch arbor-like over the water. The creek attracts muskrats and ducks; it shelters turtles and frogs. It also makes the pond. My little house, known as "the caretaker's cabin," overlooks the pond.

Long ago, back when this parcel was known as the Campbell property, someone—perhaps a "caretaker"—had scooped out a hole the size of a youth-league hockey rink and about as deep as the shallow end of a swimming pool. He then sliced two trenches into the earth, one to siphon creek water into the hole and one downstream to let the water out. So the pond is really a kind of holding tank, a pause, a still and quiet detour, but one enjoyed by me and geese and ducks, snapping turtles and sunny little bluegills. It freezes in the winter, evaporates muddy low by late summer, and gives me something to gaze at, to throw rocks into, to fish, to contemplate.

When the water is at low tide during August or Indian summer, I'll go flap around in the creek and try to divert its meager current—by angling boards and logs, rocks and sticks—to replenish the dehydrating pond. There is little evidence the task accomplishes more than a minimal amount of good, but there are the hours of carefree entertainment, the mud-slurping feet and wetness and that bare-backed concentration toward a largely pointless pursuit. It is good for me, in these hollowed, transitional years, to go outside and play, even solitary games.

The house, the pond, the creek, and the uncultured landscape all come to me for $300 per month (utilities included). I have it all to myself, though I am surrounded by the symphony of nature, the murmuring lulls and breathtaking crescendos. Down the road is "the Campbell house." It sits empty, closed off, blinds drawn. Someone died. Someone else thought a golf course to be a good use for the "vacant" property. In the meantime, I inhabit the full sweep, ranging over these acres, settled into this cabin like any homesteader establishing a place in the universe. So I know to savor these days, know to value my Walden, my Lake Isle at Innisfree. I suspected when I moved in, and still believe today, it will be the best place I ever live. I know, too, that it is only a matter of time and money before the whole thing is remodeled for golfing. Its days are numbered.

So we live together—the place and I—in patient, quiet intimacy. Together we watch each long, languorous sunset, mindful of the slow and deliberate turning, relishing the passing and the peace, when the lengthening shadows give rise to meditation and acceptance, and when you see the colors and the shapes more clearly in the dying of the light—keen, precious, deserving of attention. Abundant beauty in the details. I walk here daily, sometimes twice or 3 times a day. I sit for hours in the darkness, in quiet contemplation, remembering, recollecting, regretting, looking back. I have sat for hours watching the snow fall, looking out my window at the grey and white landscape, transfixed by memories and thoughts, or thinking nothing, conscious only of snow and wind and the patterns stenciled in the swirling world in front of me.

For neighbors I have only the creatures—the fidgety squirrels and chipmunks, woodchucks, gophers, opossum and raccoons, plenty of serene and angelic deer, an itinerant fox whose briar-patch home I finally located by following tracks in the snow. My first Christmas here two coyotes came and stayed awhile. They'd watch me cautiously, keeping their social distance, acting like a married couple still loving and affectionate, licking each other's face. Each spring the Canada geese would come squawking and honking, arguing and biting, only to settle into pairs, then mating, nesting, hatching their young, swimming in my pond before gusting up and leaving. There are loud crows and jays, wading blue heron and owls, and all kinds of smaller birds. At one point I bought a bird book and tried naming the cast of characters. But it was too difficult: male or female? chickadee or finch? No one sitting still. I finally realized I got more out of watching the show than I did from identifying the players. I did get to where I recognized the *scree* of the red-tailed hawk before seeing it. Then I would scan the sky and eventually spot it, and watch it circle lazily in the sky, banking, gracefully stroking, riding the winds higher and farther, dissolving from sight. My ears tuned in as well to the chattery drumming of woodpeckers and the many voices of crows.

In time I came to feel like one of them—just another neighbor inhabiting this place, making it my home, getting along with the others, the various tribes and nations, all of us going about our ways, peaceably aware of the kind accompaniment. I fish and walk and sometimes just stretch out on the grass, cloud-gazing, sunning, dozing, letting the wind kiss my skin. I soon learned that the best view comes from lying flat on my back, staring upward, sometimes through the branches of trees, often straight-away and unobstructed into the infinite sky. I hear no cars, no voices, no radio or TV. I have no electronic devices, no clock to notch the time of day. So I walk or sit, outside or in. In the first few weeks, after I had covered every corner of the place and seen what was there to see, it did not matter where I stood or walked or sat. While I grew fond of favorite glades and hollows, there really was nowhere else to go, nowhere I'd really rather be. I was always *here.*

Even being in the cabin has felt like being outdoors; it is so small and the outside so big and close around it. Crickets and moths seem to come and go as they please; other callers have found their way to my house. A groundhog has burrowed by the front door, a long scary snake once nested by the steps, spiders have spun webs in the corners of the window frames. Sparrows have made their homes in the attic rafters, and some loud little creatures have lived inside the walls, busily digging and scratching, nibbling, chewing, sawing incessantly all winter long. Mice have occasionally skittered across the hardwood floors. Except for the rigid, drowned squirrel I once found floating in my toilet bowl, I do not mind these occasional visits. It seems natural to me that they found entrance into this dry, warm place, using it (as I did) for shelter and comfort.

There have been other surprises. One fall Saturday, the first autumn in the house, I was startled by loud pelting upon my roof. I looked out the window for kids throwing rocks at the house but saw none. The hailstorm persisted, so eventually I went outside and saw acorns rain from above. Squirrels were in the treetops performing their high-wire harvest in the lofty oaks around my house. Acorns littered the place. Periodically the squirrels would descend and scamper about, gathering their loot. In the meantime, I went through autumn days with the sounds of bombardment thumping over my head, till the oaks were picked clean and the squirrels hidden for winter.

Another Saturday a possum caught my attention veering in circular patterns all around my house, getting nowhere, bumping into trees. He seemed oblivious to me, even when I approached close, and soon I realized the poor young thing was blind. One winter four raccoons, over a period of 3 weeks, chose to die on my doorstep. In these years I have found two deer, dead and partially eaten, their bodies, their hide and fur decomposing, leaving bones and teeth and antlers.

Eventually they—and the fallen leaves and fallen trees—became part of what was there all along. And I did, too. I became attuned to the turnings of seasons, aware of the subtle changes in the minor dramas of animals getting along on their own in the woods. I came to anticipate the arrival of fireflies, the ripening of berries, the appearance of groundhogs—and tick season. In spring the juicy, tender grasses speared up through last year's crusty shafts—flattened stalks sucked empty of moisture and color, blown crackly and brittle by winter winds. I do not like stepping on these first emerald shoots of tender grass leaping for light in the spring. But by July these grasses would be jungle-thick and chest-high, having left last year's decaying remnants far below. I remember black raspberries and the fuzz-ball sheddings of cottonwoods and the wild daffodils in spring, lemony yellow on a forest floor still brown and grey from winter. I remember how *green* it would all look in spring and how stunningly brilliant were the flashing colors of fall.

The cabin has a large floor-to-ceiling window that overlooks the pond. I often sit there, looking into space, and watch it rain, dappling pockmarks sprayed upon the surface of the pond. I'd watch the sun edge up over the eastern horizon, or stare at the moon, its glittering trail in silver swatches across the water, or look at the trees in autumn, flaming brushstrokes of shining gold, fiery red, sun-splashed yellow. Mallards and wood ducks come to the pond; deer are plentiful. One night in winter when the pond was frozen slick but blanketed in snow, 3 deer, spooked by something and in quick retreat, came bounding downhill and then onto the pond's glassy surface, slipping and sliding, their hooves flailing about, unable to fix themselves with traction, losing their balance, tumbling and skidding the length of the skating-rink pond, into a snowbank lit by the moon.

5

Moonlight on white snow, the shadows of winter, trees dolloped with fresh-fallen snow. A funny sight for such sure-footed, spry, and willowy creatures.

I remember one evening sitting at sunset on the edge of a field where a fox patrolled the many burrows and hideouts, the front doors and back doors of warrens and dens, loping from one to the next, sniffing. Occasionally he would stop and cast an eye my way, looking back over his shoulder, furtive thief. Sometimes, when he and the sunlight aligned, his bushy coat was radiant, inflamed, haloed by a shimmering orange corona at the tips of his fluffy coat. *Vulpes aureole.*

At nightfall I return to the house, like a shell I pull around me, tucking in my legs and arms and head, to fend off any chill or inclement influences. The cabin is a little like that, tight and warm. It consists mostly of two rooms. There is a bedroom and another room—a good room with knotty pine walls, that large floor-to-ceiling window, and a wood-burning stove and built-in bookshelves and hardwood floors. I have never counted the bathroom or galley kitchen as real rooms; each has space for only one person at a time. For entertainment I have only my neighbors. And storms. And star-filled skies. Sunrises. And silence.

I have spent most of my time in the good room. I have thought a lot, and written and read, and sat looking out the window. Occasionally I have sorted through the box of rocks and writings. I often sit there eating my cereal before heading off to work. And in the evenings, making dinner or sipping coffee in the darkness, I'd sit there watching shadows and ghosts, bats and stars, the lightning bugs or silhouettes creeping in the moonglow. My thoughts were idle, wide-grazing, and lazy. In time they scoured a life that had gotten off course, that had wandered—one misstep at a time—far away from intended directions.

Perhaps what has appealed to me most—apart from the immediate comings and goings of my many neighbors—has been the act of trimming life down to an acute simplicity. There have been no competing voices—neither electronic nor human. There has been little clutter; the stuff of my life has been reduced to the minimum. Much has been left behind as I stepped through that door between then and now. I have missed my sons with an ache that is palpable, the psychic pain felt in the chest, in the pit of the stomach. Most things I have been glad to be rid of, to let go of, to get along without. Like an ascetic meticulously distinguishing between wants and needs, I have sought the monk's life, the path of the holy recluse, unburdened and desireless. "In anything at all," wrote Antoine de Saint-Exupery, the author of *The Little Prince*, "perfection is finally attained not when there is no longer anything to add, but when there is no longer anything to take away."

During these days by the pond, casting my hook into still waters or watching out the window or walking the manifold grounds, even then, one by one, I have peeled away layers, drawing closer to myself, to the seed, the nut, the pilgrim's coal. To see what matters most. To see what is real and true.

I have been fortunate, I suppose, that in my middle years I have had such a sabbatical, that I could step outside my life and see it from some distance, where I had been and where I might go. The retreat, the isolation, the view from this lone cabin has been a blessing; most of us are not given such lucrative exile in the midst of our lives. In these days by the pond I have come to my own angle of repose, to that point where the rockslide comes to rest, where the tumbling boulders and stones find their state of equilibrium between the pull of gravity and the placid, sustaining slope.

It would be unfair to say I had become a stranger in my life; I was right there in the middle of it all. It would be wrong to say I had only been going through the motions; I devoted myself to all the chores and jobs, the commitments and responsibilities asked of me. I was a good and giving husband for almost 20 years. I did my share of the shopping, cooking, and cleaning. I have taught college writing courses year-round for more than a decade while working a job full-time as a magazine editor. I had freelanced some and counseled students outside of class and done some writers' workshops. Through those years I had given the most of myself to my two sons—changing their diapers and feeding them, taking them on wagon rides and zoo trips, playing, talking and reading, taking them camping, coaching their basketball and baseball teams, serving as ringmaster to the neighborhood circus, the frolicking games of kick-the-can and football. And I loved doing all of it.

In the midst of all this were bills to pay and a house to maintain, medical insurance matters, annuities and pensions, papers to grade, cars to pay for and keep running. There were doctor visits and trips to the grocery store, television and sports to watch, movies to see, weddings and funerals to attend, anniversaries and birthdays to celebrate, Christmases coming and going, vacations to plan, milestones to mark a life getting away, heading down the tracks, a roiling current carrying me along. It was not until I sat in the woods awhile that I realized how much stuff, how much clutter, how many distractions and activities had piled up between me and . . . what? What was it that had gotten covered up? That had dropped out? That was lost, obscured, or long forgotten? I no longer even knew.

Now here I am alone again, the harried traffic of that existence gone, many of those roles taken away, leaving me only this solitude in the woods, wondering what had happened, where had I been, what had it all come down to. My thoughts roamed widely, but one voice persisted through those first weeks here. It came from *Siddartha*, a book by Hermann Hesse that I had liked as a teenager, that I had read on several occasions back when I was younger. As a young man, Siddartha had been a religious ascetic of uncommon virtue, but he soon felt restless and abandoned that path for a life of comfort and wealth. Although surrounded by many earthly distractions, he again sensed a nagging void. There were some words that echoed throughout those first days by the pond, and so I dug out the book and located the passage: "At times he heard within him a soft, gentle voice, which reminded him quietly, complained quietly," until "he saw that he was leading a strange life; that he was doing many things that were only a game; that real life was flowing past him and did not touch him; that with his heart, with his real nature, he was not there. His real self wandered far away and had nothing to do with his life."

It would not be accurate, I thought at first, to say this passage fit completely, but there were surely some similarities: I *had* lost touch with something inside of me, had drifted far away from things I knew as a teenager, things I had determined in college, dreams I had had when I was younger. Where had they gone? How far removed was I from the person I had once dreamed of being?

So these 3 years here have become an exploration of landscapes, both internal and external, and a search for some things lost and some things never found. And at some point in the journey, as I reclaimed some notions from the past and discovered many new ones,

I decided to write them down—as a way to see into myself more clearly, as reminders for the future, and to have something to pass on to my sons from these long days apart. I have done so not as a philosopher, naturalist, or scientist, but as a regular guy still trying to figure it out, an earnest pilgrim with a short attention span.

So I began collecting and recollecting, retrieving memories, following newer paths of thought. Some things appeared out of the past; some have revealed themselves while I sat watching or was walking. Some came from places far away—some from far back when I was younger, back when I pursued truth and meaning, as if they (not goods, status, or financial security) were the ultimate prizes. And I remembered back in the day, hiking, exploring the world, and picking up stones along the trail, stashing them into a backpack and taking them home as souvenirs, reminders, talismans, from excursions along the way.

Those rocks, the ones I have gathered from here and there throughout the years, are with me now in my good, big room. I have taken them out of the box. Some sit in clusters on the bookshelves; others are piled by the bed, the window. I haul them out and from time to time hold them, my fingers rubbing the various surfaces, massaging their coat, my hands testing the heft and weight. They come in different colors, different shapes and sizes. They are here among the books I read, the ones with yellow highlights and ink scribbles in the margins, tattered pages and well-worn covers. Books and rocks sit side by side. Here is a little book I read from time to time. *Letters to a Young Poet,* by Rainer Maria Rilke. It was first marked by my hand 25 years ago, when I was a college senior, still growing up, staring at adulthood:

> The necessary thing is but this: solitude, great inner solitude. Going into oneself and for hours meeting no one. To be solitary, the way you were solitary as a child, when the grownups went around involved with things that seemed important and big because they looked so busy and you comprehended nothing of their doings. And when one day you perceived that their occupations are paltry, their professions petrified and no longer linked to the living, why not then continue to look like a child upon it all?

And here, just below, arrow pointing: "For him who becomes solitary all distances, all measures change." What is near fades away and

9

what is far grows very close around us. "The experiences one calls 'visions,' the whole so-called 'spirit world,' death, all those things that are so closely akin to us, have by daily parrying been so crowded out of life that the senses with which we could have grasped them are atrophied. To say nothing of God."

My story, I soon realized during this retreat into the woods, is not mine alone. It is shared by many others—and not only by people caught up in the currents of twenty-first-century living but also by a species, a race of people who have let too much accumulate between them and what they knew long ago, people heading madly in all the wrong directions, a culture gone awry. What was true in my life seemed true for everyone around me—too many tangents, too many distractions, too much stuff in the way, too many barriers between me and the heart of it all. It was time to find redemption, time to go outside and fish.

2

After the long letters
have been written, read,
abandoned, after
distances grow absolute
and speech, too,
is distance, only
listening is left.

I have heard the dark hearts
of the stones
that beat once in a lifetime.

—*William Pitt Root*

I am 51 now, I live alone, and sometimes in the evenings I go out back and fish. Here by the pond I am dwarfed by oak and sycamore. The late-afternoon air can be blue or grey, or tinted rose right at sunset. I cast my wormy, weighted hook into the languid, brown water. I can hear it plop and see the concentric circles ripple, swell, dissolve. A bullfrog watches from the sidelines. Time lingers here in the autumn dusk. Shadows stretch, then spill over the earth.

I am not a fastidious fisherman. I use this secondhand, 15-year-old Zebco hoping to snare any fish that hang out here instead of in the rapid creek that flows through this pond behind my house. But the point isn't really to catch fish; mainly I look around.

This afternoon, for example, I stand by the pond immersed in the autumn twilight, the reddened air, and watch brittle airborne leaves spin down. Squirrels scamper in busy preparation as iron-hued clouds blow southeastward, herded by wintry winds. The Canada geese, who came in spring and spawned their waddling, yellow-green young, have fled the stalking winter. The turtles, too, who spent their summer lounging on logs, have dived deeper, knowing the sun in winter will not warm their reptilian blood. Time passes; the pond will freeze over, be blanketed in snow.

I turn up my collar to the cold air. My bobber bobs unmolested. It doesn't matter. Fishing is what I do with my hands; mainly I look around. And I think a lot. I am 51 now, living alone, a man in search of themes. I do not know where the creek begins. But it flows into a river, and the river feeds a great lake that eventually goes out to sea. But here today by the pond, where the water stills before proceeding, I think a lot about time. I figure mine is at least half up.

It is hard to know what to make of time. It comes in many guises. Nature's time is cyclic, a revolving carousel of sun and stars, winters and summers, buddings and births, new moons and primeval migrations. The wheels turn and snakes emerge from hibernation, loons head north, green leaves curl up and die. Like clockwork, the spinnings of celestial spheres choreograph the ebb of tides, the movement of wolves, the repeated plantings and reapings of farmers. Upon the giant globes of creation, life goes round and round. Our biological clocks are tuned to these cosmic rhythms too. Our lives are governed by the waltz of sun and Earth, the lunar cycles, the pull of gravity on flesh and bone.

But human time is mostly linear these days. Unlike our tribal ancestors, we compute time as a passage from then to now, or from now forward. We number the days, the years, the centuries; we package time into eras and epochs, as if the human journey from swamp to space came in clear demarcations, tidy as a tape measure.

But Thomas Mann warned: "Time has no divisions to mark its passage. There is never a thunderstorm or blare of trumpets to announce the beginning of a new month or year. Even when a new century begins it is only we mortals who ring the bells or fire off pistols." Time just rolls along, oblivious to any human manipulations or incantations, despite death, destruction, and apocalyptic visions.

Often we mistake the measure of time, our calibration of it, for time itself, its nature, what it *is*. The effects of time are all around us (night falling, hair graying, heart beating, the VCR light winking), but time itself flees—phantom-like—when we try to pin it down. Time is like God or the wind: You may see evidence of its work but not the thing itself.

Of course, many of time's faces are unfathomable. When, for example, did creation's clock start? What came before that? How do you get a fix on 15 *billion* years? Scientists, looking backward, talk about "deep" time and "geologic" time as they pick and probe at a living laboratory that is incomprehensibly ancient. John McPhee, in *Basin and Range*, describes the Earth's age this way: It is the distance from your nose to the tip of your outstretched hand—with one swipe of a nail file on the tip of your middle finger eliminating all of human history.

Presented on that scale, time must certainly make one rethink the significance of one life's trials and triumphs, might inspire humility, deflate one's hubris, may even ease the guilt you feel for having spent a night watching television. And when I pull a stone from my cardboard box—my fingers clutching a 3-billion-year-old wedge of black granite—I ponder the relationship between it and me, and the meaning of lasting value.

Perhaps even more confounding are the theories of today's physicists which, when taken to their imaginative conclusion, show how time travel is possible. Only decades ago people believed—in accord with common sense and Newtonian physics—that time proceeds at a constant rate. But Einstein's theory of special relativity says the passing of time depends upon the placement of those observing events and the speed at which they move through space. Time is not constant but relative—depending upon the bodies in motion. In essence, time is merely a measure of duration, but that measure depends upon points in space, and space is not as simple as we once thought it to be.

Time today, as conceived by our tribe's visionaries and scouts, is neither circular nor linear; it deals in new brave worlds and enough coexistent universes to make H. G. Wells dizzy. But a layperson's foray into the realm of Einstein, Stephen Hawking, and their kin can lead only to the same conclusion reached by Alfred North Whitehead: "It is impossible to meditate on time and the mystery of the creative passage of nature without an overwhelming emotion at the limitations of human intelligence."

The rest of us must rely on analogies, metaphors, and other devices to explain or understand time as the bottom line accountant of the human condition. Thus time is described as money—to be invested wisely because it is limited and cannot be spent twice. Or as a river—constant, incessant, erosive, whose beginning and end are unknown. Or it is a train carrying us down the line, gaining momentum as we age, as it hurtles along the rails. Or time is, in the words of Henri Bergson, that which "eats into things and leaves on them the mark of its tooth," or it is (according to your pick of adages) the best teacher, doctor, counselor, preacher, the rider who breaks youth. And some say time heals.

My sense of it has changed here at the pond as I pass time on these clockless, solitary weekends, watching the sun's gradual arc across the sky, marking my own life's path in stages and phases. I even surveyed the local library for ways of understanding it, and I learned what a weight is time, what power it has upon the drama of mortal existence—as if time, even as a human construct, were a force acting upon the affairs of men. So time flies and marches on and goes slowly for those who watch it. Time reveals all things, does not wait. Time is on our side. Time kills. Time erases sorrow, consumes the strongest. Kill time—the moralists warn—and it will kill you. Lost time is never found. The hands of time will never turn back. Nothing is more precious than time, yet nothing less valued. He who knows most grieves most for time. "All my possessions," said Elizabeth I and countless others at death's door, "for a moment of time."

And so it is. One sure thing about time is that we don't get enough, although the world is full of elderly folk with time on their hands but not the wherewithal to make much of it. Have they, who seem only to be waiting "for their time to come," had enough of it? Would they, if they could, trade some of these lingering, surplus *years* for another *month* of sunlit juvenescence? Even in her middle years, my mother alerted me to the notion that youth is wasted on the young. Now we both hear the echoing lullaby asking time to turn backward and return us to childhood even if just for a night.

Now, with fewer demands placed on my time, no places to go, no people to meet, I think back to a life lived on the run, when each day was a game of beat the clock, and I hustled me and the kids from one deadline to the next, from soccer to baseball to Cub Scouts, grabbing fast food between. Minutes seemed precious then; now I have hours to walk, or sit, or pretend to fish. So time is a trickster, shape-shifting like a character in an old Indian myth, outwitting us with its pranks—giving us too much now, not enough then; speeding up through the good times, slowing down through the bad; leaving us to wonder where it went, never knowing when it ends. Mechanical time may be constant, methodical, systematic, but our experience of time is fitful and capricious, as though the gods delight in playing practical jokes, keeping us perpetually off guard.

Psychologists point out that an awareness of time is an important step in human development, as the child emerges from an existence locked solely in present time, "the eternal now," and gradually assimilates concepts like "later" and "tomorrow" and "when I grow up." An inability to order events in time, on the other hand, is a telltale sign of mental deficiencies in adults. And what must time mean to those afflicted with progeria, that extraordinary disease that accelerates the aging process, turning 4-year-olds into octogenarians by the age of 10?

Even under normal circumstances, the passing of time is certainly different for children eager for Christmas or teenagers eager for birthdays than for those of us facing the last turn of our lives, digging in our heels. Is it only a matter of perception that time quickens its pace the older one gets? Studies done on *this* theory of relativity (some of them examining the body's internal timing devices) can't explain why, if time is a river, its current hauls you along faster as you approach the dropping off point, as you hear the roaring waterfall waiting to carry you beyond time.

But if granted a longer lifespan, would we—in all honesty—use time more wisely? Probably not. We are, after all, more likely to waste that which comes in abundance, appreciating most dearly those properties fast running out. Even when given a reprieve, a stay of execution, some of us may take full advantage of the bonus time but most of us do not. Some while ago I was told I had malignant melanoma. My immediate reaction was a series of resolutions: Do good deeds, write long letters to my sons, finish a manuscript I'd been patching for decades, smell the flowers, repeat the mantra: "Today is the first day of the rest of my life." But after two minor surgeries, the horizon looked clear again and I went back to normal—sleeping in, doing crossword puzzles, sitting, dancing alone in the dark of my house, and singing real loud.

And sometimes I fish, and stare at autumn fading, my life now abruptly divided into then and now, before and after, yesterday and tomorrow. I think of what has brought me here. I think of what it means, and where it leads. "Life can only be understood backwards," wrote Thomas Merton, "but must be lived forward." For time, at its sharpest penetration, is finite, enclosed, apportioned out in unequal shares by God or the fates, by destiny or random occurrences as misguided and arbitrary as the bouncing, colliding balls that determine lottery winners.

We do, of course, want to squeeze out as much living as we can. But what does that mean? Live for the moment? Build for the future? How *does* one seize the day? What does the ancient proverb mean: "Live as if you were to live forever; live as if you were to die tomorrow"?

Sometimes, as dark descends and I head back to the house with nothing but muddy fingers to show for my fishing, I wonder if the time were squandered. Sometimes I think not. Sometimes I do.

✤

Down at that library are lots of books about time. Many have to do with quantum physics, space-time, wormholes—sorcerers' talk that has little to do with my life. A lot have to do with the history of time, but these mainly address ways of keeping time—water clocks and sundials, Mayan calendars and Stonehenge, ephemeris time and carbon dating (as if, in our species' quest to measure time ever more exactly, we might actually prevent it from slipping through our grasp).

These books tell you where the names of the days and months came from, what the vernal equinox is, what the effects of photoperiodism and pineal glands and papal edicts are, and what a hard time humans have had trying to figure out what a *year* really is (we are still, despite our technological precision, unable to reconcile stellar years with lunar years with solar years).

But there are four dozen other books, too, on time—those telling you how to manage it, how to control time so it doesn't control you. These books (reminding me of that part of my life governed by time and its coxswain urging) have names like *The 90-Minute Hour, Mak-*

ing Time Work for You, and *Time Is Money, Save It.* Even the titles put the pressure on—*How to Put More Time in Your Life, 365 Ways to Save Time, Competing Against Time,* and *Busy-Bodies: Why Our Time-Obsessed Society Keeps Us Running in Place*—but they are all the same. They tell you that the secret to life is to set goals, make lists, prioritize, and then just do it—now.

I had a boss once who gave me such a book and told me to keep a log of how I spent my day. He wanted me to see where my time went. He believed in stacking "blocks of time" tightly together, not a moment to spare, no time for daydreams or idle wonder. To him and many others in the workaday world, busyness itself becomes a virtue. The truly virtuous among us, according to this plan, are those whose time is filled with deadlines and commitments, those who, essentially, have the least time for the rest of us, for leisure, for fun. Those who make you wait longest for an appointment are typically seen as the busiest, hardest working, most important, most valued members of an organization. Their time is in most demand; they earn stature, prestige, and importantness for this.

This breathless existence can probably be traced to Puritan frugality, Ben Franklin's *Poor Richard's Almanac,* and the Protestant work ethic. But it was the Industrial Revolution that linked work so tightly to timekeeping. "The clock, not the steam-engine," wrote Lewis Mumford, "is the key machine of the modern industrial age."

"Before the industrial revolution," echoed Ralph Keyes in *Time-lock,* "there was no lane but the slow lane. Without clocks people worked until a job was done, not until a timepiece told them to stop." That is the one book I checked out and brought home to read. *Time-lock.* It seemed right for my days here by the pond, to this imposed reconfiguration of a life.

The work schedule of a largely agrarian society, Keyes explained, was keyed to seasons and sunlight, not 40-hour weeks. In those days, hard work was not equated with constancy, as it is today; it was a life of exhaustive labor followed by periods of rest—harvest festivals and more leisurely winters. Even professionals did their work according to the job, not parcels of time; but today even writers and mechanics, like lawyers and psychiatrists, charge by the hour.

As more people worked away from home and under a clock's gaze, extended mealtimes were curtailed, naps became extinct, and jobs were defined not so much as tasks completed but as "putting in time" after punching in, before punching out. As competition revved the engines of American productivity, time grew even more important; factories stayed open around the clock and employees supplied the power that kept industry humming, working shifts, night and day.

Time became money—a commodity to be bought, sold, and put to use, with a premium placed on haste and punctuality, lest time be "lost."

Time consciousness became so pervasive in twentieth-century America that it's embedded in our national conscience. The use of one's time has become a moral issue. Idle time, even leisure, is widely perceived as wasteful, a sign of laziness. We fear that our children will have "too much time on their hands," so we plot their lives to keep their minds and bodies engaged in "quality time" activities. We deride those who seem too casual about time. We respect those who use their time efficiently, those who cope best with the demands and stresses time imposes on their hurried, harried lives.

And now—with microwaves and fax machines, e-mail, "instant messaging," the Internet, cell phones, and overnight delivery, "drive-thru" fast-food restaurants, and live news reports from around the globe—the pace continues to accelerate. It's all immediate, *right now*. Even more pressure is exerted as the treadmill speeds up, until for many of us that hectic, pulsing schedule—in which "there are just not enough hours in a day"—has become an inescapable way of life. And time has assumed new meaning, a new power over us: that of foe, taskmaster, slave driver.

Once upon a time—at least 28,000 years ago—our ancestors notched bones to mark the phases of the moon. They were the first timekeepers, looking for patterns, rhythms, cycles. Time was duration then, marked off in long, loose intervals, measures of natural repetitions. These primitive timekeepers mostly looked to the heavens: Australian tribesmen knew it was time to hunt termites when Arcturus was on the horizon in the evening; Vega told them when to seek the eggs of the mallee hen. The Tukano Indians of Brazil planted crops when Pleiades dropped below the horizon just after sunset, because that meant heavy seasonal rains were coming.

It is no wonder that the tribe's stargazers were also the seers and shamans, that calendar-making became an art, that timekeeping had religious significance. The ancient calendars, some of which are more exact than our own, are evidence of the human longing to understand, to find patterns and reasons, to prophesy and predict, to align human activities with heavenly navigations.

About 4,000 years ago, the priest-astronomers of the megalithic culture of northwestern Europe were erecting dozens of Stonehenge-like structures to observe and interpret the heavens, still linking time-keeping with worship. The early Greeks told stories of Cronus, god of agriculture, known to later Greeks as Chronos, god of time, who carried a sickle to cut down the passing years. In Rome, emperors and popes fought over calendars, lawyers used water clocks to restrict speech-making, and sundials were used to measure the hours—prompting the Roman playwright Plautus to deride the devices which "cut and hack my days so wretchedly into small pieces."

The cutting and hacking has continued, but the technology necessary for greater precision was centuries in coming. Then, during the Middle Ages, advances with pendulum, weight, and spring drives sparked a revolution in clock-making. An impressive town clock became a source of civic pride. Shared public time brought uniformity. Business hours, religious services, and civic gatherings all demanded cooperation and punctuality. Eventually, railroads required synchronization between villages and cities—sometimes in distant countries.

Hours became important, then minutes, then seconds. Now, in the twenty-first century, quartz crystal and atomic decay are used to split seconds into infinitely smaller pieces, to measure fractions of time too minuscule to notice without artificial means. And electronic technology has given us the tools to work just that fast. The result is a rapid-firing, time-obsessed society. Hyper America. A world set in fast-forward. An MTV-*Sesame Street*-sound-bite-Attention Deficit Disorder existence.

The beat has changed in music—going from waltz to ragtime to jazz to swing, from rock to rap to hip-hop—as well as food preparation. In 1937, Kraft bragged about its new macaroni-and-cheese dinner—a complete meal in 9 minutes. Then came "minute rice" and "instant soup," the advent of frozen dinners in the 1950s and today's microwave-oven entrees, where 10 seconds of cooking time may be the difference between "still frozen in the middle" to "just right" to "tough and chewy." And White Castle diners, which once bragged about serving you food and getting you off your seat in 12 minutes, and today's drive-through operations (with touchpad computer ordering), that brag about serving billions of burgers to passing motorists who don't have time to stop and eat.

We've gone from mail to phone to fax, from bank tellers to ATMs, from daily newspapers to *CNN Headline News*. A Delaware court reporter swears that witnesses now speak 20 to 40 words per minute faster today than they did in the 1950s. We are consumed with decision making. We are overwhelmed by choices: phone services, banking opportunities, *butter*. How often would I stand before the dairy case pondering butter and margarine, soft and stick, calculating *fat*, saturated and unsaturated. In 1925 the typical "supermarket" carried 900 items; today's carries more than 10,000.

Time-saving devices only make us feel more hurried, more anxious. For one thing, they break down a lot. Though they may eliminate drudgery, they are often nuisances, agitating us with "down time" while we wait for a technician to fix the printer or a plumber to fix the disposal. Other devices—Walkmans, car phones, cell phones, even "exercycles"—have us doing two things at once (multitasking). Still others—fax machines and e-mail, microwaves and telephones—can become time-takers by demanding immediate gratification. They also become electronic "pacers," setting the tempo we live by. That tempo often feels like time is traveling at breakneck speed, cranking up our body's fight-flight thermostat to unhealthy levels.

"Another reward," writes Keyes in *Timelock*, "is that the faster we go, and the more crowded our schedules, the less likely it is that we'll have to stop and think about where we're headed. Busyness can be an effective filter. Having too many things to do provides a built-in excuse for not dealing with things we'd rather not deal with: people, thoughts, ourselves."

That is time as I've known it much of my life. Now, being here at this cabin—with no clock, no watch, no television, only the flight of the sun and the rotating of seasons and stars—has drawn me into the gears of this other timepiece, the cosmic clockwork of creation. Our species has come a long way since timekeeping meant monitoring celestial migrations and contemplating the universe in all its twinkling wonder. Yet we seem less attuned and more bewildered. Perhaps, in asking how best to spend our *time*, we have forgotten to ask, "Is this how I want to spend my *life*?" Progress is not absolute.

If time is an arrow, philosophers ask, is its trajectory upward? Assorted cultures have concocted a grab bag of answers to explain the historical dimensions of time—from believing that events repeat themselves in slowly circling epochs to believing that energy is dissipating and the clock of the universe is winding down. But for most of Western civilization's history, the belief has been persistent that the time line is marching ever upward.

For centuries it has been hard to think otherwise. Human knowledge has expanded dizzily, leading to stunning advances in science and technology, in medicine and health, in virtually every aspect of human endeavor. Writers, thinkers, and statesmen, heady with the potency of human ingenuity, were eager to unleash the power of the individual, freeing them to flourish under democratic ideals. Darwin's revolutionary theses (linking us to monkeys and tracing human advancement for millennia) underscored the idea of progress, refinement, improvement, just as America was entering an era of unprecedented power and expansion. As time unfolded, life would surely get better.

Today we are not so sure. Part of our national distress, I think, is due to a creeping feeling that things are coming unraveled, that life is *not* getting better, that the human journey through time is faltering. A look at the state of planet Earth might confirm this. The notion that we may not be leaving the world a better place for our children upsets our American optimism and faith.

We are deeply uncomfortable with the thought that time's arrow may ultimately be not upward but directionless. Just as individuals grow unhappy when they sense they are not advancing, so too do cultures and societies. It makes the meaning of human existence too wayward, too arbitrary. And that, of course, is what our species' first timekeepers were trying to overcome when they scanned the heavens for signs of guidance, indications of patterns or design or divine imprint. They were looking for God in time—for religion is, ultimately, humanity's earnest attempt to reconcile the eternal with the temporal. So you have Christians, for example, believing in a God who started the clock ticking, who entered time to redeem his creation, and who promises a place beyond time when this time-locked existence ends. I suppose such cosmologies lessen the anguish we feel as we ponder the moment when our time will be up. At my age, that is something.

🌿

What I know best of time I have relearned here in these woods—not from books or proverbs—but by seemingly wasting time, sitting still, fishing at twilight. Despite telling myself to lighten up and take it easy, it has taken awhile for the urgency and antsiness to dissipate. But I've learned the value of deep breaths, patience, and acceptance. It has reminded me of old times out on the trail, far away from the artificial pulse of modern living. The complexion of days changes when they are not dissected into compartments tagged with numbers—when there is no timekeeper pacing you, exhorting you; no deadlines, no one to meet, no other place to be. The days lengthen, stretch elastically, extending themselves into rhythm with the slow-motion sun, advancing imperceptibly, subtle changes in light and dark and shadow length, enveloping darkness, the gradual rotations of stars and moons and planets. It takes days to sense these rhythms, for the revolving continuity to feel more natural than the calibrated logic of our fabricated existence. But when it happens, it brings a truer perception of time and life, less artificial, more in step with the ultimate timepiece. After awhile you begin to live according to these rhythms rather than an electric clock.

Much of what I know of this time I learned from Walt, an older man with whom I once backpacked each October for almost 10 years. White-bearded and wise and old enough to contemplate death close-up, Walt preferred to sleep out, under no cover of tent, to watch the stars all night long. We could stand for hours staring at the nighttime sky, necks crooked back, saying nothing—before settling into our bags to watch more till dozing off . . . waking off and on as the Earth and moon drifted and danced through the cosmos. We rarely spoke of what thoughts this gazing prompted—of space and time and human insignificance, of black holes and quasars and other forms of life, and creation and God and the swimming of galaxies and planets and the shining thrill of shooting stars. The stuff to make your head spin. The vast synchronic machinations of the universe.

No matter how cold the morning (and they were cold ones those Octobers at higher altitudes, often under clear, thin-air desert skies),

Walt always woke me as soon as first light began draining the blackness of night. He wanted us up for the ceremony of sunrise. Each day was a savored celebration, filled from beginning to end, until the beginnings and ends merged into one, ceasing to be beginnings and ends, and day and night became indivisible. So he would fire up the coffee in the cosmic shadow and we would stand and stamp our feet, bundled and shivering, gloved hands cupped around steaming mugs, plumes of frosty breath visible as we awaited dawn.

I remember best one dawning in New Mexico, camped high under a bountiful sky, with the stars gleaming glassily almost within reach. It had been a cold, cold night, and Walt woke me in the cobalt blue air of dawn. Stirring, cold air biting, pulling on stiffly frozen boots, we shuffled about—day coming, water bottles frozen, high mountain wall to the east, delaying the sun's arrival this day. Our anticipation was heightened by that and the cold and the proximity of the low-ceilinged sky the night before. And I remember the persistent call of a loud-mouthed canyon wren and the updrafts of morning winds, and the gradual, ever-so-slow lightening of the land. Sunlight first reaching the summits behind us, creeping slowly down our way.

And I remember thinking, imagining the way it really was. This: not that the sun was rising from behind the Earth's edge, but that the world itself, the very globe that we were riding upon, was slowly, slowly revolving and bringing its face toward the stationary sun. I could almost sense the turning. The sun was not scaling the horizon; our planet was rotating, wheeling toward the sun. And when it did, when the jagged, silhouetted mountains gyred just one more notch around, their pinnacles became glowing tungsten filaments brilliant with flame. And then there was fire upon the mountain as a sliver of the sun peeked over the earthline and shouted its rays in golden streamers all over the land. Then I looked and saw the light and warmth reflected in Walt's reddish, worn face as he watched the sunlight splash wildly over the Sangre de Cristo range. Transfiguration.

I am but a traveler passing through, and that makes me think a lot about time, and this place, and me. And about the material of my body and how it came to be, disparate ingredients coalescing somehow, growing, shaping into *me*, to some day expire, decay, and dissipate, someday returning to what and where *it* came from. Flesh, bone, molecules, and atoms eventually dispersed, to once again be an indistinct part of it all. Dissolution of the self.

I do know the best of times are those periods when time and self are gone, when time evaporates, when its grip is loosed, when the experience itself carries us beyond time, like a child at play for whom time dissolves and, with it, that sense of self that weighs us down and makes us distinct from our surroundings. The best of times are those moments when the self is forgotten, abandoned, when the experience is so direct and full and absorbing that it wraps us right into it. The religious among us have, for ages, valued this dissolution of ego, of self, and the commensurate absorption into some Other.

Sometimes I sit and watch out the window. Some days I do nothing. Some days I move slow like a cloud, some days fast like a cloud. Some days, when I walk past my window, my eye is caught by boys—baseball caps and T-shirts—playing around the pond. For the briefest moment my heart leaps because I think they are my sons. But that time, too, has passed. My sons are now twice as big as those wraith-like interlopers; my sons would not be at my pond. Time has changed all that, though memories endure, bringing the past forward so fully I can feel it.

Sometimes I think about how time changed when I used to backpack in the wilderness, how it took me three or four days to settle into those rhythms. Sometimes I recall how important that was, to be in synch with the rolling tumblers that open nature's locks.

Sometimes I think about the month I spent in the Arctic one summer, when the sun never set. There were only four of us, far away from the world yet very close to it. The days elongated, then went away, and the time and place floated out of time somehow, as if time was of no consequence.

Sometimes I think about sacred time, about Mircea Eliade and his theory that ritual puts us in touch with what's holy, that ceremonies in which we repeat sacred events connect us to eternal things, subverting time. Sometimes I think about all these sacramental observances that create a time outside of time, and of ways to touch the holy, and what my culture has done to change the ancient, eternal concepts of time— and what that has done to us. I am older now and sometimes I think of me when I was younger. And sometimes I just fish.

Kerry Temple

3

I only went out for a walk, and finally concluded to stay out till sundown, for going out, I found, was really going in.

—*John Muir,* Journal, *1913*

I live in the Heartland. It is where I have lived and worked and homesteaded for over half my life. This corner of the Midwest is a rolling mixture of agriculture and broad-leaf woods, crisscrossing creeks, some lowlands, bluffs, and hollows. This place of mine is like a gently cresting sea whose swells and troughs, covered in grasses, elm and maple, sycamore and oak, invite some solitary walking. So I do. If I am not sitting or fishing, I am walking. I walk here a lot, at least one long hike a day. And I take my time.

I've found it best to choose direction over destination, leaving me free to change course, to wander or to follow. I keep a lookout for deer. I often scare up rabbits. I roam here to there, ambling, investigating, looking, thinking. Walking encourages thinking; it opens the mind in a way that sitting still does not. Thoughts outrun and outmaneuver concentration, finding their way in and out of an idle mind, chasing down crooked pathways like hound dogs on a scent. Walking takes me places where even my feet don't go.

I walked here even before I lived here. For 8 years I ran my dog in the woods adjacent to this property I now call my own. We didn't miss a day. No matter how surly or mean the weather, we'd get in the car and get out of town and come to these woods and fields nestled into the crescent bend of a slow, brown river. Sometimes we'd venture onto this private property, but mostly we roamed the hundreds of acres nearby. We would make a loop, a meandering circle, with my dog racing ahead, galloping after groundhogs, sniffing out squirrels, treeing raccoons. Those times together were dear to me. I still miss that dog, another good friend left behind with all the rest. I walk alone now. I have for almost three years—making more than a decade walking daily in these woods, in the golden extravagance of summer, in the harsh, grey grip of winter.

It really isn't much, as parcels of nature go. An ordinary wedge of land, common in appearance. But it is to me a hallowed place. There are houses way across the river, and a wastewater-treatment facility; and one corner is bissected by colossal skeletons with power lines strung from their fists. Far to the south is a college campus with another wide border of woods; off to the north, past some farms, Interstate 80 hums with east-west traffic 24 hours a day; and far to the east is U.S. Highway 31, which runs from the straits of Mackinac to the Gulf of Mexico. When that particular byway runs through here, it is lined with laundromats and motels, convenience stores, and a smorgasbord of fast-food franchises that make the whole strip look ugly and cheap and in a constant state of disintegration. The non-renewing and non-renewable entropy of human contrivances.

But these woods and the place I live in now are largely insulated from all that by geometrically proper sheets of cultivated fields—beans one year, corn the next—subdivided by fencerows of tangles and trees that shelter the groundhogs and rabbits who burrow there. In a sense those fields shelter me, too. They distance me from human development. They comprise a wide moat between the refuge-woods and the concrete and steel of middle America, making the people-things fall away, leaving me alone with my thoughts and the affection of this good place.

Although I prefer the woods, I like the fields, too. They bring breadth to the surroundings, a depth of vision not available in the midst of trees. When I stand on their deck, I can watch the giant thunderheads advance angrily from the west, survey the reddening sky at sunset, and lean back to stargaze on clear winter nights. I can watch the red-tailed hawks sail gracefully on soft summer breezes, and the Canada geese, in formation and unflaggingly honking, make their autumn flight. It is here that the wind blows most freely—swift and lean and undeterred by building or hill, or copse of trees.

Kerry Temple

But even these plowed fields are broken by an occasional oak, sycamore, or cottonwood tree standing as a stark vertical totem in the horizontal plane of mid-America. Sometimes I think of these deciduous creatures as the proper inheritance from a time when this whole territory was covered in wild forest, and home to bear, elk, and panther. I am grateful to those who first cleared this plot for sparing these trees; they make these fields less commercial, more personal. The solitary tree offers something of real stature to dignify the surroundings.

In the hierarchy of natural wonders, this place, and the woods where I live, would be thought by many as common and plain. But there is beauty in the details here, and rightness in the symphonic resiliency of life. Besides, it is largely left alone, and is now but a few paces from my door, and I like it here. I have an excursion every day.

I usually make the long sojourn at dusk because my workday is done and that is the best time to see the wildlife in this island of woods that blanket the gullies and bluffs along the rolling river and my creek. I like sunset—the rose-colored light that washes over the landscape, the hush that descends upon the world, the appearance of deer and fireflies and evening stars, the moment when you stop and look around and think of spheres turning, of planets and moons and the dizzying machinations of the universe . . . and what you did that day.

But I have walked at sunrise and noon and late at night, in chill, pelting rains, and on sultry, mosquitoey days, and when it was dark and 20 below, with gale-force winds that stung and numbed my face. There were three consecutive nights like that one December which I remember for their sheer extravagance. The cold was brutal, the snow knee-deep—with the wind driving it sideways and piling it into 4-foot drifts. But the jeweled sky was radiant, and the land seemed pushed right to its edge, and each night I saw a lone fox, was able to watch its silhouette romp over the frozen fields. On two of the nights I was startled by a large owl perched in a twisted tree, and once he buzzed low over my head before he stroked ghostily away and disappeared into the night. Despite the howling, needling cold, the place seemed wonderfully alive, even magical. And somehow I seemed far less lonely and insignificant on those frostbit nights as I stood and savored the stars.

Back to Earth

For a decade now, I have seen these woods daily in all their seasons and have become attuned to the rhythms of their life—even the quotidian changes one would not notice without the constancy of being here so much. And in time I have learned the animal trails, the timing of dogwood blooms and the ripening of berries, the rise and fall of the river. And I have seen this place as its moods have shifted, when it was shrouded in fog, baked by drought, and riled in storm—winds whipping, lightning crackling, and the thunder reverberating off the trees as the rain-laden clouds surged down from the sky. Sounds of the cosmic drumbeat.

Of course, on most days the walk is uneventful, but over time something meaningful comes through, is somehow absorbed through the skin, the soles of the feet. Much of this is due, I think, to the solitude, the stillness, the time free of distractions and noise and all the clutter that separates us from the living world. We are so cut off from the land from which our species emerged. Even the walls of our homes are barriers between us and the soil and winds of our beginnings, to say nothing of the genius that dwells therein. The full-throttle engine of our culture has carried us far away from here, away from the roadbed of our existence.

In the quiet here I have listened to the air rushing through the wings of geese, have watched the stilt-legged blue herons sniping fish in the shallows along the creek and riverbank, and have learned that each twilight sky is a singular expression of light and life, of cloudscape and sun. I've come to appreciate the little things here—the blaze of a cardinal against the blue-white of a winter day, the smell of the earth after a summer rain, the nervous irascibility of opossums.

Sometimes I think our infatuation with nature is too dependent on its show. Sometimes it is the ordinary that speaks most eloquently, and in the monotony of walking here daily I have at least opened myself to its voice. Being here has become a ritual; the place a part of me. But in this geography of the familiar dwell all the elements and essences of our human connections to the earth.

Sometimes I think it is more important to find those bonds here, where the geometric designs of agrarian man commingle with nature, than in the great wide open. This, after all, is our habitat. And, daydream as we might about the cathedral spires of the Rockies or the seaswept cusp of Maine, our species' place these days is mostly a

Kerry Temple

mapping of concrete and grass, malls, parking lots, and corners of nature that are unremarkable in their countenance. Too often, I think, we let the wild and special places, the pristine reservations, represent all of nature; we let the rest go, as if its meager beauty did not merit protection from bulldozers, shoppers, and condominiums, as if "the rest" is all expendable.

But it is in these neighborhoods, where the earth is largely hidden, that our need for its strength is greatest. For the more estranged we are from the earth (even in its most humble guises), the more impoverished is our existence, and the more cut off we are from the precious chords of our very nature. This place keeps my toes to the ground.

Perhaps it is the setting, but I can recall few other places where I have stopped to look at trees. But I do here. I watch them closely in summer when their leafy branches pitch and roll in the gusts of stormy winds, and in winter when their limbs are bare as whips and more exquisite than lace.

Trees, a local naturalist once wrote, are best, because they stand still and let you look at them. Yet they change: the flashing of autumn colors, the first green shoots of spring, the rotting, mossy husks that are home to mushrooms and worms. And deep in these woods, on brittle cold winter days, you can hear the old ones creak and moan, you can hear their joints pop and their spindly arms rattle like bones as arctic air rakes through them down from Canada. I like the trees, both singly and leaning all together where I can be among them. They keep the cold away.

There are footpaths in these woods and a winding loop of road— twin tire ruts with a green grass median—that make the walking easy, and quiet. But these are narrow and overarched with foliage, more like tunnels than expressways, made by the treading of feet, not by tool or asphalt. So that, when you're in these woods that rise and fall upon the bluffs here by the river, you feel immersed in them, enveloped, as if caressed. Even when you emerge into a sunlit clearing or wade through a thicket of stickery brambles, you feel the woods around you.

One night, for example, I passed beneath the raccoon tree and felt I was being watched. The raccoon tree is an old hollow oak. It has only a few remaining limbs and several knotholes that serve as doorways for the animals that live there. I had noticed a large coon there on

several winter nights and that spring I saw a family—mother sham-
bling up the scaly bark followed by four young ones at her heels, stopping to look at me looking at them. Later that summer on a moonlit
night I heard a fierce racket in the woods and followed the sounds to
the raccoon tree where I spotted a pair of teenage coons sparring rau-
cously. They were out on a limb, apparently trying to knock each
other off. It wasn't until my dog twirled and jumped below them that
they froze—mid-push—and did not budge until we had ambled off.

And so at dusk one summer evening I walked past the raccoon
tree—and stopped. I felt like I was being watched. I surveyed the tree
for signs of the raccoon I had seen there of late. But I couldn't spot
anything, so I moved on. After walking a few paces, though, the feeling tugged at me and I went back to study the tree again. And this
time I spied it. A barred owl. Perched erect as a magistrate in the oval
of a large knothole, it peered down at me. And as I stepped this way
or that, I could see its ear tufts turn as its head swiveled to follow my
movements.

Emerson wrote: "I conceive of man as always spoken to from behind, and unable to turn his head and see the speaker." I have felt that
way a lot in these woods, as if secrets were being whispered in my ear
and I couldn't quite make out the words. Sometimes some vague intuition reports a presence hiding in the shadows; sometimes I think
it's just the hushed murmurings of wind in the trees. There have been
other times, however, when I'd swear I felt a tapping on my shoulder.
I recall the day I saw a bobcat here, and the night a fox danced in the
snow. And sometimes I am convinced Elizabeth Barrett Browning
was right when she wrote, "Earth's crammed with heaven, and every
common bush afire with God."

But I am talking now of the meaning of trees—the way they form
a canopy overhead, a playground for sparrows and squirrels; the way
they filter sunlight through their fingers, until it pools at my feet; or
the way they look at midnight in winter when they're splashed with
thick, wet snow. I like to touch the trees. I like to touch the bark, to
run my fingers over their scratchy surfaces like a blind man reading
Braille. I like to rub my hands along their rough-skinned roots, the
ones that protrude from the soft, gooey mud along the river bank—
sturdy ropes coiled along the water's edge, holding fast. I find solace
in the company of trees; they can teach you how to live.

Kerry Temple

It has occurred to me, walking here these years and reading the landscape like a poem, that most anything a person needs to know can be deciphered here. The lessons are here for the taking; the glory of stars, the softness of earth, the endurance of rock—these are field guides for the living. The place becomes a melding of story, metaphor, and myth. Even here, where the visits are often commonplace and the natural wonders tryingly subtle, the narrative is unfolding. So I come here, walking out of the tedium of my life, to read between the lines.

I go by signs.

I have seen a multitude of deer here, their leaping and bounding as elegant as angel flight. They are so gentle, so fleet, so beautiful that I can watch them browse, graze, or escape, and marvel at the grace of their movements. I have seen them at night clustered in twos and threes, mere silhouettes upon the snowfields under a silvery moon. I recall a foggy night when a small herd was backlit by moonlight in the mist and they moved hurriedly past a grove of trees like soldiers stealing away under cover of dark. And I have sat and watched a mother whitetail skitter and snort to drive me away from two unwatchful fawns.

But I have encountered deer, too, in broad daylight, coming upon them up close, poised face-to-face—they as startled to see me as I to see them. On a brilliant blue-sky day in winter, with a generous white frosting spread on every trunk, branch, and twig, I came upon a large antlered buck hunched under a trellis of snow-laden vines. We stood and stared at one another for awhile, with no language to span the gap between us, except for our stillness and a respect to leave the other be.

I have been close to deer on many occasions and have often stood still enough to be approached by them—their heads bobbing and craning as their liquid black eyes try to discern my meaning. I like to stay long enough for them to mosey away, paying me little heed, perhaps glancing back occasionally to check on me. When it is clear they do not mind my presence, I feel as if I have entered their world and become part of its texture. When they run, I sense that I have disturbed the composition, that I am an interloper who has broken the spell, the uninvited guest who disrupts the pastoral contours. So I go still and softly and try hard not to disturb the animals living here. I admit, though, to a time or two springing into a pack of deer and racing with them for as long as I can, finding some joy in that sport until I feel leaden and slow—like a pelican flying with falcons—and the deer have disappeared from sight.

In these woods and fields I have also seen groundhogs in trees, opossums playing dead, and twin hawks performing an hour-long aerial show, riding the invisible wind, banking, arcing, somersaults of grace and style, playing follow-the-leader. I have watched an owl pose rigid in its nest while being scolded harshly by a dive-bombing swarm of blackbirds. I have admired the feats of acrobatic squirrels and have watched whole clans of raccoons devour mulberries while hanging from their hind feet in the lush, leafy limbs of mid-June. And I have seen butterflies and fireflies, hummingbirds and hoptoads, feisty skunks, and one autumn day a duck perched in a tree.

One cold snowy Saturday night my dog discovered something in the brush beside the trail. It was an ailing raccoon, which did not run when I approached. When I stooped to investigate, it looked up at me and watched. With my gloved hand I rubbed the spot beneath its ears as if it were the family dog. It purred. I stroked its cheek and ran my fingers along its rib cage, petting the length of its resting body. I had never touched a wild animal like this and was surprised when it rolled onto its back and let me rub its stomach in gentle tidings between species.

There were gurgling sounds in its throat and a shiver in its breath as the coon made no attempt to get away, though it never took its bandit eyes from mine. I almost took it home; I thought of carrying it to a vet; I finally decided to let nature have its way—though I carried it deeper into the woods and tucked it into a hole, a refuge from the cold and whatever else might bother it. The next morning I returned and found that it was dead.

I feel a certain kinship with the animals I see here, a recognition that we're all members of the same grand menagerie inhabiting this heartland district. But I also realize that this is their place that I enter when I leave my house. There is a kind of diffidence that comes with this. I am reminded here of my weaknesses and vulnerabilities, the limitations of my senses, my inability to last long where they thrive, my need to eventually get back home, my being somehow on the outside of their domain looking in.

Kerry Temple

There is something else about animals, and it has to do with this—with nights when I hear the sweet distant song of an owl, a melodious hooting in the air. Usually I try to follow its call until I find it, until I spy the vase-like shape, the cowlick ears, the turret head. Sometimes, when I get near, the owl will fly, revealing a wingspan surprisingly broad, a wraith-like presence, a tranquil stroke, until it fades like an apparition into the night. Just this—this fleeting brush with one wild soul—brings magic to the mundane.

Such encounters may not bring visions of the mystical kind, but to a pilgrim who treads these woods daily they bring their own kind of revelation, a sense of enlightenment, of having been paid a visit by an emissary from the other side. They are rewards for a faith in a universe that is not totally inscrutable, indifferent, opaque, but wondrously alive to those attuned to distant soundings. I have, for example, seen fox out here on perhaps a dozen occasions, but only once did one dance for me. I watched its joy in a clearing on a snowy night as it hopped and spun, jitterbugged and jigged as happy as a faun cavorting with the moon.

I have also seen a bobcat here. It emerged from a thicket some 30 yards in front of me when our eyes met, and held. We watched each other for the longest time, each afraid to move. I am sure it was a bobcat; I took inventory wanting to be certain—the spots and tufted ears and bobbed tail, the broad feline cheeks and padded paws. In time I moved closer, step by watchful step, until I thought I'd gone close enough—some flinching or tenseness in the wildcat's body told me so. Time passed and we watched each other still, until, after awhile, the cat turned slowly and, stepping easily, slipped back into the hedgerow from which it had come—in no apparent hurry to get away from me.

Whenever I walk these woods, I think of stories. I recall the bobcat sighting and the dancing fox . . . or the night some years ago when I discovered the "electric moss." It was just after dusk one damp summer night when I spied a radiance in the woods over by the river. It was an eerie glow, as if a fluorescent duffel bag had been dropped from a UFO. I moved closer cautiously, staring in amazement, creeping closer, edging nearer, half-expecting an extraterrestrial.

When I came upon the mysterious luminescence, I gazed in wonder. It was emitting a greenish light, like the glowing of sea-green embers—the color of a firefly's taillight. I bent to look closer and I still could not make out what it was I was looking at. I held my hand over the radiance but felt no warmth. I was afraid to touch it—this curious incandescence in the darkness of night—so I jabbed at it with a stick. Pieces, like charcoal or embers, tumbled about, some brighter than others. "This," I thought, "must be where the lightning bugs come to get their light." I imagined whole squadrons coming here for a refill before heading out on maneuvers.

I knew it wasn't so, although I wished it to be true. But I have grown old enough to see where science clashes with fable, where the magical often gets grounded before taking flight. I later learned it was "electric moss," a phosphorescent kind of stuff that absorbs sunlight during the day to be radiant at night. I had never seen it before and I have not seen it since. But I like to think I once found the place where the fireflies come for light, the mouth of some secret flyport that was mistakenly left uncovered one night.

Of course, the story of these woods, like that of any patch of nature, is not all splendor, whimsy, and rapture. The swift beauty of wild rabbit and the keen grace of red-tailed hawk can collide in one sudden, brutal moment. I have seen the frenzied scrambling of a rabbit laid bare in a late-autumn cornfield when a hawk is closing in. Unable to reach shelter, it dashes madly, frantically, zigzaggedly— heart popping—until the hawk pounces, talons flashing. The claws snap flesh and bones; the resistance is brief. The raptor rips apart its prey, applying beak and claw to greedily extract from the bloody mess the tough cords of steaming intestines. Clumps of downy fur wander away in the wind.

Nature does not always smile, but it does things in balance. Its complementary parts preserve an order that, watched closely, can bring an acceptance and faith in the way things are. There is beauty, then, in the interweaving of the harsh and the raw, the elegant and the unremarkable, the fleeting and the never-ending. One sees cycles here, and the constancy of life forms undergoing startling metamorphoses— decaying, ingesting, dying, thriving—until you look upon the living mosaic and see that it is all one big thing.

The river, too, could tell stories—of swollen springs and frozen winters, of mallards, heron, and wood ducks, of changing course and quicksilver fish and the holy persistence of flow. This place and its river share a history. I know just a little: that this steady brown stream was once called "the river of the Miamis" because so many of that native tribe lived along its banks. The region then was filled with elk, deer, panthers, wolves, and assorted ground mammals—otters, weasels, minks, raccoons, badgers, and bobcats. Black bear prowled the woods and buffalo roamed the grasslands. Hundreds of bird species were at home here, including several types of hawk and eagle. And a botanist, writing in 1880 and perhaps giddy with excitement, estimated that almost half of the 2,400 species of flowering plants found in the United States grew here.

The first white person to see this place, where the river tumbles out of Michigan into Indiana before bending north again to Lake Michigan, may have been Jacques Marquette. The Jesuit explorer stood on the banks of this river—maybe 2 miles from my cabin—in 1675. In 1679 the explorer LaSalle came, too, to this very bend in the river, paddling its waters upriver from Lake Michigan when trying to catch the Kankakee on his way to the Mississippi.

Today the river is called the St. Joseph, and its currents still roll along, through dams and under bridges, past towns and cities, bordered by houses and streets, and allowed to breathe and stretch itself here where I stand on its banks and listen to its song. I have canoed the length of this river, taking 4 days and portaging 7 dams, which back up the water and turn it lake-like. I prefer the river where it runs lean, wild, and free, as it does where these woods flank its path. I've been told there's an Indian burial ground here on the tall bluff where the water turns north. I have unearthed nothing there, have not turned a spade. But sometimes I long for the days when the bears and buffalo, the elk and eagles lived here. I listen for the owls to call their names. I find comfort in the company of the river.

There is another story I think of when I walk the woods each day. It has to do with a different place and a different people, on a continent far away. It is about the forest people. Like most native folk, this tribe was intimately bonded to the forest. The forest, which provided all the stuff of their lives, was also a very real presence, an all-encompassing fusion of the material and the divine. So each night they sang to the forest, and in their singing and living sought to be one with the forest, to be wholly within it. But the forest was shrinking, was being consumed by the march of progress and civilization. Its power was being diminished.

One day a developer took one of the tribal elders to the mountain-top from which the two looked down upon the valley and the forest laid as a plush green carpet on the land. "That is the forest," the developer said, to which the elder replied, "No, that is not the forest."

The developer, thinking the forest must look too tiny to be believable to someone who has never been outside its embrace, said, "Yes. Yes, it is the forest." The elder again said no. "The forest," he explained, "can be seen only from within."

I think of this story these days not only because of what it means to be immersed in such a place but also because of what it means to see from within, to be held in the grasp of that which can't be seen. Just as the forest people—or the Hopi, the Miami, or the Sioux—came to know the deity through the land, I, too, have seen glimmers of it here in these woods.

But the forest is shrinking, the golf course is coming, and all across America the wild lands are shrinking, and these woods and fields are shrinking, too. I have seen the stakes and ribbons tied to trees. I have heard the chainsaws whining in the distance. And in the woods west of here, the ones owned by the college where I've walked so long, someone has come along and put up signs identifying white oak from pin oak from sycamore and pine. More new signs proclaim the place a "nature preserve" and ask folks to please stay on the trails. And the trails have grown wider, then got covered with cinder and gravel; and now the signs proclaim the place "closed" at dusk. So I have largely confined my walks to the property where I live, though I know that here, too, the place will someday be landscaped for golf.

I wondered, years ago when I first heard of the forest people in Africa, how one would know the forest gods once the forest was dead. I think about that now here, too. What happens to the deity when its dwelling places are gone? Who will articulate nature's gleam and high spirits when the last of the wild animals are gone from here?

Until then, until the woods are tamed, I savor these walks between the holy and the plain. I favor the starlight. I think of redemption. I watch the moon. I stand still at sunset and listen to the wind. I like to hear the wind as it rolls long and fierce across the land, sails unimpeded over the fields, surges and sweeps through the trees in the woods. I like to feel the restless wind, to know its touch on its journey through this place, flying free from there to here to there. I don't

Kerry Temple

know how it is that a piece of landscape enters the blood, but I know it happens. I'm not sure why, but I think it has something to do with connecting us—over time—to something even bigger, more wondrous than itself.

When I was younger, I went looking for it in fields and haunts far and wide. I set out like a pilgrim in the woods, backpacking, hiking, covering the land on foot. I sought an education in such travel; I learned long ago there is salvation in the walking.

Back to Earth

4

By means of all created things, without exception, the divine assails us, penetrates us, and molds us. We imagined it as distant and inaccessible, whereas in fact we live steeped in its burning layers.

—Pierre Teilhard de Chardin

What she said startled me. Later I realized my surprise was more because of who said it than what was said. She said, "I would have been a better person had I lived on the water all my life."

It was a daylong family gathering, several generations of relatives who thought it would be nice to rescue me from my lonesome solitude. So the clan was turned loose at a nearby state park all afternoon. There was plenty of room to roam and everyone contributed to the fixing of food. The day was exquisite, and there were broad, grassy meadows and towering trees, wooden stands of playground devices, and creeks and wild things and spaces to explore. There was an ample lake for fishing and a small beach for swimming, deer trails through the woods, and blue skies overhead. And I felt good about it all— wiffle ball, Frisbee, kites, and kick-the-can—until I spied her sitting alone at a picnic table under a tree by the lake. She had been my only concern. My elderly aunt.

She had never married. She had started working as a bank teller during the Depression and had retired as executive vice president of a large financial institution. She had traveled to luxury hotels and posh resorts and had lived in the city all her life. She had no use for the raw gifts of nature—"unless," she said, "I'm sitting comfortably indoors and looking at them out the window," as she had done in the Alps, the Canadian Rockies, the seacoast of New England. She did not understand the lure of "roughing it" or my attraction to "rustic things." She preferred "the finer things in life." She was something of a Southern aristocrat with a keen interest in the history of the British monarchy with its royal lines and fancy ways; she liked jewelry, good books, and fine china. She was a good person, devoutly religious, culturally sophisticated, and intellectual. And to her the real aim of human progress was to elevate oneself, to rise above the primeval cauldron, to distance oneself as far as possible from our physical nature and to place as much of human civilization between us and the soil as possible. "Your aunt," my mother once said of her sister, "thinks of nature as an idea whose time has passed." That's an outlook that's guided human behavior for millennia.

Of course, I wasn't thinking all this as I approached her, sitting alone at that table, gazing silently at a big, blue lake rippling with gusty summer winds. I just wanted everyone to have fun and I figured she was miserably bored and ready to be rescued by a book, a ride into town, or a conversation. But as I approached and settled next to her, she spoke first—without removing her eyes from the lake. She said, "I would have been a better person had I lived on the water all my life." It was a conclusion drawn, I supposed, from a period of thoughtful retrospection and represented to her some profound realization—things about her life and its living that were unnecessary or impossible to explain or express. So the sentence hung in the air between us for a time. And together we watched the lake in silence, contemplating it and us and this day of familial celebration.

I do not recall how long we watched that lake or who spoke next or what was said. But I remember that moment as at least a minor epiphany in the turning of a life—mine, if not hers. I have thought about it often since.

I do not think it was an idle comment, a throwaway line let loose in a sudden gust of happy circumstance. It came from certain deliberation, the final product of some honest reflection, a dose of memory, perhaps a forgotten longing. And it was offered to me from someone not inclined to revel, like Emerson, Blake, or Wordsworth, in the bounty of natural wonders, or even to count the blessings of nature. So I savored it as an extraordinary affirmation, an acknowledgment of those blessings and power. I have often thought that revelatory confession to be a confirmation, from an unexpected source, that the landscape offers grace to those open to its gifts. If we look and touch and listen, the world can indeed make us better people.

Sitting with my aunt that day reminded me again how much I have forgotten since I was young. What I mean is, I have taught writing classes at a college for almost 20 years. Students often drop in to talk—to talk about their writing and about story ideas and their development, about themselves and their futures. With some, our conversations range from literature to life, encompassing poems and books and passions and what it all means, those dreams and fears and truths and what to live for. So often I have found myself startled by their words, reminded of things I once believed in. "I knew that," I will exclaim, and not merely mean the recollection of a line from a poem or passage from a novel. I will mean that I remember how they feel, how I once perceived the world that way, how strongly I believed in those ideals and values, those romantic notions, the beauties and glories so obvious to those in love with life and love and learning. "I knew that," I have said, excited again with discovery, with ideas, with wonder.

But these days, more than ever, I realize I must relearn what I once knew, calling forth ideas long forgotten. My life journey brought detours and distractions that obscured the heart's path, that got in the way of what's important. I got tangled in the trappings of my daily life, forgetting what I knew as a boy—how important it is to play, to imagine, to wonder, to believe in the magic all around me. We are like that as a species too. We have forgotten so much. There is so much to relearn. And much of that relearning has to do with God.

These years in the cabin have given me a strong sense of what it must have been like when our species lived close to the land. There was little between our forebears and the earth. They studied the skies and watched for signs and prayed for blessings. They were acutely aware of their dependence on the environment's resources for food and warmth, clothing and shelter. While their very survival depended on their relationship with the physical world all around them, their spiritual and religious life was similarly connected to the natural landscape. "Having become aware of objects and begun to name them, this Earliest Man became aware of something else," wrote John

Stewart Collis in *The Triumph of the Tree*. "No sooner had he looked closely at Nature than he began to concern himself, not with the physical object in front of him which he could clearly see, but with an invisible object which he could not see at all. He looked at the trees, the rocks, the rivers, the animals, and having looked at them he at once began to talk about something *in them* which he had never seen. This thing inside the objective appearance was called a god."

Today, in our civilized, concrete-and-glass world, the natural landscape is virtually silenced, carved into gardens and lawns, a distant backdrop to the more important human activities that take place in houses, boardrooms, and malls. Despite my youthful bonds to wilderness, my life, too, had relegated the natural world to backyards and city parks—put-away places on the outskirts of my real existence. Even more neglected were the spiritual qualities of any landscape. These days, in our secular, demythologized world, we consider the spirituality of our ancestors to be primitive and superstitious. Even the religious among us scoff at their beliefs and deride their worldview as pantheistic or animistic, as if so labeling their theologies dismisses them.

We have lost touch with an immanent God, no longer acknowledging the Creator behind creation. We are too knowledgeable and sophisticated for that. We have come too far. Science and technology have carried us far beyond such elemental notions, providing knowledge, constructing new environments, and explaining mysteries that have dispelled the myths and left magic and fairy tales far behind. In such a world of human triumph, some would celebrate our species' progress; others would say we have lost our way.

"The red philosophy," Russell Means once told a reporter, explaining his Native American heritage, "is that all living things come from one mother. Eons ago we looked around and saw that every living thing had a direction and a role to play in life except the two-legged creature—the human being.

"The red people decided the human beings were the weakest things on earth and were *cursed* with the power of reason. So we decided to learn from our superiors, and that is how we built our civilizations. We listened to what the eagle and the sparrow had to say. We listened to the evergreen and the cottonwood. We found our place in life.

"Now, eons ago when the white man looked around, he said he was *blessed* with the power of reason, and that's when he blew it. He said, in effect, that he was superior to all other life, that he was a god and that he had a license to exploit and manipulate. To prove that he was a god, the white man created science."

The reason for comparing these worldviews is not to disparage the triumphs of human reason, creativity, and power. In essence, science is itself an adventure, an expedition whose purpose is to discover the workings and wonders of the world. Art and architecture, health care, food production, and global communication as well as advancements in transportation, education, and human understanding, all derive from Western civilization's ride upon the mighty currents of human ingenuity, science, and technology.

By now, however, it is apparent that in the midst of astonishing advancements in human culture there are severe pathologies. The symptoms of those mental and spiritual pathologies, obvious throughout modern society, in cities, families, schools, and the media, challenge the notion of just what we mean by human progress, quality of life, issues of the heart and soul. In fact, no symptom more glaringly demonstrates the irony of this contradictory achievement than the fact that our species has so successfully thrived, adapted, and overrun the globe that the planet's very health—and ours—is severely threatened by our handiwork.

The point of Russell Means's story is not to dismiss the important advances of human resourcefulness or to advocate the return to an idyllic, romanticized past. His meaning is to remind us of things that we once knew—about humility and hubris, about harmony, separateness, and the place of humans in the world, and about the limitations of reason when looking for God. It is obvious to me, looking back at my life, that one of the most persistent tensions in trying to understand the universe is the predominant scheme that divides the universe between the material and spiritual, the body and soul, the seen and unseen—and our species' handing over to science all authority on what is and is not. I, too, have spent years looking to empirical evidence, to the outward signs drawn and quartered by our senses, to let me know what to believe and what to leave behind.

What is needed now, in this era when the profusion of knowledge has far outpaced the marination of wisdom, is a new way of seeing the world, one that melds the perceptions of past visions with the trained eye of modern explorations. Central to this is the need to reconnect, to find ourselves at home again *in* the land, and then to understand what that world, that creation has to say about a Creator.

Most of the world's religions look back to a lost and cherished age, a mythical, Edenic period—a time out of time—characterized by a more intimate union with God. The story of life on earth, then, is a story of a separation from God, of an estrangement, of a fallen race wandering in the desert, of a journey back to God, toward a reuniting, a reunion, a redemption. And what guides that return, that journey back to the eternal are improbable and enigmatic moments of clarity—fleeting signs and flashing revelations, epiphanies, illuminations, *satori*. And faith. This ancient story, retold in culture after culture, is even more relevant today for a human race whose pursuit of material, temporal gods has led it out worthwhile but ultimately unfulfilling tangents. Or whose migration has left God and the promised land behind, and frighteningly damaged.

That reunion with nature's inherent spirit *is* the coming home, I realize now. And that ancient truth is that the universe is a path, a way, a poem, a book revealing its Author's touch, and a route to the sacred not obscured by artificial human constructs—cities and shopping centers, suburbs, parking lots, billboards, highways, and industrial "parks." It is significant, I think, that the deterioration of our species' psychological and spiritual health has coincided with its gradual separation from and exploitation of the earth. A restoration of the human spirit, individually and culturally, will depend upon our reestablishing bonds with the landscape, by recognizing that we belong to it, not that the universe belongs to us.

We do still reach for connections to the natural world around us. We bring plants into our homes; we adorn offices and building interiors with greenery. We tend lawns, manicure flowerbeds, and plant gardens. And we are snapped out of our ruts by the call of a bird, the fists of a storm, the colorful bloom of a sunset. We admire the moon, canoe rivers, stroll beaches, gaze at stars, picnic in parks, hike through trees, and fish mountain streams. We do all this for pleasure, in appreciation of the world's natural wonder, to savor the beauty and order and elegance of nature.

But we do it, too, I think, because of an intuitive desire to connect with those places, to find solace in the exquisite and irrepressible life forms, and to embrace a world flooded with rightness and authenticity. We do it, I think, because of some internal desire for a relationship, to touch some elemental Other, to appease some subconscious longing for that reality we cannot see. "The comfort we need," Bill McKibben once wrote while watching the Perseids from the Adirondacks, "is inhuman." So the moon, the sun, the garden's very soil beckon us. Something in us responds to something in the rocks and trees, the mountains and the rivers, fields of grass, the soaring hawk, a liquid seascape, the Perseids. If nothing else, it is the spirit liberated from the confines of human enterprise.

I knew all this once, years ago—some things learned by playing on the land, others gathered from books and walks and conversation. But I, too, had forgotten—with life passing, with the daily drumming and distractions, job and family deserving my attention, getting lost while growing up. So it was not until these recent years, living alone in a cabin in the woods, that these truths all came together, that tangled meanings became clear, that I realized the comfort I needed was inhuman.

Somewhere in the backstretch of my life the race was lost, the purpose covered over, the accumulations gone. My life broke in two. But I moved into this cabin in the woods, with this pond and stream and rolling countryside all to myself. Exile and retreat. Just time to remember and time to gather, to explore the interior landscapes, and to catch those notes falling down around me, like leaves in autumn, fireflies on a summer's night. Recollecting themes and things from times when I was younger. Gathering stones along the way. Then to get them all down once and for all, for myself and maybe for my sons. A journal of rediscovery. Things I should not have forgotten. Things I want them to know. Fulfilling a promise made when I was 17.

I do not know if I would have been a better person had I lived on the water all my life. I do know I would have felt closer to the soul of things—and would have *had* a better life—had I lived for long in this cabin by the pond, had there been less between me and this geography of the soul. But there was so much to get in the way, to distract, to clutter my field of vision, to block the direct experience.

Still embedded in us are those ancestral genes, that lingering, nagging sense that there is something more, something nurturing, sustaining, liberating in the landscape. Years ago I first put my feet to the

Back to Earth

trail in search of what that is. I would head out, walking and listening and looking and touching and thinking, going after God. For years that seemed so important. For decades I forgot what all was at stake. I am fortunate to have made this turn in my life to remember back and try to reconnect.

Kerry Temple

5

The earth never tires,
The earth is rude, silent, incomprehensible at first, Nature is
  rude and incomprehensible at first,
Be not discouraged, keep on, there are divine things well envelop'd,
I swear to you there are divine things more beautiful
  than words can tell.

—*Walt Whitman*

I don't know how it is that a piece of landscape enters the blood, but I know it happens. I was 19 when I stood on the scrub-brush flanks of the Chisos Mountains in southwest Texas and looked south across the parched khaki skin of Mexico. I could see the razor edge of the planet. The hazy, falling-off horizon. And all around me the gnarly mesquite trees and rattlesnakes and prickly pear cactus. A delicate, self-contained microuniverse of grasses and grasshoppers, long-tailed lizards and squawking jays. And my eyes climbed from that igneous rock shelf across the scorched expanse of earth and into the sky. That was my first time. The stony landscape was for-ever changed.

Since that luminous moment there have been other times—wrapped in the stone-cold intimacy of a steep-walled canyon, struck by a sudden cast of light in a place that is big and wild and empty—when I had a sense of coming home to the land. Like that secluded cove tucked along the coast of Michigan's Upper Peninsula where some alchemist's blend of sunlight and cliff and the clear, crashing waters of Lake Superior caught me by surprise and held me there. Or

Wyoming's Big Horn Mountains, whose frosted sawtooth peaks first appeared to me as a mirage after I'd driven 3 days west on Interstate 90 across the hot flats of mid-America in the sweat of summer. I was so taken with the mountains' cold beauty and wild grace that I stopped and stayed two years, working for a little newspaper and exploring the heights that first drew me there.

Sometimes the kinship is immediate; often it comes in time. You find a good spot and go back until a relationship deepens. The plains of South Dakota, endlessly sweeping sky to sky, are like that for me. The place is so vast and seemingly uneventful, littered with billboards and tourist spots—Wall Drug and Reptile Gardens, Bear Country USA and the Corn Palace in Mitchell—that it wasn't until I took to the two-lanes, spent time on the reservations, then later slung on a pack and went into the backcountry hollows and hills that its genius settled into me. So, too, some woolly pockets in the boundary lands of Canada just north of the Great Lakes where my family vacationed for years. Some flashing moment, some ineffable presence, some memory of moose or stars or the ceremony of a sunrise brings a personal attachment to a corner of the universe that momentarily effloresces, yet remains untamed, and somehow far beyond us.

Of course, getting there is not always easy. Even those revelatory moments that seem to bloom immediately, spontaneously, require a certain preparation, some internal journey, or at least a faith-filled openness—which is not often easily attained, especially in our shuttered culture. But every homecoming requires some travel, and sometimes the beauty of the landing is proportionate to the arduousness of the flight.

When I stood on that perch in the gristly Chisos Mountains of southwest Texas, it was with rubber legs and rawbone shoulders. My boots had carved flaming notches into my feet and my throat was raspy dry. We had been rationing water in this dusty space, insufficiently, while winding our way higher and farther and wearier. But the view at my feet, as my toes overhung the promontory ledge, stirred an act of renewal. "We get our power," Jim Harrison once wrote, "from the beauty we love most." So as fatigue and stiffness settled into my legs, I learned something about spiritual sustenance, and how far is a mile, and the base importance of food. And how places look different to those who've walked far enough along.

Kerry Temple

I have driven into Yosemite Valley and stood on both the north and south rims of the Grand Canyon, and gazed from the scenic overlook at the proud, craggy spires of the Tetons. But I have hiked in none of these places, so don't know them really, cannot say I've seen them, can claim no kinship with their power—except to say that it is all one big thing: the mountains and plains, canyons and seacoasts, earth and sky and me. So I know something of their power. I have caught glimpses, to paraphrase Melville, of the face behind the mask. And I learned there are different ways of seeing and different ways of knowing, and that the landscape keeps secrets with those who listen.

We decided to stay the night atop that lofty headland, sleeping bags tossed upon the ground. The wind blew all night long, herding the wondrous stars right across the full-moon sky. The streetlamp moon was so bright we could read each other's faces, could peer out upon the softly subdued landscape, keeping a wary eye out for snakes and scorpions and tarantulas. We were novice campers then, so I was jittery about extending any warm-blooded flesh beyond the cozy confines of my Coleman bag. Early on, the distant wailing of coyotes and the up-close skitterings of ground animals made me antsy. I stayed alert to the wind sounds rustling through the dried brush and grasses. I sometimes held my breath and listened closely, trying to determine what manner of interloper might be approaching.

I slept that way through most of the night, keen to the soundings of that desert landscape. I would doze and awaken, noticing the shifts in wind, the flight of the hot-air-balloon moon, the gradual scrolling of what few constellations I know. The rises and ravines glittered, too—moonlight bouncing off some metallic ore that reflected light. These eerily glowing eyespots, the legends said, had gotten mixed with tales of Apache ghosts haunting these parts, still protecting their territory from the miners, soldiers, and opportunists coming here. So like a nervous sentry, I watched the moonshadow surroundings and cocked my ears like antennae to detect any danger lurking about.

I don't know at what time the calm came, breaking through the restlessness; but I remember waking once and having a sense that most of the night was behind me. I lay back then and looked up at the stars, the indiscernible spinning of the vast and glorious universe, and felt my body relax, as if the witching hour had passed and I could come to rest there on the breast of that gentle mountain. I could

Back to Earth

imagine then that the earth itself had just exhaled, come to rest, lay back to pass the night in easy repose. So we lay together. And the sounds, which I had been trying so hard to distinguish, to decipher, came together as one voice, in concert, one symphony of earth tones—the cosmic lullaby, the music of the spheres. And I was immersed in that nighttime serenade, the sound waves rolling over me like oceanic tides, drifting me off to sleep.

In the days that followed we made a playground of those arid spaces, for no pilgrimage should be incessantly solemn, but must be leavened with whimsy and sport and merriment. After all, creation itself can be playful, mirthful, clownish. Animals can be comical. River otters frolic; polar bears have been watched sledding down icy knolls on their buttocks while holding their sharp-claw toes. So we—4 rookie campers chasing after fun—took off on our great adventure, laughing at our inadequacies, joking about our unskilled ways, eating out of cans, playing with fire, splashing in the Pecos, swimming naked in the Rio Grande, cliff-diving at the Amistad Reservoir outside of Del Rio. We were out on the land, young and bare-backed and full of joy.

I remember how it felt when we'd left the human stuff behind, how big the land felt, how big the sky, how full our laughter. I remember driving through the middle of the night. Headlight glare on the two-lane blacktop, dotted line pulsing yellow, distant stars overhead, and radio stations coming to us in Spanish, or from Kansas City, Terlingua, and El Dorado, staticky voices and wavery music, a whole exotic universe full of wayfaring calls and anthems and sing-along choruses. The road ran straight and fast into darkness, no end in our imagination. We basked in our carefree disconnection, the anonymity of being nowhere and anywhere, buying beer at a shabby cantina in Boquillas del Carmen, just across the border. It doesn't get any better than this, better than sitting in the desert, campfire, and stars, sleeping bag tossed out on the ground, telling jokes, drinking beer, talking about girls and triumphs and trials and all the wondrous places your own particular roads would lead.

Something happened out there, in those days of running loose in the rugged terrain of southwest Texas, mostly car-camping, expanding the concentric circles of our teenaged lives. I don't know if it happened to anyone else, but it happened to me. I am not sure when it did. Maybe that translucent day on the ledge of the Chisos Mountains. Maybe that night when I slept with the earth. Maybe that late afternoon in Santa Elena Canyon.

The canyon is a work of the Creator's art. A cleft in the earth. Narrow. Sun stopping. Staggeringly deep. Steep, sheer walls immediately flanking the muddy Rio Grande. Twin walls that seem to lean toward each other as they mount to the sky. The sky just a thin blue ribbon high overhead. Wispy clouds passing like wraiths through the telescopic viewfinder. The water runs cool in the shadows here. Green reeds and grasses protrude from the rocks. Your neck will crane in awe, till it aches.

We had come to this cool, shaded sanctuary late one afternoon after a day in the searing sun. It was a welcomed refuge, and I waded alone upriver some and found a tongue of moist sand where I stretched out on my back to gaze above. The faint tinkling of the water soothed me and my breathing slowed and, after a few more moments, my eyelids grew heavy.

I must have slept then on that little beach. When I awoke I was flat on my stomach, my cheekbone pressed to the ground, and my fingers were clenched into the dirt, having gripped fistfuls of wet sand into the palms of my hands. Embarrassed at having napped there while the others were off exploring, I got to my feet, looked quickly around, wiped the grit from my hands and hair, and went to find my friends, . . . glancing back over my shoulder once to where my body had made an imprint in the sand.

Years later, reading this passage from Stephen Graham's *The Gentle Art of Tramping*, I thought of that time in Santa Elena Canyon: "And as you sit on the hillside, or lie prone under the trees of the forest, or sprawl wet-legged on the shingly beach of a mountain stream, the great door, that does not look like a door, opens."

During these weeks and months and years alone in the cabin, I have looked back at my life and been reminded of the first time I sensed "the great door" had opened. I remember back to my teenage years, to the tumult of adolescence, to the surly, angered growing up that invokes the clashing of powers, generational and new. I was 17 and I felt hemmed in by conformity and expectations, the gentlemanly customs and culture of the Louisiana South, the city life of middle-class compliance. Bristling and restless, wick burning, fuse lit,

I felt miserably alone, yet not. There were others—Jimmy, Stuart, and Mitch—who wanted out, too, who could not wait to get out of there, who burned then with the same universal rebellion.

So we played at rambling, taking off, heading out, running away, adventuring, but almost always home by curfew. Our games took us to ever-widening fields and places wilder than the last. Out past the city parks and schoolyard playgrounds, to the woods surrounding town, to the weedy pond where we swam and out to Bayou Pierre, where we waded in its marshy flanks, chasing through cotton fields, daring to play on the train trestle that spanned a deep ravine, dropping rocks and spitting through the cross-ties, lying flat between the rails, accepting dares to stand closer, closer still, to the rumbling, thundering boxcars until you could feel their *whoosh* right in your face, and the creosote and oil and iron smoked your nostrils. We ambled through pecan groves (helping ourselves to the fallen nuts whose meat tasted woody and fine), tormented coiled and angry snakes, played hide-and-seek, spied on the raggedy shanties of Louisiana's hand-me-down blacks. We romped free in the outskirts of our gobbling, swelling city, out beyond the gaze of cautious, warning-voiced adults, out beyond the watch of other teens who might think us childish and weird. Then the two-lanes took us farther—into Texas and Arkansas where we explored pine forests and red-clay hills and little-town grocery stores and diners, talking to the fire-watchers alone in their towers, the old men sitting on shabby, threadbare porches. Weekends on the run, joying in our newfound independence and mobility, the exhilaration of cars, the gritty soul of the vagabondish rural South. We just wanted out. Mostly we went to Red River.

The river is slow and shallow and thick, terra cotta in color. It slides past sandbars and flats, coursing waywardly through the flat delta country, home to cotton fields and lazy cows and all manner of bugs and snakes and ground animals like opossum, coons, and squirrel. We could drive quickly out of town, veering off the asphalt, heading out a dirt road cleaving symmetric rows of crops, trying not to raise that telltale plume of dust—wanting not to be followed, on back toward the levee where barbed wire fences stopped our car's advance. We would then tuck the car into concealing brush and slip through the fence, disappear over the levee, and hope not to be noticed. Then we would be on our own, venturing into the sun-bathed countryside, feeling liberated and alive and free from the stuff left behind.

It was out there one day, early spring, the tree leaves still that apple-green color and rustling in the coolish winds, when something happened. A day when the stuff left behind was especially troubling, had *not* been left behind, a day when the anger and turmoil of being 17 had the better of me—the way it does when you are young and willful and full of feeling and desire, when the combustible turbulence inside whirs mad as cornered badgers. I went apart from friends. I went on my own. I went to have a talk with whomever or whatever is out there, hiding atop the sky. Mainly I knew I wasn't happy, despite all the reasons I had to be happy. And I knew too, despite meeting all the criteria set out for me, that I felt hollow, vacant inside. That those achievements, the direction of my life till then had not made me happy. And that the sheltering comforts of middle-class living had not satisfied, had only made me restless.

So I walked and thought, wading in the river, floating some in the warm currents. In time I sat on a sandbar, my fingers playing in the sand, digging into the powdery, sun-bleached sand. And it occurred to me—as my fingertips dug deeper, squeezing handfuls of moist, cool, gritty earth, pulling it up from the riverbed, sifting it through my fingers—that I felt alone and alien from all that surrounded me. And I thought about that loneliness and that emptiness and that isolation and, as I thought about things, my fingers sifted the sand—sands of time and flow, permanence and impermanence, the direct touch of the earth. And I realized that what I had tried till then had not worked, had not brought me peace or contentment, and I asked—whom or what I do not know—for something somehow to show another way.

It seemed then—after awhile—as if shafts of sunlight broke through clouds bathing the landscape in a shimmering light—that the air changed and the landscape changed, and I could see more clearly, more vividly than ever before. As I sat, hands playing in the sand, it was as if a lens had been placed before my eyes to provide a cleaner, sharper vision, to reveal a truer place. It was indeed as if a doorway opened, leading right into the landscape and away from the structures of human commerce. Toward the primordial elements of creation.

What I felt then, as wind rustled in the sunlight-splashed leaves, was the symphonic hush of the earth. I heard the harmonies and

Back to Earth

detected the flow, the balance of all things one. I sensed the beauty of that interrelatedness, the dance of many parts. That is how it started; that was my born-again moment. And that is when I made the deal: vowing to tell others about it, to write about the findings, if I could be shown the way. And that is when I began collecting souvenirs—pieces of driftwood and bone, the sun-bleached skull of a cow, an old, weathered panel from a wood crate marked "SARDINES."

I knew then, could feel it inside, that answers and meanings resided somehow in the land itself, in the air and sky and in the very wonders and nubby particles of God's creation. That was the answer and that was the meaning—going directly to the source, the very things God had put into this world, not the human constructs interpreting and corrupting it all. And I began to see how much truth and meaning had been inscribed into the little dramas of nature—how the irrepressible riot of singular life forms mysteriously translate anarchy into order and symmetry, how bees come only when the flowers are blooming, how the prettiest skies are those left clean after storms have passed, how the landscape is transformed by the changing cast of light, and how powerful is the water humbly seeking a lower place, how trees, the stars, the seasons show ways to live a virtuous life, how right it is to bend, hold fast, let go.

But I learned, too, that the experience itself is fleeting, that the luminous moment doesn't last, the blossom fades. And it's those in-between times that leave you looking for more, even questioning the experience itself—caught, I would later learn, between the prayers of South Dakota and the true-false tests of Ellesmere Island. Still, I tried to have those experiences as often as I could, and for each to last as long as it would.

As the years went by, I sometimes wondered about that time on the sandy banks of Red River, would question what really happened. I would spend years looking for other doorways, other portals. That has been my affliction: I am an eager apprentice whose good intentions turn like a weather vane in wind. Those peak experiences of clarity and light have given way to the interrogation of reason and the erosive forces of doubt. Distractions have gotten in the way. Life's currents and whirlpools have carried me along. I stopped trusting the directions I was given because the light changed and what once appeared embedded in stone became indecipherable, etched in water, inscribed in cryptic shadows.

But I remember, during these middle years alone, recalling that moment in the sand of Red River, the retreat into the depths of Santa Elena Canyon, that there are answers to be heard—though for years I forgot how to listen, or lost my way, or was looking elsewhere when they came. So the great door stopped looking like a door, and faith did not come easy, even for one who wanted badly to believe.

I remember in the early days of that trip to Big Bend, as we were lunging into the land, how struck I was by the bewildering beauty. I had never seen a place so big. I had never seen light so grand. I had never known anything so wild. But I had a sense that it was all *out there* somewhere—a vista, a view, something to be looked at and admired. I felt apart from it, disconnected. And it—the landscape—seemed coolly distant and inaccessible, opaque, unfathomable, indifferent to me who had come as an intruder looking for signs.

Yearning for what I had found in the powdery sand of Red River, I can remember feeling anxious with desire early in the trip, as if I wanted somehow to get closer, to be given sure, clear signs, to have visions. I remember feeling, even when I stood in the midst of that scruffy desert, that it was all too far away. And somehow impenetrable, inaccessible.

But something happened over time during those days of play upon the land, and I don't know if *I* changed or if the landscape was somehow transformed. But eventually—when I had finally forgotten to seek it, when I had leaned on the rock until I could feel its divinity and had climbed out of the pit of myself and man—I felt like the preacher in John Steinbeck's *The Grapes of Wrath* who says he doesn't have a soul. He says his soul is part of the one big soul of the universe. And so it was. It all became—slowly, quietly—somehow different to me; I saw more than rock and radiance and crackling vegetation. The land had gotten into my blood. Without me looking, when I was no longer expecting it, I was no longer apart.

I don't know how it is that a piece of landscape enters the blood, but I know it happens. And I think that when it does, it is a blessing. It comes as grace to the unsuspecting heart, after the brain lets go, and the pilgrim ceases seeking, but sleeps upon the sand. Though it is gone too quick. Is a seductive flirtation that leaves you looking for more. Leaves you wondering what just happened. Is difficult to explain to others, unless they have been there themselves.

I don't know how it is that a piece of landscape enters the blood, but I know it happens. These years living alone by the pond have reminded me of that long-forgotten power.

Kerry Temple

6

The elemental simplicities of wilderness travel were thrills not only because of their novelty, but because they represented complete freedom to make mistakes. The wilderness gave them their first taste of those rewards and penalties for wise and foolish acts which every woodsman faces daily, but against which civilization has built a thousand buffers. . . . Perhaps every youth needs an occasional wilderness trip, in order to learn the meaning of this particular freedom.

—*Aldo Leopold,* A Sand County Almanac

We were 19 that summer—two "flatlanders," as they say—and we had flown to Denver and had walked right out of the airport terminal, backpacks only, and stuck out our thumbs. We had wanted to see mountains, had set our aim on Rocky Mountain National Park, but would take wherever the rides might ferry us. So when we stepped out of Mac's rusted, white sedan and spun full-circle, having wound around in those bounteous, big, green-tree-covered mountains for hours, Duff and I exulted, knew we were probably higher than we'd ever been in our lives. On top of the world it seemed—though we would not see that snowy range (or another human being) for almost a week.

What I remember was the green trees, whole, big mountains covered with green trees, and the blue sky and the big, green-tree-covered mountains spearing right up into that sky. And I remember Mac pulling off the dirt road—a logging road perhaps—on top of a bald ridge. And we got out of the car. And I remember how cold the air felt—thin mountain air, chilled and clean—and how it seemed then as if we had somehow arrived. That we'd made it, Duff and me. The thumping wild heart of Colorado. I had never felt air that free before, and it was all around me, wrapping me into its chilled, clean self, smelling sweet when I sucked it through my nostrils. And I remember the sun shining on everything, making it all warm, too.

And there was Mac pointing and Duff and me looking and Mac saying, "See those snow-capped peaks?"—and we did see them then, though we hadn't till he pointed them out—"Well, that's Rocky Mountain National Park. Just walk north and you'll get there in a few days." And I remember—still—how those shining summits looked: rock-rugged and forbiddingly distant, fortress-like and princely, cloud-feathered, almost celestial, like a stone-spired Valhalla beckoning. That's where Mac dropped us off and drove away. On a bald ridge. Staring at a destination that seemed far away, almost illusory, hovering out beyond the viewfinder wedge in the foliated mountains before us. No map, no trail, no tent, no stove, no clue—undaunted, free, not a worry between us.

What I remember is how heavy the packs felt—edgy straps grating the soft muscle between shoulder-bone and neck—with a 10-day supply of *canned* food—beef stew, chili, peaches and pears, tuna, deviled ham. And what an ordeal it was tramping cross-country, bushwhacking, lugging canned food, inner compass stuck on north, the terrain herding us astray. And how Duffey's feet bled—soles ground raw as skinned meat—because his boots were new and cheap and ill-fitting. And how it either rained or snowed on us every day, keeping firewood soggy, our canned food cold, our gear and clothes soaked, our tentless, trembling nights miserable. I recall the wandering, the steep grade—both up and down—of snarled mountainsides, vast mountains stacked like a repeating array of giant barricades thwarting our progress, providing—even on ridgetops—no vista, no view of our objective, not even an indication of advancement, or road, or trail. The cloud-filled sky hiding the sun in its path, leaving us unsure of north or west or east or where we'd been—two bugs in a swallowing sea of grass, each blade its own tiresome journey.

We did come upon a wooden cabin once, but it was locked and boarded up—although its slatted porch provided something of a shelter from a daylong downpour. We huddled there, wrapped tightly, shivering together, taking turns reading to each other from a paperback collection of John Steinbeck stories. I can still bring back the aching fatigue and the constant hunger, dreading nightfall and the look of dark clouds, and the thirst, and how hard it was—wanting water—to decipher between the rain and the distant call of a rushing stream and the sound of wind in the trees. But we did not complain. Not about feet or fatigue or the land and all its peevish elements.

We did argue over the last peach in the can and who got to drink the juice and whether the shared can of chili would be eaten cold or cooked and how the petty angers would erupt when one or the other of us struggled to ignite a fire, coaxing pyramids of damp twigs, totems to heat and warmth and cooked food, conscious to ration matches, watching little tongues of flame show promise, smoke, and contagion, only to sparkle, whither, and fade, pinestraw embers curling, emitting trails of cold smoke in the cold, dank mist surrounding us. Sunlight gone from the day, abandoning us to the cold mountain world.

One night the rains drove us to bed without eating. I made a kind of lean-to with my rain poncho, fastening it over me with rocks and log, tucked into the lap of a boulder on the side of a forested hill. I had beaten Duffey to the "good spot," leaving him to scrounge for cover among little pines, using only a tattered sheet of thin plastic Mac had given us when he learned we had no tent. Duff, ignoring the relentless rainfall, went to great and patient lengths to set up his little fort, positioning rocks and sticks to secure the makeshift rain fly, giving him room underneath to survive another night.

It was the lightning that woke me—an electric explosion whose flash sizzled and scorched the tree trunks around us. The clapping arrival of a storm rocking the heavens. The roaring of wind, the wind whipping our covers, driving the rain right into our faces. The deafening, percussive thunder reverberating off rock and canyon wall, filling our ears, echoing drum-like out over the landscape. Booming Olympian timpani. And lightning striking and me clenched to the earth, clinging to all my gear, my poncho a snapping, whipping sail cut loose from its moorings. *We're too high*, I thought, *too close to the sky*. I was holding on, afraid of the ferocity, of being 12,000 feet closer to the sky than I'd ever been, praying for the battle to subside. And I remember Duffey, a barrage of mutterings punctuated with the growls of

"*Goddamnit!*" and "*Shit!*" as he grappled with his wind-ripped shelter, as his plastic broke loose and danced away on the wind, leaving him fully exposed, eventually drenched, his raggedy tarp never seen again.

But the sunrise was clear and the sky was again blue and, after waking stiffly, pulling ourselves together, and ambling uphill half the morning, there were snow-laden crests just ahead, fresh and virgin-white, visible through the furry pines wet with glassy, glistening droplets. Rainbow spectra when you stopped to look very close. I remember stopping, resting, sitting in the sun, leaning back against pack and tree, and grinning at Duffey grinning.

That's what I remember about that time in the Colorado Rockies—that life was an adventure daring us to live it that way. I remember feeling so young and free, discovering what a playground the world is, the heady exuberance of that discovery, how creation flung open its doors to those who banged for entrance. And the sun breaking through the curtainy fleets of grey clouds and how the landscape lit up then and how the sun burned on my face, air scraped clean by wind-shear. And then emerging from trees, finally stepping lightly above the timberline, where you could see the alpine meadows and grassy fields and stony mountaintops all around, and a trail to follow, and that night giving up on the campfire but watching a clan of deer graze nearby, oblivious to us watching, unaware of our presence.

We finally mounted the crest, topping the saddle between summits, heading up over the Continental Divide, reaching the goal of our weeklong trek. And then, arriving at the top, being engulfed in snow—white-out, blizzard, zero visibility—and laughing at the farcical irony of it all—dodging the impetuous gods' thunderbolts and storms, withstanding the deluge, navigating their obstacle course, taking whatever they dished out. Laughing at the human comedy.

We had come here for some inarticulate reason, either pulled or compelled, college boys wanting something, looking for something, maybe only an adventure, testing ourselves, maybe holding out the hope of finding ourselves, and finding those selves descended from explorer, mountain man, seafarer, pioneer, pilgrim. Their blood in ours. Maybe, really, just looking for some fun. College boys, we had had enough of mental exercise, the regimens of schooling, the ghosts of theory and talk, the tedium of preparation for a life not yet being lived.

Kerry Temple

So in the midst of our studies, we looked up from our books, and wrote down the words of Herman Melville: "As for small difficulties and worryings, prospects of sudden disaster, perils of life and limb; all these, and death itself, seem to him only sly, good-natured hits, and jolly punches in the side bestowed by an unseen and unaccountable old joker. . . . There is nothing like the perils of the wilderness to breed this free and easy sort of genial, desperado philosophy."

And Bernard of Clairvaux: "Believe us who have experience, you will find much more laboring amongst woods than ever you will amongst books."

So inspired, the words of poets and thinkers singing in our blood, thumb-tacked to the walls where we dreamed, we went to the land. Partly what we found was not a sense of conquest or triumph over nature or the elements as much as belonging—proving we belonged. We had come to the mountains. As novice packers, we had entered the landscape to experience it firsthand, to do it right, on *its* terms, and—so tested—we had found ourselves there.

We had seen, in the absence of mirrors, away from the defining context of our lives, something true of ourselves, of the light shining in us. I maybe saw myself, as a member of the world, for the very first time. In his book *Travels* Michael Crichton explains: "Stripped of your ordinary surroundings, your friends, your daily routines, your refrigerator full of your food, your closet full of your clothes—with all this taken away, you are forced into direct experience. Such direct experience inevitably makes you aware of who it is that is having the experience. That's not always comfortable, but it is always invigorating."

What I remember, too, is Mac picking us up that first Sunday when we'd grown weary of too-short rides and paved highways. I remember his last name was McGowan and he said to call him Mac and he said do not worship nature for it is only the face of God, not God itself. And he took us for a drive and pointed us north, and in the meantime took us fishing and touring around, higher and higher, deeper and deeper into the woodsy mountains. He found us a trout stream and showed us how to fly-cast, where to look for fish, how to clean them. We hopscotched down the tumbled stones lodged in sharp-tasting mountain-stream waters, sunlight splashing off the waterway, joying in the hunt, mostly watching Duff and Mac fish, the slippery, wiggling bounty cold and slick to the grip, me just playing. Mac gave Duff some fishing line and a bottle of salmon eggs and as the days circled by he got better at catching little ones, though all nearly futile to cook up and eat. But I remember how green the grass looked that day, how brilliant the flowers, how I'd never seen the world so bright and clear.

It got that way again, days later, after the rainy season when precipitation was a mountain way of life. The world shone bright and shiny again, and inspired a liberated feeling—and not just from the wet and cold but from a planned and patterned mode of living Duff and I had grown too accustomed to. I read some semesters later a passage from Victor Frankl's *Man's Search for Meaning*, and I knew exactly what he was saying and I recalled how it was those days in Colorado.

Frankl had just reentered the world after four years in a Nazi death camp and he remembered:

> I walked through the country past flowering meadows, for miles and miles, toward the town near the camp, larks rose to the sky and I could hear their joyous song. There was no one to be seen for miles around; there was nothing but the wide earth and sky and the lark's jubilation and the freedom of space. I stopped, looked around and up to the sky—then I went down on my knees. At that moment there was little I knew of myself or of the world—I had but one sentence in mind—always the same: "I called to the Lord from my narrow prison and He answered me in the freedom of space."

That's exactly how it felt those days above the timberline in Rocky Mountain National Park. The freedom of space. It had about it that chest-swelling, yipping, yawping, liberating kind of feeling that makes you want to wrap your arms around it, or at least to scream a thank-you at the sky. I remember that feeling and I remember a deep, clear pool of mountain water where we learned that mountain water was too cold for swimming. And a night when the risk of hypothermia seemed real, balled deep into my sleeping bag, shivering uncontrollably, and how my legs ached from being curled tight for too long, but how straightening them thrust my bare head—jack-in-the-box-style—out of my bag and into the icy, pelting rain . . . and how welcome the sunrise felt that dawn.

Kerry Temple

Once or twice we dropped packs and climbed the rocks and cliffs just for the fun of it. Climbing, scaling higher on up the ladder-like ledges till the handholds were only knuckle-deep and the footholds the depth of my toes, and how it felt to look down, little stones crumbling away and falling, falling, and how scary it was then, my knees shaking, trembling, not bearing up well under my weight and my fear. Fingertips sweating. Body pressed against rock and traitor moss. But making it to the top anyway. Then having to go back down.

And one day, late afternoon, we found a place to camp and dropped packs and started sloshing and skidding up a glacier, an ice field, tossing ice balls at each other, skiing or sliding down aways on our butts, then climbing up even higher. We were on the eastern slope of a giant ridge and the sun dipped over the brim, leaving us in shadow but determined to go on, to make it to the top, almost racing, dodging the snowballs flung in our direction. Duffey was the first to get off the snow-cone slush, scooting around the glacier's edge and heading over pointy scree on up to the top. I got breathless chasing him, so slowed my pace and followed, pausing occasionally to look around, measuring my steps. I stopped short when I saw him step to the rim.

He was bathed in rosy sunlight; his gaze was to the west. The wind blew through his whipping hair; he had a smile upon his face. He was a diminutive figure made large by the stature of his surroundings, stunned into silence and stillness by the vision at his feet. Soon I joined him and had the vision, too. The sun was radiant low in the west, and everywhere in every direction there were mountaintops and snowy-crested peaks, a grand, unpeopled wilderness as far as the eye could see, awash in rose-sunlight and long-shadow, the universe at our feet. We stayed there till the sun went down, till it slipped behind the lip of earth that was purplish, jagged, and cold. The wind gusted up, sailing swift across the land, chilling us in our T-shirt skin, pores still open from our chase up the glacier.

Going down we somehow got separated, hopping rocks, no straight course. Duffey was out of sight and twilight was darkening, and I stopped on the lower edge of a talus slope I had descended till I reached a meadow rolling downhill steep as a schoolyard slide. There were truck-size boulders and stands of trees and a world in the hush of day. I surveyed my surroundings and gauged my way back home and, as I strode heavy-booted downhill, came around a stand of aspen and stumbled—surprised—into a small band of deer.

They, too, started in fright—eyes wide in wonder—and broke off away from me, fleeing madly, darting, bounding, and leaping downhill. So I also took flight, racing to catch up, following their bobbing white tails. Graceful creatures, fleet, nimble, and strong. Predator and prey. Playing tag together—till they flew into another herd just emerging from another copse of trees. Then another mad dash was on. Me behind in gleeful, clumsy pursuit, my legs flying downhill nearly out of control, my arms flailing like propellers in the air, me running faster than I could, till they had all disappeared from sight—not a warning-signal tail in view.

But as I walked on, feeling more urgent about the descending dusk and food, pressed by fatigue, I again walked into the midst of deer and together we all ran again—close enough this time to watch their flanks leap and the elegant thrill of their gait, the white softness of their muscular rumps, the quick-turn precision of their swift step. We ran that way for a little while, till they evaporated, leaving me far behind—slow-footed *Homo sapiens* rubber-legged, light-headed, winded, chest pounding. But for those few minutes, perhaps seconds only, I felt close to a beauty, finger-touch-close to a beauty so elemental, so alive, so holy I could nearly taste it. I had run with a pack of deer and I could smell the earthy fragrance.

That is what I remember about that time in Colorado, and this final thing, too.

We had been out 9 days of the 10 we had planned and we were out of food. And the rains had returned that day and the world was heavy-laden, cold and wet. We were set on making a mountain's peak that afternoon, although I forget the name. But as we trudged along uphill, knifing through the trees, intent on traversing the timberline, our clothes and faces and hair more soggily drenched, the rains beating relentlessly, we stopped and slumped against the crusted trunks of heavy-smelling pines, sitting, facing each other, wrists resting upon our knees. *One more night,* I thought. *Even without food, I can take it one more night to make it to the top.* But as we sat there facing each other, stomachs hollow, grumbling, energy depleted, and time passing, it soon occurred to me that we were done. Spent. We discussed the pros and cons.

Kerry Temple

And while we did that I remember a man stepping lively through the trees, making his way down from the top—ice axe and gaiters and jaunty hat and shorts—a day's hike for him, roundtrip from his car. He stopped, of course, and encouraged us, telling us to move on, no reason to be sitting here. He had "summited," he said, and, while the low clouds blocked any kind of view, it was important not to stop, push on; we could make it—if we hustled—to the top by dark. I do not remember Duff or me responding, saying any word, but staring straight ahead.

But when he had passed and gone his way and we figured far ahead, we got up and, without saying anything to each other, followed him on back downhill. We had found what we had come for. There would be other trips ahead.

We were soon in a motel room in Estes Park, thanks to a ride we hitched, and before long had plenty of pizza, steak, and beer. We would shoot some pool and dry our clothes and shower up clean and patch up Duffey's feet. We were young then and bold, full of spirit and naive. But we were no heroes. We had simply gone to the mountains looking for something our lives hadn't had till then, something we had read about in books.

"Go fish and hunt far and wide," Thoreau had advised. "And rest thee by many brooks and hearthsides without misgiving. Remember thy creator in the days of thy youth. Rise free from care before the dawn, and seek adventures. Let the noon find thee by other lakes, and the night overtake thee everywhere at home. There are no larger fields than these, no worthier games than may here be played."

And I can remember, after eating, sitting quiet in a shadowy juke-box bar, tired and full and satisfied, ordering one more pitcher of beer. Duffey and me looking at each other, nothing left to say, a smile of recognition between us. Pride in what we had done. My legs and shoulders stiff with wear, my hands and wrists looking somehow leathered, older, thicker. Leaning back in my chair, feeling strong and sure, having taken what those days dished out and returning it with respect and laughter. Friendly sparring. The folly of our naivete. The peace that comes from exploits well ridden. The repose of those who've happily abided. In the company of mountain, rock, and cloud. And I had then—by whom or what I do not know—but I had then a strange sense of acceptance, as if I had somehow been admitted, acknowledged, initiated . . . by what or whom I still don't know.

That is what I remember of that time in Colorado, when I was young and loose and feeling happy and invincible, my life as free and pure as that mountaintop sensation, when the stone I carried away from there told of liberation and a greeting.

I have recalled those Colorado days as the years have passed. And when I do remember, I am haunted by a statement I associate with that time, the source and exact words now lost to me, although this is a close paraphrasing: *He becomes great by holding fast and true for a lifetime to those ideals that burned in his youth.* Late at night, alone in this cabin, I recall those Colorado days with Duffey, and I wonder when I traded adventure for security and comfort. Does the settling for, the settling down, come with being husband, father, provider? With the acquiring, guarding, the need for certainty? There was a time when I figured I had nothing to lose. Sometimes these days I'm thinking I already have.

Kerry Temple

7

🌿

*It is a commonplace of all religious thought, even the most
primitive, that the man seeking visions and insight must go apart
for a time in the wilderness. If he is of the proper sort, he will
return with a message. It may not be a message from the God he
set out to seek, but even if he has failed in that particular, he will
have had a vision or seen a marvel, and these are always worth
listening to and thinking about.*

—Loren Eiseley

So here we are, sailing along U.S. 89, huddled in the bed of a pickup
truck, facing backward, watching the tanned Arizona landscape whirl
by. The sky is brilliant blue; the air is October chilled. The blue plastic
tarp bundled around our backpacks is flapping, snapping in the
wind. I am young and eager. Out of college. Into the days of youthful
exploration—the Sawtooths of Idaho, the Big Horns of Wyoming,
Moab, Monument Valley, the Bitterroots, and Wind River Range. I
am loose and unencumbered, untethered and on my way to find out.
And I've gained a better idea of what I'm doing on the trail. But right
now I munch on Wheat Thins and lean back to enjoy the ride like a
footman in the company of Ponce de Leon, looking for more than silver
and gold.

Walt and I flew 2,000 miles to be here; Alex came from Pittsburgh.
We met Joe, who lives in Phoenix, and the four of us are driving toward
Utah—north out of the desert basin and into the cool piney
hills around Flagstaff, past the San Francisco Mountains upon whose
peaks the kachina gods are said to dwell, then down again out of the

sweet-smelling juniper and pine, and across the dusty desert floor. This is Navajo land, and there are mud huts and dogs and roadside stands where jewelry and blankets are sold. But mostly there is the land—red and rocky, dry and windswept—dominated by the sky, punctuated with mesas and ruddy sandstone cliffs that watch over the earth like tribal elders from long ago.

The four of us are driving to Utah for a wilderness backpacking trip, a chance to wander the desert for a few days without encountering another human being. But this escape into the land also puts us onto the trail of a great American tradition—the journey into nature for a glimpse, a footprint, or a truth. None of us would spoil the fun by saying this, but one of the reasons to walk any patch of earth is to explore the geography of the soul.

We will drive 6 or 8 more hours before getting there, this loosely collected group, bound together mostly by our desire to be here. Our destination is Zion National Park. We don't consider, as we race through the desert with rock music splashing out the windows of our truck, that ancient Zion was the spot where David built the Temple of Jerusalem. Or that Mount Zion was the point from which Mohammed is said to have ascended into heaven. Only later do we recall that in both the Old and New Testaments, Zion means heaven, God's home. Zion Canyon, in Utah, created by the Virgin River, was named by Mormon settlers in 1861. The important thing now is that we are headed into the land, and we feel free and happy and cold. And my tailbone is numb from riding too long in the bed of a pickup.

Relief comes in Page, Arizona, when we pull into the McDonald's parking lot and I stand and stretch in the noontime sun. This will be our last touch with civilization, our last chance to eat fast food, but I am glad to be heading to a blank spot on the map. Sometimes the only way to endure the banalities of life is to go and sit in the woods for awhile.

While our desire to find freedom and fun on the land is just our way of satisfying another natural impulse, we had learned in college that "going into the woods" has been an American ritual whose grace may have lured the first people across the Bering Straits thousands of years ago. Little is known of the first wanderers who waded ashore upon this hemisphere, but there is no doubt the rest of us descended from nomads—the explorers, pilgrims, and pioneers who settled this

Kerry Temple

New World. William Bradford, landing at Plymouth in 1620, may have spoken for his cohorts (half of whom died their first winter here) when he said their new home was "a hideous and desolate wilderness, full of wild beasts and wild men." But most of the new-comers saw America as a New Eden, a fresh start bestowed by God, resplendent in beauty, bounty, and seemingly infinite space. "This country, the last found," wrote Emerson, "is the great charity of God to the human race." The rhetoric of the founding fathers reflects this sense of religious mission, that America was God's own, to be a City on the Hill, a pristine paradise whose cultivation was an act of both hubris and faith.

In our national folklore and literature, in film and on television, our heroes were placed in the natural world—Davy Crockett and Daniel Boone, Jim Bridger and Jeremiah Johnson, Natty Bumppo and Chingachook, Paul Bunyan and Pecos Bill, Ahab, Ishmael, and Huck Finn. The great American cowboy. The mountain man. The pioneers of Willa Cather and Laura Ingalls Wilder. The adventurers of Melville, Conrad, and London. Hemingway's sportsmen. Hollywood's gun-slingers. The male-defining heroes, the cultural icons were singularly independent souls removed from human society to test their wills in untamed territory, cut loose from restraint, custom, and convention to face themselves, their foes, and the elements alone. So, too, our culture's poets and thinkers—Thoreau, Whitman, Emerson—were those who sought and found in nature the gifts of insight and truth, allegory and metaphor that helped shape our national identity. It has been common, since the first Americans—in ceremonies of one—to turn away from the company of men and women to seek visions upon the hillsides, to search the landscape for meaning, to find revelation in a sunrise, on a mountain, upon the sea.

The American paradox, of course, is that nature has been both ele-vated and subdued. While many have found there the etchings of an epic worth reading, others have seen only abundant resources placed at our disposal to be spent and fashioned as we pleased. Even the civ-ilizing of the continent was ascribed religious motives, giving us li-cense to exploit the land as raw material for human commerce and industry. The effect of that is the story of America: whole territories used up and settled, prompting the seekers to leave for the next stand of woods—until footpaths become trails, which become roads, which become highways, which start the process all over again. So Americans have been, ever since the first fouled nest, heading into the woods, both running away and running toward.

Page, Arizona, was established in 1957, when work began on the Glen Canyon Dam, an admittedly impressive sight. Glen Canyon, they say, once possessed a beauty that rivaled Grand Canyon, but now much of it is buried beneath Lake Powell, which was created by the dam, a 30-story concrete monolith across the Colorado River. The dam's tourist center boasts of kilowatt hours, the number of people who use the recreation area, and the dam's role in taming the wild and flood-prone river. But the project, as with every intrusion by man into nature, is altering the natural—in this case, the water temperature and the vegetation in the Colorado as it flows through the Grand Canyon.

It is late afternoon when we wind our way into Zion National Park. Towering cliffs surround us. The road meanders snake-like, looping in and out of sunlight and shadows. Then, like a passage into some kind of mythical kingdom, it courses through two cold, dark tunnels and emerges into a magnificent, sunlit, deep-wall canyon. The road drops down then, switching back and forth, as if lowering us into the belly of the earth. We follow the Virgin River past bristly green vegetation and a pair of mule deer nibbling leaves in a gulch along the road. We gaze up at orange cliffs, scraping the azure sky like the spires of some lofty cathedral.

We drive much slower now. The music has been turned off. The canyons have silenced us. They are made of red Navajo sandstone, laid as giant sand dunes more than 150 million years ago. The walls, sculpted by wind and water for millennia, thrust skyward hundreds of feet above us. Some of the escarpments catch the golden sunlight; others appear blue in the shadows. My neck grows stiff from staring. "Better than any church I've ever seen," Walt says, and we all have a sense that we have come face to face with Creation . . . and the One whose handprints are on the wall.

The gorge narrows. At a spot called the Temple of Sinawava (named for a wolf goddess) we stop by the side of the road. We stand there, smile at each other a little bashfully, quietly. We are immersed in the shadows of this great pit, each of us revolving full circle, staring stiff-necked at the summits. Finally Alex, holding finger to thumb,

Kerry Temple

says, "I feel about this big." The cool air smells of pine; the faint rush of wind and water is like music. No words can hold this. We are here.

☙

On Monday we are up before dawn, having slept beneath the stars, and drive to the Kolob wing of Zion; no other hikers have permits to be here. The names on the topographical map—Timber Creek, Nagunt Mesa, Shuntavi Butte, Beartrap Canyon, and Bullpen Mountain—mean little to us as we tighten the laces on our boots and recheck our backpacks.

I am always a little apprehensive when I head into the backcountry. With each step you draw farther away from the conveniences, the creature comforts, the safety nets of modern existence. All you have is carried on your back—food, shelter, bedding, clothing, pots, pans, and stove, all bundled and slung onto your shoulders.

There is a vulnerability in this exercise that is unsettling. Even on trips that are not intentionally dangerous, risks present themselves. I am no daredevil, but I can remember times when I have been stilled by fear or when the possibility of death seemed real. Even less dramatic problems become troublesome when you're miles from nowhere and relief is days away.

All this, of course, makes you feel palpably alive, a sensation rarely known in our day-to-day existence. It also nurtures humility. It doesn't take long to realize that, out here, humans are not the superior species. We are slow and weak; our senses are dull compared to those species at home here. We must carry with us the means of our survival. Being out like this, even temporarily, helps you know your place in the hierarchy of living creatures.

There is beauty in this simplicity; one sees clearly the essential things. Necessity becomes a central consideration. Sometimes an extra pair of socks goes in and a chocolate bar and flask come out; sometimes the second pair of jeans is sacrificed for another bag of granola. The clutter, the stuff of our lives is eliminated. Sometimes, I think, my species' very problem is that we have simply piled too much stuff between us and the mud where we might sink our toes, divorcing ourselves from the place of our being. Wilderness travel means going bare bones, meeting the land unadorned, accepting the pilgrim's asceticism. As the Buddhist Dalai Lama once told an American audience: "Because of obstructions, we are unable to know everything. But by removing these obstructions, it is ultimately possible to know everything."

These are the thoughts that help you put your life in order, and on the trail there is lots of time for thinking. Even Jesus went into the wilderness when he needed some time to think, to listen for voices, to confront the demons within. "Now I see the secret of making the best persons," Walt Whitman once said. "It is to grow in the open air and to eat and sleep with the earth."

We spend the morning hiking, learning anew the mirage of distance. This is the hard part: tromping along like a pack animal, staring at the ground in front, the mountains far away. My boots carve blisters into my heels; my shoulders ache. We walk uphill and down, the mountains never seeming to draw closer. You appreciate distances out here, deceiving distances. The bigness is overwhelming. So is the thick, liquid blue sky. No one talks; we walk for hours, each alone in his thoughts.

The sun is high when the dusty trail drops down to a shallow creek, a small pool, and a miniature waterfall. We stop and soak our feet in the icy water. Then we follow the trail into canyon country, turning into gorges whose walls grow taller as we go. A side canyon leads to Kolob Arch, the longest natural arch in the world.

After a lunch of tortillas and cheese, we go exploring—scrambling up rocks, following creek beds. Our excuse is to ascend to the arch which is hundreds, perhaps a thousand feet above us. But, really, we're climbing and romping like kids in a playground. Water trickles out of grey sandstone walls like magical springs, irrigating clusters of bright green ferns and mosses. Stagnant pools are full of water striders and leaves; fallen tree trunks become ladders, rocks become stairs. We play here awhile, test ourselves, then (confronting a sheer 40-foot wall) decide it's time to push on up the trail—miles to go before we stop.

The trail follows the creek throughout the afternoon, coursing through small stands of maple and oak, with giant walls above us. We find a place to spend the night and watch the darkness fall. The stars are brilliant here, away from city lights and hazy atmosphere, and we begin what becomes a nightly ritual—stargazing. Like apprentice

Kerry Temple

Druids, the four of us stare heavenward, our mouths slightly open, and contemplate the universe. Alex spots a satellite; Walt and Joe point to the same constellations that ancient mariners used as guides on their ocean voyages.

After awhile my neck and legs ache, so I flop down on my sleeping bag to watch. A few minutes later, Walt, Alex, and Joe stretch out on a boulder, their backs pressed against rock, and watch.

In time we slip into our sleeping bags and doze off, spending the night, as we did every night, under the stars, without a tent. And through each night, sleeping and waking, we would look up to see the stars moving across the sky, to spot shooting stars, to track the journey of the moon. Few activities instill a sense of wonder more plainly than stargazing. The darkness, the distances, the infinite expanse of the universe, the mysteries and measures of time, questions of beginnings and ends. Some of the stars, whose light is just now reaching our eyes, burned out long ago. Others, still twinkling brightly, were firing their light into the darkness long before Earth was formed. Confronted with the awesome, literally incomprehensible dimensions of time and space, it is easy to understand the dread sense of one's insignificance, and isolation, and to connect somehow with it all. Ties of blood and bone and pieces of soul.

On Tuesday the trail follows a shallow creek which ripples over rocks in the sharp crease of a narrow canyon. The small oaks are mostly bare, their brown leaves sometimes a crinkly carpet. The maple leaves are still yellow, a slash of brightness in the deep-wall canyon that is shaded grey and home to green tamarisk, juniper, and pinyon pine. The trail crisscrosses the stream often and we teeter under packs, lurching from rock to rock as we cross. Occasionally we stop, just to stare upward. The earth is closer to us today, more intimate than yesterday when we wandered out upon the red dirt land amid the squawbush, sage, and narrowleaf yucca.

At midmorning we are greeted by a golden eagle that swoops low over our heads. It perches before soaring off again, its wings like sails, the sunlight glinting off its shoulders. A few minutes later, as Walt and I lead around a bend, we hear a ruckus up on the left. In a flash, right in front of us, a gang of deer skitters down a small rocky hill. A large buck bounds across the creek and bolts up a steep slope to our right and into thick trees. The others—females and young—clatter down the cobblestone creek, splashing water in a mad but graceful retreat.

I am inclined, when encountering such living manifestations of nature's majesty, to join the chorus of those who proclaim this realm benign, innocent, and sweet in its holiness, as if viewing the landscape through a filtered lens. It is easy to echo the Romantic poets, who took joy in the flowered universe and who saw the sky's distant orbs as faces looking down upon the affairs of man. "The aspect of Nature is devout," wrote Emerson. "Like the figure of Jesus, she stands with bended head and hands folded upon the breast. The happiest man is he who learns from Nature the lesson of worship."

But Jesus struck other poses, too, in his life's journey. And the forces of nature can be as magnificent in their brutal and indifferent power as they are inspiring in their beauty.

I am reminded of this contradiction on this Tuesday morning as the four of us stare at a deer who lies dead at our feet. It is a grey mule deer, recently killed, although there is no blood. Its black gelatinous eyes are still moist as they gaze into space. It lies beneath a rocky cliff, its head on a rock as if on a pillow, its legs crumpled under the elegant body. We stand there for awhile and say nothing.

We will see the deer again later—with the fur and meat of its flank chewed off, the red flesh exposed, shining in the sun. In the harmonious order of things this is only right, that it become a meal for something else. This is nature's way, the delicate balance, the interweaving of life forms. Darkness and light, yin and yang. Those who seek to deify the natural world are stopped short by the storms that rage at sea or the fissures in the earth that snuff out lives without pity or care. But this is life—the cycles of time, the rhythms of the seasons, of life and light and death. It is best to find one's place in the natural order of things—under the stars, amid the flowers and ferns, the beauty, power, and frailty of flesh and bone, the ancient rocks, and the water that never stops. Acceptance brings its own kind of faith in the reality of creation; the world is a mean, mysterious, and wonderful place.

It is midafternoon when we reach a grassy meadow surrounded by towering precipices and shaded by Ponderosa pine; it will be our place for the night. It feels good to be free of our packs; the sun is high and warm. Joe pulls out a hand-drawn map that shows the way to Chasm Lake, situated on a plateau high above. The map suggests we follow a shallow wash, cut through a narrow crevice, then climb a canyon upward.

We scramble up a wooded hillside and point to where we think we should be. Then we head cross-country, improvising, calculating that, from ridge to ridge, we will find our way and connect again with the suggested route. We climb higher; the ground is steep and loose; we stop often to catch our breath. We continue on, weaving through Ponderosa pines, stepping up rocks, onto a broad, shoulder-like ridge. The western horizon lies before us; we can see for miles into the distance—where brown land meets blue sky.

"We should be over there, I think," says Joe, pointing to a vast wall of red rock to our left. A rocky ridge leads that way, but between it and the sandstone cliff is an abyss.

We follow the ridge, climbing rocky outcroppings always higher, until we come to an apex—and stop. The view is breathtaking. The Kolob Canyon area lies at our feet—bold red escarpments plunging out of the earth, green forests, red earth, and vibrant blue sky. Our eyes scan the landscape; we are silent. The wind roars freely here, strong and cold. The three of us sit for a while, staring at the world before us, and I recall the words of an old Zen saying: "When you get to the top of the mountain, keep climbing."

This is what we came for—to be at a spot like this, to feel our hearts beat, to be fatigued, sweaty, short of breath, and to have earned a place among the headlands and heights where the landscape lies before us like riches spread before kings. No matter how spectacular the view from a car or scenic overlook, it is never the same as the beauty found at the end of a climb. Somehow the scenery is transformed when you have become part of it and have transformed yourself by being there.

That night we eat a dinner of mean jalapeno spaghetti, then lean against a log and watch the stars for an hour without talking. In the darkness, somewhere in the distance, a cow moos.

On Wednesday, the cows come through. Two hundred head. Right down the middle of the canyon, trampling everything in their path, a

Back to Earth

dozen cowboys yipping and barking at their hooves. The 4 of us perch on a ledge until the coast is clear.

Every backpacking trip has a surprise—a fluke snowstorm or 3 days of rain. Our surprise on this trip is the cattle drive. The Spilsbury family has been driving its cattle down this canyon since the 1800s, moving the herd between the pasture on the plateau above the park and the pasture near Toqueville, Utah. Later that day, when we have made our camp and talk about the day's events, we know we have witnessed a vestige of the American West.

On Thursday we follow the trail back down the narrow gorges, re-tracing yesterday's advance, past the pool where three days ago we soaked our feet, then into the open hills. We trudge along, new blisters form, the sun is hot, and I am sweating. I walk without thinking, listening to the wind and my feet and the rhythmic squeak-squeak of my backpack. I do not know with whom or what, but I get this strange sense that I am in step.

Early in the afternoon we stop for a rest. I lean against a weathered log beneath a grey and gnarled old tree. Joe does the same, and Walt and Alex go scouting for water and a place to stay the night. I pull off my boots and socks, dig my toes into the powdery earth. For the first time since we set out, I have no inclination to go anywhere. I'm not eager to climb or explore or hurry around the next bend; there's nowhere else I want to be.

The sun bakes my face, and my fingers lazily sift through the dirt. They eventually extract a rock—a round golf ball of red sandstone. It feels good to my fingers—grainy but solid. I remember that day on the sandbar in Red River. Years later I would recall this moment when a Lakota holy man who handed me a small rock and said, "Understand this and you will understand it all. You do not understand it now. It is too simple. Pray for understanding."

That understanding, I eventually realized, is not a conscious thing, not an intellectual concept or a belief necessarily compatible with our scientific view, but must be an understanding of the heart. I don't know what mix of soil, sky, and sun is necessary, how many miles must be walked, or how many nights slept with the earth, before this

Kerry Temple

understanding emerges within you. But it comes on its own, when you least expect it, like grace floating down from the sky, seeping into your pores or absorbed through the soles of your feet while they pad monotonously along. And then you're sure there are ways of knowing beyond mere cognition, beyond the brain, a sense that you have touched something, or have been touched by something, though it's hard to say much more than that, sitting here among the flies and sage and the dry creek bed, waiting for Walt and Alex to tell us where we go from here.

Where we go is toward the sandstone walls, along the creek bed, into the land of the overhanging peaks as if toward an opening in the earth. As we hike in the middle of the wash, the dirt changes to mud, then the mud to water. Small pools become little streams and the stream becomes bigger, deeper, faster. All around are mountain lion tracks. We stop at the first set of prints and admire the configuration, the size. Soon the tracks become many; the cat was not just passing through. This is its place.

The wind is picking up and we head deeper into the canyon to escape its cold, swift waves; the temperature is dropping. The sun begins its descent, and we drop packs to hunt a better site. The canyon narrows, steepens; we keep climbing upstream, pulling ourselves up rocks and boulders. Gradually we realize no campsite is ahead, but there's no going back—not until we get to the end. Lion tracks are all about.

Finally, we can go no further. We stand face to face with a vast wall of rock. On the limb of a nearby tree is a hawk. Sentry, sentinel. Its eyes are fierce, its golden beak curved and sharp. It looks us in the eyes for a moment, raises its body, and lifts itself. Gently stroking its wings it breezes over our heads, then sails down over the V-cut valley and out beyond where we can see.

We stand there for awhile, as if in some sacred temple, staring up at the cliffs, watching the water trickle and the greenery waving in the wind. We stand for the longest time, too reverent to speak; then, again without speaking, we find our way out again. None of us says anything about being there; it isn't on the map.

Darkness falls on us at dinner, while we're nestled among rocks trying to stay out of the cold, strong wind. There is a slight sense of foreboding on this night—as if some danger lurks in the darkness, or at least that it will be cold sleeping.

I reach into my jeans pocket to feel the sandstone rock I found this afternoon when the sun was bright on my face. I wonder at its meaning and am reminded of the coal carried by Annie Dillard's monk: "The universe was made in solemn incomprehensible earnest by a power that is unfathomably secret, and holy, and fleet. And there is nothing to be done about it, but ignore it, or see. And then you walk fearlessly, eating what you must, growing wherever you can, like the monk on the road who knows precisely how vulnerable he is, who takes no comfort among death-forgetting men, and who carries his vision of vastness and might in his tunic like a live coal which neither burns nor warms him, but with which he will not part."

It is cold as we crawl into our bags for the last time. The sky is clear and the air is chilled. The moonglow is radiant above the black canyon cliffs, silhouettes against the midnight blue sky. The moon, which should be almost full tonight, isn't quite visible to us here in the depths of this chiseled canyon. I wonder if it will appear, and where. I wonder if the mountain lion knows we are here, and if I will be cold. I wonder how long before we forget the myth about having dominion over the nurturing earth and remember that we are but stewards, or cocreators with all whose spirit we share. But I do not wonder long; I am tired and soon asleep.

Friday is the last day. We wake before dawn, as has become our routine. In the grey morning chill the first to rise fires the stove and heats the water. We stand around, sip coffee, stamp our feet and blow into our hands, driving the shivers away. We eat bagels, granola—today, hot oatmeal. Each morning Walt has given us the word for the day: friable (the rocks), mucilaginous (the spaghetti), callipygous (surely none of us). Today's word is epiphany.

This is our last morning out, and I think we're all moving slower than usual, prolonging our stay, lingering here in the sandstone canyonlands that have become home. Slowly and deliberately, we roll up our bags for the last time, load our backpacks, pull on fresh socks for the final hike out. No one talks; we go through the motions separately, yet somehow in concert. When it's clear we're all ready, we stand a moment longer, looking around, lost in private thoughts. Then, without word or signal, the packs are hoisted onto backs, straps buckled, and we set out.

As we trundle along the final passes, I think back over the moments left behind. I remember breakfast in Beartrap Canyon, a dark, damp crack in the earth. We had set out at dawn without eating and it had taken a painful half-hour of walking for my toes to unthaw. We followed the creek upstream until we were enclosed by shelves of rock and a 25-foot waterfall. We huddled on slippery ledges matted with wet leaves and ate hot oatmeal and coffee. Rarely has food tasted so warm and so good.

And I recalled one afternoon that we followed a side canyon until we were led to a small natural shrine—a waterfall of some 20 feet. Only it wasn't really a waterfall; the crystal water poured slowly over a lip of rock and oozed down the stone wall, glistening, glimmering like jewels in the sun. Or the cave scooped from the sheer stone wall where we sat as if on a throne in the mouth of the earth. These are the souvenirs we take away, the meanings, the memories. We leave nothing behind. And when we pass away, our tracks will fade, our imprint gone, our lives hardly missed in the grand scheme of things, leaving all this to carry on in its eternally inscrutable way.

Sometimes, when I measure my life against the grand lords of rock that stare blankly at the sky, I can accept my smallness. It is enough to know I am part of all this. And I am glad to know that, when my time has come, my body will return to the clay and my spirit will find its place in the earth's wild woods. And I am glad to be making friends here now.

On Friday we walk out. Back again over the red dirt ground, uphill and down, and yet it all looks different. The mountains, ridges, and crests no longer seem distant and aloof, but somehow wrap around us. On a ridge we stop to watch a pair of deer who, on a hill across a ravine, have stopped to watch us watching, then go about their business, eating and moseying along. There are those who believe animals are ambassadors from the earth spirits, and I am one. The 6 of us linger; the sun warms my back and the warm wind brushes my neck. I hear a raven call and rub sage onto my throat and neck. Then we stir again, dragging our booted feet up the trail to where the truck is parked.

Earlier in the morning I had faced in each of the 4 directions and said what prayers I say to whomever or whatever listens. It has become a practice of mine, before I set out on a trip like this, to say that I am coming and to ask God to meet me there. I have done this a fair number of times now and I have not been let down yet.

Kerry Temple

8

*You can go through contemporary life fudging and evading,
indulging and slacking, never really hungry nor frightened nor
passionately stirred, your highest moment a mere sentimental
orgasm, and your first real contact with primary and elemental
necessities the sweat of your deathbed.*

—H. G. Wells

Only his bootprints remain—tracks crisscrossing the last slushy
patches of winter's snow, a trail that disappears as it swings downhill
and west, over earth and rock, deeper into a mountain wilderness
thick with aspen and pine, scrub brush and stone, rotting stumps and
the husks of trees. We are at 9,000 feet, days away from the nearest
road, and the sun has long since died behind the mountain. And he is
gone.

It's been a couple of hours since we stopped to eat and make camp
on a questionably flat, arguably bare perch on these forested flanks of
ancient volcanic rock. And Isaac—at 17 the youngest among us—
wandered off. After dinner. After the sun had dropped behind the
undulating 10,000-foot wall to the west. To play in the snow patches
downhill. I told his dad not to worry. I'd go get him; we'd all be
rounded up by dark. But I was wrong.

There is plenty of room here to get lost in. We headed out days
ago, roaming the bountiful emptiness of southwestern New Mexico.
We spent today winding higher into the Mogollon Range of the
750,000-acre Gila Wilderness Area, which is at the heart of the 3.3-
million-acre Gila National Forest. Which is surrounded by miles and

miles of dried-out, sun-baked, windswept nothing—a wasteland so big, so strong, so beautiful that it defies human comprehension.

We didn't plan on this. We were here on a pilgrimage of sorts, to commemorate the 70th anniversary of the establishment of the Gila frontier as the nation's first wilderness area. A 5-day trek in what is still one of the nation's largest expanses of designated wilderness. A retreat from the barren vagaries of human habitation. A way of paying homage to a long-dead forester named Aldo Leopold, who helped engineer the wilderness movement decades ago and whose *A Sand County Almanac*, published in 1949, still stands as a classic masterwork in nature writing.

It was Leopold who wrote: "I am glad I shall never be young without wild country to be young in. Of what avail are forty freedoms without a blank spot on the map?"

But that blank spot, now shrouded in a deepening darkness, swallows my calls—"I-I-I-saac! I-saa-aa-aac!"—as they roll out over the coldly rugged terrain, carried off on the wings of nighttime winds, landing nowhere. Gone. No answer. "I-saa-aac?"

So I kick at his bootprints and peer into the darkening ravine and listen and look for signs of him. Then, reluctantly, I shamble back up the hillside to camp, hoping he's back so I won't have to tell his father that his son is out there somewhere, missing. As the air grows blindingly black. And the cold goes to the bone. And the landscape—a rock-ribbed playground by day—becomes a little scary by night when there is no moon and the nocturnal species are on the hunt.

I had discovered Leopold as a college student looking for writers to guide my thinking into the philosophy of backpacking, the ethos of nature, and to extend the tradition of Thoreau, Emerson, and Whitman into the twentieth century. And now, traveling years later in the place that bears his name, I carried in my backpack my tattered Leopold book to reread the passages I had highlighted.

Leopold had been born in Iowa in 1887 and he grew up just west of the Mississippi River, exploring the woods, fields, and bluffs there. As a young man, he headed for the wilds of the virgin Southwest, roamed Oregon and Utah, ventured into the gnarly terrain of old

Kerry Temple

Mexico. Invariably he traveled by foot or canoe. Later, as a scientist, pioneer, and visionary, Leopold would become the acknowledged father of wildlife conservation in America. Early in this century, when the nation was recklessly churning up the landscape, Leopold was a voice of reason and restraint, a thoughtful conscience.

He was also something of a cultural philosopher—an insightful, even prescient thinker whose central message was the need to renegotiate our relationship with the landscape. This role shift—from "man the conqueror" to "man the biotic citizen"—was a revolutionary concept in early twentieth-century America, which still saw "wilderness," Leopold commented, as "the raw material out of which man has hammered the artifact called civilization."

Leopold was good for me because his was a less euphoric, more grounded assessment of the bonds between the human race and nature. Leopold provided me with an intellectual tradition to bring ballast to my youthful enthusiasms, shining a penlight on the American psyche. While other social critics were hailing technological advances as indicators of progress, Leopold challenged that wisdom and lamented America's disintegrating relationship with the natural landscape.

"Our grandfathers were less well-housed, well-fed, well-clothed than we are," he wrote in a eulogy for the passenger pigeon. "The strivings by which they bettered their lot are also those which deprived us of pigeons. Perhaps we now grieve because we are not sure, in our hearts, that we have gained by the exchange. The gadgets of industry bring us more comforts than the pigeons did, but do they add as much to the glory of spring?"

Even back in the day of the Model A, Leopold was already worried about the automobile's impact on the environment: "Like ions shot from the sun, the week-enders radiate from every town, generating heat and friction as they go. A tourist industry purveys bed and board to bait more ions, faster, further. Advertisements on rock and rill confide to all and sundry the whereabouts of new retreats, landscapes, hunting-grounds, and fishing lakes just beyond those recently overrun. . . . *Homo sapiens* putters no more under his own vine and fig tree; ant-like, he swarms the continents."

In response to these and other symptoms of a deeper flaw in the American character, Leopold advocated a radical transformation in the way we think. It was a prophetic call that went largely unheeded in his lifetime.

✿

The first stars, along with Venus and Jupiter, glisten jewel-like in the twilight sky. But down below, here where light has fled and dark has enveloped the landscape with tidal force, there are no markers, no signs, no reference points. We are immersed in brambly trees and bush and blackness, uncertain where Isaac may have wandered. We search the shadows. We call his name. His father blows a whistle, and its shrill scream fades into the night. We bump into limbs and logs we cannot see, and finally we stumble back to our campsite.

We stand there shuffling our feet against the cold, where earlier we joked and laughed at dinner. The three of us, listening to the drumming rumble of distant thunder, speak in solemn, whispery tones. His father is sure he is hurt—a fractured leg, perhaps unconscious—or else why didn't he answer our calls? But then, we say, how easy to get lost here; the forested ridges and ravines can spin you around in a dizzy game of Blind Man's Bluff.

Some things we do not say: Fears that seem farfetched swell amid the specter of nighttime imaginings. The threat of mountain lions and bear.

✿

Typically, Isaac led us down the trail, his long strides and youthful gait carrying him faster than our steadfast plodding. At times we would come upon him waiting for us, gazing out over the landscape, smiling at our arrival. And when we gathered for a break, easing sore bones and passing bags of trail mix, he'd be off exploring. Peering around corners. Scaling precipices. Heaving boulders and rocks downhill to see what they would do, grinning as they tumbled heavily, bounding, bouncing airborne, crashing with thuds and splashes. It was right, in our days on the trail, that each of us found his own way to interact with the earth.

On the day before we lost Isaac we had covered a lot of ground, mostly uphill, mostly steep grades, sometimes wading through snow, always higher, monotonously. We learned again the deceptions of distance and traveled in time to individual heartbeat and breathing, stringing out along the trail, drifting out of sight of each other. It was the day I saw the rangy wolf loping happily through a meadow and the day when two of us had to add a 4-mile detour to a spring to replenish our water supply. It was a day full of flitting birds and skittish squirrels and a solar eclipse that cast an eerie radiance upon the earth as distant orbs passed like burning shields in the sky.

It was also the day when, about the time rubber legs and hollow stomach said "no more," Isaac and I spiraled higher among aspen and ponderosa pine toward an imposing summit lashed by winds, cold winds buffeting our bodies as we neared the top. Then, just as the sun broke forth from cloud cover and bathed the landscape in light and warmth, we stepped into an open expanse atop this neighborhood's highest peak. All of New Mexico, it seemed, lay at our feet.

We stopped there for lunch—tortillas, cheese, and chicken soup—then stretched out, backs to the ground, sun on our faces, wind whipping lightly through the waving grass. I watched the billowing clouds sail across the sky and listened to chatty birds and whisked an occasional fly from my face. It had been work getting here but now, surrounded by the place, I knew I'd found a foothold.

Leopold knew this was the only way to learn what the land had to teach, and he knew that such learning is essential if the human race is to find its proper place amid the cosmos.

"Conservation is getting nowhere," he wrote in 1948, one month before his death, "because it is incompatible with our Abrahamic concept of land. We abuse land because we regard it as a commodity belonging to us. When we see the land as a community to which we belong, we may begin to use it with love and respect."

"Shhh!"

We are poised, transfixed by a distant sound. Is it human? A yelp? A cry? We return the call. "Isaaaac?" Urgently: "Isaaac?"

Five, ten, twenty minutes go by. All is quiet. Flashes of lightning flare in the west.

Then again, out of the darkness, we hear a call. Then nothing. The last yell of the night—and something haunting about that voice, a call from beyond our reach, out there alone. Somehow those calls, engulfed by the enduring silence, sharpen the loss, echo into the hollow drum of the cosmic immensity.

Flashes of lightning pop in the distant sky, barely discernible through the trees. I say nothing, not wanting to heighten our alarm, but I recall warnings of the electrical ferocity upon these summits— and a passage from Leopold: "When I hear anyone say he does not fear lightning, I still remark inwardly: he has never ridden The Mountain in July.

"The explosions are fearsome enough, but more so are the smoking slivers of stone that sing past your ear when the bolt crashes into a rimrock. Still more so are the splinters that fly when a bolt explodes a pine. I remember one gleaming white one, 15 feet long, that stabbed deep into the earth at my feet and stood there humming like a tuning fork.

"It must be a poor life that achieves freedom from fear."

At last we concede there is nothing more to be done. Wherever Isaac is, he is there for the night. It is just too dark to navigate these woods. Surely, we tell his father, his son has settled in. He will spend a long and shivery night but, we assure the father, his son will survive. And we'll search again by light of day.

Whether writing about pine trees or cranes, Silphium, marshlands, or the grizzly, Leopold examined the land and all its inhabitants as if each piece of the mosaic contained truths demanding translation. Every woodland, he wrote, offers up not only lumber, fuel, and fence-posts but also "a liberal education" to those who look and listen. "This crop of wisdom never fails," he added, "but it is not always harvested."

So we have spent our days here walking, sometimes sitting, watching sunsets and sunrises and starry skies and squawking jays and valleys scoured by mountain winds. I remember a squadron of crows flying way high, arcing and dog fighting, dive bombing and sailing out of sight as the afternoon thermals provided a wind-surfer's joyride through space. I remember the cold nights and some rain, tough up-hill hauls, and snow showers during dinner, aspen groves so illuminatingly holy we stood in awe. A lush green meadow. Elk bones. Quartz crystal. A rocky outcropping where we watched thunderheads stampede across the land, bearing snow and rain and winds that made us shiver.

These tutors taught us much, although we didn't talk about that; our conversation was about where the next waterhole was, and the difference between meteors and shooting stars, and the condition of boot-bruised toenails and blistered feet. I don't know what my companions thought or felt about this land that Leopold considered a sacred text, but one thing surely comes through when you're out here like this: humility, derived from an inevitable and sometimes jarring awareness of human vulnerability. It's a humility that brings respect, even admiration, for places and creatures you once thought inferior, surmountable, domitable. And when you look out upon the indifferent, self-sufficient corners of the world, you know your place.

This, essentially, was the thesis of Leopold's life's work: that the human species develop a revolutionary appreciation for the land by entering it; that the human race realize it must be a responsible member of this living community, and not an imperious lord over it.

"It is a century now since Darwin gave us the first glimpse of the origin of the species," Leopold wrote. "We know now what was unknown to all the preceding caravan of generations: that men are only fellow-voyagers with other creatures in the odyssey of evolution. This new knowledge should have given us, by this time, a sense of kinship with fellow-creatures; a wish to live and let live; a sense of wonder over the magnitude and duration of the biotic enterprise."

Leopold was not optimistic that this approach would be widely embraced. Despite the good intentions of government and the shining rhetoric of business and industry, Leopold knew overriding economic ambitions would continue to derail any environmental movement—unless the indoctrination included a full immersion into the wilderness experience. As Stephen Jay Gould once wrote, "We cannot win this battle to save species and environments without forging an emotional bond between ourselves and nature as well—for we will not fight to save what we do not love."

On the night we lost Isaac, we slipped into tents wrapped in heavy darkness. The cozy goose-down bag felt especially good, but I have always liked nightfall in the woods. The earth goes still, as if snug in a blanket of darkness pulled to its chin. Overhead the nightlights come on, and down here a certain serenity settles in—despite the creatures who stalk prey under cover of night.

Thinking of Isaac out there on his own, with no tent or bag, made me question the romantic notion that the landscape is forgiving to those who honor it, that it blesses those who seek its benediction. I once debated with friends and colleagues whether nature is benevolent or malevolent, a recurrent theme in the American mind and literature. Now, after years of watching it, I've come to know that some things just are, neither good nor bad, and to try to take them as they come.

I wake in the blackness to a clattering outside the tent—footsteps, rustlings, the glare of a bobbing flashlight illuminating the brown rip-stop nylon of the tent. Someone is pawing through a backpack, clanging tin cups and crackling paper. It is Isaac's sleepless father, frantic to be up and going. And so we rouse groggily to resume the search. But first we put together a pack of survival items in case we find Isaac hurt or hungry.

As we head out among the trees, the first hint of light emerges along the eastern horizon. The earth turns. The stars fade. The air is damp and still. A thick gray light blooms over the world. Now is the time to find him.

We yell, stop, listen—we walk on. The father blows his whistle and we pause, our ears poised like antennae. But the only whistle we hear in return is that of a morning bird hailing the dawn.

We go this way and that, uphill and down, calling. Sunlight spills onto the summits around us, flashes off the tallest trees, then slides down the mountainside until it pools at our feet. It is full morning and there is no sign of him. We circle, go back to camp, look at one another. No discouraging words, but the feeling sinks in: What now?

Kerry Temple

How long do we look before we go for help? Do we give it till noon, then risk going another night without finding him? Our car is parked a tough day's run away, and then a drive of several hours to contact authorities. Rangers on horseback? Helicopters? It all seems so preposterous. But here we are, wondering what to do.

✿

One image of Isaac on the trail persists, vivid in memory. He is ahead of me up the trail at midmorning and we are atop a ridge with a spray of aspens downhill to our right. I hear it before I see it—fallen limbs cracking, branches snapping, thundering hooves—then the bright rump of an elk, that is all, vanishing downhill.

With a second crash, Isaac bounds out from the bushes up ahead. He grins at me, and in that grin is a flash of recognition connecting us. We pause, suspended for just a moment, and then, as if on cue, we sling off our packs and bolt downhill after the elk. We bound down the steep slope, arms extended like wings. The flying elk's tracks lead us on a merry zigzag chase through grasses and thickets, the branches stinging our faces and arms until—panting—we stop.

Again we exchange grins, then more slowly we follow the elk's trail, glancing here and there, staring into the sunlit valley before us. After several minutes of cheerful stalking, we give up the chase, knowing we have been outrun, outsmarted, outmaneuvered.

As we head back uphill, I think about our chase and what exactly we were after. A lot of things perhaps; or maybe nothing more than to see an animal wild and fleet. Or to somehow be in contact with something elemental, holy.

It was late in the day when I saw them. A cloudy gloom had settled over the deep, deep woods; light was gone from the land. A moving blackness caught my eye ahead on the right, and I saw her—a large black bear—maybe 15 yards away. Then a cub, chocolate brown, cute as a cartoon, up on its hind legs looking at me. Poised on a log looking back at me.

I wanted Isaac, on the trail up ahead, to see too, so I called his name. The mother turned and the cub, startled by my voice, spun once and looked back, mouth and eyes wide open. Then they lumbered downhill and out of sight. Once again Isaac and I gave chase, though not with the same abandon with which we tailed the elk. But mother and cub were too quickly gone.

❧

It is full daylight now and, my stomach insists, long past breakfast-time, but we decide to look some more—this time splitting up. The father goes one way, I head downhill, past the snow patches, into the ravine; the third member of our party heads west. We urge each other not to get lost; that would be funny, I think, and a fine line between comedy and tragedy.

So I navigate my way into the canyon, down the steep grade into thicker brush, a seemingly bottomless drop into the Gila wilderness. As I descend over logs and through thickets, spotting rock walls, I fully expect to find only signs of him, or else to come upon a sight I cringe to imagine. Did he fall climbing a rock face? Did he tumble and bash his head? Did he fall victim to some meaner fate? I tread warily, scanning the tangled landscape, my heart throbbing in my chest.

❧

Leopold wanted something more. National parks were fine but were intended for mass use and so designed with roads and facilities to accommodate major intrusions by humans. The national forests were established as multiple-use areas which support lumbering and grazing as well as recreation. National monuments were established to preserve natural and native heirlooms, from unique rock formations to prehistoric cliff dwellings. What Leopold wanted to protect was a different national treasure—the American wilderness.

He wanted to set aside vast tracts of unspoiled landscape and to leave them that way. He would minimize human impact on the land: no roads, no facilities—not even outhouses or water pumps. These were places to be seen on foot or by pack animal; camp where you wish but leave no mark. He wanted the places to remain wild.

This begged a change of perception in the mind of the American who "must possess, invade, appropriate," wrote Leopold, who further explained: "Hence the wilderness that he cannot personally see has no value to him. Hence the universal assumption that an unused hinterland is rendering no service to society. To those devoid of imagination, a blank place on the map is useless waste; to others, the most valuable part."

Leopold knew that these wilderness areas would not be accessible or appealing to everyone. But that was the point—the landscape dominates, not man. It also circumvented one of the great paradoxes of wilderness travel: In the simple act of entering the land, humans alter it, and the more fully we interact with it, the greater the abuse. Such was the sentiment expressed in perhaps his most famous line: "Man always kills the thing he loves, and so we pioneers have killed our wilderness."

In 1922 Leopold wrote a brief but provocative proposal arguing for the establishment of the nation's first primitive area—an attempt to make sure that America's wilderness would not die. Two years later, half a million acres were set aside as the Gila Wilderness Area, preserving Leopold's vision, etching it into the face of the land he loved.

And now 70 years later, we search that "blank spot on the map" for any sign of Isaac, who is lost here, swallowed up, absorbed, gone from us. We have all but lost hope of finding him safe.

*

I stop at last in my solo hunt for Isaac, having gone about as far out this tangent as seems prudent. In the distance I still hear the periodic call of his father's whistle. I listen also to a canyon wren, watch a gray squirrel twittering among the trunks of trees. The earth seems alive with the microcosmic bustle of its flitty creatures. Shafts of light spear through the canopy of trees, forming a mottled array of sunspots and shadows on the forest floor. I am somehow soothed with a sense of resignation, of acceptance. It will be all right.

I listen to a father blowing a whistle. In response I hear only the wind, a chipmunk skittering through dried leaves, a crow calling from upper space. Then I hear another sound. More distant.

A whistle.

Then the father again; then the son's answer. Two short bursts—two shorts in return. Contact.

A mountain duet.

My heart feels as if it fills my chest. I listen to the playful whistles continuing to call back and forth, lean back against a pine, breathe deeply and, after a thank you, pull a bagel from my pocket. After a few chews I sit on a log and look around and take it all in. A happy reunion is taking place here in these woods.

Later I learn we guessed right about Isaac. He had gotten turned around and, near dark, realized he could do nothing but settle in for the night. So he arranged some logs into a triangle, cleared the ground, used pine straw and bark for kindling, and built a fire. It took a while to get it started but he kept it going all night, waking periodically to add sticks and to rake the coals into a pile where he nestled. He'd had matches and his whistle and an Instamatic camera with him. He had turned his camera into a flare by firing the flash into the nighttime sky—the flashes we misread as lightning.

Isaac had been fine—just separated from us for awhile. So it didn't take us long that morning to get back on track. It was good to be all together again, heading down the trail. It made me rethink some things. Like what it means to be lost. And who really is. And how do we get back home.

Kerry Temple

9

My book, O philosopher, is the nature of created things, and any time I wish to read the words of God, the book is before me.

—Anthony of the Desert, fourth-century monk

By the time I turned 30 I had lived in Wyoming for a couple of years and had moved to Indiana. I had a wife and two young sons. I had gone places and seen things, but there was a lot I didn't know. I was bothered, too, by the riddles of spirit and matter, body and soul, the seen and unseen elements of my understanding. I had been taught to believe in spirit, miracle, and mystery, and in God. But these had largely faded from the modern world in which I lived. And it seemed more and more that the educated and the worldly among us had left those other notions behind, as if they were quaint or childish ideas from a less sophisticated time. I did not want to live under any delusions, and it seemed naggingly fundamental to me—as I tried to figure out how to live my life, what to do, and where to go from here— that I needed to get some basics down before proceeding, that I needed to find some answers before I could make proper sense of it all. I wanted to know the truth: What am I? What is the universe all about? How do I fit into it? And I wanted to know if the cosmos told a story—and if it had a Storyteller.

So when a group of scientists asked me to come along to the High Canadian Arctic, on a monthlong expedition to the last rocky reaches this side of the polar ice cap, to the Canadian archipelago of Ellesmere, then Devon, then Baffin Island, I said "yes," and the 4 of us went to the top of the world. And there, in one of the most incomprehensibly vast, barren, and invigoratingly rich frontiers left on Earth, we stood face-to-face with the primal universe at its purest. Far north of the magnetic north pole, just beyond the final outposts of human habitation, we confronted the unadorned and elemental landscape, with me tagging along, watching, looking, reading, asking questions, taking notes. Exploring, examining, collecting specimens. Hunting insight and nuggets of truth.

And now, years later, I have the memories, pictures, and notes of a time and a place where the sun never sets, where the ice never melts, where trees cannot grow, and where a compass can only spin and bob maybe north, maybe south—within dreaming distance of all that is.

We came to Ellesmere by airplane, a DeHavilland STOL Twin Otter. It skated to a stop on the ice in Alexandra Fiord. We jumped into knee-deep snow; our gear, bags, boxes of food, and equipment, two rifles were thrown overboard. "What are those for?" I asked, thinking it unlikely we'd be hunting walrus or seal. "For the bears," I was told. "For protection. One to take whenever you go out; the other to keep in the cabin if a bear comes for the food." I stood in polar bear tracks as the plane took off, leaving the 4 of us alone, no town, no road, no one else for hundreds of miles. I no longer felt like the least threatened member of the cosmic food chain. It wasn't till later we realized our radio didn't work.

It took several trips to lug our stuff up to the cabins, built in 1953 by the Royal Canadian Mounted Police, a shelter that is serviceable for perhaps a month or so each year. We unlocked the doors, unboarded the windows, threw down our gear, and surveyed the kitchen and the beds, the stove and shelves stacked high with books left by those who came before. Then we stepped back outside and cast long, broad looks at the awesome beauty surrounding us, the brimming silence, the exquisitely white landscape. I no longer felt alone. We were not in the middle of nowhere; we were centered on top of the globe.

For almost a month we explored there, hiked there, looked around, made it home. Olga, Jack, and Bernd did what scientists do, and I tagged along. Jack, one of the few scientists in the world studying how insects "overwinter" and adapt to subzero temperatures, was here to study *Gynaephora groenlandica*, the world's most northerly distributed member of the butterfly and moth family. Olga is his grad student. Bernd is a friend of Jack's, an internationally known biologist who's written about beetles and bees, butterflies and ravens. They would be my guides, showing me how science is done, opening windows to the sweeping vistas and intricate vessels that inspire wonder and awe, bringing me to the bony edge of creation.

The old-timers said it had not snowed like this for 15 years. It was waist high when we arrived, traversable only by snowshoe, but blanketing all the specimens we'd come to collect. So we tried to build an igloo and hiked across the sea ice to an island called the Sphinx. For two days the wind, gusting at 70, 80 miles an hour, screamed down the mountain face, swept across the lowland, and hammered our cabins. It drove snow through the cracks in the outhouse, then it snowed some more.

We baked bread, played darts, and painted. We also had time to read—*Arctic Dreams* by Lopez, *Cosmos* by Sagan, *Gatsby*, *Walden Two* by B. F. Skinner, *The Magus*, *The Razor's Edge*, Kilgore Trout, Farley Mowatt, Hoagland Abbey and McPhee, poring over what others have found and thought and said: That the Earth travels through space at 66,000 miles per hour; that all the Earth's surface land masses once combined to form the continent of Pangaea, which broke apart 200 million years ago; that 20 continental plates move several inches each year; that a caterpillar like the *Gynaephora groenlandica* contains dormant cell clusters that remain tiny and inactive until it pupates—when the giant cells die and the once-dormant cells divide rapidly and nourish themselves on the soup of the disintegrating caterpillar, virtually eating itself, as wings sprout and encoded legs and a new body, radically different, are built—and breaks forth fully grown and sails off, in that single-minded quest to mate, thus perpetuating the species.

I also gathered these things: "The most ancient paintings are thought to be about 30,000 years old," wrote David Attenborough in *Life on Earth*, noting that art began as an act of worship to gods, to a Creator. "It is this talent which ultimately transformed the life of mankind."

And this from Descartes: "Those who seek the direct road to truth should not bother with any object of which they cannot have a certainty equal to the demonstrations of arithmetic and geometry." It was Descartes who proclaimed, "*Cogito ergo sum:* I think, therefore I am," launching an era in human development in which reason became the consummate characteristic of human nature, the sole path to knowledge and understanding. But he wasn't the first. "Whenever it is possible to find out the cause of what is happening," wrote Polybius, the Greek historian who lived a century before Jesus, "one should not have recourse to the gods."

"Our whole business in this life," wrote Augustine, centuries later, "is to restore to health the eye of the heart whereby God may be seen."

So I write: "Dueling quotes, and each one opinion. Do you believe in something Other, or not? Is it 'faith' or 'delusion'? What proof is there that something exists beyond these things we touch and see? Am I applying scientific methods—the search for quantifiable, physical evidence—to something beyond the reach of science? *Is* there something beyond the reach of science? Who knows? I don't. But mostly this: What does it all mean?"

The days blended easily together, ripe with the golden sweetness of a summer romance. Images, impressions persist. I remember the day Jack and I hiked up Twin Glacier, when the edges of the sunlit clouds became a rainbow prism, and the night Olga and I went looking for caterpillars, when sunlight, shadow, and crystalline snow put on a light show I can still envision. And I remember the day Bernd, then a 45-year-old scientist/little boy, was on his hands and knees watching spiders scramble across the icy tundra. Or fishing for arctic char through an ice hole at midnight. Or—butterfly net raised high—galloping after bumblebees through thigh-deep snow. Or skiing in the white-field distance, a water spider stroking across the sea ice from seal hole to seal hole where fellow mammals basked in the nighttime sun.

And I thought of another night, later in the expedition, when we went to look around on Devon Island. Bernd, intrigued by the foraging of ravens and amazed they stay here through winter ("What do they eat? How do they stay warm?"), wants to find a raven's nest. So Olga, Jack, and I go along. The day is grey, the clouds low. Our feet slosh in the snow, squish in the spongy tundra.

The ridge before us is Precambrian granite, probably a billion years old. Beyond that is the world's third largest ice field. The ravens' nest, we had been told, is up ahead—not far from the polar bear tracks (a mother and two cubs). A golden plover races along the ground mimicking a lemming to draw us away from the nest; when that doesn't work, it scuttles about, faking a broken wing. The willows, now with crimson blooms, are only a few inches high; some are a century old. The loons are back for summer; they mate for life and have flown thousands of miles to be here. A lemming lies dead on the ground, its belly open, blood red. It is steaming. A jaeger waits till we pass, then returns to eat her prey.

Across a blue frozen inlet are blackish cliffs spotted with orange lichens, green vegetation, and a storm of swooping, resting gulls, ivory white. The ice is breaking up and we hesitate to cross the inlet. "If there's a raven's nest over there, I'm going," says Bernd. We follow, carefully choosing our steps. The ice is deep blue, opaque. Yet transparent. It is like walking on the sky.

We arrive at the base of the cliff. The acrobatic gulls dive bomb and soar, sing and screech. Bernd listens. He makes his way along the wall until he hears the cry. Ravens have dozens of calls in their repertoire; Bernd discerns, amid the cacophonous gulls, a raven's begging call.

We watch the cliffs; minutes pass. Then Olga spots the ravens, high above. Young. Three tiny black blades. They flit from ledge to ledge; one teeters then tumbles off a shelf, gains an awkward balance. They are trying to fly. Their parents return; they feed their young. They are a family, enjoying summertime in the valley of the Truelove River, nestled onto the safe, wet cliffs. Bernd wants to climb, but decides their home is out of reach.

And I remember one day at Alexandra Fiord on Ellesmere Island when I went alone on snowshoes across the lowland, across the frozen river, which would soon be a torrent of icy water from the glacial melt. I clamber up a ridge I'd been eyeing for 4 days.

After a couple of hours, I reach a point in the ridge crest where I could sit, dry my socks, and contemplate the universe. The sky is cloudless and deep blue; the terrain is low and flat and white, marked by some mountains, some sandstone ridges, peninsulas extending like arms into the sea ice. The Earth is indeed a ball of rock, and life on Earth a marvel. In the spring before I came here a Yale scientist found the skull of a flying lemur, 55 million years old. Lemurs, with whom we share a common ancestor, live only on Madagascar these days—an island off the coast of Africa.

Back to Earth

Today on the sea ice there are seal holes and black dots where the seals lie, and the tracks of polar bears making their rounds. Ice edges are jagged turquoise, aquamarine, Coke-bottle green. The blurry line on the eastern horizon, where sky-blue meets sea-white, may be Greenland; maybe not. Below is Skraeling Island. Above is the sun. The sky is extraordinarily blue. It is also 78 percent nitrogen, 21 percent oxygen. In the distance I think I see a polynya; maybe not.

Polynyas are like oases in the Arctic's ice-locked seas. They are areas which, because of currents, tides, winds, and upwelling, do not freeze solid, even in winter. Because they stay open and because the upwelling keeps the nutrients swirling around, polynyas are popular feeding grounds for arctic mammals—walrus, whales, seals, bear.

Forty, maybe fifty million years ago the Arctic was temperate. Lemurs, crocodiles, and three-toed horses inhabited its forests; sequoia and ginkgo trees grew here. Then it got cold. It is mid-June now and everything is frozen, ice-locked, although the temperatures are slightly above freezing and the summer sun is warm.

Skraeling Island protrudes through the sea ice like a mountaintop below the ridge where I sit. It looks like Gibraltar sitting there at the fiord's mouth. Though it appears to be a stone's throw away, it is several miles distant. In 1977 some scientists went there to look around and found 40 prehistoric stone dwellings. The Thule people, seagoing hunters of walrus, whale, and seal, flourished there for 7 centuries. They came about 1000 A.D. and built houses of stone, whale ribs, and sod. They lit their homes with seal-blubber lamps and made clothing and boots from sealskin, pants and mittens from polar bear skins. They hunted with dogsleds, kayaks, and skin-covered boats called umiaks. They carved pottery from soapstone and fashioned harpoon heads from ivory and bone.

The scientists kept digging and found there on Skraeling rivets from a Viking ship. Sections of oak boxes. Parts of barrel bottoms. A chain of armor. European-style knife blades and spear points. A piece of woolen cloth. Had the Norse lived here too?

In 986 A.D. (when the Earth was flat and people were afraid of falling off the edge), Eric the Red founded 2 farming settlements on Greenland, which is 25 miles east of here. These pioneers came from Scandinavia by way of Iceland, which they had settled a century before. By 1300 their Greenland farms supported 3,000 people—all of whom had disappeared by 1500 (a short half-century before Coperni- cus said the Earth circled the sun and about the time Columbus "dis- covered" the Bahamas trying to find the Orient). By 1650 the Thule were gone too.

In 1977 archeologists excavated Skraeling, scraping away at the stubborn permafrost, and found only pieces of the puzzle, the mun- dane paraphernalia of human life. The diggers looked around on nearby Bache Peninsula and in 8 days uncovered more than 150 pre- historic dwellings—the northernmost human settlements ever dis- covered.

The scientists came back to Ellesmere in 1978. On Knud Peninsula they found the remnants of a Thule community of 100 persons, the bones of geese, fox, arctic hares, seals, walrus. They uncovered ivory and bone carvings—of caribou, polar bears, ducks, geese. The work of artists.

The Thule were not the first to inhabit Ellesmere. Arctic small- tool people, called pre-Dorset, lived here as early as 2300 B.C. (about the time Stonehenge and the Great Pyramid of Khufu were being built). The Dorset evolved from this cultural group about 600 B.C. and were replaced by the Thule. Their descendants are commonly called Eskimo, an old Indian word for "eaters of raw flesh." They pre- fer to be called Inuit, "the people."

All descended from Asians who may have crossed the Bering land bridge as long ago as 33,000 B.C. Some scientists say the first wave didn't arrive until 23,000 years ago, a people bearing flaked stone and bone tools similar to those carried by Neanderthal man. The second wave came 13,000 years later. Their more advanced tools resembled those crafted by Cro-Magnon man. These people were big-game hunters— bison, ground sloths, woolly mammoths.

Now we are here—in a strange and wondrous juxtaposition— small-game hunters chipping, picking, probing each piece of the mo- saic, measuring this, testing that, trying to decipher the secrets hidden in the landscape, both ancient and new. And I, now standing in their place, wonder: "Were they smart? Were they wise? Why did they come here? What were they after? What did they think of the moon and the sun?"

The sun is 93 million miles away. It burns my face; I must wear sunglasses to protect my eyes against its ultraviolet rays. Its blinding rays take 8 minutes to get here from there, where temperatures range from 6,000 to 40 million degrees. It has been on fire like this for about 5 billion years; it is a young star, and a minor one. The Milky Way, which is one of billions of galaxies in the universe, contains more than 100 billion stars. Our sun is about three-fifths of the way from the Milky Way's center to its outer edge, and it circles the center, speeding along at 43,000 miles an hour, every 225 million years.

My face is also being bombarded by neutrinos. Neutrinos come from the sun. They weigh nothing and travel at the speed of light, but they are not a kind of light or a photon. Matter is transparent to neutrinos. So when I look at the sun for 1 second, a billion neutrinos pass through my eyeball, through the back of my head, and through the earth—as easily as light passing through clear glass.

Today's "people" aren't sure what neutrinos do except change chlorine atoms into argon atoms. So scientists have poured huge amounts of chlorine bleach into a mine in the Black Hills of South Dakota (near Bear Butte, Harney Peak and Deadwood, once home to Calamity Jane and Buffalo Bill) to learn more about neutrinos and what they say about nuclear fusion in stars.

"We are made of starstuff," Carl Sagan proclaimed in *Cosmos*. "All the elements of the Earth except hydrogen and some helium have been cooked by a kind of stellar alchemy billions of years ago in stars. The nitrogen in our DNA, the calcium in our teeth, the iron in our blood, the carbon in our apple pies were made in the interiors of collapsing stars." In fact, all the matter in our sun, all the matter that has coalesced into the ball we call Earth, has been through one or two previous cycles of stellar alchemy.

Scientists tell us that our sun poured its ultraviolet radiation into our atmosphere (swirling clouds of hydrogen, carbon monoxide, ammonia, and methane), that its warmth generated lightning, and that these energy sources sparked the complex organic molecules (sugars, amino acids, nucleic acids) that led to the origin of life.

And life has been running almost exclusively on sunlight ever since that one-celled progenitor of bacteria and algae emerged from the primeval soup 3 billion years ago. These early life forms were fruitful and multiplied—from protozoa to sponges to jellyfish, worms, mollusks, and squid. The first land plants appeared 400 million years ago, then came forests and flowers, sharks, dragonflies and toads, pterodactyls and turtles, snakes, eagles, mammals. Kangaroos and giraffes, aardvarks and bats, the Great Blue Whale. Primates. Today 200 species of primates eat, think, climb, search, mate, raise families, and die.

One primate species, *Homo erectus*, emerged about a million years ago. It eventually evolved into *Homo sapiens*, a species with an unusually large cerebrum; 10,000 years ago they numbered 10 million. Today more than 6 billion of them cover the globe. Some have reached the polar caps, have been to the moon. Yet they are part of a grand family of more than 4 million species of living organisms, related by birth and design—all virtually made of the same ingredients, which are all driven by the same interplay of chemistry, electricity, and physics. And all depend on sunlight and each other to live.

Plants gather the energy-packed photons (units of light that travel in waves and, curiously, have the characteristics of waves, matter, and energy simultaneously) and, within their cell walls, change solar energy to chemical energy. Animals eat the plants, and we eat both, harvesting the converted sunlight as the fuel which makes us go—some 15 billion years after the Big Bang.

Who knows where that came from? Who knows what, if anything, awaits us at the mountaintop or hangs in the blue nitrogen air? Or what might hover out beyond the universe, on the other side of that lifegiving spark, that has—through the countless millennia—orchestrated the events that led to today? Evolution? God?

I shut my notebook, put it away. My socks are dry; I pull them on and look around. I can see for miles. The view is immense from this stone ridge high above the lowland of Alexandra Fiord: snow-crested peaks in the distance, rock and ice, sun and sky. Then I see it, inches from my hand. *Gynaephora groenlandica*. The little beast for which we came. And, as I will learn during these days far north of the Arctic Circle, the richness of creation in microcosm, folded into each little one.

For almost all of its existence *Gynaephora groenlandica* is a fuzzy, three-eyed, rust-and-black striped caterpillar. Every June it comes out of hiding, out of hibernation; it grazes on willow, Dryas, and saxifrage, and browses in the sun. After three weeks in action, it slips back into hiding and snuggles through another winter. It does this for about 15 years (most insects go through a life cycle in a year or less, many in two weeks), slowly growing up, gradually passing from one larval stage to the next, through maybe 6 stages, shedding its skin each time.

Finally, one summer, cued by hormonal changes (akin to those that tell a teenage boy to sprout hair and zits), it laboriously spins its silky cocoon. A few days later, after one of creation's little miracles, a dull grey moth struggles out of the pupal sheath, emerges, and flies. Is airborne. Flitting and dancing in pursuit of a mate somewhere on the arctic tundra. The female (which cannot fly) quickens this amorous quest by releasing a pheromone, a chemical lure that males can sniff out and track for miles. They find each other, mate, and die—shortly after the female lays about 150 eggs, starting the process all over again and thus enabling the species to carry on.

Gynaephora groenlandica has a heart that pumps blood, a brain, and a central nervous system that function at the cellular level like mine— electrochemical synaptic transmissions surging across thousands of nerve cells, each one touching a thousand others. Each cell in its body has the genes, chromosomes, and DNA to replicate itself; and, like animals everywhere, they grow and develop because of the ebb and flow of hormones, mostly steroids. Yet they can freeze and survive even the man-killing cold of arctic winter. Some insects—like *Gynaephora*—are freeze tolerant; they literally freeze, then thaw out in the spring. Others use antifreezes—alcohols (like the ethylene glycol you pour into your car) and proteins—to hibernate in a supercool state.

Gynaephora have only two enemies: a tachinid fly and an ichneumonid wasp. The fly lays eggs on the caterpillar; the wasp injects one egg into it through its stinger. The larvae then burrow in and eat them from the inside out. It is a gruesome ending, one which prompted Charles Darwin to write in 1860: "There seems to me too much misery in the world. I cannot persuade myself that a beneficent and omnipotent God would have designedly created the *Ichneumonidae* with the express intention of their feeding with the living bodies of caterpillars."

I watch the little caterpillar at my feet, watch his earnest trekking, wonder what he is doing up here, when food and friends are so far below. But I wonder, too, at all these phenomena, the order and elegance of the cosmos, the big and little miracles that astound me as I sit here on the front porch of creation, locate myself in the lap of this amazing universe.

Kerry Temple

In time there were bare patches. Winter let go; the patches grew. More caterpillars came; the bumblebees buzzed. The wildflowers, cast like calico dots across the tundra, bloomed purple, yellow, and red. Bernd chased the bees. Jack monitored one *Gynaephora* for 36 hours straight, recording its movement, its behavior, and the environmental factors that affected it. I can still see Olga on skis in the distance, sliding from bare spot to bare spot, stooping to pick up a caterpillar, plucking it into her container, then rising to search some more.

Sometimes we went out alone, sometimes the 4 of us together. We would patrol the lowland for hours, always within talking distance but saying very little. Occasionally, and without signal, we would stop and gaze around, absorbing the beauty, the glistening moment. Then a fox would cry in the distance, or we'd hear the muted rumble of a rock slide. Then we'd continue without talking, as if words would corrupt the mood.

"Our Science, which we loved above everything, had brought us together," wrote David Hilbert, memorializing a colleague. "It appeared to us as a flowering garden. In this garden there were well-worn paths where one might look around at leisure and enjoy oneself without effort, especially at the side of a congenial companion. But we also liked to seek out hidden trails and discovered many an unexpected view which was pleasing to our eyes; and when the one pointed it out to the other, and we admired it together, our joy was complete."

We collected 1,500 *Gynaephora*. They were kept in a snow corral before being transported to a lab in the States. Meanwhile, Olga and Jack put them through a series of experiments, mostly focusing on thermal regulation and how they orient toward the sun, trying to unweave these threads, these possible cues—magnetic field, sun position, light intensity, wavelength, spectral composition. Basking in the sun helps *Gynaephora* raise their body temperatures 25 degrees Celsius above the surrounding air. How do they do that?

My notes observe: "Here we are the weak ones; animals thrive where man can only fabricate the means of his survival. The fox trots easily where I climb. I fear the bear; I dread the cold. They are part of it all. What makes us 'superior'? What are we? One of them? Or master-designate? The apex of creation?"

I wrote these things one day when I had climbed a ridge to the southwest. I meandered considerably on the ascent, struggling against snow and rock, switching back, looking for passages upward. When I thought I had reached the top, I saw that it rolled back higher, that there were ridges, higher still, that I hadn't been able to see from below. I walked some more and realized it would go on like this indefinitely, that I would not reach a summit. So I sat and looked around, and I saw my tracks in the distance—over there, over here, wayward, bumbling tracks.

The footprints of a fox, lightly impressing the snow, had cut a straight line from there to here and on beyond what I could see. And I wondered, if someone did indeed watch from above, if my wandering looked as aimless and as insignificant as the movement of that caterpillar Jack was watching down below. And if my view of the universe were similarly microscopic.

And I reread the passage I had copied from *The Magus*, where Urfe says, "I'd enjoy it all more if I knew what it meant." And the Magus replies, "My dear Nicholas, man has been saying what you have just said for the last ten thousand years. And the one common thread of all the gods he has said it to is that not one of them has ever returned an answer."

During those days and nights on Ellesmere I listened to Olga, Bernd, and Jack throw the questions back and forth. I watched the interaction of teacher and student. I saw how science is driven by questions and why answers really aren't anything but doorways to more questions. We'd sit around a large wooden table in the morning over coffee and late in the bright night when it seemed wrong to go to bed. The conversations (ranging from ball lightning to barometric pressure, from nucleators to abstract thought) mostly went beyond me, but some things I managed to write down.

Chickadees can be trained to find caterpillars by spotting leaf damage; some caterpillars, in turn, disguise the evidence. In discussing a focus for her dissertation Olga said, "Their behavior is much more interesting than their physiology," and Bernd said, "But it's the physiology that drives the immediate behavior." There was talk of westerlies and trade winds, Arctic terns and animal migration, the chemistry of love, the mechanics of fish gills, and the evolution of language. We talked of God and brains and neuropharmacology, of

Kerry Temple

space and time and multiple coexistent dimensions, of ghosts and souls and the nature of energy, what "supernatural" means, and what can and can't be known empirically.

Sometimes the talk went on and on, late into the darkless nights, one question spawning a multitude more. Each one began unraveling the strands of a thousand natural wonders, only partially explained. Sometimes, when we sat in silence, talk seemed superfluous and questions an invasion of privacy. Sometimes, usually when all was quiet, there were hints of more than meets the eye. "We look not at the things which are seen," says the Bible, "but at the things which are not seen; for the things which are seen are temporal; but the things which are not seen are eternal."

"From time immemorial the distinctive human problem," countered Ernest Becker, "has been the need to spiritualize human life, to lift it onto a special immortal plane, beyond the cycles of life and death that characterize all other organisms."

"Science doesn't concern itself with things that can't be tested," Jack told me one night when I asked about the borderlands of body and soul, matter and spirit, death and immortality. "If someone could discover a test for this other, then we might try to determine if such things exist." But ultimately, as Auden wrote: "All proofs or disproofs that we tender/of His existence are returned/Unopened to the sender."

I looked out the window, up at the peaks of Twin Glacier. *Perhaps God is a scientist,* I thought. *And all this is an experiment.* Given the sublime (some would call it "divine") beauty, precision and magnificence of the universe, that theory may not be far off—and that we have been placed here like laboratory animals simply to see how we go about solving the puzzle. And all of us—scientists, pilgrims, shamans, saints—are bound together in that quest, each bringing a distinctive looking glass for the trip. And as I imagined humans dispatched as cosmic explorers—of truths and of the Truth—I recalled a passage in Elie Wiesel's *Night*:

> "Man raises himself toward God by the questions he asks Him," Moche the Beadle was fond of repeating. "That is the true dialogue. Man questions God and God answers. But we don't understand His answers. We can't understand them. Because they come from the

depths of the soul, and they stay there until death. You will find the true answers only within yourself."

"And why do you pray, Moche?"

"I pray to the God within me that He will give me the strength to ask Him the right questions."

Is it possible, I then wondered, still searching for answers on the arctic tundra where so little stood between me and the holy firmament, that all the parts are really one? Is it possible that I have been asking the wrong questions, that I have been trying to find by taking apart? Perhaps all along it's ultimately been futile to tweeze a spirit out of matter—not because there is nothing there, but because the whole is one? Indivisible. Seamless. No boundaries between this and that. "Integrity is wholeness," wrote the poet Robinson Jeffers. "The greatest beauty is organic wholeness, the wholeness of life and things, the divine beauty of the universe. Love that, not man apart from that."

Resolute Bay on Cornwallis Island is home of the Polar Continental Shelf Project, a Canadian government program to facilitate research in the North. It is an Arctic crossroads through which 400 scientists are funneled northward each year to do research at various sites. It is a polynya for *Homo sapiens*, a barracks-style meeting place where biologists, archeologists, geologists, oceanographers describe their finds, ask questions, learn more about the puzzle pieces they don't know that well. You can see the minds firing on all pistons, intellects in action, as each scientist outlines the intricate detail of his one piece of the vast portrait on which they all work.

Storytelling is an art treasured in the High Arctic. Hours are passed swapping tales of polar bears, caribou and wolves, airplane rides, and Eskimos. Close calls are recounted; the old days are remembered. Then at the Truelove camp on Devon Island, we would stay up till 2 or 3 in the morning listening to bearded Don Pattie, camp manager, elder and chief, tell of wildlife photographers being attacked by bears, or scientists running for their lives, a step ahead of a musk ox horn.

And as I listened, I thought of ancestors sitting around campfires, spinning yarns, contributing to a body of knowledge, adding to the folklore that bound the clan together, reinforced tribal values, told the truth. And I thought how far we've all come and all we've learned, and I wondered what it all really adds up to.

And I thought of a day on a rock beach on Devon Island when the four of us—Jack, Olga, Bernd, and I—stood where centuries before a family had made a home—of large stones and whale bones, big, white slabs of bone. There was a sleeping platform and an underground entranceway that once served as a cold air trap. And there was a kayak rack and a fox trap, built of stones, still standing. No one had lived here for *800* years.

That afternoon it rained and I sat in a small hut with the head of the Northern Heritage Society excavating the site. From small containers he pulled artifacts found here and at other sites in the North. Harpoon heads and fine bone needles used for sewing clothes. A delicately carved doll and a comb. Microblades carved from chert, models for instruments now used in surgery. And bone plugs, used by pre-Eskimos to seal wound holes in walrus and whale. The plugs would conserve the blood for later use and hold in the air so the heavy animals would remain afloat and be easier to haul through water.

It was impossible, then, not to sense the bonds with those who lived here centuries ago. Were they smart? Were they wise? What did they think about? What did *they* do on rainy days? I sat in the damp summer chill, drank coffee, and turned these relics over and over in my hands. And felt a profound respect for these people who lived here and asked the spirits for help in hunting and healing. "It is not only species of animal that die out," said the Magus. "But whole species of feeling. And if you are wise, you will never pity the past for what it did not know, but pity yourself for what it did."

That night, quite late, Bernd, Jack, and I set out in the rain to find a musk ox. The musk ox emerged 2 million years ago on the steppes of central Siberia. They came across the Bering land bridge 125,000 years ago and have survived all the ice ages of North America. Their companions—the mammoth, the short-faced bear, the North American camel—did not. Musk oxen were depicted in cave paintings; the golden fleece of their only living relative, the takin of northern Tibet, was the Holy Grail sought by Jason and the Argonauts.

Today there may be 40,000 musk oxen in Canada's far northern territories. They have changed little, if at all, since the Pleistocene

Epoch when a series of monster glaciers covered the North and extended below what is now Chicago. Musk oxen, browsing on the heather, grass, and sedge of Devon Island, appear like time-travelers from another realm, a world that exists only in the imagination. They stand and snort and trot along, as woolly reminders of a time when our ancestors stalked them for food. Standing face-to-face with these creatures, in the mist-shrouded valley between dark fists of rock, evoked in my mind a profound sense of awe . . . and an eerie feeling of kinship with all who take their name from the Latin *humus*, the earth.

I have a rock from that night, and the tooth of a polar bear, and this final image to share:

We are stuck here in Pond Inlet, a tiny Inuit village on Baffin Island. We would sleep on the floor of a pre-fab air terminal and hope to get a flight out tomorrow; but we weren't sure. Weather had grounded planes in the North for days. I had been told my ticket was no longer good; I had no cash, no credit card to buy a trip south. In the meantime, there was no bar in town. The clouds were low and thick; it was damp and cold. I pulled from the pocket of my goose-down jacket a can of beer I had saved for this moment, for a toast to our polar expedition, and to the predicament we were in.

We walked quietly out the gravel runway, trading swigs; the fog was really rolling in. We kept walking past the village dump (snow-mobiles and bathtubs, caribou heads and sealskins) and out along a rocky ridge above Pond Inlet. We had gone to look around once more . . . when Bernd saw the ravens walking, and I thought back to that day when ravens were just out of reach, and so we went running after them, wanting to get closer, to see. And I won't forget that one exultant moment when Bernd blurted, "One's hurt. I can catch it," and he ran around the ravine and out again onto the ridge, chasing the raven walking. Then it ran along the rocky ground as he ran behind it, down the hill with the green-blue mountains behind him. His arms flying as he ran downhill faster, gaining speed, and the raven took off gracefully and Bernd kept running, his legs bounding wildly. He was like a boy racing down a slope too fast, down toward the ice-white bay, his arms open wide to the bird and the air and the Arctic mountains rooted in the bay, with peaks shrouded in misty clouds.

Kerry Temple

For one transfigured second I thought he might take off and sail out over the bay and soar skyward there before me, with the snow and cloud-covered peaks surrounding him. A figure of loving pursuit. An earthbound descendant of *Homo erectus* running like hell to catch a bird.

10

seeker of truth

follow no path
all paths lead where

truth is here

—*e.e. cummings*

I am alone, wedged between two boulders in a scramble up to a ledge above the tree line, an aerie from which I can look around. But the next move is not easy. It's a 10-foot drop into a crevice and onto a ragged platform of stone, then up the other side to the cliff. So I squat on this primeval shelf, calculating distances, measuring the fall. I inch closer to the edge and brace against the granite boulders, trying to figure where to go next.

I hesitate here, but there is no going back. I can do this. My fingers clasp onto the cold, ragged rocks and I slide cautiously toward the edge.

One arm here; one hand there. One foot set; the other toeing its way along the scraggy stone. *Stuuussh!* My body falls as if . . . *Aaargh!* plummeting, splatting onto the . . . *My arm is wrong!* With my right hand I squeeze the arm and shove it upward, pushing, twisting, until the bone slides back into the shoulder socket. I hold my shoulder, burning with pain, then slump into a broken bundle and hunker there, my back against the wall.

My arm, hand, and fingers are trembling. I cradle the arm to my stomach and look up at the great stone faces above me. They are in shadow, overarching. The deep blue sky is far away. I lean my head back upon the rock and breathe deeply.

I'm in a fix. The only way out is up. And I have only one good arm for the climbing.

❦

This wasn't the first time I wondered what I was doing here. We had been dropped off several days ago, handed a couple of maps, and pointed south. All we had—bedroll, food, cooking gear—we carried on our backs. The trail was sometimes difficult to follow, meandering and splicing into deep-rutted logging roads, then swerving again into the woods. Up then down. Across dirt roads. One blistered foot ahead of the other. On the first day we followed a splintered wooden flume from a century-old gold-mining operation. On the second day we skirted a lake at sunrise and headed into the hills. Sometime that day we saw the mountain. We also learned that maps can lie.

The three of us—husbands and fathers on this back-to-nature retreat—were almost on empty when the October sun neared the horizon. We had been at it all day and were hungry and thirsty and ready to make camp. But we were virtually out of water; we couldn't stop without replenishing our supply. "The map shows a spring in the shadow of the mountain," we agreed, trying to convince ourselves we were practically there, not here.

We came upon a hilltop then and stood amid the carcasses of trees. It was a logged out, deforested patch of ground, crisscrossed by roads, plotted with stakes, marked with spray paint, and littered with cellophane paper and aluminum cans. It looked like a dump for ATV drivers or paintball warriors. But there in the distance was the mountain, out on the horizon like a hazy blue triangle against the sky—days away. Then, too, I wondered what I was doing here.

This isn't the way it's supposed to be, I thought—hiking over parched and stubbly ground with water and our day's destination so far away. But I was really mad after another hour's walk when we came to a two-lane asphalt highway. Two days of walking and we still hadn't escaped concrete, cars, and other people-things. And according to the map, this was a highway we should have crossed hours ago.

Kerry Temple

We stopped to review our choices: hitch a ride on the blacktop, stay on the trail but go without water, or take a chance of finding water down a dirt road we saw veering from the highway. It bore the encouraging name Twin Springs Road, so we took it—thirsty, dragging our legs, straining under 40-pound packs. It didn't help that the map showed the road led to a town called Oblivion.

A car rumbled toward us—a rusted brown Oldsmobile with an old man driving. We flagged him down and explained our problem—half lost, near sunset, miles to water. "What the hell," the man exclaimed, popping open the car trunk, "I've got *water*." He passed out plastic jugs of fresh well water as if it were champagne for a wedding feast. Slugging down the first in about a minute, we refilled our containers and took two extra jugs for the road. Our good fortune replenished our spirits, too. "What the hell," we'd mimic, laughing, walking along. "I've got *water*."

Then, at sunset, the air turned golden-red and streamers of salmon-colored clouds stretched across the sky. In time the darkness descended with a hush and the mountain was a black silhouette to the south. We camped in a grassy meadow and watched the stars come out; Venus was dazzling in the southwest. We bundled against the night cold, stuffing our hands into jeans pockets and stomping our feet while we stargazed, naming constellations, spotting shooting stars, trying to fathom the incomprehensible glory of the nighttime sky—the billions of heavenly bodies, the billions of miles in between, the billions of mysteries unfolding as they have for billions of years.

So that night, as the coyotes howled and we slept amid the giant rocks with only a bedroll between us and the earth, I wondered again what I was doing here. And what it's all for. And what it all means. And that night, like every night on the trail, we would half-wake and look up to see the stars travel across the sky, to spot the flaming meteors, to track the journey of the crescent moon—knowing that this expanse of wilderness was a good place to be.

[image of small leaf/sprig symbol]

I massage my shoulder and find it tender but intact, so I stand to plot my escape. The best route is the large boulder to my left. Though it's taller than I am, I think I can manage to scuttle up its sloping face.

Back to Earth

But when I lift my left arm, pain sears through me and I look for another way out. There is none.

So I start to scale it. I pull and push, squiggle like a worm and—slowly, deliberately—ascend the broad and craggy stone, my belly pressed tight against the rock. My fingers and feet work like little flippers, scooching me along.

When I reach the top, I see the maneuver hasn't helped much with my ascent but drops quickly down the other side—into another pit, a cleft axed into the rimrock. And I am stuck, lying face down, my body flopped over the top of the boulder like a deer on a fender, as I stare at the ground below.

Floundering, wiggling, I am practically immobile unless I want to budge forward and drop like a bag of bones onto the rocks below. Headfirst.

I do. And land with a crash.

It hurts, but my shoulder is still in its socket. My feet, however, are sticking up over my head. This hole is deeper than the last one. Things aren't getting any better.

We were up before sunrise after our night in the meadow. The stars were fading when I heard the camp stove being fired up for coffee. Frost had glazed the grass and our sleeping bags white, and there was ice in our water containers as we rattled around in the first glow of dawn. By the time we were sipping our coffee and jawing on chewy bagels, the sun had nosed its way over this edge of the planet and was pouring its light down the ridges before us.

It's hard to comprehend that Earth, as we ride upon its rugged hide, is hurtling through space at 66,600 miles per hour, spinning as it goes. But there we were as Earth rolled over and into the warmth of the sun whose golden glow crept down the mountain, flamed through the trees, and nestled into radiant puddles on the meadow. Then the sun shone on us too.

Being out like this makes you think about things, like the value of sunlight for visibility and warmth in a world without walls or roof or space heater. That there's not much between your feet and the ground—nothing to separate you from the place, no distractions, no barriers between you and the dusty world. It's a simple life: You walk, eat, walk, sit, and sleep. It is tiresome, monotonous, often boring. But when you've covered some miles, you realize you've learned as much about yourself as about the land you've crossed. It's a good thing to be doing now, at this time in our lives. I was glad I had learned the ropes when I was younger.

I was a boy growing up in Louisiana when I first went to the woods, playing along Bayou Pierre and later exploring the banks and waters of the Red and Sabine Rivers. As I got older and spread my reach, my thoughts took flight. They no longer fit inside a building, no matter how high the ceiling or how lofty the spires. I looked for God instead in the things he made, and I took seriously the words of Leopold and Dillard, Black Elk and Thoreau, the Zen and Taoist mystics, and others who knew where to look for the fingerprints left behind. But mostly I've walked. Sometimes I sit. And occasionally I've encountered guides along the way who unlocked the mysteries of the universe in a cottonwood, an eagle, or a stone.

So here I am, lodged in the Church of the Big Hole. I am propped against one boulder with another towering above me, eclipsing the sun. The air smells of pine; a gnarly dwarf juniper grows through a crack in the rock. In another crevice—a hairline fracture splitting noticeably wider each millennium—are spears of grass and the leafy exuberance of a pair of ferns. The granite boulders, exquisitely shaped by wind and water, are probably 2 billion years old, first boiled and stirred in the bowels of the fiery earth, then cooled here—having since erupted through the earth's skin like a subterranean giant's fingers grasping for the sky.

The rocks are painted with lichens, which could stand for all the world's tiny microcosms of beauty and order, a reminder that little wonders can inspire awe as readily as great ones. With my fingernail I scrape off a scratchy patch and put it to my lips, my tongue. Green, grey, and vibrant orange, these splotches of gritty life are part fungus, part algae. A lichen thrives because of the give-and-take between its two parts. The fungus provides support, water, and minerals, while the algae chips in the food, which it concocts

Back to Earth

through photosynthesis, the brewing of sunlight, carbon dioxide, and water.

So lichens grow anywhere—in the bleached skulls of dead animals, in the freezing Antarctic waters, above 18,500 feet in the Himalayas. One species travels on the wind. Some Arctic lichens are 4,000 years old; another variety furnishes two-thirds of a reindeer's diet. Lichens have been used as a medicinal against superficial wounds, chest ailments, tuberculosis, scarlet fever, and pneumonia. And some say lichen tea isn't bad.

A chipmunk skitters down the great rock before me, stops halfway, looks at me. It hangs there, perpendicular to the ground, as if gravity holds no sway. Then it abruptly bolts to the right, scurrying along the rock face. I should be so nimble, so agile, so swift.

We had hiked all morning, climbing higher, ascending the initial slopes of the mountain. By noon we had reached a broad shoulder of earth whose most ambitious outcroppings offered a panoramic view of the green, tree-covered valleys, the bold rock escarpments, the sun-bathed pinnacle looming before us. We found the spring, a delicious trickle of water emanating from a rocky glade in the mountainside. We stopped for a lunch of soup and jerky, then decided to stay the afternoon and night. It was good to move without packs, to air out our socks, to sit in the sun. We'd make our last push to the mountaintop in the morning.

But I soon grew impatient and restless, as if what I wanted was out there somewhere, across the way, up above. Unable to sit still, wanting to fill the daylight hours, I scrambled up some rocks, mounting one formation then another, driven by a heady urgency, goaded by a restive bravado—until I fell.

My shoulder throbs now; the sun is sinking. I can see the tops of ponderosa pines stirring in the breeze and a flurry of sparrows flitting, twittering, skimming away like a school of quicksilver minnows. I feel trapped in this rocky cove, broken, alone, grounded, knowing I should get out of here. But I really don't feel much like moving. I am comfortable leaning back against this rock, my arm folded to my stomach. I rest my head against the stone, take a deep breath, and try to relax.

I try to be content here, to sit still, to lean on the cold, silent rock. But it isn't easy. I am antsy and impatient, anxious. I try to settle myself. But I come from the band of predatory gatherers—even of ideas and facts and beliefs; I am accustomed to moving, pursuing, stalking. I want to see what's over the next rise, get beyond the next bend in the road. I am a product of my culture.

Perhaps no element is more central to the American character than movement. Our nation began on the move. Many of the world's societies trace their heritage back to ancient civilizations that had occupied the same geographical space for centuries. We trace our cultural lineage back to explorers, pilgrims, and pioneers who cut ties with a past in search of a better place—in the distance, in the frontier, in the future. Our cultural icon is the cowboy—restless, rootless, always in the saddle, riding into sunsets.

The frontier pushed west, then farther west, and we as a society never stopped moving. North to Alaska. West to California. South to the Sunbelt. Out to the suburbs—where we became a nation of the automobile—celebrator of mobility, power, and speed. Off to Colorado, Montana, Oregon, the paradise of someplace else. Then into space.

We are still a nation on the run, commuting to work or driving from school to the mall to the grocery store—a nation of fast-food joints with drive-through windows. Even when we stop, we are not still. We play, ride stationary bikes, climb mechanical stairs, or jog; our bodies push and pulsate to fill our leisure time. At home we turn on the TV, the radio, the CD player. We read the paper; we immerse ourselves in a swirl of media—from video games to movies to Internet explorations—to keep our mind active even when our body is not. We find noise to drown out the awful silence. We do not stop to think; we do not sit still. We choose a feast of facts and knowledge and information over the quiet solitude that makes room for wisdom and peace.

We are a restless nation precisely because we have not found that peace. Even out on the land, we are scalers of mountains, heroic in triumph, conquerors of cliffs and peaks, ignoring Robert Pirsig's warning in *Zen and the Art of Motorcycle Maintenance*: "The only Zen you find on the tops of mountains is the Zen you take up there." We are a nation of movers and shakers, of people with get up and go, and we have always looked outside ourselves for the graces that would nurture the soul. Our literature reflects this quest motif, as if God or gold or truth were out there somewhere liked buried treasure at the end of a rainbow. As a Christian nation, we are religious descendants of the wandering Jew in search of the Promised Land; we are heirs to the Arthurian legend and the quest for the Holy Grail; Ahab set sail in search of the whale and all it meant; Hemingway's old man went out to sea; Huck Finn rafted the river then "lit out for the Territory ahead of the rest."

Peter Matthiessen wrote a book about a snow leopard he didn't find. His quest took him to Nepal, deep into Buddhist thought. He did not find the snow leopard, he maintains, because he was not worthy. It was not that he hadn't earned it—he hiked for weeks in the snow and cold, spiraling ever higher into the lofty Himalayan wilderness; it was because he was not spiritually ready. The snow leopard comes not to those whose bodies have covered the miles, but to those whose souls have journeyed far enough along.

"All my life," he writes, "I have hurried down between these walls, the sun crossing high over my head, voice swept away in the din of this green flood. The river, and life going: why do I hurry?"

Trapped here, slumped in a darkening corner of this mountain range, I am reminded of my own hikes and times I rushed up trails in hope of better views, higher vistas, as if beauty or revelation waited only at the summit. But it comes only after time, I am reminded time and again, from sitting still and listening. That's an Eastern thought, not Western, that truth comes in the stillness, through contemplation and solitude, mindful receptivity. We are not a contemplative society, so we search the desert for God of the Mountaintop. We go there to find God; we do not learn how to draw God to us. Annie Dillard had it right when she wrote in *Pilgrim at Tinker Creek:* "Although the pearl may be found, it may not be sought. The literature of illumination reveals this above all: although it comes to those who wait for it, it is always, even to the most practiced and adept, a gift and a *total surprise.*"

Or, tired of not finding God or truth or enlightenment in all the wrong places, we have ceased exploring themes so big. We substitute, instead, life's little rewards to fend off the *angst* that threatens us: the fleeting moments of instant gratification, the illusions of status and fame, the opiates of popularity and power, the allure of material wealth, the adrenaline rush of triumph. We chase them; they offer momentary satisfaction, temporary escape. But they are dead ends all.

Kerry Temple

They leave us restless, doom us to a perpetual search, send us after God as if he—or truth or grace or wisdom—were somewhere else, hiding in the clouds, lurking in the shadows, waiting at the mountaintop. He isn't necessarily there either.

As the great Oriental philosopher Lao Tzu wrote in *Tao Te Ching*:

> Without stirring abroad
> One can know the whole world;
> Without looking out the window
> One can see the way to heaven.
> The further one goes
> The less one knows.
> Therefore the sage knows without having to stir,
> Identifies without having to see,
> Accomplishes without having to act.

These thoughts in the company of rock are eventually arrested by a sudden chill, the throbbing of shoulder, the absence of sunlight. It is time to move on; I cannot stay past sundown. So I stand and survey my surroundings, looking for a corridor. I search about, trying various routes, but there, hidden behind a tumble of boulders, is a narrow cleft. It is the only possible passage out, so I take it.

It isn't easy, but after a few precarious moves and one more fall and some patient persistence, I stumble onto relatively flat ground. I rig a sling with my belt and head back to camp, hoping the others have dinner ready.

That night the wind wailed like a banshee, whistling through the granite outcroppings around us and roaring with a fury through the trees, making the pines, birch, and aspens toss like stalks of wheat. I woke up often, heard the wind boring into cliffs overhead, watched the swaying trees, and felt blessed that it was a warm wind with no rain, ice, or snow in it. The night stayed starry clear, but as first light bloomed the wind had still not subsided. Unable to keep the flames of the camp stove sheltered, we had trouble boiling water for breakfast coffee. It was the morning we hoped to make it to the top.

Back to Earth

I'd been wondering about my shoulder. It wasn't the pain now that bothered me so much as feeling broken, vulnerable, flawed—and a little off balance as my pack was hoisted onto my back. But we trundled steadily uphill throughout the early morning, appreciating the cool air as the sun first splintered through the trees to cast elongated shadows. Once I spotted my own shadow striding along beside me, its arms and legs disproportionately long—like an El Greco painting, I thought.

By late morning we emerged upon a ridge and, noticing an opening in the trees to the south, left the trail for a look around. We were high; the landscape was spread at our feet. Craggy peaks were all around us; the wind was fierce. The mountain, looking higher and more distant than ever, seemed to hover against the azure sky.

The trail wound more steeply then, with switchbacks that taxed the legs and lungs. The air got thinner and the trees grew smaller, their roots clawing into the scant soil. As we walked, our bodies buffeted by the constant winds, we looked for the mountain goats and bighorn sheep reported to patrol these heights. But we saw none, though tracks and droppings were plentiful.

Up the final ridge we followed the steep and winding trail. Occasionally I glanced up, spying the summit over here, then back over there, always hanging over the next rise, around the next bend. I stepped steadily, rhythmically, bent under the weight of my pack, my knees a little shaky. Then we were close—close enough to drop packs and scramble the last few hundred feet.

The ascent to the top wasn't difficult. The last passes were easy, and dropping the pack gave my body an airy, weightless feeling, as if the wind could blow me away. It came in fists and sheets and gusts that knocked me off balance, unnerved me, had me bracing against its gale force pounding—as violent as the breakers that hammer rocky coasts. It roared in my ears and surged around me, leaving me dizzy and light and afraid.

The view from the top was staggering, exhilarating, unnerving. We scanned the horizon in every direction: to rocky peaks jutting skyward, to the woolly green carpet draped over the crests and valleys of the mountain range, to the parched brown high plains way off to the east. The sky was blue and high with ship-like clouds. Our view, standing on the edge of the precipice, was unimpeded everywhere.

Kerry Temple

After awhile I asked, "What do we do now?" The answer: "Let's eat lunch." So we clambered back down out of the wind, taking refuge at the base of a stone wall, and shared our lunch with a pair of chipmunks and a gray jay who had discovered us and our food. We agreed to spend most of the afternoon here, each going his own way, exploring the upper reaches.

The mountain was sacred to the People, before the others came. There were holy men among the People who said this was the center of the universe, a place of visions. The others found gold here, and timber to cut, fences to build, roads to pave, water to harness . . . and buffalo to slaughter. I am one of the others but I don't think of lumber when I look out upon these forests. I don't see hydroelectric power in the river valleys, nor prime real estate in the rolling grasslands.

I have come here, after my fall, to make amends, to find my place among the rocks and trees and things of which I am a part. I recall Augustine's line: "If our hearts are restless, our hearts are made for Thee, and they're restless till they rest in Thee." Such is the course of our redemption: to be one with the seen and unseen reaches of the world.

So I curl onto a bench of rock and look out upon the wind-combed landscape. From here the towering ponderosa look like dwarf grasses blanketing the land, a shag carpet tossed over the earth. Bear Butte, which remains a ceremonial site in the twenty-first century, appears on the horizon like a volcanic pyramid. The cathedral spires, the rocky points, and the crags are rough-hewn nuggets of stone breaking the bounds of nature—the sun splashing off their faces. And I want to stretch my hand upon it all, to rub the surfaces, touch the rock, caress the rolling hillsides, valleys, plains. From this place, this distance, it is all one.

The wind blows freely, washing over my body in waves. Bright-colored prayer flags whip in the wind. I watch the bare spots, the stony outcroppings, for mountain goats. But see none. I finger the stones, the dirt around me, squint into the sun as it arcs across the sky.

I try to memorize the view, to lock this feeling inside my head. Whatever God I have is in these mountains, in the forests and fields

Back to Earth

I've walked, the rivers, woods, and deserts I've known. It is bad, I think, that the places we might find the divine are fewer and smaller, more corrupted. Cut off from the land that nurtures us, we grow more estranged from the soul of our universe.

It is time to move on, so I stash a rock in the pocket of my jeans and stand. I face in the four directions: to the north from which comes the cleansing wind, the power to make pure; to the east from which comes the morning light, the power of insight, knowledge, and wisdom; to the south from which summer comes the power to make warm, to grow and bring life; and finally to the west from which the Thunder Beings come. They are the spiritual guides, and I ask them again to point the way.

Turning to leave, I spot an eagle riding the thermals high, then dropping down before banking again, swooping toward me. Its blade wings knife the air and the sun shimmers on its shoulders as it strokes gracefully into the valley, flapping and sailing before disappearing from sight.

Later we gather again to sling on our backpacks and start down the trail. We walk slowly down the shadow-side of the mountain, descending to the lap of the earth. The air is cool and moist as we follow Grizzly Creek and the canyon it has carved out of the mountainside. The narrow-gorge ravine is forested with aspens and pine sprouting from the banks of the meandering stream. We find a place to nestle in till morning, sleep on a mat of yellow leaves, pine straw, and grass, and listen through the night to the spring water tumbling along the chasm. We hear an owl there, too.

We pass the next few days wrapped in a kind of intimate tranquility, slowing our pace, taking time to wander where we wish. Sometimes we'd follow the stream, examining the design and construction of beaver dams and marveling at their industry. Or we'd climb around on the ancient rock sculptures, walk the woods, laze in grassy meadows. The trail glistened with mica and quartz crystals and the silvery speckles and veins of unknown minerals—as if the whole landscape had been transformed.

We took pleasure, too, in each other's company, in the moss on the trees, in the fish that slithered in the sunny pools of Grizzly Creek.

Kerry Temple

But mostly what I recall from these days was going—individually or together—to the rocks to sit. One early morning we mounted a ledge and looked out upon the distant green valleys still draped with a heavy grey fog. We stared at the peaks lunging skyward and waited for the sun to burn the valley clean. One afternoon we found a glade whose leaf-strewn floor was mottled with patches of sunlight filtering through the aspen trees. We stayed there for the longest time, basking on the flat, sunny-hot boulders and watching the cirrus strands pass overhead. We stood in an open meadow at sunrise to see the first red glow of dawn strike stony crests, illuminating the world. And we delighted in the exotic rock grottoes, the texture of the granite, the abundance of the lichens holding fast.

One evening as we waited for dinner to cook, one of us mentioned an experience he'd had that day on the trail. It was a feeling he was bashful about discussing, but I understood when he described it—something about "the mountain speaking"—and then said, "It's the kind of feeling that comes on its own, when you least expect it." Sometimes I think it comes only when you stop looking, when you lose yourself in the landscape, momentarily forgetting to observe it. Sometimes I think it comes when you've hiked far enough along, or been out long enough, blending unself-consciously into it. When it comes, you would swear that grace is real. That you've just been handed the rarest of gifts.

I remembered, then, the day we broke for lunch in a meadow—the first day out, when a warm and powerful wind suddenly whooshed over us. We stopped what we were doing and stood there facing it, letting it brush our faces and whip our clothing, hats, and hair. We joked about spirits and prayers.

Later in the trip we found an old, dried-out skull of a huge horse. The teeth and jaws were intact, and the bones clean and gray. We carried the skull into camp, perched it on a boulder, toasted it with Gatorade, and put trail mix in its mouth. In the darkness of night we put a flashlight inside the hollow head to give it a ghostly look, and we called on the headless horse to come and retrieve its skull.

On the last night I awoke from a dream with pain in my shoulder. Perhaps it had grown stiff in the nighttime cold, or maybe it hurt because of the position I'd been sleeping in. I sat up in the blackness and felt a warm breath of air roll over me. After massaging the shoulder I lay back down and looked up through the black tree limbs into the starry sky laced with fingery clouds. It was the middle of the night and we were camped atop a small hill littered with boulders. It was good to lie there, flat on my back, watching the twinkling stars one last time. Then I heard a strange sound that I first interpreted as the snarl of a mountain lion.

I heard it again. Closer.

A few seconds passed and I heard the noise again, now only a few feet away. I held my breath and, without twitching a muscle, listened intently. There it was—the snort again, then the thud of heavy hoof beats bounding downhill. It stopped and I heard more wheezing, a heavy breathing in the distance. Then the hoof beats again galloping back up the hill and into camp.

I could hear the animal breathing close to me—panting, exhaling, the air blowing forcefully through dampened nostrils. I couldn't, I wouldn't budge.

From the lusty snorting and the power of the hoof beats, I knew it was a horse, a buffalo, or an elk—probably an elk, given our altitude. I knew, too, that if I rolled over for a look, I would not see it in the darkness; I would only hear its ghostly breathing and feel its thundering presence—as if some phantom beast was favoring us by dancing in our camp.

Then it rumbled away, hooves pounding the earth, the thumping and snorting fading until the sounds, carried on the wind, evaporated into the night. I lay listening for its return and heard a soft rhythmic throbbing. I realized it was my own heart beating.

The wind gusted then, jostling the trees, threatening a storm. But I, bundled in my bedroll spread upon the ground, savored the aroma of pine and the scent of rain in the air, then drifted off to sleep. And while the moon rolled slowly around the earth, I slept through the night like a rock.

11

The first peace is that which comes within the souls of men when they realize their relationship, their oneness, with the universe and all its powers, and when they realize that at the center of the universe dwells Wakan-Tanka, and that this center is really everywhere, it is within each of us. This is the real peace, and the others are but reflections of this.

—Black Elk, Lakota holy man

This small stone reminds me of a dream. It is a dream I still see when I sit alone in my cabin. I was younger then. There were things I wanted to know. So I got in my car and I went to find out. Sometimes I think I got very close to something important. Sometimes I think not. Sometimes I think I was young then and I got carried away. But it all starts with this dream.

I am sitting on a rocky ocean cliff overlooking sea and sky. Before me, across a circle of stones surrounding campfire ashes, an old man sits and talks of eagles. "The eagle," the man's voice says, "not only flies but is one with the wind. Crosscurrents, hot air shafts that lift him, cold air funnels that drop him like a rock—he must know them all. And not just as a pilot checking radar and instrument panels—he must sense them well enough to ride the wind as though his spirit and it were one." And a long-haired woman, sitting to my right, answers each of my questions with, "The value cherished most is an honest sincerity, a sincere honesty." That is what the woman says to all my questions.

And the next thing I know I am swimming in that sea-blue sky, soaring then plummeting. Turning somersaults, tumbling happily upward, out of control, sailing through space. And as I do so, I try only to spot that eagle—sometimes close, sometimes distant—flying above and below me in that liquid-blue sky; sometimes right next to me, sometimes pinpoint high, often eclipsed by the sunlight blinding me, shafts of radiance flung off its wings.

Images of that eagle remain today, and the glory of effortlessly flying I can still recall. I see it every time I step from my cabin to spy a red-tailed hawk. I can see it in every sky.

The dream I had one night on my way to South Dakota. I had read the histories and studied by book the ways of those native to this place. Here was a people, I thought, whose belief system was inseparable from the land, whose Great Spirit filled the universe, whose culture embodied the faith I had been seeking. So I got in my car and went to see what legacy survived among those still living here. I was in my early 30s.

The road west veers out of the city, out through the suburbs, fast-food strips, and malls. It skirts along the grungy edges of Chicago, past the steel, smokestacks, and rust, then out to the cornfields of fenced-in Illinois to the undulating green of homestead Iowa where the towns and farms grow farther apart—greater distances between people and passing cars—until you begin to feel the land. A strong wind sweeps over this grassland sea and red-winged blackbirds fly into the air. And when you exit the interstate and take the two-lane across southern South Dakota, on the other side of the dammed up Missouri River (passageway for Lewis and Clark) with the colossal power lines strung out in every direction, you feel something different coming on. The earth and sky are so big here, and people-things so small.

You drive for miles across the vast treeless landscape only occasionally punctuated by the last outposts of human detritus: the fences and poles stringing wire and the final few billboards and farm implement dealerships, the Tastee Freezes and bars in out-of-the-way places like Bonesteel, Burke, and Colome. And as you approach the Rosebud Reservation, rolling on from Winner to Okreek, the sky is full of wind and the horizons are all far away. It is easy then to imagine when no roads led here—just the land as far as you could see. Just you and the plains rising and falling like the tanned, curving body of a sleeping woman. Here the land breathes, I was told; the ridges and hills rise and sink from one month to the next. Young Mother Earth.

I drive slower now with the wind flapping through open windows, then pull off onto a dirt road, tires rumbling underneath. I stop the car, get out, and stand beneath this different sky, where the wind blows forever and the clouds pass like ships. I turn slowly, facing in each of the four directions, seeing only land and sky, sagebrush, dirt, a hawk. And as my eyes scan the mesas and ravines, I want to run my hand over the textured contours of the earth like a lover gently tracing the lines down his girlfriend's throat, breast, then hip.

"There was no such thing as emptiness in the world," Luther Standing Bear once said, recalling the old days of his Lakota people. "Even in the sky there were no vacant places. Everywhere there was life, visible and invisible, and every object gave us a great interest to life. Even without human companionship one was never alone. The world teemed with life and wisdom."

I cannot help but think of a time when all this was theirs, this *and* the land it's taken me two days to cross; I could drive for days in any direction and not leave what once was theirs. It was a time before state lines or reservation boundaries, before the whole vast continent was drawn and quartered, when the coastal forests became the seaboard mountains and the grasslands must have seemed infinite to those on foot or horseback. They say that before the white man came wild buffalo stretched from horizon to horizon here. One man told of riding more than 100 miles through one herd. People lived here, too—for 10,000 years before whites arrived. The buffalo, whom they held sacred, sustained them.

Evidence suggests that the continent's natives were first called Indians by Columbus not because he had set out for India (which was then known as Hindustan) but because he found them a people in God, *in Dios*. After these people had surrendered more than half the continent to the invading whites, and about the time developers were building railroads and towns and saying things like "the only good Indian is a dead Indian," these plains were laden with buffalo bones.

A paper trail of broken treaties had pushed the Native Americans halfway across the continent by 1840 when another "Permanent Indian Frontier" was established. But whites continued to advance, blazing the Oregon Trail in 1842 and streaming westward during the California

Gold Rush of 1849. Late in the summer of 1851 some 10,000 Plains Indians—Sioux, Cheyenne, Arapaho, Crow, and more—converged at Fort Laramie and signed a treaty in which they divided their diminishing hunting grounds among themselves and pledged peace with whites, to whom they offered safe passage through their land.

But that treaty, too, was broken, and over the next few decades the Sioux, also known as Lakota, defended their land against encroaching whites, most notably in the late 1860s when U.S. troops tried establishing a series of forts throughout Indian country. Then, in 1874, gold was discovered in the Black Hills and the floodgates opened. Black Elk, who would fight Custer at Little Big Horn and survive the massacre at Wounded Knee, recalled years later: "When I was older, I learned what the fighting was about that winter and the next summer. Up on the Madison Fork the *Wasichus* had found much of the yellow metal that they worship and that makes them crazy, and they wanted to have a road through our country to the place where the yellow metal was; but my people did not want the road. It would scare the bison and make them go away, and also it would let the other *Wasichus* come in like a river. They told us they wanted only to use a little land, as much as a wagon would take between the wheels; but our people knew better. And when you look about you now, you can see what it is they wanted."

By the winter of 1890 the "Indian problem" had been virtually eradicated. The last defiant Sioux had been killed or rounded up onto reservations—their land gone, their lifestyle destroyed, their religious practices outlawed and punishable by force. In the three decades following the treaty of 1851, Indian country was reduced from roughly half the continent to the backwater reservation-plots we know today. "Once we were happy in our own country," Black Elk recalled, "and we were seldom hungry, for then the two-leggeds and the four-leggeds lived together like relatives, and there was plenty for them and for us. But the *Wasichus* came, and they have made little islands for us and other little islands for the four-leggeds, and always these islands are becoming smaller, for around them surges the gnawing flood of the *Wasichus*; and it is dirty with lies and greed."

In that winter of 1890, a band of Sioux held prisoner on reservation land after surrendering to the 7th Calvary was attacked. Mostly elderly, women, and children, they had just wanted to dance; they believed it would restore the old way. A shot rang out; they were slaughtered, mutilated. Rapid-firing Hotchkiss cannons were turned on children huddled in a ravine; women and children were chased down and murdered—200, maybe 350 killed in the snow along Wounded Knee Creek—not very far west of where I have stopped to look around. Over near Pine Ridge. There is a highway marker.

The frozen bodies were buried in a heap on New Year's Day 1891, about a century ago. "There was a big blizzard, and it grew very cold," Black Elk recalled later. "The snow drifted deep in the crooked gulch, and it was one long grave of butchered women and children and babies, who had never done any harm and were only trying to run away."

They called it the Ghost Dance. And they sang *"Wanbli galeshka wana ni he o who e."* "The Spotted Eagle is coming to carry me away." *Wanbli Galeshka,* The Spotted Eagle. His feathers described as rays of the sun, whose feathers hold the real presence, *Wakan-Tanka,* the Great Spirit.

I am coming here but two generations after those voices—singing of the spotted eagle—were drowned in the winter wind. I had met a young Oglala Lakota, Fernando Dreaming Bear, living in Indiana, in a square room in a rectangular dormitory. The powers of the universe move in circles, his ancestor Black Elk had said. All time is cyclical. The moon, sun, and earth are round; our drums and lodges are round. Birds build their nests in circles, the wind swirls in circular patterns and a man's life is a complete cycle. When the *Wasichus* confined us to reservations, Black Elk had said, he put us in square houses. And there is no power in a square.

It was Fernando Dreaming Bear who led me—who had only read the books and wanted to know more—to South Dakota, to Leonard Crow Dog and Sam Moves Camp and Little Soldier. "I am caught between three worlds," he told me once. "The white way. Traditional Lakota values and beliefs. And the third is . . ." His voice trailed off; he could not describe the limbo, the purgatory of reservation life.

On February 27, 1973, several hundred armed Indians seized a church and a trading post at Wounded Knee. Under siege and exchanging gunfire with FBI agents, the Indians held the town for 71 days. On a hill overlooking the battle and equipped with a telescope and a transistor radio, Fernando Dreaming Bear had watched as two

FBI agents and an Indian fell dead from gunshot wounds. When the agents finally stormed the building, they discovered that the last of the occupiers had slipped their siege line and headed for the hills.

One not so fortunate was Leonard Crow Dog who, along with Russell Means and Dennis Banks, was a leader of the occupation and a principal in the American Indian Movement. Crow Dog spent 23 months in federal penitentiaries for assault and robbery during the takeover—for handcuffing postal inspectors and confiscating guns.

When I met him he lived along the banks of the Little White River where his family has lived for 12 generations. It was a formidable homesite, remote and fenced and defended by large, hand-painted signs that read, "NO TRESPASSING" and "WHITES KEEP OUT." Prayer flags hung from posts and trees; a sun dance area and *tipis* stood out back. Farther on, in the green valley of the winding river, his grandfather's remains rested upon scaffolding in a tree, wrapped there with his things, in the traditional Lakota way, so that his spirit might join his ancestors. On the morning we met he stepped from his log house and tossed a small bird into the air.

"He is my messenger," Crow Dog said. "The birds, buffalo and deer are close to us. The eagle speaks with the whistle sounds of the echoes of the powers of this land. The face of the land is sacred. Nature is sacred. This is our Lakota way. Nothing has changed that. We are the richest people because of what comes from the land."

"It is simple," Crow Dog told me. "It is time to make relations to everything."

Those memories, those voices echo in my head as I stand along the roadside, reorienting myself from one world to another, the city-place I left behind and this landscape breathing with mystery and possibility and, as well, the devastating poverty, alcoholism, unemployment, and suffering also found here. It is summer now, and hot, though the wind here never stops. Storm clouds approach in the distance and I walk slowly back to the car.

"What were you doing?" asks Casey, my son. He is now 9. I had asked him to come west with me. For two days he has quietly stared out the window at America passing by. For two days he has listened to this history, and to stories of pioneers and mountain men, and of Red Cloud's War, the Sand Creek massacre, and the murders of Crazy Horse and Sitting Bull—a legacy better not forgotten.

Kerry Temple

"Just looking around," I tell him.

"What were you looking for?" he asks.

"I'm not sure," I say. He watches out the window.

I had asked him to come along with me this time because I wanted him to see for himself this land and its people, and I hoped (though I did not tell him so) that this trip might be one of the most important things I could give to him. As I start the car and turn it back toward the two-lane, Casey blurts, "Look, there's deer." So there is. And as we drive on I know we have arrived, although we have not yet reached our destination.

I have been here before—7 years prior to this trip back with my son. Seven years had passed since I first came upon Little Soldier's home on the vast and gently rolling plains of South Dakota, great sky overhead, shadowy cabin. Little Soldier had sat across the table from me and tied a red bandanna around his head "to think right thoughts" as we spoke. We talked long through that summer afternoon—of traditional Lakota ways, the meaning of the pipe, the sanctity of the earth and all its creatures. Sam Moves Camp, who had come from Oglala then to help Little Soldier prepare for a vision quest, was there, and we drank coffee and talked; but in the silences, too, were stories I tried hard to understand.

It was that afternoon in Little Soldier's cabin, 7 years ago, while his wife in the shadows prepared the tobacco pouches to protect him on his vision quest, that the Lakota seer placed his fist upon the table and unrolled his palm to reveal a small stone. "Understand this," he said, handing it to me, "and you will understand it all. You do not understand it now. It is too simple. Pray for understanding."

Our eyes met and locked. His dark eyes smiled from beneath the bandanna. I took the rock from his hand—it is round, opaque, and smooth—and slipped it into my jeans pocket where it felt good amid the flat quarters and dimes. Sam, sitting to my right, his long hair down his back, looked at me and grinned.

After a silence, as twilight deepened and shadows settled into the room, I asked about *Inipi*, the rite of purification, the sweat lodge. Robert Stead, described as one of the most powerful medicine men in South Dakota, had asked me to join him on this night. I had read of the intense heat, the possibility of passing out and falling into the coals, the coming of the spirits who enter the lodge and dance in the darkness.

Back to Earth

To ease my apprehension Sam said, "The sweat has one purpose only and that is to pray, and to pray you must be sincere and honest. Think of the rocks whose steam you will breathe. They come from Grandmother Earth. Listen, for they have much to teach. Breathe in their spirit and it will drive the poisons from your body. Be sincere. Be honest. And you will not know it is hot."

Quiet filled the room and Sam added, "Be sincere. Be honest." And I looked hard at Sam and at Little Soldier and at the woman in the corner looking down, silently preparing the pouches and the sweetgrass braids and the colored prayer flags to bring good medicine on Little Soldier's vision quest when the hidden spirits come. And I remembered my dream then, and I figured it was time to go to Robert Stead's, an hour's drive away.

So we moved outside where the sun hung orange over the long, flat earth line to the west. Children scampered through the dirt yard. Dogs trailed after. This was Ring Thunder, Little Soldier's camp, where a band of Lakota, called Sioux by the French, lived the traditional way.

"What do you think when you see storm clouds in the sky?" Sam asked as I stepped to my car.

I said, because I thought this then, "I wonder what spirits are shaking up the universe."

"It is the Thunder Beings," he replied. "They come to protect you. With thunder and lightning they guide you on your way. So too will this," he said, handing me twin feathers still joined bloodily at the quills. "These are feathers from a spotted eagle. The spotted eagle will help you see clearly 15 years into the past and 15 years into the future. They will show you the way. With the rock and the feather, pray tonight in Robert Stead's sweat lodge."

I am soon ripping down the dirt-and-gravel washboard road from Ring Thunder to Stead's place, running late and raising dust. Other than the rumbling road, there is no sign of man as far as I can see over the sweeping Dakota plains. For the first time, glancing in my rearview mirror, I notice the western sky blue-black with clouds. I speed on and notice the wind picking up. Dust covers the lower sky, and the grass and sage whip like waves on a choppy sea. Tumbleweeds careen in front of me. Huge shoulders of darkened clouds stampede low across the sky. Thunder booms, lightning crackles. A

Kerry Temple

yellow light casts an eerie pallor upon the landscape, then the clouds cut loose and flood the waiting earth. The rain comes in torrents, pelting my car while the windshield wipers flap madly, beating themselves, but do little to clear my underwater view.

By the time I reach Stead's place, the downpour is but a sprinkle. I climb from the car and see the sun glowing golden in the west. A double rainbow—one bright spectrum curving atop the other—shines brilliantly against the dark eastern sky, stretching from north to south, announcing a vapory portal into the sky. The clouds are herded on.

By nightfall the sky is ink black, glittering with a universe full of stars. Lightning flashes like silent bombs on the horizon. Around a wind-whipped fire—our shadow-streaked bodies orange in the fire glow—I strip with 7 Lakota men and crawl naked into the sweat lodge. The lodge is a shallow dome framed with willow saplings and layered thickly with canvas. We crowd thigh-to-thigh ringing a small pit inches from our toes and knees. Although hunched, our backs scrape the heavy canvas.

Soon the stones, glaring red-orange from the fire burning outside, are brought in and raked off the pitchfork with elk antlers. They tumble into the pit, sometimes stinging toes with cinders. Immediately the lodge is warm. My face is flushed. When the sacred pipe and a bucket of water and dipper are handed into the lodge, the doorway is sealed. No shadow of light remains. There is no getting out. The prayers, in English and Lakota, begin, and 4 dippers of water, representing the four directions, are poured over the stones. Hissing steam floods the lodge. The sweating has begun. The steam fills my mouth and lungs, suffocatingly oppressive.

Remembering Sam's words, my dream, I pray to the rocks, cliffs, and mountains I have known. As steam fills my mouth, I envision the dream eagle soaring in the clear blue sky. I recall the buffalo clouds, the rainbows, and the cold, drenching rain. I think of the meaning of the sweat lodge, the rite of purification, and how the lodge represents the universe with the rocks at its center and the willow saplings aligned to the four directions.

Soon the others are singing, chanting, their voices wailing Lakota songs, and more water is poured over the stones, assaulting my throat, driving the poisons from my pores. Sage is used to mop the

Back to Earth

perspiration running freely. Normally the door is opened 4 times during the ceremony but tonight, because we are helping prepare a young man, Steven Red Buffalo, for a vision quest, the door is left closed. The heat, the darkness, and the mash of bodies are stifling. I pray.

More prayers are followed with singing. The singing grows louder until it fills my ears. Then a rattle spins throughout the lodge, weaving, and dancing. The rattle throbs in my face. It is close but I cannot touch it. The spirits are dancing.

As the singing mounts to a crescendo and I see myself standing beneath the arching rainbows, a draft of cool air washes over my legs. Drops of cold rain plop onto my hot back. I pray in wonder and thanksgiving. The singing is louder yet—rolling, scaling rivers of words I do not know but which send chills down my neck. And when finally I emerge from the steam bath canopy and move naked and wet into the nighttime chill, I see the stars and the lightning popping and flaring, illuminating the place where earth meets sky.

We go then—joined by many others—in the ghostly darkness to a singular hilltop in the middle of nowhere. Steven Red Buffalo stands alone, holding the pipe, facing west. Four flagged poles surround him, marking the four directions. Tobacco pouches are strung around the poles to ward off evil spirits. Braided sweetgrass is burned, and the ashes are sprinkled over the string to erase any human smell. A few songs are sung, and soon he is left alone on his vision quest. He will stand there for 4 days and 4 nights without sleeping, eating, or drinking. Crying for a vision. Listening to the coyotes, eagles, and rattlesnakes that will visit him. Defying the evil spirits with his courage and his pipe. Praying to the Grandfathers in a manner passed on for generations. On a hill in the Lakota territory of South Dakota, a young man cries for a vision that comes only to the holy.

The rest of us withdraw. We gather in a house at Stead's homeplace. In a circle we sit and pray, maybe 30 or 40 of us, men and women and children. The fires and the lights are extinguished and in the darkness drums beat and the spirits are beckoned. It is the *Yuwipi* ceremony, time for praying and healing. Stead enters the spirit world of which the physical world is just an image. It thunders and rains and the roof leaks, but the spirits dance again. Much happens that I cannot explain—flashes of light, the walls thumping and jarring, meteor-like flares flaming through the pitch darkness, phantom visitors . . . and me, caught somewhere between skepticism and awe.

"I wouldn't call the Indian way 'religion,'" said Father Bill Callahan, a Jesuit priest I had met the day before at Red Cloud School in Pine Ridge. "There is no dogma, no structure, no mimeograph machine.

"It is spirituality. They believe in the sacredness of the created world and the spiritual ideal of personal and family holiness.

"I have a theory," he added, "that at about the same time as Pentecost, when the Holy Spirit came to Christ's followers after his death, that the primary religions throughout the world received the same gift of the spirit. But talk to many Christians about the manifestation of the spirit or anything that smacks of spirits, and it is considered evil. Too many got stuck on the crucifixion, stopped short of the resurrection, and so have never come to Pentecost."

The next day I return to Ring Thunder, to talk again with Little Soldier and Sam Moves Camp, trying to explain why I have declined Stead's invitation to sweat again tonight, hoping they can help me understand why. "It just doesn't feel right" is all I can say.

"I have friends," Little Soldier says, "who chew peyote in their sweat lodge. One evening I started a fire for a sweat and these friends asked me to join them. 'No,' I said, 'I have a fire burning too.'"

Then it grew quiet as we each read the others' face. I felt suspended in time, waiting for something to move. Through the silence I said, "Maybe I have a fire burning too."

"You should pray to your grandfather," Little Soldier said after a time. I peered into his deep brown eyes; his crow's-feet crinkled in a smile. I waited for him to say more. After a moment he said, "Your grandfather sent you here. He has sent you here to learn what he knew, but which he didn't have a chance to teach you in his lifetime. Pray to him."

I sipped my coffee and stared into his eyes. I thought of my mother's father. He had left his wife and daughters in Louisiana, had headed to Colorado looking for oil, for adventure, for something more. He had not returned until he was destitute and dying of cancer. He wanted a place to die, then he wanted his ashes strewn over Nevada. His name was not invoked favorably in my house when I was growing up. As a teenager with a rebellious streak, I was told often how much I resembled him, how like him I was. There was a bond there, an affinity. I was given to think this was not a good thing; I yearned to know more of my grandfather who went west seeking what he could not find at home. He had died before I was born.

"Let's spark it up," said Sam. "Let's spark it up and pray together. It's time you learned to build the sweat lodge fire.

"Two logs facing east and west," he said, placing the logs before the lodge. "And two facing north and south." We are outside now, out back, behind the cabin, not far from the outhouses, surrounded by junked cars and scraps of corrugated metal. There is no running water here, no electricity, no plumbing. The sweat lodge is here where the dogs run, where firewood is piled high and mounds of large earth stones have been gathered for ceremony. I can see the western horizon. Two dozen rocks are placed one-by-one on these logs and a te-pee of logs is piled over them. The fire is lit. The pipe is placed in the forehead of the buffalo skull facing the lodge. The earth unfolds as far as the eye can see, and above the flat horizon the sun is aloft in the sky. In time the fire builds and rages, popping and snapping, its heat shimmering in the late-afternoon air.

Any talk is now subdued. We undress slowly and move into the lodge. We pray over the rocks as they are brought in. I am given the sacred pipe to hold toward the west. Sam pours 4 ladles of water over the stones and the sweat begins.

We pray, in Lakota and English, for health, understanding, gen-erosity, fearlessness, fortitude, and wisdom. We sing and pray some more. The door is opened 4 times. It is shut 4 times. My friends pray for me and on the third closing Sam, in his quiet, steady voice, inter-prets a vision the spirits have revealed to me through him. It has to do with the path of the heart's desire, the red road, the holy way. On the fourth and final closing we pass the pipe and smoke it.

We emerge from the lodge. The prayer has been good. There has been no show, no rattles, no sparks, but the effect is more deeply pro-found. The sun, now gone from the land, has left a red rim in the western sky. We move slowly and silently—getting dressed, watching the sky, returning to the house. There, three generations of Lakota and I sit in the glow of a kerosene lamp and talk. They share their meal of warm pumpkin pie and I feel a staggering peace. It grows late and I rise to go. Time to move on. The clan's grandfather, his lined face craggy in the soft light, asks, "How do you like our land?"

"It's beautiful," I say. "You are close to many things."

"No pollution," he says. "Here you have breathed the Great Spirit. You may go and be free."

In a few days—by the time I would be back home—Little Soldier would go into the hills where he would stand and pray for days without food or water, holding his pipe and calling upon the Grandfathers to bless him with a vision, to bring him health and understanding, to give him strong medicine with which to help his people. But now, as I stepped out his door and into the black South Dakota night, he said to me, "You'll be back." A multitude of stars glimmered overhead and the wind blew strong and free. And the land was much alive. We each raised a hand in farewell.

Seven years have passed since that night and now Little Soldier, who is 60, surprises me with a question: "So by now do you understand it's an individual thing?" I don't know what he means. We are sitting in his house drinking coffee and the question comes out of the blue. He watches me stare at the floor, then adds, "That each of us must find his own way."

I can hear Casey outside laughing. He is playing with the children—Babe Reed, Troy, B.J., Keith, and Gwendolyn—who live here in Ring Thunder, a huddle of homes made of logs or plywood and sometimes sheets of tar-paper roofing. There are dogs and a basketball hoop attached to a telephone pole and tiny red tobacco pouches strung around a tree to protect the house from evil spirits. In a field to the southeast is the sun dance place, an arbor-like ring of 28 posts and branches surrounding a tall central pole—usually a cottonwood, representing the axis linking earth and heaven. The ceremony has been called *Wiwanyag wachipi*, "dance looking at the sun," and it is a dance of sacrifice and restitution, denying the flesh, submitting to the spirit. Each August the dancers pierce their chests with skewers that connect them by rope to the top of the central pole. They will dance that way for 4 days in the baking sun, singing and praying and seeking visions until the flesh breaks free. I have seen the scars on Little Soldier's chest.

It is shadowy inside where Little Soldier and I sit and talk about things. "It's hard," I say finally, "in my culture to speak of spirits and signs." I look at Little Soldier who is watching me as I add, "Whenever I am ready to say 'yes,' everything around me says 'no.'"

"People ask me how I talk to spirits," he says. "But I am speaking to one now, as I talk with you." It is true that in the times he and I have been together he has spoken to something inside of me. There is an understanding never talked about, perhaps impossible to articulate; it hovers in a realm our culture scoffs at, has lost touch with, or refuses to believe in. Black Elk often talked of going "into the world where there is nothing but the spirits of all things. That is the real world that is behind this one, and everything we see here is something like a shadow from that world." I know Little Soldier has been there; sometimes I think I've gotten glimpses.

On this evening as darkness falls, Little Soldier talks of his vision quests—going into the hills for days, waiting in a pit, pipe in hand, for the spirits to come. Days spent praying without food or water. The burning sun and gnawing hunger. Every summer he goes, seeking a vision, *Hanblecheyapi*. Suffering, thinking he is crazy to be there. Then hearing hoof beats, the thundering rattle, snakes with black tongues, and a woman who offers strong medicine and places it into his hands before vanishing. The medicine used for healing, for those who come to him.

Little Soldier speaks slowly and I try to understand. I think of the secret of the rock, and the spirit of the land. And I hear him talk of "God, Power, Transcendence, Oneness—*Wakan Tanka*, the Great Spirit." He speaks, too, of the Grandfathers—those who have gone before and are now one with the earth and sky and its spirit. *Tunkashila.* The Grandfathers, to whom he prays for strength and understanding. An understanding of the heart.

"For us Indians," John Lame Deer once explained, "there is just the pipe, the earth we sit on and the open sky. The spirit is everywhere. Sometimes it shows itself through an animal, a bird or some trees and hills. Sometimes it speaks from the Badlands, a stone or even from the water."

The conversation continues. Little Soldier tells me I'm a good listener. "It's good to be attentive to all that is around you," he says, and I tell him I have much to learn. He says it's time to sweat, time to pray, to purify, to cleanse myself of the debris of living. Little Soldier rises and I go, too, out back beyond the outhouses and the wall of corrugated tin, where you can see forever, the long flat line where the earth and sky touch. The western sky is a deepening blue and the stars are twinkling above and the wind blows in waves, whipping the fire in an orange-glow dance. We undress then and climb naked into the sweat lodge, calling out *"Mitakuye iyasin"*—"All my relations"—as we crawl in.

Pieces of antler and brightly colored strips of cloth hang from the willow frame: red for the east from which comes light and understanding, white for the north and its cleansing wind, yellow for the south from which comes summer and the power to grow, and black for the west from which come the Thunder Beings. At the center of the womb-like dome is a small pit into which the rocks, heated in the fire until they are glowing red, are placed to signify Mother Earth and the beginning of time.

Four of us sit cross-legged around the shallow pit as the rocks are handed in. My bare back scrapes against the willow frame and I can feel the heat of the rocks radiate into my face. Little Soldier takes sweetgrass straw, braided into a golden rope, and touches the rocks. The grass flares red, smokes, and fills the lodge with a sweet scent. Already it is hot. I can feel my heart pounding. Finally, the last of the rocks, orange as embers, tumbles into the pit, splashing off cinders, and the bucket is handed in by the doorkeeper, who seals up the opening behind him, leaving us in an infernal darkness.

"The rocks are life. The water is life and this steam is life," Little Soldier says as he ladles water over the stones. The water sizzles and fries, filling the hut with a suffocating steam—the breath of Mother Earth. Sweat streams out of my skin as Little Soldier pours more water over the steaming rocks. The air is stifling. I pray for strength, that the steam fill my lungs, that the bad be driven from my body. The singing begins—loud and soaring, deep-voiced, rising and falling like hawks on wind. They are sung in Lakota—as they have been for millennia on these sea-like plains in ceremonies like this one long before the white man came. But the songs, the voices rising and falling, fill the sweat lodge with a primal music that penetrates my skin.

My heart pounds in my chest, throbs in my ears. The heat is enormous. I resist the urge to bolt from the lodge by praying for strength, by envisioning that dream eagle, *Wanbli Galeshka*, and thinking of the rock, the feathers given me so long ago. Little Soldier prays in

Back to Earth

Lakota while the others continue singing, and in time, after I have subdued my desire to flee, the door is opened as it will be four times. "*Mitakuye iyasin*," we all say as we pass the water ladle, drinking and washing our bodies. "All my relations"—for here we are all one people, of one blood, wrapped together in one spirit. The water is incredibly cool and refreshing.

The door is shut again and the singing swells to a crescendo. We take turns praying, some of us in English, to *Tunkashila*, the Grandfathers, for family, health, and the wisdom to see rightly. And as the door is opened and closed and the singing fills the lodge, my body is both strong and limp, lifted and at rest. On the final opening the pipe is passed and we smoke, drawing deep into our lungs the smoke of the willow bark. "That smoke from the peace pipe," John Lame Deer explained, "it goes straight up to the spirit world. But this is a two-way thing. Power flows down to us through that smoke, through the pipe stem. You feel that power as you hold your pipe; it moves from the pipe right into your body. The pipe is not just a thing, it is alive."

In time it is over, and we crawl out and dress. I am absolutely drained, yet I feel a lightness, a peace. I walk alone in the darkness, spotting shooting stars in the half-moon sky. I find Casey, now alone in the house and waiting patiently for me. He looks at me and I smile and he says, "Can I touch you?" I am surprised by the question but reach out and take his hand in mine as he gets to his feet. "You feel different," he says. "I know," I reply, and we walk together to the car holding hands.

The next day we drive to Wanblee, a small town north of Wounded Knee on the Pine Ridge Reservation, an hour or so from Ring Thunder. To the home of Sam Moves Camp, who 7 years ago had given me the eagle feathers. He is younger than Little Soldier. He has small eyes that close when he smiles and a ponytail and muscular bronze arms. He sits at his kitchen table while we talk and eats a lunch of eggs, meat, and potatoes fried up together.

He speaks slowly, choosing the right words, and he gestures to make a point or to say what words cannot—like when I ask him how he knew the spirits had come and he touches his chest, or when he points skyward when I ask what happens when people die. Sometimes he watches me, smiling, after he's spoken, as if his words are gifts and he's waiting for them to land and settle inside of me. For 3 hours we talk of the sun dance and the importance of fasting, of his ancestors and the way his people are treated today. He answers my questions about spirits and the meaning of animals, the sacred pipe, medicine bundles, and discerning the truth. And I come to understand his fierce loyalty to family, his disregard for worldly things, and his emphasis on prayer.

I ask him who he prays to and he replies, "*Tunkashila*, the Grandfathers." I ask him what that means. "Your boy here is your life and your purpose, and you would do anything for him." I nod. "Protect him, teach him, show him the way. You try to give him strength and understanding, but you cannot preach. You do by example." I nod again and he says, "So too with the Grandfathers."

We talk more about spirit beings and the Grandfathers and what happens when people die, and about other things hard to commit to paper. Sometimes you see just a rock. Other times not. It's hard to explain the difference. "Sometimes you doubt," Little Soldier had said. "So you pray for strength and the Grandfathers offer signs. So too will you, after you die—for those who come after, trying to find the way." His eyes again mirthful. "As your grandfather guided you."

At Sam's house dogs walk in and out the open door; children lounge on wobbly couches watching TV. And when the room has grown quiet and all talk is gone, Sam concludes, "Our way is simple. But it's hard."

We step out to the car and Sam follows. "Will you be with us at Little Soldier's tonight?" he asks.

"I think so," I say.

"Tell him to get a fire going," he says. "We'll have a good sweat. Nice and hot."

Sometimes, when the road you are on trails off into the forest and the light in the sky grows soft but alive, and you could swear that you've been surrounded though you know that what you feel might not even be there, it is then that you begin to wonder if something invisible lives in the air. And sometimes the feeling persists until your head cannot make it go away. Or the road won't let go. And then you know.

A storm is in the air. Far off to the west, dark clouds billow skyward. It is evening and the wind is cool and gusty as we drive, windows down, west on 18 then north on 83, west on the gravel road. Then I stop.

Sitting on a fencepost is an eagle. Brown, with pale splotches on its chest. It looks right at us; we stare back. Frozen moment. Then it arches its wings, leaps, and sails out over the car and banks round to the west, gliding low alongside the road. The sun lights its graceful shoulders and its easily stroking wings, and we follow it in its flight, rumbling down the road until it lifts itself up over some trees and disappears. Casey looks at me and smiles. I ask him if he knows what he just saw and he says yes.

The wind is blowing harder now, the western sky gone dark. Tumbleweeds skitter across the road and the cottonwood trees bend and whirl. Some fine storm is brewing; the air is grey. As we ease down the road to Ring Thunder, huge glops of rainfall splatter on the bug-smeared windshield. The air is fragrant with rain. Storm clouds in all directions, their peaks seeming to scrape the sky. Then jagged lightning—flashpoint fissures in the plane between heaven and earth. And the children play, oblivious to the thinly falling rain.

Little Soldier and I go out back to build the sweat lodge fire as scattered thunderheads roll across the vast Dakota sky. We wait for the rocks to get hot and for Sam to arrive. Night falls and the wind blows. Thunder rumbles and the lightning sometimes throws light across Little Soldier's shadowy face. And as we talk, he says I will see signs as guides along the way; but that I must pay attention, and see, and believe. I ask if the thunderstorm is just a coincidence; he smiles and says it's time to sweat. Sam emerges from the darkness; he says he hopes the sweat is very hot. Little Soldier laughs; he knows Sam likes it very hot. "For a good sweat," Sam says, almost beaming as he pulls off his shirt and pants.

I undress slowly and silently until Casey tells me that he will be the doorkeeper's helper. His solemn voice lets me know I don't need to say anything, so I get on my knees and follow the others into the lodge. "*Mitakuye iyasin*," each of us says. Six of us tonight, sitting in a circle thigh-to-thigh. The stones are passed in; the sweetgrass is burned, and the bucket is handed through the door. Casey and Babe Reed seal up the opening and soon the singing begins.

Again the heat is stifling and the voices loud. The sweat floods from my body and my heart pounds in my head. And again I think of

Kerry Temple

the eagle and the meaning of the thunder and rocks and of the Grandfathers flying across the landscape, souls sailing along the Milky Way, laughing spirits in the sky. And I think of signs and of things I have seen, of understanding and faith and that old idea that you can't understand until you believe, that it's the believing that brings the understanding. And then I am up there, too. Carried on cold sheets of air. Surrounded by tumultuous clouds. And I hear my voice joining into the singing, singing out from deep inside me while I feel the rain and the wind.

Then the door is opened and the ladle is passed around and I see Casey standing outside by the buffalo skull, his face turned up toward the sky. He, too, drinks from the ladle and the door is resealed and the sweating begins again. The heat rises up, scorching my skin, and I fasten my hands to the ground to steady my body. And again I go there—singing and praying and smoking the pipe—buoyant until the ceremony ends. And we crawl out. "*Mitakuye iyasin.*"

I stand there for several moments, feeling the wind wash over my bare skin. Lightning flares like bombs on the horizon and stars have returned to the sky. And I place my hand on Casey's shoulder and hope that he feels what he sees.

After I dress and say goodbye, Casey and I drive slowly back toward town. The singing was beautiful, Casey says; he could hear it so loud and clear. And he and Babe Reed smoked the pipe together, remembering that it is a holy thing. And in the sky across the plains, he says, were buffalo he could see.

Then up ahead, just beyond the headlight glow, a coyote is standing. It stops and looks at us, then trots off to the side. I ease the car forward to get a closer look and it scampers up the hill to the right, then stops and turns again. It watches us. I can see its ghostly form in the darkness and its eyes twinkling like stars in the sky, reflecting the headlight glare. We watch each other for the longest time—until it is no longer there.

So Casey and I drove on out of there that night and talked little of it afterward. But I have thought about these people and events often through the years. I have thought about them a lot during my time here by the pond. I went there for the first time many years ago to see what remained of the old Indian ways. I was drawn then to a people whose existence clung so close to the land, to a belief system

Back to Earth

and ceremonial life devoted to the earth and all its creatures . . . and to an invisible world as real as the one that I could touch and see.

There were years then when it faded into a fine and curious vapor, when it all seemed so far away and implausible, the stuff of delusion and imagination. As the years passed and I traveled the city streets of my life, I considered those people and events too strange to have happened in a universe of strip malls and cityscapes, houses and cars, mowed lawns, the Internet and ATMs. So I let go, the way you let go of teenage summers, of a past seen through the patina of nostalgia.

There are times now when I sit alone in the dark of my cabin or when walking on a cold, star-rich winter night (sword-wielding Orion straight overhead), when those days and ways don't seem so distant. There is mystery in the air, a wisp of holy jesting upon the shuffling wind. Trickster hide-and-seek. A riddle of faith and vision. Sometimes the cosmic text reads like free verse, leaving us to supply the meaning and connections, like ancient astronomers seeing constellations in a scattering of stars.

I did make more trips to Ring Thunder, found it overgrown and abandoned. Little Soldier had moved into the little town of Mission, lived in a trailer on a street where he was recovering from heart surgery. "Still strong," he said one afternoon, puffing his chest and smiling, mirthful glimmer in his deep brown eyes. Still sun dancing, he said, still sweating. Sam too. Fernando I lost touch with. Crow Dog was still there, charging tourists $25 apiece to watch the sun dance at his place each August. Robert Stead had gone, headed to California. But there were still plenty of kids running loose and drunk people and loping, long-tongued dogs and shambly old buildings falling down, some government housing. And other folks just trying to hang on. A funny place for the miracles of nature. An incongruous setting for those mysterious acts of God.

Kerry Temple

12

You do not have to be holy to love God. You have only to be human. Nor do you have to be holy to see God in all things. You have only to play as a child with an unselfish heart.

—Matthew Kelty, a Trappist monk

"Have you ever seen God?" he asks, untying the ribbon around his teddy bear's neck.

The question was simple enough; it reached for a direct answer. But when you talk theology with a little child, you have to choose your words carefully. Like knowing which stones on a beach to keep and which to leave be.

"No, I've never actually seen him," I say.

He slid the green ribbon from the bear's neck and handed both to me; I retied the bow and returned the bear—a bedtime ritual for this serious little boy with the knitted brow.

"God is like the wind," I say. "You can't see him, but you can feel him. And you can see the way he works, like watching clouds cross the sky or trees blowing. You can't see the wind, but you know it's there when it blows through your hair or carries your kite to the sky."

What else could I say? Do I dare tell him that sometimes I think the wind is nothing more than molecules in motion? That sometimes your hands, wanting to be sure, will never hold it? That some nights are so still and so empty you'd swear even the slightest breezes have left you alone? When you talk theology with your children when they are very young, it is probably best to keep it simple, to speak in metaphors, to be an arrow pointing down the path of faith. Who knows what may be found there.

I have spent years looking for God to show himself. There have been times when I'm sure he has. Other times I feel I have arrived at the place right after he has left—as if I can still sense his presence, catching some faint scent lingering in the air, that telltale sign snatched away too quickly, a phantom visitor who leaves no trace when you've answered the doorbell an instant too late. I have felt this way coming over a ridge in the mountains, when an evening sun splashes its rose-colored light upon the land. I have felt this way after a storm has cleared through this property, just before sunrise when I lie awake in the night listening. I still look for footprints, or feathers caught on a limb. Whispers fade on the wind.

On other days I have wondered if he isn't absent from here. Figment of imagination, a product of my own longing. There is a thin edge between belief and wishful thinking, faith and delusion. There is no direct evidence, no proof, no empirical documentation. Besides, I sometimes question the existence of the "intercessory" God, the one who takes a personal interest, who answers prayers, who does more than observe the mechanism he wound up 15 billion years ago, who stands idly by while there is human suffering and tortured children and innocent lives lost randomly, arbitrarily to "natural disasters" and other "acts of God." And I wonder about the world's religions and the institutional churches and all the human fabrications intended to explain this stuff. I told a friend once—only half joking as we talked by the fire one cold night, the sky and stars a cold and scary infinity above—that the trouble with religion is that it attempts to organize and align the thinking of more people than you would take on a backpacking trip. And that number would be 4.

A priest friend of mine, whose wisdom I cherish, once lamented the cat-and-mouse games God plays with his children seeking him. When I asked him what to tell my kids about God and religion and my own doubts, he talked about his mother. Her wisdom, he said, was keeping faith simple. "Just don't tell them things you don't believe," he said. "Don't give them baggage they must discard later."

That won't be so difficult, I thought; there is so little I really believe, and that mainly has to do with the world around us. So years ago, when I spoke to my sons of God and life and meaning, I stayed with the fundamentals, speaking in story, seeking to give hopeful foundation to their own excursions and doubts.

"God made everything," I tell my sons. "The stars, the trees, the grass, the rivers. He made all the animals, the bears, lions and tigers."

"Did he make Cookie Monster?" asks the 3-year-old, referring to his cuddly, furry partner, a rumpled beneficiary of nighttime hugs and squeezes.

"The men at the store made Cookie Monster," I answer.

"No, they didn't," he says. "Santa Claus made Cookie Monster."

"Oh yeah," I say. "Right." Santa Claus and God. But I continue. "And God put a piece of himself into everything he made. So God is everywhere and inside everything. He's inside the trees and rocks, and inside you and me."

"I thought I came from mommy's stomach," he says.

"God helped," I say, thinking it best to steer clear of theories about birds and bees, sperm and egg, the origins of life and evolution. I could see him picturing God of the Delivery Room, Santa Claus in a green surgical gown.

"What does God look like?" he asks.

"You don't ever see him," I say. "He's like the wind, like the air. He's a spirit."

"Like a ghost?"

"Sort of like a ghost."

"Like Casper?"

"Not exactly like Casper."

"Casper can walk through walls. He can walk through anything but metal. Metal's too hard."

"It's the other way around with God," I say. "He's the air, the space that everything else is in. And he's inside everything. Higher than the sky, inside everything he made; all one big ball of God."

"Why don't we go to church?"

"We do."

"No, we don't."

"You probably never realized it," I say, "but every Sunday morning we go to a park or to the woods or the beach. That's when I take you to church. To be with all the things God has made so you could feel him. Some people feel God in a building. I feel God outside."

Back to Earth

It's more than a feeling, I want to say. God wove into his world countless things for us to know, like respect for life, harmony and humility, the knowledge that—as a Lakota holy man named Black Elk once said—a person's life is but a blade of grass upon a hill. The lessons are there for the learning, for those who listen easy.

One Christmas Eve, Jack Kerouac, at the time an enthusiastic young man on the road to find out, sat in New York with a bottle of wine and watched Midnight Mass at Saint Patrick's Cathedral. He saw, he later wrote, "bishops ministering, and doctrines glistering, and congregations, the priests in all their lacy snow vestments before great official altars not half as great as my straw mat beneath a little pine tree I figured."

"I figured," wrote Kerouac. Who really knows?

I knew that wasn't good enough for a serious little boy. It wasn't good enough for me. But it wasn't time then to talk about *my* nights in the Garden of Gethsemane when I called on the God of my intuition to make himself known. It wasn't time, on the eve of my sons' journey, to express my own doubts about the possible destinations.

"You know when you're so happy you just feel like running through a field? Or you feel so full you want to just hug your teddy bear or me?" I ask.

"Uh huh," he says, looking down at his bear.

"It's God you feel inside you then," I say. "God can make you feel so full. It's times like that you live for, to have those times as often as you can for as long as you can. But you know they cannot last."

"Why not?" he asks.

"I don't know," I say.

The room grows quiet and dark; a nightlight glows in the corner. "I'll tell you one more story before you go to sleep," I say, wondering what I could say about Jesus. "Once there was a man named Nikos Kazantzakis who lived in a land far away," I begin. "He spent his life looking for God, and one cold, winter day he came upon an almond tree in the frozen desert. He wrote, 'I said to the almond tree, "Sister, speak to me of God." And the almond tree blossomed.'"

I wasn't sure exactly what the story meant, so I was relieved when the boys didn't ask. But it seemed like a good place to end; I was just about out of things I believe in.

Kerry Temple

Still, that Sunday we went to the woods again. It was a grey, windy day, the kind to make your spirit soar. The trees were in bloom. Clouds sailed across the sky.

"God is an experience," I wanted to say, "a fullness of feeling." But words would have spoiled the mood. So we walked among the trees, looking for animals as if they would come out talking and singing like they do in Disney films. We tried to be quiet; we walked into the wind. We saw nothing but tracks, but sometimes it's enough to know you're on the trail.

I know there are many paths to God; it's the hiking that's important. But sometimes I long for a marker to point the way. I wish I had truths to hand my sons like stones from the beach. Sometimes I do not.

When we were leaving the woods, getting into the car, my younger son said, "It's been a good day. I saw God peeking out of a rock."

"Oh yeah," I said, not quite sure what to make of this. Did he mean it? Was he trying to please me?

Dark clouds were rolling in. I thought: But will God turn the stones to bread to feed the starving millions? And will he throw some answers down to those of us still looking? Nobody knows for sure what is really going on; no voice will ever boom from the heavens like thunder beckoning the rain.

"It's the Thunder Beings," a Lakota holy man once said to me. "They've come to guide you on your spiritual way." Didn't he know that thunderclouds are nothing but intense electrical fields and powerful updrafts and downdrafts? That the cloud's colder upper region is positively charged; its lower region negatively charged? And that when the imbalance is great enough, it overcomes the air's insulating capacity, and lightning flashes and thunder cracks because of an electrical discharge? Was it coincidence that thunder boomed just then, carried over the earth on gusts of wind?

Is that what they mean when they talk about faith? Is there a God? Do we have souls? There is so much to life, but sometimes it makes so little sense. There is no certainty; nobody knows for sure. You discover your own truth to make life worth living. Or you don't.

I spent many years looking for God to show himself, but never quite got hold of the proof I was looking for. Still, I thought it best to show my sons how to watch and listen, how to sit and how to walk,

Back to Earth

finding those places where all goes silent except for the cosmic heart-beat, where little is left but the muddy, wondrous planet itself. That is enough. And better than more.

So through those years, as the boys grew ready for expanding horizons, we found the fields and woods and corners where they could be set loose upon the playing fields God made for their benefit and mine. I rarely evangelized, thinking it better to put them where God could talk, get out of the way, and let the deities work. We were happy pitching tents, telling stories by firelight, waking to birdsongs, swatting mosquitoes, cooking in the rain, putting up with the good and the bad and the hardships that come with such adventure.

Then one day at work, when some of us were swapping vacation talk, a friend said, "I don't know why you go to that place. There's nothing there."

"You're wrong," I told him. "Everything is."

It's a matter of perspective, I suppose, that enables one to see what is and isn't there. The stars shine in the daytime too; the sun's radiance just upstages them. Even city lights dull them at night, but it doesn't mean they're not all up there, like lanterns beaming in the cosmos.

My friend and his family had just returned from Disney World, Epcot Center, and Busch Gardens, with a swing back to the Midwest through the nation's capital. He talked about Space Mountain, the Smithsonian, and the dancing dolphins at Marineland. So I understood his reservations about my low-budget vacation retreat into the woods with my two sons. What's there, he asked, to entertain or educate two eager boys ready to spring into the world? After all, we hadn't been to the Tetons, Yosemite, or the Grand Canyon. Just a patch of woods along Lake Superior.

So in a sense he was right when he said there's nothing there—except for rocks and trees, the crystal beauty of clean, cold water, mud and grass and sand and the solitary nest of a lordly bald eagle. There are no museums, no amusement parks, no golden arches or showers or televisions sets to turn on at night. That's precisely why I took them: to see the stars far, far away from the glare of the city lights. They are so much brighter there.

I remember one night and a towering summer sky and a cool, damp wind blanketing us. We had driven that day far out a dirt road to the forested shore of Lake Superior, where we pitched a tent and made ourselves at home. At dusk we began walking along the beach, the cold, dark water slapping against sand and stone. We walked until night fell, until the stars came out, until we stopped and stared. Then we listened to water and wind and beheld the cosmic wizardry.

No one talked—not even when shooting stars flamed across the sky. Not even as time passed and the constellations slid down the galactic dome. Then a toad appeared, a dark, leggy blob hopping along the moonlit beach. Another. Then a third.

The trio was soon corralled by two barefoot cowboys, caressed and belly-stroked, played with, and confined in a hole dug especially for the occasion but from which they easily escaped—only to be recaptured. Set loose. Observed. Seized and, for purely experimental purposes, flung into the frigid depths of the largest of the five Great Lakes.

In time each toad reemerged from the tidal foam to be tried again and again—until a whip of a snake slithered into view and distracted the merry scientists from their toad study. The boys set upon the snake, which also showed an impressive ability to boomerang ashore—until one final hurl from which it never returned. After a sullen vigil knee-deep in the toe-numbing waters, we agreed the snake must have outflanked us in order to take a less Sisyphian passage to land.

I don't know what time it was when we finally tumbled into our tent and zipped our bags against the chill, but I remember thinking about things—about what makes the water cold, and how long it takes for rocks to be ground to sand, and how many stars are out there, spiriting their light across the mysterious cauldron of life we call the sky. And I weighed something my son had asked: "If the universe is expanding, what is it expanding *into*?" And I thought about God. And the rightness of toads. And the solace of the garden.

And I realized how, when all the stuff that's been close around you gets pushed far away, what has been distant draws very near—until you can look upon nothing and see everything.

We brought home four newfound rocks in the glove compartment of my car. They're in my box now, talismans reminding me of places where we played. One is as big and as red as a human heart. It feels good in my hand. I remember when I saw it—bold red amid the earth-tone stones lodged under 4 feet of water at the edge of Lake Superior. It gleamed. When I bent to snag it, my face splashed into the cold, clear lake as my hand plunged deeper than I had anticipated. Rarely does water run so clear so deep.

We were on an island. No one else was around, and we had wandered the woods all day. It was hot and close and buggy, and as fatigue enveloped us we saw a bear.

It was a big, black bear high atop a bare, dead tree. We were tired and hot from walking all day when Ross said, "There's a bear." We could see its pink tongue licking, needling at the tree, then it stopped and we looked at each other for a minute or two. The bear seemed surprised to see us, as if it had been caught with its nose in the honey jar. It shimmied down a few feet—its cleat-like claws scrattling over the brittle bark—then stopped and looked at us again. We were all fixed like that for a moment: alien creatures watching apprehensively across some great divide, with no language to span the chasm. Then the bear dropped to the ground, looked once over its shoulder, and disappeared into the dense green foliage. We ran the opposite way.

We were still flushed and breathless when we made it to the water's edge. The sun was low and we could see a couple of smaller islands across the water to the west. We stood on the cusp of a gentle inlet flanked by tawny cliffs and riddled with boulders and nice climbing rocks scattered along the shore. Despite the water's frigid grasp, I could not resist the urge to swim. So we stripped down to our underwear and plunged into the lake.

We played there a long time, climbing on the rocky shelves, exploring beach and cliff and secluded grotto until the yellow sun eased into the lake. There was no place else we needed to go, no one waiting for us. We could stay out all night if we wished. Our camp was set up in an orchard of birch trees on a tongue of land some ways down the shore. It would be there whenever we arrived. Our excursions had an air of boundlessness about them, an immunity from any limits of time or space.

I watched my barebacked sons in their idle wanderings, watched them derive games out of driftwood and imagination, watched them dodge deer flies and chase seagulls and lose themselves in this lavish playground of earthwork and whimsy. I like to watch these boys turned loose upon the land. They seem at home, joyously engaged in a sporting life that possesses the heart, the kind of engagement Steve McQueen meant when he said, "I'd rather wake up in the middle of nowhere than in any city on Earth."

⚘

It was a meaningless and futile activity, and I'm not sure why we started it—except that I wanted to dig my fingers into the earth.

I had been sitting and watching long enough. It is good to observe, waiting for the quiet pieces of landscape to come to you, but sometimes a restlessness sets in when you've been looking too long. And sometimes you can't know a place by what you see.

The boys had been out all morning, climbing mountains of sand, bowling rocks downhill, skipping stones over the lake. Sunlight glinted off their bare shoulders as they, stickmen in the distance, tiptoed in the lake.

I sat by a clear, spring-fed stream that crashed out of the woods and crossed a strip of sand and stone before flowing into the lake. I was enchanted by the raucous whitewater, the liquid brilliance, the way the weaving waters surged and spun and rolled around rocks and whitewashed slabs of wood. Sunlight glistened off its surface, pock-marked with ripples and eddies. Sunlight splashed off the multicolored cobblestones embedded in the bottom. Sunlight made rainbows in the bubbles.

I was entranced by the currents, the wave patterns of rapids and falls, the spiraling showcase of whirlpools that drowned sticks and leaves, only to spit them out later and shove them out to sea. And I thought about the persistence of water. The fluidity of living. The interminability of flow. The liquid confluence of sunlight and stone. The Zen of H_2O.

The stream, emerging from the woods, splayed into three rivulets as it cascaded toward the lake. When the boys came back, I flopped a log across one of the tributaries to serve as a bridge. But with a big splash it landed halfway down in the water and became more of a dam. I decided to finish the job. The boys and I set to work.

We recruited the largest rocks first, packing them snugly between the stream bed and log dam. The water was largely undeterred; in fact, its pace seemed to quicken as it broke into a thousand silver fingers, finding the holes, opening new routes, perforating our dam. We worked quickly to plug the leaks, jamming rocks into any cavities we could see. The water level rose.

Encouraged, we redoubled our efforts. We stationed one stone layer at the dam site while two gatherers waded upstream, seizing softball-sized rocks and tossing them back to the builder. Occasionally, having learned that surface area counts, we would enlist hunks of driftwood and wedge them into the stone wall. But the water found our gaps, and when Casey tried sealing the crevices with sand he learned he couldn't count on that shiftless material.

Eventually, dripping sweat, I stood to survey our progress and admire the irrepressible ingenuity of water. It was going over the top. It was eroding the banks at each side. It was burrowing underneath. There was no holding it back. What it couldn't dislodge or penetrate, it simply outmaneuvered.

So we moved upstream and tried again at a site more conducive to dam-building. And we applied what we had learned about materials and placement and structure. Two dams would be better than one. When that failed to work, well, we turned to the other tributaries and adjusted their configurations—removing impediments, rerouting the current—so they'd handle more of the river's volume. "We are changing the course of the universe," I said triumphantly as I dug out new channels by hand.

By now the boys were just watching. Hungry, they no longer shared my obsession. But I was having a blast, as happy as a toddler in a sandbox, oblivious to anything beyond the fringes of my imaginary little world—at least until the boys jumped me and we tumbled into the water and rolled around wrestling and roughhousing in a tickling-ticklish heap of arms and legs and laughter. They have grown too large for me to handle two-on-one, so I was the one who cried uncle. I do not like to be tickled; I didn't mind the sand in my face. And I didn't mind that the river was still carrying on as if our engineering were a minor disruption in the natural order of things.

We dismantled the dam and rescattered the rocks. I stashed one in my pocket to keep—as a reminder of the day I spent all day doing nothing—then we walked away to let nature run its course.

Kerry Temple

This was the day of rain. We woke to the sound of it drumming on the tent, to the drop of it into the tent, and to a heavy gray sheath subduing the earth. I poked my head out and guessed that it would rain all day. The day proved me right.

The rain—steady, incessant, depressing—presented two choices. The leaky tent left us with one. So we pulled on slickers and ponchos, fired up the stove and had breakfast under water. Then we went for a walk. A wade.

The plan was to scout out a bald eagle's nest, following some loosely diagrammed directions provided by a fisherman. We eventually found the nest after several hours of meandering, but by then the quest was secondary—it was enough to be traipsing through the wet, wet woods, as soggy as river otters on a spree. We were happy. We were drenched. Our shoes had the texture of sponges.

We would have been miserable if we had stopped so we kept moving, following a trail and an old twin-rut logging road, skirting a pair of inland lakes, heading toward Lake Superior. We had been walking north for a while and were just beginning to drag when we heard it— the sound of breakers on rock. We raced ahead. Here is what we found.

The big lake was no longer a turquoise and aquamarine lullaby but a raging beast of charcoal swells and frothing whitecaps. We stood on a cliff, our toes clinging to sandstone and shale, and gazed down perhaps 200 feet into the surging, abysmal vat of angry water. Our bodies were buffeted by a cold wind that drove the dark clouds low across the sky. Huge fists of water hammered the rocky shore, sending crystal sprays high in the air. I moved the boys away from the cliff's edge and we stood in awe of the power resounding in nature's temper.

We were hypnotized by the constant smack and suck of the waves, by the speed of the low-flying clouds, and by the fragility of the human form in the midst of such violent forces. I shuddered to imagine one of the boys adrift in these turbulent waters, their kindling bones pitched into the ancient, unyielding walls, then dragged into the depths.

We spied a slender crescent of beach, found a passage down to it, and flung rocks into the bellies of the crashing waves. Then we saw— offshore, bobbing along the surface, spinning like a candy-colored top—a beach ball. It rode the undulating crests as it made its fitful way to the beach, where we snagged it out of the water: a toy spewed

Back to Earth

from the mouth of the cosmic fury.

So we played. We ran and chased each other in games of hotbox and dodgeball—always mindful of the lake's grim threat and the danger of getting too cold. Then, from some combination of sunset and storm cloud, the world grew dark and the heavens opened up. The rains came harder, drilling the air and stinging us. Thunder cracked and rumbled across the water. Lightning bolts lit up the sky, crackled, flared all around us, snapping at the earth in a torrent of blinding flashpoints. We took cover in a hollow of rock, bundling together to watch the show.

We waited out the storm. The sun eventually returned to the western horizon and illuminated the glassy landscape, just before sinking into the lake. The air was cleaned out, cool and still. We tromped back to the tent in the deepening twilight, put on warm, dry clothes, and ate. Then we watched the straggler clouds pass like ghosts across the stars, and we nestled into our tent for a good night's sleep. And I put away another rock, this one stolen from a day when we said yes to a world that was moody and mean, for this night when it was so good to be together.

The fourth and final rock came from paradise.

There was a beach where we played home-run derby with a tennis ball and driftwood bat. There was a river where we raced sticks, and some steep foothills where we tracked wildlife. At one end of the beach were rocky cliffs beautifully sculpted by wind and water. Lively breakers exploded at the foot of these walls, the water shattering into sun-catching jewels.

With courage you could jump into the water from the cliffs. The freefall was scary and exhilarating. The water was deep green, almost pure emerald-green, and when you landed, the water hugged you in a frigid embrace, absorbing you into the liquid greenness. Swimming underwater with my eyes open, I felt I could glide into that greenness forever.

It was late afternoon when the stick races were over and the batting title had been settled. I told the boys it was time to head back to the tent for our last night in the woods. We started out, walking ankle deep in the lapping water. We were the only ones there and it felt like paradise. The sun was an orange ball hanging out over the water near the cliffs, which by now were silhouettes. Orange slivers danced upon the water in a trail leading to the sun.

"Can we go back?" the boys suddenly asked. "Can we jump off the rocks one more time?" I looked out over the water and thought of my shivery body and the chilled air and the hunger in my stomach and what it felt like to be 12 and what it would feel like back in my office in two days. I said yes.

The boys hustled back down the beach but I, somehow drawn to the sun and its luminous path, walked into the lake. The water was cold enough to contract my muscles and steal my breath, and I swam toward the cliffs in an urgent breaststroke, occasionally dipping my face into the water. And when finally I arrived at the jumping rocks, the tides nudged me into the cliffs like a bear nuzzling its young.

The boys arrived and we all jumped—over and over again, until we were trembling white prunes of goosebumps and chattering teeth. Until dark descended and the world became a restful place. I took a stone from there. It is loden-green, with a forest-green vein all the way around it, as if it were two parts somehow fused together.

I am glad now that I said we could go back. That was the last night of the last trip we took—all three of us together. I miss them now with an ache that is palpable. I am glad I said yes to that one time.

I had told the boys that the world is a poem whose meanings are there to be deciphered by those who will see. I had told them that there are different ways of seeing. I had tried to leave it at that.

It is hard sometimes to resist the urge to impose my meanings on things, to explain, for example, the importance of water, the significance of sand, the lessons of rock. I did not always refrain from such instruction, but I tried. Look closely, I told them: Everything you need to know to get along in the world is right there. Read the poem. The meaning of life is all around you. The lessons are there in the woods. But in the long run it is probably better, rather than telling them *what* they should see, to help them learn *how*.

So I have kept the rocks as keepsakes, reminders of a time and a place and a family on the loose, playing tag among the wild things, looking for the Artist's signature on the rocky universe, humbled in the knowledge that these stones may be as close to the eternal as we'll ever come. And I listen to the stories they have to tell, to the songs that were sung those last carefree days together.

Back to Earth

13

Apprehend God in all things, for God is in all things.
Every single creature is full of God and is a book about God.

—Meister Eckhart

I am mostly alone these days, a family of one. I walk the grounds and fish the pond and I sit a lot. I have these rocks and things, some books and notes collected in my bundle. But mostly I sit and think. I think about the events in my life that have led me here, the good and the bad, the memories that make me smile and the memories that make me cringe, injecting their guilt and regret. When you are alone long enough, there is nowhere to hide. You see who you are and you see what you did—maybe not sins committed as much as acts of omission or neglect, that brought about this isolation and this loss. For far too long I sort of let life happen to me, caught up in the masquerades of modern living, rolling along with whatever seemed right or easy or expedient, until I looked around and wondered how I'd ever gotten way out here, so distant from those youthful destinations.

These days by the pond, living in solitary contemplation, I've had a chance to get my bearings back. I've replayed those hearty excursions, rediscovered some of the ideals and good sense of my younger days. I've also revisited some of the crossroads, located some of the markers that I missed, figured out some of the places where I went wrong. There's no going back, of course, but it does a person good to see where mistakes come from, and then to redirect a life in need of fixing. So much I knew back then. It's been good to retrace those steps along the trails, to re-create those times when I was close to something sacred. More and more, with the weeks sliding by, it feels like "back then" and "now" are coming together again; it's the intervening years that ache with separation.

But I have been here long enough now for it to feel like home. I feel a part of things, one element in a spectrum whose color bands have no edges. This is my place. I walk through these leafy woods, I sit by the wind-stroked pond. The deer have grown accustomed to me. Rodents share my house, scampering into darkened corners upon my arrival, but persisting nonetheless. The birds get my stale and leftover bread. I leave nuts for the squirrels, toss apple cores to the gophers. I pick berries, but there are plenty for us all. I am grateful for my place here, my apportionment, for the beauty, the harmony, the apparent simplicity in a world so incomprehensibly complex. A sense of wonder still guides my days. Really, it is all quite beyond me, and yet, here, I fit in.

Over time, as the seasons have turned one to the next, I stopped being a guest. The woods became familiar, the cabin part of the natural landscape, wrapped in vines, bathed in rain, the heaving spring breezes breathing through open windows. Even the cabin's walls have been more membrane than partition, a border easily traversed, travelers commuting back and forth. The affairs of animals became routine, their comings and goings flowing into a pattern of our mutual existence.

I have learned a lot about animals while living here, but they have taught me as much, if not more, about humans. They have cut me down to size, put me in my place. I cannot forage for food, gather, and hunt as they do. I cannot stand the outdoors in winter, cannot move as easily through the natural landscape. I am nowhere near as self-sufficient, not nearly as attuned, never so much a part of the whole. The neighbors I have here in these woods, the creatures with whom I share this place, demonstrate daily their skill and prowess, their own familial bonds and generational teachings. They represent the mosaic of life in all its textured harmony. Here I am one small fragment in that mosaic. None of us is truly independent; we all rub against the other. I cause trouble if I think or live otherwise.

Much of what I have learned here and in other expeditions into the real world contradicts what I was taught as a boy. And there is grave, even lethal danger in those lessons. I was taught in school and church that all of creation was made for the benefit of humans. Our species, according to the Bible, was given "dominion over the fish of the sea, the birds of the air, and all the living things that move on the earth." Humans were instructed to "fill the earth and subdue it." So we have. Throughout modern Western culture animals were seen as inferior beings whose primary function was to serve the human race, providing food, clothing, companionship, and entertainment, and were otherwise disposable. This philosophy largely persists today.

For centuries we have depicted our species as the pinnacle of evolution, with all previous earthly activity (epochal games of "survival of the fittest") engineered for man's ascension to the top of the squirming, leaping, writhing, roaring mud heap: humankind as the apex of creation. Those shaping Western social, political, and religious thought, subscribing to this view of *Homo sapiens* as king of the hill and enamored of the rapid expanse of technology, fostered this self-absorbed and arrogant attitude that led ultimately to estrangement from the environment as well as widespread destruction of it.

This air of superiority and the European surge across America in the nineteenth century prompted Chief Seattle to ask Congress in 1854, "What is man without the beasts?" His answer was both poetic and practical: "If all the beasts were gone, men would die from a great loneliness of spirit. Whatever happens to the beasts, soon happens to man. All things are connected." Scientists over the past 150 years, studying ecology and the interdependence of all life forms, have learned just how true that admonition was. They've also learned enough about natural history to know that the mechanisms of evolution were not designed for the singular purpose of producing human beings.

Those indigenous to this continent understood all this well. They were mindful of the interrelatedness of all life. They knew man's place in the natural scheme of things. They sensed a value in all the earth's creatures, knew powers of intelligence far beyond the intellect. "We listened to what the eagle and the sparrow had to say," Russell Means once said, explaining his Native American heritage. "We found our place in life." The two-leggeds and the four-leggeds and the wings of the air, they said, all come from one Mother, one Father. Animals, they believed, could possess special powers, could come as teachers, as messengers, as reflections in material form of divine principles.

"*Mitakuye oyasin!*" the Lakota would exclaim in prayer and wonderment, when confronting other life forms. "All my relations!"

Like most aboriginal cultures, their lives intimately twined with the other creatures inhabiting their landscape, Native Americans watched closely their neighbors, knew their habits and pathways and idiosyncrasies. The depth of this knowledge inspired a respect for the unique qualities of animal life, and the inevitable taking of that life was most often carried out reverently, with prayers said in honor, gratitude, and humility, with a belief that the animal's spirit was passed on with its flesh, its presence woven into the very clothing and tools and ceremonial objects its body became—the wild and mundane becoming sacred, being sacred. All life, in this scheme, was a growling, flowing, snarling mandala of the Creator's art, the Great Spirit's immanent domain.

"He is not set up as lord over the earth," wrote Karl Barth in *The Doctrine of Creation*, "but as lord on the earth which is already furnished with these creatures. Animals and plants do not belong to him; they and the whole earth can belong only to God." These years in this cabin have instilled in me such a sense of community, a oneness, a solidarity with the other species living all around me.

Of course, I am a stranger, interloper, guest where animals are right at home. By their very nature they meld into the landscape. It is their place, not mine. I am never more aware of this than when walking the woods, backpacking, or bushwhacking cross-country. Animals slip so easily into and out of eyesight, blending in, responding instinctively, their sensory and motor skills so keen, always so extraordinarily tuned to their surroundings. We modern humans, entering the natural world as visitors and observers, are removed from it all in a way that animals are not. Not only do we thrump and tromp around, but we also cannot help but come as tourists, visitors passing through. Animals are so keenly and thoroughly engaged in reading the landscape through their senses that they fully inhabit the land in a way we simply cannot.

I wish I had such a kinship with the landscape; I wish I could get closer to it. "What I want," wrote Robert Finch, explaining this desire, "is to go silently and smoothly into the maze, without a rustle, as the light fox bounds with inborn agility across the rounded stone walls; as the soft rabbit threads itself surely and painlessly through the briar.

Kerry Temple

"Those creatures tease me with their unconscious competence, a sureness that implies not so much prowess as belonging, of knowing where and who they are, of being local inhabitants in a way I am not."

We are inescapably aware, so conscious of ourselves being there, witnessing, observing that we never become fully at one with our surroundings. This is due largely, I think, to our being so conscious of a self in a way animals are not. Animals move in sensory fusion with their surroundings; humans filter so much cerebrally. It is ironic, a whimsical twist in the Creator's scheme, that the very quality that elevates humans—our self-consciousness, our ability to step back, to analyze, to reason, to remove ourselves from the immediacy of stimuli and sensory activity and fight-flight responses—is the very characteristic that does indeed set us apart. It is this awareness of self that acts as a barrier, that extracts us, that prevents us from being truly joined to the landscape. It is only by forgetting ourselves (like children at play) that we find ourselves there, in the land—as participants, not as observers walking through.

It is crucial—just as saints, mystics, and monks through the ages have prescribed dissolving the ego, the self, to find God—to lose oneself in the landscape in order, ultimately, to find oneself there. And yet animals, long perceived by Westerners as inferior beings, are already there. They are real citizens of a universe we want to join, a realm we have become alien to.

That is why, as Russell Means explains, the Lakota believed humans to be "cursed with the power of reason" and why "every living thing had a direction and a role to play in life except the two-legged creature," thus making it necessary "to learn from our superiors" in order to bring about a unity with the Great Spirit, the Creator, God— and the original harmony of Eden.

It is significant, I think, that even biblical teachings suggest this. Was it not the human ambition and pride of Adam and Eve—their desire to lift themselves above their given place—that tempted, then drove them to eat from the Tree of Knowledge, wanting to be like God, thus prompting the "fall" of the human race? Banishment from paradise. Leaving their descendants burdened with the original sin of wanting to be God, saddled with self-conscious reason, ailing from this chronic estrangement, destined to scour the wilderness for a promised land, a way to get back home. Seeking guides along the way.

Back to Earth

"But ask now the beasts," God tells Job, "and they shall teach thee; and the fowls of the air, and they shall tell thee." Forget oneself, release the ego, and find communion here.

"We need another and a wiser and perhaps a more mystical concept of animals," Henry Beston once wrote. "In a world older and more complete than ours they move finished and complete, gifted with extensions of the senses we have lost or never attained, living by voices we shall never hear. They are not brethren, they are not underlings; they are other nations, caught with ourselves in the net of life and time, fellow prisoners of the splendour and travail of the earth."

So animals have became both real and metaphorical. I see in them meanings beyond their physical attributes, incarnations of a wilderness spirit, powers too difficult to define. They show the way, and so I look for them when I walk or hike. I watch for red-tailed hawks, listening for the distinctive *scree!* Or for the call of an owl in the dark. When I backpack I have been on the lookout for deer and moose and elk and bear. And bobcats. I still take great pleasure in chance meetings, especially when I am weary after days on the trail. Other creatures animate the landscape, appearing before me, snapping me out of the hypnotic monotony of hiking. In some ways, animals put a face on nature; they are the eyes looking back at me as I study the realm they inhabit, and represent. I have often thought of them as emissaries, teachers, and guides, a greeting from some other side— stepping out of the wilderness and into my frame of reference—each appearance an act of blessing.

As a boy growing up down South, I dreamed of seeing bobcats in the woods. In a land of squirrels, raccoons, and opossums, they—not wolf, lion, or bear—were the wild things. The solitary carnivore. Meat eater and mystic. A deadly blend of elegance and cunning, tooth and claw, ferocity and grace. The bobcat is a remarkable creature whose shadowy presence loomed large in our landscape and in my imagination, informing both with the scent of elemental danger, predatory wildness, beguiling apparition.

Its wraith-like nature had prompted some old-timers to call it "wood ghost," for it is a reclusive, almost secretive animal so rarely seen that many doubt that it prowls their neighborhood—until they hear its banshee cry. As a teenager backpacking in Texas or canoeing in Arkansas, I would lie awake at night listening for that other-worldly wailing, the caterwauling that Thackeray described as "a shriek and a yell like the devils of hell." But I never heard it, and in time I began to wonder if any such creatures were still out there in the few remaining wild spots east of the Rockies.

It was important to me then, and still is, to think that such elemental wildness still vitalized the countryside where I lived—however curbed, fenced in, or civilized. So I delighted in hearing of the occasional sightings of this pint-sized descendant of the saber-toothed tiger—though these were usually reports of something lurking in the shadows before dissolving from sight, glimpses of the haunting amber eyes blazing in the twilight. Still, the idea that this distant cousin of the panther, this wily remnant of untamed America, might roam my boyhood's rolling, piney hills infected that landscape with a hint of joy and peril.

Lynx rufus traces its lineage to an ancestral lynx that prowled the Asian high country 4 million years ago. About 200,000 years ago these cats crossed the Bering Straits eastward to give rise to the Canada lynx, the bobcat's closest relative but clear subordinate in territorial war games. The bobcat's reputation as a ferocious predator had an immediate impact on the whites who descended upon this continent 500 years ago. To colonists who must have been fidgety about all the strange and fearsome creatures lurking in the woods, the wildcat made a singular impression.

"The wilde cat," wrote William Wood in *New England's Prospect: A True, Lively, and Experimental Description of That Part of America*, "is more dangerous to bee met withall than any other creature." The chronicler also expressed admiration for the bobcat's hunting technique which it "useth to kill Deare": "Knowing the Deares tracts," he explained in 1634, "hee will lye lurking in long weedes, the Deare passing by he suddenly leapes upon his backe, from thence gets to his necke, and scratcheth out his throate."

Tales of bobcats bringing down 200-pound deer are told by those who admire the cat's bold venery. Aware of the game trails within its territory, the bobcat will climb a tree (usually on the side away from the trail in order to conceal its claw marks) and wait for a passing deer. Pouncing on its prey, it will go for the throat. The relentless snapping action of its jaws, which has been likened to the rapid firing of a sewing machine, enables an adult bobcat, wrote one naturalist, "to pulverize the throat, including the major blood vessels and trachea, in a matter of seconds."

Because of its fierce and independent nature, its wild and crafty ways, the bobcat rests prominently in the anthology of our national folklore, its snarling visage on the same pages as Daniel Boone, Davy Crockett, and other pioneer heroes. Its reputation has prompted some observers to exaggerate the animal's size. As early as 1637, Thomas Morton wrote warily of bobcats and said they were as "bigg as a great Hound."

In truth, the bobcat is slightly larger than a housecat and usually weighs about 25 pounds. Although vicious when cornered, the wildcat's relatively small size makes its ability to prey upon deer all the more impressive. More often the bobcat, who cannot supplement his diet with plants because his stomach physiology is so specialized for meat, settles for smaller game—rabbits, mice, squirrels, chipmunks, gophers, and such. But it is also admired for its ability to survive by taking third and fourth choice—snakes, frogs, birds, fish, cave bats, lizards . . . whatever it takes to get along.

Where humans have cultivated its territory, bobcats have shown an appetite for livestock, most notably poultry. Its notoriety as a raider put a price on the bobcat's head long before the American Revolution and almost cost the bandit its very existence. But it wasn't the only animal so threatened. Americans have never really known what to do with the wild animals that flourished here before the European migration. Some were taken for their meat, some for their pelts, and others—like the wolf, the bear, and the wild cats—were killed like outlaws. They were thought to threaten the safety and well-being of those carving a civilization out of the great American wilderness.

Other animal populations were decimated over time by a reduction in habitat; others killed as a nuisance. Still others were killed for the fun of it, for the sport, even to accelerate the genocide under way. The great hordes of bison—said to stretch across the plains from horizon to horizon, their thundering hooves shaking the very earth— were thus slaughtered wholesale, their carcasses left rotting, strewn across the landscape, their bones bleached white by time and wind and sun.

By the end of the nineteenth century the bobcat had become more of a character in our cultural mythology than a main player in the territory once its own. Still, in 1915, a government agency was created within the U.S. Department of Agriculture to eradicate the "predator" populations, and over the next several decades half a million bobcats were killed (along with thousands of wolves and mountain lions) through a carefully orchestrated poisoning program.

As a young forester, Aldo Leopold was a foot soldier in the government's efforts to eliminate wolves and other predators from the rangelands of the West. Later he wrote sadly about what was sacrificed in that effort: "We reached the old wolf in time to watch a fierce green fire dying in her eyes. I realized then, and have known ever since, that there was something known only to her and to the mountain. I was young then, and full of trigger-itch; I thought that because fewer wolves meant more deer, that no wolves would mean a hunters' paradise. But after seeing the green fire die, I sensed that neither the wolf nor the mountain agreed with such a view."

In an eloquent eulogy for the last bear killed upon Escudilla, a mountain in the American Southwest, Leopold conveyed a sense of the ambivalence Americans have felt toward the continent's wild things—and the loss of something precious and irrevocable, ineffable yet real: "The Congressmen who voted money to clear the ranges of bears were the sons of pioneers. They acclaimed the superior virtues of the frontiersman, but they strove with might and main to make an end of the frontier. We forest officers, who acquiesced in the extinguishment of the bear, knew a local rancher who had plowed up a dagger engraved with the name of one of Coronado's captains. We spoke harshly of the Spaniards who, in their zeal for gold and converts, had needlessly extinguished the native Indians. It did not occur to us that we, too, were the captains of an invasion too sure of its own righteousness.

"Escudilla still hangs on the horizon, but when you see it you no longer think of bear. It's only a mountain now."

So the bobcat has become for me a symbol of the diminishing wildness that vitalizes the landscape, infusing it with a primal, fearsome, yet sacred presence. And I have imagined that the pure, predatory spirit still lingers here. I like to think one might prowl these woods and fields where I now live, for the bobcat has indeed survived, although its habitats have been radically reduced and although it is still hunted as a threat to livestock and trapped for its pelt. Give credit for this hardy resiliency to the cat's belligerent nature, its knack for being there one moment and gone the next, and for its gritty adaptability. For while the grizzlies, wolves, and panthers have receded into the closets of America's frontier, the bobcat dug in its claws and hung on.

Though it prefers scrubby country and broken forests, the bobcat has made a niche for itself in each of the lower 48 states. The "wood ghost" has persisted because it has made a home in soggy swamplands, throughout the arid Southwest, even amid this Midwestern farmland. It is, in essence, all around us—somewhere between 700,000 and 1.5 million of them, although its reclusive nature makes the census hard to figure. Even naturalists who study the creature may go a lifetime without spotting one. It has largely faded into the modern American landscape like a phantom prowler depositing signs of its sweet trespassings, somehow eluding the noose of *Homo sapiens*.

When I was younger, exploring the fields of my ever-widening universe, I was on the lookout for wildcats in the backcountry of Colorado and Utah, in New Mexico, Wyoming, South Dakota, and the Adirondacks. I saw their claw marks near the bases of trees, which they use to sharpen their claws and mark their territory; their scat, which is similar to a dog's but which they bury during summer to conceal their presence; and their tracks, which also resemble a dog's. But I found no bobcat on these travels.

And yet, as I sought the elusive wildcat and hiked its uncultured domain and read about its habits, I learned a lot about the cat and its country and my place in it. I learned, for example, that the cat places its hind feet into the tracks of its forepaws, a practice biologists attribute to its instinct to stalk unnoticed.

I learned, too, that the bobcat can spring 8 feet into the air, that it makes its den in rocky ledges or caves, in abandoned fox dens, even hollow logs. Male and female find each other in early spring, spend some courting time together (howling wantonly), and mate. The male then wanders freely off to continue his solitary existence. The kittens, usually 3 or 4 in a litter, appear about two months later and stay with the mother throughout the summer, learning bobcat ways. By late fall the young will also wander off, will first mate when they're about a year old, and will live about 15 years. Their isolated existence makes it easy for them to evaporate into the landscape, upholding their ancestral charm.

They are largely but not exclusively nocturnal. They get their name from their bobbed tail, and their ear tufts help them gather sounds. They use their whiskers as a navigational device when stalking, and females are much more combative than males when defending their territory. Their eyes glow in the dark because wildcats are eerie, phantom-like creatures—and also because light hits a reflective layer behind the retina, called the tapetum, which bounces the light back, enabling the eye's rods a second chance to absorb the dim nighttime rays.

Except for man and his dogs, which really are no match for it, the bobcat has no serious enemies. If tracked, the cat may vault into a tree and wait in ambush. Or may loop back, appearing behind its hunter, reversing the predator-prey relationship. Such is the stuff of myth and fact, fable and truth, both literal and figurative, which tell of bobcats.

At some point I learned, as anyone does who watches animals long, a certain humility in the presence of bobcats. They are so fast, their senses so keen, their genius so remarkable that humans, turned loose upon the land, seem clumsy and dumb in comparison. To say nothing of their beauty and grace. Their power. Their rightness. Their capacity to slip into the landscape and to live there unencumbered. I envy them their intimacy with the earth. I have looked for bobcats everywhere.

I walk here mostly at dawn or dusk, because that is when the animals are out and when there is enough light to see by. Some days the woods and fields are busy with activity, and I sense I am in the company of cohorts, and I think about what our forebears, what all aboriginal people knew all along: Our well-being—physically and spiritually—depends upon the health of all life, and a balance must be found for the mutual benefit of all God's creatures. Recognizing the intrinsic value of each traveler aboard the ark we call Earth is fundamental to our prosperity. "When we try to pick out anything by itself," John Muir once wrote, "we find it hitched to everything in the universe."

I saw the bloody remains of a rabbit first. It was daybreak—the dried blood, the tufts of hair, the ivory bone. After a few moments I walked on. Then, emerging from a copse of trees, I looked across a grassy clearing when an animal appeared some 30 yards in front of me, having stepped out of a hedgerow—as surprised to see me as I to see it. So we watched each other for a moment while I, stunned by its appearance, took inventory—and assured myself that it was indeed a bobcat staring back at me. The broad paws and ears and bobbed tail. The proper coloring and size.

Although I stepped several paces closer to it, it did not appear threatened. In fact, I had a sense that it was content to meet there like that, to stand face-to-face, to hold one another in a gaze, before moving on, easing into the thicket from which it had come, in no apparent hurry to get away.

Since that morning I have thought of that encounter many times. It seems significant now, as I recall that meeting, that the bobcat appeared after all these years and came to that place, those woods, to that intersection of my world and his.

Kerry Temple

14

The same God who is in us, and upon whose tree we are the buds, if not yet the flowers, also is all about us—inside the Spirit; outside the Word. And the two are ever trying to meet in us; and when they meet, then the sign without, and the longing within, become one in light, and the man no more walketh in darkness, but knoweth whither he goeth.

—George MacDonald, *Thomas Wingfold*

I came then as a visitor, a guest, a sojourner. I was a traveler passing through. I came to this cabin some years ago knowing it to be a temporary existence, that the time would come when I had to move on from here. But then life is a perpetually shifting enterprise, a hazardous trip riddled with abrupt turns and sudden endings. My particular journey has also included some restful travels in this cabin, the tours of interior and exterior landscapes. I have tried to use this quiet time to discern what really matters, when all is said and done, what's important, what's of value, right and true. What it is that lasts in a persistently changing world.

For awhile it seemed strange living here without television, music, or radio. I rarely went to movies, only occasionally read a newspaper or a magazine. For awhile this new neighborhood of mine seemed too quiet, too still, and I felt left out, cut off from all that was happening in the world. Sitting alone in the quiet darkness of night made me feel as if I were missing out, exiled here in this remote corner untouched by the lights and excitement of the living. People at work would talk about TV shows, celebrities, the hottest fads, something in the news, and I would think important things were happening without me, without touching my life. That disconnection felt wrong, disorienting. But as the weeks and months and years went by, the workplace conversations turned to newer TV shows, different trends, and different famous people, and the dreary recycling of the same news reports but from different spots around the world. I realized I got along fine without the topics and the latest trends left behind, that much had come and gone without my knowledge, and that I was doing quite well never learning what I had missed. So much just really didn't matter anymore.

When set against mountains and the nighttime sky and the intricate, always surprising wealth of life unfolding, the sparkle and glare of popular culture seemed false and fleeting, inane and superficial. Although it took some patience to break the habit, to get past the initial restlessness and boredom, I eventually lost my appetite for modern entertainments and was happy to trade in sit-coms, football games, and talk shows for the quiet blush of sunset, the flight of hawks, the beauty of trees. In time the whistle and bang of the societal apparatus grew faint, distant, flaccid. In its place came the quiet, subtle, but genuine geography that uplifted me, settled me, put my feet to the good and lasting earth. The shallow and transitory had given way to something richer, more eternal.

When I was younger, I set out to learn about myself, that universe, and God. I wanted to know the nature of each, and if and how the three elements fit together. I never tried finding answers for anyone else but me; I believe there are many routes to God. But I knew enough to clear out the obstructions, to go to the source, not to an intermediary or the kinds of human fabrications that would delude, distract, get in the way. Right to the earth itself, to the basic, fundamental book the Creator laid before us. Gave to us to know him.

Of course, our modern culture is engineered otherwise. The natural landscape is ignored, if not exploited; it is the raw material for our acquisitive, materialistic society. We build up, add on, spread out, consume, want more. We hunger and thirst for things—goods, possessions, status symbols, the stuff we hope will meet our needs, as if the add-ons would actually fortify the self. But I have seen how acquiring fails to satisfy, how taking doesn't fulfill us. If there's a hole at the center, it doesn't matter how many layers you put on, the building up and accumulating only surrounds the central emptiness. It covers up, patches over, conceals the hollow at the heart. And sometimes it seems the bigger, the fancier the apparatus, the bigger is the hole. "One should from the very first renounce acquisitions and heaping up and building," said the ancient Lama Milarepa, "and set about reaching the truth." *Discover* that truth, I realized long ago, and you'll get to the heart of the matter, and maybe find God along the way.

But these days I have finally stopped searching for signs of God and glory. I no longer look for God because he is here, all around me, permeating every little thing. As the countenance of this wild place stopped being a sign of something other, I forgot to look for him, to seek his tracks or any reassuring signals. And with that came a sense of calm, of *being here.* Siddartha by the river.

The significance of that literary allusion did not occur to me until much time had passed, but I do not know how I could have missed it all these years. After all, *Siddartha* had been a favorite book of mine when I was younger, one of those apparently simple books that carry good weight and seem to come into our lives right when we need it. The novel by Hermann Hesse had given sage guidance when I was a college student, and now my life seemed to be a late but poignant re-alization of its message.

In the book, Siddartha spends many years searching about and trying different lifestyles—from austere to extravagant, from world-denying to worldly, from mendicant to rich man—until he ends up on a river, stopping there and staying long enough to eventually find some contentment and real peace. He becomes a ferryman, acquaint-ing travelers with the river, taking them to the other side. He has found what he needed there by the river; there's no reason to go look-ing elsewhere again.

I have made a home along the creek on this property, going to the creek often, wading in the cold stream, with jeans rolled to my knees. I sit on its banks and watch its rippling flow. It is a shallow creek but spring-fed and clear. Sometimes it narrows and deepens, its waters pausing, collecting itself in pools; sometimes the creek bed broadens, sometimes the water stills, is ankle-deep and resting. The creek has been a companion, a pathway, a self-revealing metaphor to me these past few years.

In autumn, I would stand and watch the leaves fall and float atop the creek, waltzing as a regatta of bronze and golden boats, as weightless as crinkled crepe floating downstream. In spring the fish would come, in winter the ice. Sometimes I have tried catching tadpoles, blue gills, and minnows by hand—something playful to do while I sat there, bare feet plunged into the brink, lulled by gentle breezes and summer sky. The creek was always changing; yet it always remained the same. It all depended on the moment, the weather, the mood, the lighting, for water itself is ultimately mutable, clean, clear, invisible.

One thing I liked was how the light dressed it up or down. The sunlight played on its waters, sparkled on its face, penetrated to the creek's sandy bottom, casting shadowy lines and squiggles dancing on the floor. Reflected light bobbled and winked in patches on the surface; moonlight glistened like jewels at night. Sometimes I raced sticks, as I had done as a boy, dropping a few twigs into the water to watch them chase the current, bobbing and weaving, twirling, stalling, getting hung up, or shooting rapids ahead of the rest (idle games that made nature an interactive playmate). Once I walked the length of the creek as far as I could go, beginning to end, strolling thigh-deep from one edge of the property to the farthest reaches, wading its liquid path, just to do it.

The creek and the choreography of this land have taught me how important is confluence. I have come to believe in the value of flow. Like dancers in ballet, musicians in symphony, or athletes at the height of their game, life has its currents and its concerts, and it is best lived within those unseen streamways, those arteries, graces, and rhythms. Fluidity, synchronicity. The convergence of channels blending mysteriously, harmoniously, simultaneously for an effect that sometimes baffles, sometimes charms, sometimes helps you intuitively sense the undercurrents that carry us along—the flow, the way, the Tao. The path of the heart's desire. Red road, holy road, the Navajo *Hozho*. I would sit by the creek, watch fish in the current, light on the surface, water in transit, and blend into the wholeness, wade in the current, absorbed into wonder.

Something else I witnessed in that creek. Most days it ran with clarity; its clear waters cascading over sand, stone, and rock. Yet the stream is mostly bordered by muddy embankments and the gnarled intricacies of tree roots, leafy soil, and sticks and moss. And when

Kerry Temple

the rains come—cloudburst upon the darkening hills—sheets of water wash the earth. The power of the deluge, the downpour, the turbulence stirs up the mix, washes the soil and sticks and leaves into the stream, turning it muddy, brown, and thick. I see it happen. The creek is churned up, roiling, inflated, and muddled with commotion.

For awhile it is troubling, unsettling, these new ingredients muddying the waters, throwing the mixture out of kilter, upsetting your life. You cannot see clearly any river rocks or sandy bottom; the water is opaque. It will take time, but eventually the waters integrate these new things, mull them over, swallow the rainfall and its debris, bearing much away. Or, using logjams, stones, and distance as filters, the waters purify themselves, clarifying, cleansing, washing away the rubbish and the silt until all is in equilibrium again. And clear.

Then there, on the bottom, brilliant as Easter eggs, hard as bone, the rocks shine again in sunlight. A tumble of stones shimmering. A nest of rocks reflecting sunlight, animated with dancing shadows. These are offered up. And when I reach for them, when I plunge my hand into that stream—a stream so clean and clear it is invisible to the eye—I will get not only the hard, round stone worth keeping but also that splash of cold, pure water I could not see, that I had not thought to ask for. Cold on the wrist, wet to the touch, ultimately ungraspable.

Such cleansing does take time; I have lived here for 3 years. I have spent many long nights, lying awake in bed, looking into myself, untangling my head, listening to the quiet. Healing, like art, does not respond well to pressure but to patience, as the poet Rilke explains, "not reckoning and counting, but ripening like the tree which does not force its sap and stands confident in the storms of spring without fear that after them may come no summer. It does come. But it comes only to the patient who are there as though eternity lay before them, so unconcernedly still and wide. I learn it daily, learn it with pain for which I am grateful: *patience* is everything." The morning does come, but not without the full examination of the night.

This is the best I can do to convey this place, my time here, the transparency in this world I see. So I have stopped thinking of the world as a place divided. I stopped seeking spirits and the supernatural, stopped yearning for the magical, the mystical. I let go of the rigorous demands of science. I often lose track of myself while walking or wading, fishing or sitting, inside or out. There are few profound moments of revelation, only rare flutters of epiphany, and the companionship that comes from subtle entertainments. The change came slowly, imperceptibly; it settled over me when I wasn't looking, wasn't thinking, until these woods by the pond and all of its inhabitants became indistinguishable, inseparable, one. A singular wholeness. No other way to explain it. So much a matter of perception. Ways of knowing, of seeing.

There on the talus slope of my existence, having learned something about which stones to keep and which ones to leave be, I decided to set down a record of these findings along the way, these soundings of depth, these memories, these specimens collected upon this holy ground. So here I have found again the joy of play, the flight of discovery and wonder, the liberties of being out among the wild things. The indispensability of sitting. The generosity of solitude. The gifts delivered by patience, by watching. Mindful exploration and order and continuous harmony. Here I have found faith in the lens of science, the desire to seek and to know, to say yes to the truth in whatever raiment it may come. Here I have found the power that comes when the self accepts, submits, dissolves into the whole. And a vision of the universe as sacred.

Many years ago I was taught by stones, stones collected from south Texas and rocky Colorado, Michigan's Upper Peninsula and the sun-blazed cathedrals of Zion National Park, Wyoming's Big Horns and the plain-dressed woods of rural Indiana. A shaman's stone from South Dakota. Leopold's wilderness prophecies and a fall while climbing that taught me to sit still.

I also remember a trip to New Mexico, a trip recalled not for stones collected and kept, but for pieces of pottery found then given away. That trip brings me back to green mountain woods, overcast skies, and sleet. And sleeping in a sunless deep canyon, shivering through the night, water-bottles frozen solid at dawn. I remember endless blue skies, rattlesnakes and tarantulas, cactus, and looking down upon a distant Rio Grande, a meandering mud ribbon at the bottom of a dry-wall canyon. We had gone from pine-draped mountain to desert, past cliff dwellings and ancient altars to gods and ghosts, past pueblos abandoned centuries ago, and back again into the forested mountainsides with views of the earth and sky and horizons far away.

The two of us—Walt and me—were there alone, crossing paths with no one. Out five days. Silent, sweaty, and dusted. Solemn among the holy spirits. Laughing around campfires, stiff and surly at sunrise. I remember finding shards of pottery here and there, broken pieces from a jug or bowl, relics from a prehistoric potter, hand-shaped and sun-baked, painted, by fingers caressing clay, mud, human hands, hands like mine. Fragments and hands I jammed deep into blue-jean pockets.

I also remember the handprints on the walls of a cave near where we camped a final night, elemental drawings of the hunt, two-leggeds and four-leggeds and the wings of the air. I stood before the paintings, pulled the pottery pieces from my pocket, and placed my offerings there. There were pieces of ivory skulls. Water vessels. Handprints upon the walls of the cave. *I am here.* My hands matched theirs. *I am here too.* Twilight, the tinkling water from a creek nearby, sunset, darkness, and stars. We sat in humble silence. The winds stirred. Moonlight upon the landscape. Reverence, communion, and life. Smoky prayers.

How does one extract the spirit from this place? Separate the soul from an encasing? Tell me those hands are not mine too. There are stars overhead and trees rustling in the nighttime and campfire smoke ascending to heaven. There are memories here and dreams in my blood and the voices of those praying forever. The earth spins on its axis, the Sangre de Cristos are not far from here, a coyote wails in the distance. Sand, rock, dried wood burning sweetly. My eyes scan the creamy girdle of the Milky Way, and I watch here, propped against rock, wind in my face. Am I not a chord, a note, a tone in the symphonic oneness of the universe? The sound, at least, of a bow drawn once across the strings of a violin in orchestra? A singular oscillation folded into the music of the spheres. Into the chorus of woodwinds and sea, percussion and fire, meadowlark and baby's cry. And is God not to his creation just as waves are to water? Am I—and everything else—not swallowed up into this ocean of mystery and wonder? Coming from, returning to the river.

There was smoke from ancient fires caked black onto the ceiling of this dwelling place. And stones worn smooth from use, from footfall, from human wear. Moonlight shone off the rock facing. An occasional meteor flared across the desert sky. Canopy of stars. We bedded down there, inhaling the scents of cedar and pine, listening to animals scuttle in the brush, wrapped into the landscape embracing us. The pieces of clay I had found scattered across the desert were now returned as an offering to that backcountry shrine carved into the canyon wall.

In these years by the pond I remembered such moments of enlightenment, and I thought about how distant I had grown, how far away from home I had wandered, how far from that original Eden. All of us are looking for our way back home, for a reuniting, a reunion of souls. That is the human story. From the beginning— ever since we pressed our handprints onto cave walls—we have been trying to connect to the immanent, to the Other, the Presence, to God.

Some healing has come during these years of solitude as I have rediscovered some elemental truths about my place in the natural landscape. Unteachable wisdom has come from mute or illiterate masters, appearing with the quiet force of sunrise, as sudden and bold as the first light of dawn breathing over the sleeping landscape—the earth read as text. Like most of us these days, I had grown largely estranged from the spiritual aspects of creation. Despite the infatuation in my younger days, I, too, had gotten misplaced. I had gotten snared by the forces of Western culture, trying to choose between spirit and flesh.

I had been raised in a religion that had divided me into body and soul, that had cleaved creation into matter and spirit, and that had encouraged people not to embrace the natural world but to overcome their physical and temporal nature in order to seek future kingdoms, a spiritual ascendancy and salvation. But in time, having gone off to school and college, having absorbed the intellectual themes of modern society, I had come to doubt that any such supernatural realm existed. Our scientific and technoindustrial culture has focused its attention on the material world, disregarding those elements of creation that cannot be seen, touched, or measured, dismissing talk of the spirit as largely naive, superstitious, unsophisticated. I had spent years dismissing the invisible, viewing things from this mechanistic, reductionist approach. The years passed and I took on the mind of this existence.

Kerry Temple

My time here has shown me again what I discovered as a teenager loose on the land but had forgotten in those intervening years—that the landscape does offer spiritual sustenance, a sense of grace, an avenue to the divine. Perhaps those two—the land and its spirit—are not that different. And the human race, in order to find redemption, to locate itself, to be at rest in the world, must find again the union of the two.

But for me, there is one more place to tell about, one more place to return to, before I can get all the way back home.

Back to Earth

15

The only real voyage of discovery consists not in seeking new landscapes but in having new eyes.

—Marcel Proust

It is dark and I am driving. I have been driving now for two days, heading west across Iowa, South Dakota, into Wyoming, into the Big Horn Mountains where I used to live. It is dark, and it has been years, but I remember these mountain roads pretty well. They wind and veer; they switch back and forth and wheel around and climb higher. They are narrow two-lanes, and all I can see is what my headlights show me. It's been years, but the hairpin turns and rocks and chasms come back to me, and I know I'm getting close. *Ah yeah, I remember now*, and I soon spy the rutted dirt road I was looking for. I ease the car off the asphalt and head out into the inky, bumpy night. I have been here before. First time about 25 years ago. I was young and free then, all my possessions packed into a car—a little blue Ford Pinto.

I roll my window down, nighttime air sucking in, follow the lumpy road as it rises and falls and meanders. I am at 9,000 feet, a rock-studded meadow, high above the timberline. When I have driven far enough, I stop. Turn off the engine, turn off the lights, step out into the chilled night air, mountain air. No glimmer of light in any direction—except for the stars overhead, an awesome, vast, sweeping sky full of stars. Glimmering. Twinkling. Seemingly within reach, but also dizzyingly untouchable, like tiny twinkling nightlights at the farthest outposts of creation.

I turn slowly, rotating full circle, eyes upon the horizon, where black earth borders near-black sky. The circle is a jagged pantheon of mountains and peaks, an irregular line of vaulting summits, notches, raggedy formations. I am alone here. The rock in these mountains is billions of years old. No one can see me; no one knows where I am. I stretch my legs, bend over, stretch out my stiff back. Then I climb onto the hood of my car and lean back against the windshield, looking up at the infinite sky. The hood is still warm, the mountain breeze is loose and cool.

This place is a repository of memories for me, although it is hard to know what to make of them. Sometimes memory is a landscape you rediscover; it reveals itself as you go. Sometimes memories fall right out of the sky, plopping you on the head like cold, wet beads of summer rain. It is only in hindsight we see the truth in themes.

The first time I came here I was maybe 25. These mountains first appeared as clouds upon the horizon. I had been driving three days west that August, across the sun-dried, oceanic flats of middle America. Tanned hide. No trees. Hot winds beating in the windows. Sagebrush and thirst and nothing on the radio. My car loaded with all my stuff. And me on the run from my scalded young life, cut loose from the moorings of my existence. Close relationship gone bad. Unemployed and out of school. Out on the land but lost at sea. I had long dreamed of heading West and seeking a home there. So here I came.

The mountains I mistook for clouds at first—the hazy, billowing, bluish-white kind that hover far, far distant just above the waterline when you look from shore at the vast ocean exhaling, inhaling, bending off the edge of the earth.

I had known clouds like that living by the beach for two summers during my college days. I'd watch the Gulf of Mexico in the evenings after long days working pipeline in the soggy marshes and prickly, snaky woods of southern Mississippi. Clouds at sea. Piles of clouds. Never coming landward. Heraldry of heaven way far away. Sometimes stacking up tall—sky skimmingly tall—great thunderheads brushing their feathery crowns on the sloping dome-roof of the world.

I would sit in the summer evening after work, body hot and sore from a day on the pipeline, lean and strong then, and watch tide pools and gulls, sandpipers, plovers, and those mighty cumulus clouds passing like ghost ships seeming never to approach. In time darkness would settle over the sea—deepening blues, streamers of scarlet, indigo bleeding to violet, bruised plums, clouds now gone to vapor. Blackness. And the hovering stars would be matched in their twinkling radiance by the lights of the shrimp boats plowing Gulf waters. The peace of all things in their place. The rotation of spheres, the moon-pulled tides, heat-lightning sometimes flaring in the distance, the briny winds stirred lightly or sternly by the spinning of heavenly orbs in motion. A mobile hanging above the baby's crib. I watched the show.

That is what I thought about when I was 25 and first saw the Wyoming cloudscape poised upon the western edge of the sunburnt world. I was parched by the baking heat of the day, by the unblinking wrath of the sun crossing Dakota, the desolate moonscape of eastern Wyoming. I expected to meet those distant clouds by nightfall. I was hoping to drive into them, into a cooling, sheltering dusk of rain and thundering percussion and the spark and flash of cloud-snapping lightning. I anticipated a spirited change in the monotonous, mile-a-minute journey—something good to be running toward, having grown weary of the leaving.

Miles passed and I relished the names driving from Spearfish to Sundance, past Devil's Tower, Rockypoint, and Lightning Flat, across the Powder River and Crazy Woman Creek, through Spotted Horse and Recluse. The West of myth and memory and dreams. Both empty and brimming. Landscape coming alive with wind and ghost. And as I drove on, the clouds became less distant, seemed to be piling up, slowly rising as I rattled on from Gillette toward Buffalo. They appeared as a sleeping leviathan stirring. Eventually, they became more distinct until I realized they were not cloud, but mountain. A whole vast range of mountains—cloud-crowned and snow-capped, even in the melting heat of late summer. Mounting before my eyes as I approached. Rising right out of the earth. The Promised Land.

My car—that old, blue Ford Pinto, worn-out and rusted—did not like the climb into the foothills, with their steep grades, the switchbacks wheeling and striving onward and upward. Pedal braced to the floor, decelerating, straining against the pull, the winding path of ascent as we entered the mountains, finally arriving, by virtue of climbing thousands of altitude feet. But once there, once among the barrier headlands, I spied a dirt road diverging, and took it, meandering briefly through undulating meadows. I stopped the car and got out and breathed in deep. The air was cold and clean and fresh, and wildflowers dotted the grassy hillsides like a calico print on a lush field of deep emerald green. The sky overhead was as blue as a sky can get. I stood there and spun around, thinking I had found my Elysium, and knew that this was no visit.

So now I have come back to the very spot, a 50-year-old seeking solace and reunion, driving in the night to this high mountain meadow where—a quarter century before—I first arrived as a boy in the Big Horns. The mountain air has grown colder; it fingers at my neck. I rustle a bit, figuring it time to get off the hood of my car. My back is achy and stiff, my legs and shoulders sore and fatigued from driving all day. I pull my sleeping bag out of the backseat. I toss it on the ground, among the grass and sage, and pull on my hooded sweatshirt, yank a black knit cap upon my head. I take a little walk before bedding down, brush my teeth, pull off my shoes. I stretch out flat on my back and stare up at the stars above. I listen to the wind. I gaze at the mountains all around.

I lived at the base of these great mountains for two years—watching the Big Horns from my second-story window, eyeing them as I walked to work, venturing into them when I could, going to favorite spots, going back again, looking for new places to see.

It is a smallish range, a sleeping dragon's back in profile, a rugged backbone exposed and running north and south. A few summits top 12,000 feet and the highest, Cloud Peak, reaches 13,175. They are rocky, proud, and snow-covered year-round. They are accessible and friendly, with flowery alpine meadows and many clear lakes and frothy, cold-running streams. Fortunately, the Big Horns are little known, and most travelers make the slow and scenic drive through them on their way to Yellowstone and the Tetons on across Wyoming to the west, or around them—on up Interstate 90 past the Little Bighorn River and Custer battlefield, through the Crow Reservation and into the big sky country of Montana.

They are quiet, unpretentious, but self-assured mountains, less showy than other spots, the kind of celebrity scenery showcased on calendars. Like many corners of the world, the Big Horns let you come to them and are best seen on foot. So I have walked here a lot and they somehow became mine, and I theirs. On weekends I would often take off alone, drive as far as I could, and walk the rest. Sometimes I'd feel urgent about seeing more, heading over ridges, hotfooting down trails, getting past one more bend in the road. And sometimes I'd be content just to be there, to be *in* the mountains, leaning against a rock, basking in the sun, watching wildflowers and grasses nod and wave in the clean mountain breezes.

Before I came to live here in Wyoming I had seen other ranges, had backpacked with Duffey in Colorado and romped through Big Bend in southwest Texas, had even gotten a glimpse of the magnificent Alps and Dolomites in Europe; but I had never had mountains in my own backyard before. So like a lover sometimes liking the thrill of newness, exploration, and discovery, but also liking the comfortableness that comes when you know it's real and lasting, I sometimes sought and sometimes made myself at home.

The stories we tell of the human pilgrimage are threaded with these twin quests—the metaphor of hunting for God at the mountaintop and the complementary search for the God that comes to those who wait. In the Big Horns years ago I learned there is virtue in both: You travel to the place where you can be found.

In summer I would make it into the Cloud Peak Wilderness Area, up above the timberline, the dragon's very backbone, where the rocky ridges are close and all around you, and you can bushwhack off trail and scramble here and there, pitching a tent by nightfall or lie there exposed, star-canopy overhead, nestled into the cupped hand of a valley, surrounded by summits. You can walk to the top of Cloud Peak without any skill as a climber, if you know the route. In the months when light lingered longer in the air I could drive up in the evenings after work. There were rocky ridges on which I'd perch, lean back, and watch the shadows spill like melted wax over the land as the sun fell behind the jagged silhouette of Cloud Peak, Blacktooth, and Bomber mountains. The deer would come out and graze, and I'd sleep among them in a grove of aspen.

But even on those days when I wasn't up there—which was most of winter because the killing cold keeps you away—I would look up from the streets of town and see rocky, snowy mountains waiting in the west. It was good to see them there. I felt connected to them— touching the sky, promising space and height and freedom, pointing to the heavens. Two and three and four billion years old. With me, standing at the door of the church, threshold to the kingdom.

One weekend late the second summer I lived out there I back-packed up to Geneva Pass and spent an afternoon fooling around there on the stony crest, leapfrogging rocks, squishy tundra under-foot. There were rock formations to climb and fresh animal trails (the hoof prints of deer, elk, or bighorn sheep) and the grass was a soft, cushiony green. And up there where I was playing was a silvery, splashing spring, a stream deliciously cold and sweet, no wider than a stride—and an old board sign that said, "Goose Creek." At those heights Goose Creek was narrow but gathered snowmelt and swelled, was joined by other rivulets, emptied into mountain lakes, drained out the lower ends of those lakes, was herded by gravity and stone, tumbling downhill, gaining momentum and power, cascading in tor-rents off boulders and rocks, eroding the earth, with imperceptible patience, cutting canyons and valleys through the granite in its path.

Back in town I lived on Bellevue, a few houses down from Goose Creek, which I crossed on a bridge to get to the city park shaded by tall cottonwoods and cruised by high school kids looking for laughter and a friend. Once out of town Goose Creek enters the Tongue River, which joins the Yellowstone, which joins Lewis and Clark's Missouri, which bleeds southeastward through South Dakota to eventually en-ter the massive Mississippi (upon whose levees I often walked as a graduate student in Baton Rouge and into which the Red River of my teenaged years flows after cutting a diagonal across Louisiana, finally emptying into the brackish, familiar Gulf of Mexico, basin floor to those summertime clouds of my pipeliner days—the clouds I recalled on my first drive out here). From here to there, I thought, my finger tracing this journey on a map to confirm how one silvery splash of water might make its way from Geneva Pass in the Big Horns to the Gulf Stream currents merging with the cold and incomprehensibly vast Atlantic. The unifying principle of this little universe.

Then I thought about how much of that silvery splash of water might remain intact, self-contained, might actually make that jour-ney. And I wondered then what constituted that splash—a molecule, drop, or tiny droplet? Like splintered glass shattering over stone, crys-tal beads of water splash off rock in momentary flight before falling again to rejoin the flow. How did it then differentiate itself from the current consuming it, in which it was immersed, all one flowing, living thing? How do we perceive, define a drop of water? By watery bead or by hydrogen and oxygen atoms? Adhering, stirring, splashing, separating, blending, and reblending. Or did it? Would it evaporate perhaps, becoming airborne, consumed into rain clouds in the Heartland, falling later as raindrops somewhere in the Ohio Valley where, by some other tributarial passage, it would reunite with the Mississippi on its way to the Gulf. And then what? Rider of Gulf Stream currents, swimmer of ocean depths, hoisted into the air again as vapor? What constitutes a splash of water? Drop, molecule, or all-consuming sea? Perhaps no distinct drop at all, just *water* within the long and living stream.

And what of us? Are we so different?

We, too, are as temporary as a splash in geologic time, emerging airborne from a mother's womb as a singular drop of water, distinct as individuals thrust out of the living stream, the randomly stirred mix, reconstituted from gloppy matter as old as the birth of stars. Each of us but a recent concoction of those tiniest particles, those charges and atoms, those complex carbons and bone, rib and foot, water and teeth and amino acids, the essential building blocks of matter, hormones and spit, coalescing, forming, and reforming a particle of life we label human. Even then we merge from one permutation to the next, in a continual state of flux, immersed in the world around us, sopping up sunlight and air, cracked wheat and fruit, animal meat and splashes of water, shedding hair and skin and waste as we go, in some ways a transient receptacle of life forms passing through us, flowing into and out of us—as many organisms living in us and on us as there are humans on earth. Drop of water in a stream? Prayer beads of water flying?

And what of the self? What really is ours? Are even our thoughts our own? Am I not my parents, and their parents, and genetic coding from time immemorial? Electrical circuits, neurons and chemical impulses, childhood traumas wired into me? Star stuff coalescing in the shape, fiber, and design of me. Particles of reality passing into and out of me.

How is it we each come together as we do, thinking, breathing, sculpted loosely—by the magic of DNA and protein—as some individual consciousness, to stand amid the peaks at Geneva Pass

Back to Earth

contemplating God and life and one bead of water on its way from here to the Gulf? Our lives but a passage, a moment in time, a shape-shifting intersection of fleeting matter, perforated by heaven-sent neutrinos, an indistinguishable droplet in the bloodstream of the grand and holy universe. So that death comes, too, as a passage, a flight out of time, a bridge joining before and after—introducing us to the Yellowstone or the Missouri or the Gulf, where water is consumed by sea. Indistinguishable. One.

So what are we but the very universe itself?

Of course, I did not think much about death or endings or the passing of time in those days. I was in my 20s then and full of living, covering 12 or 15 miles in a day, eating little as I went, striding along from lake to lake. My good life spread before me; my feet were square with the earth. And the land was all around—big, wonderful Wyoming as far as the eye could see. Holy drop of water swimming happily at sea.

It's not real clear to me just how memory works. Sometimes memories seem to drop right out of the sky, like the first few warning shots of summer rain; images fall into your head from some place far away. Sometimes memory is like a landscape you rediscover, unfolding its secrets as you retrace your steps one turn or corner at a time.

But time carries memories away and in their place come other thoughts and doubts. Shortly after that trek up to Geneva Pass toward the source of Goose Creek, I moved back east. There was work there and a house, a family growing up around me, the nagging demands of middle-class living, errands and pursuits that seemed important because they were close at hand and time is a ticking clock. And excursions into the Big Horns were replaced by Saturdays cutting the grass, by Little League baseball games, the affairs of human ambition, and I got lost.

Still, one spring when a friend and I were walking through woods in northern Michigan and he said it was the most beautiful place he'd ever seen, I asked him if he'd been west and he said no. And I stopped there in my tracks and thought for a minute, and I listened to a distant longing, to a time and a place and a person I once knew, and I said, "You need to see the Big Horns. We can get there in two days if we drive there long and hard." So we did. But I had forgotten that spring comes late in the mountains, where the trails start at 8,000 or 9,000 feet.

Kerry Temple

We found the trails blanketed deep in snow, lakes frozen shut, frosted air numbing fingers—making the finger-bones ache with cold when we'd cook, hunched over our little gas stove, reluctant to fire up, with us shivering and cursing, bundled even at midday, cold winds blowing the chilling air off snowfields, spidery dark clouds coursing overhead always threatening. We'd shiver and move around, stomping our feet while eating, knowing we had come ill-prepared for what we had found, sometimes not wanting to stop to eat, despite the hunger, because we'd be warm only when walking—or nestled into tent and bag.

We did not get lost only because I had a good idea where the trails led, even though snow blocked our passage. At times the snow was knee-deep or more; at times we'd slosh in and be up to our waists, struggling to pull ourselves and our packs upright, dog-paddling, sometimes more horizontal than vertical. But our sights were set on Geneva Pass.

Foolhardy and without 4-wheel drive, we thought we could go from Tensleep Lake to Misty Moon then down to Solitude over to Te-pee Pole Flats and up to Geneva and back in the brief time allotted, fending off cold and pelting rain, slopping through drifts of knee-deep snow, hiking for days seeing no one, wading three streams hip-deep with snowmelt and runoff, with no dry jeans or boots or socks to change into, stumbling and slipping because of rocky bottoms and frenzied currents, hardly stopping to look at the beauty of the land, much less contemplate its power, determined to reach Geneva Pass, me wanting to get back to Geneva Pass.

I remember a few sunlit days. I remember the placid presence of Lake Solitude, the forbidding countenance of Cloud Peak, the tumultuous roar of waterfalls and streams with the jailbreak of spring. I remember occasional fissures in the clouds, exposing blue sky, when we'd optimistically spread out wet sleeping bags and hang out the tent to dry so our bedding wouldn't be soggy when we climbed into it again at nightfall. There was some occasional misery as well as some confident measures of fortitude, and an elk and a porcupine, some deer and an eagle we surprised out of its aerie when we pulled ourselves up onto a cliff at sunset, wanting to absorb the last wedge of sunlight—shadows swallowing the landscape—before another chilling night.

Back to Earth

I also remember a bad night we had. Late in the afternoon, we traipsed back and forth along the bank of a thick and careening stream flush with snowmelt. We were looking for safe passage for crossing and found none, so we finally splashed on to the other side. We crossed and marched on, feet spongy, jeans squishy, the scowl of rain overhead. We persevered, launching our ascent toward Geneva Pass, until darker clouds closed in, snuffing the twilight out of the sky, prompting us to drop packs and make home for the night.

We found no good, flat place. Bedrolls and tent were wet. Clothes were wet. The rains arrived in the midst of us cooking our dinner. We frantically stashed our things, the deluge soaking us to the skin. We lay in the darkening twilight, with the winds wildly ripping at our tent, lightning snapping all around us, light flaring in the tent, rain driving against the sides, soaking through the thin layers of nylon— tiny, storm-assaulted skiff at sea in a cyclone, sinking.

Perhaps I dozed; I know time passed. The cold and wet startled me awake. All was deep dark now. My sleeping bag was soaked. Water pooled in the tent, a tent soggy and sagging down around us. Feeling agitated, trapped, and claustrophobic, I broke out of the tent into the cold night air. The torrents of rain had calmed to a steady drizzle but—with penlight halo scouring the ground and tent—I saw the rivulets streaming around and under the tent, infiltrating and flooding. The tent was virtually collapsed, essentially worthless, hardly responsive to my attempts to get it upright, to get stakes to hold anew.

Cold and chilled, I had no choice but to crawl back in where I began to shiver—uncontrollably. I had the shakes, cold rivers trembling up and down my spine, teeth chattering, muscles shuddering. No source of warmth, no escape, no warm, dry place to offer refuge. I fought the urge to bolt, knowing there was nowhere to go—days from any road, surrounded by the wet and hostile darkness.

As I tossed and turned, trembled, and curled into a ball, tremors rippling through my body, I knew that I was in danger. I also realized Tim was awake. He asked if I was OK; I asked him—the rapid trembling almost preventing speech—if he knew what time it was. He turned on his penlight and pointed it toward his watch. "About 3 a.m.," he said, rolling up onto his elbows. *OK, OK,* I thought. *I can make it a couple of hours till first light.* Then he said, "Oh, sorry. Never mind. It's about 9:30." *9:30? It's only 9:30?* A shock of panic surged through me. "Yeah," he said. "Sorry. I was looking at my watch upside down." *I can't make it, won't make it*, I thought. *The night will be too long.* Again I fought the urge to run.

I tried to settle myself. Tim said he was cold and shivery, too— "the kind of shivers," he said, "that come from inside and don't stop no matter how many layers you put on." I knew there was danger. I knew our bodies had had little food and were threatened by the long exposure to wet and cold. I knew the dangers of hypothermia. I knew there were worse predicaments to be in. I knew the sun would rise again tomorrow. I talked myself down and through.

Nature is not always kind. You take it as it comes. You do the best you can, knowing that life, too, dispenses fair and unfair shares of trouble. You tap your reserves then, your measures of strength and faith and ingenuity. We lay there, back pressed to back, hoping any body heat would get us through the night. There was no other source of warmth; we just had each other. But we made it, dozing, sleeping, tossing and turning, throughout the labored night.

The next day was rainless, though overcast and cool. So we were able to cook some breakfast and we hung our wet stuff from the limbs of trees and from the long noses of rocks, and stiffly we stalked on up the trail, a packless hike in search of Geneva Pass. Long and urgent strides carried us into the realm of rocky ledges, pointy escarpments, the approximation of that place. We didn't have much time. The journey's roundtrip called for a quick return.

It was pretty but not stunning. Sometimes it is the light that transforms a place. Sometimes it isn't the eyes that see. We didn't have long to stay. We looked around some and I wondered if Tim thought it worth it, this single-minded quest that left us blind to stuff along the way. After loping around on the rocks and summits there for awhile, we headed on back downhill. We had a long return trip yet ahead of us, with many streams to cross.

I have never gone back to Geneva Pass. I learned not to try to re-create what I once had had before. I learned not to miss the journey because my eyes were so focused on the destination. I learned you first need to get yourself right, if the view is going to please. And I marked this passage in Robert Pirsig's *Zen and the Art of Motorcycle Maintenance*: "Mountains should be climbed with as little effort as possible and without desire. The reality of your own nature should determine the speed. If you become restless, speed up. If you become winded, slow down. You climb the mountain in an equilibrium between restlessness and exhaustion. Then, when you're no longer thinking ahead, each footstep isn't just a means to an end, but a unique event in itself. . . . To live only for some future goal is shallow. It's the sides of the mountain which sustain life, not the top." So, too, with life: There's a path, a pace, a flow to be found.

I am 50 now and I have come back again to the Big Horns, have slept in the meadow I discovered a quarter century ago. I have pulled on my backpack and taken a favorite hike into the midst of the summits, the formidable headlands, the grassy meadows, with heavy clouds draping the landscape. A placid lake awaits me there, though it's a climb to get to its rocky shores. Snowmelt and waterfall keep it full to overflowing, draining to the east. The lake is cradled there by steeply rising stone and scree. The wind blows hard and cold there nearly all the time. It reminds me of a mystical, primeval place unaffected by the march of time.

I stay here a night and the next afternoon I climb rocks alongside the waterfall, mounting higher, the spray of blowing mist and splash cooling my sunburned face. I stop to guzzle mouthfuls of water and keep on scrambling higher till I ascend up over a shoulder where the land begins to level out. I follow the water flow steadily upstream, walking gradually uphill now, bounding from rock to rock, until I come to vast and gently sloping, marbly slabs of rock—pinkish, blue, beige, or dark slate grey, sculpted by wind and water into beautiful works of art. The water tumbles and slides over the hard surfaces, large as banquet tabletops, shining with sunlight, liquid magnificence. I hasten my step in search of the source.

I come, a few minutes later, to yet another lake, smaller, shallower, a radiant turquoise green, pooled into the basin formed by surrounding summits emptying their winter ice into the dish where I now cool my feet. I stare at the water and the beds of rock and the sky close and blue overhead. I lean back then, flattening my spine to the stone, shut my eyes, and feel the sun bake my skin. My feet dangle in the purest, chilled water; my body feels the heat close around it, the sun's rays penetrating my skin, with my shoulders and hips pressed bone to stone.

The mountains form a bowl around me and I, flat on a pillow of rock, lay at the bowl's base, pistil at the blooming flower's center, seed

Kerry Temple

in the palm of a hand. The sun's rays come from far away and the sounds of wind and water come from far away, and I feel close to the marrow, as if I've found the center, the vortex, the still point of it all. And yet all around me, even down into the rock and root and earth beneath me, the landscape comes alive—the mountains breathing, rising, teeming. I daydream and doze and forget myself, absently merging with the breezes and the liquid gurglings and the sunlight shining down. It and I and the Other—it is all one thing. I have finally found what I've been coming for.

On the northwest corner of the Big Horns is a towering shelf of mountain—wind-seared, grass-coated, plunging above the timberline, head in the sky. It is called Medicine Mountain, and from there the landscape drops precipitously to the west, plummeting from almost 10,000 feet, onto the expansive rawhide flats of central Wyoming. Vision extends incomprehensibly far in many directions; the ice-castle summits of the Beartooth range, off toward Montana, the Tetons and Yellowstone, the Wind River range show faintly on the horizon.

Of course, the sky is immense here, indescribably distant and broad, yet close, as near as an arm's length. At night the stars are within reach, yet they point beyond the edges of the universe. The wind blows here in sheets, in waves, in boisterous, rollicking gusts, driving hard across these flinty open spaces before splashing into this giant seawall of stone and canyon, mountain peak and ancient headland. Sunsets fill the sky, dying light rising off the earth's distant floor, as the sun slides over the western ledge of the planet. Reds and salmon colors, crimsons and the hues of flamingoes and salt seas and iron. It is a geography that both screams and whispers with the power of creation.

Here, too, is the giant Medicine Wheel, an array of stones, 245 feet in circumference, laid out carefully with 28 spokes, cairns marking the primal directions—a kind of Stonehenge, a kind of colossal bicycle wheel made of stones to mark the passage of time, the movement of constellations, the drift of the sun, the circle of seasons. It was constructed, archeologists say, sometime between 1200 and 1700 A.D. The hoop structure is significant, of course, those native here believing in the power of the hoop and the sanctity of the Sundance Lodge or Medicine Lodge aligned to the anchor directions. It was not unusual for these people, whether Lakota, Crow, or Cheyenne, to seek visions on sacred heights, to make prayer offerings on holy summits.

But explanations for the origin of this place hide among the myths and tales of those who speak in myth and tale. And yet they still come, native peoples still having prayers, rituals, and ceremonies here, with ribbons and flags left behind flapping in the wind, tobacco pouches dangling, medicine bundles and sweetgrass woven, and prayer feathers offered to the spirits who dwell here. I saw an eagle here once and a sunset I'll never forget and one night sat here late, looking for shooting stars and watching the sky scroll overhead and thinking about what life lurks in the universe. This is holy ground. I am reminded of that each time I come to this place.

It is surrounded now by chain-link fence; only Native Americans are permitted inside the enclosure. And you can almost drive to this majestic promontory, hiking the final couple of miles to the plateau 9,642 feet above sea level. Yet when I am here, I marvel at the pilgrimage made by those who preceded us on this continent, coming on foot, long days of approaching, carrying their food and shelter, their offerings and petitions, to stand here and pray and to look out upon the vast, distant, and intimate cosmos. I can stand here, too, and feel close to what they felt and saw and must have wondered.

There are other places around the earth, many similar constructions, stones of various sizes, pyramids and etchings, altars and carved rock tablets linking the human species to the celestial machinations, indicating a need to discern, to correlate, to map somehow the mysterious and awesome secrets of creation, looking for a higher power's hand in it all, believing in the spirited intelligence that beckons from just beyond the horizon of human comprehension. We come and leave our offerings upon the landscape, too—our own prayer feathers, medicine bundles, and humble pouches of tobacco.

I marvel, too, at the other belief systems, as old as the human race, that looked for the meaning of life in nature and sought truth in the patterns there. Native cultures and Eastern ones, the Christian mystics and the Transcendentalists, the aborigines in Australia and the physicists puzzled by the essence of matter and the origins of existence. Pilgrims all. Seekers of truth exploring, examining the evidence all around them.

Kerry Temple

I have learned much from my time in the Big Horns, through the years as I have come and gone from here, first arriving as a 25-year-old and now returning after many years away. I am different each time. The years have done some of that to me, of course, the changes that come from decades passing. But what I mean is, I have come here in different frames of mind, my soul in different places, different angles of receptivity and repose, urgency or impassivity. I have, for example, arrived fit and ready to square myself with the expedition ahead. But I have also come, head filled with distractions, internally cluttered, and slow to shake the hounds of living.

Once I had spent 5 days in the Big Horns, hiking around, scrambling on stone and scree, but it wasn't till the end of that trip, when I stopped off at the Medicine Wheel, that I realized what I had missed. I had forgotten so much. I wanted to go back then and do it again, but to embrace the second chance more mindfully. But the obligations of my life dictated that I turn the car toward home. Sometimes we get no second chance.

It is so easy, immersed in city or suburban life, to distance oneself from that which is all around us, but not as apparent as the things that consume our lives. We are tangled in the nets of our cities, burdened by the demands of modern survival—a kind of living that alienates us from the spirit of life. As a culture, we have divorced ourselves from that, have become estranged from that which prompted others to ascend a summit 10,000 feet, inaccessible but for a few months each year, to make a pilgrimage to a place that inspires both faith and awe. And it shows in the way we live.

Ever since that day on the sandbars of Red River so long ago I have been looking for the supernatural, for the soul inside creation, for God, for tangible signs of the mystical, for that spirit world said to co-exist with the material one, for indications that such a realm exists. I have believed in signs; I have followed one to the next, thinking myself right on God's heels. I have examined the weeping Madonnas, the enigmatic apparitions, trying to locate the border between miracle and matter. And I have watched shamans talk to ghosts, evangelicals speak in tongues. I have held myths to the fire of science and have studied the texts of the world's religions, the stories of faith and belief, and I have spent other years believing only in what can be seen and touched and measured, proud of the advance of human civilization and its ability to explain and understand, dispelling ignorance and superstition, dismissing whatever might be holy from this silent, rocky ground. And I have come and gone, believing, disbelieving, dusting each corner of the universe for the fingerprints of God, then often doubting such telltale signs exist.

Finally tonight, sitting with the stars atop the Medicine Wheel plateau, I wonder about this desire to divide the spirit from the flesh, that age-old hypothesis that the world is split in two. I puzzle over this enduring compulsion to cleave the world in halves, to draw the supernatural from the natural, to extricate somehow the unseen from the seen—as if it is only some internal, spiritual realm that raises creation to a sacred plane.

Such has been the twin-engine turbine of Western culture—the scientific mind looking only for what can be seen and tested, logically analyzed, measured, calculated, and empirically proven, eliminating those slippery and elusive clouds of the heart, spirit, soul, and mind, and, on the other side, the religious who talk of other kingdoms, who have sought salvation by leaving this world behind, by overcoming human nature, trying to free the soul from flesh, by seeking a spiritual purity and self-denial apart from the animal drives and instincts characteristic of our species. Thus the two priestly castes of Western culture see the other as a rival, and exclude, disregard, or diminish the other's half, leaving me caught in the middle, trying to decide between sides.

But tonight, here with the stars atop the Medicine Wheel plateau, I remember sitting with Little Soldier on those visits to his place. I would ask and listen, and he would tell stories, recount things that had happened, try to find answers for me. Things he said tested my preconceptions, stretched my imagination. And yet he spoke matter-of-factly about what I perceived as extraordinary events, as if the occurrences were not that unusual, mystical, or magical. It was all just plain and simple, this casual coalescing of the fantastic and mundane. Plants had healing powers. The weather could—through prayer and incantation—be altered. Animals spoke to him on vision quests.

"The snake *spoke* to you?" I would ask, and he would look at me as if to say, "Well *of course* it spoke to me," as if to say, "how else would it have told me . . . ," as if I were somehow too thick to fully comprehend, as if the meaning were too obvious to explain. He seemed as amused and surprised by my finding this episode remarkable as I was surprised to learn that snakes could speak.

In time I realized his definition of speaking may be different from mine, but that didn't make his or my concept of speaking any less real. His world was inhabited by animals that could talk, animated by life forces affecting the affairs of human beings. His worldview had no room for conflict here, no boundary being crossed, no need for resolution or exclusion between one realm and another. It was all a singular landscape where the wind blew and the sagebrush grew and humans cooked and ate, told stories and made love, and where animals appeared and the Thunder Beings came out of the West bringing rain. I also came to understand that a snake or buffalo or deer speaking to humans—however they did so—was as real to him as theories of relativity and "string" and black holes are to me. And I came to consider what is real and what is not, what exists and what does not.

Native peoples have known for millennia that a spirit world coexists with the world we touch and see. Scientists these days are beginning to explore a whole universe *within* the material world they once believed to be the basic, fundamental, atomistic essence of reality. All religions, all belief systems, require a certain faith. Religions have their miracles and mysteries; even science has its theories, hypotheses, and myths. There are ways of knowing beyond the five senses and much to be known that reason cannot grasp. "It is only with the heart that one can see rightly," wrote Antoine de Saint-Exupery. "What is essential is invisible to the eye."

If I wondered at the stories Little Soldier told me, I marveled, too, at how comfortably he dwelt in a world with no borders, how easily he accepted a transparent reality with no margins, no divisions, no separation between what I would call the mystical and the plain, the natural, and the supernatural. It came to him as a coherent whole; he accepted it the way it came to him—the world as he knew it. He did not need to put his fingers into the wounds to believe in the resurrection; he accepted what he knew to be true.

So this time under the stars on Medicine Mountain, as I sit and watch the stars scroll slowly across the sky in the night, the lens finally dissolves and the night's shielded landscape comes alive. The silhouette mountains are fairly breathing and the sky teems with firefly stars and there is no inanimate object, nothing that is not living, and the edge of the universe folds over me and in the flickering leap of my imagination this realization seeps into me. There is no division, no two realms. It is all one thing. The Presence dwells within it all and it all dwells within the Presence. It is all one thing. *The rock is alive.* It comes to me then, fleeting as a meteor whose blaze flares in the sky: *The ground, the earth, the mountain is alive. The wind, the trees, the sky—alive. And Little Soldier's stone as well. All and everything, alive.* Alive with the life force breathed into all creation.

I realize I could no more peel a spirit out of nature than I could extract a soul out of myself. I look at the stars overhead and the mountains all around and the nighthawks flitting past and the wisps of clouds floating by and then at me. Fingers and thoughts, hair, heart, and self, wind-stroked skin, the cosmos close around me. And I see myself not as some physical creature with a soul loose inside, animus housed in a husk, but as a continuous harmony of mind and brain, genetic soup and muscle and bone and self and spirited whole enveloping me. Creation, too, not some physical manifestation of some hidden, underlying specter, but all one thing inseparably wrapped together in splendor. Making no distinctions, no partitions, indivisible, celebrating the unifying oneness of it all.

Once upon a night in the Big Horns, when the stars were close enough to touch and yet infinitely sky-high, a connect-the-dots ladder out of myself and a fractured universe best left behind, I see more clearly than I have in years and years. And I see more sharply, too, my own life in memory, all that's happened to lead me here, the waywardness and detours, the persistence and the faith, leaving me to wonder why it took me so long to find my way back home.

Kerry Temple

EPILOGUE

Man's days are like those of grass;
like a flower of the field he blooms;
The wind sweeps over him and he is gone,
and his place knows him no more.

—*Psalm 103*

The eviction notice came by registered mail. It came sooner than I had wanted but—as it is with many endings—I had been expecting it since the day that I first arrived. It was late fall. The leaves were down, crackling around my feet, giving off their thick, musty smell, the scent of dissolution and decay. A mailman came and I signed on the line to acknowledge I'd gotten the word. There was a sharpness in the air. The evenings were shorter now, the golden sunsets coming sooner, fading quicker, followed by the chilling breath of winter coming. I watched the deer who watched me back. I walked the grounds in quiet contemplation, trying to memorize this place and that. I tended fires in the woodstove, sipped cider, boxed books.

I did not want to leave. I would've stayed forever if I could. But I have thought that about other places and other times when letting go was like removing part of me. I tried to find reasons it was good to be moving on. Having been reclusive for this long, it was probably time to find again the company of humans, to live in another kind of neighborhood, to enter into the affairs of fellow leaf-rakers, dog-walkers, snow-shovelers, saying hello over the fence, lending a ladder, giving a neighbor's car battery a jump, taking in mail and newspapers for the ones on vacation.

Even in the past it had occurred to me, when I'd return from a week of backpacking, that it is easier to live according to one's good senses out there in the solitude of nature. There is beauty out there and certain liberties, flush harmonies, the honesty of stone and sun and star, the divine revelations concealed elsewhere by human contrivances, the starkness of seeing oneself alone in the landscape of doubt and faith and hope, the simplicity and comfort and humor that comes from being among a few good friends, like-minded, true, and generous. I'd come home from those days on the trail with stones in my pockets, new wealth, and good intentions.

It has also occurred to me that these truths and hopes and good intentions are of little power if they do not last, if they are not incorporated into the affairs of human interaction, if they are not brought along and shared, integrated into the lives of those around us. It is one thing to revel in the beauty and order of creation; it is another to find it here among the people, the many nations with whom I live. So I learned to bring back stones as keepsakes and reminders, as teachers and as totems. They have helped me remember the importance of turning theory into practice, translating idea into action, to take my prayers beyond the monastery walls and to the full community of the human race and all its many relations. The ultimate measure of a human being, after all, rests in his ability to love, and now it was time to go and love again.

The earth tells us when it is time to move on, when an ebbing or a ripeness signals the coming of new pathways and horizons, when it is right to bundle up one's stuff and get on down the road, looking homeward, become companion to the others. That time had come. So I loaded up my car, boxes of rocks and books, feathers, and bone on the passenger seat beside me.

I have made my place here and now I go, disappearing, dissolving from view. That is as it should be: The doorway seals behind us, the place eclipses us, is left the way we found it. It is good to slip into the scenery, traveling undetected, grass growing over whatever tracks we might have made. One thing I do take from here is a sense of acceptance. I am not sure it is faith really, and it's a long way from peace, because the dull pain endures and serenity is not yet mine. Nor is it a grim fatalism or bleak sense of reality. What I mean is that the woods and seasons and my time here have taught me that life comes in different colors, different shades of lightness and dark, that it defies the logic of fairness or reason, that there are problems without resolution and questions without answers ultimately mysterious, but that it is all a good and beautiful thing, a wondrous thing really, and a richly textured gift that I have accepted smiling.

I leave here, too, with many good memories and with these rocks, and I have written all this down so that I will remember, perhaps so others might know—because the bulldozers have now come and the trees have been cleared, and the pond filled in, and the creek rerouted to make room for a big, handsome clubhouse. People will pay $75 each to play a round of golf here, and a chain-link fence crowned in barbed wire will guard the periphery, keeping the place animal-free and protected. Of course, I am glad the acreage has stayed mostly green and has not been turned into a subdivision, parking lot, or mall; but the wildness will be missed. I am grateful I did not come here too late. I am glad this piece of landscape got into my blood, that this place brought me home to myself and to creation. Here I learned what the forest people meant when they said the forest could be seen only from within. And here I finally learned what Little Soldier and his prayer stone had to say so long ago—and that we now have come about as far as words can take us.

Back to Earth

ACKNOWLEDGMENTS

This book really did start because of a pact I made on a sandbar in the middle of Red River in northwest Louisiana when I was 17. So, to one degree or another, it's been a work in progress for 35 years. It is true that the main labor of fashioning these ideas and words into a book took place in that very small cabin in the woods of northwest Indiana, but some of the stories had appeared previously, and it took almost another decade of writing and rewriting, reshaping, reworking, and repeatedly resubmitting before the text was accepted for publication.

Over that decade, my sons Casey and Ross and I worked hard to find each other again. I am grateful to them for their love, strength, and understanding, and I am immensely proud of the men they have become. While each has made his own way into the world, we have again hiked and camped together, have backpacked in favorite old haunts, and the three of us eventually made a return trip to the woods along Lake Superior where we once had the best of times together. Wherever we go they are deep and big inside of me, and their presence permeates this book.

Anyone who has traveled much (particularly those who have put up with the trials of backpacking) knows that the wear of fellow travelers is as crucial as the scenery. I am grateful to all those with whom I have backpacked through the years—Jimmy Walker, Dan Duffey, Tim Truesdell, Don and Isaac Nelson, Paul and Andrew Wieber, Chuck Cealka, and especially Walt Collins. Walt has been a mentor and friend, a boss and an editor of mine, an absolutely ideal trail companion, and a quiet but expert guide—through the world and through life. He was right there for a lot of this book.

Because of Walt, Bill Sexton, and Dick Conklin at the University of Notre Dame, I have had at *Notre Dame Magazine* an almost perfect job, with great travels, great assignments, great stories to tell, and all the encouragement to tell those stories in the magazine where I have worked since 1981. The first piece I did on staff took me to South Dakota to learn more about Lakota spirituality, and a good portion of the stories in this book were first told in the pages of *Notre Dame Magazine*.

There are others to whom I am indebted—my parents who sacrificed to give me the education and opportunities I've enjoyed; all who have written about the natural world, serving as guides, scouts, and wise elders for those of us who have followed; John Soisson at the University of Portland for his encouragement and who published in *Portland Magazine* the narrative that became chapter 7; Jack Duman, Bernd Heinrich, and Olga Kukal, who took me along to the High Canadian Arctic when my only qualification for being there was my ability to pick up a caterpillar and pop it into a jar; Liz Nagle, whose rejection letter was so nice I decided to try one more time; and the good people at Rowman & Littlefield who saw the merit in publishing this, especially Jim Langford, whose enthusiasm, support, and editorial insights helped considerably as we moved from manuscript to book. For years all I wanted was to find an editor who believed in the potential of this manuscript and who could then help me shape it into a book. Jim Langford, through happy serendipity, proved to be that editor and also a good human being who made the process feel right.

I also need to thank Sam Moves Camp and Little Soldier. They took me in and shared their lives, their teachings, and their traditions when I showed up as a stranger at the door. I knew them as wise and holy men and I am grateful for their gifts. I am pleased they approved what I wrote about their Lakota ways. I am sorry that Little Soldier passed on to the Grandfathers before he could see this book.

Finally, I must thank Jessica for coming into my life and for bringing her love and faith, her sweetness and vision to the road we've taken together. She brought light into my darkness and her gifts have been a blessing of inexpressible grace. The world is persistently beautiful, but the experience is always grander when loved ones share the view. Her heart and soul have transformed the landscape of my life.

Kerry Temple

MONOGRAPHS OF THE SOCIETY FOR RESEARCH IN CHILD DEVELOPMENT
Serial No. 246, Vol. 61, Nos. 1–2, 1996

CONTENTS

ABSTRACT

CASE, ROBBIE, and OKAMOTO, YUKARI, in collaboration with GRIFFIN, SHARON; McKEOUGH, ANNE; BLEIKER, CHARLES; HENDERSON, BARBARA; and STEPHENSON, KIMBERLY MARRA. The Role of Central Conceptual Structures in the Development of Children's Thought. With Commentary by ROBERT S. SIEGLER and DANIEL P. KEATING; and a Reply by ROBBIE CASE. *Monographs of the Society for Research in Child Development*, 1996, **61**(1–2, Serial No. 246).

In this *Monograph*, we present a new theory of children's conceptual development and the empirical research on which that theory is based. The main construct in the theory is the notion of a central conceptual structure. These structures are defined as networks of semantic nodes and relations that represent children's core knowledge in a domain and that can be applied to the full range of tasks that the domain entails. Major transformations are hypothesized to take place in these structures as children enter each new stage of their development. Once formed, the new structures are hypothesized to exert a powerful influence on all subsequent knowledge acquisition. The process by which they exert this effect is believed to be a dynamic one, in which general conceptual insights and more specific task understandings become reciprocally coupled, each exerting a bootstrapping effect on the other.

In the first chapter, the general theoretical framework that underlies this conception is spelled out in broad strokes and compared to other contemporary views of conceptual development. In subsequent chapters, more detailed models of children's central conceptual structures are presented for three different domains: number, space, and social interaction. These models are then tested using a mixture of new and previously designed cognitive tasks, which are administered to children from four different age groups (4, 6, 8, and 10 years), three different social classes (high, medium, and low), and four different countries (the United States, Canada, Japan, and China). The results of a 6-year program of instructional research are also summarized and used to clarify and refine the theory. Analytic tools that are employed include computer simulation, item analysis, and linked growth curve analysis. Statistical techniques include latent structure analysis, factor analysis, and Guttman scaling. Problems with previous versions of the theory and implications of the present version are discussed in the final chapter.

I. INTRODUCTION: RECONCEPTUALIZING THE NATURE OF CHILDREN'S CONCEPTUAL STRUCTURES AND THEIR DEVELOPMENT IN MIDDLE CHILDHOOD

Robbie Case

The first theorist to articulate a general theory of intellectual development in the post-Darwinian era was James Mark Baldwin (1894/1968). According to Baldwin's theory, children's thought progressed through a sequence of four universal stages, which he termed the stages of "sensorimotor," "quasi-logical," "logical," and "hyperlogical" thought. In any given stage, Baldwin believed that new experience was "assimilated" to the existing form of thought, much in the manner that the body assimilates food. He saw transition from one form of thought to the next as driven by "accommodation," a process by which existing habits or schemata are broken down and then reorganized into new and more adaptive patterns.

Although Baldwin was the first to articulate a general theory of cognitive development, it was Piaget's (1960, 1970) reworking of Baldwin's theory that had the greatest impact on the field. The most important feature that Piaget added to Baldwin's theory was the notion of a "logical structure," that is, a coherent set of logical operations that can be applied to any domain of human activity and to which any cognitive task in the domain must ultimately be assimilated. Piaget hypothesized that the form of children's operational structures is different at different stages of their development and that this gives their thought at each stage a unique character. To highlight the importance of these operational structures, he relabeled Baldwin's second and third stages of development, calling them the stages of "preoperational" and "operational" thought, respectively. He also divided the stage of operational thought into the "concrete" and "formal" periods.

Piaget spent a good deal of effort explicating the process that Baldwin had labeled "accommodation": that is, the process by which low-level opera-

1

tional structures are transformed into higher-level ones. He suggested that this process is a dynamic one, involving at least three phases: (1) an initial phase of disequilibrium in which the inadequacy of a current operational structure is recognized; (2) a phase in which children actively search for a higher form of equilibrium but still remain trapped by the contradictions of their current structure; and (3) a phase in which children gradually abstract a more satisfactory operational structure from the patterns that are implicit in their current mental activity. Piaget assumed that the process of stage transition is necessarily a slow one because it depends so strongly on children's own activity. He also assumed that the process cannot easily be modified by external interventions such as instruction.

For many years, Piaget's account of children's conceptual growth was the only one to be given much attention. During the late 1960s and early 1970s, however, a reaction against it set in. Particularly in North America, investigators began to articulate a view of conceptual development that was less monolithic than Piaget had proposed. Theorists began to assert that children's conceptual development was less dependent on the emergence of general logical structures than Piaget had suggested and more dependent on the acquisition of insights or skills that are domain, task, and context specific. They also began to assert that children's thought is more responsive to external influence than Piaget had suggested and more dependent on the sort of social interaction that had been described by Vygotsky (1962).

In support of this view, a new generation of researchers gathered a variety of experimental data. From the point of view of the present *Monograph,* the most important studies were those that showed (*a*) insignificant correlations between developmental tests that Piaget had claimed tapped the same underlying general structure, (*b*) substantial asynchrony in the rate of development of concepts that Piaget had claimed depended on the same underlying structure, (*c*) large effects of short-term training on logical tasks such as conservation (tasks that were supposedly dependent on the gradual emergence of a general operational structure and thus impervious to such transitory influences), and (*d*) transfer of such training to other tasks having the same conceptual content but not to other tasks whose conceptual content was different but that were supposed to depend on the same underlying operational structure. Although these data did not call into question the epistemological underpinnings on which Piaget's system had been founded, they did run counter to the notion that children's intellectual development is dependent on the gradual acquisition of a universal system of logical operations. Thus, even investigators who were Piaget's close colleagues and collaborators began to deemphasize the importance of these structures in their account of children's intellectual growth (Cellerier, 1972; Inhelder, Sinclair, & Bovet, 1974).

CURRENT VIEWS OF COGNITIVE STRUCTURES
AND THEIR ROLE IN CHILDREN'S DEVELOPMENT

During the early 1980s, researchers interested in modifying or replacing Piaget's theory took a number of different directions in response to the criticisms that had been leveled at it. The first direction, which became known as the "neo-Piagetian" one, was to introduce a stronger set of assumptions about the specificity of children's cognitive structures and their environmental dependence. Rather than focusing on system-wide logical structures, neo-Piagetians focused on concepts, control structures, and skills that were a good deal more specific in nature (Biggs & Collis, 1982; Case, 1978, 1985; Fischer, 1980; Halford, 1982; Pascual-Leone, 1970, 1988). Their general premise was that cognitive structures are acquired in a fashion that is local and dependent on specific experience; what gives development its generality, according to their view, is that the complexity of these structures is subject to a common ceiling, a ceiling that can be attributed to the existence of age-linked constraints on children's information-processing capacity and/or working memory.

A second general theoretical direction drew its impetus more directly from Chomsky's theory than from Piaget's. According to Chomsky (1957), children's acquisition of language is governed by an innate neurological system, or "module," that operates in a relatively autonomous fashion. Drawing on this notion, several investigators suggested that the mind is best conceived as a loosely connected set of modules, each of which is specialized for executing its own particular function (Carey, 1985; Fodor, 1982; Gardner, 1983). Although children's performance may well be underpinned by a universal set of structures, these structures are module specific rather than general. For any given module, children begin their life "prewired" to pay attention to certain features of their environment and to relate these features in particular ways (Spelke, 1988). As they grow older and more experienced, their original naive or "prewired" structures are reworked into more sophisticated "theories" (Carey, 1985). This reworking may be "strong," in which case it results in a new theory that is "incommensurate" with its predecessor; alternatively, the reworking may be relatively "weak," in which case it results in a theory that is more elaborate or complex but still based on the same general set of principles (Carey, 1985, 1988). Stagelike change is possible within any given module whenever a strong reworking takes place. However, it is unlikely to occur across modules since each theory follows its own unique developmental trajectory and develops at its own unique rate (Carey, 1985; Gardner, 1983; Keil, 1986; Spelke, 1988).

A similar conclusion was reached by a third group of investigators who

3

had been working in the tradition of learning theory. Although this group was not particularly interested in structures of a biologically based or module-specific sort, they *were* interested in structures that are specific to particular content domains such as physics, chemistry, medicine, or chess. They were also interested in how the structures of "experts" differ from those of "novices" (Simon & Simon, 1978) and in the process by which an individual moves from novice to expert status. In fact, they viewed the novice-to-expert transition as a good model for most of the intellectual changes that take place in the course of children's cognitive growth (Chi, 1988; Chi & Rees, 1983). Although these investigators' epistemological position differed from that of modular theorists and their interest in external influences was much greater, they agreed with modular theorists in suggesting (*a*) that one of the most important changes in children's development is the change that takes place in the structure of their conceptual knowledge and (*b*) that this change takes place in a fashion that is not general to the entire cognitive system but is domain specific (Chi, 1988; Chi & Rees, 1983).

A similar conclusion was also reached by a fourth group of theorists who were working in the sociohistoric tradition. Following Vygotsky's (1962) lead, this fourth group saw children's cognitive development as critically dependent on the linguistic and conceptual frameworks that they inherit from their culture and on the physical and social technology with which these frameworks are associated. Although one branch of this school of thought viewed mastery of these tools as producing extremely general changes in children's mental capabilities (Olson, 1977), the majority opinion was that these effects are domain and context specific (Frake, 1985; Scribner & Cole, 1980). Most sociohistoric theorists thus concurred with modular and learning theorists that Piaget's general system perspective on cognitive development should be abandoned.

THE NOTION OF COGNITIVE STRUCTURES ON WHICH THE PRESENT *MONOGRAPH* IS BASED

The work reported in this *Monograph* is based on a controversial hypothesis, namely, that Piaget's notion of a general cognitive structure has been abandoned prematurely and that what is needed is not to reject this construct but to rework it in the light of the theoretical developments just cited. The data that led to this conclusion were generated as the result of a second-order analysis: one that pooled a number of neo-Piagetian analyses of local conceptual developments and arranged them into broad groups (Case, 1992a). When the data were arrayed in this fashion, it became apparent that development showed much stronger evidence of generality within task groups than across them. To account for this pattern, a new construct was proposed: the *central conceptual structure* (Case, 1992a; Case & Griffin, 1990; Case & Sandieson, 1988).

Central conceptual structures were originally defined as networks of semantic nodes and relations that have an extremely broad (but not system-wide) domain of application and that are central to children's functioning in that domain (Case, 1992a). In subsequent elaborations of the construct, it was suggested that such structures are actually "central" in at least three different senses. First, they are central in that they form the conceptual "center" of children's understanding of a broad array of situations, both within and across culturally defined disciplines or content areas. Second, they are central in that they form the core elements out of which more elaborate structures will be constructed in the future; in effect, they constitute the conceptual kernel on which children's future cognitive growth will be dependent. Third, they are central in that they are the product of children's central processing: although the content that they serve to organize is modular, the structures themselves reflect a set of principles and constraints that are system-wide in their nature and that change with age in a predictable fashion. They thus possess certain general commonalities in form that transcend the specific domain to which they apply. In order to understand these hypothesized commonalities in form, it is useful to take a brief look at three central conceptual structures that will be described in greater detail in subsequent chapters.

CENTRAL CONCEPTUAL STRUCTURES UNDERLYING CHILDREN'S QUANTITATIVE THOUGHT

As Starkey (1992) has shown, 4-year-olds possess a good deal of knowledge about quantity that is not numerical in nature and that permits them to answer questions about "more" and "less" as well as to understand the consequences of such operations as addition, subtraction, and spatial transformation. Figure 1*a* lays out the major semantic nodes and relations that appear to underlie this set of competencies.

As Gelman (1978) has shown, children of this age also possess a good deal of knowledge about quantity that is numerical in nature. They can reliably count a set of objects by the age of 4 years. They can also understand that the answer to the question, "How many objects are there in this group?" is the final number tag assigned to a set. Although there is some disagreement as to whether this capacity stems from a conceptual or a procedural knowledge base (Gelman, 1978; Siegler, 1990), there is no disagreement that it implies the existence of a complex knowledge network. One possible way of representing this network is illustrated in Figure 1*b*.

Although children assemble knowledge structures for generating num-

CASE, OKAMOTO, ET AL.

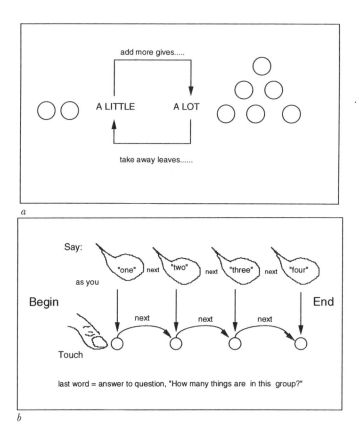

Fig. 1.—The central numerical structures hypothesized at the preliminary stage of the dimensional period, roughly 4 years of age. *a,* The global quantity schema that permits children to answer questions about "more" and "less." *b,* The counting schema that permits children to state how many objects are in a set.

ber tags and for making nonnumerical judgments of quantity during the preschool period, they appear to be incapable of integrating these two competencies (Resnick, 1989). Thus, when asked, "Which is more/which is bigger, 4 or 5?" they respond at chance level, even though they can successfully count to five and make relative quantity judgments about arrays containing five versus four objects (Siegler & Robinson, 1982). It is as though the two sets of knowledge are stored in different "files" on a computer and the two files cannot as yet be "merged."

As children move from age 4 to age 6, they gradually become capable of answering such questions. It seems reasonable to hypothesize, therefore, that these two earlier structures have merged and that a new conceptual

6

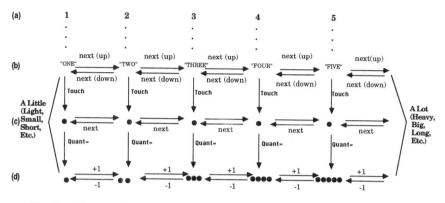

FIG. 2.—The central numerical structure (the "mental number line") hypothesized to emerge at around 6 years as a result of the elaboration and merging of the two earlier schemas shown in Fig. 1 above. The four rows indicate, respectively, (a) knowledge of written numerals, (b) knowledge of number words, (c) a pointing routine for "tagging" objects while counting, and (d) a knowledge of cardinal set values. The vertical arrows indicate the knowledge that each row maps conceptually onto the next; the horizontal arrows indicate an understanding of the relation between adjacent items. The external brackets indicate the knowledge that the entire structure can be used as a vehicle for determining the relative amount of quantities composed of identical units (weight, height, length, etc.).

structure of the sort illustrated in Figure 2 is now available (Case & Griffin, 1990; Case & Sandieson, 1988).

Since the structure that is illustrated in Figure 2 will be treated as a prototype for the rest of the present *Monograph*, it is worthwhile to explicate the notation used in the figure at some length. The top row of entries in the figure (row *a*) indicates that children can recognize the written numerals from 1 to 5 and that these written symbols are "grafted on," as it were, to a structure that is more fundamental, which appears below the dotted lines. This more fundamental structure has three basic components, which appear as interconnected rows below the dotted lines.

The first of these rows (row *b*) is the "verbal labeling" line. What the notation is intended to indicate is that children can recognize and generate the number words *one, two, three,* etc. The row immediately below this (row *c*) is the "mental action line." What it is intended to indicate is that children have a routine for pointing at or "tagging" a set of objects as they say the number words, in such a fashion that each object is tagged once and only once in the process. Initially, this routine is a sensorimotor one, which can be applied only to real objects. Eventually, however, the routine becomes a purely cognitive one, which mentally simulates the more primitive sensorimotor activity. The bottom row in the figure (row *d*) is the "conceptual interpretation" line. What the entries in this row are intended to indicate is that children understand that each act of tagging an object is equivalent to

7

forming a set that has a certain number of objects in it and that also has a certain characteristic perceptual form (as displayed on dice or with certain finger constellations). Finally, they understand that movement from one of these characteristic forms to the next involves the addition or subtraction of 1 unit.

Consider next the arrows in the figure. In each case, the horizontal arrows indicate the "transformations" or "rules for movement" that allow children to move from one item to the next in any row and back again. The vertical arrows signify children's understanding that there is a one-to-one mapping between each row and the next. Thus, movement from one item to the next in any row must necessarily be accompanied by a similar movement from one item to the next in all other rows as well. Finally, the wide brackets at the edge of the figure indicate children's understanding that movement forward or backward along the four rows is simultaneously a movement toward "more" or "less." Thus, counting can be used for making predictions or assessments of quantity along a wide variety of dimensions such as weight or length.

Once it is formed at about the age of 6, the "mental counting line" depicted in this figure forms a sort of lens through which children view the world. It also constitutes a tool that they use to create new knowledge. Children use the mental number line to build models of the conceptual systems that their culture has evolved for measuring such dimensions as time, space, and musical tonality. They also use it to understand their culture's rules regarding the fair distribution of material resources and its medium of commercial exchange. Finally, they use it to make sense of any direct instruction that they may receive regarding the particular systems that their culture has evolved for arranging numbers into groups and for conducting numerical computations.

Children's mastery of these systems progresses through three recognizable phases. Between the ages of 6 and 8, they become sufficiently fluent in using single mental number lines that they can focus on, and tentatively begin relating, two mental number lines. As a consequence, certain new properties of numerical systems—for instance, the relation between the "tens" column and the "ones" in the base-ten number system—become more apparent to them. With further growth and practice, by about age 10 years, they become capable of formulating the relation between two quantitative scales in an explicit fashion and of generalizing this understanding to an entire system (e.g., tens = ones × 10; hundreds = tens × 10; thousands = hundreds × 10; etc.; Case & Griffin, 1990). As a consequence, they gradually piece together a good working understanding of the entire whole number system and of the sorts of operations or "moves" that are possible within it (Case & Sowder, 1990).

Note that the number line does not function simply as a tool for making discoveries about the world; it also functions as a "core conceptual element" in the developmental progression that these discoveries produce. Structures that are formed early in this stage are constructed from a single number line, albeit one that may stretch from 1 to 100. Structures that are formed in the middle of the stage involve two mental number lines or scales, albeit ones whose relation is incompletely understood. Structures that are formed toward the end of the stage involve two or more mental number lines whose relation is explicitly understood and represented.

CENTRAL CONCEPTUAL STRUCTURES UNDERLYING CHILDREN'S SOCIAL THOUGHT

A great deal of research has been conducted in recent years on pre-schoolers' "theory of mind." What this work has shown is that, by the age of about 3 years, preschoolers possess some rudimentary understanding that people *have* minds and that, by the age of 4–5 years, they understand the way in which mental states can be modified by external events (Asting-ton, 1994; Astington, Harris, & Olson, 1989). Another understanding that is in place by this age is that of "scripts": 4–5-year-old children understand how familiar sequences of events unfold and the way in which one event can cause or prepare the way for the one that follows it; they can also describe these familiar "scripts" in language (Nelson, 1978). The content that is represented in this first knowledge structure is depicted in Figure 3*a*, that represented in the second is depicted in Figure 3*b*.

Although 4-year-olds are quite skilled at operating within each of these domains of knowledge, they are much less skilled at moving across them. Thus, for example, if asked why a mother performs some particular action in a familiar action sequence, they have no trouble referring to the key element in the previous event that causes her to do so or extrapolating forward and predicting what event will come next. But, even if probed with further questions, they do not spontaneously shift their focus and refer to the role of the mother's internal state in motivating her action (Goldberg-Reitman, 1992). As was the case with numerical understanding, one could say that children of this age have their knowledge of familiar scripts and their knowledge of familiar mental states stored in separate "files," which they have great difficulty "merging." Between the ages of 5 and 6 years, children become capable of answering such questions in an "intentional" fashion. One can therefore suggest that they have now merged the two original files and have formed a superordinate structure such as that illus-trated in Figure 4. As the figure suggests, children can now think of any familiar human activity as a coordinated sequence of events involving two components: a "landscape of action," which is the behavioral component of

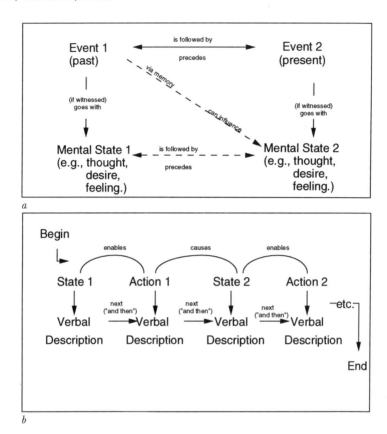

FIG. 3.—The central narrative structures hypothesized at the predimensional period, roughly 4 years of age. *a,* The inner state ("theory of mind") schema that permits children to infer the thoughts or feelings of others and to solve the classic "false belief" task. *b,* The event sequence ("theory of action") schema that permits children to verbalize the social scripts with which they are familiar and make causal statements and/or predictions about what will happen next.

any event sequence, and a "landscape of consciousness," which is the internal or "intentional" component (Bruner, 1986).

As a comparison of Figures 2 and 4 will reveal, there is a similarity in the general form of children's narrative and numerical thought at the age of 6, notwithstanding the many differences. In effect, the structure depicted in Figure 4 may be viewed as a mental "story line" that corresponds in its general form to the mental "number line" with which children of this age approach quantitative tasks. This parallel between 6-year-olds' social and numerical understanding applies at older ages as well. Between the ages of 6 and 10, there is a progression from uni-intentional to bi-intentional and

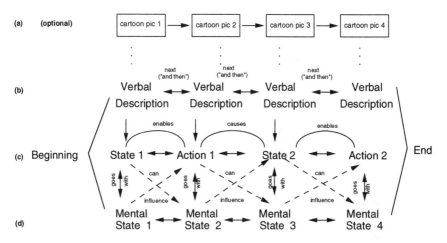

FIG. 4.—The central narrative structure (the "mental story line") hypothesized to emerge at the unidimensional stage (around 6 years of age) as a result of the elaboration and merging of the two earlier schemas shown in Fig. 3 above. The four rows indicate, respectively, (a) the (optional) knowledge that cartoon pictures can be drawn for states and action descriptors, (b) the knowledge of sentence forms for describing familiar events and actions, (c) the knowledge of familiar states and actions, together with the causal or "enabling" relations that they bear to each other, and (d) the knowledge of the role that those events play in influencing mental states, and vice versa. The external brackets indicate that the entire structure is understood to have a characteristic beginning, middle, and end.

then to integrated bi-intentional thought that directly parallels the corresponding progression in the domain of number, that is, the progression from unidimensional to bidimensional to integrated bidimensional thought (Griffin, 1992; McKeough, 1992a).

CENTRAL CONCEPTUAL STRUCTURES UNDERLYING CHILDREN'S SPATIAL THOUGHT

A similar progression also takes place in children's spatial cognition during the same time period. By the age of 4 years, most children (or at least most Western, middle-class children) have developed a general schema for representing familiar three-dimensional objects on a two-dimensional surface. This representation correctly captures the shape of these objects, as well as the shape of their most salient component parts, and the adjacency and inclusion relations that obtain among them. Thus, a tree is typically represented as a circle (for the branches and the leaves) with a line extending downward from the bottom (for the trunk). Similarly, the human

11

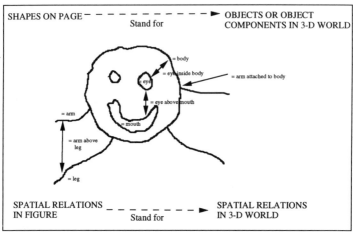

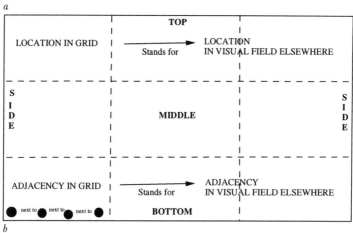

FIG. 5.—The central spatial structures hypothesized at the predimensional stage, roughly 4 years of age. *a*, The object shape schema, which permits children to symbolize the constituent two-dimensional shapes of which a three-dimensional object is composed and the relations among them. *b*, The object location schema (grid), which permits children to represent the general shape of a rectangular field and the location of objects within it.

figure is typically represented as a circle for the body, with two dots and a semicircle inside for the eyes and the mouth, and lines extending out from the circle for the arms and legs (Kellogg, 1969; Luquet, 1927). The implicit knowledge that underlies these representational capabilities is illustrated in Figure 5*a*.

At the same age, children also learn to represent the location of any familiar three-dimensional object on a two-dimensional surface by noting its position vis-à-vis the scene of which it is a part. As this knowledge develops, they become capable of reproducing the position of a single dot that is placed on a 3 × 3 grid, such as is depicted in Figure 5*b* (Crammond, 1992), or a line of dots that goes along some particular edge (Halford & McDonald, 1977). They also become capable of placing predrawn "stick figures" in the correct position in a scene and of locating objects in a three-dimensional room by noting the position of these objects as depicted in a two-dimensional photograph or drawing (DeLoache, 1989). The emergence of these competencies suggests that children are simultaneously acquiring a primitive "object-location" or "map" schema, whose elements are indicated in Figure 5*b*.

Once again, although preschool children possess both these sorts of knowledge, they have great difficulty integrating the two in any systematic fashion. Thus, if asked to draw a picture of two people standing side by side on the grass, they tend to represent the internal relations of each person correctly but ignore the relations that obtain between two people and between the people and their general environment (Dennis, 1992). By the age of 6 years, this task poses little problem. One may therefore infer that children have merged the two lower-order structures into a superordinate structure in which each individual object can simultaneously be seen as a configuration of two-dimensional shapes with its own internal structure and as one component in a broader spatial field with a structure of its own: typically one in which each object's position is referenced to a common ground line or "reference axis." The knowledge that permits them to do so is illustrated in Figure 6.

Between the ages of 6 and 10, children's ability to set up this sort of "mental reference window" increases in a systematic fashion. By the age of 8, they appear capable of mentally dividing any overall scene into two subscenes, each referenced to a different axis. Finally, by the age of 10, they appear capable of examining any set of objects in a spatial array and noting the position of those objects with regard to two orthogonal reference axes simultaneously. This "conjoint referencing capability" can be used for understanding the system of Cartesian coordinates that is used in graphs or the system of projective representation that is used to render perspective in Western art.

PARALLELS IN CENTRAL CONCEPTUAL STRUCTURES ACROSS DOMAINS

As will I hope be apparent to the reader, there is a strong similarity in the general form of children's numerical, narrative, and spatial develop-

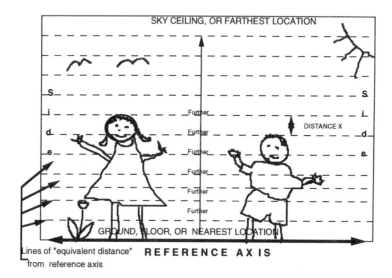

Fig. 6.—The central spatial structure hypothesized to emerge at the unidimensional stage, roughly 6 years of age, as a result of the elaboration and merging of the two earlier schemes shown in Fig. 5 above. Note that the structure permits children to represent the relations of object components (head above body etc.) as well as the relations of objects to each other (girl taller than flower etc.). Note that the latter judgments can be made only with reference to the ground line. It is the construction of this line, and the referencing of all objects in the window to it, that gives the schema its name (the *mental reference axis*).

ment—or at least in our models of this development—between the ages of 4 and 10 years. In each domain, 4-year-olds appear to possess two separate structures, each of which represents a fairly elaborate set of first-order symbolic relations. In each domain, an integration or "merging" of these structures takes place between the ages of 4 and 6 years, with the result that children begin to construct a system of second-order symbolic relations. Finally, in each domain, there is a similar progression between the ages of 6 and 10 as children move from partial to complete mastery of such a system. The structures that are constructed at 6 years all appear to be "line-like" ones, which integrate knowledge regarding the internal components of an individual object or event with knowledge about its position in an overall sequence or field. The second-order structures that are assembled between 7 and 8 years of age all appear to be ones in which two line- or field-like structures are integrated in a tentative fashion. Finally, the structures that are assembled at 9–11 years appear to be ones in which multiple line- or field-like structures of this sort are integrated, with more explicit rules that can be generalized to an entire system. These general characteristics, and the way in which they are embodied in different domains, are summarized in Table 1.

TABLE 1

Hypothesized Progression in Children's Conceptual Competencies between 4 and 10 Years of Age

General Competence	Manifestation in Domain of Number	Manifestation in Domain of Narrative	Manifestation in Domain of Space
Level 1: Two sets of relations, one linear (A) and one less so (B), can be conceptualized and assigned appropriate symbols	A. Global quantity schema B. Object counting schema	A. Inner state schema B. Event sequence schema	A. Object shape schema B. Object location schema
Level 2: Merging of two schemas into supercoordinate unit, often one with a "line-like" character	Mental counting line	Mental story line	Mental reference line
Level 3: Two superordinate (often line-like) structures differentiated and tentatively related	Two mental counting lines related; e.g., understanding of tens and ones in base-ten number system	Two story lines related; e.g., understanding of two-character interaction; understanding of main story plus complicating events	Two spatial reference axes related; e.g., first understanding of maps, Cartesian grids, and perspective
Level 4: Ability to formulate relations among different dimensions and scales in an explicit fashion as well as to generalize to an entire system	Multiple counting lines related; e.g., understanding of whole number system	Multiple story lines related; e.g., well-integrated action stories	Two or more reference axes related; e.g., understanding of orthogonal layout in maps and perspective in pictures

FACTORS PRODUCING STRUCTURAL PARALLELS ACROSS DOMAINS

The reason for these similarities in the form of children's conceptual structures across domains is less clear than the similarities themselves. Several general factors, however, may be suggested as relevant.

1. *Maturation.*—The first factor is simply maturation. Important neurological changes take place in the human cortex between the ages of 4 and 10. The tracts connecting the two hemispheres become increasingly myelinated, for example (Yakovlev & Lecours, 1967), and the activity in the two hemispheres becomes better differentiated and integrated (Witelson, 1983). Since all the structures that have just been described involve the integration of sequential and parallel components, and since the two hemispheres are generally regarded as playing differential roles in these two types of activity, this sort of change could be one important potentiator of, or constraint on, the changes that take place in children's central conceptual structures during this age range.

Another important maturational change takes place in the fibers connecting the frontal with the posterior lobes. These fibers show a strong pattern of dendritic growth during this period. Moreover, as this growth takes place, there is a gradual synchronization of electrical activity across the frontal and posterior regions (Thatcher, 1992). As the reader will no doubt be aware, the frontal lobes are generally regarded as the seat of the function that is crucial in making new mappings between existing knowledge networks (Stuss & Benson, 1986). They are also generally regarded as the seat of "working memory" (Goldman-Rakic, 1989a, 1989b), which grows from 1 to 4 units during this period. (A working memory of 2 might be an advantage if one wanted to make new mappings between two existing networks or files since it would enable one to keep both files "open" while one did so. Higher levels of working memory would also permit a more elaborate mapping process.) The increased "connectedness" of frontal and posterior activity could thus constitute a second, general potentiator of, or constraint on, children's conceptual progress across domains during this age range (Case, 1992b; Thatcher, 1992).

2. *Social experience.*—Since the structures that have been described all have referents in the external world, maturation by itself could not produce the central conceptual changes just delineated. This internal change would have to be accompanied by some common form of external experience. In certain nonliterate cultures, two-dimensional representation of space is rare, and no formal system exists for making those sorts of mappings. In other cultures, numeration of the sort developed in the Hindu-Arabic tradition is unheard of. In the modern era, however, both these forms of representation have become increasingly standard, as has the experience that is pre-

are more likely to be concerned is *how* children's knowledge structures become more differentiated and integrated (Chi, 1988; Siegler, 1995).

In an attempt to answer this latter question, Pascual-Leone (1970) proposed the existence of two basic processes. The first of these he labeled C-learning because of its presumed importance in the process of *conditioning*. The second he labeled M-learning because of its presumed importance in the sort of rapid learning that takes place under the influence of *mental attention*. According to Pascual-Leone, what happens in C-learning is that an existing schematic node (e.g., the node representing "a lot") receives a high degree of activation every time that a subject performs a particular action in a particular context (e.g., playing a board game in which a high number is rolled). If, at the same time, some other mental element (say, the particular pattern of dots on one die) receives a weak degree of activation, then a connection will gradually form between the weakly activated and the strongly activated unit (thus, this pattern will tend to become associated with the representation of "a lot"). If, in addition, the weakly activated element varies from one trial or subcontext to the next (e.g., because five dots appear on some trials that are classified as "a lot" but other times six dots appear), the result will be a gradual differentiation of the two situations. A similar process can also lead to schematic integration, the only difference being that the elements to be connected both already exist in the subject's repertoire as part of two preexisting schemas (as might be the case for the word *five* and the pattern formed by five dots, once this pattern has been differentiated from other patterns).

According to Pascual-Leone, the principles governing C-learning are similar to those that were first articulated by Hebb (1949) and that have been incorporated by modern neural network theorists in their learning algorithms (see McClelland, Rumelhart, & Hinton, 1987). A different process must be invoked, however, to account for the sort of rapid and flexible learning that takes place when children are engaged in active problem solving. This second form of learning, which Pascual-Leone calls M-learning, takes place whenever two schematic elements are *both* highly activated; in turn, this happens whenever someone attends to both elements simultaneously or in immediate succession (as might occur, e.g., if a child became interested in the patterns formed by different constellations of dots and began actively to scan back and forth between two dice, one showing five and one showing six dots). Under these conditions, a new connection is formed between the two units much more rapidly; in addition, the new connection is much more likely to be formed with conscious awareness, to be bidirectional, and to lead to a differentiation or an integration that can be more flexibly applied in other contexts.

A detailed account of C- and M-learning is beyond the scope of the present *Monograph*. The point that I would like to make in the present context, however, is that *both* sorts of learning are likely to be at work in the formation of new central conceptual structures and that the two processes are likely to feed on each other in an iterative manner. Whenever associative (C) learning takes place, existing connections are likely to be strengthened, and attention is likely to be freed up for learning of an attentionally mediated (M) sort. Similarly, whenever attention expands, new opportunities are likely to open up for C-learning to do its slower but equally vital work.

This sort of iterative feedback loop is likely to be present in all of children's learning, whether or not it is conceptual, and whether or not it is central (Case, 1985). A second feedback loop is likely to be present in children's central conceptual learning, however, one that draws on the hierarchical structure that any such learning entails. As an illustration, suppose that a 5-year-old child is playing a board game with an older sibling and that—in this context—she improves her understanding of the standard number patterns for the numerals from 1 to 5 as they appear on dice. Suppose further that she also improves her ability to count from 1 to 5 along a path that is divided into rectangles. When these advances take place, the specific connections that are formed and strengthened will also constitute a step—no matter how small—toward creating a more general structure of the sort illustrated in Figure 2 above. Moreover, as this general structure is formed, it will have a positive influence on the child's understanding in other specific situations, such as those presented by money and time. Finally, as further learning takes in these other specific contexts, there will be a further differentiation and integration of the more general structure, which will lead to further opportunities for specific learning. In short, a *hierarchical learning loop* will be established in which specific learning and general learning will exert a reciprocal influence on each other.

Such hierarchical learning loops have a number of interesting properties. One of the most important is that they tend to standardize the rate at which conceptual development takes place across specific contexts, even those to which children have a very different degree of exposure. Another is that they tend to accelerate children's intellectual development and bring it much closer to whatever limits may be set by maturation. These properties will be described in more detail in subsequent chapters. For the moment, the important points are simply these. (1) New central conceptual structures are almost invariably formed by the differentiation, integration, and consolidation of existing structures. (2) The process by which this occurs is one in which both associative and conceptual learning are involved. (3) The process is also one in which both specific and general learning are involved. (4) Finally, whenever these pairs of processes are involved, they feed on each

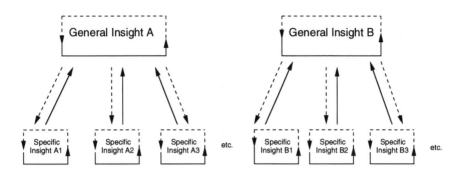

FIG. 7.—The hierarchical learning loop. What this diagram is intended to illustrate is that children's associative learning and their conceptual learning in specific situations "feed" on each other in an iterative feedback loop. A similar feedback loop connects children's learning in specific situations with their more general (structural) understanding. One result of this hierarchical feedback process is that the rate of learning in low-exposure situations is faster than one might otherwise expect since it is mediated by general understanding (which in turn is "fed" by insights acquired in high-exposure situations).

other in a reciprocal and highly dynamic manner. An overview of the general process is presented in Figure 7.

THE RELATION BETWEEN THE PRESENT VIEW OF CONCEPTUAL STRUCTURES AND THOSE PROPOSED BY OTHER THEORISTS

At the beginning of this chapter, I provided a brief sketch of Piaget's theory of conceptual growth and of the alternative views proposed by contemporary theorists. Before concluding, it seems worthwhile to compare the present view to these other views in a systematic manner.

The Relation to Piaget's Theory

As will I hope be apparent, the structures that have been delineated in this chapter bear a great many similarities to those that were described by Piaget. Like the latter, the present structures are viewed as playing a central role in organizing children's experience across a wide range of problem types and content domains. They are also seen as having different characteristic forms at different points in children's development. Finally, they are conceived as resulting from a very similar process. This process is one in which both maturation and social experience play a facilitating role but that is also driven by the child's natural curiosity and that involves the differentiation and coordination of his or her existing schemes, in a reflexive fashion that involves the active application of attention.

In addition to these general similarities, there are a number of more particular similarities as well. In the numerical domain, the structures that have been described are ones that move children from a "logic of functions"—that is, a logic that can be characterized by the formula $X = f(Y)$—through a transition phase in which they are able to make decentrations of the form $X = f(Y, Z)$ to a final and more equilibrated phase in which they can apprehend compensatory relations of the form $X = f(Y \times Z)$. This sort of characterization played an important role in Piaget's model of conservation and many other quantitative tasks.

In the domain of narrative, there is a similarity between the structures proposed in the present *Monograph* and Piaget's hypothesized structures as well. In the present account, children's movement is from a focus on action to single and then multiple intentions. The shift from action to intention-based accounts of social interaction played an important role in Piaget's early account of children's moral development; the shift from single to multiple perspectives played an important role in his theory of children's social development in general.

Finally, in the spatial domain, the hypothesized progression in the present account is one that moves children from a representation that is essentially topological to one that permits space to be represented in either a *Euclidean* or a *projective* fashion. This sort of characterization played an important role in Piaget's model of children's spatial development.

Since the central conceptual structures that we have hypothesized are similar to Piaget's in so many ways, it is important to stress that they are not identical. In contrast to Piaget's structures, the structures that we have described contain content that is semantic, not syntactic. For example, for Piaget it was the acquisition of the "logic of functions" that allowed children to establish a one-way mapping between one quantitative variable and another at the age of 5 or 6 years. In the present formulation, this relation is reversed. It is the acquisition of the notion of a numerically quantifiable variable—a semantic construction—that permits children to think in a fashion that can be described by the logic of one-way functions.

A second way in which our central conceptual structures differ from Piaget's operative structures is that their content is symbolic and represents the product of years of cultural learning. It may well be the case that humans have interpreted the quantities in their environment in terms of a mental number line from time immemorial and that they do so in all cultures throughout the world today. However, it is certainly *not* the case that human beings have always understood the relations between single and double digits in the way that 9- or 10-year-olds do in our modern industrial culture. Nor is it the case that children in all cultures grow up learning these relations today (Saxe, 1988). The same may be said with regard to the representation of space. At least since the era of cave art, human beings have been capable of representing the profile of objects in their environment on a two-dimensional surface and referencing the height of different objects to a common ground line. However, they have not always gone on to represent these objects in the way we do in Western art today. Nor do all children today grow up in Western cultures. The general point is a simple but important one: the semantic/procedural structures that we have postulated and analyzed have a strong cultural component, that is, a component that depends on being initiated into a particular set of ways for thinking about, talking about, and acting on the world. The acquisition of these structures may also require initiation into a system for representing those thoughts, words, and deeds on a two-dimensional surface (Gardner, 1991; Olson, 1994).

A final difference between the present model and Piaget's lies in the characterization of structural change. In Piaget's theory, change was seen as taking place centrally and as involving a process that Piaget labeled "reflective abstraction" rather than just simple maturation or experience. Increasingly as children grew older, their reflective processes were viewed as becoming conscious in nature and as operating in a general rather than a specific manner. In the present theory, conscious central processes are also assigned great importance. However, equal importance is assigned to processes that are more specific, unconscious, and associative in nature, even at older age levels. In addition, as was illustrated in Figure 7, a necessary and reciprocally facilitative relation is postulated between change that is context specific and change that is more general in nature.

The difference in the way that structural change is thought of in the two theories is perhaps most clearly evinced by the way in which school learning is treated. In Piaget's theory, school learning was seen as being dependent on cognitive development but not as contributing to it. In the present view, the relation between conceptual development and school learning is seen as being reciprocal. General conceptual development may influence specific school learning, but specific school learning may also influence general conceptual development in powerful ways. The nature of this process will be considered in greater detail in subsequent chapters.

The Relation to Other Contemporary Conceptions of Cognitive Structure

As they are formulated in textbooks, most modern theories of cognitive development are seen to challenge the classic structural view in certain fundamental ways. Different contemporary schools of thought are also seen as challenging each other in fundamental ways or as being incommensurate. As we have just seen, however, there are strong similarities between the notion of a central conceptual structure and Piaget's notion of a general operative structure. There are also important similarities between the notion of a central conceptual structure and the structural notions implied by other contemporary theories. The notion of a central conceptual structure bears a strong resemblance to the modular notion of a "theory," for example, in the breadth of domain to which it is presumed to be applicable. It bears a strong resemblance to the "knowledge networks" proposed by modern learning theorists in the way in which its content is defined and in the way in which learning processes are proposed to affect it. Finally, it bears a strong resemblance to the "conceptual/linguistic frameworks" of modern sociocultural theorists in its reliance on culturally defined symbols and forms of representation.

Because it bears a strong resemblance to each of these other constructs, it seems likely that many of the theoretical propositions that have been advanced for these other constructs may ultimately be shown to hold true for central conceptual structures as well. The following three propositions appear to hold particular promise in this regard.

Proposition 1 (from modular theory).—During the first few months of life, children parse their experience into a set of basic categories or "domains" whose origin lies in the evolutionary history of the human organism and the modular structure of the cortex to which this history has given rise. These domain-specific features then constitute the raw material from which the first central conceptual structures are assembled and the foundations on which all subsequent structures must be erected. As children develop further, these first structures are periodically reworked in major or minor ways. Any time a major reworking takes place, the form of children's thought appears to undergo a conceptual "revolution"; any time a minor reworking takes place, children's existing form of thought appears to undergo a process of conceptual refinement or elaboration.

Proposition 2 (from contemporary learning theory).—Central conceptual structures may be more profitably represented as knowledge networks—that is, as sets of nodes and relations among them—than as formal theoretical systems. With such a representation in place, it may be possible to show that both the content of the nodes and relations and their *strength* are subject to influence by children's physical and social experience. Both these experiential factors may also exert a strong influence on the cognitive strategies that children employ and/or the rate at which change of a higher order takes place.

Proposition 3 (from contemporary sociohistoric theory).—Beginning during middle childhood (if not sooner), one focus of children's activity is mastering a set of central conceptual structures whose content has been the product of a long process of cultural evolution and that cannot be easily represented without the higher-order system of symbols that their culture has evolved for dealing with this content. In the modern era, certain notational systems have also been invented for depicting these symbolic systems on paper, and the institution of schooling has evolved to help children master these notational systems. Wherever this institution is present, a stronger parallel will be found across different central conceptual structures than would otherwise be apparent.

The foregoing propositions are not explicitly tested in the research that we report in the present *Monograph*. As will be seen, however, they have exerted a considerable influence on the general direction of our work and constitute a useful background against which the results of our research may be evaluated.

OBJECTIVES OF THE PRESENT PROGRAM OF RESEARCH AND OF THE PRESENT MONOGRAPH

Three general objectives were pursued in the present program of research.

1. *Provide stronger empirical support for the theory.*—The first objective was to provide a more rigorous empirical demonstration that central conceptual structures actually exist and have the properties we have imputed to them. When we first hypothesized the existence of central conceptual structures, we presented a broad array of findings that we felt were consistent with this hypothesis (Case, 1992a; Case & Griffin, 1990; Case & Sandieson, 1988; Case & Sowder, 1990). Although the hypothesis was generally well received (Fischer & Hencke, 1993; Johnson, 1993), it was pointed out that there were certain problems with the database that had been marshaled to support it (Bickhard, 1994; Halford, 1993a; Lewis, 1994). In particular, the conceptual changes on which we had focused tended to covary with changes of a more subtle sort. By focusing on these other changes, it was possible to interpret the same pattern of data without presuming the intervention of structures with the degree of generality that we had hypothesized. Our first goal in the present program of research was to address this problem. To do so, we conducted a variety of new studies. Some of these replicated our earlier studies, but with stronger controls. Others used new measures, new

designs, and new analytic techniques. These studies are reported in the next three chapters.

2. *Extend the range of situations to which the theory is applicable.*—Our second goal in the present program of research was to extend the range of domains, tasks, and children to which our theory was applicable. In our previous work, we had examined only two spatial tasks, and our speculations regarding children's central spatial structures had been confined to one paragraph. In the present program of research, we conducted the more elaborate theoretical analysis of children's central spatial structures that has been summarized in the present chapter. We then conducted a series of three studies that were designed to test this analysis. Finally, once the results of these studies were available, we extended our investigations to children from other cultures, particularly those whose educational values and curricula are different from our own. These studies are reported in Chapters V and VI.

3. *Refine the theory itself.*—Our third goal was to refine the theory itself. In particular, we wanted to be able to present a more detailed theoretical description of (*a*) the content that central conceptual structures typically embody in different domains, (*b*) the manner in which they are applied to particular problems within these domains, and (*c*) the process by which they are acquired and the constraints to which they are subject. The techniques that we used for this purpose included rational task analysis, computer simulation, and linked growth curve analysis. The results have been adumbrated in the present chapter; they are spelled out in greater detail in Chapters II and VII.

In any ongoing program of research, new problems and/or questions emerge as work progresses. In the final chapter, we summarize the progress that we feel we have made in pursuing the three objectives listed above. We then outline a number of new questions and/or problems that arose in the course of our investigation and attempt to answer them in the light of our new understanding.

II. EXPLORING THE MICROSTRUCTURE OF CHILDREN'S CENTRAL CONCEPTUAL STRUCTURES IN THE DOMAIN OF NUMBER

Yukari Okamoto and Robbie Case

Of the three central conceptual structures that were described in the previous chapter, the one to which the greatest amount of attention has been devoted is the first, the one representing children's understanding of number. This understanding has been hypothesized to play a central role in producing the developmental changes that are observed on four different kinds of task, namely, (1) tests of *scientific reasoning*, including Siegler's (1978) Balance Beam and Shadows and Noelting's (1982) Juice Mixing tasks (Marini, 1992); (2) tests of *social cognition*, including Damon's (1977) Distributive Justice and Borke's (1973) Birthday Party tasks (Marini, 1992); (3) tests requiring an understanding of *cultural artifacts* such as money, clocks, or musical scores (Capodilupo, 1992; Griffin, Case, & Sandieson, 1992); and (4) tests of *arithmetic computation and estimation* (Case & Sowder, 1990; Griffin, Case, & Siegler, 1994).

The hypothesis that successful performance on these tasks depends on the development of a central numerical structure is a reasonable one. However, as yet the evidentiary base on which this claim rests is not a strong one. With one exception, which will be discussed in Chapter IV (Griffin et al., 1994), all previous attempts to investigate this hypothesis have followed the same general procedure. First, a version of some existing task has been developed for which the items can be classified as falling into one of four categories:

Category 1.—No precise quantification is necessary. (Questions can be answered by some form of polar classification.)
Category 2.—One dimension must be quantified precisely.

Category 3.—Two dimensions must be quantified precisely, but they need not be related in a very precise fashion.

Category 4.—Two dimensions must be quantified precisely, and the (additive or subtractive) rule that relates them must be explicitly formulated.

Next, these four classes of items have been administered to children of different ages, and the passing age for each class has been determined. Finally, the empirically determined passing ages have been compared with those predicted by our models: namely, 4, 6, 8, and 10 years of age, respectively.

In each case, the results from this comparison have been the same: the empirically determined passing ages have closely matched those predicted by the theoretical models. As a number of authors have pointed out, however, these results are far from definitive (Bickhard, 1994; Halford, 1993a; Lewis, 1994). The strongest criticism of the studies has been the one advanced by Halford (1993a). Halford's claim is that the four levels of items constitute what he calls a "measurement sequence," that is, a sequence for which the requirements of tasks at lower levels are embedded in those of higher levels. Whenever this is the case, he asserts, one will necessarily obtain a positive developmental gradient. If, in addition, the new test items are modeled on existing ones for which the passing ages are already known (in this case, 4, 6, 8, and 10 years of age), then the passing age of the new items can be predicted as well.

Halford's measurement criticism seems to us to be too severe. The item classes that we created in past studies rarely met his measurement criterion in any strict sense. Children were rarely required to do everything at higher levels that they were required to do at lower levels. Rather, they were required to demonstrate some higher understanding, one that—according to our theoretical model—required the combination of two lower-level understandings or some elaboration of that understanding (Griffin et al., 1994). To say that the developmental gradients *had* to be uniform, then, or even that they had to be positive, is to grant the validity of our theoretical analysis. In principle, such sequences could show much less regular patterns than we found, ones that contain temporary regressions as well as progressions. Yet all the sequences show the same general rate of development, namely, the one that conforms to our model.

A similar point may be made with regard to Halford's second criticism. It is true that many of our previous tasks were based on existing ones, such as Siegler's Balance Beam task. However, the surface resemblance of the second set of tasks to the original tasks was never a close one. Indeed, an effort was always made to ensure that there was as little surface resemblance as possible and that the only commonality was in the underlying conceptual structure that the tasks required. If our tasks were not tapping a common underlying conceptual sequence, then there would be no basis for predicting a common set of slopes. In fact, Siegler has not always obtained a common set of slopes himself when he has generated a set of tasks based on his original measure (Siegler, 1978). Once again, then, we see the correspondence between our theoretical analyses and our empirical results as providing considerable support for the general model, on which the theoretical analyses were based.

Although Halford's criticism seems to us to be too severe, we would be the first to admit that the results that we have reported to date do not establish the validity of our models in a definitive manner. This is the point made by Bickhard (1994). While it is true that the existing tasks all appear to require the application of a common set of numerical insights, they also share a good many other features in common, and these features could possibly be cited as the locus of the common developmental pattern. For example, all the task sequences mentioned above put a higher load on children's working memory at the upper levels than they do at lower levels. Since children's working memory is known to increase from 1 to 4 units during this age range (Case, 1972; Pascual-Leone, 1970), the results could be explained entirely on this basis, without any reference to their common conceptual underpinnings. By the same token, all the task sequences require more numerical computation for high- than for low-level items. Since children's computational ability also increases during this age range—owing primarily to the instruction and practice that they receive in school—this factor could be cited as the main source of the common developmental pattern. Finally, even if one is prepared to acknowledge that increased conceptual understanding is important for moving through the various task sequences, one might reasonably argue that this conceptual growth takes place in a much more task-specific fashion than we have suggested and that children's understanding never assumes the central forms that we have hypothesized.

Our position with regard to these counterinterpretations is a subtle one. The working memory explanation for the existing data is congruent with contemporary neo-Piagetian theory, to which we by and large subscribe. The next two explanations are congruent with contemporary sociohistoric theory and/or learning theory, which we also see as having great merit. We do not deny, then, that these three factors (working memory growth, growth in computational facility, and growth in task-specific knowledge) are important contributors to the pattern that we have isolated. We simply deny that they are sufficient to account for this pattern in its entirety.

How might we buttress this position? Although a variety of studies will be reported in this and succeeding chapters, the one with which we begin is the one that tackled the problem most directly.

STUDY 1: THE DEVELOPMENT OF CENTRAL NUMERICAL UNDERSTANDING FROM 6 TO 10 YEARS OF AGE

Perhaps surprisingly, no study has yet been reported in which the primary objective was to investigate the development of central numerical structures directly: by asking children questions about numbers and by evaluating the extent to which their answers to these questions at any given age can be accounted for by a single underlying structure. To be sure, a good deal of work has been devoted to exploring different aspects of children's numerical understanding—both in our own research (Case & Sandieson, 1988; Case & Sowder, 1990; Griffin et al., 1992; Griffin et al., 1994) and in research conducted by others (e.g., Baroody, Ganon, Berent, & Ginsburg, 1985; Carpenter, Moser, & Romberg, 1982; Gelman, 1978; Siegler & Robinson, 1982). However, no study has yet been reported in which an attempt was made to explore all these various aspects together and to see if they assume the coherent pattern that we have hypothesized.

That was our objective in the first study. The general methodology that we used was as follows. (*a*) First, we selected a number of items from previous studies of children's numerical understanding that seemed to us to target key elements of the structures that we have hypothesized. (*b*) Next, we supplemented these items with new items of our own creation, items that were derived directly from our models. (*c*) Next, we administered both sets of items, as a group, to elementary school children at several different grade levels, in order to see if the items were passed at the ages hypothesized by our models. (*d*) Finally, we conducted a latent structure analysis, to see if the pattern of correlations among the items could be accounted for by a set of underlying structures of the sort that we had hypothesized.

Development of the Test Items

Items Reflecting Unidimensional Thought

All the items at our first level were designed to probe for the presence of the "mental number line" structure whose components were diagrammed in Figure 2:

Item 1: One and two numbers after 7.—On this item, children were first asked, "What number comes after 7?" and then, "What number comes two after 7?" The idea behind this item was to test for the presence of the "next" arrows that connect the number nodes depicted in row *b* of Figure 2 above. Note that being able to count does not necessarily imply having an explicit representation of what number comes after any other number. It is this latter knowledge that Figure 2 presupposes and that this item is designed to assess.

Item 2: Forward counting.—On this item, children were shown a card with several numerals on it (8, 5, 2, 6) and asked, "Which number comes first when you are counting?" and, "Which number comes last when you are counting?" The background knowledge that this item requires is indicated in the top two rows of Figure 2. To respond correctly, children must be able to recognize written numerals and must also know their position in the counting sequence. In addition, they must be able to go through the counting sequence mentally while monitoring the visual display to see which numbers are and are not depicted on the card.

Item 3: Backward counting.—On this item, children were asked which number comes first when counting backward, 6, 4, 2, or 9. They were then asked which of these numbers comes *last* when counting backward. The rationale for these questions was the same as for the previous item, except that the direction of counting was the reverse.

Item 4: Bigger/smaller.—The type of problem represented by this item was originally designed by Siegler and Robinson (1982). In our version of the task, children were asked, "Which of these two numbers is bigger, 5 or 4?" and then, "Which of these two numbers is bigger, 7 or 9?" These two questions were followed by two parallel questions for "smaller" in which the number pairs were 8/6 and 5/7. The four items were summed to control for guessing and/or confusion in terminology between the terms *bigger* and *smaller*. Our intention in using this item was to get a sense of children's ability to use the ordinal information depicted in row *b* of Figure 2, in order to make cardinal judgments of the sort indicated in row *d*.

Item 5: Which is closer?—This is an item originally designed by Baroody et al. (1985) and adapted by Case and Sowder (1990). In our version of the item, children were presented with a card on which three numerals had been drawn at the points of an equilateral triangle: 5 (at the top), 6 (bottom left), and 2 (bottom right). The children were asked, "Which is closer to 5, 6 or 2?" Our intention in using this item was to assess children's knowledge of numerical adjacency in a novel context. If one knows that 6 comes next after 5, one should be able to infer that 6 is closer to 5 than to 2. Two items were used at this level to reduce the possibility of success due to guessing. The question in the second item was, "Which is closer to 7, 4 or 9?"

Items Reflecting Bidimensional Thought

According to the general theory, children at this substage become capable of coordinating two number lines in order to reason about a variety of new problems (Case, 1992a). Assuming that they receive some sort of further exposure to numbers, we argue that this should enable them to acquire two further conceptual understandings. The first is an understanding of the (additive) relation between the ones column and the tens column in the base-ten system. The second is the understanding of a numerical "difference." Children should be able to compute a difference with a simple number line structure (Case & Sowder, 1990). However, to think of a difference as a "mental object" (Greeno & Resnick, 1993; Riley & Greeno, 1988), we argue that they must be able to do more than simply decrement a number by a specified amount. In addition, they must be able to use one mental number line to represent the position of two numbers and a second to compute the difference between them. Two groups of items—Group A items (understanding the relation between tens and ones) and Group B items (use of "double counting" to construct a difference)—were presented at this level, one to assess each of these hypothesized conceptual understandings:

Group A Items

Item 1: Four numbers before 60.—The question for this item was, "What number comes four numbers before 60?" When counting backward, children show a clear hesitation when they come to the "decade breaks." Our interpretation of this phenomenon is that, although children have overlearned the "backward" number sequence from 9 down to 1, they have not overlearned the full sequence from 100 down to 1. Thus, at each decade break, they must pause, switch their attention from the ones to the tens column, and decrement the tens column by 1 unit. The ability to switch meaningfully from the tens to the ones column and back is one of the most important competencies that we see as emerging at the bidimensional stage, and this item was designed to test for it. The item also requires a short period of "double counting"—that is, counting backward while counting how many times one has counted backward—which is the second major bidimensional competence that we hypothesize.

Item 2: Five numbers after 49.—Another question of this same type was, "What number comes five numbers after 49?" It seemed possible that this item might be solved by one of two strategies: (1) the school-taught strategy of adding 5 to 9 and carrying, which would require a bidimensional capability (owing to the requirement for breaking 14 into 4 and 1 and dealing with each number separately), or (2) a "counting" strategy, which would present the children with the same bidimensional difficulties as they moved across the "decade break" that were mentioned in the discussion of item 1 (four numbers before 60) above.

Item 3: Backward counting.—A third question in this group was, "When you are counting backward, which number comes first, 49, 81, or 66?" To control for guessing we also asked, "When you are counting backward, which number comes first, 71, 46, or 69?" These items do not require that children actually count backward; however, they do require that children focus on the tens column and make a judgment about it that is not influenced by the value of the ones column.

Item 4: Bigger/smaller.—This item was presented in the same fashion as the corresponding item 4 at the previous level, the difference being that the numbers that children were asked to compare were two-digit rather than one-digit ones. For the "bigger" items, the number with the lower overall value was assigned the higher value in the ones column so that children who could not sustain a bidimensional focus would be misled into picking this number. For the "smaller" questions, the same sort of misleading cue was established in the opposite direction. The specific number pairs for the "bigger" question were 69/71 and 32/28; for the "smaller" question they were 27/32 and 51/39.

Item 5: Which is closer?—This item was also parallel to the corresponding item 5 at the previous level. However, once again, the item utilized two-digit rather than one-digit numbers, and the numbers were chosen so that, if children focused only on the ones column, they would be misled. The specific questions were, "Which number is closer to 28, 31 or 24?" and, "Which number is closer to 25, 21 or 18?"

Item 6: Biggest/smallest two-digit number.—This item was taken from Baroody et al. (1985). Children were asked, "What do you think is the biggest two-digit number?" and, "What is the smallest two-digit number?" The assumption was that they could answer correctly only if they could view a two-digit number as containing two one-digit numbers and understand that the highest value that each of these numbers could assume was 9 and the lowest 1 (or 0).

Group B Items

Item 1: How many in between?—On this item, children were asked, "How many numbers are in between 3 and 9?" The intention behind the item was to tap the second general competence mentioned above, namely, the competence for treating one sequence of numbers as a set of mental objects and the other as an operator that can be used to count along this sequence and compute differences. To control for guessing, several trials were presented; the other number pairs were 2/6 and 7/9.

Item 2: Numerical difference.—On this item, children were shown two cards, each with a different numeral printed on it (8 and 3 in the first trial, 7 and 9 in the second). Then they were asked, "What is the difference between these two numbers?" We saw this item as being similar to the previous one, except that the term *difference* had to be understood as well. The potential importance of this verbal capability has been treated at some length by Gelman and Greeno (1989) and Riley and Greeno (1988).

Items Reflecting Integrated Bidimensional Thought

As children move into the final substage of the bidimensional period, our hypothesis is that they should become capable of constructing and comparing two sums or differences rather than just one. One capability that this is hypothesized to give them is the potential for constructing a more integrated conceptual understanding of the whole number system: that is, for understanding that the *same* additive principle applies to each successive pair of columns (ten 10s equal one 100, ten 100s equal one 1,000, etc.). Another capability that is hypothesized to result is for understanding situations where two variables "trade off" or "compensate" for each other's operation in a subtractive manner. We also tested to see whether children could apply their capability for understanding additive rules to the understanding of two other systems: time and money. The three groups of items presented at this level were Group A items (understanding the structure of multidigit numbers), Group B items (understanding the relation between two differences), and Group C items (understanding other numerical systems):

Group A Items

Item 1: Ten numbers after 99.—Recall that, at the bidimensional level, we asked children what number comes five numbers after 49, on the assumption that they would have to decompose the number into tens and ones as they crossed the "decade break." At this level, we asked children which number comes 10 numbers after 99, on the assumption that they would have to decompose the number into hundreds, tens, and ones as they crossed the "hundred break."

Item 2: Nine numbers after 999.—The question here was identical to the previous one, except that the break children had to cross was from three to four rather than from two to three columns.

Item 3: Biggest/smallest five-digit number.—This item was the same as at the previous level, except that children were asked to state the biggest and smallest five-digit numbers, to see if they could generalize their bidimensional competence to a larger number of columns.

Group B Items

Item 1: Bigger/smaller difference.—At the previous level, we asked children to compute a difference between two numbers. At this level, we asked them which difference was bigger, the difference between 6 and 9 or that between 8 and 3. A second item (to control for guessing or positional responding) asked the same question for two different pairs of numbers, 6/2 and 8/5. Two further items asked which of two differences was "smaller." The form of the question was, "Which of these two differences is smaller: the difference between ——— and ——— or the difference between ——— and ———?" The items were (*a*) 99 and 92 or 25 and 11 and (*b*) 48 and 36 or 84 and 73.

Item 2: Numerical difference in +/− direction.—This final item also built on the item at the previous level that asked children to compute a difference between two numbers. This time children were shown two cards: one with a numeral on it and one with a question mark on it.

The experimenter said, "This number is 4, and we don't know the other number. The difference between the two numbers is 3. What number is this [pointing to the question mark]?" Children were scored as correct if they answered "7 or 1." If they responded with only one of these two numbers, a probe was presented to see whether they understood that there was a second possibility.

Group C Items

Item 1: 90 min = hour + half.—The first item required children to understand that 90 min was the same as an hour and a half.

Item 2: Which is closer?—The next item asked children, "Which is closer to $25.35, $20.00 or $30.00?" To control for guessing, several other questions were also asked—"Which is closer to $46.55, $46.00 or $47.00?" "Which is closer to $40.00, $29.99 or $61.05?" and, "Which is closer to $15.00, $9.95 or $19.95?"

Basal and Ceiling Levels

Although the children we assessed were 6–10 years of age, it was necessary to have at least a few items on our scale for picking out children who might be functioning above or below the levels that are characteristic for this age range. Our items for assessing predimensional functioning drew on the analysis by Case and Khanna (1981) and included such questions as, "Which of these two piles of chips [one pile of five chips, one pile of two] has more?" "How many blue chips are there in this array [of three red and four blue chips]?" and, "How many triangles are there in this array [of eight triangles and seven circles]?" Our items for assessing postdimensional functioning were a series of mental multiplication and division questions as well as two questions involving rational numbers. The specific items in each group are listed in Appendix A.

Method

Subjects

Children from kindergarten and the first, second, third, and fourth grades participated in the study. The children were students in two private schools in the San Francisco Bay Area, one denominational and the other nondenominational. Both schools served predominantly middle to upper-middle socioeconomic status (SES) families of European-American origin. All but one child were monolingual and English speaking. There were 60 children altogether: 7 kindergartners (3 boys and 4 girls), 18 first graders (6 boys and 12 girls), 4 second graders (3 boys and 1 girl), 21 third graders

(11 boys and 10 girls), and 10 fourth graders (4 boys and 6 girls). The mean ages were 6-3 (SD = 5 months), 7-0 (SD = 5 months), 8-4 (SD = 2 months), 8-10 (SD = 6 months), and 10-2 (SD = 3 months), respectively. The study was conducted near the end of the school year.

Procedure

Children met with the first author individually, in a resource room or other private space made available by the school. After a brief introduction, they were given the Number Knowledge test, beginning at the lowest level and working up until the majority of the items at a level were failed. The testing time varied, depending on the age of the child, but rarely lasted longer than 20 min, even at the oldest age level.

Scoring

Scoring criteria were established prior to testing. All the responses were classified as either correct or incorrect. Since the test did not require qualitative judgment, only one scorer was deemed necessary. A full protocol for administering and scoring each item is presented in Appendix A.

Results

A preliminary analysis revealed that, as anticipated, no subject failed any of the predimensional items and only a few 10-year-olds passed a few of the postdimensional items. Accordingly, the main analysis was conducted on the dimensional items described above. For these items, a further analysis indicated that there were no sex differences in performance (F = 1.99, df = 1, 58, N.S.). Consequently, boys and girls were treated as one group in all subsequent analyses.

Proportion of Correct Responses for Each Item

The first analysis that we conducted was an item analysis. The proportions of correct responses for all dimensional items were displayed for each age level, to see if they met the criterion of being passed by the majority of subjects at the age when structures of that level are hypothesized to be acquired. As may be seen from Table 2, all the items at the unidimensional level met this criterion, as did seven of the eight items at the bidimensional level. At the integrated bidimensional level, the majority of items still met the criterion. However, the overall "hit rate" was not as high.

TABLE 2

Proportions of Correct Responses on the Number Knowledge Test by Age Group

Item	6-Year-Olds	8-Year-Olds	10-Year-Olds
Unidimensional			
1. One and two numbers after 7	1.00	.95	1.00
2. Forward counting	.85	1.00	.95
3. Backward counting	.85	1.00	1.00
4. Which is bigger/smaller?	.90	1.00	1.00
5. Which is closer?	.85	.90	1.00
Overall level	.89	.97	.99
Bidimensional			
Group A (10s and 1s):			
1. Four numbers before 60?	.30	.70	.90
2. Five numbers after 49?	.60[a]	.60	.75
3. Backward counting	.25	.75	.95
4. Which is bigger/smaller?	.35	.75	.75
5. Which is closer?	.25	.50	.75
6. Two-digit number	.15	.60	.90
Group B (differences):			
1. How many in between?	.25	.75	.90
2. Numerical difference	.11	.65	1.00
Overall level	.28	.66	.86
Integrated bidimensional			
Group A (full structure of number system):			
1. Ten numbers after 99?	.15	.70[a]	.75
2. Nine numbers after 999?	.15	.25	.50
3. Largest five-digit number	.00	.00	.35[b]
Group B (difference comparison):			
1. Two differences: bigger/smaller?	.00	.25	.50
2. Numerical difference in +/− direction	.00	.25	.65
Group C (other number systems):			
1. 90 min = hour + half	.00	.15	.40
2. Which is closer (decimals)?	.00	.10	.25[b]
Overall level	.04	.24	.49

[a] Passed by more subjects than hypothesized.
[b] Passed by fewer subjects than hypothesized.

In examining the two items that proved easier than we had predicted, we noticed a pattern. The bidimensional item that was easier than we had expected was the one that required children to say what number comes five numbers after 49. The integrated bidimensional item that was easier than expected was the one that asked what number comes ten after 99. We interpret both these predictive failures in the same manner. Quite early in children's careers as mathematicians, they learn the patterns that are associated with counting forward by fives or tens, very probably because their fingers come in these denominations (Yoshida, 1991). When counting forward by fives or tens, therefore, children do not really have to break a number down into its components at the decade or hundred break (as we had hypothesized). They can simply count forward, using their fingers as a guide, or (if the number is 10) draw on the decade pattern that they have memorized (29 + 10 = 39). They therefore find these items easier than we had predicted. This interpretation is supported by the fact that the backward counting items, as well as the items requiring that a different number of counting units be used in the forward direction, did behave in the predicted fashion.

Two other items—both at the integrated bidimensional level—proved to be too difficult. For the item, "Which is the largest five-digit number?" the difficulty appeared to be that children had not yet learned the strategy for assigning numerical labels to large numbers—not that they had failed to acquire the general insight that the largest number of any size is the one composed entirely of 9s. To avoid this problem, we recommend that, in future versions of the test, children be asked to state the largest four-digit number.

The other item that proved too difficult at the integrated bidimensional level was, "Which number is closer to $25.35, $20.00 or $30.00?" In subsequent studies, we have attempted to show that, any time two bidimensional systems must be coordinated (as is the case for dollars and cents in this item), the task is not solved until the formal period (Case, Krohn, & Bushey, 1992). We therefore recommend that a "closer" judgment with three or four digits, and no decimal notation, be used in subsequent versions of the test.

Notwithstanding the four predictive failures, the data shown in Table 2 are in good general correspondence with our predictions.

Latent Structure Analysis

To assess the coherence of the three categories of item, we next conducted a latent structure analysis of the data using the Maximum Likelihood Latent Structure Analysis (MLLSA) developed by Clogg (1977). Latent structure analysis provides a method for determining whether an observed relation among manifest variables can be explained by postulating the existence of one or more latent variables (Goodman, 1974, 1975). The technique is analogous to factor analysis in many ways, but it is more appropriate for dichotomous items (Green, 1952). In the present instance, we treated the items on the Number Knowledge test as manifest variables for the analysis and the three levels of thought that we had hypothesized (unidimensional, bidimensional, and integrated bidimensional) as latent variables. Since it is necessary to have a certain minimum number of subjects per response category in order to ensure the reliability of the results, it was necessary to collapse some items on the Number Knowledge test so as to reduce the number of response categories. At the unidimensional level, five items were used to generate two response categories: pass (three items or

TABLE 3

Observed and Expected Frequencies Generated by MLLSA

Response Patterns for Substages of Dimensional Thought			Frequencies	
Uni	Bi	Integrated	Observed	Expected
F	F	F	2.00	.81
P	F	F	9.00	9.77
F	T	F	.00	1.11
P	T	F	14.00	13.31
F	P	F	.00	.00
P	P	F	14.00	14.00
F	F	T	.00	.03
P	F	T	.00	.39
F	T	T	.00	.04
P	T	T	1.00	.53
F	P	T	.00	.00
P	P	T	9.00	9.01
F	F	P	.00	.00
P	F	P	.00	.00
F	T	P	.00	.00
P	T	P	.00	.01
F	P	P	.00	.00
P	P	P	11.00	10.99

Note.—P stands for pass, T for transition, and F for fail.

more correct) and fail (two items or fewer correct). At the bidimensional level, the eight items were pooled to yield three response categories: pass (five items or more correct), transitional (three or four items correct), and fail (two items or fewer correct). At the integrated bidimensional level, the seven items were collapsed to three response categories: pass (four items or more correct), transitional (three items correct), and fail (two items or fewer correct).

The observed and expected frequencies for each of the response patterns are presented in Table 3. The index of fit of the model was .961,[1] which is considered excellent. The fit was further supported by the two chi square ratios provided by the program: the Pearson goodness-of-fit chi square was 3.812, and the likelihood ratio was 4.803. Comparing these ratios to a test statistic with degrees of freedom of 5, one finds both ratios to be nonsignificant.

[1] This index is computed by dividing a chi square ratio by its degrees of freedom. A likelihood ratio was used to compute this index because it is more robust than a chi square ratio for small sample sizes.

TABLE 4

FINAL CONDITIONAL PROBABILITIES FOR THE NUMBER KNOWLEDGE TEST

RESPONSE CATEGORY	LATENT CLASS		
	Unidimensional	Bidimensional	Integrated Bidimensional
Unidimensional items:			
0–2	.0770	.0000	.0000
	(.1000)	(.0000)	(.0000)
3–5	.9230	1.0000	1.0000
	(.9000)	(1.0000)	(1.0000)
Bidimensional items:			
0–2	.4234	.0000	.0000
	(.8000)	(.0000)	(.0000)
3–4	.5766	.0007	.0007
	(.2000)	(.1000)	(.1000)
5–8	.0000	.9993	.9993
	(.0000)	(.9000)	(.9000)
Integrated bidimensional items:			
0–2	.9620	.9620	.0000
	(.9000)	(.9000)	(.0000)
3	.0380	.0380	.4347
	(.1000)	(.1000)	(.2000)
4–7	.0000	.0000	.5653
	(.0000)	(.0000)	(.8000)

NOTE.—The estimated conditional probabilities are reported in parentheses.

The conditional probabilities for the model are presented in Table 4. According to this calculation, children with unidimensional thought have a probability of .92 of passing Level 1 and no chance of passing Levels 2 or 3. Children with bidimensional thought have a probability of 1 of passing Levels 1 and 2 and no chance of passing Level 3. Children with integrated bidimensional thought have probabilities of 1, 1, and .57 of passing Levels 1, 2, and 3, respectively. Overall, the results show that the three levels of conceptual structures are qualitatively distinct and internally coherent. In other words, the test items representing the concepts specified for each knowledge structure are found to form coherent structures, as hypothesized.

Scalogram Analysis

Our final analysis was concerned with the developmental sequencing of the three structures that our a priori analysis had suggested and that the latent structure analysis confirmed. In particular, we were interested in knowing whether our assumption about the necessary ordering of these structures would be confirmed. Accordingly, we established a "developmental level" score for each child, using the highest level passed (according to the same passing criteria as the latent structure had suggested) as a subject's level.

With these criteria, both the coefficient of reproducibility and the coefficient of scalability were 1. In short, the Number Knowledge test was a perfect Guttman scale. While our testing procedure guaranteed that the items would form some sort of Guttman scale, it did not guarantee that the scale would be a perfect one. Thus, we took this result as further support of our model.

Discussion

Our predictions for the passing age of items were by no means perfect. This should not be surprising, however. Without a detailed empirical analysis of the way in which children respond when faced with a particular test item, one can never be certain what test features they will find most salient or what strategy they will adopt. That they reacted to 80% of the items in the fashion that we had predicted, and at the age that we had predicted, is an encouraging sign, as are the facts (*a*) that our predictive errors seemed explicable, after the fact, in a fashion that can be tested in future versions of the test and (*b*) that the latent structure analysis yielded such a strong and simple solution.

The goal of the first study was to demonstrate that children really did acquire the numerical knowledge that we had hypothesized, in the order and at the ages that we had hypothesized. We feel that this goal was achieved and that the overall picture that resulted was consistent with the view that, although in all probability children's knowledge networks grow incrementally, they nevertheless assume one of three functional patterns. At any point in time, the probability that any aspect of a given network can be accessed is far from certain. What is certain, however, is that a child will not be able to access the majority of items at a higher level if she cannot also access the majority of items at a lower level.

Before proceeding, one final point is important to mention. The percentage of children who reach the integrated bidimensional stage by the age of 10 years was smaller than the percentage of subjects at ages 6 and 8 who reached the unidimensional and bidimensional stages, respectively. This result appeared both in the proportional analysis of individual items and in the latent structure analysis. The first time that we encountered a result like this, we took it as a refutation (albeit a minor one) of our general model. However, as Dennis (1992) has pointed out, the datum should actually be taken as a confirmation of the model. The reason is that the underlying variable against which our task analyses are calibrated is working memory capacity, not age, and that the same slowdown of growth occurs in this variable during this age range as well. On the Counting Span test, for example, the percentage of children who have spans of 2, 3, and 4 at the ages of 6, 8, and 10 are approximately 90%, 80%, and 50%, respectively (Dennis 1992; McKeough, 1992a). These values are close to the overall values for the three levels that appear in Table 2 above.

We return to this point at several further places in the present *Monograph;* for the moment, we simply want to flag this aspect of the data as being of significance and to indicate that we find Dennis's argument to be persuasive.

STUDY 2: SIMULATING THE PROCESS BY WHICH A CENTRAL NUMERICAL STRUCTURE IS APPLIED

The methodology of the first study was designed to demonstrate that children possess the conceptual structures for representing numbers that we had hypothesized and that these structures are acquired in the order and at the ages that we had proposed. The methodology of the second study was designed with a different goal in mind, namely, providing a model of how numerical structures of this sort might actually be applied to the solution of mathematical tasks. For this purpose, the class of task that we selected was arithmetic word problems, and our method of investigation was computer simulation.

Arithmetic Word Problems and the Competencies They Require

Although often decried by reformers in math education, arithmetic word problems have a long history in the teaching of mathematics, one that goes back to the ancient Greeks, if not earlier (Hoyrup, 1994). While they may not be the most interesting or useful sort of problem that children encounter in the modern mathematics curriculum, they are still present in virtually all programs and thus constitute a class of problems with which most children have considerable familiarity. They are also a class of problems for which the numerical structures that we have described should, in principle, be relevant.

Children's performance on arithmetic word problems has already been the object of a good deal of scrutiny. Consider the following two examples: "Tom has six marbles. He gives away two. How many does he have left?" and, "Tom has six marbles, and Joe has two. How many more marbles does Tom have than Joe?" These two problems involve similar, if not identical, arithmetic operations, namely, subtracting 2 from 6. However, the majority of 6- and 7-year-olds are successful in solving the former but not the latter version (Carpenter, Hiebert, & Moser, 1981). This difference in difficulty, and others like it, has captured the interest of cognitive scientists and mathematics educators alike and led to a considerable body of research.

On the basis of a theoretical analysis of their semantic structure, researchers have divided word problems into three general categories: (1) those that involve *changes,* of which the first problem above is an example; (2) those that involve *comparisons,* of which the second problem above is an example; and (3) those that involve *combinations* (e.g., "Tom has six marbles; Joe has two. How many do they have altogether?"). A further breakdown has been based on which of the three quantities in the problem is unknown. Prototypes of the problems included in previous studies are shown in Table 5, following the terminology used by Riley and Greeno (1988).

How do children solve the problems in each of these general categories? Previous analyses have suggested that they go through the following general steps (Mayer, 1985). (1) First, they extract some form of meaning from the verbal statements. (2) Next, they form some representation of the problem that is congruent with their mathematical knowledge. (3) Next, they establish a goal and determine a procedure to get the answer. (4) Finally, they execute the operations that their plan calls for and report the result.

Over the past ten years, a family of cognitive models based on this procedure has been developed and used to simulate children's performance on a computer (Briars & Larkin, 1984; Dellarosa, 1986; Fletcher, 1985; Kintsch & Greeno, 1985; Nesher, Greeno, & Riley, 1982; Riley & Greeno, 1988; Riley, Greeno, & Heller, 1983). Among the most successful of these simulations is one developed by Riley and Greeno (1988). In their model, the first step in the foregoing process (i.e., meaning extraction) is accomplished by applying a simple text interpreter of the sort developed by Kintsch and Greeno (1985). This interpreter parses sentences into words and phrases and builds a semantic network of the meaning that each sentence conveys. The second step (mathematical representation) is accomplished by setting up models that represent the actions referred to in the semantic network, using sets of blocks. The third and fourth steps are accomplished by applying actions on the blocks, actions that are specific to each problem type and each unknown.

The critical step in the Riley and Greeno model is the second one, that in which children build mental models of the mathematical relations that can obtain among sets of blocks. Children's cognitive development is simulated by assuming that, at each developmental level, children have a more explicit representation of the sort of problem that is involved (change, compare, combine) and of the part-whole relations that obtain among the elements of each problem. To test the adequacy of their developmental model, Riley and Greeno have compared the difficulty of problems as experienced

TABLE 5

SCHEMA USED FOR CLASSIFICATION OF WORD PROBLEMS

Combine

Combine 1 (combination unknown):
Joe has 2 marbles.
Tom has 6 marbles.
How many marbles do they have alto-
gether?

Combine 2 (subset unknown):
Joe has 2 marbles.
Tom has some marbles.
Joe and Tom have 6 marbles together.
How many marbles does Tom have?

Change

Change 1 (result unknown, increase):
Joe had 2 marbles.
Then Tom gave him 6 marbles.
How many marbles does Joe have
now?
Change 2 (change unknown, increase):
Joe had 2 marbles.
Then Tom gave him some marbles.
Now Joe has 6 marbles.
How many marbles did Tom give him?
Change 5 (start unknown, increase):
Joe had some marbles.
Then Tom gave him 2 marbles.
Now Joe has 6 marbles.
How many marbles did Joe have in the
beginning?

Change 2 (result unknown, decrease):
Joe had 6 marbles.
Then he gave Tom 2 marbles.
How many marbles does Joe have
now?
Change 4 (change unknown, decrease):
Joe had 6 marbles.
Then he gave Tom some marbles.
Now Joe has 2 marbles.
How many marbles did he give Tom?
Change 6 (start unknown, decrease):
Joe had some marbles.
Then he gave Tom 2 marbles.
Now Joe has 6 marbles.
How many marbles did Joe have in the
beginning?

Compare

Compare 1 (difference unknown, more):
Joe has 2 marbles.
Tom has 6 marbles.
How many more marbles does Tom
have than Joe?
Compare 3 (compared quantity un-
known, more):
Joe has 2 marbles.
Tom has 6 more marbles than Joe.
How many marbles does Tom have?
Compare 5 (referent unknown, more):
Joe has 6 marbles.
He has 2 more marbles than Tom.
How many marbles does Tom have?

Compare 2 (difference unknown, less):
Joe has 6 marbles.
Tom has 2 marbles.
How many fewer marbles does Tom
have than Joe?
Compare 4 (compared quantity un-
known, less):
Joe has 6 marbles.
Tom has 2 fewer marbles than Joe.
How many marbles does Tom have?
Compare 6 (referent unknown, less):
Joe has 2 marbles.
He has 6 fewer marbles than Tom.
How many marbles does Tom have?

by their computer program at different levels of sophistication with the difficulty of problems experienced by children in grades K–3. Children's performance has been shown to correspond quite well to that exhibited by the computer, with one important exception. For Compare problems, the model of part-whole relations fails to predict the relative difficulty of differ- ent types of problem. For real children, however, certain problems within this general class are much more difficult than others and are not solved until a much later point in their development.

Given the success of Riley and Greeno's general approach, in developing a model of our own we decided to use a text interpreter and a general system architecture that was similar to the one that they had developed. Given the problems that their program had experienced in simulating children's performance on Compare problems, we decided to substitute our own model of central numerical structures for Riley and Greeno's model of sets and set relations.[2]

Conceptual Analysis

A detailed comparison of the present model with Greeno's earlier model is available elsewhere (Okamoto, 1992, in press). In the present chapter, we focus on the way in which our model embodies the structures that were described in the previous chapter. We then report an experiment in which the performance of the model was compared with that of real children who were assigned to developmental groups on the basis of the measure that was described in Study 1.

Basic architecture of the program.—As mentioned above, the general approach that we used was the same as that devised by Greeno and Riley. That is to say, the architecture of the general system was similar, as were the set of production rules for simulating children's parsing of the text, their construction of a semantic network, and their setting of problem-solving goals. For each problem, the current program reads the problem statement, constructs a semantic network, and then sets up a conceptual model of the situation. It then repeats this process until a goal is identified and finally solves the problem by operating within the context that the conceptual model provides. The general flow of the program is shown schematically in Figure 8. This figure should not be taken as an algorithm that the program follows since production rules fire whenever they match the content of memory. Rather, it should be taken as a general indication of the way in which control moves from one function to another, as different production rules are matched and fire.

Simulating Children's Construction of a Mental Representation

The major way in which the current computer model was distinctive was in the form of representation that it used to build a model for each problem. Three different forms of representation were set up, as follows.

Level 1: Unidimensional structure.—At the unidimensional level, the pro-

---

[2] James Greeno was the one who originally suggested developing a model of this sort and was an active collaborator in the process. We wish to acknowledge his participation and thank him for his assistance.

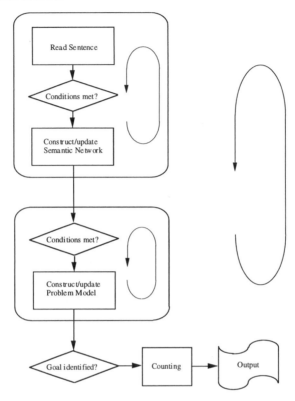

F<small>IG</small>. 8.—The basic architecture of the computational model for solving arithmetic word problems.

gram that we created was endowed with a single "mental counting line" that was 10 units in length and that could be used to represent any set of objects specified in its semantic network. In setting up this sort of linear array, the program (*a*) recognized the existence of a quantity in the text representation, (*b*) represented this quantity as a line of objects that could go from 1 to 10, and (*c*) counted the number of mental objects actually present in the line. In effect, the program behaved in much the same way as children might when they put out a certain number of fingers to represent a set of objects.

Once the number of objects stated in the word problem had been specified in this fashion, the program treated any additional information that was entered in its semantic network as a request to add a specified number of mental objects to the existing line of objects or to take a specified number of objects away. As an illustration, consider the following problem (Combine 1): "Joe has two marbles. Tom has six marbles. How many marbles do Joe and Tom have altogether?" First, a semantic network like the one shown in

PROBLEM (Combine 1)
Joe has 2 marbles.
Tom has 6 marbles.
How many marbles do Joe and Tom have altogether?

STEP 1:

Current sentence ⟶ "Joe has 2 marbles"

A. Semantic Representation

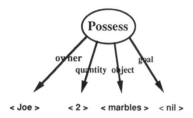

< Joe >   < 2 >   < marbles >   < nil >

B. Numerical Representation

Joe: ● ● ○ ○ ○ ○ ○ ○ ○ ○
        1-2

FIG. 9.—Representations of the first sentence in a word problem. When the program reads the first sentence, it sets up the semantic representation indicated in panel *a*. Then, as soon as this semantic representation is set up, it goes on to set up the numerical representation indicated in panel *b* by accessing its mental number line, tagging the objects on it as belonging to Joe, and counting out two of them, beginning at the left.

Figures 9*a* and 10*a* was constructed. These networks represent the main ideas of the first two sentences, that is, that two different people each possess a particular quantity of the same sort of object. The pieces of information necessary to complete each mental representation are identified by the program and the appropriate "slots" filled (i.e., the particular person, the particular object, and the particular number are filled in for each statement).

As soon as each semantic network is set up, a corresponding conceptual model of the situation is set up, within the context that the number line provides. Thus, the network representing the sentence "Joe has two marbles" is modeled by counting out 2 units from the origin of the number line and placing a pointer in this location, as illustrated in Figure 9*b*. The same procedure is followed for the second sentence, as illustrated in Figure 10*b*.

47

STEP 2:

Current sentence ——➤ "Tom has 6 marbles"

A. Semantic Representation

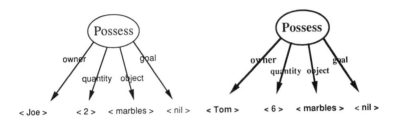

B. Numerical Representation

Tom: ●●●●●● ○○○○
1-2-3-4-5-6

FIG. 10.—Representations of the second sentence in a word problem. When the program reads the second sentence, it sets up the semantic representation indicated in panel *a*. Then, as soon as this semantic representation is set up, it goes on to set up the numerical representation in panel *b* by accessing its mental number line, tagging the objects in it as belonging to Tom, and counting out six tokens, beginning at the left. (*Note:* Two semantic representations are now present, one to represent each sentence.)

When the question "How many marbles do Joe and Tom have altogether?" is read, in order to make sense of this sentence a semantic network is set up that identifies Joe and Tom as the individual referents to which the phrase "Joe and Tom" refers and that takes the word "altogether" (or any other similar word) to signify that the objects that the two individuals own must be put together. The phrase "how many" is used to set finding the number of this combined group of objects as the goal of the problem. These two operations are illustrated in Figure 11*a*. To find out what this number is, the program now goes through the procedures indicated in Figure 11*b*. Using the number line as the conceptual context, it re-counts 2 units from the origin (i.e., Joe's two marbles), adds 6 units in sequence to the same mental object line (i.e., Tom's six marbles), and finally obtains the answer by counting from the beginning of the line to this position, getting a new number as its answer (8).

The foregoing set of procedures may seem cumbersome. However,

STEP 3:

Current sentence: ⟶ "How many do Joe and Tom have altogether?"

A. Semantic Representation

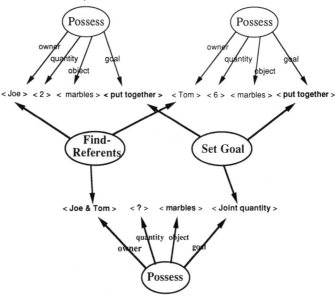

B. Numerical Representation

1. **Joe & Tom:** ●● ●●● ●●●○ ○

       1-2 1-2-3-4-5-6

2. **Joe & Tom:** ●● ●●● ●●● ○ ○

       1-2-3-4-5-6-7-8

Fig. 11.—Representations of the third sentence in a word problem. Once the program has set up the representation in Fig. 10 above, it reads the third sentence in the problem and sets up the further representations indicated in bold. The semantic representation is set up in two steps. In the first, the referents for the phrase "Joe and Tom" are found by scanning the existing representations in semantic memory. Next, the phrase "altogether" is interpreted via "Find Referents" as a request to put together the quantities possessed by Joe and Tom. Since this combined quantity is not given, the phrase "how many" is interpreted as a request to make finding this quantity the goal. This is done by setting up a numerical representation of the sort indicated in panel *b*. First, Joe's marbles are counted out, along the number line, from the left. Next, Tom's marbles are counted out, beginning where Joe's left off. Finally, the amount that Joe and Tom have "altogether" is found by (re)counting all the active tokens in the mental number line.

they do correspond quite closely to the procedure used by most 5- and 6-year-old children. Using the same general procedure, the program can generate the correct answer to two other types of problems as well, namely, Change 1 and Change 2.

Level 2: Bidimensional structure.—At the bidimensional level, the program retains all the competencies that it had at the previous level. However, it is now endowed with a second mental counting line and can manipulate this line with respect to the first. The problems solved at the previous level (which used a single mental object line) are now solved by operating on two mental counting lines. One feature that the second line adds is the one that was assumed in the construction of the Number Knowledge test (described in the previous study), namely, the capability for using one number line to count the number of units that intervene between two groups of objects that are represented on the first number line. Another feature that the second line adds is the capability for executing a "reflection" operation. This may be thought of as a mentally imagined "displacement" of one linear representation onto another.

As an illustration, consider the following problem (Combine 2): "Joe has two marbles. Tom has some marbles. Joe and Tom have five marbles altogether. How many marbles does Tom have?" In solving this problem, the program sets up two separate semantic networks, one for Joe (with two marbles) and one for Joe and Tom altogether (with five marbles). Each of these semantic networks is instantiated on a separate number line. Then, once a semantic network and a goal are set up for the final sentence, the program begins its solution by "reflecting" the line with two marbles onto the one with five marbles, in much the same way that one would were one to put up two fingers on one's right hand and use them to touch two of the five fingers on one's left hand. Once the two objects are marked on the same number line as the one indicating the five objects, the second number line is now freed up and can be used to count the number of units between 2 and 5 on the first line. This value (3) is presumed to represent the marbles that must belong to Tom.

As described above, the critical features that distinguish Level 2 capabilities from Level 1 capabilities in this program are (1) the ability to set up a second mental counting line, (2) the ability to reflect this line on the first, and (3) the ability to use this counting line, when it is not otherwise engaged, to count from one point to another on the first counting line. These same capabilities permit the program to solve simple comparison problems such as the following: "Joe has two marbles. Tom has six marbles. How many more marbles does Tom have than Joe?" (Compare 1). They also permit it to solve a wide range of other problems with similar structures, including Combine 2, Change 3, Change 4, Change 5, Change 6, Compare 1, Compare 2, Compare 3, and Compare 4.

Level 3: Integrated bidimensional structure.—The program at this final level has all the competencies of those at the first two levels plus one additional capability. Psychologically, this additional feature may be viewed as derived from the capability for comparing two differences and noting their quantitative equivalence in spite of a difference in their direction. In effect, children at this level are presumed to be able to understand that Tom having four fewer marbles than Joe is the same as (and automatically entails) Joe having four more marbles than Tom. Computationally, what the program does is to substitute one of these formulations for the other if it cannot otherwise proceed. This additional operation allows it to solve Compare 5 and Compare 6 problems.

Empirical Procedure

The arithmetic word problems that we studied were those listed in Table 5. As noted in the preceding discussion, the predictions with regard to the new problems that should be solved at each stage were as follows: at the Unidimensional stage, Combine 1 and Change 1 and 2; at the Bidimensional stage, Combine 2, Change 3–6, and Compare 1–4; and, at the Integrated Bidimensional stage, Compare 5 and 6. Since only two types of problems could differentiate Level 3 from Level 2 knowledge, an alternate version of each of these items was presented at Level 3 to increase the reliability of the measure. Sixteen word problems were then constructed, each of which was placed in a unique context (i.e., with its own owners and/or objects). The quantities used in the problems were all less than 10, and their sum was also always less than 10.

Filler problems, in which no arithmetic questions were asked, were also constructed. One of the filler problems was the following: "Mary got up at 6:30 in the morning and went to school 1 hour later. What time did she get up?" The reason for presenting problems such as this was to prevent establishment of a "cognitive set" that would permit the children to adopt some mechanical strategy for answering the problems in which we were interested rather than bothering to set up a genuine mental representation.

The 16 word problems, along with four filler problems (asked after every three target items), were presented in a predetermined fixed order. Each problem was read orally, and a card with the problem printed on it was concurrently presented to the child. In grades K–2, the cards contained a verbal form of the problem supplemented with icons; for grades 3 and 4, they contained only the verbal form. No concrete objects were presented. All children began with the Level 1 items and worked until they had failed more than half the problems at a higher level, at which point testing was discontinued. Children's responses were scored as correct or incorrect for all problems; computational errors were scored as incorrect.

TABLE 6

PROPORTIONS OF CORRECT SOLUTIONS OF 14 TYPES OF ARITHMETIC WORD PROBLEMS
SOLVED BY CHILDREN

Problems by Level	Proportions of Correct Solution	Problems by Level	Proportions of Correct Solution
Level 1 problems:		Level 2 problems:	
Combine 1	.950	Change 6	.617
Change 1	.900	Compare 1	.650
Change 2	.867	Compare 2	.683
Level 2 problems:		Compare 3	.467
Combine 2	.533	Compare 4	.500
Change 3	.633	Level 3 problems:	
Change 4	.683	Compare 5	.300
Change 5	.633	Compare 6	.233

NOTE.—Two problems were given for each of Compare 5 and Compare 6. The proportions of children who solved both problems correctly for each type are reported here.

Subjects

The subjects were the same 60 children who participated in the first study; the problems were given to them in a second session that was conducted in a similar fashion to the first and that took place a week or two later.

Results

Preliminary analyses showed no sex differences in children's word problem–solving performance ($F = 1.96$, $df = 1, 58$, N.S.); consequently, boys and girls were treated as a single group in all subsequent analyses.

Overall Pattern of Correct Solutions

In our first analysis, we examined the general pattern of correct solutions to the 16 word problems. There were large differences in the proportions of correct solutions among the three levels of word problems (Table 6). Within each level, however, the proportions were quite close to each other in magnitude. As expected, the majority of children correctly solved all three types of unidimensional problem. Bidimensional problems were solved by approximately 50%–70% of the children. Integrated bidimensional problems were solved by fewer than one-third of the children. Although some variations in the proportions of correct responses could be observed within each problem level, lower-level problems were solved correctly by many more children than higher-level problems. These results support the proposition that the difficulty of problems differs considerably from one grouping to another, even within the same semantic category.

Pattern of Correct Solutions by Levels of Number Knowledge

In our second analysis, we examined the relation between performance on word problems and performance on the Number Knowledge tasks that we used in Study 1. We expected that children who possessed a particular level of number knowledge would be able to solve word problems at the corresponding level on the Word Problem test. Recall that, although it contained a few questionable items, the Number Knowledge test nonetheless allowed us to classify children as possessing one of the three general latent structures with a reasonable degree of confidence. Relying on this classification, we conducted an item analysis of the different types of word problems; the proportions of correct solutions obtained by children in each of the three different latent structure groups are listed in Table 7. In general, the results were congruent with our prediction. That is, the majority of children with a unidimensional level of numerical understanding correctly solved unidimensional word problems and gave wrong answers to bidimensional as well as integrated bidimensional word problems. The majority of children with a bidimensional level of numerical understanding correctly solved unidimensional and bidimensional word problems and failed to solve integrated bidimensional word problems. Children with integrated bidimensional understanding of number were expected to solve all the 14 types of word problems, and the majority of them did so. Given the data in Table 7, it is hardly surprising that the mean scores on the two tests were strongly correlated ($r = .794$); a scatter plot of individual subjects' performance on each measure is shown in Figure 12.

Discussion

The fact that our central conceptual structures could be used as a guideline for writing a program that would model children's representations at three different age levels was gratifying, as was the fact that the program was able to solve all 14 types of problems. Even more satisfying was the fact that the program's performance on the problems corresponded more closely with the performance of real children than previous simulations in which children's conceptual understanding was modeled in terms of mathematical sets and set relations.

In and of themselves, these results do not prove that children really do set up the sorts of representations that we impute to them, of course, nor do they prove that children go through the sorts of operations that we

TABLE 7

PROPORTIONS OF CORRECT SOLUTIONS OF ARITHMETIC WORD PROBLEMS ACHIEVED BY
CHILDREN CLASSIFIED BY LEVELS OF NUMBER KNOWLEDGE

	Unidimensional ($N = 24$)	Bidimensional ($N = 23$)	Integrated Bidimensional ($N = 11$)
Unidimensional problems:			
Combine 1	.92	1.00	1.00
Change 1	.79	.96	1.00
Change 2	.79	.92	1.00
All Level 1	.83	.96	1.00
Bidimensional problems:			
Combine 2	.25	.71	.90
Change 3	.38	.83	.90
Change 4	.46	.83	1.00
Change 5	.38	.79	1.00
Change 6	.33	.79	1.00
Compare 1	.42	.79	1.00
Compare 2	.42	.88	1.00
Compare 3	.21	.54	1.00
Compare 4	.21	.67	1.00
All Level 2	.34	.76	.97
Integrated bidimensional problems:[a]			
Compare 5	.17	.52	.90
	(.08)	(.30)	(.82)
Compare 6	.10	.35	.75
	(.04)	(.26)	(.64)
All Level 3	.14	.44	.83

[a] Two problems were given for each of Compare 5 and Compare 6; the average proportions are listed, and the proportions of children who solved both problems correctly are given in parentheses.

specified. However, the results do establish this as a strong possibility. This possibility gains additional support from a recent study by Fan, Mueller, and Marini (in press) in which the "mental counting line" model was assessed in a different fashion: by observing the strategies that children reported in solving the various problems and the explanations that they offered. Fan, Mueller, and Marini found that these explanations and strategies directly correspond to the general forms that we have hypothesized. In effect, then, we can say that three different forms of methodology (the two reported in this chapter and a more direct, observational strategy) now converge on the same general conclusion: that children reason in terms of a single mental counting line at the age of 6, in terms of two counting lines at the age of 8, and in terms of two counting lines with the capability of comparison and reversal of differences at the age of 10.

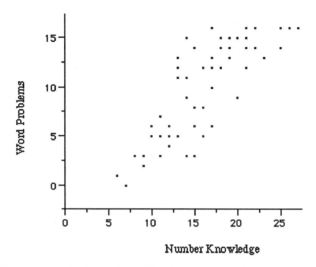

FIG. 12.—A scatter plot indicating subjects' scores on word problems as a function of their scores on the number knowledge test.

GENERAL DISCUSSION

The problem with which we began the present chapter was that the evidence of the existence of central numerical structures is for the most part indirect. On a wide variety of scientific, cultural, social, and mathematical tasks, children appear to move from a predimensional, to a unidimensional, to a bidimensional, to an integrated bidimensional form of response. In and of itself, however, the presence of this general pattern does not demonstrate that children are constructing "mental number lines" and using them to solve the problems that they encounter in these various domains. The common gradient that is observed on these tasks could just as easily be ascribed to a general increase in working memory, to the acquisition of increased facility in counting, or to the acquisition of task-specific knowledge.

We do not deny that these factors play a vital role in children's conceptual development. We do not believe that they are sufficient to account for children's conceptual development entirely, however, and we see the two studies that we have reported in the present chapter as taking us one step closer to verifying the proposition that central conceptual structures play an equally important role in mediating children's performance on these tasks. For the first time, we were able to demonstrate (a) that children do possess most of the elements of numerical knowledge that we have hypothesized, at each of the three age levels with which we have been concerned (6, 8, and 10), (b) that this knowledge is organized in a coherent fashion,

(c) that, if applied to the solution of mathematical word problems in the fashion that we have specified, this knowledge yields a pattern of performance very similar to that actually observed, and (d) that a good correspondence exists between the central numerical knowledge that children display on two different empirical measures.

Even taken together, these results do not guarantee that central numerical structures play the more general role that we have hypothesized, that is, that they mediate children's performance on other, less mathematical tasks. However, they do at least establish this as a credible possibility and suggest that work on this broader problem is worth conducting. In the next two chapters, we report several studies that were designed with precisely this goal in mind. Before proceeding to these studies, however, we wish to list several more specific conclusions that we feel are warranted on the basis of the two studies reported in the present chapter.

1. Not only do children possess a conceptual system for understanding numbers that is analogous to a "mental number line"—as we and a number of others have hypothesized (e.g., Resnick, 1983)—but the elements and relations also appear to be verbally "tagged" in the fashion that is indicated in Figure 2 above. If they were not tagged (or at least "taggable") in this fashion, it seems unlikely that children could answer questions that use these tags as prompts (e.g., "What number comes 'next' when you are counting?"). The role that verbal tags play in children's conceptual understanding of number is not known but deserves to be investigated further.

2. The central conceptual structure whose development we have studied and simulated is a procedural system as well as a conceptual one. Children can use the system to mentally simulate the act of adding or subtracting real objects as well as to answer general conceptual questions about relative magnitude. The computer program also uses a set of such procedures for creating semantic representations of the problems that it is posed. Rather than using the term "mental number line" (Resnick, 1983), then, it might be preferable to use *mental counting line*. And it might be worthwhile to explore the relation between children's procedural and conceptual understanding of number a good deal further.

3. As children develop the capability of switching their focus from one number line to another and back, they also develop the capability for creating new mental objects: objects such as "differences" and "sums." The creation of mental objects of this sort has been hypothesized to play a major role in certain accounts of children's mathematical development (Greeno & Resnick, 1993). This being the case, the present account of how this transition takes place should be further explored. To restate our model as it applies to the construction of a difference, our contention is as follows. (1) Children first acquire the counting schema: a motor routine with a set of verbal tags to accompany it. (2) They next learn how to map this routine

onto a set of conceptual categories that correspond to it and that have been developing in parallel. (3) At about the same time, they acquire a set of verbal tags for describing the integrated structure and a set of numerical symbols with which to represent the results. (4) Finally, they acquire the capability for applying their newly integrated structure, recursively, to the new numerical symbols that they have acquired; they can thus think of numbers as themselves something that can be counted and the "difference" as the second-order number that they create when doing so.

In future work, it would be interesting to determine what aspects of this process are general and can also be detected in children's construction of other mathematical objects such as fractions. In other work (Case et al., 1992), we have found that teenagers find it hard to understand what is meant by the question, "What is a half of a third?" This question, which is directly analogous to the request to count the number of numbers between 5 and 8, may make sense only once a similar process has been completed and the operation of division has become something that can be applied to its own products.

4. Although each level of mathematical development has its own distinctive structure or set of structures, the underlying development of children's knowledge can nonetheless be modeled by the simple addition of elements and the exploitation of the new capabilities that these elements provide. This is indicated both by the change in the problems that children can solve (which become more complex but do not change radically in kind) and by the changes that one must introduce to one's program for simulating their performance (which involve the addition of elements rather than their transformation). The two higher levels of structure are thus better thought of as elaborations of the first structure, or as points in a continued growth process that have particular (discrete) utility, rather than as radically different structural entities. Again, it would be of interest to see if this same conclusion applies to mathematical development at higher (or lower) stages.

5. Finally, it is worthwhile to point out that, although the operation of the mental "counting simulator" may appear quite trivial at first glance, a more detailed inspection reveals that it is a cognitive tour de force. Within one simple representation, the simulator succeeds in honoring all three of the major constraints diagrammed in Figure 2 above simultaneously. (1) Whether real or imaginary, the overlearned motor routine that is executed has the same ordinal property as the number tags in row *b* of the figure. (2) This set of actions is always timed precisely to saying (or imagining) the number words, as it would be were one actually touching objects of the sort indicated in row *b*. (3) Finally, the simulator always keeps the previous tokens that have been put in place in a fixed position as one continues one's motor routine, thus forming sets of the sort indicated in row *d* of the figure. The net result is that, as it moves from one token to the next in mental

counting, it is simultaneously representing (1) an object that is being counted, (2) an ordinal tag that is being applied to this object (the word *three*), and (3) the cardinal value of the set that is formed. This capability for conjoint representation seems to distinguish 6-year-old mathematicians from 4-year-old mathematicians quite sharply.

The foregoing conclusions fit with the results of both studies that were reported in the present chapter. In our opinion, they also fit with the work of many others who have studied children's early conceptions of number and counting (e.g., Baroody et al., 1985; Davidov, 1982; Greeno, 1991; Piaget, 1952; Resnick, 1983, 1989; Siegler & Robinson, 1982; Siegler & Shrager, 1984; Starkey, 1992). Finally, they fit with recent observations of children's strategies and explanations in solving the sort of word problems that were used in the second study (Fan, Mueller, & Marini, in press). In subsequent chapters, we will not examine these issues further. At this point, however, we do wish to indicate that we regard the foregoing conclusions as worthy objects of further inquiry (i.e., we regard them as raising as many questions as they answer) and that we believe that a parallel set of questions could be generated for all the other central conceptual structures and structural sequences that we will consider in subsequent chapters.

III. EXPLORING THE MACROSTRUCTURE OF CHILDREN'S CENTRAL CONCEPTUAL STRUCTURES IN THE DOMAINS OF NUMBER AND NARRATIVE

Robbie Case, Yukari Okamoto, Barbara Henderson,
Anne McKeough, and Charles Bleiker

In the introductory chapter, we suggested that structures such as the mental counting line and mental story line are central to children's understanding of a broad array of tasks, both within the domains with which they are normally associated (i.e., mathematics and story composition) and outside them. In Chapter II, we conducted a detailed investigation of the mental counting line and concluded that it does, in fact, play a central role in mediating children's performance within the domain of mathematics. The studies that we report in the present chapter were designed to investigate two of our broader claims, namely, (1) that this structure plays a similar role in mediating children's performance on a wide array of other quantitative tasks and (2) that a similar role is played by children's central narrative structures in organizing their understanding of social tasks.

In a previous series of studies, we had already taken a first step toward achieving these two objectives. What we had shown was that children's performance on a broad range of social and nonsocial tasks goes through one of two patterns: either the four-substage "counting line" pattern that was described in the previous chapter or a parallel four-substage pattern that involves the understanding of human motives (Case, 1992a). These data provided good prima facie evidence that the structures in which we are interested do play the central role that we have hypothesized. However, as was mentioned in the previous chapter, they were also open to other interpretations. The four-step pattern could conceivably have resulted from children's increasing ability to handle complexity, from their increasing familiarity with specific tasks in the domains in question, or from a variety of other factors, such as increasing computational facility.

How might one demonstrate that each group of tasks really does tap a central conceptual structure? One of the standard methods for answering this sort of question in psychological research is to conduct a factor analysis. Perhaps surprisingly, such a study has never been attempted with our tasks. Indeed, as Halford (1993a) has pointed out, very few of our tasks have even been administered to the same subjects, and thus their correlational structure has never been examined. The one exception to this generalization is a study conducted by Marini (1992), in which four tasks that were hypothesized to tap children's central numerical structures were administered to a group of 80 subjects who ranged in age from 4 to 10 years. The tasks in question did show substantial correlations with each other. Unfortunately, however, there were too few tasks to conduct a factor analysis and too few subjects to determine how high the correlations were within any age group. In addition, no other tasks were administered, to see if they showed a different pattern of correlations. In our first study, therefore, we decided to conduct a correlational investigation in which these problems were rectified.

STUDY 1: FACTOR ANALYSIS OF CHILDREN'S PERFORMANCE ON A BATTERY OF QUANTITATIVE AND SOCIAL COGNITIVE TASKS

The tasks that we administered in our first study formed two broad conceptual groups. The first consisted of quantitative tasks that had been used in previous studies and shown to demonstrate the four-step developmental pattern described in the previous chapter (predimensional thought at 4 years, unidimensional thought at 6 years, etc.). The second consisted of narrative tasks, many of which had also been administered in previous studies and shown to demonstrate a similar pattern (preintentional thought at 4 years, uni-intentional thought at 6 years, etc.). To control for method and/or content variance, we included tasks in the quantitative battery whose content was social and introduced some sort of numerical content into two of the tasks on the social battery. The age group that we selected for study was 6-year-olds because this is the age for which our existing measures are most reliable.

Since the tasks that we selected had never been administered as a set, we had no empirical basis for predicting what factor structure would emerge. However, since they all fell into one of two broad conceptual categories—at least according to our analysis—we did have a clear theoretical basis. Our predictions were (1) that two distinct (although correlated) factors would emerge, (2) that all our quantitative tasks would load on one factor while all our social-cognitive tasks would load on the other, (3) that the Number

Knowledge test described in the previous chapter would show a high loading on the quantitative factor (because the items on this test were developed to reflect the workings of the central numerical structure), and (4) that, for similar reasons, the Storytelling test would show a high loading on the narrative factor.

Methods

Subjects

A total of 148 subjects (71 boys and 77 girls) participated in the study. The mean age of the full sample was 6-6 (SD = 8.6 months); for boys it was 6-7 (SD = 8.1 months) and for girls 6-6 (SD = 9.0 months). The sample was drawn from kindergarten and first grade classrooms in six different schools located in the San Francisco Bay Area. Three of these schools were private and three public. Two of the public schools and one of the private schools served middle to upper-middle socioeconomic status (SES) families of European-American origin. The remaining schools drew from low to middle SES populations of mixed ethnic backgrounds. All but a few children spoke English as their first language.

Criteria for Task Selection

In selecting individual tasks for the study, we used the following criteria: (1) The task had to have substantial face validity as an index of numerical or narrative thought. (2) Children's responses to the task had to be classifiable as reflecting one of the four patterns that we postulate (e.g., predimensional, unidimensional, bidimensional, or integrated bidimensional thought). (3) The task had to have a high degree of reliability when scored in this manner. In deciding on the final set of tasks, we used the following additional criteria: (1) Within each battery, the set of tasks, as a whole, had to tap content from more than one domain or "subject area." (2) Within each battery, the tasks also had to involve a range of assessment methods (e.g., pictorial vs. verbal stimuli, responses that do and do not require verbal justification, etc.). (3) The surface content of at least some of the tasks within the numerical battery had to fall in the realm of social cognition, and vice versa.

Six of our existing numerical tasks and four of our existing narrative tasks fit these criteria. To equate the number of tasks included within the two batteries, we designed two new tasks for inclusion in the narrative battery. Extended descriptions of the administration and scoring procedures as well as of the origins of each task are provided in Appendices A and B. The brief descriptions we give here focus on characteristics that are relevant for evaluating the correlational structure of the two batteries.

Tasks Constituting the Numerical Battery

1. *Number Knowledge.*—This task was described in some detail in the previous chapter. Before administering it to the current sample, we added a few mental addition and subtraction items, in order to tap children's procedural as well as conceptual knowledge. These items, like the ones described in the previous chapter, were designed to reflect the operational definitions of the central numerical structure. A central numerical structure at the unidimensional level should allow children to move forward or backward on a mental counting line a specified number of units from a referent number; accordingly, the items that we added were $2 + 4$ and $8 - 6$. Bidimensional thought should enable children to understand the meaning of digits in the tens and ones columns and to keep track of mental computations on two separate counting lines. Accordingly, the items that we added were $12 + 54$ and $47 - 21$. Integrated bidimensional thought should allow children to trade back and forth between digits in the tens and ones columns while keeping track of mental computations in each; the items that we added were $13 + 39$, $36 - 18$, and $301 - 7$.

2. *Balance Beam.*—On this task, children are presented with a wooden beam balanced on a fulcrum, with a stack of weights at each end. After a period in which the operation of the balance is demonstrated, they are asked a series of questions about which side of the balance will go down when weight stacks of varying sizes are placed at varying distances from the fulcrum.

The first two items are ones where the weight stacks are placed at equal distances from the fulcrum and their difference in magnitude is readily apparent. Since numerical quantification is not required to establish which stack is bigger, these items are classified as *predimensional*. On the next two items, the weight stacks remain at equal distances from the fulcrum but differ by only one weight. Since careful enumeration is now required, children who pass these items and justify their answer in some sort of numerical fashion (e.g., "This one because it's got five") are credited with thinking at the *unidimensional* level. The next two items are ones where the stacks have the same number of weights but are placed at different distances from the fulcrum. Children who pass these items and justify their responses by referring to the second dimension (distance from the fulcrum) are classified as functioning at the *bidimensional* level. On the next two items, the weight stacks are again placed at slightly different distances from the fulcrum, but the magnitude of the weight stacks is no longer equal. Children who pass these items and justify their responses in some sort of numerical fashion (normally by comparing the size of the weight difference with the size of the distance difference) are classified as functioning at the *integrated bidimensional* level.

From the viewpoint of the present study, the major strengths of the balance beam task were (a) that it has a long history of being used to investigate children's scientific and/or logical reasoning (Inhelder & Piaget, 1958; Siegler, 1976, 1978), (b) that the different levels of dimensional thought are clearly reflected in the items, and (c) that children's thought has been shown to be reliably classifiable as being at one of these levels (Marini, 1992).

3. *Distributive Justice.*—On this task, subjects are shown a picture of two siblings and their parent. They are then told that the parent wants to distribute a specified number of prizes to the two children, as a reward for their performance on a recent spelling test. The subjects' task is to say how many of the prizes each child should get. On the first two items, one child has made a large number of errors, and the other has made almost none. Subjects who remember this difference and take it into account in allocating their rewards receive credit for thinking at the *predimensional* level. On the next two items, one child has got one more correct than the other. Subjects who notice this difference and take it into account are credited with thinking at the *unidimensional* level. On the next two items, each child has made the same number of errors, but the father's expectation (based on previous performance) is that one child should have done much better than the other. Subjects who notice this difference and take account of it in some fashion are credited with thinking at the *bidimensional* level. Finally, the next two items are ones where the children's previous record on spelling tests suggests that their performance should differ subtly, and it does, but not in the expected direction. Subjects who notice both dimensions in the task and develop a principled procedure for assigning some weight to each are credited with thought at the *integrated bidimensional* level.

From the viewpoint of the present study, the major strengths of the Distributive Justice task are (a) that its surface content is social (indeed, tasks with very similar content are normally considered to tap children's conceptions of *distributive justice;* Damon, 1973; DeMersseman, 1976), (b) that the different levels of dimensional thought are clearly reflected in the items, and (3) that previous work has shown that, when children's responses are tape-recorded and transcribed (as they were in the present study), the responses can be scored with high reliability (Marini, 1992).

4. *Birthday Party.*—On this task, subjects are shown a picture of two children who are having birthday parties. Each picture shows the number of marbles that each birthday child is hoping for, in a "thought cloud." The number of presents that each actually receives is also indicated, by laying

out a set of marbles under the picture. The subjects' task is to decide which of the two children in the picture is happier and why. Once again, items on this test increase in complexity, with predimensional items showing a large difference in the number of presents received by the two children and subsequent items showing more subtle differences along one of two dimensions: the number of gifts received and the number of gifts hoped for. Like the previous task, the major advantages of this task are (a) that its surface content is social, (b) that the different levels of dimensional thought are clearly reflected in the items, and (c) that children's (transcribed) responses to the task have been shown to be reliably classifiable as exemplifying one of these four levels (Marini, 1992).

5. *Money Knowledge.*—On this task, children are asked a series of questions involving money. Once again, the problems are presented in increasing order of complexity and in such a fashion that they require a focus on an increasing number of quantitative dimensions. At the *predimensional* level, the problems are ones involving large and readily apparent differences (e.g., "Which is worth more, a dollar or a penny?"). At the *unidimensional* level, some sort of numerical focus is necessary (e.g., "Which is worth more, this pile of money [containing three 1-dollar bills] or this [containing a single bill of higher denomination]?"). At the *bidimensional* level, the child must evaluate and/or compare quantities along two quantitative scales (dollars and cents). Finally, at the *integrated bidimensional* level, subjects must not only focus on two different scales but also perform some sort of conversion operation to move from one to the other. From the perspective of the present study, the major strengths of this task are (a) that the content of the task is neither social nor causal/scientific, (b) that the varying degrees of dimensional thought are clearly reflected in the items, (c) that children's responses to the task can be reliably classified as exemplifying one of our four developmental levels (Griffin et al., 1992), and (d) that the test uses a variety of different question formats, including those that do not rely on verbal explanations.

6. *Time Telling.*—On this task, the children are asked a series of questions about time and clocks. Once again, items vary in complexity and are presented in ascending order of difficulty, from those that can be answered by some sort of global quantification to those that require a careful evaluation along two quantitative scales (hours and minutes). From the present perspective, the advantages of the task are much the same as for the Money Knowledge task: (a) the test taps content that is neither social nor scientific; (b) the varying degrees of dimensional thought are clearly reflected in the items; (c) children's responses to the task can be reliably classified as falling into one of our four levels (Griffin et al., 1992); and (d) the test uses a variety of different question formats, including those that do and do not rely on verbal explanations.

Tasks Constituting the Narrative Battery

All the tasks in the narrative battery were designed to assess children's progression through the central conceptual sequence that was hypothesized for the social domain, that is, the sequence that goes from preintentional to uni-intentional to bi-intentional to integrated bi-intentional thought.

1. *Storytelling.*—On this task, children are asked to tell two stories, one about two prespecified characters (a little child and a kind old horse) and one about a child of their own age who has a problem. Stories are tape-recorded, transcribed, and scored as a function of the "plot structure" that they contain. According to the analysis that was summarized in Chapter I, *preintentional* children can generate an account of a social situation that contains a familiar event sequence. What they cannot do is link this sort of "scripted action" with a consideration of human motives. At the *uni-intentional* level, children can create plots in which events unfold in the same sort of scripted fashion but center around the desire or goal of the central character. At the *bi-intentional* level, children can produce a plot that contains a "chain" of two or more event sequences. Both event sequences typically flow from the same motive, but the first does not lead to goal satisfaction, while some subsequent one typically does. Finally, at the *integrated bi-intentional* level, children can produce plot structures involving multiple attempts at resolution that are integrated into a nested series, with the result that the overall story assumes a more coherent form than a simple "chain." From the perspective of our current study, the major strengths of this task were (*a*) that responses to the task have been subjected to extensive task analysis and used as a criterion for defining children's central narrative structures and (*b*) that a reliable coding scheme has been developed for classifying children's responses as falling into one of the four levels described above (Case & McKeough, 1990; McKeough, 1992a).

2. *Mother's Motives.*—On this task, children are shown a cartoon sequence of two sisters at the beach. In the last frame of the sequence, the older sister is pushing the younger sister's head under water. The children are asked (*a*) what they think the mother will do and (*b*) why they think she will act this way. After they have responded, they are presented with a further series of verbal probes that focus on the mother's motives. Children's responses are tape-recorded and transcribed for later scoring. *Preintentional* responses are ones that focus solely on the events that take place in the story, without making any mention of the mother's motives. *Uni-intentional* responses refer to the most probable consequence of the sister's actions and the mother's concern and/or intentions with regard to this consequence. *Bi-intentional* responses are ones that focus on two separate thoughts, feelings, or desires of the mother; alternatively, they make some mention of the children's internal state as well as the mother's. From the

perspective of the present study, the advantages of this test are (*a*) that children's responses have been shown to be capable of being reliably classified as falling into one of the four levels of intentional thought (Goldberg-Reitman, 1992) and (*b*) that the task involves a format and content that are different from that of the Storytelling task.

3. *Empathic Cognition.*—On this task, children are shown a short film in which a 10-year-old actress is playing with her dog in a park. In the first scene, the young girl is clearly having fun, telling her mother that she considers her dog to be her best friend. At the end of the scene, the dog chases a ball out into the street. A loud screech of tires is heard, and the camera cuts to the next scene, where the girl is sobbing on her mother's shoulder and saying, "It's hard to believe that Harry [the dog] is dead; I will miss him so much." Following the film, children are asked a series of probing questions that are designed to assess their ability to deduce the feelings and thoughts of the girl and to respond to these thoughts and feelings in an empathic manner. Children's responses to these questions are scored in the same general manner as for the Mother's Motives task. Responses that focus entirely on the action in the film are considered to be at the *preintentional level.* Responses that take account of the girl's feelings for the dog and/or her thoughts about the future are considered to be at the *uni-intentional* level. Responses that focus on two thoughts or feelings are considered to be *bi-intentional,* etc. From the viewpoint of the present study, the advantages of this task are (*a*) that it utilizes a format that is grounded in the literature on empathy (Feshbach & Roe, 1968; Hughes, Tingle, & Swain, 1981; Mood & Johnson, 1973), (*b*) that it involves a different sort of stimulus from that used in any of the other narrative tasks (i.e., a film), and (*c*) that it has been shown to be capable of assigning children's thinking to one of our four general developmental levels with high reliability (Bruchkowsky, 1992; McKeough, Yates, & Marini, 1994).

4. *Definition of Feelings.*—On this task, children are shown a hand puppet and asked to explain to the puppet what it means to be (1) *happy,* (2) *proud,* and (3) *embarrassed.* For each word, several probes are presented after the child's first attempt at explanation, in order to prompt further reflection. *Preintentional* explanations are those that center on actions or external events. *Uni-intentional* explanations include some mention of internal states. *Bi-intentional* explanations make reference to two internal states, often a feeling and some sort of evaluation. At the *integrated bidimensional* level, explanations typically involve two logically related episodes or concepts, which are juxtaposed against each other in some fashion. From the perspective of the present study, the advantages of this test are (*a*) that it utilizes a different testing format from any of the other social tasks and (*b*) that a coding system has been developed for assigning children's responses to developmental levels in a reliable fashion (Griffin, 1992, 1995).

5. *Psychological Verbs.*—On this test, which was created for the present study, the child is presented with a series of sentences of increasing complexity and difficulty. As each sentence is read, a card is presented on which four cartoon-style drawings appear. The child's task is to pick out the drawing that most accurately represents the sentence that is read by the experimenter. At the *preintentional* level, the sentences refer to a single activity and use simple action verbs (e.g., "In this picture, Betty *is climbing* the stairs to see her four sisters"). At the *uni-intentional* level, the sentences focus on some internal state and use verbs that reflect this (e.g., "In this picture, Jennifer *is planning* to go up the walk to play with her two friends"). At the *bi-intentional* level, the sentences make mention of two internal states (e.g., "In this picture, Ashley *is thinking* about going up the hill to show her four grandparents her *bad* report card). At each level, the distractors include items designed to ensure that, if the children fail to process the critical semantic features, they will not be able to choose the correct card with any certainty.

From the perspective of the present study, the advantages of this task are (*a*) that it utilizes a different response format from the other social tasks (children do not need to provide an elaborate justification of their response; they simply need to point to the picture that best represents the sentence), (*b*) that previous work (Astington, 1985) has shown that the task can be used to assign children to one of the first two levels reliably (the higher levels were added for the present study), and (*c*) that the task is an easy one to which to add surface numerical content, as illustrated above.

6. *Affective Change.*—This task was also created for the present study. Subjects were shown two cartoon sequences, each of which was accompanied by a brief story in which some sort of affective change took place. (For example, "[Picture 1 is presented.] Here's Joey. His three friends called him up to play four-square. You need four people to play this game. He was very excited about playing. [Picture 2 is presented.] When he got to the playground, his three friends decided they would rather go to the movies and left. [Picture 3 is presented.] Now there were no other kids on the playground. [Picture 4 is presented.] Joey went home with a frown on his face.") Following each story, children were asked a series of questions that probed their understanding of the initial affect, the final affect, and the reasons for the change. Children's responses were classified according to their focus, with responses that focused exclusively on actions being classified as *preintentional,* responses that mentioned a single internal state being classified as *uni-intentional,* responses that mentioned two internal states being classified as *bi-intentional,* and responses that mentioned and explicitly related two internal states being classified as *integrated bidimensional.*

Since this task was a newly developed one, its psychometric properties were not known. The idea behind the task, however, was to present children with a second social task on which some sort of extraneous numerical information was present and to classify their responses as a function of how many affective states they identified and how well they integrated their description of these states into their overall response.

Administration and Scoring

Training of interviewers.—Ten graduate students in educational psychology served as interviewers; in a 3-day training program prior to the interviews, all of them were trained to administer all 12 tests. This training program covered the following agenda: (1) rationale behind the test items; (2) test administration; (3) probing procedures; (4) typical and atypical responses; (5) feedback on administration; and (6) scoring. After an introductory period, the trainers practiced giving all the tests to a group of children and received feedback on their performance from experienced testers. A further period of practice took place in a school before the testing proper began.

Task administration.—Children were interviewed individually on three separate occasions. Each session was conducted by the same interviewer and lasted approximately half an hour. The tasks were grouped in sets of four per session (two quantitative and two narrative) and administered in a fixed order. The three sessions were completed within 2–3 weeks near the end of the school year. The order of task administration was as follows: *Session 1:* (1) Balance Beam, (2) Storytelling, (3) Birthday Party, and (4) Psychological Verbs; *Session 2:* (1) Mother's Motives, (2) Distributive Justice, (3) Affective Change, and (4) Money Knowledge; and *Session 3:* (1) Time Telling, (2) Definition of Feelings, (3) Number Knowledge, and (4) Empathic Cognition. All interview sessions were audiotaped. Interviewers also wrote down children's responses on the coding sheets.

Scoring.—A score of 1 was awarded to responses at the predimensional level; scores of 2, 3, and 4 were awarded to responses at the unidimensional, bidimensional, and integrated bidimensional levels, respectively. If a response met all the criteria for one level and some but not all of the criteria at the next level, it was scored halfway between the two. For example, a score of 2.5 signified a response that met all the criteria for unidimensional thought and some but not all of the criteria for bidimensional thought. On most measures, possible scores for each measure ranged from 0 (indicating a failure to meet the criteria for predimensional thought) through 4 (indicating the presence of integrated bidimensional thought).

For three of the tasks on the quantitative battery (Number Knowledge, Money, and Time), and for the Psychological Verbs task on the narrative battery, scoring was relatively straightforward. Accordingly, children's responses were scored by the interviewer who had administered the test. For the remaining tasks, a more careful and lengthy examination of responses was required. Accordingly, two trained raters independently scored all the children's responses on these tasks. The criteria that were used for the rating are given in Appendices A and B. The percentage of interrater agreement ranged between 87% and 90%. Disagreements were resolved by discussion.

Results

With one exception, the general pattern of children's responses to all the tasks was the one that we had anticipated, that is, the one already reported in the literature. The one exception occurred on the Distributive Justice task. On this task, approximately 15% of the children treated numerical performance on the spelling test as irrelevant to the task of distributing rewards. They did count the number of rewards and distribute them evenly. However, they insisted that this was the only way to distribute the rewards, no matter how well or poorly the two siblings had done on the spelling test, no matter what the father's purpose was in distributing the reward, and no matter what his expectations were. There is, of course, nothing wrong with this response. Since it did not fit our preexisting coding scheme, however, we were initially at a loss as to how to classify it. In the end, we decided to award it a score that was intermediate between the predimensional and the unidimensional levels. Still, we got the impression that several children whose numerical cognition was in other respects quite sophisticated were responding at this level for other reasons.

Problems of reliability also surfaced on both new measures, namely, Psychological Verbs and Affective Change. Both tasks employed cartoons that we had drawn especially for the purpose of the present investigation. While many of the children responded to the cartoons in the fashion that we had expected, many also focused on small details that we had not meant to be of relevance. Although we did not feel that this invalidated the tasks completely as measures of narrative thought, we did feel that this feature added a great deal of unwanted noise. To bring the reliability of the new measures in line with that of the old ones, therefore, we decided to average children's scores on these two tasks. We called the new variable that resulted from this procedure "Pictures."

Before conducting a statistical analysis, we first examined the distribution of mean scores for the batteries as a whole. These distributions are shown in Figures 13 and 14. As may be seen, the distributions were approximately normal in each case. When the distributions of scores for individual measures were examined, they were somewhat less smooth, but the pattern was generally similar.

69

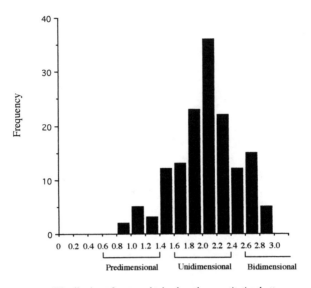

Distribution of scores obtained on the quantitative battery

FIG. 13.—The distribution of total scores obtained on the quantitative battery

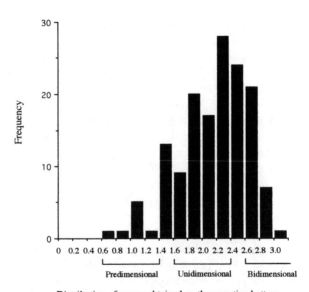

Distribution of scores obtained on the narrative battery

FIG. 14.—The distribution of total scores obtained on the narrative battery

TABLE 8

MEAN PERFORMANCE ON EACH TASK
(Scores Reflect Performance at Hypothesized Levels 1–4)

Tasks	M	SD	Range
Numerical tasks:			
Balance Beam	2.05	.75	0–3
Birthday Party	1.99	.75	0–3
Distributive Justice	1.83	.51	0–3
Money Knowledge	2.01	.61	.67–3
Time Telling	2.07	.58	.58–3
Number Knowledge	2.21	.45	1.14–3
Average score on battery	2.03	.44	
Narrative tasks:			
Storytelling	2.01	.89	0–3
Mother's Motives	2.14	.73	1–3
Definition of Feelings	2.20	.63	0–3
Empathic Cognition	2.37	.71	0–3
Pictures	1.90	.44	.75–3
Average score on battery	2.12	.47	

Our first statistical analyses were of mean scores. A preliminary analysis of variance showed no significant sex differences; hence, boys and girls were combined for all subsequent analyses. The means and standard deviations for the entire sample on the eleven tasks are shown in Table 8. As may be seen, the mean scores ranged from just under 2 to just over 2 points on all measures. This means that the average level at which children were functioning was the unidimensional level, which is what one would expect from a group of children at this age.

Table 9 presents the Pearson product-moment correlations among the various measures. As may be seen, most of the quantitative tasks showed correlations of intermediate magnitude, which were of statistical significance. The general pattern for the narrative battery was similar, although the absolute value of the correlations was lower. As expected, the Distributive Justice task showed the lowest correlations with the other tasks in the quantitative battery. The lowest correlations on the narrative battery were shown by the tasks that used a cartoon format, namely, the Pictures task and Mother's Motives. Finally, modest correlations among the two clusters were present, but the pattern was less regular, and the majority of the correlations were statistically insignificant.

The correlation matrix was analyzed using a variant of alpha factor analysis with orthogonal factors and varimax rotation, applying Kaiser's (1960) criterion for determining the total number of factors (i.e., eigenvalues > 1). As might be expected, given the pattern of scores in the correlation matrix, the initial statistics from this analysis indicated a two-factor solution.

TABLE 9
Correlations Among Numerical and Narrative Tasks ($N = 148$)

	Numerical Tasks						Narrative Tasks				
	1	2	3	4	5	6	1	2	3	4	5
Numerical tasks											
1. Balance Beam											
2. Birthday Party	.41										
3. Money Knowledge	.46	.45									
4. Time Telling	.49	.54	.75								
5. Number Knowledge	.37	.47	.72	.70							
6. Distributive Justice	.25	.26	.21	.22	.21						
Narrative tasks											
1. Storytelling	.23	.35	.38	.39	.29	.12					
2. Mother's Motives	.04	.15	.28	.28	.19	.11	.36				
3. Definition of Feelings	.16	.22	.20	.24	.12	.08	.43	.31			
4. Empathic Cognition	.23	.38	.45	.43	.29	.14	.47	.30	.41		
5. Pictures[a]	.13	.27	.23	.21	.18	.13	.26	.28	.21	.27	

NOTE.—$r > .21$, $p < .01$; $r > .27$, $p < .001$.
[a] Combination Psychological Verbs and Affective Change.

TABLE 10

FACTOR LOADINGS: VARIMAX AND OBLIQUE ROTATIONS OF PRINCIPAL COMPONENTS

	FACTORS			
	1, Numerical		2, Narrative	
TASKS	Varimax	Oblique	Varimax	Oblique
Numerical tasks:				
Time Telling	.77	.78	.30	−.09
Money Knowledge	.74	.77	.30	.05
Number Knowledge	.72	.74	.16	−.10
Birthday Party	.62	.67	.29	.11
Balance Beam	.62	.61	.08	−.13
Distributive Justice	.30	.30	.11	−.03
Narrative tasks:				
Storytelling	.25	.09	.64	−.64
Empathic Cognition	.31	−.08	.58	−.62
Definition of Feelings	.09	−.06	.58	−.58
Mother's Motives	.10	.16	.55	−.56
Pictures	.19	.09	.38	−.37

Given the significant first-order correlations among certain of the narrative and numerical tasks as well as our expectation that the two factors in which we were interested would be correlated (since both are hypothesized to be subject to the same central limitations), we next conducted an oblique rotation. The factor loadings resulting from both rotations are given in Table 10. As may be seen, the two solutions revealed similar patterns of loadings: all six of the quantitative variables showed their primary loadings on the first factor, and all five of the narrative variables showed their primary loadings on the second factor.

Our final analysis was designed to determine whether the children's overall mean scores on the two batteries—which reflect their hypothesized developmental levels in each domain—would be equivalent. The joint distribution of scores on the two batteries is presented in Figure 15. As may be seen, there was a statistically significant correlation of moderate magnitude between the two sets of mean scores ($r = .476$, $p < .001$). For individual children, the general pattern was also one of synchronous rather than asynchronous performance: 69% of the children scored within half a substage (i.e., within half a point) across the two batteries, and 29% scored within a half to one substage (one point). Only three children (2%) showed a discrepancy of more than one substage between their average numerical and narrative scores.

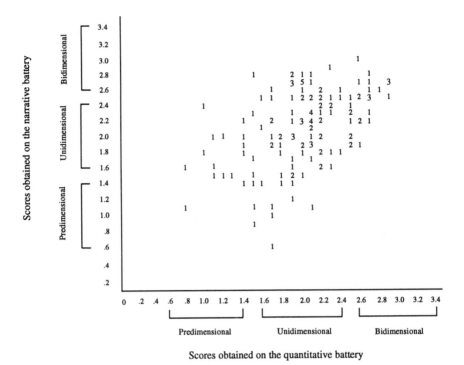

FIG. 15.—A scatter plot indicating subjects' total scores obtained on the narrative battery as a function of their total scores obtained on the quantitative battery.

Discussion

Correlations of similar magnitude have been found among Piagetian tasks by a number of other investigators in the Piagetian or neo-Piagetian tradition. What is distinctive about the correlations in the present study is that their pattern was in such good agreement with our conceptual analysis. This pattern was not extracted using any sort of procrustean transformation—that is, any statistical manipulation designed to force the data into the best possible agreement with our predictions. Consequently, we interpret its presence as support for our general theory.

Of course, the support is far from definitive. One of the dilemmas of factor analysis is that it is usually possible to identify more than one set of features that are shared by the tasks that load on any given factor. In the present case, this problem is reduced since social and numerical content was built into both batteries, as was the requirement for rating by means of qualitative scales. Still, it would be too strong to say that *no* set of features—other than those that we intended—ties each group of tasks together. For example, the tests that show their strongest loadings on the numerical factor are those with the "crispest" scoring procedures and the least reliance on the use of verbal protocols, while those that show their highest loadings on the narrative factor are those with the highest dependence on this sort of evaluation. Thus, differences of method may be partially responsible for the clarity of the solution.

Although the results may not be definitive, they are clearly congruent with the theory that led us to gather them. Moreover, they gain strength when they are compared with previous attempts to gather data of this sort in the context of Piaget's theory. As was mentioned in the introductory chapter, a persistent problem for Piaget's theory was the failure to confirm his conceptual analyses of cognitive structure by means of correlational methods. To be sure, some of his tasks did show strong intercorrelations; however, others did not, and the correlational clusters did not seem to bear any relation to his hypothesized logicomathematical structures. This could equally well have happened in our own case. The factor analysis could have extracted any number of factors, and the pattern of children's performance across them could have fallen along any number of lines that would have been quite different from those that were actually obtained.

The fact that they did not is significant. In our view, this predictive success is a joint result of several factors. First, we are standing on Piaget's shoulders and have the advantage of being able to use his insights and methods, modified as time has shown to be necessary. Second, we are also standing on the shoulders of other neo-Piagetians, most notably Pascual-Leone. In his early work, Pascual-Leone (1969) analyzed the full corpus of Piagetian tasks in great detail, highlighting the salient perceptual factors that they entail, showing how these are related to children's cognitive style, and making detailed (and successful) predictions about how they would be reflected in the factor structure of a large test battery. Informed by this work, we were able to prevent such factors from overshadowing those in which we were interested in the present test battery. Finally, and perhaps most important, the form of analysis that we conducted was intended to capture the structure of the knowledge that underlies children's performance across tasks. This sort of structure is, we believe, more likely to be reflected in the structure of children's performance than some more abstract logicomathematical competence.

The fact that the correlational structure was tighter for the quantitative tasks than the narrative tasks is an interesting one. As already mentioned, this may be partly a factor of method. Of equal importance may be the fact that a greater emphasis is placed on training children's quantitative reasoning than on training their narrative reasoning, at least in our culture. Although implicit narrative training is present in many forms of early education (e.g., in the form of the questions and answers that go on with regard to stories), it is not nearly as standardized as it is in the quantitative realm. Nor is the form of thought as standard, either.

One final point forms the bridge to the next study. As reported earlier, the mean score on each battery and the distribution of scores on the two batteries were virtually identical. This finding is congruent with the position that we outlined in the introductory chapter, namely, that central conceptual structures tend to have the same form in different domains at any given age, owing to the common constraints to which they are subject. On the other hand, it is not consistent with results from other studies or with the account of conceptual development that has been offered by theorists in the neonativist and/or "modular" traditions. Accordingly, we decided to conduct a second study in order to determine whether the same pattern would be present in other age groups.

STUDY 2: DETERMINING THE RATE AT WHICH DIFFERENT CENTRAL CONCEPTUAL STRUCTURES DEVELOP

The object of the second study was to chart the development of children's narrative and numerical structures from age 4 to age 10 and to determine whether these structures develop at the same general rate.

Subjects

A total of 89 children participated in this study. These included 20 4-year-olds (12 boys and 8 girls), 22 6-year-olds (11 boys and 11 girls), 23 8-year-olds (8 boys and 15 girls), and 24 10-year-olds (10 boys and 14 girls). The mean ages of these children at the time of testing were 4-1 (SD = 1.6 months), 6-0 (SD = 3.5 months), 8-1 (SD = 4.3 months), and 10-5 (SD = 6.1 months). The youngest children were drawn from three preschools, all of which served middle- to upper-middle-class families of European-American origin. The older children were drawn from two elementary schools, one parochial and one public, both of which served middle-class populations of mixed ethnic backgrounds. The parochial school, located in the San Francisco Bay Area, served mostly European- and Mexican-Americans with approximately 10% Asian- and African-Americans. The public school, located in the Los Angeles area, served predominantly European- and Mexican-Americans, although it also included some children from African- and Asian-American backgrounds.

Tasks and Procedures

The two task batteries were identical to those used in Study 1. As in Study 1, children were interviewed individually on three occasions to complete all 12 tasks contained in the two batteries. The task administration procedure was identical, with one exception; the order of task administration was slightly modified to include the Number Knowledge task in the first session. The tasks were administered in the following order: *Session 1:* (1) Balance Beam, (2) Storytelling, (3) Number Knowledge, and (4) Psychological Verbs; *Session 2:* (1) Mother's Motives, (2) Birthday Party, (3) Affective Change, and (4) Money Knowledge; and *Session 3:* (1) Time Telling, (2) Definition of Feelings, (3) Distributive Justice, and (4) Empathic Cognition. A total of eight individuals conducted the interviews; six of them were the same interviewers who had participated in Study 1; the other two were newly trained prior to the actual interviews, using the same training procedure. The elementary school children were interviewed at the end of the school year; interviews with preschoolers were conducted in the summer of the same year.

Scoring

The general procedure for scoring was the same as for the first study in this series, although certain refinements were introduced, as indicated in Appendices A and B. For the numerical battery, the percentage of agreement between raters ranged between 91% and 98%; for the narrative battery, the percentage of agreement ranged between 73% and 90%. In each case, disagreements were resolved by discussion.

Results

Since preliminary analyses indicated that there were no sex differences, boys and girls were treated as one group. The mean scores obtained on each task by each age group are reported in Table 11. As may be seen, mean scores obtained by the 6-year-olds were similar to those reported for the sample in Study 1, and the age-related progression on each task was similar in magnitude to what we reported for the Number Knowledge test in Chapter II.

Turning to the correspondence of overall performance across the two batteries, the pattern at all ages was very similar to what we obtained in Study 1. The correlation between the two batteries was .83, and a repeated-measures analysis found no significant difference in mean battery scores ($F[1, 85] = .25, p < .61$). The majority of individual children also scored at the same level on the two batteries; no child showed a difference greater than one level at age 4, and only one child at each of ages 6 and 8 years showed a discrepancy of this magnitude. The 10-year-old group showed a sizable percentage of the discrepancies of this magnitude; however, even at this level, only two of the children showed a discrepancy greater than 1.5 points. The most common

TABLE 11

MEANS, STANDARD DEVIATIONS, AND RANGES OBTAINED FOR TASKS ON THE NUMERICAL AND NARRATIVE BATTERIES

	NUMERICAL BATTERY							NARRATIVE BATTERY					
	Number	Money	Time	Balance	Birthday	Justice	Overall Quant.	Story	Motives	Feeling	Emp. Cog.	Pictures	Overall Narrative
4 years:													
M	.98	.73	.75	1.05	1.10	1.50	1.03	1.34	1.30	1.26	1.24	1.28	1.28
SD	.33	.26	.32	.50	.70	.70	.30	.64	.52	.61	.49	.39	.41
Range	.4–1.4	.4–1.2	0–1.4	.5–2	.5–2	.5–2	.53–1.6	.5–2.5	.5–2.5	.5–3	.8–2.5	.8–2.3	.8–2.4
6 years:													
M	1.82	1.66	1.82	1.90	1.84	2.00	1.75	2.04	1.63	1.98	1.88	1.95	1.90
SD	.31	.47	.42	.42	.51	.30	.25	.78	.41	.49	.62	.57	.38
Range	1.2–2.6	1.2–3.2	.8–2.3	1–3	.5–3	1–3	1.2–2.5	.5–3	.9–2.5	.9–3	.8–3.3	1–2.8	1.3–2.7
8 years:													
M	2.90	2.17	2.87	2.39	2.21	2.50	2.70	2.63	2.17	2.65	2.81	2.88	2.63
SD	.30	.43	.63	.58	.89	.74	.33	.58	.57	.60	.69	.45	.40
Range	2.3–3.5	2.3–3.8	1.8–4.7	1–3	.5–4	2–5	2.1–3.7	2–4	1.1–3.5	1.6–4	1.6–4	2–3.7	2–3.2
10 years:													
M	3.92	4.19	3.88	3.35	3.34	3.91	3.78	3.45	2.94	3.45	3.46	3.37	3.31
SD	.69	.61	.59	.63	1.50	1.12	.66	.67	.91	.85	.69	.60	.55
Range	2.6–4.9	1.8–5	2.95	2–4.5	.5–5	1–5	2.3–4.9	2–4.5	1.8–4.8	1.6–4.5	2.3–5	2.3–4.5	2.2–4.1

NOTE.—Scores of 1–4 are defined by substages 1–4.

pattern was thus one in which conceptual development appeared to be taking place in the two domains at the same general rate.

Discussion

The data from Study 2 confirmed the finding from Study 1 concerning the parallel pattern of development in the numerical and narrative domains. Both in the population as a whole and in individual children, development appeared to go through the same general conceptual progression in each domain. Moreover, it appeared to go through this progression at the same general rate. This being the case, it is important to examine the considerable body of literature in which a different pattern of data is reported or in which a different conclusion about the likelihood of such a pattern has been reached. These studies normally differ from the present one along one or more of the following dimensions.

1. *Presence of a common metric.*—The first feature that unites the majority of studies in which conceptual development appears to take place in different domains at widely different rates—and that distinguishes them from the present study—is that they have no common metric for measuring a child's conceptual sophistication on the different tasks or different domains in which development is being assessed. In the classic Piagetian literature, for example, there is often a surface commonality across tasks, in that subjects can be classified as being at substage A, B, or C on each. As a number of investigators have pointed out, however, Piaget never intended these designations as more than ad hoc ways of classifying the steps along the road to the structures in which he was interested (Chapman, 1988). Since he did not define substage A on task X and substage A on task Y in the same manner, the fact that subjects are often found to be functioning at different levels on two different tasks—even though both are tests of the same general operational structure—is not surprising.

A similar point can be made with regard to tasks designed to measure children's conceptual development in the modular and/or neonativist tradition. As Keil (1986) has pointed out, there is a universal progression in children's conceptual development, in the sense that children invariably begin by defining any new concept in terms of its surface or perceptual features and end up by defining it in terms of its deeper semantic features. When one looks at the age at which this progression takes place, however, one finds a wide difference from one task to the next. From the present point of view, the important point to note is that, since the concepts have not been scaled in terms of a common metric, the conclusions that one can draw from this finding are limited.

The same may be said for the less formally documented but frequently cited findings on the rate of cognitive change across tasks that are known to have a different neurological substrate. It is widely believed, for example, that the most important period of development for musical ability is the preschool period, whereas the most important period of development for logicomathematical ability is the school years. The claim has also been made that the spontaneous development of musical intelligence ends by the age of 7 or so, whereas spontaneous development of logicomathematical thought extends considerably beyond that period (Gardner, 1983). Once again, however, it is hard to know what to make of this claim since there in no common basis for deciding what is important and what is "rapid." Certainly, there are many objective tasks where untrained children continue to show great improvement in musical cognition after the age of 7 (Serafine, 1988). Moreover, in the one study that we know of where an attempt was made to develop a common metric, development was found to be proceeding in this domain at the same general rate as in others (Capodilupo, 1990).

2. *Lack of attention to misleading task features.*—If we focus on studies where some sort of common conceptual metric *is* present, we will still find many examples where development appears to be taking place across different tasks or task domains at a different rate. A second factor that distinguishes many of these studies from the present one is that no attempt is made to eliminate misleading task factors or to control the extent to which such factors are operative across different tasks. A great deal of work has been conducted on this problem by Pascual-Leone (1969), as has already been mentioned. Many other important lines of work have also begun by isolating some important misleading factor in a Piagetian task, then systematically examining its effect (e.g., Markman, 1984). Informed by this work, however, we were able to prevent such factors from overshadowing those in which we were interested in the present study, by the way in which we designed our test battery. This constitutes a second possible reason that the results that we found were more comparable across different domains than those reported by other investigators.

3. *Failure to distinguish specific from general variance.*—Although tests of cognitive development are perhaps unique in the extent to which they involve misleading task factors, a general measurement problem in psychology is that one can never control all the specific task factors that might influence a subject's response and prevent one from forming an accurate assessment of some more general disposition, trait, or structure. When such a state of affairs obtains, the standard procedure in most subfields is to present a battery of tests that includes a large number of specific tasks and then to eliminate the effects of local task factors by averaging.

As Rushton, Brainerd, and Pressley (1983) have pointed out, however, this procedure is almost never used in developmental psychology. Thus, most studies can make statements about the rate of development only from one context or task to the next, not from one general conceptual domain or structure to the next. This is perhaps the most important reason that our findings differ from those reported by others. If one examines the mean scores in Table 11 carefully, one will see that there is still a substantial amount of variability from one task to the next, notwithstanding our attempt to control extraneous factors. What is equally clear, however, is that this variability is present in both test batteries to the same degree. Since both test batteries also have the same central tendency, the general pattern that is observed is one where children find it considerably easier to apply their central conceptual structures in certain task situations than in others but where the overall pattern of their development looks very similar in both the numerical and the narrative domains.

In the past few years, studies have begun to appear in which the above distinction has been made and an effort has also been made to disentangle specific from more general structural variance. By and large, these studies have shown results that are quite like those reported here (Demetriou, Shayer, & Pervez, 1988; DeRibaupierre & Pascual-Leone, 1979; Lautrey, DeRibaupierre, & Rieben, 1985; Marini & Case, 1993). The present study thus joins these studies in suggesting that development often proceeds across different conceptual domains at a relatively constant rate.

Before concluding, we would like to mention two sets of data that we believe are compatible with the foregoing conclusion but that might be taken to be incompatible with it were they not scrutinized quite closely.

1. In research conducted on a variety of tasks—including the Balance Beam, Estimation of Time, and Estimation of Area—it has been reported that children are capable of integrating information about two separate dimensions in making quantity judgments by the age of 5 years (Anderson & Cuneo, 1978; Wilkening, 1981). By contrast, we repeatedly found them *incapable* of doing so until the age of 9 or 10. The important point to note here is that Anderson and his colleagues were not trying to assess the presence of a central numerical structure: they were merely trying to assess children's ability to utilize information from two different quantitative dimensions. As a consequence, most of the judgments that they asked children to make could be made by simple visual inspection and did not require careful enumeration. In our terms, then, they did not require a level of numerical sophistication beyond the predimensional level. On several tasks that we have designed for preschoolers ourselves, we have predicted and found similar findings (Bruchkowsky, 1992; Marini & Case, 1993).

2. Consider next a set of data reported by Siegler (1981). These data are congruent with ours in showing that, in general, bidimensional thought does not emerge until the age of 7–10. They are also consistent in showing considerable evidence of cross-task consistency in development; thus, for example, approximately 70% of the children studied by Siegler used the same-level rule in approaching the Balance Beam task as they did in ap-

proaching Inhelder and Piaget's (1958) Shadows task. There is one task, however, on which a finding emerged that was similar to the one reported by Anderson and his colleagues. On the Conservation of Number task, children appeared to be using a bivariate rule (Rule 2) at the age of 5 or 6, a good 2 years before they used the corresponding rule on most other tasks. Once again, it is important to point out that Siegler was not trying to assess the presence of a central numerical structure. He was trying to determine the age at which children used a formally similar rule in several different perceptual and conceptual contexts. As we pointed out in earlier work, the conservation of number problem can be solved by applying a single mental number line (Case, 1972, 1977). By contrast, Rule 2 usage on the Balance Beam, the Shadows, or the Conservation of Liquid task cannot be attained until children have assembled a bivariate numerical structure. When data obtained in these tasks are recoded for the level of numerical reasoning that needs to be applied, the level of understanding that children demonstrate turns out to be quite similar across these various situations.[3]

CONCLUDING COMMENTS

In contrast to the data from the previous chapter, the present data were not intended to provide a more detailed look at the internal workings of children's central conceptual structures for number. Rather, they were intended to demonstrate, both analytically and empirically, that the operation of these structures can be identified on quite a wide range of tasks and contexts, including those that have been interpreted in the literature as indexing competencies that are quite disparate, such as scientific reasoning and social competence. A second goal of the present chapter was to demonstrate that a similar general pattern can be observed in the domain of children's narrative.

In and of itself, correlational data such as those reported in the present chapter do not allow one to conclude that the development of children's central conceptual structures plays a causal role in determining the pattern of reasoning that they display on the various specific tasks that have been studied. Nor do they allow one to conclude with any certainty that children's central conceptual development across different domains is subject to the same limitations. They do add a certain degree of intuitive plausibility to both these suggestions, however, and they provide an extremely important general context within which experiments aimed at drawing causal inferences must be interpreted. It is to studies of this latter sort that we turn in the next chapter.

[3] We are grateful to Robert Siegler for making his data available to us for the purpose of this analysis.

IV. EVALUATING THE BREADTH AND DEPTH OF TRAINING EFFECTS WHEN CENTRAL CONCEPTUAL STRUCTURES ARE TAUGHT

Sharon Griffin and Robbie Case

Since the central conceptual structure hypothesis was first proposed (Case & Griffin, 1990; Case & Sandieson, 1987, 1988), a great deal of work has been devoted to increasing the precision of the theoretical framework and testing its core components. Thus, for example, several studies have focused on showing that children's central conceptual structures for representing number have the content that had been originally suggested and that they emerge at the postulated point in development (Chap. II). Other studies have been devoted to showing that children's quantitative and social-cognitive competencies form two coherent factors and that the Number Knowledge test is one of the principal tests to define the quantitative factor (Chap. III).

The studies reported in the present chapter were designed to test a stronger hypothesis, namely, that children's central numerical structures play a causal role in the development of competencies in other areas. In order to test this hypothesis, it is not enough to demonstrate that a wide range of developmental tests correlate with tests of children's central numerical knowledge, nor is it sufficient to show that children's number knowledge loads on the same factor as such tests as the Balance Beam, Time Telling, and Money. In addition, one must demonstrate that, when children's central numerical structures are changed, these other competencies will change as well.

Some previous work does indicate that this may be the case. Case and Sandieson (1992) found that exposure to a training program designed to teach elements of the central numerical structure led to substantial gains on the Number Knowledge test as well as transfer to a range of other quantitative measures. McKeough (1992b) found that a similar pattern pre-

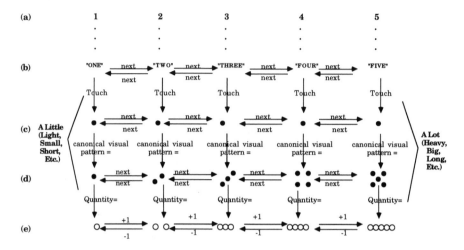

Fig. 16.—The expanded representation of the number line used for instructional purposes. The top row indicates knowledge of written numerals. The second row indicates knowledge of number-word sequence. The third row indicates knowledge of appropriate motor routine for counting physical objects. The fourth row indicates knowledge of canonical visual patterns for small sets of numbers as they appear, e.g., on dice. The fifth row indicates knowledge of the cardinal values of these sets and the "increment/decrement" rule that connects them.

vailed when elements of the central narrative structure were taught to children in the same age range (4–5 years). There are a number of problems with these early studies, however, and the authors themselves have urged caution in interpreting their findings. These problems include (*a*) small sample size, (*b*) interventions that were impromptu in many respects and only partially documented, (*c*) the absence of controls that would permit the locus of the effects to be identified, and (*d*) transfer effects that were demonstrated only in the laboratory (if central conceptual structures really are central, some sort of effect should be found in children's everyday learning as well).

The current studies were designed to eliminate the foregoing difficulties. The set of questions that they were designed to address can be summarized as follows: (1) Can the knowledge specified in the 6-year-old central numerical structure and illustrated in Figure 16 be taught to children who are at an age when they should have acquired it but for some reason have not? (2) If so, will this knowledge have an effect on children's performance on a broad range of developmental tasks for which no specific training has been provided? (3) If so, will this knowledge also have an effect on children's learning outside the laboratory—for example, in school mathematics? (4) Is the current specification of the 6-year-old central numerical structure adequate to capture its core meaning, or do some elements of this structure carry more of this core meaning than others and thus contribute more to development in other areas?

STUDY 1

The first training study was designed to provide an initial answer to each of the questions posed above. To address the question of whether central numerical knowledge can be trained (question 1), a set of measurable learning objectives was constructed for each component of the central numerical structure, and a curriculum ("Rightstart") was developed to teach each of these. To address the question of transfer (question 2), the battery of quantitative tasks that was described in the previous chapter, as well as in Griffin, Case, and Capodilupo (1995), was administered both before and after training. To address the question of whether certain components in the structure are more important for transfer than others (question 4), a mathematical "control" program was developed and administered to another group of children. This program was designed to teach a partial set, but not all, of the components specified in Figure 16. A second control program that taught none of these components but engaged children in a set of games and activities that were similar in their general form to those used in the treatment program was also developed. Finally, to address the question of transfer to school learning (question 3), children in all three training interventions were presented with several standard school "mini-curricula" immediately following the transfer tests; the extent of their learning was then evaluated.

Methods

Training Interventions

Core training: The number knowledge program ("Rightstart").—The content covered in the main training program consisted of the set of nodes and relations that were postulated to compose the central numerical structure illustrated in Figure 16. These were partitioned into instructional units as follows:

    1. Number sequence going up from 1 to 10 (row *b*);
    2. Number sequence going down from 10 to 1 (row *b*);
    3. One-to-one mapping of numbers onto objects when counting in either direction (rows *b* and *c*);
    4. Mapping of each number onto a canonical set of appropriate size (rows *b* and *d*);

5. Increment rule (i.e., knowledge that each number up one in a sequence represents a set that has been incremented by one [+1]; row e);

6. Decrement rule (i.e., knowledge that each number down one in a sequence represents a set that has been decremented by one [−1]; row e);

7. Mapping of relative numerosity onto number sequence (i.e., since this set [XXX] has more than this set [XX], one can say that 3 is "more" than 2; rows b and d);

8. Use of information regarding relative numerical magnitude to make dimensional judgments (e.g., A is longer than B since A contains three identical objects and B contains only two identical objects; outer brackets in the figure);

9. Mapping of numbers onto symbolic representations (rows b and a).

The principles followed in devising materials to teach this content were as follows:

Affective engagement.—Each exercise should be affectively engaging.
Representational congruence.—The visual props for representing numerical change should be congruent with children's internal representation of number. This means that they should indicate numbers of increasing magnitude as lying along a line that increases in length.
Representational diversity.—A variety of external forms of representation should be utilized (e.g., thermometers, board games, "number lines," rows of objects, etc.).
Developmental sequencing.—The concepts to be covered should be sequenced in their normal order of developmental acquisition.
Multiple levels of learning.—Wherever possible, multiple levels of understanding and learning should be facilitated. Thus, in the early exercises where the explicit activity is counting, the props and general context should be such as to permit some implicit learning of the higher-order concepts by the more capable children; in the later exercises, children who are still consolidating their counting should have the opportunity to do so, and they should be able to get some fun and knowledge out of the exercise.

The materials that were developed to help children acquire each of the elements of knowledge listed above and integrate them into a coherent structure were assembled into a set of 20 lessons that teachers were asked to follow. To maximize affective engagement, the majority of the activities included in these lessons were set in a game format, and the majority of the games were designed to be played by small groups of children under the teacher's guidance (for a sample lesson, see App. D). The instructions for following the lessons that were given to teachers always stressed two objectives, namely, (1) helping children acquire the number line structure and (2) helping them realize that numbers can be fun.

Control Program 1: Traditional Math Readiness

The math program developed for the first control group was a traditional one that incorporated some, but not all, of the components of the Rightstart program. The components that were included were forward and backward counting, mapping of numbers onto objects, cardinality, and recognition of numerals (i.e., elements 1, 2, 3, 4, and 9 of the core program). The reason for selecting these components is that they form the backbone of the typical math readiness program found in American schools today.

Control Program 2: Reading Readiness

The second control program was a reading readiness module designed on the hypothesis that a major component of reading readiness is phonemic awareness (Adams, 1990; Bradley & Bryant, 1985). The program that we developed was based loosely on a sound categorization program developed by Bradley and Bryant (1985). It provided systematic training in sound categorization as well as ample opportunity for children to map sounds (e.g., beginning word sounds, final word sounds, rhyming sounds) onto words, letters, and pictorial representations of objects and events in the real world. To ensure comparability across treatments, the three instructional modules were identical in length and comparable in the sort of participation structures employed for the games and other activities (copies of all these programs are available on request from Sharon Griffin).

Subjects

The training programs were implemented in three public kindergarten classes serving middle- to low-income families who had immigrated from rural Portugal to Toronto. Although Portuguese was the dominant language in most of the children's homes, the vast majority had attended prekindergarten and were proficient in English. The few children who lacked minimal oral comprehension of English were excluded from the sample, and the remainder ($N = 60$) constituted the treatment and control groups. When the Number Knowledge test (Griffin et al., 1995; Chap. II above) was administered to this sample in the middle of the kindergarten year (November), the majority of children performed at or below the predimensional level and appeared to be missing many of the components of the central numerical structure.

The total sample of 60 was divided into three matched groups on the basis of the children's Number Knowledge pretest scores. A rank-ordering procedure was used to assign children to groups, with the child receiving the lowest ranked score assigned to the Rightstart group (i.e., the treatment group), the child receiving the second lowest ranked score assigned to the traditional math group (i.e., Control Group 1), the child receiving the third lowest ranked score assigned to the reading readiness group (i.e., Control Group 2), etc. This method was adopted in order to provide a conservative rather than a liberal estimate of the effectiveness of the training as well as to give the "neediest" children the benefit of the Rightstart program. The mean chronological ages of the three groups were 5.23, 5.26, and 5.30 years, respectively.

Training

Training was provided by Sharon Griffin and two graduate students in education. Each trainer was assigned to one of the three classrooms and was responsible for the training of all the children it contained in small groups. Since children from each of the three intervention groups were represented in each classroom, each trainer provided training in all three instructional programs. This design permitted us to assess the effectiveness of the Rightstart program not only in relation to the other two training programs but also across classrooms and across trainers. Each child received 40 small-group training sessions, with each session lasting approximately 20 min. The size of each training group was five children. For the most part, training was conducted in a corner of the regular classroom, and visual distractions were minimized by the use of room dividers; however, auditory distractions were quite frequent and could not be controlled.

Assessment Instruments and Procedures

A battery of quantitative tasks was administered individually to all children participating in the study in November (pretest) and in April (posttest) of the same school year. Children were tested in the language with which they were most comfortable (i.e., English or Portuguese); in most cases (93% on the pretest, 100% on the posttest), English was the preferred language. The test battery included the *Number Knowledge* test (which provided a direct measure of the effectiveness of the Rightstart program in teaching the central numerical structure) and five transfer tests drawn from the quantitative domain, namely, the *Balance Beam* test, the *Birthday Party* test, the *Time Telling* test, the *Money Knowledge* test, and Piaget's *Number Conservation* test. The first four transfer tests are described in Chapter III as well as in Griffin et al. (1995). The last test is familiar to most readers. Note that no specific training was provided for any of the transfer tests. In fact, mention of balance beam concepts, time concepts, money concepts, etc. was carefully avoided in all the instructional programs.[4]

To assess children's posttraining ability to profit from conventional instruction in subjects typically taught in school, three postinstructional units were designed to teach children symbolic content that had not been included in any of the three training modules but for which the mental counting line structure was hypothesized to be a prerequisite. These units (described below) were taught in a quiet room to small groups of three to four children, 1 month after training was completed. Each took a total of 45–60 min to implement, over a period of 2–3 school days. As a partial control for teacher bias (i.e., teacher's expectation that the treatment group would show superior learning), each group was composed of children from each of the three training groups. Within this constraint, the groups were matched for ability levels as much as possible. Teaching was performed by the same teachers who had administered the three treatment programs over the course of the school year. The three units introduced children to addition, subtraction, and music sight-reading as follows.

The Addition unit.—Children were introduced to a "story" of the typical "Change 1" variety (Riley & Greeno, 1988; Table 2 above). The teacher manipulated objects as she told the story and then wrote the numerals and sizes under the objects that had been moved to summarize what had happened. Eventually, she faded out the props and gave the children formally stated problems to solve without props or a story. The whole sequence proceeded in carefully graded steps, as is customary in first grade instruction. At the end of this instructional unit, children were presented with four criterion problems written in traditional notation (e.g., $4 + 3 = $ ————). They were given an opportunity to solve each problem with no prompts and, if unsuccessful, were given a prompt in the form of a story (e.g., "Suppose someone gave you four candies, and then they gave you three more"). Children were credited with understanding the material if they

---

[4] The one exception to this generalization is that, in a few of the games, the bingo chips that children used were referred to as "money" in order to improve the story line (see App. D). This exception is more apparent than real, however, since the situations depicted in the games did not bear any direct relation to those described in the Money Knowledge test, and no money concepts from the test were illustrated or referred to in the training.

provided the correct answer to three of these four problems, with or without prompts.

The Subtraction unit.—This unit followed the same format as the Addition unit, with the story line and the problems adjusted to teach subtraction. Passing criteria were also identical.

The Music Sight-Reading unit.—This unit was a modified version of an instructional program developed by Capodilupo (1992). Children were told a story about a spaceship that wanted to go to the moon. The spaceship was represented by a sticker that looked like a flying saucer; one such sticker was placed on the middle C on the piano and one on the music staff. The moon was represented by a sticker of the "man in the moon," and one copy of this sticker was affixed to the F immediately above middle C on the piano and another on the music score. The notes in between C and F were referred to as "stations" on the way from the spaceship's ground base to the moon. At the end of the unit, the children were given six test melodies to play without any stickers and were credited with passing if they played four of these melodies without error.

To provide a control condition for these number-based posttreatment instructional units, and to assess the effectiveness of the language module in facilitating children's first formal learning of reading, three language-based miniunits were also developed and taught to all children in the sample immediately following the number-based units. Each of these units was taught individually and took approximately 15 min to complete. The first was a set of *Sound Categorization* exercises (see Bradley & Bryant, 1985) that required children to listen to a sequence of four words and to choose two that sounded most alike. The second was a set of *Rhyming* exercises that provided several warmup examples before children were required to generate rhyming words when familiar words were presented. The third was a *Word Reading* unit, which is described below.

The Word Reading unit.—This unit consisted of a sequence of steps designed to prepare children to read four simple words (i.e., *mat, sat, pat,* and *rat*). The word *cat* was used for instructional purposes, and children were (1) shown a picture of a cat and asked to name it, (2) given practice in sounding out this word with respect to its beginning and ending sounds (i.e., *c-* and *-at*), (3) given practice in mapping these sounds onto letters (i.e., *c-* and *-at*), and (4) given practice in blending the sounds into a single word when the letters were combined. Children were next presented with cards depicting a new beginning letter (*m-*) and the same ending letters (*-at*). They were then asked to read the word when the letters were combined. For this and all following criterion items, children were given assistance in identifying any letter they didn't know as well as the sound each letter makes. Passing scores (0–4) were assigned on the basis of children's ability to read the new word (i.e., blend the sounds into a single utterance).

TABLE 12

PERCENTAGES OF CHILDREN PASSING THE NUMBER KNOWLEDGE TEST AND PERCENTAGES
PASSING THE NUMERICAL BATTERY TRANSFER TESTS AT THE UNIDIMENSIONAL LEVEL
PRE- AND POSTINTERVENTION

TEST	CONTROL GROUP 1 ($N = 19$)[a]		CONTROL GROUP 2 ($N = 20$)		TREATMENT GROUP ($N = 20$)	
	Pre	Post	Pre	Post	Pre	Post
Number Knowledge	15	37	15	35	15	80
Balance Beam	5	37	5	35	20	65
Birthday Party	21	42	15	25	5	65
Time Telling	15	37	10	45	10	45
Money Knowledge	10	31	10	30	5	50
Number Conservation	10	16	10	30	10	40

[a] One child moved during the intervention, reducing the pretest sample from 20 to 19 on the posttest.

Results

Our data analysis was designed to determine whether the Rightstart program (1) taught children the knowledge that it was designed to teach, (2) produced the transfer to the developmental tasks on our quantitative battery that we had predicted it would (Balance Beam, Time Telling, etc.), and (3) enabled children to profit from instruction in the sort of content to which they are exposed in the typical school curriculum (i.e., addition, subtraction, and reading). The most useful form of analysis for all these purposes was to establish some criterion for success and then to examine the percentage of children who reached it. The criterion selected to assess the first objective was passing six of the seven items on the posttreatment Number Knowledge test at the unidimensional level. The criterion selected to assess the second objective was passing the majority of items on the five numerical posttests at the same level. Table 12 shows the percentage of children in the treatment and control groups who demonstrated this level of competence, before and after treatment.

As the data in the table indicate, very few children in the overall sample passed any of the tests at the unidimensional level prior to training. After training, the majority of the treatment group passed the Number Knowledge test as well as most of the developmental transfer tests at the unidimensional level. The majority of the control group subjects failed to demonstrate this level of postintervention competence on any test. The size of the effect clearly differentiated the treatment group from the others on four of the transfer tests (the Balance Beam, Birthday Party, Money Knowledge, and Number Conservation tests); the absence of training effects on the Time Telling test might have been due to the complicated wording of some of

TABLE 13

PERCENTAGES OF CHILDREN PASSING THE INSTRUCTIONAL UNITS IN THE THREE
NUMBER-RELATED AND THE THREE LANGUAGE-RELATED SCHOOL SUBJECTS

Instructional Units	Control Group 1 ($N = 19$)[a]	Control Group 2 ($N = 19$)[a]	Treatment Group ($N = 20$)
Number related:			
Addition	53	42	75
Subtraction	42	26	85
Music sight-reading	50	47	75
Language related:			
Reading	37	65	50
Sound categorization	16	40	25
Rhyming	37	40	30

NOTE.—Passing was defined as succeeding on the majority of items on the test constructed for each unit (with the exception of the Rhyming test, where a two of four criterion was used).

[a] Sample size was reduced from 20 to 19 prior to this year-end assessment when one child moved from the school district.

the test questions, a particular problem that may result in indexing general intelligence rather than quantitative understanding for a population for whom English is a recently acquired, second language. A repeated-measures analysis of variance indicated a significant difference between the treatment group and the control groups on the overall battery of tasks ($F[1, 45] = 38.46$, $p < .001$). No significant difference emerged across the two control groups: no trainer, classroom, or sex effects emerged either.

Table 13 shows the percentages of children in the treatment and control groups who mastered the instructional units that were taught at the end of the school year (with mastery defined as passing the majority of the postintervention test items). In the number-related school subjects, the majority (75%–85%) of the treatment group demonstrated an ability to profit from the instruction that they had been given; the majority of children in the reading group (Control Group 2) demonstrated the lowest level of competence, and the traditional math readiness group (Control Group 1) showed an intermediate level of performance. By contrast, on the language-related measures, it was the performance of the children who had received the reading readiness program that was superior to that of the other groups. In summary, the differences between the training groups were clearly related to the form of treatment that each had received and hence suggest that each training module had its intended effect.

Discussion

Given the pattern of strengths and weaknesses that the three training groups demonstrated on the posttest battery and the concurrent absence of trainer and classroom effects, it seems reasonable to conclude that the Rightstart program achieved its effects because its content enabled children to develop a deeper understanding of numbers, not because it exposed children to games or taught them a more "test-like" or "school-like" way of relating to adults. This conclusion is further supported by the fact that Control Group 1, which was exposed to some, but not all, of the content implied in the central numerical structure, showed a pattern of performance on the numerical posttests that was intermediate between those of the Rightstart group and the reading readiness group (i.e., Control Group 2).

What conclusions can be drawn with regard to the four questions that we posed at the outset of the study? First, the results indicate that the knowledge specified in the 6-year-old central numerical structure and illustrated in Figure 16 can be taught to a group of children who give little evidence of possessing this knowledge prior to training. Second, they suggest that acquisition of this knowledge facilitates children's performance on other developmental tasks for which no specific training is provided. Third, they indicate that this knowledge enhances children's ability to profit from instruction in school-type tasks (and also in music sight-reading). Finally, they suggest that the components of the numerical structure that we had listed as 5–8 (i.e., the increment and decrement rules, relative quantity, and use of this information to make variable estimates) are critical.

STUDY 2

As is evident from the findings of Study 1, the results of our first trial of the Rightstart program were promising, and they suggested that we were well on our way toward creating a program that could teach children the knowledge implied in the number line structure. However, several limitations of the first study suggested a need for caution in interpreting the findings. First, the effects had been achieved with a sample of children whose background history was unique (recall that all came from Portuguese immigrant families). Second, although the "school learning" effects were substantial, they were achieved under conditions that were somewhat artificial (recall that instruction in first grade subjects was extremely brief and was provided at the end of the kindergarten year). Third, although the transfer effects on the quantitative battery were significant, they were not as large as we thought might be possible if the components noted above were given greater emphasis and the program fine-tuned to make sure that all its objectives could be met.

Accordingly, we decided to replicate the first study on a different population and with an improved Rightstart program. We also decided to follow the children in this new sample through their first year of formal schooling, to see whether the treatment versus control group differences would be reflected in school performance in mathematics.

The questions in the second study were stated as follows: (1) Could the effects established in Study 1 be replicated with a sample of children drawn from a range of different cultural backgrounds? (2) Could learning effects be established in a more naturalistic setting, namely, in children's arithmetic achievement following a year of traditional schooling? (3) Would an improved Rightstart program produce larger transfer effects? Our theory predicted an affirmative answer with regard to the first two questions and was neutral with regard to the third.

Method

Subjects

Three inner-city schools in a central Massachusetts city were chosen as sites for the second study. These schools had the largest proportion of minority students (i.e., African-Americans, Hispanics, and Southeast Asians) in the city, and children in these schools generally came from low to middle-low socioeconomic families. In the second half of the school year, all kindergarten children in these three schools were given "parent permission slips" written in their native language; of the 161 slips taken home, 112 were returned signed, giving the parents' consent to participate in the study. The Number Knowledge test was administered to all children who had returned with signed consent forms; 55 of these (49%) failed the unidimensional level of this test and were used to constitute the study sample.

As in the previous study, children were rank ordered on the Number Knowledge test prior to being assigned to the treatment or the control group and then matched in pairs on the basis of (a) cultural group, (b) school, and (c) home classroom. Whenever two otherwise matched children differed in their Number Knowledge scores, the one with the lower score was assigned to the Rightstart group. Seven children for whom a match could not be found were eliminated from the sample. The resulting groups contained 24 children each. At the end of the pretest period, the mean chronological age of the treatment group was 5 years, 7 months, and the mean age of the control group was 5 years, 10 months.

Training

For instructional purposes, the 24 children in the treatment group were divided into six groups of four children each. Two groups of children received training in each of the three sites; this training was provided by two research assistants who had been trained by Sharon Griffin to teach the Rightstart program. Each of these trainers assumed sole responsibility for teaching both groups of children at two of the sites; at the third site, each trainer taught one of the two groups.

As in the first study, 40 group-training sessions were provided, with each session lasting approximately 20 min. Some children were present for all sessions, and others were absent for several of them. Instruction was provided in a separate room within the school; which room was used on any particular day was determined by availability. The library and the cafeteria were frequent training sites. These locations, as well as the variability in sites that were used across sessions, did not make for ideal training conditions. However, they did provide conditions characterized by frequent distractions, a situation that reflects the prevailing reality in many inner-city schools in the United States today.

To increase the possibility of obtaining substantial treatment effects, the Rightstart program was modified and expanded prior to commencement of training. The revisions included (1) reordering several lessons so as to provide a learning sequence that was more natural for children and that permitted better hierarchical integration of knowledge, (2) rescripting several lessons to include teacher-posed questions (e.g., "How did you figure that out?"), (3) eliminating activities that were not sufficiently multileveled and/ or affectively engaging, (4) creating new activities that addressed components of the numerical central structure that had been found to be critical in the previous study (e.g., relative quantity estimates), (5) creating new activities to address content objectives that had proved difficult for children to master (e.g., counting backward from 10), and (6) creating more cooperative (as opposed to competitive) games, which permitted greater participation for the less capable students.

Children in the control group received no special intervention beyond their regular classroom instruction. On the other hand, children in the treatment group received little or no mathematics instruction from their classroom teachers, who claimed that this subject was adequately covered by the Rightstart program. Consequently, the absolute quantity of mathematics instruction was roughly comparable across groups, although it differed in content as well as instructional format.

Assessment Instruments and Procedures

Kindergarten Assessment

The pre- and posttest assessment included the Number Knowledge test and the five other tests constituting the quantitative battery described in

Chapter III. The entire battery of tasks was administered individually to all children in the treatment and control groups in whatever language they were most comfortable with; for the majority of children this was English, but a sizable number of children were tested in Spanish and a smaller number in Vietnamese or Laotian. Pretesting was conducted in January and February of the kindergarten year, posttesting in May and June of the same year, in any quiet spot in the school that could be found. All tests were individually administered to each child, in a single session for most children and in two sessions for children who showed fatigue partway through the first session. It is important to note that the revised Rightstart module still provided no specific training for any of the transfer tasks. Thus, the tasks still provided an indication of children's ability to apply the concepts that they had learned in the program to new contexts.

Follow-Up Assessment

Subjects..—The sample comprised all children in the original group who completed first grade in the same general geographic area (i.e., within a 50-mile radius of the treatment sites) during the school year following training. This included 11 children from the treatment group (original $N = 23$) and 12 children from the control group (original $N = 24$) who were attending 14 different first grade classrooms at a total of six different urban schools (the remaining children had moved outside this geographic area and/or were classified in school records as "current address unknown").

Instruments and procedures.—To capture a broad assortment of numerical competencies deemed to be typical in the first grade, a four-part assessment battery was administered in May and June of the school year following treatment. This included the *Number Knowledge test* (described in Chap. II) plus the following three tests.

The *Oral Arithmetic test* presented children with four small addition and subtraction computations to perform in their heads (e.g., "How much is 2 plus 4?" "How much is 8 take away 6?"). A "pass" was assigned if the child produced correct answers for all four problems.

The *Written Arithmetic test* was a more standard arithmetic test that required children to solve four single-digit addition and subtraction problems that were presented using traditional, vertical, formal notation. Children were required to read each problem and write their answers in the space provided. No penalty was imposed for correct responses in which the numerals were reversed or partially formed, and a "pass" was assigned if the child produced correct answers for all four problems.

The *Word Problems test* was adapted from one used by Riley and Greeno (1988). The first four items are instances of "combine" and "change" problems and were assigned to Level 1 (i.e., the unidimensional level) and Level 2 (i.e., the bidimensional level) on the basis of normative data reported by Riley and Greeno (1988) as well as a conceptual analysis of task demands from the perspective of our theory. The fifth item is an instance of a "compare" problem and was assigned to Level 3 (i.e., the elaborated bidimensional level) on the basis of the analysis reported in Chapter II. Each of the five word problems was read aloud to the child and repeated as often as necessary. The child was required to produce an oral response. One point was assigned for each item passed, and a separate score was computed for each level. The pass criteria for Levels 1 and 2 was success on both items.

Additionally, we used a *Teacher Rating* scale that included seven items that were taken directly from the report cards used in the school district. For each item, teachers were requested to determine whether the child was average, above average, or below average on some particular quality or skill with respect to his or her classroom peers. The skills on which children were to be ranked included number sense, number meaning, number use, addition, subtraction, accuracy, and speed. All teachers were blind to the treatment status of the children they were rating.

The four tests were administered in May of the school year by two of the project staff, one of whom was blind to the child's treatment status. Testing was usually completed in one session. If two sessions were required owing to fatigue on the part of the child, they were spaced a few days apart. The rating scale was given to the child's classroom teacher on the first day of the follow-up testing.

Results

Using data obtained from the pretest, our first analysis focused on establishing which items on the Number Knowledge test proved to be among the most difficult to pass at the unidimensional level. Recall that all children in this sample ($N = 55$) had failed to meet the pretest pass criterion established for this test (i.e., five of seven items correct at Level 1). However, within this global criterion, there was room for considerable variation in the error patterns demonstrated by individual children. An item analysis of the data revealed that the items posing the greatest difficulty for the greatest number of children were those that indexed components of the structure that had been identified in the earlier study as being critical, namely, knowledge of relative quantity and of the generative rule. On the two items that assessed this knowledge, only 36% of the sample were able to tell which of two numbers was bigger or smaller, and only 13% were able to tell how many objects they would have if they received four objects followed by three more. While difficulty on the first item suggests the absence of the general

TABLE 14

PERCENTAGES OF CHILDREN PASSING THE SECOND ADMINISTRATION
OF THE NUMBER KNOWLEDGE TEST AND THE FIVE NUMERICAL
TRANSFER TESTS AT THE UNIDIMENSIONAL LEVEL

Test[a]	Control Group (N = 24)	Treatment Group (N = 23)
Number Knowledge (6/7)	25	87
Balance Beam (2/2)	42	96
Birthday Party (2/2)	42	96
Time Telling (4/5)	21	83
Money Knowledge (4/6)	17	43
Distributive Justice (2/2)	37	87

[a] Number of items out of the total used as the criteria for passing the test is given in parentheses.

conceptual knowledge inherent in the mental number line structure, difficulty with the second item indicates the absence of the particular aspect of this knowledge on which the solution of first grade addition and subtraction problems is most directly dependent.

Turning to the effects of treatment, Table 14 shows the percentages of children in the treatment and control groups who performed at the unidimensional level on the Number Knowledge test and the five transfer tests at the end of the kindergarten year. A strong majority of the treatment group (87%) passed the Number Knowledge test, whereas only a minority of the children in the control group (25%) achieved the same level of success (recall that, at the pretest, no child in either group had passed this test at this level). A similar pattern of differential performance was obtained on each transfer test. On four of these, the difference between the groups was substantial, and the proportions of children who passed were commensurate with the proportions passing the Number Knowledge test. Results of a multivariate analysis of variance indicated a significant difference between the treatment group and the control group on the overall battery of quantitative tasks (i.e., the Number Knowledge test and the five transfer tests; $F[1, 70] = 23.46, p < .001$).

In the present study, the percentage of the research sample passing the Number Knowledge pretest was lower than in the previous study (0% vs. 15%). However, as the data in Table 14 indicate, the proportion of the treatment group passing the posttest was higher than in the previous study (87% vs. 80%), and the proportions passing the transfer tests were also higher (87% vs. 51%). Overall, then, the training given in Study 2 appears to have been more effective than that provided in Study 1. Training effects were consistent across the three school sites on the composite scores that

TABLE 15

PERCENTAGES OF CHILDREN IN THE FOLLOW-UP GROUP PASSING THE NUMBER
KNOWLEDGE TEST AND ARITHMETIC LEARNING/ACHIEVEMENT MEASURES
AT THE END OF GRADE 1

Test	Control Group (N = 12)	Treatment Group (N = 11)	Significance of Difference
Number Knowledge test:			
Level 1 (undimensional)	83	100	N.S.
Level 2 (bidimensional)	0	18	*
Oral arithmetic	33	82	*
Written arithmetic	75	91	N.S.
Word problems:			
Level 1	54	96	*
Level 2	13	46	*
Teacher rating:			
Number sense	24	100	*
Number meaning	42	88	*
Number use	42	88	*
Addition	66	100	N.S.
Subtraction	66	100	N.S.
Accuracy	59	63	N.S.
Speed	42	75	N.S.

* Significant at the .01 level or better.

were computed for each school, although they varied somewhat in specific content domains. No significant sex differences were obtained.

Turning to the results of the follow-up study (displayed in Table 15), we found that, by the end of the first grade, 83% of the control group now demonstrated unidimensional number knowledge on the Number Knowledge test. However, the comparable percentage in the treatment group was 100%, and quite a number of children in this group had moved onto the bidimensional level (18%). Moreover, the treatment group outperformed the control group on every other measure included in the first grade battery. The difference between the groups was significant in a multivariance analysis on (a) Level 2 of the Number Knowledge test, which assessed the ability to solve double-digit number problems that were normed at the 8-year-old level and are not typically taught in the first grade ($F = 7.26$, $p < .01$), (b) the Oral Arithmetic test, (c) the Word Problems test at Level 1 and Level 2 ($t = 3.59$, $p < .01$), and (d) the three items on the Teacher Rating scale that most directly tap the conceptual knowledge that the Rightstart program was designed to teach, namely, demonstrates number sense, understands the meaning of numbers, and understands the use of numbers.

In all, these findings suggest (a) that the knowledge acquired in kindergarten through the treatment program was still available to the children when they started the first grade, (b) that many children in the control group acquired this knowledge at some point during their first grade experience, and (c) that the treatment group still maintained an advantage over the control group in many areas, presumably because these children arrived in school with the conceptual structure necessary for further mathematical learning already in place.

Discussion

All three of the questions posed at the beginning of Study 2 may be answered in the affirmative on the basis of its results. (1) The effects of the Rightstart program are clearly not unique to children who have immigrated to North American cities from other, more rural environments. (2) The improved learning of formal arithmetic that was demonstrated in Study 1 is not unique to the sort of short-term training situation to which we exposed children in that study. It is also demonstrable in the more naturalistic setting of the school and continues to operate up to a full year later. (3) The second version of the Rightstart program does appear to have a stronger effect than the first did, both with regard to what is learned and with regard to what is transferred.

Additional Studies

The questions addressed in the two studies reported in this chapter by no means exhaust the list of those that could be asked from either a theoretical or an educational standpoint. Among these, a further question one could ask is whether the effects produced by the Rightstart program are unique to children's central conceptual structure for number or whether they are also manifest in structures such as those discussed in other chapters—the narrative structure, for example, or the structure for representing space. There is no a priori reason why one instructional program could not have an effect on several different central conceptual structures. However, if such multiple effects were found invariably, this would run counter to the hypothesis that central conceptual structures are modular.

The question of cross-structural transfer was investigated directly in a recent study of a group of low-income children in California. In this study, the first version of the Rightstart program was used for one group, and a treatment that had been developed for teaching narrative structure (McKeough, 1992b) was used for another. The results indicated that children receiving the narrative training showed transfer to most of the tasks on the narrative battery but no transfer to any of the tasks on the quantitative battery, whereas children exposed to Rightstart showed the opposite effect, transfer to all the tasks on the quantitative battery (as in the present studies) but no transfer to the narrative tasks (Case, Okamoto, Henderson,

TABLE 16

PERCENTAGE OF CHILDREN PASSING THE NUMBER KNOWLEDGE
TEST AND THREE NUMERICAL TRANSFER TESTS AT THE
UNIDIMENSIONAL LEVEL

TEST[a]	CONTROL GROUP ($N = 36$)		TREATMENT GROUP ($N = 36$)	
	Pre	Post	Pre	Post
Number Knowledge (6/7)	6	14	8	53
Balance Beam (2/2)	[b]	33	[b]	70
Time Telling (4/5)	[b]	22	[b]	67
Money Knowledge (4/6)	[b]	8	[b]	22

[a] Number of items out of the total used as the criteria for passing the test is given in parentheses.

[b] Not administered.

& McKeough, 1993). The "modularity" of these structures was thus supported.

A further question that one might ask concerns the importance of the individual attention and of the game-like exercises that children in the Rightstart program received. How important are these elements of the program in producing the success that we reported? The performance of the control groups that we introduced in Study 1 suggests that the treatment group's success cannot be *solely* attributed to the game-like format or small-group attention (since the control groups received these as well). However, it does not rule out the possibility that these aspects of the treatment program played a crucial role. To address this question directly, the Rightstart program was converted to a "whole-class" format in a further follow-up study. Because the program was administered to a whole class of children in this study, games and individual attention of necessity played a smaller role. As indicated in Table 16, although the results were considerably weaker, they were still significant. We interpret these findings as indicating that small-group formats and game-like activities are, in fact, a valuable part of the program, presumably because they enable children to acquire and utilize the knowledge contained in the central numerical structure more easily. On the other hand, these activities are not absolutely necessary, as long as children get some introduction to the requisite knowledge.

CONCLUDING COMMENTS

Considering the pattern of data across all four studies (i.e., the two studies that we reported in detail and the follow-up studies that we summarized), the following theoretical conclusions appear to be warranted:

1. The knowledge specified in Figure 16 is crucial for achieving a 6-year-old (unidimensional) level of success on a broad range of developmental tasks that involve a quantitative component: both on tasks such as are typically used by developmental psychologists to assess children's level of cognitive development and on tasks that constitute the formal learning experiences to which children are typically exposed at this age. If the knowledge depicted in Figure 16 is not present, children do not perform at the level normative for their age group.

2. Of the components specified in Figure 16, the last to be acquired yet the most crucial for success on unidimensional tasks are (a) the components that link ordinal judgments that are made on a purely verbal basis (three, four, etc.) with those that link cardinal judgments about set size, (b) the components that link adjacent items in the ordinal series (i.e., the "increment or decrement by 1" rule), and (c) the components that link judgments of numerical magnitude with judgments involving other dimensions such as height, weight, etc.

3. These components are often absent for environmental reasons (e.g., insufficient opportunity in the preschool years to use numbers in contexts that would make these links salient). They can be put in place by an appropriate instructional program, however, and—when they are—children's performance rises to age-level expectations on a broad range of tasks within the quantitative domain while remaining unchanged in other domains.

Several additional conclusions of an educational nature appear warranted. The first is that a surprising proportion of children from low-income North American families—at least 50% in our samples—do not arrive in school with the central cognitive structure in place that is necessary for success in first grade mathematics. The second is that, if nothing is done to intervene, the school may act as a "magnifier" of what otherwise might be very small differences in the children's initial "number sense." For some, their first learning of addition and subtraction may be a meaningless experience and may lead to strategies for "surviving" in school math rather than "thriving" in it (Biemiller, 1993).

Finally, it appears that this situation need not persist: with a relatively small investment, a curriculum that does a better job of meeting children at their own level can be put in place. Children at every level of skill can be enabled to construct the conceptual structure that they need and to use it to profit from the sort of instruction to which they are typically exposed in the first grade. Further curricular changes may be necessary at higher grades (see Griffin, in preparation), but the cycle of school failure will at least have been broken at the most crucial point, namely, the point at which it normally gets started.

V. CENTRAL SPATIAL STRUCTURES AND THEIR DEVELOPMENT

Robbie Case, Kimberly Marra Stephenson, Charles Bleiker,
and Yukari Okamoto

In the previous four chapters, our main focus was on children's representation of number and social interaction. In this chapter, we focus on children's representation of space. The history of research in this domain is similar to that in the previous two domains. Early in the century, certain spatial tasks (e.g., drawing, figure copying, handwriting) were established as classic indices of development in this area, and the performance of different age groups on them was chronicled. When Piaget and Inhelder (1956) became interested in children's representation of space, they interpreted these classic data in terms of their theory and gathered a wealth of new data to support their interpretation.

According to Piaget and Inhelder's analysis, certain elementary spatial features of objects (e.g., size, contour) are apprehended during the "sensorimotor" stage. The location of objects in space is also apprehended during this stage, first in a fashion where each object is referenced to the infant's own body, and later "allocentrically," that is, in a fashion where the position of each object is referenced to its surroundings. At the beginning of the representational stage, both sorts of spatial properties (i.e., relation to self and relation to surrounds) are represented in a symbolic rather than a "sensorimotor" format. Three stages are then traversed, in which children represent these features: first, in a topological fashion (2–7 years); second, in a projective or Euclidean fashion (7–12 years); and, third, in an explicit, formal fashion that permits them to master systems of representation such as plane geometry (12–18 years).

Piaget and his colleagues designed a number of new tasks that were intended to demonstrate this developmental progression and highlight some of its most important features (Piaget & Inhelder, 1956; Piaget, Inhelder, & Szeminska, 1960). As these tasks became known, they were standardized and administered to larger groups of children (Laurendeau & Pinard, 1970). Although the individual tasks did show the general progression that Piaget had described in his studies, the overall pattern did not appear to be nearly as coherent, as monolithic, or as stage-like as he had proposed. Attempts to resolve these difficulties took two directions in the 1970s and 1980s. One was to explore the properties of Piaget and Inhelder's tasks in greater detail and to show how their norms were affected by such variables as training, presentation format, and perceptual salience (e.g., Accredolo, 1979; Flavell, Omanson, & Latham, 1978; Flavell, Shipstead, & Grofit, 1978; Liben & Down, 1989). The other was to use the tools of modern cognitive science to model children's representations of spatial tasks with greater precision (e.g., Freeman, 1972, 1980; Halford & McDonald, 1977; Morra, Moizo, & Scopesi, 1988; Olson, 1970; Olson & Bialystok, 1983; Simon, 1972).

During the late 1980s, our research group conducted two studies of children's spatial cognition, using the new form of structural analysis that we had developed. In the first study, Dennis investigated the changes in children's drawing between the ages of 4 and 10. On the basis of previous research, she already knew that 4-year-olds are able to depict certain global features of objects in drawings but that they do not attempt to capture the second-order relations that prevail among them. By the age of 6, children do represent these second-order relations; as a consequence, they tend to situate the main object that they are drawing in a graphically defined context or "scene." At 8 years of age, children often draw two such scenes, one in the foreground and one in the background. Finally, at age 10 years, children will often include an "intermediate" or "middle ground" in their drawings and produce scenes in which space appears continuous rather than discontinuous (Case, Marini, McKeough, Dennis, & Goldberg, 1986).

In keeping with neo-Piagetian theory, Dennis interpreted this pattern as reflecting a broader four-stage progression in children's thought. (1) At the end of the relational stage, children consolidate certain fundamental schemas (in this case, schemas for drawing objects). (2) During the first period of the dimensional stage, they coordinate these schemas with each other, thus creating some form of higher-order structure (in this case, the "scene"). (3) As they progress through the dimensional stage, they differentiate different forms of this new structure from each other (hence the foreground-background differentiation). (4) Finally, as they reach the end of the stage, they integrate these newly differentiated structures into a coherent system (a unified picture).

To test her hypothesis, Dennis (1992) asked children to draw a set of pictures with prespecified foreground and background relations. In one such task, children were asked to draw a picture of "a mother and a father holding hands in a park, with their little baby playing on the grass in front of them and a tree far off behind." The drawings that emerged indicated that the general pattern was as hypothesized (see Fig. 17).

Soon after Dennis completed her study, Reid (1992) examined children's gross motor development during the same age range (i.e., 4–10 years). On the basis of preliminary work, she advanced the following developmental hypothesis. (1) At age 4 years, children cannot yet track the incoming movement of a ball along some particular axis and then direct it back with a racquet or bat along the same axis. (2) Six-year-olds are capable of this sort of coordination because they can construct a "mental corridor" in space. (3) Eight-year-olds can differentiate the incoming corridor of flight from an outgoing corridor and switch their attention from one to the other at the moment of impact. (4) Finally, 10-year-olds can sustain a focus on two potential corridors or axes simultaneously and hit a ball along a trajectory that goes forward an equal distance along both (i.e., a diagonal).

The task that Reid used to test her hypothesis involved batting a sponge ball back across a 2.5-foot-high tennis net from a distance of 5 feet when the ball was tossed to them. As illustrated in Figure 18, three variants of this task were created. In the first, children simply had to hit the ball back along the same trajectory as the one that it had traveled to reach them. In the second, they had to track the ball as it came along one trajectory and then hit it out along another that was set at 90°. In the third, they had to track the ball along one trajectory and hit it out along a diagonal. As she had predicted, Reid found that these three tasks were mastered by children at 6, 8, and 10 years of age, respectively. In a manner similar to Dennis's, she interpreted her findings to indicate that, at 6 years of age, children construct a new form of mental unit (the mental corridor, or "axis"). At the age of 8, they are able to differentiate two forms of these new units from each other, at least in a tentative fashion. By the age of 10 years, they are able to generate a performance in which these differentiated units are integrated in an "on-line" fashion.

As described by Dennis and Reid, the similarities between the development of children's drawing and their skill at tennis are quite abstract. A question that therefore arose was whether some other form of commonality, one that is more concrete and/or substantive, might not prevail among these tasks. In short, the question that arose was whether there might not be some sort of central conceptual structure that might underpin children's performance on both tasks. This possibility was raised but not explored in our previous work (Case, 1992a, p. 227).

a

b

c

d

FIG. 17.—Typical pictures drawn by children from four different age groups in response to the request, "Draw a picture of a mother and a father holding hands in a park, with their little baby on the grass in front of them, and a tree far off behind." (From Dennis, 1992.) *a*, Four-year-old. *b*, Six-year-old. *c*, Eight-year-old. *d*, Ten-year-old.

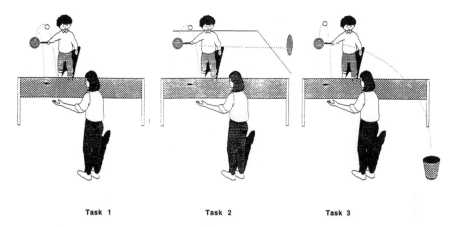

Task 1   Task 2   Task 3

FIG. 18.—Three tasks presented to young children. In the first, the ball must just be hit back over the net. In the second, the child must hit the target stationed laterally to her left. In the third, the child must hit the bucket stationed to the experimenter's right. The expectation (which was confirmed) was that these tasks would be appropriate for children aged 6, 8, and 10, respectively. (From Reid, 1992.)

SPECIFYING THE CONTENT OF CHILDREN'S
CENTRAL CONCEPTUAL STRUCTURES FOR SPACE

What sort of central conceptual structure might underlie 6-year-olds' performance on motor and/or spatial tasks? To answer this question, we began by asking ourselves the prior question as to whether there was any commonality in what is needed to direct a ball along a "mental corridor" with a racquet and to draw a flat "scene" of the sort that characterizes a 6-year-old's art. Although many possible answers might be ventured (including that no commonality exists at all!), the idea that occurred to us was that both tasks require children to calibrate the distance from one or more objects to a ground line in a very careful fashion. On the tennis task, children must note the height at which the ball arrives in front of them relative to the ground on which they are standing—if they do not, they will fail to make contact with the ball. Concurrently, they must also be conscious of the height of the net—otherwise, they will be unable to direct the ball back with the sort of "sweep" that will ensure that it clears the net (this is, in fact, the most common mistake made by 4-year-olds; they quite often manage to hit the ball with the racquet but fail to direct it in such a fashion that it goes over the net). Although most of the specific requirements needed to succeed on Dennis's drawing task are quite different, awareness of relative heights remains a central condition: children must position each individual object that they are asked to draw so that the relative height from the objects to the bottom of the page mirrors the relative height of the same objects in the real world. Thus, the grass must be drawn along the bottom of the page and the sky at the top. The father's head must then extend the furthest up from the ground line, the mother's head just a little less, and so on.

This same general requirement appears to characterize a good many of the other tasks that children master in this age range, including those that are normally regarded as assessments of children's logical capabilities rather than of their spatial cognition. One of these is the test of seriation, a task in which a set of dowels must be placed in descending order of height with regard to some real or imagined ground line. Another is the pretest for conservation, in which children must note the height of two columns of liquid in order to make sure that they are exactly "the same."

If a central conceptual structure that permits this sort of calibration does exist, it might also be useful for performance of certain school tasks such as learning to print letters along an imaginary baseline while maintaining their correct relative height. In fact, one could hypothesize that, just as children's construction of a mental counting line is facilitated by school experience with numbers and numerals, their construction of a "mental reference line" may be facilitated by exposure to school copybooks and the task of neatly printing words along the lines that these books contain. The structure's acquisition might also be facilitated by computer games in which a character moves along a baseline and must be "jumped" to hit targets at different heights (as in the Nintendo game Mario Brothers).

In Chapter I, we included a figure to illustrate our first attempt to specify the various elements that such a "mental reference axis" might entail (Fig. 6 above). What the figure was meant to suggest is that children can look at any scene—be it in the three-dimensional world or on paper—and encode the various relations that they see there as though they were being projected on a window, that is, as though the objects were lying in a flat plane. Not only can children who possess such a structure note the internal shapes of any object, but they can also locate the object within the rectangular contours of the imaginary window: they can specify the general "sector" in which the object lies (e.g., near the top, the bottom, side A, or side B), and they can also specify with precision how far each object extends from one edge of the window. It is this imaginary edge that gives the structure its name: the *mental reference line*.

In the everyday world, the reference line that children use for calibrating relative distance is normally the ground. In tasks that are encountered in the "world on paper," the reference line is normally the side of the paper that is nearest to the child (which we call the "bottom" of the page). In other tasks, the reference line can be an edge where the ceiling meets the floor of a room. The key point is that children can construct a rectangular plane and then reference the location of any object within that plane to one of its edges while simultaneously taking account of the object's own internal spatial features.

In the example depicted in Figure 6 above, the two objects were people. The expectation is that children should be able to calibrate the relative height of the people quite precisely, both with regard to the ground in the three-dimensional world and with regard to the bottom of a piece of paper. We do *not* presume that children can calibrate the lateral distance between the two people as precisely, at least not without losing track of the calibration from the ground. Thus, in the illustrated example, the person on the right would probably be encoded as being just "over to the side" of the person on the left, whereas the relative height could be given a precise analogical value (i.e., "this" much higher, with the fingers indicating the amount).

If the structure that we postulate really exists, then it should be possible to identify two or more precursor structures that give rise to it and that are present in the repertoires of younger children. Figure 5 above (also in Chap. I) represents our first attempt to suggest two likely candidates. The first of the schemas illustrated in this figure enables children to represent—with a tool such as a pencil or their forefinger—the outlines of familiar objects and the shapes of their major parts. It is this schema that produces the universal pattern that is observed in children's drawing at this age: the "tadpole" man, a form created with a circle and lines that radiate out from its circumference (Kellogg, 1969; Luquet, 1927).

The second schema that appears to be available at 4 years of age is one that is used for specifying the general location of any object with regard to the field of which it is a part. We conjecture that this schema underpins children's developing ability to use photos or models as representational devices that can help them find an object in a room (DeLoache, 1989). It also enables them to encode, remember, and retrieve the location of a spot of color on any part of a familiar grid (Crammond, 1992) or to arrange a set of small objects in a straight line within a frame (Halford & McDonald, 1977). Finally, we hypothesize that, between 4 and 6 years of age, children's object-shape schemas and their object-location schemas are further differentiated and integrated with each other. The result is the uniaxial mental reference window that is illustrated in Figure 6.

Our final proposal concerns development after the age of 6. We propose that, at the age of 8, children become capable of referencing the objects in a rectangular grid to two different reference lines or axes rather than just one and that, at the age of 10, they become capable of referencing any single object to two reference lines simultaneously. In our culture, this latter structure is of particular importance for mastering the system of Cartesian coordinates and the system for representing perspective. Accordingly, we propose that both these systems should be apprehended and used—at least in a qualitative fashion—by the age of 10 years. The overall developmental progression we hypothesize is illustrated in Figure 19.

CREATING A BATTERY FOR ASSESSING CHILDREN'S CENTRAL SPATIAL STRUCTURES

As a prelude to conducting an empirical study, we first created a battery of nine spatial tasks. Following the same methodology that we had used in studying children's numerical development, four levels of item were created for each task, one corresponding to each of the hypothesized levels of structure.

1. *Seriation.*—This task was based on Piaget's task in which the experimenter shows the child a drawing depicting a set of sticks. The drawing is then removed, and the child is asked to arrange a set of real sticks of varying lengths into the same pattern. Our presentation differed only in that we substituted white pieces of cardboard to which dowels of several lengths were glued.

Sample items for each level are illustrated in Figure 20. The rationale for these items was as follows. (1) The *preaxial* items show a simple array of three objects, with a big stick on one side, a small one on the other, and a mid-sized stick in between. No careful linear arrangement by height is necessary to reproduce this pattern; the child simply has to treat the sticks as though they were in a grid and place each one in approximately the right position. (2) The items at the *uniaxial* level require that a larger set of sticks—which differ only slightly in height—be arranged so that their tops form a decreasing or an increasing series and their bottoms form a straight line parallel to the bottom of the page. For this item, it is necessary to align the bottom of each stick with some sort of ground line and make sure that each successive stick protrudes just a little more (or less) than the previous one. (3) At the *biaxial* level, the test items require that a set of sticks be ordered so that the top edge forms a decreasing and the bottom edge an increasing series by height. The position of the two series can be referenced to an implied horizontal line through the middle of the array or two lines, one running parallel to the top and one parallel to the bottom edge of the page. In either case, it is necessary to use two mental reference axes rather than just one. (4) Finally, for the two items at the *integrated biaxial* level, the sticks have to be ordered not just with respect to the top and bottom edges of the frame but also with respect to the side edges. This requires the use of two orthogonal reference axes.

2. *Checkers.*—The Checkers task that we developed was based on prior work by Olson (1970) and by Halford and McDonald (1977). In our version of their test, children were shown a set of small checkers

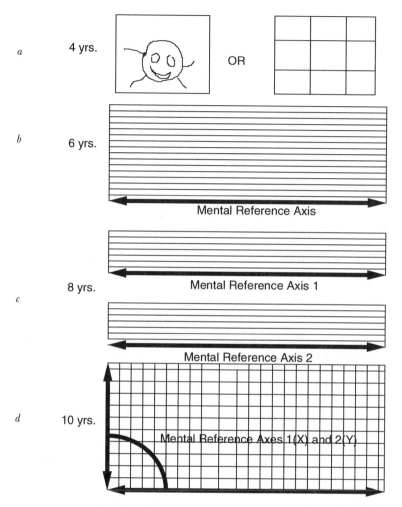

FIG. 19.—The hypothesized progression in children's central spatial competencies between 4 and 10 years of age. Panel *a* indicates the preaxial schemas possessed by 4-year-olds for representing the component shapes of an object and the location of an object in a rectangular field (see Fig. 5 above). Panel *b* indicates the uniaxial schema possessed by 6-year-olds, which can conjointly specify an object's internal shapes and spatial relations and its location relative to the edge of a field (see Fig. 6 above). Panel *c* indicates the new biaxial capability acquired by 8-year-olds, i.e., the capability of setting up two discrete representations in different locations, each referenced to a different axis. Panel *d* indicates that 10-year-olds can now conjointly reference a whole field of objects to two discrete mental reference axes that are orthogonal to each other.

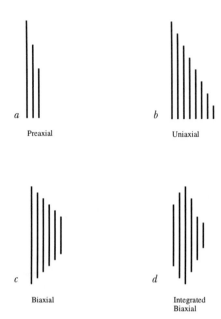

FIG. 20.—Examples of items presented at each of four levels (*a*, preaxial; *b*, uniaxial; *c*, biaxial; *d*, integrated biaxial) on the Seriation task. The child's task is to reproduce the pattern of sticks indicated at each level with a set of sticks of his or her own.

(plastic rings) glued on a piece of cardboard on which a grid had been ruled. This initial display was then removed, and the children were asked to reproduce the pattern that they had seen by placing a second set of rings in the empty grid drawn on an identical piece of cardboard.

Once again, the items were presented in hypothesized order of difficulty, as illustrated in Figure 21. The rationale for classifying the items was as follows. (1) Items at the *preaxial* level required the child to put the rings in a straight line that goes across the middle of the board or down one edge: as long as they get the line in the right general location on the grid and put each successive checker next to it, they are scored as correct. Thus, all they need to succeed in is the preaxial grid schema. (2) On *uniaxial* items, the children have to construct a series of diagonal rings, with each end of the line anchored in a corner. Our interpretation of this task is that it is much like the seriation task. Each successive checker must be placed "next" to its predecessor but also 1 unit further up from the baseline. (3) Items at the *biaxial* level require children to break the overall display into two halves, each containing the same sort of diagonal pattern as they constructed at the uniaxial level. Accordingly, we hypothesized that two mental reference windows must be used instead of one. (4) Finally, items at the *integrated*

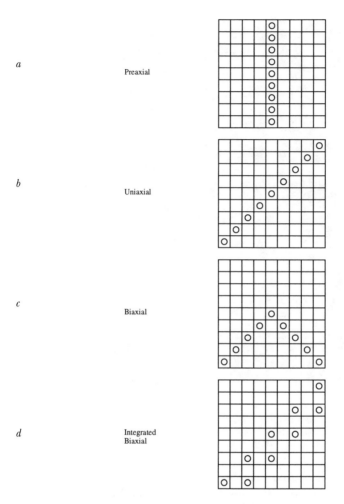

FIG. 21.—An example of items presented at each of four levels (*a*, preaxial; *b*, uniaxial; *c*, biaxial; *d*, integrated biaxial) on the Checkers task. The child's task is to look at the patterns indicated, then reproduce the pattern with a set of small rings ("checkers") in an empty matrix.

biaxial level require careful and simultaneous calibration of each ring with regard to its distance from each of the two orthogonal axes.

3. *Map Drawing.*—This task was based on a task designed by Liben and Down (1989). The scoring criteria were developed by Berg (1991). Children were shown a map of their kindergarten classroom and told that the experimenter had pretended that she was up in an airplane looking down into the classroom at the time she made the drawing. Each symbol on the map was pointed out and labeled (e.g., "See? Here is the rug; here is the chalkboard; here is the teacher's desk"). The

113

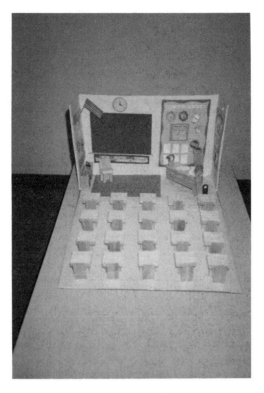

FIG. 22.—The model classroom shown to young children on the Map Drawing task. The child's task is to draw a map of this classroom "as though you were a bird, looking down on it." Children's maps are then classified according to the system described in the text, as either *preaxial, uniaxial, biaxial,* or *integrated biaxial.*

children were then told that this wasn't a regular picture but a map. Finally, they were asked to draw their own map of the model classroom depicted in Figure 22.

In scoring the children's drawings, it was assumed that those who were functioning at the *preaxial* level would draw recognizable objects whose shapes and approximate sizes might be correct but whose position relative to the walls would not be accurately represented. *Uniaxial* children were expected to use a reference line, such as a wall, in aligning the objects that they drew but not to reference any object to two orthogonal walls simultaneously. Children with *biaxial* capabilities were expected to lay out two uniaxial drawings: one to represent the plane formed by the main floor plan of the classroom and one to represent the plane formed by the front wall. Alternatively, they were expected to reproduce the "rows and columns" layout of the desks in the main floor section, but with some considerable drift, owing to the absence of the ability to locate each desk with regard to two orthogonal

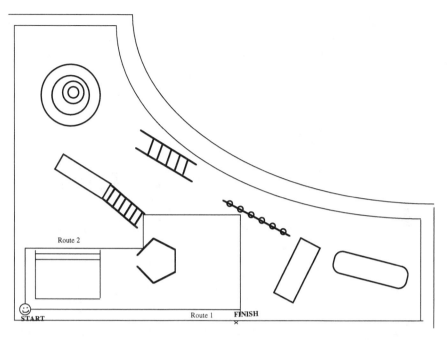

Fig. 23.—A map of the playground at school in which the spatial study was conducted. Children were asked to walk along the straight path (Route 1) for practice, then along the irregularly shaped route among the various pieces of apparatus (Route 2). The route that they actually walked along was recorded by the experimenter and its match to the prespecified route coded according to the system described in the text.

axes simultaneously. Finally, children using *integrated biaxial* structures were expected to depict all the objects in the classroom, as though they were conjointly referenced on a Cartesian grid.

4. *Map Following.*—For this task, children were taken to the sandbox area of their school playground. A previously prepared map of this area that had been mounted on a piece of thick cardboard (see Fig. 23) was then shown to them. The experimenter first explained this map to the children, pointing out the objects whose position it indicated. She then asked them to follow a simple route going from their existing position along the edge of the playground to an object indicated on the map (Route 1). After the children had attempted this task (usually successfully), they were then given the map and asked to take the more circuitous trip indicated on it.

The path actually taken by the child was recorded by the experimenter. Owing to the simplicity of the first route and its designation with clear beginning and ending markers, it is not necessary to use a mental reference axis in order to follow it. Accordingly, we assumed that children with *preaxial* structures would be able to navigate it successfully. *Uniaxial* children were expected to be successful in following

115

the global contour of Route 2. This expectation was based on the assumption that they would be able to scrutinize the overall contour of the route and encode it as going "up and away" from the baseline of the playground, then "over" for a while, then back down toward the baseline. They should also be able to represent a physical path that actually followed this route by winding through the indicated set of objects in the way that a ship might pass between the port and starboard buoys in a channel, going "forward" and "over" the required distance on each leg of the journey.

At the *biaxial* level, we assumed that children would be able to hold an original course that was parallel to the vertical side of the map (i.e., one edge of the playground) until they touched the first object indicated on the map, then alter course with a right-angled turn, set out on a course parallel to the second (orthogonal) boundary of the playground until they reached the second indicated object, and continue on in this manner until arriving at the final point on the map. In effect, we assumed that they would be able to navigate the entire route using a right-angled "tacking" strategy in which each successive "tack" was referenced to a different edge of the playground. Finally, we presumed that children with *integrated biaxial* capabilities not only would be able to "tack" from one object to the next (alternating between two reference axes, as it were) but would also be able to hit the precise point indicated on each object, even if the object were located diagonally to their charted path of movement and thus had to be conjointly referenced to the two right-angled axes simultaneously.

5. *Still Life Drawing.*—This test was originally suggested to us by Ellen Winner, for reasons that are outlined in the next chapter. The scoring criteria were developed by Bleiker (1995). Children were shown a display consisting of a coffee cup standing on a table with an upside-down toothbrush inside it and a tube of toothpaste lying in front of and next to it. They were then provided with a set of colored pencils and a blank sheet of paper and asked to draw the display.

In scoring the drawings, we presumed that children at the *preaxial* level would be able to indicate the general shape of the most salient part of each object as well as the adjacency relations among them. Thus, for example, they should be able to depict the cup as a circle (for the opening) and the handle as a sort of U shape and place the second shape (the toothpaste tube) so that it is very close to (ideally, touching) the first. At the *uniaxial* level they should be able to view the objects "in side view," that is, as though they were projected on a vertical plane whose bottom edge is in line with the top edge of the table. With this edge as the reference line, they should be able to draw the basic shapes that the objects present, as seen in Figure 24*b*.

Children at the *biaxial* level should be able to depict the projection of each object onto two different planes. As at the previous level, the cup should be rendered as a rectangle (its side view), but it should now have a circle (its top view) indicated at the top of the rectangle as well.

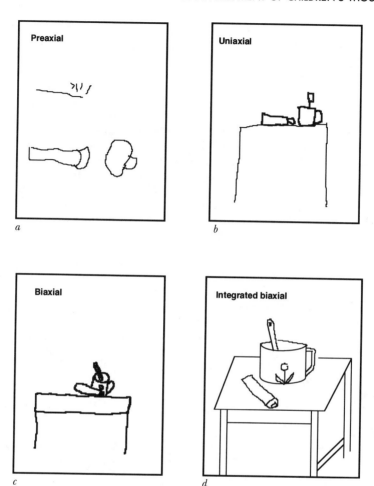

FIG. 24.—Examples of still life drawings drawn by children that would be classified at each of the levels indicated (*a*, preaxial; *b*, uniaxial; *c*, biaxial; *d*, integrated biaxial). The objects presented are a cup, a toothbrush, and a tube of toothpaste. The most faithful representation is the one classified as *integrated biaxial*.

This form of drawing is sometimes referred to as "characteristic view rendering." Finally, as at the previous level, we presumed that children at the *integrated biaxial* level would be capable of coordinating the depiction of each of the two separate planes of the object but that they would now be able to do so in a more integrated fashion, that is, with the shapes the way they would appear when seen from a single viewpoint. In operational terms, this means that the children should draw the opening of the cup more as an oval than as a circle (as in Fig. 24*d*).

6. *Picture Drawing.*—This test was taken directly from Dennis's

(1992) study. Children were asked to draw a picture of a mother and a daughter holding hands in a park, with a little baby in front of them and a tree far off behind.

The pictures that the children created were scored as *preaxial* if there was no implied ground line, *uniaxial* if there was a single implied ground line, *biaxial* if there was a different implied ground line for foreground and background objects, and *integrated biaxial* if there were a foreground, background, and unifying middle ground in between (see Fig. 17 above).

7. *Handwriting.*—Children were told that the experimenter had a little dog at home named Gargoyle, a name selected because it was unlikely to be familiar to children and because it had lowercase letters with descenders projecting below the implied baseline axis (as in the letter *g*) as well as ascenders extending above the x-height (as in the letter *l*). They were then shown a card with this name printed on it and asked to copy it on a blank sheet of white paper.

Children at the *preaxial* level were expected to be able to reproduce the general configuration of most of the letters but not to align the overall name with the horizontal edges of the paper. Children at the *uniaxial* level were expected to place the letters along a single implied axis in such a way that a straight line could be drawn through all the letters. Children at the *biaxial* level were expected to be able to arrange the small letters along one implied line and the capital letters and other large letters (e.g., *l*) along a second one. Finally, children at the *integrated biaxial* level were expected to be able to reproduce the name in cursive writing and to succeed in drawing the diagonal lines connecting letters in a neat and appropriate fashion.

In addition to these seven core tasks, we used two other tasks drawn from the classic Piagetian tradition, to supplement the Seriation test.

8. *Beakers.*—This was a judgment-of-quantity task in which two partially filled beakers were shown to the child, who was asked to judge which of the two contained more water.

Beaker pairs aimed at the *preaxial* level had a substantial difference in beaker diameter and a correlated difference in the height of the liquid columns that they contained. The child had to scan the array globally, pick the correct beaker, and justify the choice by referring to some aspect of the display (e.g., "Because it is up here"). Beaker pairs at the *uniaxial* level were equal in diameter, and the height of the liquid columns differed very little. Children had to choose the correct beaker on two out of three trials and mention height as the reason for their choice. At the *biaxial* level, the liquid columns of the beaker pair were of the same height, and the difference in the beakers' diameters was small. Children had to choose the correct beaker (in two of three trials) and justify their answer by mentioning diameter in some fashion (e.g.,

"This one's wider/fatter/etc."). Finally, beaker pairs at the *integrated biaxial* level differed in both liquid column height and diameter and were constructed so that the higher liquid column contained less liquid than the shorter one. Children did not have to be correct on all items, but they did have to analyze each one carefully and make some sort of compensation argument to justify their response (e.g., "Well, this one looks a little wider, but this one is a lot taller, so I think this one probably has more").

9. *Judgments of Length.*—This task was adapted from Piaget's work on conservation of length. Children were asked to pick out the longer or shorter of two lines that were drawn on paper; the difficulty of this judgment was increased from one trial to the next by offsetting the lines by differing amounts (Piaget & Inhelder, 1956). A subject's score was the total number of correct judgments made in this situation.

STUDY 1: EXAMINING THE COHERENCE OF THE TEST BATTERY

The objective of our first empirical study in this series was to determine whether the tasks in our test battery formed a coherent correlational cluster and could therefore be construed as assessing a common underlying factor.

Method

Subjects

Fifty-seven kindergarten and first grade children were recruited from two parochial elementary schools located in the San Francisco Bay Area. There were 34 kindergartners (11 boys and 23 girls) and 23 first graders (10 boys and 13 girls); their mean ages were 5-9 (SD = 5.2 months) and 7-2 (SD = 3.9 months), respectively. Both schools served middle-class communities of families of diverse ethnic backgrounds. In one school, approximately half the children were European-Americans, with Hispanics and Filipinos and a few Asian- and African-Americans making up the other half. In the other school, the children came from European- and Mexican-American families with approximately 10% Asian-Americans and a few African-Americans.

Procedures

Children were tested individually. All tasks but the Map Following task (which was presented in the schoolyard) were administered in an empty schoolroom. Each child was tested in two separate sessions, lasting approxi-

TABLE 17

INTERRATER RELIABILITIES FOR SPATIAL TASKS ($N = 59$)

	Correlation (r)	% Agreement
Checkers		100
Seriation		97
Map Drawing	.91	
Map Following	.96	
Picture Drawing	.82	
Still Life Drawing		98
Name Writing	.84	
Beakers		95
Length Judgment		95

mately 30 min each. The order of task administration varied from child to child in order to accommodate the school's schedule and the time that was made available. Two research assistants who had been trained to administer the spatial battery conducted the sessions.

Results

Preliminary Analyses

All tasks were scored independently by the two research assistants who administered the test battery. As may be seen from Table 17, the interrater reliabilities proved satisfactory for each measure.

A preliminary analysis of variance indicated no significant sex differences on any of the tasks separately or for the battery as a whole. Accordingly, boys and girls were treated as a single group in all the analyses that followed. Table 18 presents the mean scores and medians for each age

TABLE 18

MEAN AND MEDIAN SCORES OBTAINED BY THE 6-YEAR-OLD
SAMPLE ON THE SPATIAL BATTERY ($N = 57$)

Tasks	M	SD	Median
Seriation	1.87	1.02	2.0
Checkers	2.28	.91	2.0
Map Drawing	2.00	.77	2.0
Map Following	2.23	.84	2.0
Picture Drawing	2.16	.87	2.5
Still Life Drawing	1.90	.70	2.0
Handwriting	2.61	.74	2.5
Beakers	2.28	1.23	2.0
Length Judgment	2.45	.47	2.5
Spatial battery score	2.20	.89	2.0

TABLE 19

GUTTMAN COEFFICIENTS OBTAINED FOR THE MULTI-ITEM SPATIAL TASKS

Task	N Items	Coefficient of Reproducibility	Coefficient of Scalability
Checkers	4	.93	.70
Beakers	4	.91	.67
Length Judgment	4	.96	.71
Seriation	4	.98	.90

group on each measure (the numerical values reflect Levels 1–4). As may be seen, the scores ranged from 1.87 to 2.61, with a mean of 2.2 and a median of 2.0. These values are within the range that we had expected on the basis of our general theory since the mean age of the children was 6½ years and a mean score of 2.0 indicates the presence of unidimensional thought. They are also similar to the scores that we obtained on the tasks included in the numerical and narrative batteries for children in this age range (see Table 8 above in Chap. III).

On tasks where multiple items were presented, children were awarded a pass or a fail at each level, and a Guttman analysis was conducted on these data. As shown in Table 19, none of the scales were perfect according to Guttman's criteria. However, the coefficients of reproducibility and scalability all fell in the acceptable range.

Factor Analysis

To address the question of coherence, we submitted the entire battery to a factor analysis. The first-order correlation matrix among the tasks is presented in Table 20. The factor structure that resulted when this matrix was submitted to a principal components analysis is displayed in Table 21. Of the two factors that emerged, Factor 1 accounted for 47% of the common variance. All but the Beakers and Length Judgment tasks (two of the three Piagetian tasks) showed their primary loadings on this first factor. The Beakers task also showed a secondary loading on this factor. We interpret the first factor as a general one, which indexes children's acquisition of the central spatial structure in which we are interested.

Factor 2, which accounted for 10% of the variance, is less easy to interpret. The factor was defined by the Piagetian Length Judgment and the Beakers task. Seriation (the one other task taken directly from Piaget) and Map Drawing also showed secondary loadings on this factor. Both the Beakers and the Length Judgment tasks require that children focus very carefully on the perceptual dimension that the experimenter mentions. Both tasks also require some active "overcoming" of the structure of the visual

TABLE 20
CORRELATIONS AMONG THE SPATIAL TASKS ($N = 57$)

Variable	Checkers	Seriation	Map Drawing	Map Following	Name Writing	Picture Drawing	Life Drawing	Beakers	Judgment of Length
Checkers									
Seriation	.64								
Map Drawing	.63	.64							
Map Following	.46	.39	.58						
Name Writing	.51	.52	.71	.50					
Picture Drawing	.50	.46	.65	.40	.39				
Life Drawing	.29	.44	.44	.39	.40	.40			
Beakers	.29	.35	.42	.36	.24	.33	.41		
Judgment	.23	.29	.36	.12	.19	.18	.12	.31	

NOTE.—$r > .230$, $p < .01$; $r > .300$, $p < .001$.

TABLE 21

FACTOR LOADINGS: VARIMAX SOLUTION

Task	Factor 1 (Central Conceptual Structure for Space)	Factor 2 (Resistance to Misleading Field Effects)
Map Drawing	.76	.47
Handwriting	.75	.21
Checkers	.74	.21
Map Following	.72	.12
Still Life Drawing (entire scene)	.74	.09
Picture Drawing	.65	.27
Seriation	.62	.49
Still Life Drawing (cup only)	.57	.22
Beakers	.37	.49
Length Judgment	.02	.91

field as it is given, before a successful response can be generated. One possible interpretation, therefore, is that the second factor indexes the subject's ability to overcome misleading field effects. As Pascual-Leone (1969, 1974) has pointed out, Piaget explicitly built such a factor into many of his tasks, so as to be sure that subjects' "operativity" was genuinely taxed. While desirable for Piaget's purposes, the inclusion of such features is not essential for our own purpose, and it may indeed constitute an impediment in structural assessment.

Discussion

All the tasks on the battery could be reliably scored in terms of the conceptual progression that we hypothesized. They also proved to index a common underlying factor, as we had hypothesized. While this factor may well be related to the one in which Piaget was interested, it is not identical to it since two of the three Piagetian measures showed only weak loadings on it. Thus, in future use, we recommend that the battery be streamlined and reduced to the six or seven tasks that defined the first factor. In keeping with this recommendation, we reanalyzed the data using only the first seven measures (i.e., Map Drawing, Map Following, Checkers, Still Life Drawing, Picture Drawing, Seriation, and Handwriting). Only one factor emerged from this analysis, and all tasks showed a substantial loading on it.

In any factor analysis, one's conclusions must always be tempered by the possibility that method variance, rather than structural variance, may be responsible for the results. One must also acknowledge the possibility that alternative interpretations are possible. This having been said, it should be pointed out that many other patterns would have been possible, but the pattern that did emerge fit our hypothesis clearly. At the very least, then, we can claim that the pattern of the data was congruent with the hypothesis that we proposed and supportive of it.

STUDY 2:
TRAINING THE ELEMENTS OF THE UNIAXIAL SPATIAL STRUCTURE AND TESTING FOR TRANSFER

The objective of our second study in this series was to determine whether the elements of the uniaxial structure could be trained and, if so, whether training would transfer to all the tasks included in the assessment battery. In view of the limited time available and the many tests that we wished to administer, we decided to use a single subject design. Accordingly, we administered the "streamlined" battery of six tasks to three children who were attending a child-care program in a public school located in the San Francisco Bay Area. This school was bilingual and served children from low-income Mexican-American families. We selected one of these children as our "treatment subject"; the other two children served as controls.

Method

Subjects

The subject for our study, whom we will call Ramon, was 5-9 and in his second month of kindergarten at the time we began the training. His social adjustment and physical development were normal, and he was an engaging and enthusiastic child with whom to work. Since the training was conducted in Ramon's home, we were able to note that he lived with his two siblings and his mother in a small apartment near the school and that this home environment was warm and nurturing. It was not one that was oriented toward preparation for school, however, and it did not contain any pictures, books, or writing implements. Ramon's mother had not been to school herself and was functionally illiterate.

Pretest

One of the research assistants who took part in Study 1 administered the spatial test battery. (For a detailed description of this battery, see App. C.) The assistant was also responsible for the training. On the pretest battery, Ramon scored at or below the preaxial level on most of the spatial battery items. On the numerical and narrative batteries, his performance was at the predimensional and preintentional levels.

The two control children lived in the same community as Ramon, spoke the same language (Spanish), and attended the same kindergarten. On all three batteries, their pretest scores were within a few tenths of a point of Ramon's.

Training

The training was conducted in Spanish, with both Ramon's siblings present for most of the sessions. Sometimes Ramon's mother used our presence as a baby-sitting opportunity, but more often than not she was also present and supportive of our efforts.

The training consisted of a series of drawing games requiring the application of preaxial and uniaxial structures that were described earlier. In the first few exercises, our objective was simply to get Ramon to place (and then draw) figures on a piece of paper, locating them in the same general positions as those that we displayed for him on a felt board. Discussions with him centered on the size and the position of his figures and introduced the terms for the top, bottom, and sides of the page. In subsequent exercises, our emphasis expanded to include encoding and reproducing the height of the figures that were drawn, relative to each other. Finally, in the later sessions, training focused on the coordination of figure placement with height evaluation, as referenced to the bottom of the page. For this final purpose, the prop that we used most often was an acetate sheet, ruled with dark parallel lines. In one such game, Ramon saw several of his favorite puppets on a stage, which had a lined, acetate curtain in front of it. Ramon's task was to draw each puppet in its correct position and height on a piece of blank paper. This paper was placed over another acetate sheet whose dark parallel lines showed through the paper; thus, it provided a frame exactly like that which was provided by the stage curtain and that could be used for reference purposes.

Training lasted for about 1 hour per session, and there were a total of 11 sessions spread across 8 weeks. A full account of each training session is available on request.

Results and Discussion

Ramon's drawing showed a dramatic change during the course of the study. His favorite characters were Batman and Robin, and his pictures of them steadily increased in complexity and in the sophistication of their spatial arrangement. When the figures were scored for complexity at the beginning and the end of the training period (using the Goodenough Draw-a-Man criteria), his score had increased from 100 to 170 points.

At the end of the 8-week training period, Ramon was retested on the full battery of six tasks. Figure 25 illustrates the change in his performance on the Picture Drawing tasks; the mean scores that he obtained on this and on the other tasks are reported in Table 22. As may be seen, on each measure there was an improvement of at least half a point, which corresponds to about 1 year of mental age. The mean improvement was approximately three-quarters of a point, which corresponds to about 1.5 years in mental age.

With a single subject design, and especially one involving a low-achieving student, the obvious concern is that any change that one finds would have occurred anyway, owing either to exposure to kindergarten or to regression toward the mean. With regard to the first point, it should be noted that Ramon showed no progress whatever on the number knowledge battery from pre- to posttest. With regard to the second point, it is important to note that the progress of the two control subjects (whose scores are included in Table 22) was minimal and of the magnitude that one would expect given the 3-month interval between the tests. Had Ramon's improvement been due simply to his exposure to kindergarten, coupled with the passage of time, or to regression to the mean, one would have expected at least one of these two other indices (i.e., his numerical competence or the spatial competence of his peers) to have shown a substantial change as well.

STUDY 3: EXAMINING THE MEAN SCORES ON THE BATTERY ACHIEVED BY SEVERAL DIFFERENT AGE GROUPS

The objective of our third study was to determine whether the general structural progression—that is, from preaxial to uniaxial to biaxial to integrated biaxial thought—took place at the same rate as did changes on the other two batteries that we had developed for this age range.

Method

Subjects

The subjects for this study came from the same parochial school that had participated in our numerical and narrative studies and whose children had scored closest to the group mean. This school was located in the San

FIG. 25.—Pictures drawn by Ramon in response to the Picture Drawing task, before (*a,* pretest) and after (*b,* posttest) receiving weekly instruction for a 3-month period. (For a comparison with drawings of other children, see Fig. 17 above.)

a

b

TABLE 22

Pre- and Posttest Scores by Ramon and the Two Control Subjects
on the Spatial Battery

TEST	TREATMENT (Ramon)		CONTROL 1		CONTROL 2	
	Pre	Post	Pre	Post	Pre	Post
Seriation	.5	1.0	1.0	1.0	1.0	.5
Checkers	.5	1.5	1.0	1.0	1.0	1.5
Map Drawing	1.5	3.0	1.0	1.0	1.0	1.0
Map Following	.5	1.0	1.0	1.1	1.0	1.5
Picture Drawing	1.5	2.5	1.0	1.0	1.0	1.5
Handwriting	2.0	2.0	2.0	2.0	1.0	1.5
Mean spatial	1.1	1.8	1.2	1.2	1.0	1.3
Goodenough Draw-a-Man	100	170	80	80	113	120

Francisco Bay Area; it served a middle-class community with the majority of families of European- and Mexican-American background and approximately 10% Asian-Americans and some African-Americans. In all, 96 children were tested, 16 in kindergarten (mean age = 6-1, SD = 4.1 months), 29 in grade 3 (mean age = 8-6, SD = 5.3 months), and 30 in grade 5 (mean age = 10-6, SD = 5.6). An additional 21 high-SES subjects were tested in a university nursery school located in the San Francisco Bay Area (mean age = 4-5, SD = 4.2). Each subject was tested individually, in a room on the school premises, by the same research assistants who participated in Study 1.

Results

Once again, the great majority of children's responses could be classified quite easily as belonging to one of our structural categories or to a transitional point in between two adjacent categories. Once again, too, the performance of children in each of the four age groups was in accord with our theory and with previous empirical studies. We were therefore able to proceed directly to our quantitative analysis.

The possibility of sex effects was examined first. Analyses indicated no significant sex differences on any of the six tasks or on the overall battery mean. Therefore, boys and girls were treated as one group in all subsequent analyses. The mean scores for each age group on each spatial task are presented in Table 23. As may be seen, the majority of the mean scores at each age level fell within the same range as had those of tasks within the narrative and numerical batteries (Table 8 above). The overall battery mean at each age was also within a half point of those on the other batteries.

TABLE 23

MEANS (and Standard Deviations) OBTAINED ON INDIVIDUAL SPATIAL TASKS AT EACH AGE LEVEL

Age (N)	Map Drawing	Picture Drawing	Seriation	Checkers	Map Following	Handwriting	Overall M
4 years (21)	1.21	1.21	1.45	1.33	1.64	1.57	1.40
	(.51)	(.44)	(1.12)	(.60)	(.64)	(.58)	(.42)
6 years (16)	1.81	1.94	1.59	2.09	2.22	2.19	1.97
	(.57)	(.79)	(.84)	(.71)	(.89)	(.31)	(.43)
8 years (29)	2.77	2.88	2.83	3.22	2.98	3.98	3.11
	(.58)	(.81)	(.97)	(.70)	(.54)	(.09)	(.36)
10 years (30)	3.32	3.53	3.27	3.22	3.27	3.95	3.43
	(.53)	(.61)	(.74)	(.47)	(.61)	(.27)	(.29)

Two differences from expectations may be noted in the table. The first occurred on the Handwriting test, which yielded much higher scores than expected at the 8- and 10-year-old levels. We interpret this as being due to the fact that (*a*) children typically receive extensive training in and practice on this skill and (*b*) our scoring criterion was quite global. If this test is to be used in future studies, we think that it would be a good idea to develop a more refined set of criteria, in which the problems involved in drawing diagonal lines in particular letters are examined in greater detail and a scoring index for them is developed.

The second way in which the scores obtained on the spatial battery differed from these on other batteries was in their variance, which appeared to be 50%–100% greater than the variance obtained on the other two batteries. We have no explanation for this finding. However, we do note the possibility, which has been suggested by DeRibaupierre (1993) and Lautrey (1993), that, whereas both narrative and numerical tasks must be solved by processes that are "digital" in nature, spatial tasks may be solved by processes that are "analogical." It is possible either that analogical processing is inherently more variable or that some subjects use one form of processing and some another, thus generating more variable performance.

In sum, the general conclusion that we draw from these data is the same as we drew from the developmental data reported in Chapter III: the underlying structural progression on the spatial test battery appears to conform to the pattern that we hypothesize, and development through this progression appears to take place at the general rate that we hypothesize as well.

VI. CROSS-CULTURAL INVESTIGATIONS

Yukari Okamoto, Robbie Case, Charles Bleiker,
and Barbara Henderson

No evidence has yet been presented on the development of children's central conceptual structures in any culture other than that of North America. In the present chapter, we present data that were gathered in two other cultures. First, however, we provide a brief review of the problem that cross-cultural work has posed for research in the classic Piagetian tradition and of our own position on this problem.

CROSS-CULTURAL VARIABILITY IN CHILDREN'S INTELLECTUAL DEVELOPMENT

Of the various difficulties that beset Piaget's theory in the 1960s and 1970s, one of the most interesting was the difficulty posed by cross-cultural investigations. The basic data are easily summarized. (*a*) Children in other cultures do not always pass Piaget's tests at the same age as European or North American children. In certain traditional cultures, for example, certain conservation tests are not passed until the age of puberty, and others are not passed at all (Bruner, Oliver, & Greenfield, 1966; Dasen, 1972). (*b*) Virtually none of Piaget's formal tasks are passed in traditional oral cultures at any age or stage of development (Dasen, 1972). Even in modern postindustrial societies, certain subcultures can be found in which adults' passing rates on these tasks are extremely low. (*c*) In countries where the opportunity for schooling is limited, children who have not been to school normally perform much worse on Piaget's tasks than those who have, whether these tasks are concrete or formal (Cole, Gay, Glick, & Sharp, 1971; Fiati, 1992). (*d*) Finally, some of the most sophisticated intellectual activities in which nonliterate, nonschooled, and/or non-Western adults engage are difficult to classify within the context of Piaget's theory—they do not seem to be "formal" in the sense in which Piaget used that word, yet they are clearly complex, subtle, and well beyond the capabilities of young children (Dasen, 1972).

For a theory that purports to describe a universal progression in the development of human thought, as Piaget's did, the foregoing data are problematic. Are Piaget's logical operations really a cultural creation, dependent on formal schooling for their acquisition? Do they describe just one of the many diverse pathways that intellectual development can take? Or is the problem simply one of measurement? Are concrete and formal operations universal but difficult to demonstrate on Piaget's particular tests owing to the background knowledge that the tests require? In the end, Piaget (1972) argued in favor of the latter conclusion. He continued to view concrete and formal operations as universal attainments but acknowledged that certain of his measures might be valid only for children from Western backgrounds.

Other investigators preferred a more relativistic interpretation, however. To assert that the problem lies in Piaget's tests is to imply that concepts such as "the isolation of variables" are universals and that one merely needs to find a particular set of variables that is of local relevance and a familiar situation where isolating one such variable would be desirable in order to demonstrate this fact. Yet the more relativistic conclusion—that these concepts themselves are the creation of the Western scientific tradition—is equally plausible on a priori grounds. It is also equally consistent with the data.

Regardless of how one interprets Piaget's measures, it seems to us that most of the tests that we have developed for 8- and 10-year-olds are best viewed in a relativistic fashion, that is, as tests of concepts and conceptual frameworks that are cultural creations. There are a wide variety of culturally differing ways in which number systems can be constructed using a mental counting line as the basic element. There are a large number of ways in which human interaction can be depicted using motivated actions as the basic elements. There are a wide variety of ways in which three- and two-dimensional space can be represented, using the edges that frame the space as lines of reference. The particular systems that we use in our culture—such as the base-ten system for representing numbers or the Cartesian system for plotting coordinates—all have their own unique properties. Each of these systems has also had its own unique history of development (Gombrich, 1960; Hagen, 1986; Olson, 1994). As children struggle to master these systems, we suggest that they are not simply passing through a universal set of cognitive stages. Rather, they are setting out on a unique cognitive journey, one whose properties are just as much a function of the conceptual system that has to be mastered and of the social resources that are available for assistance in this process as they are a function of children's general stage of development and/or their cognitive style.

Of course, in the twentieth century, certain basic conceptual systems have become relatively standard. The base-ten system of whole numbers, the system for representing perspective, and the form of narrative where a hero must face certain challenges before his goals can be met—all these have become familiar in literate societies throughout the modern world. The institution of schooling has also become relatively standard. Thus, what vary among cultures are such factors as which conceptual system is most highly valued and what sort of educational philosophy is adopted—not the existence of these systems themselves or of formal institutions for teaching them. This being the case, it seems likely that the central conceptual structures that we described in previous chapters may well develop in much the same manner throughout the modern world and that their cultural specificity may be demonstrable only by means of studies of premodern groups.

In a previous volume, Fiati (1992) reported one such study. The particular group that he studied lived in the Volta region of central Africa, in remote villages of no more than 15–30 households. Access to the villages was by footpaths through dense bush. The villagers lived in traditional mud huts with grass roofs and were dependent for their livelihood on subsistence farming. Virtually all the amenities that we have come to associate with Western civilization—such as electricity, running water, clocks, and radios—were lacking in the villages. Daily life was a traditional one, in which the pattern of activity was determined by the rising and setting of the sun. After sunset all community activities ceased completely except for storytelling around a common fire. No books were present, the adults were not literate, and the children did not attend a formal school of any sort.

Of particular interest for our purposes is that children's exposure to numbers was quite different from that of schooled children in the West or even unschooled children growing up in commercial cultures such as those studied by Caraher and his colleagues (Caraher, Caraher, & Schlieman, 1985). The Western (base-ten) system of measurement was not used by the villagers, and their trade involved direct barter rather than money. Local markets were difficult to reach by foot and were visited only rarely; moreover, children were not taken on these trips since the journeys were long ones and involved dangers (such as snakes) to which the adults did not want to expose them. As might be expected under these circumstances, computation was neither a highly practiced nor a particularly valued skill.

Without daily exposure to numerical tasks involving clocks, money, or school mathematics, one might expect that children's quantitative development would follow a very different path than it does in cultures in which such tasks play a prominent role. In fact, this appeared to be the case. On local adaptations of our narrative tasks, the children in these isolated communities displayed the same sort of insight and sophistication as children in the nearby towns. On adaptations of quantitative tasks such as the

Balance Beam, however, they were much less effective. Although they clearly understood the questions and were interested in the problems, they rarely solved any of the problems involving two variables, even in adolescence. Both their working memory for numbers and their counting speed were similar to those of children many years their junior who were receiving schooling in the nearby towns. In fact, no quantitative task was found on which children's development proceeded beyond the unidimensional level.

STUDIES REPORTED IN THE PRESENT *MONOGRAPH*

Fiati's study clearly needs to be joined by others before any strong conclusion about the cultural specificity of high-level central conceptual structures can be drawn. In the present series of studies, however, our objective was a different one. What we sought to do was chart the development of children's conceptual structures in other modern cultures and test our notion that development in such contexts proceeds in a much more uniform fashion. In order to make this test as stringent as possible, we deliberately selected for comparison societies that were as different as possible from North American society in (*a*) the value that they place on certain classes of tasks, (*b*) the techniques that they use for teaching these tasks, and (*c*) the amount of time that they devote to teaching them. Our hypothesis was that such differences would exert a strong effect on the rate at which children come to understand the tasks in question and on the richness of their understanding but that they would have much less effect—if any—on the development of their central conceptual structures.

Before describing these studies, it is worthwhile to explain the rationale for our interest in this hypothesis in more detail. Each one of the central conceptual structures that we have studied is relevant to, and is supported by, performance on a wide range of more particular tasks. Although the problem-solving experiences that a child typically encounters in the course of schooling or everyday life constitute the most likely grounds of her central conceptual learning, our model holds that the central concepts learned in one particular context are equally relevant to successful performance in other contexts—and hence are equally learnable from a broad range of specific experiences (see Chap. I). An implication of this is that, unless one culture places a higher value than another does on *all* the tasks that contribute to the growth of a central conceptual structure and devotes more time to training all these (as in the case studied by Fiati), the effect on the rate at which children's central conceptual structures are acquired is unlikely to be large. To be sure, the emphasis on different tasks will alter the context of children's central conceptual learning. However, it will alter neither the content of that learning nor the rate since central conceptual learning will simply be "fed" by some other set of specific experiences to which the child is exposed on a more frequent basis.

How might one test this proposition? The problems of cross-cultural assessment are less severe in modern societies than in premodern ones. However, they are still of the same general nature. Unless the measures are designed by individuals who are thoroughly familiar with life as lived in both cultures that are being contrasted, it is likely that the test items will have different meanings to the children in the two cultures and that their responses will be difficult to compare or to interpret. If one's objective is to determine whether the same mental structure is present in two groups or whether it emerges at the same age, the situation can be particularly difficult since any cognitive measure always requires background knowledge of some sort and this knowledge may be differently valued and/or accessible in the two cultures under investigation.

Although it is never possible to solve these problems entirely, it is possible at least to reduce their influence. In the studies that we report, we took care to employ tasks for which someone could serve as our local "guide" and ensure (a) that the background knowledge required by our tasks was available to the children whom we wished to study and (b) that the tasks were presented in a form and context that the children would find congenial. We also took care to have children's responses to our tasks evaluated by someone who was familiar with the local culture and with the lives that children lead in it. Finally, we introduced a feature in our testing that—to the best of our knowledge—is quite rare in studies of this sort. Wherever possible, we evaluated children's performance on each task in two different ways: one that would reveal the cultural specificity of their responses and one that would reveal their cultural universality. The advantage of this methodology is that, when differences are found, they cannot be ascribed to children's general understanding of the test or the test situation and must therefore be given some other interpretation.

STUDY 1: THE DEVELOPMENT OF SPATIAL STRUCTURES IN CHINA AND CANADA

The first domain on which we chose to focus was spatial cognition. The task on which we chose to focus was drawing, and the two countries that we compared were China and Canada. The reason for these choices was that relatively little emphasis is placed on teaching drawing in Canada—time for art is allotted in the elementary school curriculum, but this is because opportunities for artistic expression are thought to stimulate children's creativity, not because teachers are expected to train children's drawing skills per se. The standard approach is to provide children with drawing materials about once a week, perhaps with some general suggestion regarding a topic or style, but then to let them create whatever they wish within these broad constraints. In China, by contrast, a substantial amount of effort is devoted to training the skill of drawing itself, and the curriculum provides specific instruction on how to render certain objects, such as the human figure, in a traditional fashion. According to Winner's (1989) analysis, the cumulative result of this experience is substantial. As they develop, children in China become much more adept at drawing than their North American peers, at least when the objects to be drawn are ones for which some preexisting schema has been taught and mastered.

The situation with regard to the task of "perspective drawing"—which is what we evaluate in our central conceptual battery for space—is different. Neither culture devotes much attention to teaching the laws of perspective, at least in the early primary grades. The rules of perspective are also quite complex and may be more difficult to master than those for drawing particular objects. For our first study, then, we decided to contrast two aspects of children's drawing: perspective drawing (i.e., spatial layout) and drawing a well-known object, the human figure.

Method

Subjects

The Canadian sample consisted of 116 middle-class children who participated in a study conducted by Dennis (1992; see also Chap. V above). The sample included 26 4-year-olds (13 boys and 13 girls, mean age = 4-6, SD = 2.5 months), 30 6-year-olds (13 boys and 17 girls, mean age = 6-6, SD = 3.5 months), 30 8-year-olds (12 boys and 18 girls, mean age = 8-5, SD = 3.7 months), and 30 10-year-olds (12 boys and 18 girls, mean age = 10-5, SD = 4 months). The school-aged children were sampled from three elementary schools in the suburban communities near Toronto, which served predominately middle- and working-class SES families. None of the schools emphasized art in their curricula. The preschool children were sampled from day-care centers in Toronto that served a similar population.

The Chinese sample consisted of 94 children from Nanjing. The sample included 25 4-year-olds (13 boys and 12 girls, mean age = 4-2, SD = 3.3 months), 26 6-year-olds (13 boys and 13 girls, mean age = 6-0, SD = 3.1 months), 21 8-year-olds (12 boys and 9 girls, mean age = 8-2, SD = 4.8 months), and 22 10-year-olds (12 boys and 10 girls, mean age = 10-2, SD = 4.7 months). These children were selected from six schools whose art program was judged to be weak, intermediate, or strong (two schools in each category) according to standards set by the Ministry of Education of the People's Republic of China.

Task

The task instructions, materials, and procedures were taken directly from Dennis's (1992) original study. In their original form, the instructions given children are the following: "Draw a picture of a man and a woman holding hands in a park. Their baby is in front of them and a tree is very far away behind them."

Our "local guide" in China was a professor of elementary art education in the province of Nanjing. After examining the instructions, she assured us that their general form would not present children in her province with any problems.

Procedures

The children's drawings in Canada were collected by Dennis (1992) and were lent to us for this study. The children in her study were given the drawing task individually, by her, in a quiet room and/or a private workplace. The Chinese data were collected in class by our collaborator. All children in Canada and China were given a chance to draw a picture that conformed to the specifications. The instructions were repeated halfway through the drawing and once again at the end.

Scoring

Using the axial classification system described in Chapter V, the overall spatial layout of the children's drawings was classified as preaxial, uniaxial, biaxial, or integrated biaxial (more detail on scoring is available on request). The human figures in the children's drawings were scored using the criteria proposed by Goodenough (1926) and a more global set of criteria proposed by Berg (1991). According to these latter criteria, "tadpole"-style figures receive a score of 1, "sausage" figures a score of 2, figures with clothing a score of 3, and figures with contoured clothing a score of 4.

Several graduate students served as raters for the drawings, three from our research group and two from a comparable group in Nanjing. Of the five scorers, one from our research team scored all the drawings, and the rest formed two pairs, with each pair scoring half the drawings. Interrater reliability using the Pearson product-moment correlation coefficient procedure for the two pairs ranged between .83 and .92 for the figural complexity scores and between .83 and .94 for the spatial layout scores.

Predictions

Given the different value that is placed on the skill of drawing in the two cultures and the different educational practices, our predictions for the

TABLE 24

Mean Scores (and Standard Deviations) Obtained on Two Measures of Figural Complexity: Canada versus China

		CANADIAN DATA (Toronto)				CHINESE DATA (Nanjing)	
Age	N	Goodenough Score	Berg Score	Age	N	Goodenough Score	Berg Score
4-6	26	8.50 (7.3)	1.70 (.61)	4-2	25	11.52 (7.4)	2.14 (.43)
6-6	30	15.30 (6.5)	2.68 (.56)	6-0	26	19.9 (7.0)	3.03 (.40)
8-5	30	20.90 (6.4)	3.03 (.39)	8-2	21	22.3 (8.3)	3.09 (.46)
10-5	30	24.90 (7.5)	3.16 (.36)	10-2	22	26.9 (8.7)	3.57 (.54)

Note.—Standard deviations are given in parentheses.

measure of figural complexity were that children in both groups would show substantial developmental progress with age but that the rate of this progress would be considerably faster in the Chinese group. Our predictions for the measure of spatial perspective were that children in both groups would show progress through the same general developmental sequence and that the rate of progress would be roughly the same since it would be determined primarily by children's central conceptual structures rather than by differential emphasis on drawing.

Results

Preliminary analyses indicated the absence of sex differences within each nation on any of the scoring systems; consequently, boys and girls were treated as one group.

Figural Complexity

From a qualitative point of view, the difference between the two groups was striking. At the younger ages, figures drawn by Chinese children were more complete, more likely to be wearing clothes, and drawn with better line control. At the older ages, they showed more movement and better form. The quantitative analysis confirmed this difference; the mean scores and standard deviations for each age group on each of the two figure drawing indices are presented in Table 24. As assessed by an analysis of variance procedure, there was a strong age effect ($F[3, 198] = 155.77$, $p < .001$)

FIG. 26.—Typical pictures drawn at each of four age levels by children in Nanjing, China, in response to the instructions, "Draw a picture of a mother and a father holding hands in a park. A baby is in front of them and a tree is very far away behind them." *a*, 4-year-olds. *b*, 6-year-olds. *c*, 8-year-olds. *d*, 10-year-olds.

and a substantial effect due to country ($F[1, 198] = 24.99$, $p < .001$) that favored the Chinese. Within the Chinese sample, an analysis was conducted to see whether there were any school effects or effects due to parents' occupation. No effects of either sort were found.

Spatial Layout

Chinese children's general representations of space, as reflected in the overall composition of their drawings, are illustrated in the examples shown in Figure 26. As may be seen, the observed developmental sequence conformed to the one that we expected (see Fig. 17 above, Chap. V). The means and standard deviations for each group are presented in Table 25. Again, as assessed by an analysis of variance procedure, there was a strong

TABLE 25

MEANS AND STANDARD DEVIATIONS FOR PERSPECTIVE DRAWING SCORES:
CANADA VERSUS CHINA

| | CANADIAN DATA (Toronto) | | | | CHINESE DATA (Nanjing) | | | |
STAGE	Age	N	Mean Score	SD	Age	N	Mean Score	SD
Predimensional	4-6	26	1.25	.53	4-2	25	1.50	.87
Unidimensional	6-6	30	2.63	.51	6-0	26	2.94	.50
Bidimensional	8-5	30	3.25	.63	8-2	21	3.22	.51
Integrated bidimensional	10-5	30	3.48	.64	10-2	22	3.35	.53

age effect ($F[3, 198] = 124.77, p < .001$) but no statistically significant effect due to country ($F[1, 198] = .15, p > .70$); the interaction of age and country was also not significant ($F[3, 198] = 2.64, p > .05$). Within the Chinese sample, analysis by school and by parents' occupation again failed to reveal any effects.

Discussion

The general pattern of results conformed to our expectations: Winner's hypothesis with regard to schematic complexity was confirmed, as was our own hypothesis with regard to the overall organization of space. The only surprise was the absence of any cross-cultural difference on the measure of spatial perspective. Although we had expected that the developmental patterns on this measure would be similar in the two countries, we had not expected them to be statistically indistinguishable. This surprise notwithstanding, what we see as being the important points are as follows. There are substantial cultural differences between China and Canada with regard to the value that is placed on drawing and in the training provided for rendering the human figure in a realistic fashion. Presumably as a result of this cultural difference, there are also differences in the rate at which children master this skill and in the complexity and sophistication of their drawings. In and of themselves, however, these cultural differences do not appear to exert any major effect on the stages through which children progress in their understanding of perspective. Mastery of this system develops in the same fashion in the two countries and at the same rate. We interpret this finding as supporting our notion that emphasis on a single task, or training in its performance, will not greatly affect the general rate of development of the central conceptual structures on which execution of that task is dependent.

STUDY 2: THE DEVELOPMENT OF SPATIAL STRUCTURES
IN JAPAN AND THE UNITED STATES

Given the results obtained in the first study, we decided to conduct a similar study to contrast children's performance in Japan and in the United States.

Method

Subjects

Sixty-one Japanese children in this study attended two public schools located in the Tokyo area that served middle-class families. The Japanese sample consisted of 19 6-year-olds (10 boys and 11 girls, mean age = 6-5, SD = 1 month), 22 8-year-olds (13 boys and 13 girls, mean age = 8-3, SD = 4 months), and 20 10-year-olds (10 boys and 10 girls, mean age = 10-5, SD = 2 months). The U.S. data were collected from two schools in California. One of these was a public school located in the Los Angeles area that predominantly served European- and Mexican-American families as well as some African- and Asian-Americans. The other was a parochial school located in the San Francisco Bay Area that served mostly European- and Mexican-American families with approximately 10% Asian-Americans and some African-Americans. The U.S. sample consisted of 19 6-year-olds (7 boys and 12 girls, mean age = 6-2, SD = 4 months), 28 8-year-olds (17 boys and 11 girls, mean age = 7-8, SD = 6 months), and 22 10-year-olds (10 boys and 12 girls, mean age = 9-9, SD = 4 months).

Procedure

The drawing test was prescreened by several consultants in Japan, including the children's teachers. By and large, their reaction was the same as the reaction that we encountered in China; our local experts assured us that children would understand the instructions and enjoy the challenge that they presented. The one modification suggested was that the figures who were holding hands in a park be described as a mother and her child— this would be a more common occurrence in Japan and one that would be deemed more socially appropriate. Accordingly, the instructions were presented in this modified form to both the Japanese and the U.S. groups.

Predictions

On the measure of figural complexity, we expected that Japanese children would be more advanced than American children since drawing re-

TABLE 26

MEAN SCORES (and Standard Deviations) OBTAINED ON MEASURE OF FIGURAL
COMPLEXITY: UNITED STATES VERSUS JAPAN

AGE	UNITED STATES (Los Angeles and San Francisco)			AGE	JAPAN (Tokyo and Chiba)		
	N	M	SD		N	M	SD
6-2	19	17.16	7.0	6-5	19	20.89	6.3
7-8	24	23.33	5.4	8-3	21	31.43	5.2
9-9	17	30.00	6.5	10-5	16	36.69	3.3

ceives much the same emphasis in Japan as it does in China while it is treated in the same "hands off" fashion in the United States as it is in Canada. On the measure of spatial perspective, we expected to find the Japanese and American groups to be roughly equivalent.

Results

Figural Complexity

There were noticeable differences in the appearance of the drawings obtained in the two countries that echoed those found in the previous study. For example, at age 6, Japanese children typically drew scenes that included many more objects than requested; American children drew only the requested objects, and their landscapes were much more sparsely filled as a result. At age 10, Japanese children drew more elaborate figures, whereas the American children's figures were less elaborate and more two dimensional.

The overall impression of greater complexity in the Japanese drawings was confirmed by comparisons using the Goodenough Draw-a-Man test index. Means and standard deviations achieved across age and country on this measure are indicated in Table 26. Significant main effects were found for age ($F[2, 104] = 62.58$, $p < .001$), country ($F[1, 104] = 33.32$, $p < .001$), and sex ($F[1, 104] = 14.90$, $p < .001$). None of the two-way and three-way interactions was significant. Further analyses were conducted to examine the main effect of sex differences. Significant differences were found only in the Japanese data ($F[1, 50] = 17.88$, $p < .001$), none in the U.S. data. (It should be noted that a few drawings—nine in the United States and five in Japan—did not show a front view of human figures, which made them impossible to score using the Goodenough criterion. These drawings were therefore excluded from this section of the analysis.)

TABLE 27

Means and Standard Deviations on Perspective Drawing Task:
United States versus Japan

	UNITED STATES (Los Angeles)				JAPAN (Tokyo and Chiba)			
STAGE	Age	N	Mean Score	SD	Age	N	Mean Score	SD
Unidimensional	6-2	19	2.26	.82	6-5	19	2.39	.52
Bidimensional	7-8	28	2.91	.56	8-3	22	2.93	.22
Integrated bidimensional	9-9	22	3.41	.63	10-5	20	3.43	.41

Spatial Layout

No sex differences were found in either country. The means and standard deviations obtained at each age level and in each country are indicated in Table 27. There was a significant effect for age across all subjects ($F[2, 118] = 31.66$, $p < .001$). However, there was no significant effect for country or for the interaction between age and country.

Discussion

The findings of the second study, combined with those of the first, suggest that the conceptual understanding of space that is reflected in children's drawings differs from the level of skill that they display in drawing figures. Although Asian children were able to draw impressively complex figures, complete with exaggerated features, movement, and depth, they still tended to arrange them in their drawings in ways that were markedly similar to those used by children in North America. We interpret this as evidence in favor of the proposition that children's execution of specific tasks on which they are trained is more likely to show cross-cultural variability than is the general understanding on which the execution of those specific tasks is dependent. Were China and Japan to develop programs for teaching perspective, we would predict that they would be successful in their quest and that the spatial arrangement of objects drawn by children in these countries would become more advanced than what would be seen in North America. If the full battery of other spatial measures were administered, however, we would predict that there would still be relatively little effect on the overall spatial scores—unless, of course, the training was aimed at developing the central conceptual structure itself, by focusing on a broad range of more specific tasks and situations.

STUDY 3: THE DEVELOPMENT OF CONCEPTUAL STRUCTURES FOR REPRESENTING NUMBER IN THE UNITED STATES AND IN JAPAN

In recent years, a good deal of attention has focused on differences between America and Japan in the domain of mathematics. Cross-cultural studies have shown that Japanese parents place a far higher value on mathematics than do American parents and that they monitor their children's progress far more closely (Stevenson, Lee, & Stigler, 1986; Stigler, Lee, Lucker, & Stevenson, 1982). Japanese elementary school teachers are also far better prepared in mathematics than their American counterparts; they spend a far greater number of hours every year teaching mathematics, and their lessons are more coherent and more strongly focused on conceptual understanding (Stevenson & Stigler, 1992). The cumulative result of these differences is that, on virtually every sort of measure that has been devised to date, Japanese children have outperformed their American peers in mathematical achievement. The differences have been so strong, in fact, that students in the lowest-achieving schools in Japan have often outperformed those in the highest-achieving schools in the United States (Stevenson et al., 1986; Stigler et al., 1982).

Given the magnitude of the differences that have been reported, we decided to undertake a comparison of Japanese and U.S. children's numerical thinking similar to the one that we conducted between Asian and North American children for the domain of space. Accordingly, we developed two types of tests: (1) one that assessed the specific kinds of mathematical knowledge on which the elementary school curriculum in both countries focuses and (2) one that assessed children's general conceptual understanding of the base-ten number system and their progress from predimensional through bidimensional thought in understanding that system. Once again, our assumption was that cross-cultural differences in general conceptual understanding would be a good deal smaller than those in specific mathematical skills or concepts.

Method

Subjects

Data were collected from 69 American and 67 Japanese children drawn from the same schools that we had used in each country for our work on spatial development (see above). Since our study was limited in scope, we decided to focus exclusively on children who came from middle- to upper-middle-class homes. The American sample comprised 22 6-year-olds (11 boys and 11 girls, mean age = 6-0, SD = 4 months), 23 8-year-olds (8 boys and 15 girls, mean age = 8-1, SD = 4 months), and 24 10-year-olds (10 boys and 14 girls, mean age = 10-5, SD = 6 months). The Japanese sample consisted of 21 6-year-olds (10 boys and 11 girls, mean age = 6-5, SD = 1 month), 26 8-year-olds (13 boys and 13 girls, mean age = 8-5, SD = 2 months), and 20 10-year-olds (10 boys and 10 girls, mean age = 10-5, SD = 2 months). For reasons of scheduling, the test of mathematics achievement was administered to a different group of children in the same schools. For this comparison we used 34 U.S. fifth graders (20 boys and 14 girls, mean age = 10-11, SD = 5 months) and 29 Japanese fifth graders (17 boys and 12 girls, mean age = 11-2, SD = 4 months).

Measures

The test of Number Knowledge and the Balance Beam task—two of the measures used in the study—are described in Chapters II and III. Data on the Number Knowledge test were obtained at all ages. Unfortunately, the data on the Balance Beam were obtained only from children at the 6- and 10-year-old levels. Japanese 8-year-olds could not be tested.

Mathematics achievement.—The test that we used to measure children's scholastic achievement was an abbreviated version of the fifth grade assessment device that had been constructed by Stevenson and his colleagues for their comparisons of mathematics learning in the United States, Japan, and Taiwan (Stevenson et al., 1986; Stigler et al., 1982). The primary reason for using this index was to measure achievement on the topics that are actually taught to children in all three countries, and the Stevenson et al. test was constructed on the basis of a thorough analysis of the mathematics curricula used in these countries. Moreover, it had already been used in cross-cultural comparisons and shown to differentiate the performance of U.S. and Japanese children. The subset of items that we selected from the Stevenson et al. test consisted of 36 problems; 23 of these assessed children's computational skills in addition, subtraction, multiplication, and division, seven were geometry problems of a simple nature, and six were word problems (the complete set of problems is available on request).

Procedures

All three tests were originally constructed in English and then translated by researchers fluent in Japanese. The Japanese children's schoolteachers were also consulted on the appropriateness of translation. For the Number Knowledge and Balance Beam tests, children were seen individually and interviewed in their native language. These interviews took place in a quiet room provided by each school and were conducted by research assistants (native speakers) trained to administer these tasks. The achieve-

TABLE 28

MEAN SCORES (and Standard Deviations) ON NUMBER KNOWLEDGE AND BALANCE BEAM
TESTS: UNITED STATES VERSUS JAPAN

| | | UNITED STATES | | | | | | JAPAN | | | |
| | | Number Knowledge | | Balance Beam | | | | Number Knowledge | | Balance Beam | |
AGE	N	M	SD	M	SD	AGE	N	M	SD	M	SD
6-4	22	1.82	.31	1.91	.42	6-5	21	2.52	.73	2.00	.83
8-1	23	3.04	.31			8-5	26	3.33	.77		
10-5 ...	24	4.23	.68	3.35	.63	10-5 ...	20	4.05	.76	3.23	.41

ment test was group administered by the homeroom teachers in each
country.

Results

Preliminary analyses indicated an absence of sex differences within
each nation on any of our measures. Consequently, boys and girls were
treated as one group within each nation.

As expected, there was a substantial difference between the two cultural
groups in the percentage of correct responses on the mathematics achievement test. On the average, American fifth graders solved 50% of the problems correctly, whereas Japanese fifth graders solved 77% of the problems.
Because this test consisted of three subsets of problems (see the previous
section), a multivariate analysis of variance was carried out. This analysis
revealed a large and statistically significant difference between the performance of the two groups ($F[3, 59] = 57.57, p < .0001$).

Children's performance on the Number Knowledge test was subjected
to a 2 (nationality) × 3 (age group) analysis of variance. The main effects
of nationality and of age group were both significant ($F[1, 130] = 7.51$,
$p < .01$, and $F[2, 130] = 131.94, p < .001$, respectively). The two-way
interaction also yielded significant differences ($F[2, 130] = 6.37, p < .01$).
The Tukey-Kramer method was then used to determine which pairs contributed to the overall significance. The result of the between-country comparison at each age group indicated a significant difference ($p < .05$) in
favor of Japanese children at the 6-year-old level but none at either the 8-
or the 10-year-old level. On the Balance Beam task, no significant differences were present at either the 6- or the 10-year-old level. The mean scores
on the two tasks are presented in Table 28.

Discussion

The pattern of findings for 8- and 10-year-olds was identical to that in the previous study of space. Focusing on middle-class U.S. and Japanese children, we found large and consistent differences favoring the Japanese in the mastery of elementary mathematics but no differences in their understanding of the way in which quantitative variables may be related in general or of the particular way in which they relate within the whole number system. In short, we found striking differences in particular numerical skills and concepts but not in central numerical structures.

The data for the 6-year-olds were different. Here, no significant difference was found on the Balance Beam test, but a statistically significant difference was found, in favor of the Japanese children, on the Number Knowledge test. Whereas American 6-year-olds' performance was consistent across the Balance Beam and the Number Knowledge tests and in line with age-level expectations suggested by our general theory, Japanese 6-year-olds performed at a higher level on the Number Knowledge than on the Balance Beam test, and their performance on the former was more in line with our theoretical expectations for 8-year-olds.

Why was this the case? If the reason lay in the school curriculum, one would expect the Japanese advantage to be maintained at the 8- and 10-year-old levels—just as it was in the case of the mathematics achievement test—but the data show that it was not. One possible explanation is that Japanese mothers value mathematics more highly than American mothers and actively teach their children more about it before they go to school (Hess, McDevitt, & Chang, 1987; Mordkowitz & Ginsburg, 1987; Stevenson et al., 1986). In effect, the Japanese 6-year-old might arrive at the first grade with more extensively trained skills than her U.S. counterpart. Another possible explanation—not incompatible with the first—is that the Japanese language makes the structure of the base-ten number system more explicit and thus easier to master than does English. The numbers 11, 12, and 13, for example, are expressed in Japanese as "one 10 and one 1," "one 10 and two 1s," "one 10 and three 1s," respectively. By contrast, in English, the same numbers are expressed with single words whose relation to the base-ten system is opaque (Miura, 1987; Miura & Okamoto, 1989). Many of the 8-year-old-level items on our Number Knowledge scale require an elementary understanding of the base-ten principle, and it was on these items that the Japanese 6-year-olds excelled relative to their American counterparts; thus, we favor this latter explanation and think that it should be explored further.

Turning to the more general pattern, what we found at the other age levels as well as on the Balance Beam test at the age of 6 was the absence of major differences in general quantitative structures, in spite of large and

147

significant differences in the specific concepts and skills that are trained in school. Our explanation of the apparent paradox is that, although specific instructional opportunities differ widely across the two groups, more general educational opportunities do not. The everyday lives of children in both cultures provide ample opportunity to encounter quantitative problems in such domains as time, money, and distributive justice. These problems constitute equally valid contexts in which to learn about numbers and to reflect on the way in which the base-ten system is structured. Thus, the advantage that Japanese children have in the specific domain of school mathematics is not reflected in their acquisition of these more general structures.

STUDY 4: THE DEVELOPMENT OF CONCEPTUAL STRUCTURES FOR REPRESENTING NARRATIVE IN JAPAN AND IN THE UNITED STATES

Our final study focused on the development of social knowledge and its expression in narrative. In contrast to the systems of mathematics or perspective drawing, modern systems for engaging in, understanding, and talking about social interaction vary greatly from one culture to another. In addition, although the activity of telling stories appears to be universal, it is less valued in some cultures than in others. Indeed, in some cultures, storytelling is considered an unnatural activity for children to engage in (e.g., Heath, 1984). Given that this is so, we were not sure that our narrative measures would yield results comparable to those that we obtained in the other two domains.

Nonetheless, it did seem possible that similar results might emerge. Structural analysis of folktales suggests that differences in the specific forms of social interaction that are depicted in stories and the ways of understanding such interactions may not be reflected at the level of story structure (Propp, 1922/1968). It is on story structure that our measures focus. Moreover, the particular form of structure on which we focus is a very basic one, namely, a narrative that reflects some understanding of the role of motives and other intentional states in generating action. This understanding may be so basic as to underlie human narratives in all cultures.

The particular contrast in which we were interested lay once again between Japan and the United States. There is a good deal of literature indicating that the social life of young children in these two cultures is very different, both at home and at school (DeVos, 1973; Hamilton, Blumenfeld, Akoh, & Miura, 1989; Rohlen, 1985, 1995; Tobin, Wu, & Davidson, 1989). One dimension along which a strong difference exists is the value that is placed on individual expression. In the United States, children are encouraged to express themselves from an early age, using language as a tool. For example, in the preschool activity Show and Tell, an individual child brings something from home and is encouraged to tell the group about it. No comparable practice exists in Japanese preschools, where more emphasis is placed on helping children adapt to group life and develop a shared social purpose. There may also be a difference in the amount of time that young children in the two countries spend listening to stories and responding to questions that their teacher poses about story events. This being the case, we thought that it would be interesting to examine the development of children's central structures for narrative in the two cultures.

Method

Tasks

The two measures that we selected were the Storytelling task and the Mother's Motives task, both of which were described in Chapter III. No alteration of the task instructions was deemed necessary for administration to the Japanese children. However, the Japanese 10-year-olds seemed much more comfortable with writing their stories out than with telling them to the experimenter orally; hence, they were allowed to proceed in this fashion.

Subjects

Data were collected from 46 American and 41 Japanese children. These children were drawn from the same schools that we had used for our work on spatial development (see Study 2, this chapter). The American sample consisted of 22 6-year-olds (11 boys and 11 girls, mean age = 6-0, SD = 4 months) and 24 10-year-olds (10 boys and 14 girls, mean age = 10-5, SD = 6 months). One American 10-year-old was absent when the Storytelling task was administered; therefore, the story data were collected from 23 children at this age level. The Japanese sample consisted of 21 6-year-olds (10 boys and 11 girls, mean age = 6-5, SD = 1 month) and 20 10-year-olds (10 boys and 10 girls, mean age = 10-5, SD = 2 months).

Procedures

Both the Storytelling and the Mother's Motives tasks were administered in the standard fashion (see Chap. III), with the one exception already noted.

Scoring

The children's audiotaped protocols were transcribed in both countries. Next, Japanese protocols were translated into English by a native speaker of Japanese. All the Storytelling and the Mother's Motives protocols were then scored by two raters: one who had grown up in Japan and one who had grown up in the United States. Each was a trained elementary school teacher in her country of origin, and each had a degree in educational psychology. The criteria to determine children's levels of central narrative structures were the same as those presented in Chapter III. The interrater reliability was .80 for the Storytelling task and .85 for the Mother's Motives task.

In addition to analyzing the plot structures of the stories, we also analyzed the children's stories in terms of the sorts of problems with which they dealt (recall that the children are instructed to tell about a child their age who has a problem and what he or she did to solve it). For this analysis, the two raters both reread all the stories of each group and suggested a set of possible categories. These categories were then clarified by discussion, and a common set of categories and way of defining each were agreed on. The final categories selected were interpersonal conflict, bullying (or *ijime*—note that this word refers to both physical and psychological harassment), achievement, drugs, family conflicts, and (a residual category) problems faced by a single individual.

Results

Preliminary analyses indicated an absence of sex differences within each nation on any of our measures. Consequently, boys and girls were treated as one group within each nation.

Story Themes

Interestingly, Japanese 6-year-olds were unwilling to participate in the Storytelling task, a clear indication of a cultural difference since all our American subjects did so with considerable enthusiasm. For the 10-year-old sample, there were quite a number of differences in story content between the two groups. Children from the United States created a more humorous group of stories than did their Japanese counterparts. Whereas Japanese 10-year-olds were almost unanimous in leaving their protagonists unnamed or referring to them by a single letter (e.g., A, B, C), American children typically named their characters.

In addition to these differences, there were also differences in the types of settings, problems, and themes with which the stories dealt. Most of the Japanese stories took place in a school setting, whereas the setting of the American stories was more varied. A majority of the American stories were about peers, but there was also a high percentage of stories in which adults

TABLE 29

PROPORTIONS OF DIFFERENT THEMES IN STORIES COMPOSED BY
10-YEAR-OLD CHILDREN: UNITED STATES VERSUS JAPAN

	United States ($N = 23$)	Japan ($N = 20$)
Interpersonal conflict among peers	.22	.40
Bullying or *ijime*	.00	.35
Drugs	.18	.00
Within-family conflicts	.18	.00
Individual problems	.30	.10
Achievement in academics or sports	.18	.15

figured prominently and in which an adult or a child faced an individual problem outside school.

When the children's stories were classified according to category of the problem that had been selected, Japanese 10-year-olds were almost twice as likely to tell stories about interpersonal conflict within the peer group as were their American peers (see Table 29; since the Japanese 6-year-olds proved unwilling to engage in this task, contrasts can be made only at age 10). Only the Japanese children told stories where the action was clearly and centrally about being teased or bullied. Almost 20% of the 10-year-old children from the United States told stories where the central problem was related to drug addiction. American children also told stories that involved family conflict, including events such as disobeying parents, jealousy among siblings, and struggling to find privacy. Although only a relatively small percentage of the American 10-year-olds told such stories (13%), these stories portrayed such family problems openly, believably, and in a fully elaborated manner. A few of the Japanese children used their family members in stories. However, these typically were peripheral characters, and no conflict within the family was ever portrayed. Nearly one-third of American children told stories about an individual dealing with some problem of a realistic nature on his or her own. By contrast, only 10% of Japanese 10-year-olds told such stories, and these stories were moralistic tales probably taken from the school curriculum. The Japanese and American 10-year-old children were equally likely to tell stories about success in sports or school achievement, and the concern of the characters in each case centered on how one appeared to peers.

Development of Central Narrative Structures

Using the criteria described in Chapter III, the children's responses to the Storytelling and Mother's Motives tasks were classified as falling into

TABLE 30

MEAN SCORES (and Standard Deviations) OBTAINED FROM CLASSIFICATIONS OF
STRUCTURAL LEVEL OF TWO NARRATIVE TASKS: UNITED STATES VERSUS JAPAN

	UNITED STATES			JAPAN		
	N	Mean Score	SD	N	Mean Score	SD
Storytelling:						
10-year-olds	23	3.46	.68	20	3.60	.92
Mother's Motives:						
10-year-olds	24	3.83	1.09	20	3.55	1.00
6-year-olds	22	2.23	.75	21	2.10	.63

one of the four intentional levels; the scores 1, 2, 3, and 4 refer to the preintentional, uni-intentional, bi-intentional, and integrated bi-intentional levels, respectively. Mean scores for the Storytelling and Mother's Motives tasks obtained for each subgroup are presented in Table 30. There were no significant differences between the Japanese and the American samples on either task ($F[1, 39] = 0.25, p > .62$, and $F[1, 79] = 1.20, p > .27$) for the Storytelling and Mother's Motives tasks, respectively.

Discussion

Although we had anticipated that there might be differences on the Storytelling task between Japanese and American children, we had not anticipated that these would take the particular form that they did at the 6-year-old level, namely, the youngest Japanese children's unwillingness to tell or "shyness" about telling stories. In future work, it may be possible to circumvent this problem by introducing the task in a different manner, perhaps with the child's parent or teacher as a collaborator.

The differences in story content between the two groups of 10-year-olds were in line with our original expectations as well as with the differences in how children's lives are lived in the two cultures—each group created stories that reflected their cultural experience in all its richness and distinctiveness. In view of these differences, we found it particularly significant that there were no differences in the structure scores that the two cultural groups obtained on the Mother's Motives test or the Storytelling tasks. We see these results as congruent with those that we obtained in our other cross-cultural studies, in that they indicate significant cross-cultural differences in aspects of tasks that reflect activities that differ in two cultures but commonalities on these same tests in aspects that require a more general and common set of understandings.

TABLE 31

MEAN SCORES FOR 6-YEAR-OLDS ON NUMERICAL AND NARRATIVE
BATTERIES: BREAKDOWN BY SOCIAL CLASS

SES	Numerical Battery	Narrative Battery	Number Knowledge Test
High	2.23	2.27	2.36
Medium	1.81	1.96	1.94
Low	1.42	1.72	1.75
Very low			1.40

SOCIAL CLASS DIFFERENCE IN CENTRAL CONCEPTUAL STRUCTURES

Taken together, the results from the four studies that we have just described are reminiscent of those obtained by Demetriou et al. (1988), who administered a large battery of Piagetian measures to children from several different age groups in five modern industrial countries. The children in all the countries studied were found to move through the same general sequence of stages and substages, with only modest differences in their rate of progression. Within each country, however, there were major differences among socioeconomic status (SES) groups, with regard to both the rate of progress and the final level that was attained; these differences were always in favor of high-SES subjects.

Since these investigators' cross-national findings were very similar to our own and their findings with regard to SES are similar to those of other studies conducted in the United States (Gaudia, 1972; Lesser, Fifer, & Clark, 1965), we decided to examine our American database for similar social class effects. The most useful data for this purpose were those collected from our 6-year-old subjects on the numerical and narrative batteries (see Study 1, Chap. III) since the children in this study were drawn from six different schools that served a broad range of socioeconomic groups. Accordingly, we reanalyzed these data as a function of the socioeconomic status of the community served by the school; the results of this reanalysis are shown in Table 31. The same table includes the results from a supplementary study that we conducted, in which children from a very low income group were tested on one measure: the Number Knowledge test (Griffin et al., 1994). For certain test items, the differences were even larger than the means suggest; for example, for the four items that had the general form, "Which is more, this number [e.g., 5] or this number [e.g., 4]?" the passing rate was 89% for kindergarten children in the highest-SES school but only 6% in the lowest-SES school.

The general pattern, then, is similar to the one reported by other research groups. Although cross-cultural differences on central conceptual structures are small and statistically insignificant, social class differences are large and statistically significant, at least for American and European groups.

SUMMARY AND CONCLUSION

In Piaget's system, the development of children's cognitive structures is seen as progressing through a universal sequence from sensorimotor, to concrete, to formal logical thought. The data that have been obtained on his measures are problematic in their support for this view, however, because they indicate that adults in traditional societies often fail his formal tasks. Piaget's (1972) interpretation of such findings was that they indicated a problem with his measures, not his theory—if appropriate measures were available, he believed that formal logical operations would be found in all cultures and social groups. Our own interpretation differs. While we acknowledge that adults in all cultures are capable of thinking in a fashion that is more sophisticated, subtle, and complex than that of young children, we see the highest forms of thought as being dependent on the mastery of systems that are cultural creations and not universal human attainments— and we see Piaget's system of formal operations as being just one example of the sort of system that can be created by a culture and passed on from one generation to the next.

In a previous investigation, Fiati (1992) studied children who were growing up in isolated, agricultural villages in the Volta region of West Africa. In these communities, life was still a traditional one, and children's experiences with time, money, and mathematical computation were considerably different from those of children who were attending schools in the nearby towns. Under these conditions, Fiati found that village children's skill in using numbers or in thinking about quantitative variables did not develop to a very high level as compared to that of their peers in the towns or as compared to their own thinking about social issues. In the terms used in the present *Monograph*, it appeared as though children's central conceptual structures for number—in contrast to their central conceptual structures for narrative—did not advance much past the unidimensional level.

Are unidimensional structures, at least, universal? Very probably the answer to this question is yes. Although systems for counting, for example, vary widely, no culture has yet been found in which counting does not play some role or where young children fail to pass Piaget's conservation of number test (Saxe, 1988). It seems highly likely, therefore, that a mental counting line of some sort is a universal construction. The situation in the domain of narrative is quite similar. Although folktales vary widely from one culture to the next, no culture has been reported in which folktales play no role whatever or where the story line of existing folktales does not have some form of intentional component (Propp, 1922/1968). The mental story line may thus be a universal construction as well. Finally, no culture has been reported in which some form of decorative art is not present or in which no technology exists for launching a projectile along a desired trajectory. If these activities require a mental reference line of some sort, then this would be a candidate for universal conceptual attainment as well.

In the present series of studies, our investigations were confined to societies that are modern, highly literate, and schooled. Thus, our interest was in demonstrating a universal progression well beyond the unidimensional level, in the sorts of structure that are crucial to life in a modern industrial culture. In fact, this was what we found in each of our studies. On our tests of central conceptual structures, children progressed through the same stages and at the same rate. By contrast, on our tests of more specific understanding, especially on those dealing with issues on which different cultures place different emphasis, we found large and significant cross-national differences. From this we conclude that, if a culture values a particular task or set of tasks and invests a great deal of effort in teaching them, it is likely that the training will pay off. Children growing up in that culture will very likely be more skilled at the activities in question. They will also develop a deeper understanding of these activities and display this understanding at a younger age than children in other cultures. However, in and of itself, this advantage is unlikely to produce any great acceleration in the central conceptual structures to which the activities are related and on which their development is dependent.

These findings are of interest in their own right. They assume a particular significance, however, when juxtaposed to the findings from the SES comparisons. At least in our American sample, large and consistent SES differences in the rate of development were found on all types of tasks, that is, on tasks that tapped specific understanding or skill as well as on tasks that tapped more general conceptual understanding. While it is true that our studies involved small numbers of children and samples that were gathered in an unsystematic fashion, the SES findings were similar to those that have been obtained by many other investigators. Thus, a question that we think must be addressed is why cross-cultural differences—which often seem so dramatic and pervasive—should have such a small effect on the development of children's conceptual structures while social class differences—which often appear to be relatively limited and restricted to the economic sphere—should have such a large one. This is a question to which an answer will be proposed in the next chapter.

VII. MODELING THE DYNAMIC INTERPLAY BETWEEN GENERAL AND SPECIFIC CHANGE IN CHILDREN'S CONCEPTUAL UNDERSTANDING

Robbie Case

The two fundamental questions with which the study of cognitive development is concerned are (1) how best to characterize children's cognition at different points in their development and (2) how best to characterize the process by which children move from one of these points to the next. Throughout the present *Monograph,* our prime concern has been with the first question. What we have attempted to show is that, unless one presumes the existence of central conceptual structures, one cannot fully understand the general pattern of children's understanding at 4, 6, 8, or 10 years of age. In the present chapter and the next, I take up the second question, namely, how to model children's movement from one level of understanding to the next.

THE CLASSIC CONFLICT BETWEEN GENERAL AND SPECIFIC ACCOUNTS OF CONCEPTUAL DEVELOPMENT

In the context of Piaget's theory, children's general level of cognitive development was presumed to set a ceiling on the specific learning of which they were capable. However, specific learning was not seen as affecting their general level of cognitive development in any fundamental way (Piaget, 1964). In the context of classic learning theory, the opposite assumption was made, namely, that children's intellectual development was the direct result of their specific learning and had no other source (Gagne, 1968). It was this difference that led Bruner (1966) to characterize Piaget's position as one where development was presumed to occur "from the inside out" and the learning position as one where development was presumed to occur "from the outside in."

Neither of these classic positions is easily squared with the full set of data that have been reported in the developmental literature in recent years or in the present *Monograph*. The classic Piagetian position fits well with the finding that development proceeds at the same general rate across a broad array of tasks during the period of middle childhood. However, it is not easily squared with the fact that large and significant differences are found in the rate of this development as a function of direct instruction, schooling, and/or social background. The classic learning position fits well with these latter data, but it is less easily squared with data showing that children perform at the same general developmental level in certain circumstances, across tasks to which they have had a widely different degree of prior exposure.

The data from the quantitative battery may be used as an illustration of this latter phenomenon. In the case of arithmetic word problems, children receive a great deal of training and practice in school. In the case of time telling, they do not receive a great deal of training, but they do receive a great deal of practice: clocks are prominently displayed in school classrooms and are eagerly checked as recess or any other break approaches. Practice in dealing with money may be a bit less frequent, but it is still available on a weekly if not a daily basis in many middle-class homes. Practice in distributing rewards is, in all probability, less frequent still. Finally, practice in solving the sort of torque problem presented by the balance beam is extremely rare, if it is encountered at all. Were specific experience the only factor that is relevant to children's understanding of specific tasks, one would expect that their rate of conceptual development would vary widely from one of these tasks to the next. At least as scored by our criteria, however, children's rate of development appears to be remarkably constant across these different situations and contexts.

The tension between general stage theories and specific-learning theories, and the inability of either group to account for the full pattern of data gathered by the other, was one of the major factors that led to the creation of neo-Piagetian theory. Neo-Piagetian theorists accepted the general epistemology of constructivism that was inherent in Piaget's work. They also accepted the notion that children of different ages have different cognitive powers. However, they attempted to take a more balanced stance with regard to the importance of general and specific factors in children's development and to assign task-specific learning a more important role.

In Pascual-Leone's system, for example, learning was defined as being of two sorts, conditioned (C) or mentally mediated (M). Specific task variables deemed relevant to M-learning were (*a*) the complexity of the mental coordination that has to be achieved in order to learn a new concept or rule, (*b*) the extent to which this mental coordination is facilitated or interfered with by previous learning, and (*c*) the extent to which the cues that are relevant for problem solution are perceptually salient or concealed (Pascual-Leone, 1970; Pascual-Leone & Smith, 1969). General developmental variables that were specified as relevant to M-learning were (*a*) the size of children's mental power or working memory, which sets a limit on their ability to coordinate their existing schemes into a more sophisticated pattern, and (*b*) children's cognitive style, which can influence the degree to which they are influenced by perceptual and/or previous learning factors (Pascual-Leone, 1970; Pascual-Leone & Smith, 1969).

Since neo-Piagetian theory synthesized elements from both classic positions, it offered a more satisfactory basis for explaining both aspects of the general pattern that was described above. The explanation for cross-task consistency turned on the following three points. (1) The tasks for which this state holds true tend to be ones that have been carefully equated in complexity, that is, in the number of schemes that must be attended to simultaneously in order to arrive at a solution. (2) Misleading task effects are also absent or else carefully controlled by the task designer from one situation to the next. (3) A warm-up or pretraining period is normally provided for each task to make sure that all children have the specific requisite schemes necessary to solve it in their repertoires. Under these (atypical) conditions, evenness in developmental profile may be shown to be the norm. The more typical pattern in development, that of an uneven level of performance across tasks, is explained in the context of neo-Piagetian theory by recourse to the same factors, that is, by pointing to naturally occurring differences in task complexity, in misleading task properties, or in task familiarity (Pascual-Leone, 1970; Pascual-Leone & Smith, 1969).

REEXAMINING THE CLASSIC CONFLICT
FROM THE POSITION OF THE PRESENT THEORY

The present view of learning and development is one that accepts the general neo-Piagetian position but goes beyond it. The basic notion is that, if we are to explain the full pattern of children's cognitive development, it is not sufficient to think in terms of local schemes whose coordination is limited by the general growth of mental power and/or processing capacity. In addition, we must reintroduce a construct similar (although not identical) to Piaget's notion of a general operative structure. The reintroduction of such a construct gives us the ability to predict the sort of factor pattern that was reported in Chapter III and the sort of transfer pattern that was reported in Chapter IV; neither of these patterns could have been predicted otherwise. In addition, the reintroduction of this sort of construct provides us with an interesting new perspective on the question of how children move from one point in their learning and development to the next. The basic idea is that each classic school of theorists was correct about the developmental factor whose influence it studied and wrong only about the factor whose influence it did not study (and that it sought to dismiss). General conceptual structures *do* exert a strong influence on children's specific learning, and specific learning *does* make a strong contribution to children's general conceptual development.

In and of itself, this assertion may seem rather straightforward. Certainly, it is the most obvious way to resolve a historical controversy of the sort that has existed up to this point. The assertion does have a set of entailments, however, that are not at all obvious. If children's developing general structures exert a positive influence on their specific learning, and if specific learning also exerts a positive influence on children's level of general understanding, then it follows that a feedback loop must be present in which each of these variables influences the other in an iterative manner.

As many readers may be aware, iterative feedback loops are the cornerstone on which modern dynamic systems theory is based. They have also played a central role in theoretical attempts to apply this theory to development (Lewis, 1994, 1995; Thelan & Ulrich, 1991). In his later years, Piaget argued strongly that the process of development was a dynamic one. Pascual-Leone (1970, 1988, 1994) also devoted a great deal of time to arguing this case and to building a system in which this sort of dynamic interaction played a prominent role. By focusing on the feedback loop that connects specific and general understanding, the present model provides us with a specific context in which one aspect of this dynamic interaction can be studied and modeled.

The particular feature of the hypothesized feedback loop that makes it interesting is that it is hierarchical, as was illustrated in Figure 7 above (see Chap. I). In turn, one of the most interesting properties of a hierarchical feedback loop is the "standardizing" influence that it exerts across different tasks. To illustrate this influence, consider the case of children's central numerical structures and their relation to performance on specific tasks such as handling money, telling the time, or solving word problems in elementary arithmetic. Whenever genuine progress takes place in children's understanding of numbers in some specific task (say, handling money), this change should have the potential to precipitate a small change in children's general numerical structures (e.g., their understanding of the base-ten system). By the same token, whenever a small change takes place in children's understanding of the base-ten system, this change should have the potential to induce a small but noticeable change in their understanding of a wide range of specific situations. When this sort of reciprocal process repeats itself in an iterative fashion, a process of intellectual "snowballing" or "bootstrapping" should be set in motion. One consequence of this is that the pace of development should accelerate. Another is that the cross-task profile of development should even out because the general conceptual benefits obtained in high-exposure situations should be "passed on" to low-exposure situations via the mediation of the general structure.

There are several implications of these two effects with regard to the demographic data that were presented in the previous chapter. The first is that children who have different styles or backgrounds may arrive at the same general level of general development and exhibit the same even pattern of performance across several tasks as a result of quite different sorts of specific experience. The diligent schoolchild who invests a great deal of attention in learning the math that she is taught by her teacher, the lazy schoolchild whose prime interest is in checking the clock to see how soon his school lessons will be over, and the unschooled child who sells candy in the streets of Brazil—each lives in a highly distinctive environment. Nevertheless, each of these children must work at understanding the same general numerical system. Moreover, as progress is made in understanding this system, this progress should in each case inform the child's performance in a broad range of contexts, including those to which they have relatively little exposure or to which they have not bothered to apply themselves. In effect, different developmental pathways should all lead to the same general end point, namely, that all three children should be able to answer novel questions at the same general developmental level in all three task domains (school math problems, time problems, and money problems).

In effect, this is the explanation that we advanced to explain the fact that children from Japan and America showed such similar rates of quantitative development, even though the Japanese children received so much more training in school math. The notion was that children's general quantitative understanding is fed from many sources and that, even though American children may receive less adequate experience in school math, their opportunities for numerical thinking in other areas are little different and may even be superior. If one culture emphasizes specific task A and another emphasizes specific task B, the general result should be the same. Perhaps more important, if one culture emphasizes one task out of a group of eight and the other has no compensating emphasis, the results should still not be very different.

What about the lower level of development that was obtained in our low-SES samples? In order to explain this phenomenon, consider the possibility that social class differences may produce small differences in the amount and quality of exposure to *all* the tasks that are valued by a culture in contrast to cultural differences, which primarily affect the emphasis that is placed on certain tasks within a general conceptual group. If one is willing to accept this as a possibility, then the logical consequence is this: if hierarchical feedback loops really do exist, then they should magnify these small differences and parlay them into substantial differences in children's general level of cognitive development.

A final implication is that the developmental profile of low-SES children should be the same as for high-SES children, notwithstanding the different experience that they encounter. The even developmental profile of low-SES children is a phenomenon that is difficult to explain within the context of existing neo-Piagetian theory. Explaining the failure of low-SES children to attain their full developmental potential is not a problem: one can simply postulate differences in schematic repertoire and/or differences in schematic activation weights (Case, 1975; Globerson, 1983). Explaining the equivalent performance that such groups exhibit on tests of working memory is also not a problem: one can simply postulate that their cognitive systems mature at the same general rate and thus exhibit equivalent mental power (Bentley, Kvalsig, & Miller, 1990; Case, 1975; Globerson, 1983; Miller & Pascual-Leone, 1981; Miller, Pascual-Leone, Campbell, & Juckes, 1990).

But how can one explain the even cross-task profile? For high-SES groups, this even profile has usually been explained by asserting that, although exposure to different tasks may vary, all children "bump their heads" against the same common ceiling in mental power. This explanation cannot be used for low-SES children, however, because they are so clearly functioning below their optimum level. This being the case, one would expect that, on tasks where they had almost no experience, they would exhibit an extremely low level of performance. By contrast, on tasks for which they had a good deal more experience, they should come closer to their optimum level. The net result of this sort of influence should thus be greater variability in developmental profile, not the same even level that is exhibited by high-SES children. Yet this is not the case, as our own data and the data of others (e.g., Demetriou et al., 1988) amply demonstrate.

With the notion of a hierarchical learning loop in place, a straightforward interpretation of this phenomenon becomes possible, namely, that the same "averaging" effect takes place in low-SES as in high-SES populations owing to the mediation of the general structure. For both groups, insights gained in high-exposure situations are passed on, via the mediation of central conceptual structures, to situations that are encountered with a much lower frequency. Thus, a relatively even developmental profile is produced regardless of the absolute level of performance or the relation between this level and the optimum.

In order to understand how this sort of influence operates in greater detail, it is useful to model the dynamics on which it depends with a set of mathematical equations. For the balance of the present chapter, therefore, I shall devote myself to this task.

DEVELOPMENT AS MODELED BY MATHEMATICAL FUNCTIONS:
THE CASE OF THE EXPONENTIAL GROWTH CURVE

Before I can begin, I must first make a brief digression. In a recent series of studies, Van Geert (1991, 1994) has shown that many developmental functions can be modeled as a set of dynamically linked growth curves. The particular curve on which he has focused is the "logistic growth curve." Although this curve will not be familiar to most readers, its first few terms may well be. They are as follows:

$$Q(X)_{t+1} = Q(X)_t + Q(X)_t \times \text{GR}(X), \tag{1}$$

where $Q(X)_{t+1}$ represents the quantity (Q) of some developmental variable (X) at time $t + 1$, $Q(X)_t$ represents the quantity of that same variable at some earlier time t, and $\text{GR}(X)$ represents the growth rate of the same variable.

The foregoing expression is the discontinuous form of the exponential growth curve. What it asserts is that the quantity of any variable at some time, $t + 1$, is equal to its quantity at some earlier time, t, plus an amount that has been added to that quantity in the interim. In turn, the quantity that has been added in the interim is equal to the earlier quantity multiplied by the variable's growth rate.

An example may help illustrate how this sort of exponential process operates. Consider the case where the variable X represents the size of one's bank account during a lengthy period during which one makes no deposits or withdrawals. What the equation asserts is that, after an interval such as a year, the amount of money in the account will be equal to the amount that was present at the beginning of the year plus an additional amount that is equal to the annual accrued interest. In turn, the annual interest will be equal to the amount present in the account at the beginning of the year times the annual interest rate. If one makes no deposits or withdrawals during the second year, the same process will occur again. The balance at the end of the second year will thus be equal to the size at the end of the first year plus an additional amount equal to that size times the annual interest rate. Over long periods of time, what will happen is that the initial interest will be "compounded" in subsequent time periods, with the result that growth will eventually begin to accelerate in a dramatic fashion. This effect is what investment counselors refer to as "the miracle of compound interest."

Unfortunately for us, bank balances are unlikely to exhibit this sort of dramatic acceleration during the course of a single lifetime, given the annual interest rates that they offer. Figure 27a shows the different rate at which the growth of an account into which 5 cents was deposited might accelerate with two different growth rates: 9% and 7%. As may be seen,

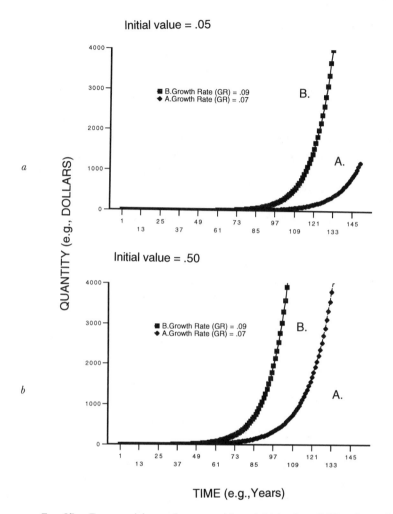

FIG. 27.—Exponential growth curves with an initial value of .05 and monthly growth rates of 7% (A) or 9% (B). The example in the text is that of a dormant bank account with an annual interest rate of either 9% or 7% and an initial deposit of 5 cents (panel *a*) or 50 cents (panel *b*). The general equation is $Q(X)_{t+1} = Q(X)_t + Q(X)_t \times GR(X)$.

both curves have the same general shape, and neither shows a very rapid acceleration during the first 100 years of growth. However, the faster growing curve (B) does begin to grow quite rapidly after about 100 years, the more slowly growing curve (A) about 20 years later. If the initial value were 50 cents instead of 5 cents, the two curves would show their inflection at an earlier point in time, as is illustrated in Figure 27*b*.

DEVELOPMENT IN SITUATIONS WHERE RESOURCES ARE LIMITED:
THE CASE OF THE LOGISTIC GROWTH CURVE

Consider a second example, the case where two rabbits migrate to an uninhabited meadow and establish a new warren. Let $Q(X)_t$ represent the quantity of rabbits in a meadow at the beginning of a breeding season, $Q(x)_{t+1}$ the quantity of rabbits at the end of the breeding season, and $GR(X)$ the growth rate of the ensuing rabbit population. Were no other factor at work, one would expect that, as one generation succeeded the next, the increase in the size of the rabbit population would begin to escalate quite sharply after a few generations. What this example also makes clear, however, is that the exponential curve would not be the best function to model this process because the number of rabbits in the meadow would soon exceed the capacity of the meadow to sustain life and the rate of growth would decelerate.

To model situations where growth is subject to some sort of natural limitation, the function that is normally used is the "logistic" growth function (Van Geert, 1991). In its unreduced and discontinuous form, the function may be expressed as follows:[5]

$$Q(X)_{t+1} = Q(X)_t + Q(X)_t \times GR(X) - [Q(X)_t \times GR(X)] \times Q(X)_t/K, \qquad (2)$$

where $Q(X)_{t+1}$ represents the magnitude or quantity, Q, of some developmental variable, X, at time $t + 1$; $Q(X)_t$ represents the quantity of that same variable at some earlier time, t; $GR(X)$ represents the growth rate of the variable X; and K represents the external limit or "carrying capacity" to which the growth of this variable is subject.

At first glance, this new equation may appear to be rather daunting. In actual fact, however, it is quite simple. The first two expressions to the right of the equals sign are the same as those for the exponential function. The first part of the third expression (which has been placed in brackets) is identical to the second, except that it is negative rather than positive and is multiplied by a "damping parameter" represented by the ratio $Q(X)_t/K$. When this ratio assumes a value of 1, the quantity that is subtracted by the third term becomes identical to that added by the second term. The third term thus cancels the second term out exactly, and the function stays at its original level. Needless to say, the ratio $Q(X)_t/K$ can assume a value of 1 only when its bottom term, K, is exactly equal to its top term. In short,

---

[5] Throughout this chapter, I use the unreduced form of the logistic equation. Although this form is less elegant than the reduced form from an algebraic point of view, the relations that it embodies are more transparent.

growth can be terminated only when the size of the variable in question reaches the carrying capacity to which the process that it models is subject.

The typical chain of events that unfolds in the course of a simple logistic growth process is as follows. At the beginning of the process, the size of the variable that is growing is small, compared to the carrying capacity of the environment. The ratio of $Q(X)_t$ to K is also very small, and very little is subtracted during each compounding interval by the third term. Initial growth thus proceeds in a fashion that is similar (although not identical) to the exponential case. As further growth takes place, the ratio $Q(X)_t/K$ increases, and a substantial quantity is now subtracted each year, relative to the quantity that is added. Finally, as $Q(X)_t$ begins to approach the carrying capacity, the ratio $Q(X)_t/K$ begins to approach 1, and the amount subtracted during each compounding period approaches the amount that is added. The result is that there is a rapid deceleration of growth and an equilibrium point or asymptotic level is reached.

Under conditions of extremely rapid growth, a more turbulent set of events can take place as $Q(X)_t$ approaches K. However, the chain of events just described is by far the most common one as well as the most relevant to the sort of intellectual growth that has been considered in the present *Monograph*. The pattern of growth reflected by a simple logistic function is illustrated in Figure 28. As does Figure 27, this figure also presents two curves, one of which (B) has a growth rate of 9% and the other (A) a growth rate of 7%. Both curves also have initial values of .05. The difference from Figure 27 is that both curves are now subject to a resource limit, which has been set arbitrarily at 4,000 in Figure 28a. Note that, since the first curve rises more rapidly than the second, it also reaches the point where it is strongly affected by this resource limit more rapidly. In contrast to the second curve, then, the first curve looks more sigmoidal, or S shaped, than it did in the previous figure (Fig. 27a). Figure 28b shows the same two curves with the carrying capacity reduced from 4,000 to 10. As may be seen, both curves now exhibit the sigmoidal shape, and both reach asymptotic level at the same value (i.e., 10).

GROWTH AS MODELED BY DYNAMICALLY LINKED LOGISTIC FUNCTIONS: THE SIMPLE COMPOUNDING MODEL

Not all variables that we study in cognitive development exhibit the regular pattern of growth that is indicated in Figure 28. What makes Van Geert's analysis interesting is his demonstration that a large number of other developmental curves can be modeled by a dynamically linked combination

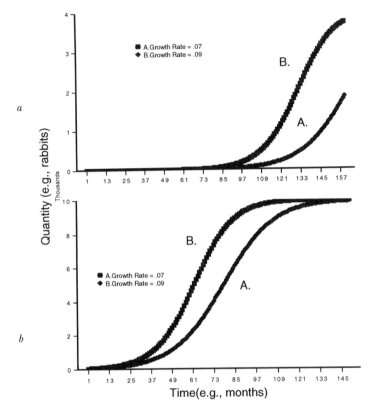

FIG. 28.—Logistic growth curves with initial values of .05 and monthly growth rates of 7% (A) and 9% (B). In panel a, the carrying capacity (K) has been set at 4,000. In panel b, the carrying capacity has been set at 10. Note the difference between these curves and those in the previous figure. This difference results from the fact that the logistic growth curves have a third term that the exponential curves do not: this term subtracts an amount equal to the second term times $Q(X)_t/K$. As $(X)_t$ approaches K, this ratio approaches 1, and the amount subtracted in any growth interval approaches the amount added. The result is that the curve asymptotes at $Q(X)_t = K$ and its shape is sigmoidal rather than exponential.

of these more basic curves. In the present section, I present three examples in which one curve makes a contribution to another.

The Floating Capacity Model

Consider first the case where, owing to overcrowding in the old breeding ground, the original two rabbits who migrated to the new meadow are followed by other rabbits in subsequent years. If the net "inflow" from this older population is 5%, and if this older population (A) is also growing logistically, then the size of the new "hybrid" population (H) may be represented as follows:

$$Q(H)_{t+1} = Q(H)_t + Q(H)_t \times \text{GR}(H) - [Q(H)_t \times \text{GR}(H)_t] \times Q(H)_t/K$$
$$+ Q(A_t) \times .05,$$

or, more generally,

$$Q(H)_{t+1} = Q(H)_t + Q(H)_t \times \text{GR}(H) - [Q(H)_t \times \text{GR}(H)_t] \times Q(H)_t/K$$
$$+ Q(A_t) \times k_{A>H}, \tag{3}$$

where $Q(H)$ represents the growth of the "hybrid" variable that is under consideration (in this case, the number of rabbits in the new field), $Q(A)$ represents the variable that makes the contribution (in this case, the older, original population of rabbits in some other field), and $k_{A>H}$ represents the percentage of the second variable's magnitude that is added to the first variable during any given time interval (.05 in the above example).

As in the previous case, this formula is much less complex than it might appear at first glance. The terms in the first line are identical to those of equation (2). The second line, $Q(A_t) \times k_{A>H}$, has only two components: (a) the value of the second variable at the beginning of the time interval in question ($Q[A_t]$) and (b) a constant indicating the percentage of the second curve's value that is to be taken, and added to the first, during each growth interval. As will no doubt be apparent, the additional quantity of rabbits that are added each year as a result of the immigration is "compounded" in each subsequent year because it becomes a part of the hybrid population and indistinguishable from it.

This situation is illustrated in Figure 29a. As may be seen, the hybrid curve "floats" to a new level, one above that specified by the original carrying capacity, owing to the extra influx of mature rabbits that is received each year from this other source. Were this other source to dry up, as it were, the population would drop back down to its original level. As it is, it continues to grow until the old carrying capacity is sufficiently exceeded (hence the ratio $Q[H]_t/K$ sufficiently greater than 1) that the amount being subtracted each year counterbalances the amount being added from both sources ("exogenous" and "endogenous").

The Fixed Capacity Model

Not all environments are so "elastic" that they will permit this sort of artificial enlargement of a population beyond its normal limits. To model the situation that would obtain in environments with a more rigidly fixed carrying capacity, one would need to add a damping parameter to the "ex-

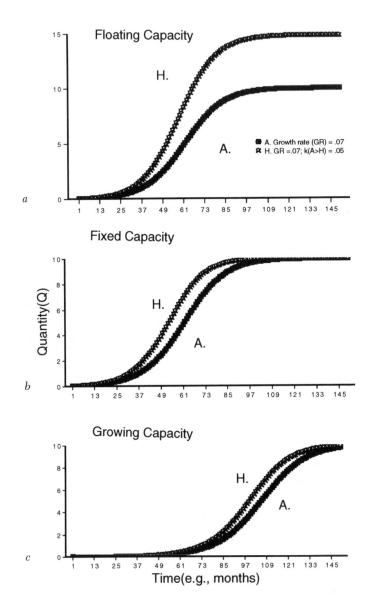

FIG. 29.—Linked growth curves: simple compounding model. In all panels, the bottom curve (A) is a simple logistic function, with an initial value of .05, a carrying capacity of 10, and a growth rate of 7%. The top curve (H) is a "hybrid" growth curve with the same initial value, growth rate, and carrying capacity as A, but receiving an additional monthly contribution of 5% from it. In panel a, although the endogenous carrying capacity of the top curve is 10 units, it "floats" to a higher value as a result of this additional contribution. In panel b, a parameter has been added that "dampens" the additional contribution as the curve approaches the original carrying capacity. The result is that the curve H now asymptotes at the same level as A, although it reaches this level more quickly. In the bottom panel, the carrying capacity for both curves has been changed from a fixed value (10) to a variable value, K_t. K_t has then been allowed to grow from .05 to 10 in a logistic fashion.

ternal" source of growth like that already added to the "endogenous" source. The new equation would be this:

$$Q(H)_{t+1} = Q(H)_t + Q(H)_t \times GR(H) - [Q(H)_t \times GR(H)] \times Q(H)_t/K$$

$$+ Q(A_t) \times k_{A>H} \qquad (4)$$

$$- [Q(A)_t \times k_{A>H}] \times Q(H)_t/K.$$

This expression is identical to equation (3), with the exception of the addition of a new term, $[Q(A)_t \times k_{A>H}] \times Q(H)_t/K$, which subtracts a quantity equal to the term in the second line multiplied by the ratio of H divided by K. Figure 29b shows the curve that would be traced by this equation, with all parameters held identical to those in Figure 29a. As may be seen, the new curve, H, still grows considerably faster than A; however, it now reaches asymptotic level at the same absolute level.

The Growing Capacity Model

One final case worth considering is the one that obtains when the carrying capacity itself is a logistically growing variable whose size is exogenously determined, that is, determined by factors other than those modeled in the two primary growth curves. Such a situation might obtain in the present example if the meadow was originally quite a marginal one owing to extremely arid conditions. Should the annual rainfall start to increase, equation (4) would have to be modified in such a way that K is a variable rather than a constant. The resulting function may be expressed as follows:

$$Q(H)_{t+1} = Q(H)_t + Q(H)_t \times GR(H) - [Q(H)_t \times GR(H)] \times Q(H)_t \times GR(H)_t/K_t$$

$$+ Q(A)_t \times k_{A>H} \qquad (5)$$

$$- [Q(A)_t \times k_{A>H}] \times Q(H)_t/K_t,$$

where K_t is a variable that grows in some fashion.

Figure 29c illustrates the pattern of growth that results from this function when K grows logistically at a rate intermediate between that of H and A and everything else is held constant. As may be seen, the overall effect of letting K vary in this fashion is to shift the growth of both curves to the right. In the limit, as the carrying capacity of the overall system increases more and more slowly, both curves grow at a rate that is identical and equal to the rate set by the carrying capacity, just as they did before. It is just that they bump up against this limit earlier (because the carrying capacity is initially lower) and thus are strongly shaped by the carrying capacity at an earlier point in the growth process, not just at the asymptotic level.

GROWTH AS MODELED BY DYNAMICALLY LINKED LOGISTIC FUNCTIONS: THE MULTIPLICATIVE COMPOUNDING MODEL

Floating Capacity Model

In all the examples considered so far, the amount that one curve adds to a second curve has been computed by multiplying the magnitude of the first curve during the previous interval by some constant $k_{A>H}$ and then adding this to the second curve. One can imagine a situation, however, in which the amount added by one variable to another would depend on the value of the hybrid variable that was receiving the contribution (H) as well as the value of the variable that was making it (A). Consider what would happen, for example, if some chemical started to accumulate in the water table of the meadow that increased the average number of baby rabbits born to every female. The total increase in the rabbit population during any breeding season would now be greater by an amount that would depend, not just on the amount of the chemical that had accumulated in the meadow, but also on the existing size of the rabbit population. The new expression would be

$$Q(H)_{t+1} = Q(H)_t + Q(H)_t \times GR(H) - [Q(H)_t \times GR(H)_t] \times Q(H)_t/K$$
$$+ Q(A)_t \times k_{A>H} \times Q(H)_t. \tag{6}$$

This equation is identical to equation (3) except that the first two terms in the second line, $Q(A)_t \times k_{A>H}$, are multiplied by the value of $Q(H)$ at time t. The curve that would be generated by this equation (with all other values held the same as previously) is shown in Figure 30a. As may be seen, the effect of adding the chemical is much more dramatic than was the effect of adding "immigrants" from the neighboring field, owing to the geometric increase in the amount added to the population during each successive breeding interval. In effect, growth is now subject to a "double compounding" effect.

The Fixed Capacity Model

The increase in Figure 30a is so dramatic that one might wonder whether the overall carrying capacity of the meadow would really be increased in the dramatic manner indicated, especially since the amount of food in the meadow would remain unchanged. Perhaps a better model would be one in which the external carrying capacity remained constant. To model the case where a carrying capacity is externally fixed, a new fifth term—similar to the one added to equation (3) in order to produce equation (4)—must be added to "dampen" the effect of the fourth term, as the carrying capacity of the sys-

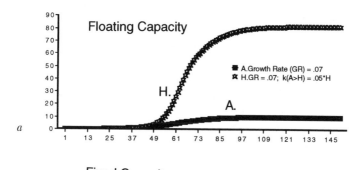

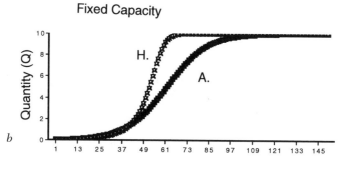

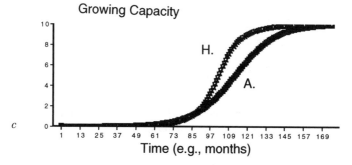

FIG. 30.—Linked growth curves: conjoint compounding model. All the curves in this figure have been generated in the same fashion as those in the previous figure, with one exception. This is that the hybrid curve (H) in each panel has been generated by making the contribution from the bottom curve equal to 5% of $H \times A$ rather than 5% of A. As with any product, there is a geometric increase in the size of the result over time. In comparison to the curves in the previous figure, therefore, the compound curves in this figure show a more explosive pattern of growth.

tem is reached. The new equation for this situation is

$$Q(H)_{t+1} = Q(H)_t + Q(H)_t \times GR(H) - [Q(H)_t \times GR(H)] \times Q(H)_t/K$$

$$+ Q(A)_t \times k_{A>H} \times Q(H)_t \tag{7}$$

$$- [Q(A)_t \times k_{A>H} \times Q(H)_t] \times Q(H)_t/K.$$

171

Equation (7) is identical to equation (6) except that the amount added during every growth interval by the term in line 2 has been dampened in the same manner as specified for the curve's own endogenous growth in line 2. That is to say, the terms added in line 2 have been matched by an identical set of terms in line 3, times a "damping" parameter" equal to $Q(H)_t/K$. The new curve that would be generated by this equation (when all other parameters are held the same as previously) is shown in Figure 30b. The function still shows a dramatic inflection; however, it now reaches asymptotic level at the same point as the other variable.

The Growing Capacity Model

One final model is worth presenting: namely, the model for a carrying capacity that is externally determined and growing. The equation for this case, under conditions of conjoint rather than simple compounding, is the same as equation (7) except that K is now itself a logistic variable:

$$Q(H)_{t+1} = Q(H)_t + Q(H)_t \times \text{GR}(H) - [Q(H)_t \times \text{GR}(H)] \times Q(H)_t/K_t$$

$$+ Q(A)_t \times k_{A>H} \times Q(H)_t \tag{8}$$

$$- [Q(A)_t \times k_{A>H} \times Q(H)_t] \times Q(H)_t/K_t.$$

The resulting growth curves are illustrated in Figure 30c.

MODELING THE PROCESS OF GROWTH IN A HIERARCHICAL SYSTEM WHERE MANY SPECIFIC VARIABLES ARE LINKED TO ONE GENERAL VARIABLE

The Floating Capacity Model: Simple Compounding

So far I have not considered the situation described at the beginning of the present chapter, where several specific variables contribute to the growth of one more general variable. The equations just developed may be extended to deal with this case in a straightforward fashion, however. Let us assume (*a*) that five specific variables, S_1, S_2, S_3, S_4, and S_5, may each be modeled with its own logistic growth curve, (*b*) that there is an additional, more general variable, G, that may also be modeled with its own logistic curve, and (*c*) that the general curve G receives a contribution from each one of the more specific curves. Under these conditions, the equation for each specific curve would be a simple logistic function with its own initial value, growth rate, and carrying capacity. The curve for the general equation would be a good deal more complex and would include either five or 10 additional terms depending on whether each term that was added also had its own damping terms.

For the floating capacity model with simple compounding, the equation for the general curve would be the most straightforward, namely,

$$Q(G)_{t+1} = Q(G)_t + Q(G)_t \times GR(G) - [Q(G)_t \times GR(G)] \times Q(G)_t/K$$

$$+ Q(S_1)_t \times k_{S_1 > G}$$

$$+ Q(S_2)_t \times k_{S_2 > G}$$

$$+ Q(S_3)_t \times k_{S_3 > G} \tag{9}$$

$$+ Q(S_4)_t \times k_{S_4 > G}$$

$$+ Q(S_5)_t \times k_{S_5 > G}.$$

This curve is illustrated in Figure 31a. The growth rates of the specific curves have been set at 4%, 5%, 6%, 7%, and 8%. The growth rate of the general curve has been set at 0% (i.e., it gets all its growth from the specific curves).

The Fixed Capacity Model: Simple Compounding

For the fixed capacity model, equation (9) would have to have a damping parameter added to each of the terms, thus:

$$Q(G)_{t+1} = Q(G)_t + Q(G)_t \times GR(G) - [Q(G)_t \times GR(G)] \times Q(G)_t/K$$

$$+ Q(S_1)_t \times k_{S_1 > G} - [Q(S_1)_t \times k_{S_1 > G}] \times Q(G)_t/K$$

$$+ Q(S_2)_t \times k_{S_2 > G} - [Q(S_2)_t \times k_{S_2 > G}] \times Q(G)_t/K$$

$$+ Q(S_3)_t \times k_{S_3 > G} - [Q(S_3)_t \times k_{S_3 > G}] \times Q(G)_t/K \tag{10}$$

$$+ Q(S_4)_t \times k_{S_4 > G} - [Q(S_4)_t \times k_{S_4 > G}] \times Q(G)_t/K$$

$$+ Q(S_5)_t \times k_{S_5 > G} - [Q(S_5)_t \times k_{S_5 > G}] \times Q(G)_t/K.$$

This curve is illustrated in Figure 31b.

The Growing Capacity Model: Simple Compounding

For the growing capacity model, the equation would be the same as equation (10), except that K would itself be a logistic variable rather than a

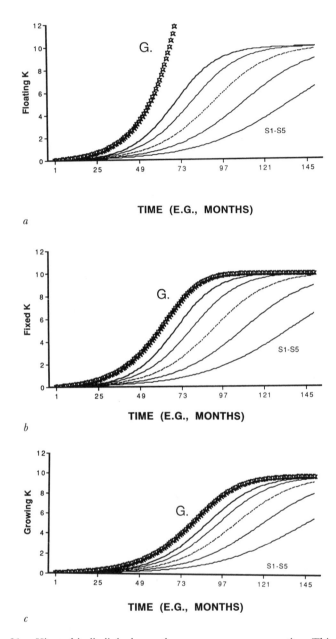

FIG. 31.—Hierarchically linked growth curves: one-way connection. This figure depicts five specific logistic curves ($S_1, \ldots, S_5$) that feed a more general curve (G) under various conditions. The five specific curves grow at rates that range from 3% to 7%. The contribution of each specific curve to the general curve is 1% less than its growth rate.

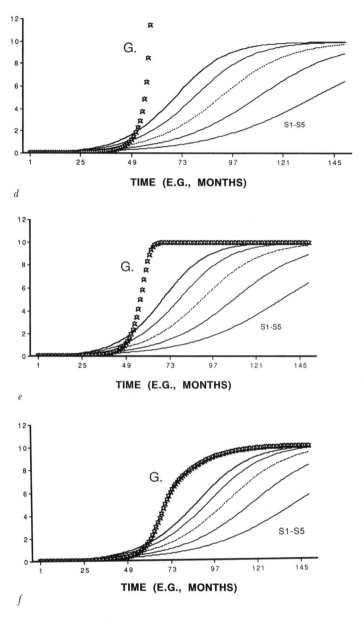

FIG. 31 (*Continued*).—The conditions include two different forms of compounding (simple vs. conjoint) and three different assumptions about the carrying capacity (free to float, fixed at a value = 10 units, and growing logistically from .05 to 10 units). Note that the effect of conjoint compounding is to make the growth of the general curve more explosive while the effect of limiting the carrying capacity of the general curve is to decrease the rate of its growth and its terminal level.

constant. Figure 31c shows the pattern of growth that would be expected for this model.

The Floating Capacity Model: Conjoint Compounding

The same basic set of equations could also be used to model the case of conjoint compounding, the only difference being that the term $Q(H)_t$ would have to be inserted as a multiplier in each additional term. For the case of the floating capacity model, the new equation would be

$$Q(G)_{t+1} = Q(G)_t + Q(G)_t \times GR(G) - [Q(G)_t \times GR(G)] \times Q(G)_t/K$$

$$+ [Q(S_1)_t \times k_{S_1>G}] \times Q(G)_t$$

$$+ [Q(S_2)_t \times k_{S_2>G}] \times Q(G)_t$$

$$+ [Q(S_3)_t \times k_{S_3>G}] \times Q(G)_t \qquad (11)$$

$$+ [Q(S_4)_t \times k_{S_4>G}] \times Q(G)_t$$

$$+ [Q(S_5)_t \times k_{S_5>G}] \times Q(G)_t.$$

The Fixed Capacity Model: Conjoint Compounding

For the case of the externally determined carrying capacity, a damping term would be added to each additional term; thus, the equation for the general curve would be

$$Q(G)_{t+1} = Q(G)_t + Q(G)_t \times GR(G) - [Q(G)_t \times GR(G)] \times Q(G)_t/K$$

$$+ Q(S_1)_t \times Q(G)_t \times k_{S_1>G} - [Q(S_1)_t \times Q(G)_t \times k_{S_1>G}] \times Q(G)_t/K$$

$$+ Q(S_2)_t \times Q(G)_t \times k_{S_2>G} - [Q(S_2)_t \times Q(G)_t \times k_{S_2>G}] \times Q(G)_t/K$$

$$+ Q(S_3)_t \times Q(G)_t \times k_{S_3>G} - [Q(S_3)_t \times Q(G)_t \times k_{S_3>G}] \times Q(G)_t/K \qquad (12)$$

$$+ Q(S_4)_t \times Q(G)_t \times k_{S_4>G} - [Q(S_4)_t \times Q(G)_t \times k_{S_4>G}] \times Q(G)_t/K$$

$$+ Q(S_5)_t \times Q(G)_t \times k_{S_5>G} - [Q(S_5)_t \times Q(G)_t \times k_{S_5>G}] \times Q(G)_t/K.$$

The Growing Capacity Model: Conjoint Compounding

Finally, for the growing capacity model, the equation would remain the same, but K would be a logistically growing variable rather than a constant.

The compound curves that would result for each of these cases are illustrated in Figure 31d–f.

MODELING THE PROCESS OF GROWTH IN A HIERARCHICAL SYSTEM WHERE THE LINKAGE BETWEEN GENERAL AND SPECIFIC VARIABLES IS RECIPROCAL

The final situation that must be considered is one where the general curve (G) makes a reciprocal contribution to each of the specific curves $(S_1, \ldots, S_5)$. To represent this reciprocal relation, the equation for each specific curve must be rewritten as well. For the case of simple compounding, with a constant and externally fixed carrying capacity, the full set of equations would be as follows:

$$Q(G)_{t+1} = Q(G)_t + Q(G)_t \times \mathrm{GR}(G) - [Q(G)_t \times \mathrm{GR}(G)] \times Q(G)_t/K$$

$$+ \, Q(S_1)_t \times k_{S_1 > G} - [Q(S_1)_t \times k_{S_1 > G}] \times Q(G)_t/K$$

$$+ \, Q(S_2)_t \times k_{S_2 > G} - [Q(S_2)_t \times k_{S_2 > G}] \times Q(G)_t/K$$

$$+ \, Q(S_3)_t \times k_{S_3 > G} - [Q(S_3)_t \times k_{S_3 > G}] \times Q(G)_t/K$$

$$+ \, Q(S_4)_t \times k_{S_4 > G} - [Q(S_4)_t \times k_{S_4 > G}] \times Q(G)_t/K$$

$$+ \, Q(S_5)_t \times k_{S_5 > G} - [Q(S_5)_t \times k_{S_5 > G}] \times Q(G)_t/K,$$

$$Q(S_1)_{t+1} = Q(S_1)_t + Q(S_1)_t \times \mathrm{GR}(S_1) - [Q(S_1)_t \times \mathrm{GR}(S_1)] \times Q(S_1)_t/K$$

$$+ \, Q(G)_t \times k_{G > S_1} - [Q(G)_t \times k_{G > S_1}] \times Q(S_1)_t/K,$$

$$Q(S_2)_{t+1} = Q(S_2)_t + Q(S_2)_t \times \mathrm{GR}(S_2) - [Q(S_2)_t \times \mathrm{GR}(S_2)] \times Q(S_2)_t/K$$

$$+ \, Q(G)_t \times k_{G > S_2} - [Q(G)_t \times k_{G > S_2}] \times Q(S_2)_t/K,$$

$$Q(S_3)_{t+1} = Q(S_3)_t + Q(S_3)_t \times \mathrm{GR}(S_3) - [Q(S_3)_t \times \mathrm{GR}(S_3)] \times Q(S_3)_t/K$$

$$+ \, Q(G)_t \times k_{G > S_3} - [Q(G)_t \times k_{G > S_3}] \times Q(S_3)_t/K,$$

$$Q(S_4)_{t+1} = Q(S_4)_t + Q(S_4)_t \times \mathrm{GR}(S_4) - [Q(S_4)_t \times \mathrm{GR}(S_4)] \times Q(S_4)_t/K$$

$$+ \, Q(G)_t \times k_{G > S_4} - [Q(G)_t \times k_{G > S_4}] \times Q(S_4)_t/K,$$

$$Q(S_5)_{t+1} = Q(S_5)_t + Q(S_5)_t \times \mathrm{GR}(S_5) - [Q(S_5)_t \times \mathrm{GR}(S_5)] \times Q(S_5)_t/K$$

$$+ \, Q(G)_t \times k_{G > S_5} - [Q(G)_t \times k_{G > S_5}] \times Q(S_5)_t/K.$$

The equations for the other models would all have to be rewritten in a parallel fashion. Figure 32 shows the growth curves that would result with the reciprocal contribution of the general curve to all specific curves set at 5% and all other parameters held constant. The important thing to note is the difference between this figure and Figure 31 above. The two major changes—which indicate the effects of the reciprocal linkage—are (1) that the development of all the curves is accelerated (since they all receive additional input) and (2) that the specific curves are more closely "tied" together (since the rapid growth that takes place in the faster-growing curves is passed on, through the mediation of the general curve, to the more slowly growing curves).

MODELING THE PROCESS OF GENERAL AND SPECIFIC GROWTH AS CONCEIVED IN THE PRESENT MONOGRAPH

With the foregoing mathematical models in hand, I now return to the psychological question with which I began the present chapter, namely, how to model the relation between specific and general growth in development. In the model that I proposed, each of a number of specific understandings (e.g., time, physical causality, social causality, commercial transactions, school math, etc.) makes a contribution to the growth of a central conceptual understanding (e.g., of number), and this central conceptual understanding in turn makes a contribution to each of several more specific understandings. Clearly, the equations necessary to embody this model are those in which there is a reciprocal linkage between a number of specific curves and a general curve. The only questions are, Which of the six mathematical models that I have described best captures the assumptions of the psychological model? and, What values should be chosen for the various parameters that the equations contain?

Selecting a Mathematical Model

The psychological model that I favor is one that, in the neo-Piagetian tradition, assumes that the child's information-processing capacity is limited and that it grows in a fashion that is independent of any specific or general understandings that are being modeled. For this psychological model, the most appropriate mathematical model is the growing capacity model. Whether the simple or the conjoint version of this model is used depends on what assumptions one makes about the contribution of the general and specific processes at different levels of development. If one assumes that, once the unidimensional structure is assembled, the child's ability to profit from specific experience undergoes a profound transformation, the conjoint compounding model might be most appropriate. One might want to make the "top-down" contribution a joint function of the two levels so that it would accelerate as the child's general understanding level climbed from a predimensional to a unidimensional value (i.e., from 1 to 2 units). If one assumes that the general structure makes an important contribution to all the specific structures, even in its predimensional form, then one would want to use the simple compounding model for both the bottom-up and the top-down contributions.

The most conservative assumptions are those of the simple additive model. However, the multiplicative model is also a reasonable possibility. Thus, in the sections that follow, I consider both cases.

Selecting Parameters for the Models

With a general mathematical model in mind, one must next select a set of parameters to plug into it. Consider first the carrying capacity (K). In the examples that were developed in the previous section, the carrying capacity for the growing K models was arbitrarily set at 10 for the constant capacity models and at a value that grew from 1 to 10 in a logistic fashion for the growing K models. In the context of neo-Piagetian theory, the carrying capacity of a developing system is identified with its information-processing capacity or mental power, which in turn is presumed to be estimable from the size of its working memory. As shown in Appendix E, children's working memory grows during the age range of interest and is well fit by a curve whose carrying capacity is 1 at the age of 4 and 3.7 at the age of 10 and that shows a monthly growth rate of 4.5% during the interim. Accordingly, it is these values that I plug into the set of equations specified in equation (13) for the value of K_t.

Consider next the growth rate that is assumed for the general curve, GR(G). In the present model, what this parameter represents is that part of the growth of children's general understanding that is independent of any specific understanding, for example, the sort of growth that might occur if children consciously reflected on their general knowledge of numbers, without any specific instantiation in mind. Piaget hypothesized that this sort of general reflectivity did not appear until the teenage years. Since I have seen no data to suggest anything different, I have followed Piaget's lead in this regard and set the growth rate of the general function at 0. From a psychological point of view, the effect of this decision is to guarantee that growth in children's general understanding takes place *only* when it is prompted by some more specific form of conceptual activity.

Consider finally the weights that should be assigned to the contributions

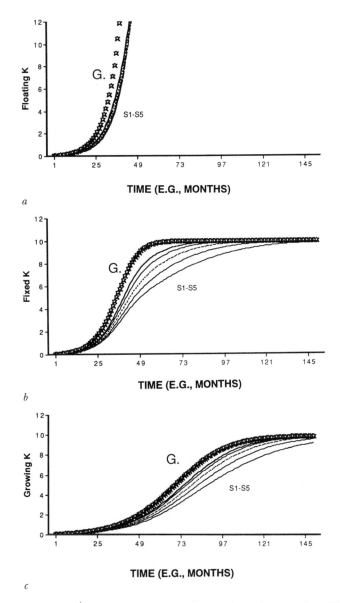

FIG. 32.—Hierarchically linked growth curves: reciprocal connection. This figure depicts five specific logistic curves ($S_1, \ldots, S_5$) that feed a more general curve (G) under various conditions. All the specific parameters are the same as those depicted in the previous figure (Fig. 31 above); the only difference is that the general curve makes a reciprocal contribution to all the specific curves ($K[G > s]$), which is equal to 5%. Note that there are two major consequences. First, growth of all functions occurs more rapidly. Second, specific curves that would otherwise show widely different growth rates get "bound together" more closely.

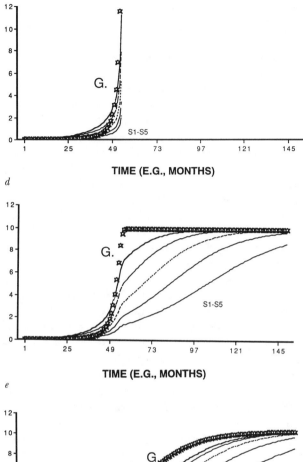

d

e

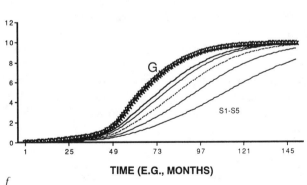

f

FIG. 32 (*Continued*)

that the general curve receives from the specific curves (formally represented as $k_{S_1>G}$, $k_{S_2>G}$, etc.). According to the psychological model, (a) specific structures for which the level of understanding is high should have a greater influence on general understanding than those for which this level is low, and (b) the absolute level of general understanding should not exceed that of the highest specific function. One way to ensure that the first condition is obtained is to let k for any specific curve be a function of its own growth rate. In the present case, k will be set, somewhat arbitrarily, at GR(S) − 1. In order to ensure that the second condition is met, the reciprocal contribution that the general structure makes to the more specific structures ($k_{G>S_1}$, $k_{G>S_2}$, etc.) will be set at a value that is equal to the average of the specific growth rates. This value will be assumed to be the same for all curves so as to reflect the fact that the influence of the general function is presumed to be constant across specific tasks. (Being able to count mentally, e.g., should make just as big a contribution to a task that a child is thoroughly familiar with as it does to one of lesser familiarity, providing that both tasks require this competence.)

Finally, consider the rate at which the specific understandings are acquired, GR($S_1, S_2, \ldots, S_x$). There is no available theoretical basis for making decisions about the absolute values of these parameters; however, as indicated in the earlier discussion, it is clear that these values must vary substantially from task to task. For convenience, I use the same values that were used in explicating the mathematical models, namely, 8%–4%.

Entering all these parameters into the first mathematical model (i.e., the model for growing K with simple compounding) yields the pattern of specific and general growth shown in Figure 33a. Substituting the same parameters into the second mathematical model (i.e., the "mixed" model with simple bottom-up compounding but conjoint top-down compounding) yields the pattern of growth shown in Figure 33b. As may be seen, the two patterns are quite similar. The difference between them lies in the rapidity of acceleration of all curves during the preschool period and the extent to which the specific curves diverge from each other during the dimensional period.

COMPARING THE THEORETICALLY DERIVED GROWTH CURVES TO THE EMPIRICAL DATA

Figure 34 compares the fastest- and slowest-growing specific curves generated by the model (i.e., those with growth rates set at 8% and 4%) to the mean scores that were reported in Chapters III and V for the numerical, narrative, and spatial batteries. As may be seen, the great majority of means obtained at each age (total $N = 60$) fall within the bounds specified by the

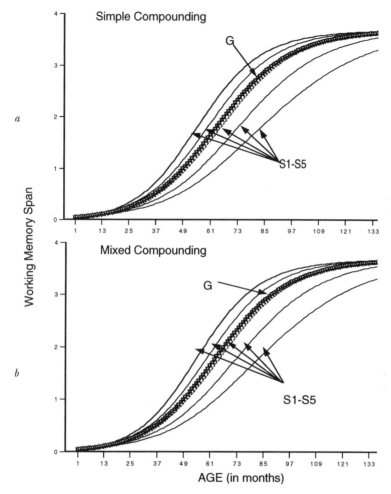

Fɪɢ. 33.—Theoretical models for a situation where several different specific numerical understandings all contribute to the growth of a central conceptual understanding but are limited by a working memory capacity that grows from .05 to 4 units. The model that has been used in panel *a* is the simple compounding model with an externally fixed carrying capacity that grows in the same manner as the (empirically derived) constraints on children's working memory (see Fig. 39 below and App. E). Panel *b* depicts a similar situation, where the reciprocal contribution of the general understanding is not simple but conjoint.

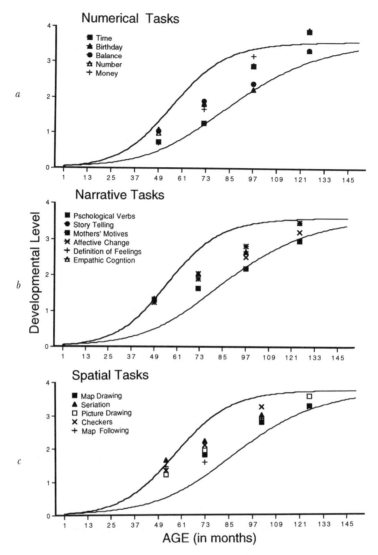

FIG. 34.—Empirical data from the three test batteries, plotted on the same graph as the fastest- and slowest-growing theoretical curves from Fig. 33 above. Note that most of the means fall in the predicted range. *a*, Numerical tasks. *b*, Narrative tasks. *c*, Spatial tasks.

fastest and slowest growth curves, and those that fall outside this range can easily be brought into it by assuming slightly faster or slower levels of growth.

That the magnitude of the empirical means should be of the same order of magnitude as those of the theoretical means may at first glance seem a tour de force. In fact, however, this aspect of the match between theory and data results from the choice of growth rates and should not be treated as either supporting or refuting the model. What *is* encouraging—and not guaranteed by the choice of parameters—is the fact that the general shape and spread of the theoretical growth curves are similar to those that were obtained empirically. Indeed, of the six models, the two that seem to make the most psychological sense are also the two that provide the best fit to the data. That is not to say, of course, that no other model could be fit to the data. A data set as simple as the present one could be fit by a variety of other models. For example, they could be fit with a model that assumed a simple process of linear (as opposed to logistic) growth, with no linkage among the different curves. The real question that must be addressed, therefore, is how easily other models can embrace the data on the effects of social class and culture.

Recall that, in the opening sections, I argued that, whereas cultural differences in the modern world would have a large effect on the children's relative exposure to different specific tasks within the same general conceptual set, social class distinctions should have a small effect on the rate or quality of children's exposure to all tasks within these sets. The final figure illustrates the consequences of these assumptions for the theoretical model. As depicted in Figure 35, increasing the rate of exposure of the lowest-exposure task by 5% so as to mimic the cross-cultural case produces very little change in the central conceptual structure (although it of course produces a change in the growth of the specific curve). By contrast, reducing the rate of growth of all specific tasks by 1% (Fig. 36a) produces a change in the central conceptual structure much like the effect that was found to be associated with social class distinctions. Figure 36b shows the pattern of growth that would be expected with a second difference as well, namely, a difference in K, of a magnitude that could be expected owing to differences in the automaticity of basic operations. I take the match between this theoretically generated pattern of growth and the empirically measured pattern of growth as an indication that the mathematical models have some promise.

SUMMARY AND CONCLUSION

In introducing this chapter, I pointed out that traditional theories of learning and of cognitive development were in conflict with regard to the

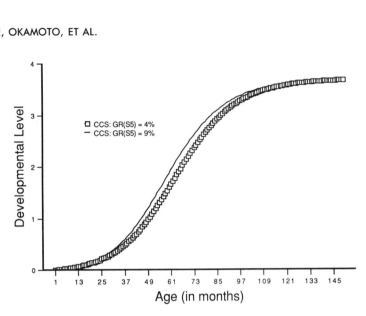

FIG. 35.—The difference in the growth rate of two general curves, one of which receives input from a set of other curves, $S_1, \ldots, S_5$, whose individual growth rates range from 4% to 8%, and the other of which receives input from a set of tasks, one of whose values (S_4) has been changed by 5%. This change in the growth rate of an individual task is presumed to be analogous to the sort of change that one culture introduces with regard to another culture, by changing the value that is ascribed to a category of task and the time that children devote to mastering it.

effects of specific learning. Developmental theorists saw general structures as influencing specific learning but not being affected by it, whereas learning theorists took the opposite view—that general structures (if they existed) were affected *only* by specific experiences. In the formulation of neo-Piagetian theory, both general and specific effects were acknowledged; however, general effects were assigned to mental capacity and specific ones to the child's schematic repertoire. Thus, the possibility of reciprocal influence did not emerge (or at least was not explored).

In the present chapter, I have proposed the existence of such a reciprocal influence and explored its consequences. At a general level, the two consequences that follow are (1) that the overall pace of development is accelerated and (2) that the profile of development is evened out because benefits obtained from high-frequency learning experiences are passed on, via the mediation of the central conceptual structure, to low-frequency ones. These two effects were then advanced as one possible explanation for the difference in the data obtained between different cultures and different social classes. In the former case, the explanation utilized the notion that the benefits of high-frequency learning could be passed on to low-frequency situations via the mediation of general structures; in the latter case, the explanation drew on the notion that experiential loops can accelerate or

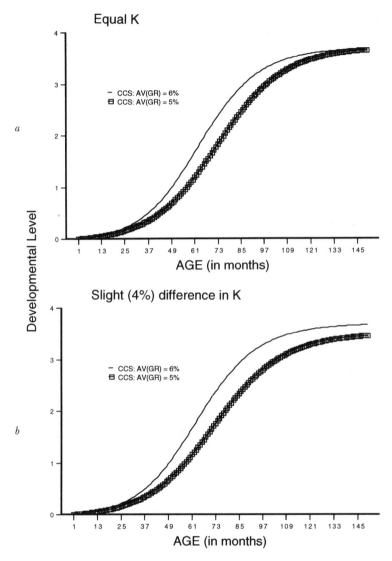

FIG. 36.—The difference in the growth rate of two general curves, one of which receives input from a set of specific curves, $S_1, \ldots, S_5$, whose individual growth rates range from 4% to 8%, and the other of which receives input from a set of tasks, all of whose values have been changed by 1%. This small change in the growth rate of an entire set of tasks is presumed to be analogous to the sort of advantage or disadvantage that one social class receives with regard to another, with regard to the amount or quality of exposure to culturally valued tasks. Figure 36a assumes equal K. Figure 36b assumes a small difference in K, owing to differential automization of basic operations.

decelerate development by magnifying experiential differences that are relatively small but that prevail across most of the tasks that a child encounters.

The last half of the present chapter was devoted to specifying the dynamics of this sort of interaction in mathematical terms. The data that were obtained in Chapters III and V were extremely regular and showed an even pattern of development across different tasks; hence, they could conceivably be modeled with single curves or even straight lines. The mathematical model chosen to fit these findings was much more complex, however. Each growth curve was generated by an expression that contained a dynamic tension between two opposing categories of effect: those whose tendency is to make different developmental pathways disperse (different growth rates and the effect of compounding) and those whose tendency is to hold development to a single course (the constraints imposed by a growing carrying capacity and the "binding together" or "squeezing" effect generated by the reciprocal feedback loop).

The disadvantage of this sort of modeling is clearly its complexity. An equally clear advantage, however, is that it allows one to provide a unified explanation for a set of data that might otherwise seem quite disparate and to express relations in quantitative rather than merely qualitative terms. This, in turn, permits one to check the entire set of proposed relations for their consistency, and to explore the dynamic pattern of their interaction, by conducting "intellectual experiments" and checking them against common sense and/or existing data sets. In the present chapter, this approach has been used for the effects of social class and of culture. In principle, however, it could potentially be used equally to explore the effects of other variables, such as those that underlie intellectual retardation and/or "giftedness." At least for the moment, then, the mathematical modeling approach looks promising.

VIII. SUMMARY AND CONCLUSION

Robbie Case

CLASSIC AND CONTEMPORARY MODELS OF CHILDREN'S COGNITIVE STRUCTURES: A BRIEF OVERVIEW

Of all the constructs in Piaget's theory, none has been subjected to more persistent criticism than the notion of a general logicomathematical structure, that is, the notion of a general and universal system of logical operations to which any new situation must ultimately be assimilated. In the context of Piaget's theory, such structures were viewed as being acquired by an autoregulative process in which children reflect on the adequacy of their existing logical structures and assemble new ones by differentiating and recoordinating their elements. Piaget believed that, in the course of cognitive growth, children construct three or four general classes of such structure, each of which has greater intellectual power than its predecessor, and each of which propels their thought to a new level of abstraction. It was this recursive reconstruction process, he asserted, that moves children through the four classic stages of cognitive growth.

As Piaget's theory became widely known, his emphasis on the active nature of children's thought was welcomed, as was his suggestion that children represent familiar situations and actions with internal structures (schemas and schemes). His hypotheses regarding children's logicomathematical structures, however, were seriously questioned. As new data were collected and existing data examined in more detail, it became apparent that children's intellectual processes were far more content, context, and culture specific than he had suggested. The challenge confronting subsequent theorists, therefore, was to construct a new theoretical system, one that would capture this specificity without losing the capability for characterizing the general properties of children's thought at different ages and distinguishing it from the thought of adults.

189

Several different proposals were advanced in response to this challenge. Neo-Piagetians proposed that children's structures be viewed as sets of specific schemes and schemas that could not yet be integrated because children's general processing capacity was too limited (Case, 1978; Fischer, 1980; Halford, 1982; Pascual-Leone, 1970). Neonativists proposed that infants' cognitive structures be viewed as module-specific theories that need to undergo two or three successive revolutions before they become commensurate with those of adults (Carey, 1985; Spelke, 1988). Learning theorists proposed that children's structures be seen as domain-specific conceptual networks that are less integrated than those of adults and that fail to capture certain essential features of the domains that they represent (Chi, 1988; Siegler, 1978). Finally, sociohistoric theorists suggested that adult thought be seen as depending on the acquisition of several different symbol systems (words, numbers, gestures, etc.), together with the conceptual frameworks, forms of notation, and patterns of activity that permit these systems to be put to full use (Bruner, 1964; Gardner, 1991; Olson, 1994; Scribner & Cole, 1980). In this final view, what distinguishes the thought of children from that of adults is that children have not as yet been fully initiated into the symbol systems and activity patterns that have been developed by their culture and can thus participate but peripherally in its daily practice (Lave & Wenger, 1991).

The foregoing proposals are quite diverse. It is important to realize, therefore, that they all share the following core features. (1) All the new conceptualizations deemphasize or eliminate the notion of a system-wide cognitive structure, replacing this notion with the notion of a structure that is specific either to a neurological module, a content domain, or a symbolic system. (2) All the new proposals abandon the attempt to model children's cognitive structures as systems of logical operations, focusing instead on their symbolic and/or conceptual content. (3) While not denying the importance of autoregulative processes, all the new theories assign much greater weight to children's physical and/or social experience in characterizing the process of structural formation.

MODEL OF CONCEPTUAL STRUCTURES EXPLORED IN THE PRESENT PROGRAM OF RESEARCH

The present research program was based on a controversial assumption, namely, that Piaget's notion of a general logicomathematical structure has been jettisoned prematurely. Rather than eliminating that construct, we proposed that it should be revised in the light of the insights and data that more modern theoretical views have generated. The core features of Piaget's theory that we retained in our own theoretical work were as follows.

(1) Young children's cognition is underpinned by a relatively small number of universal cognitive structures. (2) These structures play a powerful role in organizing their thought. (3) Major changes take place in these structures as their elements are differentiated and coordinated. (4) Children's thinking progresses through four general levels as a result of this process.

The features of Piaget's theory that we deemphasized were the same as those that other modern theorists have called into question, namely, (1) the notion that cognitive structures are system-wide in their domain of application, (2) the notion that cognitive structures are best modeled as systems of logical operations, and (3) the notion that autoregulative processes should be assigned a greater weight than physical or social experience in modeling the process of structural change.

To replace these notions, we advanced the following four proposals. (1) As learning theorists have suggested, children's structures are best understood as rich networks of concepts and conceptual relations. (2) As neo-nativists have suggested, these structures are module-wide (not system-wide) in their span of application and undergo periodic revolutionary change. (3) As neo-Piagetians have suggested, the timing of these changes is codetermined by children's experience and by changes in their general processing capabilities; thus, revolutionary changes often take place in several different conceptual networks during the same general time period. (4) Finally, as sociohistoric theorists have suggested, the content of children's central conceptual structures becomes increasingly distinctive with age since it becomes increasingly linked to the conceptual and notational systems of their own particular culture.

The name that we assigned to structures with these four properties was *central conceptual structures*. In the introductory chapter, I described two such structures in considerable detail. The first pertained to the domain of quantitative thought. The hypothesis was that, at the age of 6 years, children construct a structure in which numbers are viewed in a new manner, namely, as lying along a line that extends from small numbers to large numbers and that proceeds along this continuum in 1-unit steps. As this structure is acquired, children's strategies for solving a broad range of quantitative tasks all change in a similar manner. By the age of 8–10 years, children become capable of understanding that two number lines or scales can be involved in any problem and that these may bear a lawful relation to each other. This new capability allows them to construct a more complex conceptual system in which two numerical scales are differentiated and related. One of the most important of these systems, at least in the modern era, is the structure that represents the workings of the base-ten system of whole numbers. As children begin to understand this system, their answers to a broad range of quantitative tasks change in a predictable fashion. The structural progression to which this leads is illustrated visually in Figure 37.

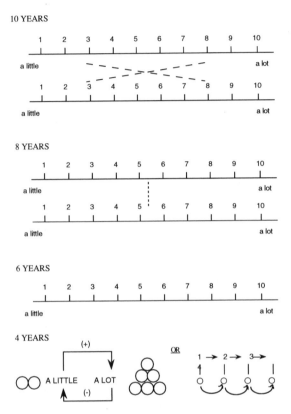

Fig. 37.—The hypothesized progression in children's central numerical competencies between 4 and 10 years of age. The bottom row indicates the predimensional schemas possessed by 4-year-olds for representing quantity and number (see Fig. 1 above). The next row above that indicates the unidimensional schema (the mental counting line) that emerges at 6 years and that can conjointly represent number and quantity. The next row up indicates the "bidimensional" capability that emerges at 8 years and that can represent two qualitative dimensions or scales and their relation. The top row represents the integrated bidimensional capability that emerges at 10 years and that can represent the (reversible) relation between two scales and generalize this to an entire system.

The second central conceptual structure that was analyzed in Chapter I was in the domain of social cognition. Between the ages of 4 and 6 years, children for the first time construct a structure in which the internal states of the protagonists—states such as desires, beliefs, or feelings—are seen to play a central role in motivating the event sequences with which they are familiar. As a consequence, the way in which they explain these events changes, across a wide range of tasks and contexts. By the age of 8–10 years, children's interpretations of social events reveal an understanding that two sets of desires or beliefs, as well as their relation, must often be taken into account in explaining why a particular sequence of events occurs. This more complex understanding allows them to construct a model of the narrative forms that are used in our culture and of the psychological explanations that are favored. One of the most important narrative forms in our culture is one where the central protagonist wants to achieve a particular goal but encounters a series of obstacles that he must overcome before he can do so. Acquisition of this structure is once again associated with a broad range of changes in children's thought.

PROBLEMS WITH THE PREVIOUSLY EXISTING DATABASE, VIS-À-VIS THE PRESENT MODEL

At the time the present program of research was initiated, two general sorts of data had been gathered to support the foregoing analysis. The first set showed that, when new social and quantitative tasks are created, the age at which they are mastered can be predicted on the basis of the central conceptual structure that must be applied to the problem: tasks that can be solved without a number or story line are passed by the age of 4; tasks requiring a single number or story line are passed at the age of 6; and those requiring two number or story lines are passed at the age of 8 (Bruchkowsky, 1992; Capodilupo, 1992; Goldberg-Reitman, 1992; Griffin, 1992; Griffin et al., 1992; Marini, 1992; McKeough, 1992a). The second set of data showed that, when children who have not yet acquired one of these age-typical structures are taught its elements, they will begin to respond in an age-typical fashion on the full range of tasks for which that structure is relevant (Case & Sandieson, 1992; Griffin et al., 1994; McKeough, 1992b).

These data were seen as promising by many investigators (Hencke & Fischer, 1993; Johnson, 1993). However, they were regarded by others with a good deal more skepticism (Bickhard, 1994; Halford, 1993a; Lewis, 1994). Although a number of criticisms were advanced, the one most relevant to the present program of research was Bickhard's (1994). While acknowledging that our hypotheses about central conceptual structures had some intuitive plausibility, Bickhard pointed out that the data could not be regarded as definitive until one had a sense of the interpretations that might be advanced to explain them from other contemporary points of view.

Although Bickhard did not specify in detail just what such alternatives might look like, the following two possibilities seemed both possible and plausible. (1) Within the context of neo-Piagetian theory, the regular progression from predimensional (or preintentional) thought to integrated bidimensional (or integrated bi-intentional) thought could be explained by postulating an increase in complexity across the tasks on the one hand and an increase in processing capacity across age groups on the other. Although a structural analysis was used to generate the original tasks on which this progression is observed, it could be argued that the main function that this analysis had served was simply to scale the set of test items in terms of their complexity. (2) Within the context of learning or sociohistoric theory, the same data could be interpreted in a different manner. One could point out that, as children enter the first grade, they encounter daily instruction in arithmetic (which affects their numerical structures) and in reading (which affects their narrative structures). Since reading and math are both highly valued skills, they both receive roughly the same amount of training (i.e., about an hour per day); as a consequence, improvement in mathematical and narrative thought takes place at roughly the same rate, not because two central conceptual structures are being constructed, but because children are acquiring the bits of conceptual and procedural knowledge that they need in each domain at approximately the same rate.

The instructional data could be interpreted in a similar manner. One could suggest that the children were taught relatively specific facts, concepts, and procedures in the course of their training, each of which improved their performance on a different particular posttest. Training did influence children's conceptual understanding according to this argument; however, it did not do so by providing children with any mental entity of a general sort. Rather, it did so by providing a wide variety of specific mental elements. Alternatively, one could argue that the children who were trained did acquire something general but that this general competence was a set of test-taking skills, not a central conceptual structure.

NEW DATA GATHERED IN RESPONSE TO EXISTING PROBLEMS AND CRITIQUES

Our first goal in the present program of research was to gather a new set of data: one that would provide stronger evidence for the existence of central conceptual structures and rule out alternative interpretations of the existing data such as those outlined above. Several new lines of inquiry were conducted with this aim in mind. In the first (Chap. II), we devised a more direct test of children's central numerical knowledge than had been available previously. In addition to testing specific skills such as counting and quantity comparison, the new test required children to answer novel questions that could be dealt with *only* if they understood the conceptual relations that we had hypothesized. For all the new items that we devised at the 4- and 6-year-old levels, and for the majority of new items at the 8- and 10-year-old levels, children responded in the manner that we predicted. Moreover, in the case of the discrepant items, children's anomalous performance appeared to result not from the absence of the structure that we had hypothesized but rather from the presence of some feature in the task whose salience we had not anticipated. We therefore interpreted the data as providing additional evidence in favor of the structural hypothesis.

In the work reported in Chapter III, we presented the results from a large correlational study, the first of its kind that we have conducted. Here, we showed that tasks that share a common conceptual structure also show a coherent pattern of correlations and load on a common factor, even when they have different surface content. We also showed that our two tests that assess children's numerical and narrative knowledge most directly (the Number Knowledge test and the Storytelling test) show strong loadings on the expected factors. Once again, we took this new evidence as shoring up our original interpretation of the developmental data by ruling out (or at least rendering less likely) the notion that children's development can be seen as stemming exclusively from the acquisition of a set of unrelated concepts and skills.

In the third set of studies (Chap. IV), we reported a new series of instructional interventions. In the first, two treatment groups were used, each of which was taught a different central conceptual structure. Since transfer was found within but not across conceptual domains, it was possible to rule out the possibility that the training was merely giving children some sort of general test-taking sophistication. In the second training study, a single treatment group was given additional instruction on the network of numerical relations that we hypothesized as relevant; the control group was exposed to a conventional readiness program that stressed only a subset of these numerical relations. Compared to the first study, the treatment group showed increased transfer, while the control group showed transfer of a much more modest nature. We therefore concluded that the network of concepts that we had originally isolated—not some different network or a subset of this network—was what had produced the original transfer. Finally, in the third study, children were taught in a group situation that did not permit as much active involvement via games or other small-group activities. Although the extent of transfer was somewhat reduced, it was still highly significant. This result suggests that children's success in the posttest cannot be ascribed to our novel instructional methods, independent of their conceptual content.

When viewed from a different theoretical perspective, any one of the foregoing studies could perhaps still be assigned some valid counterinterpretation. It is much more difficult, however, to see how any of the existing counterinterpretations could be applied across all three types of studies. As a minimum, then, we see the new studies as shifting the onus of proof to those who do not think that central conceptual structures have any psychological reality or to those who maintain that the structures do not play the role that we have hypothesized in children's cognitive growth.

CHANGE IN THE GRAIN OF THEORETICAL ANALYSIS

If our first goal in the present program of research was to demonstrate the existence of central conceptual structures, our second goal was to provide a more detailed account of their nature and of the way in which they operate in specific task situations. The study most directly relevant to this goal was the computer simulation reported in Chapter II. At the time this study was initiated, the most successful computer model of children's thinking on math word problems was one that had been proposed by Riley and Greeno (1988). In these authors' model, children's performance was seen as stemming from the acquisition of a conceptual structure of a classic nature, namely, a "part-whole" structure that represents the relation between superordinate and subordinate mathematical sets. While the data on certain problem classes were reasonably well fit by simulations that instantiated this model, the data on other problems (especially Compare problems) were not.

To remedy this problem, we decided, with Greeno's assistance, to construct a new model, one in which children were conceived as representing each set of objects in a problem as though it had been laid out on a mental number line. The line itself was composed of an ordered array of tokens, each element of which contained the following elements: (a) a specification of its position in an object sequence (object 1, object 2, object 3, etc.); (b) a specification of its number name (one, two, three, etc.); (c) a specification of its cardinal numerical value (1, 2, 3, etc.); and (4) a free slot or "pointer" indicating whether the token was or was not currently representing an entire group of objects. The main mathematical operation that children were conceived as possessing was counting. Using counting, they could move forward along the line of tokens (if one set was added to another) or backward (if one set was taken away from another). In order to make use of this number line, the children were also endowed with linguistic operations that enabled them to interpret any problem as requiring one of these two forms of movement. Finally, they were endowed with certain problem-solving operations that allowed them to set themselves some particular operation or combination of operations as a goal.

Once these basic capabilities were specified, 6-year-old thought was modeled by endowing the system with a single number line. Eight-year-old thought was modeled by endowing the system with two number lines and the capability for reflecting one onto the other (thus transposing a total to a new location) or counting the difference between two existing pointers. Finally, 10-year-old thought was modeled by endowing the system with the capability for conducting two inverse reflection operations. As it turned out, the new model did an excellent job of predicting performance on Compare problems, without sacrificing predictive accuracy for other classes of problems. The new model also proved capable of predicting the way in which the items clustered (Okamoto, 1994, in press) and the nature of the relations between these items and children's performance on our new Number Knowledge test (Chap. II).

EXTENSION OF THE MODEL INTO NEW AREAS

The third goal of the present program of research was to push the analysis of children's central conceptual structures into new substantive areas.

Modeling Children's Understanding of Spatial Tasks

According to the view of spatial cognition that was proposed in Chapter I, children's structures for organizing two-dimensional representations of space develop in much the same fashion as the structures that they use for representing quantity or social interaction. At the age of 6, children begin to see a set of small objects—each one of which has its own internal requirements for two-dimensional representation—as being part of a higher-order configuration in which the position of each object is referenced to some common external "frame." At the age of 8–10 years, they become capable of creating a pattern in which each object is referenced to two such familiar frames, first separately and then conjointly. Two spatial systems that this progression allows them to acquire are (1) the Cartesian grid structure, in which each object is set at a particular distance from an X and a Y axis, and (2) the structure for drawing a set of objects "in perspective." This progression was illustrated graphically in Figure 19 above (see Chap. V).

Three general sorts of data were presented to support this proposition. The first set of data showed that age norms across a wide range of spatial tasks can be predicted by this analysis: preaxial tasks are generally solved at 4, uniaxial tasks at 6, biaxial tasks at 8, and integrated biaxial tasks at 10. The second set of data showed that conceptually similar tasks show a strong pattern of correlation and load on a common factor, even when they have different surface content. The third set of data showed that training on the uniaxial structure leads to transfer across a wide range of conceptually similar spatial tasks but does not produce transfer to the domain of number.

Charting Children's Development in Different Social Contexts

A second way in which we sought to expand the scope of our existing database was to gather data on children growing up in different cultures. In a previous study, Fiati (1992) had already shown that children's quantitative structures develop at a much slower rate and reach a different terminal level when the children grow up in a traditional agricultural society, one in which trade does not play a major role and the physical world is not parsed into bivariate dimensions such as hours and minutes, feet and inches, etc. In the present study, we sought to demonstrate the obverse of this proposition, namely, that children who grow up in modern industrial societies develop central conceptual structures at a similar rate, in spite of wide variations in the value that their own particular culture ascribes to different quantitative or spatial tasks and the equally wide variation in the forms of training that each culture provides.

In Chapter VI, pairs of tasks were selected from the test batteries that we had developed in previous studies and were used to compare the performance of children from North America (Canada and the United States) and Asia (China and Japan). In each instance, the general pattern of results was the same. On the task that tapped content characterized by differential cultural emphasis, the rate of development was faster in the culture that assigned this task a greater value. However, on a similar task that required transfer of some sort or else assessed some more general understanding, no cross-cultural differences were apparent. Since many contemporary theorists in the sociohistoric tradition view cultural differences and social class differences as equivalent, several social class comparisons were also conducted. Here, the results were quite different. At least within North America, social class differences were strong and consistent across all the tasks that we have developed.

MODELING THE PROCESS OF STRUCTURAL FORMATION

A fourth goal in our present program of research was an extension of the second, namely, to develop a preliminary model of the way in which central conceptual structures are formed. In the past, the classic (Piagetian) model of children's cognitive development assumed that general cognitive structures exert a constraining influence on the child's specific learning but that learning does not affect development. The classic learning model assumed just the opposite, namely, that the formation of general structures is the natural consequence of specific experience and has no other source. In keeping with our general strategy of theoretical integration, the model that we proposed was a bidirectional one, in which new specific structures were presumed to have a positive effect on the formation of new general structures, and vice versa. The result of this "reciprocal coupling" is to set up a hierarchical feedback loop that accelerates the pace of development— within whatever limits are set by maturation—and also standardizes the role of development on specific tasks to which children have different degrees of exposure.

Within the framework of this model, one can explain the broad structural similarities across different cultural groups in the modern era by assuming that, although these groups provide different sorts of experience on different tasks, the tasks still span the same general set of universal categories (number, space, social narrative, etc.). Thus, although highly emphasized tasks may show cultural differences, tasks that receive less emphasis will tend to show small or insignificant differences since the benefits of learning on the highly emphasized tasks will be passed on, via the mediation of the general structure, to all other tasks in the same general group. The assumption that the model makes about socioeconomic status (SES) is different. Here, it is assumed that, the higher one's position on the socioeconomic scale, the greater one's allocation of scarce resources—financial, social, educational—across an entire *group* of tasks. Under these circumstances, the same hierarchical feedback loop will serve to augment, rather than diminish, differences that are originally quite small in magnitude.

Although no new data were presented, the hierarchical feedback model was embodied in a set of mathematical formulas and shown to provide a reasonable fit to all the data in previous chapters. At least indirectly, it was also shown to fit well with data from previous research on the growth of information-processing capacity and/or working memory.

NEW QUESTIONS RAISED BY THE PRESENT PROGRAM OF RESEARCH

Although the present program of research has answered many of the questions that we set out to explore, it has also raised a number of new ones: particularly those that bear on the relation between the notion of a central conceptual structure and other notions that have played an important role in neo-Piagetian theory and research. Two of these questions seem important to address before concluding.

The Relation between Central Conceptual Structures and Executive Structures

The work reported in the present *Monograph* had its origin in a line of work that was begun some time ago and that was devoted to exploring the development of children's executive control structures (Case, 1985). In that work, I presented an extensive series of task analyses and empirical investigations that led to the conclusion that children's control structures go through four general levels of abstraction, each of which has at least three levels of complexity within it. Transition within each stage appears to depend on the growth of working memory, on the one hand, and the learning of more complex executive processes, on the other. Transition across stages appears to occur by a process of hierarchical integration, that is, a process in which the functional relation between two qualitatively different structures is abstracted and gradually brought under conscious control. The overall shape of development that this theoretical view implies is illustrated in Figure 38.

The work on children's central conceptual structures grew directly out of this earlier work. Moreover, the age ranges that were cited for particular transitions and the general sort of tasks that were modeled remained unchanged. This correspondence has led a number of investigators (e.g., Halford, 1993a) to ask what the relation is between executive control structures and central conceptual structures, on the one hand, and between the current view of children's cognitive development and the previous one, on the other.

The simplest way to address the first question is to consider the executive control structures that must be assembled by children in order to succeed at the 6-year-old level on such quantitative tasks as (a) telling the time (Chap. III), (b) making predictions about the operation of a balance beam (Chap. III), (c) learning to sight-read a music score (Chap. IV), (d) making judgments regarding distributive justice (Chap. III), (e) performing mental computations in arithmetic (Chaps. II, III), and (f) solving word problems in arithmetic (Chap. II). The particular dimensions that children consider on these tasks are quite different (hours, tones, weights, etc.). The way in which these dimensions must be represented are also quite different (via a clock, a music score, a weight diagram, etc.). The specific strategies that children must execute are different, too ("reading" the nearest numeral to the long hand on a clock, stepping up or down a series of imaginary "steps" on a musical scale, counting and comparing the numerical magnitude of two weight stacks in a weight diagram, etc.). Given these differences, one can assert with considerable confidence that children need a different executive control structure for each. Table 32 shows the executive control processes that were postulated previously as underlying two of the tasks. Similar processes—each with its own unique features—would be necessary to master the other tasks in the group.

Although all the executive control structures that would be required to master each of the tasks would be different, the central conceptual structure that we have hypothesized in the present volume is the same. The data support this hypothesis: when the various tasks are administered to the

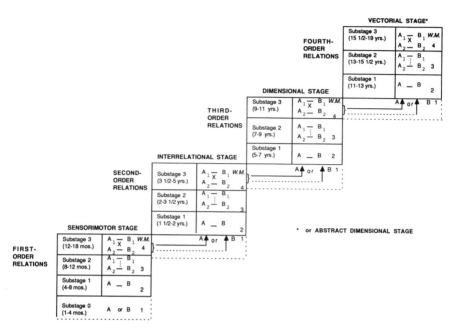

Fig. 38.—General stages and substages in children's cognitive development, as described in Case (1985). The structural diagrams indicate the way in which existing control structures (represented by letters) are used as elements in the construction of higher-order control structures. In the transition from substage 0 to substage 1 (bottom left), a new control structure is formed from two previously separate control structures A and B. The new structure is symbolized as A-B. In the transition from substage 1 to substage 2, two control structures of the new sort (A_1-B_1 and A_2-B_2) are differentiated and then integrated with each other. Since the integration is tentative, it is symbolized with a dotted line instead of a solid line. In the transition from substage 2 to substage 3, no new units are added, but the integration becomes more solid, and children become capable of oscillating back and forth between the two component structures at will. (This more elaborate and flexible integration is indicated by replacing the dotted line with an X.) Finally, in the transition to the next major stage, each one of these elaborated units is treated as a single element, and the entire process recycles. Beside each structural form, the characteristic working memory demand (noted as W.M.) is given; as may be seen, this progresses from 2 to 4 within each stage.

same subjects, they all load on the same factor; when the central conceptual structure is taught, children's performance on all the tasks shows spontaneous improvement. I believe this state of affairs to be quite general: for every central conceptual structure that children develop at any age, I believe that they must develop a whole family of executive control structures if they are to deal with the full range of tasks for which their central conceptual structure is relevant. This is the first relation that I would propose between the two constructs.

The second relation has to do with the process of structural acquisition.

201

TABLE 32

EXECUTIVE CONTROL STRUCTURES FOR TWO DIFFERENT TASKS AT TWO DIFFERENT AGE LEVELS

TASK

AGE	Balance Beam	Birthday Party

Balance Beam

Age 4

PROBLEM SITUATION
Balance beam with object on each arm →

OBJECTIVE
Determine which side will go down

STRATEGY
1. Look at each object; if one looks much heavier, predict that that side of beam will go down

Age 6

PROBLEM SITUATION
Balance beam with stack of objects on each arm →

Each stack is composed of a number of identical units →

OBJECTIVE
Determine which side will go down

Determine which side has larger number of units

STRATEGY
1. Count each unit in stack; note which stack has larger number
2. Pick side with larger number as heavier; say it will go down

Birthday Party

Age 4

PROBLEM SITUATION
Picture of 2 children with presents →

OBJECTIVE
Determine which child is happier

STRATEGY
1. Scan each picture; if one child has bigger smile (or has a lot more presents), say he is happier

Age 6

PROBLEM SITUATION
Picture of 2 children with presents →

Each child has set of presents composed of a number of identical items →

OBJECTIVE
Determine which child is happier

Determine which set has larger number of items

STRATEGY
1. Count each set; note which set has larger number
2. Pick child with larger number of presents as happier

SOURCE.—From Case (1985).

In certain cases, a new central conceptual structure may arise before a new executive control structure has been developed. When this occurs, the odds become higher that a child will use a new executive structure for a broad range of tasks because the conceptual structure will draw her attention to certain features rather than to others and serve as a guide to her problem solving as she struggles with the task's particular requirements. The new central conceptual structure will thus serve as a sort of "invitation" to the formation of a broad range of new executive structures. It will not guarantee that a new set of executive structures will be deployed, however, since there are a host of other factors that can intervene.

In other cases, a new executive structure may arise first. For the same social, contextual, and/or experiential reasons, a child may stumble on the solution of a problem before he or she has a sound conceptual understanding of why this solution works. The more strongly this solution is prompted by the situation on subsequent exposures, and the more highly consolidated his new strategy becomes, the more likely it is that the child will become curious about and/or stumble on the new conceptual relations that make the strategy an effective one. A successful executive control structure in one or more areas may thus constitute an "invitation" to form a more general conceptual understanding. This is the second relation that I would propose between the two constructs, namely, that their acquisition is reciprocally coupled. It was this general assumption that underpinned the model of structural formation presented in Chapter VII.

Given that there is a general correspondence between levels of conceptual abstraction and levels of executive control and that development of either sort of structure can be the stimulus to development of the other, it follows that the four-stage model of development in Figure 38 above may be retained and that the present work may be seen as expanding on this model rather than replacing it. This is true both with regard to the specification of what develops, which must now be expanded to include central conceptual structures, and with regard to the specification of how these structures develop, which must now be expanded to include the sort of hierarchical learning loop that was modeled in Chapter VII.

The Role of Working Memory Growth in Cognitive Development

A second question that the present program of research raises concerns the role of working memory in children's conceptual development. As I indicated at the beginning of this chapter, neo-Piagetian theorists have for years maintained that children's information-processing capacity increases with age and that this increase plays a strong role in facilitating and/or constraining the other changes that take place in their cognitive systems

(Case, 1978; Fischer, 1980; Halford, 1982; Pascual-Leone, 1970). In our previous work (Case, 1985), we showed that changes in the overall speed of children's information processing have a strong effect on the size of their working memory and that the size of their working memory in turn exerts a strong influence on the size of the "goal stack" that they can maintain in an active state and hence on the complexity of the executive structures that they can assemble at any point in their cognitive growth.

If children's executive structures and their conceptual structures are reciprocally coupled, a question that naturally arises is whether the increases in children's working memory also exert a facilitating effect on their conceptual structures or whether such effects as may exist are only indirect ones, which operate through the mediation of the executive system.

For years, Halford (1982, 1993b) has argued that the conceptual system in general and the process of conceptual mapping in particular are extremely sensitive to changes in children's working memory. We have gathered no direct evidence on this question in the present project. Such indirect evidence as we have obtained, however, fits well with this assertion. Recall that children were found to have two relatively distinct conceptual schemas at the age of 4, in each of the domains that we considered; by the age of 6, however, they had a single schema, one that mapped the elements of its two predecessors onto each other in a coherent fashion. During this same time period, children's working memory for the sort of information that these schemas contain goes from 1 to 2 units.

It seems highly likely that these two phenomena are connected. Although one could imagine mapping the elements of one schema onto those of another via purely associative processes (what Pascual-Leone has termed C-learning), such connections would require hundreds of trials to make and would not be nearly as efficient as those made by attentionally mediated processes (what Pascual-Leone has termed M-learning). Moreover, if the present model is correct, *both* processes are always involved in central conceptual learning. A corollary is that children's cross-schema mapping should be severely constrained as long as they have a working memory of only 1 unit and should get an important boost as their working memory goes to 2 units. In order to see why this is so, one need only consider the situation that we experience as adults, in trying to work back and forth between two different files on a computer system and merge their elements. Although it is possible to perform this task on a system that does not have enough RAM to keep both files open at the same time, the task becomes much easier on a system that does have this capability.

The empirical data that have been gathered with children support the notion that working memory growth facilitates the process of conceptual mapping. In a recent series of studies, Griffin (1994) examined the working memory for numbers of children who were participating in our conceptual training program for number (Chap. IV). What she found was that there was a correlation between the size of a child's working memory and his or her ability to profit from the training; children with a working memory for numbers of less than 2 units had great difficulty profiting from the sort of conceptually based instruction that we were providing, whereas those with a capacity of 2 units or more found the training much easier. On empirical as well as theoretical grounds, therefore, it seems reasonable to conclude that the growth of children's information-processing capacity in general, and their working memory capacity in particular, exerts a strong facilitating influence on the growth of their central conceptual structures.

Before concluding, it is worthwhile to consider three possible objections that have been raised to this conclusion.

Working Memory Growth as an Effect, Not a Cause, of Conceptual Development

In an important analysis of working memory development, Chi (1976) suggested that the correlation between working memory growth and conceptual development might actually result from a causal connection that goes in the reverse direction. The acquisition of a more elaborate conceptual structure might actually produce a change in the measured size of working memory, not vice versa, because of the improvements in schema-accessing speed that any more advanced conceptual network offers. This possibility is an important one; not only does it offer an alternative way of viewing the data on working memory growth and conceptual development, but it also offers an alternative way of viewing the growth of information-processing speed and its role in cognitive development.

Unfortunately for Chi's argument (or fortunately for the present one), such data as have been gathered in the past few years do not provide it with much empirical support. For example, what Griffin (1994) found in the study just cited was that children who, as a result of her training program, acquire more sophisticated conceptual structures for number show no concomitant improvement in the size of their working memory or in their speed of counting. Thus, it seems more likely that an increase in working memory capacity facilitates the acquisition of central conceptual structures than that central conceptual structures produce an increase in working memory capacity. (For a more detailed treatment of this issue and a consideration of the possibility of reciprocal influence, see Case, 1995.)

Difficulties with the Theoretical Analysis

A second objection to the notion that working memory growth plays an important role in facilitating and/or constraining children's conceptual

development is that there is no method of analyzing the growth of conceptual structures that generates an unequivocal estimate of the working memory load that they impose (Campbell & Bickhard, 1992; Flavell, 1978; Halford, 1993a). Depending on their method of analysis, different investigators
may come up with different estimates. Even using the same method, they
may come up with different estimates, depending on the assumptions that
they make about children's strategies, their representation of the task, and/
or the way in which their knowledge base is organized.

In a response to this criticism, Pascual-Leone (1994) has pointed out
that this dilemma stems from the fact that children's mental models of and/
or their executive strategies for approaching a given task may vary widely,
both from child to child and from time to time within a single child. One
should not expect, therefore, that the problem can be solved simply by
inventing more powerful methods of task analysis or forging an agreement
among investigators on the nature of children's cognitive systems; rather,
one must accept the problem as a fundamental property of children's cognition and its dynamics.

I believe that this argument is a sound one. There are two points,
however, that I would like to add to it. The real question, it seems to me,
is not whether different investigators can agree on the working memory
load of particular situations or tasks. Nor is it whether children experience
the same memory loads with different strategies or at different points in
time. Rather, the real questions are (1) whether different investigators can
agree on whether an *increase* in working memory should be an advantage
for moving through a development sequence that involves an increase in
conceptual complexity and (2) what the empirical data indicate on this point.
So far, there is complete uniformity among different investigators on the
first point. On the second point, the evidence is also powerful and consistent, with one possible exception.

Conflicting Evidence from Dual Task Paradigms

There is one set of empirical data that has been cited as problematic
for the working memory hypothesis: namely, the data from dual task para-
digms. For example, in a recent study by Halford, Mayberry, Hare, and
Grant (1994), it was reported that, when children's short-term memory is
"preloaded" with novel information, performance on working memory
tasks sometimes interferes with retrieval of this information and sometimes
does not. Halford and his colleagues assert that the fact that children can
sometimes remember a "preload" with almost perfect recall raises serious
questions as to whether working memory capacity really does constitute the
conceptual bottleneck that so many investigators have claimed it to be.

The phenomenon to which Halford has drawn our attention is an important one. However, I believe that it is problematic only if one conceives of children's working memory limitations as being due to the size of the "loop" that they can sustain by the sort of verbal/articulatory process that has been studied by Baddeley and Hitch (1974). Were this the primary source of working memory limits, it should not matter much what sorts of elements were in this loop—the presence of a preload should interfere with the ability to maintain subsequent items in an active state. The fact that certain material seems to be so well retained, then, would be a serious problem for the working memory argument.

Most theorists agree, however, that the working memory system is strongly affected, not just by temporal factors and "loop size," but by factors relating to interference. If one conceives of children's limitations as being primarily due to the number of elements that they can attend to simultaneously in the face of potential interference, then one would expect that, when the preloaded items and the working memory items were similar, span would be radically reduced; when the similarity was low, it would not be.

In Halford's own data, this appears to be the case. The tests on which no preload effect is found are those where the preloaded items consist of letters or words and the items to be stored are numbers. In the case where the preload is a set of numbers that are presented orally and the working memory test is the test of counting span, children's functional span is invariably decreased—indeed, approximately one preloaded number is forgotten for every item on the working memory test that must be recalled. We have found a similar effect in our own work. When we presented children with a Spatial Span test, followed by a Musical span test or a Verbal Span test, and then by a Number Span test, performance on all these tests stayed quite near ceiling. However, when we presented two trials of the Number Span test in succession, performance fell off sharply and immediately (Case, Marini, et al., 1986).

While further work remains to be done on this problem, then, it seems likely that the outcome will be a more refined conception of the working memory system and its neurological substrate, not a rejection of the notion that working memory limits constitute a serious bottleneck to, and their relaxation a powerful facilitator of, children's conceptual growth.

OLD PROBLEMS AND CRITICISMS REVIVED BY THE PRESENT PROGRAM OF RESEARCH

In addition to the new questions that are raised by the present program of research, a number of old questions are raised as well, questions that have their origin in the classic program of Piagetian research and the criticisms that have been leveled at it. Before concluding, I consider two of these criticisms, at least briefly.

The Overemphasis on Logico-Mathematical Processes and Their Significance in Human Development

One classic criticism that was leveled at Piaget's theory was that it provided a view of human cognition that was too "rational" and that placed too heavy an emphasis on closed systems of logic. According to this view, little room was left for other forms of intelligence, especially those that have been developed more highly in other cultures or at other points in time in our own cultural history. The present program of research is part of a broader attempt to expand the forms of human intelligence whose development we study and to expose the important role that is played in all forms of intellectual activity by the invention and transmission of culturally based systems of understanding. Still, it could be argued that, because it revives the emphasis on general cognitive structures and proposes a hierarchical model of their growth, the present form of analysis also reintroduces the classic overemphasis on forms of thought that are logical and forms of development that are hierarchical and/or linear in nature.

This criticism is not without its merit. There are undoubtedly forms of human cognition that do not develop in the four-tiered way that has been described by Piagetian and neo-Piagetian theorists. There are undoubtedly forms of cognition whose importance is not their generality but their specificity and whose nature is not well captured by the form of semantic analysis that we have employed in the present project. Still, I feel that we have made considerable progress in showing that social and spatial understanding do share certain commonalities with mathematical understanding. And I feel that we have also made progress in showing that these commonalities stem, not from a common underlying logic, but from a common semantic process, one that involves the differentiation and integration of existing structures and their incorporation into hierarchical learning loops.

Of course, if further substance is to be given to this claim, we will need to examine other structures as well. And the questions that we will have to confront as we do so include (a) how many other central structures may exist and (b) what these other central conceptual structures might look like.

In order to address these two questions, we will need to take a very broad look at the human landscape, one that considers its biological as well as its cultural underpinnings. On the basis of one recent analysis of this sort, Gardner (1983) has concluded that there are six general "frames of mind": (1) *logicomathematical;* (2) *verbal;* (3) *spatial;* (4) *social;* (5) *musical;* and

(6) *motor*. In more recent work, he has suggested that a seventh frame of mind, which he labels *intrapersonal*, may exist as well. Gardner's first category (i.e., logicomathematical thought) is one that I would prefer to see broken down into two more basic categories, one for numerical and one for logical analysis. As a preliminary hypothesis, then, I would suggest that there may be eight distinct domains, for each of which a unique central conceptual structure—or set of structures—may develop.

Given a list such as this, how might one decide what conceptual structures are central to each domain? I know of no other way than to conduct some sort of rational task analysis of the various competencies that children develop at different ages, in a given culture, and to search for their commonalities. Given the importance of the 4–6-year-old transition and the work that has been reported in the present volume, a good age to start with might be the age of 6. One could begin by laying out the general sorts of real-world tasks that children master in each of these domains at this age and the conceptual commonalities that these tasks contain. Having done so, one could then proceed in the same fashion as we did in Chapters I–IV, that is, by specifying the precursor structures from which these structures are assembled and their sequelae, then gathering new data of a developmental, correlational, and experimental nature.

Candidate structures for such an investigation might include the following:

1. *Number.*—The mental number line (already investigated) and the halving/doubling schema (Confrey, 1994).
2. *Logical analysis.*—The category hierarchy (Inhelder & Piaget, 1964), the matrix, and the analogy (Demetriou, Efklides, & Platsidou, 1993).
3. *Language.*—The mental sound line (vital for profiting from instruction in phonics, for generating rhyming couplets, for appreciating puns, and for changing one's pronunciation of words in an intentional fashion—all 6-year-old accomplishments).
4. *Space.*—The mental reference line (already investigated).
5. *Social.*—The story line (already investigated), the social hierarchy (a linear hierarchy in which social dominance and role assignment are coordinated; Case, in press), and the role-based script (Fischer, Hand, Watson, Van Parys, & Tucker, 1984).
6. *Motor.*—The mental corridor (vital for making a first stab at mastering the basics in most sports, another 6-year-old accomplishment; although related to the spatial reference line, this structure may well have its unique properties).
7. *Musical.*—The mental tone line or "scale" (Capodilupo, 1992).
8. *Intrapersonal.*—A model of self that spans all the other categories and that may include information that is dimensional (e.g., I am smart),

narrative (I came to this country from Poland), and/or role related (I am a daughter, a wife, and a senior editor of this journal).

In future work, then, it would seem desirable to see whether data that are parallel to the data that have been reported in the present *Monograph* could be gathered for these other conceptual structures.

Underemphasis on Individual Differences and Their Significance in the Process of Intellectual Growth

Another frequent criticism of Piaget's theory was that it did not take individual differences in intellectual development into account. One of the primary goals of neo-Piagetian theory was to rectify this situation. Indeed, considerable progress was made in this regard. Within the context of Pascual-Leone's theory, an explanation for several different types of cognitive style became possible, and a wide variety of new hypotheses about such styles were successfully tested (e.g., Pascual-Leone, 1969, 1974). Within the context of Fischer's theory, an explanation became possible for several demographic differences, for example, those due to gender and ethnicity. These explanations also led to new hypotheses that were successfully tested (Fischer, Knight, & Van Parys, 1993).

Since the present theory has reemphasized the role of general structures—albeit ones that are somewhat different from Piaget's—it is natural to ask whether it has also brought with it a return to the classic Piagetian impasse. Does it constitute a step back from existing neo-Piagetian theory in this regard or a step forward? This question has been brought into focus by a recent critique of the present theory by M. D. Lewis (1994). As Lewis views the matter, the present theory is incapable of dealing with individual pathways in cognitive development because it is insufficiently dynamic.

Like Lewis, I am attracted to dynamic theories. Like Lewis, too, I think that such theories (including the one that he has proposed) provide an interesting and novel perspective on the problem of individual pathways. Finally, like Lewis, I am committed to supplementing the structural aspect of the present theory with a dynamic one (see Chap. VII and the discussion there of individual differences in social class and culture). Where I disagree with Lewis is in his assertion that individual pathways cannot be accounted for by the present theory until such a dynamic component is added.

As an illustration of the theory's potential, even in its present form, consider the fact that each of the structures that was described in Chapter I has some 50 or so separate components, at the 5–6-year-old level alone. As long as one assumes, as I do, that each one of these components can be acquired independently, it follows that there must be some 50 factorial pathways for assembling each structure. If one takes into account the different components at other levels, this number becomes much larger. If one takes into account all seven structures, it becomes larger still. Finally, if one accepts the possibility of slight variations in content or affective valence at each level, the number of pathways that can be expected becomes so high as to elude computation.

Of course, as DeRibaupierre (1993) has pointed out, it is unlikely that many of these individual pathways would be of much theoretical significance. It may be a mistake, as she suggests, to leap directly from analyzing a single, supposedly universal pathway to a set of pathways that is so diverse as to be completely idiosyncratic. One does not have to move from one unfortunate extreme to the other, however. The notion of a central conceptual structure was designed to provide a level of analysis that is intermediate between the general and the particular. Thus, it seems best suited for illuminating a set of pathways that have an intermediate status also. One way to exploit this potential is to hypothesize that each central conceptual structure constitutes a "preferred developmental pathway" for a large class of individuals.

Is there any evidence that individual differences of this sort actually exist, or is this possibility, too, just a theoretical one? One of the most reliable sets of individual differences is those that emerge as "group factors" on factor analyses of psychometric tests. In the context of classic Piagetian theory, these factors cannot be explained—indeed, they are often summarily dismissed. In the present theoretical context, however, the factors can be seen as resulting from the fact that each central conceptual structure has its own content, its own type of operation, and its own developmental trajectory. The child whose spatial ability develops in advance of her verbal or numerical ability is one whose spatial operations are unusually efficient and who constructs the central conceptual structures in this domain in advance of others. Very probably she will also be the one who will first attempt to understand a situation in spatial terms when more than one conceptual model of that situation is possible. Of course, psychometric tests may tap additional aspects of children's spatial ability, aspects that are not tapped by our tests of central spatial structures. Nevertheless, if the foregoing analysis is correct, the two sorts of test should load on the same group factor in any investigation that combines both developmental and differential measures.

Were the foregoing prediction confirmed, we would be one step closer to integrating the views of the mind that have been developed in the psychometric and developmental traditions. In fact, two serious steps in this direction have already been taken. The first emerged out of a program of research conducted by Demetriou and his colleagues. What this group did was (a) convert a broad range of Piagetian measures into a psychometric format, (*b*) administer the tasks to children from several different cultures and social classes, and (*c*) analyze the resulting data using Gustafsson's (1988) structural modeling techniques. Five factors emerged in their early work, each of which was presumed to represent a different "capacity sphere." In their more recent work, they have labeled these capacity spheres "specific structural systems" (Demetriou et al., 1993) and postulated a sixth system that is responsible for building a superordinate representation of the other five. The names given to the original five systems were (1) the *quantitative/relational,* (2) the *linguistic/propositional,* (3) the *imaginal/spatial,* (4) the *qualitative/analytic,* and (5) the *causal/experimental.* The name given to the newly proposed monitoring system is the *hypercognitive* system.

The correspondence between Demetriou's notion of "specific structural systems" and our own notion of "central conceptual structures" will no doubt be apparent. There is a general theoretical parallel in the way that the concepts are conceived and labeled and a correspondence of a more specific, substantive sort as well. Two of Demetriou's specific structural systems, namely, the systems for quantitative/numerical and spatial/imaginal thought, have direct counterparts in the numerical and spatial structures whose content we have analyzed. Several of his other systems also have direct counterparts in central structures whose existence we have hypothesized, using Gardner's classification scheme as a heuristic. The qualitative/analytic system corresponds to the logical/analytic structure, the verbal/propositional system corresponds to the linguistic structure, and the hypercognitive system corresponds to the "intrapersonal" structure. In recent work, Demetriou has even suggested the existence of a specific structural system for analyzing social problems, in which our narrative structure might play an important role (Demetriou et al., 1995).

Of course, the correspondence is not perfect. There are two items that appear on our list that do not appear on Demetriou's, namely, the central conceptual structures for music and motor control systems. There is also one system that appears on Demetriou's list that does not appear on ours, namely, the causal/experimental system. Still, as a question for future research, it would seem important to compare the two classification systems in more detail and to see whether the theoretical parallels that exist between them would translate into a set of empirical correspondences as well.

As we consider how best to parse the mind's conceptual systems and how to forge a synthesis of developmental and differential conceptions, a second body of work that is important to consider is that of Lautrey and DeRibaupierre (Lautrey et al., 1985; DeRibaupierre et al., 1991). Using classic Piagetian tests of logical and infralogical reasoning and a variant of factor analysis, this group identified a factor that they believe derives from individual differences in analogical as opposed to propositional processing. Just as Demetriou's core "capacity spheres" may be related to the classic group factors identified by psychometric theorists, so Lautrey et al.'s factor may relate to the classic "hemispheric" factor isolated by Das and his colleagues (Das, Kirby, & Jarmon, 1975; Kaufman & Kaufman, 1983). Following Luria (1966), these investigators refer to this factor as "sequential" as opposed to "simultaneous" processing.

If DeRibaupierre's "propositional" and Das's "sequential" factor turn out to be the same (or even members of the same family), then this factor might be thought of as being orthogonal to the factors suggested by our work and by Demetriou's. The structural systems that have been traditionally associated with left hemisphere processing are number, language, and narrative (and possibly categorical analysis). These could be thought of as being optimally suited to propositional and/or sequential analysis. The structural systems that have been classically associated with the right hemisphere are space, music, fine motor movement, and certain aspects of socioemotional functioning. These could be thought of as being optimally suited to analogical and/or "parallel" processing.

The foregoing suggestions are of course highly speculative. However, the general assumption on which they are based—namely, that the time is ripe for an integration of differential, developmental, and neuropsychological perspectives—is one that differentialists have been advancing for some time (Demetriou et al., 1988; DeRibaupierre, 1993; Keating, in press; Reuchlin & Bacher, 1989; Snow, Kyllonen, & Marshalek, 1984). One of the major factors that has stood in the way of such a three-way integration is that we have not had any form of analysis that is applicable across these different disciplines. In particular, we have not had any analysis that would show how the broad categories into which neuropsychology divides cognitive functioning and the broad categories into which differential psychology divides cognitive functioning could be mapped onto those into which developmental psychology divides cognitive functioning.

This is the potential contribution that I view the structural component of the present work as offering. It is an advantage that stems from the fact that we have moved away from the sort of general "logical" analysis used by Piaget and yet stayed at a more general level than the task-, process-, or context-based analyses with which Piaget's analyses were first replaced. Far from preventing any progress in the understanding of individual differences, then, it seems to me that the structural component of the present theory should actually make this sort of progress a good deal easier.

CONCLUDING STATEMENT

We began the present program of research with the goal of gathering stronger empirical evidence that central conceptual structures actually exist and that they play the role in children's cognitive development that we had hypothesized. A second goal was to develop a more detailed analysis of the content of central numerical structures, of the way in which these structures are applied to novel task situations, and of the mechanism by which they develop. Finally, a third goal was to extend our analysis of central conceptual structures to new content domains and/or new populations. In the course of pursuing these three objectives, a number of new questions came into focus, especially those that bear on the relation of the new construct to previous constructs in neo-Piagetian theory and the extent to which, because it revives many of the classic Piagetian claims with regard to general cognitive structures, the new construct may also be subject to the same general criticisms.

In the present chapter, I have attempted to summarize the progress that we have made pursuing our three original objectives and to sketch out one possible set of answers to the new family of questions that have arisen. I am under no illusion that these answers will constitute the last word on these questions or that new criticisms will not emerge from other quarters, particularly from the other general schools of contemporary developmental thought whose contributions have been mentioned throughout the present volume. Still, my hope is that researchers and theorists in these other traditions will find the present line of inquiry to be a productive one and that together we can move forward in answering both the classic questions with which our field has been concerned and the new questions that have emerged as a result of our diverse investigations.

APPENDIX A

ADMINISTRATION AND SCORING
OF THE NUMERICAL TASKS[6]

BALANCE BEAM

This task was originally introduced into the literature by Inhelder and Piaget (1958), who used it to study the development of the concept of a ratio. It was later converted into a more objective form by Siegler (1978), who used it to study younger children's encoding and integration of quantitative variables. The version of the task that we used was designed by Marini and Case, who used it to assess children's movement from predimensional through to integrated bidimensional thought in understanding the way in which two opposing variables can affect the operation of a physical system (Marini, 1992; Marini & Case, 1993).

Children are presented with a wooden beam balanced on a fulcrum, which is bearing a stack of weights at each end and which is kept up by supports. They are then asked (*a*) to predict which end will go down when the props are removed and (*b*) to explain their judgment. The two quantitative variables that determine which side will go down are the number of weights and the distance from the fulcrum. The four developmental levels determined for this task are as follows. At Level 1 (*predimensional*), children can focus on the overall size of the two stacks of weights when one side clearly bears a large number of such weights and the other only a few. At Level 2 (*unidimensional*), children can focus on the precise number of weights on each side as long as distance is kept constant. At Level 3 (*bidimensional*),

---

[6] For certain tests, improvements were made from year to year. The versions described here represent the final ones. Items indicated with an asterisk (*) were not given in the correlational study described in Chap. III. Items indicated with a dagger (†) were not given in the instructional studies reported in Chap. IV. Items indicated with a double dagger (‡) were not given in the simulation study described in Chap. II. The score sheet and the tester protocol are available on request.

children can notice the second, less salient dimension, that is, distance. Finally, at Level 4 (*integrated bidimensional*), children can resolve problems in which both the two stacks of weight and their distance from the fulcrum differ by applying addition or subtraction strategies (Furman, 1981; Inhelder & Piaget, 1958; Marini, 1992).

Administration

Children are shown a balance beam and given an explanation of how it works. They are given a warm-up question in which they are asked to place weights on one side of the beam; they observe what happens to the beam and are given an explanation of what happened. Following this question, children are given a series of problems. Two problems are given at each level. Administration continues until children fail to answer both problems at a level.

Test Items

Predimensional Level (Level 1)

1. Two weights on the left and 6 on the right (second peg).
2. Seven weights on the left and 1 on the right (third peg).

Unidimensional Level (Level 2)

3. Three weights on the left and 4 on the right (seventh peg).
4. Seven weights on the left and 6 on the right (third peg).

Bidimensional Level (Level 3)

5. Four weights on the left (seventh peg) and 4 on the right (sixth peg).
6. Five weights on the left (fourth peg) and 5 on the right (fifth peg).

Integrated Bidimensional Level (Level 4)

7. Five weights on the left (fourth peg) and 3 on the right (seventh peg).
8. Six weights on the left (sixth peg) and 4 on the right (seventh peg).

*Vectorial Items (Level 5)—If Necessary**

9. Two weights on the left (fifth peg) and 6 on the right (first peg).

10. One weight on the left (fourth peg) and 3 on the right (second peg).

Scoring

Children's responses to each problem are scored as correct or incorrect on the basis of their explanations as well as their predictions: the general criterion for scoring an explanation is that it should indicate the presence of the underlying structure that we are seeking to assess. Thus, Level 1 (predimensional) explanations are scored as acceptable if any sort of global assessment is mentioned (e.g., "It was more"). Level 2 (unidimensional) explanations are scored as acceptable if children demonstrate any evidence of counting, either on their fingers or with words (e.g., "This side will go down because it has four," or, "Because it has four and the other one has three"). Level 3 (bidimensional) items are scored as correct if children made any reference to distance (e.g., "Because these weights are further from the end," or, "Because these ones are on the third peg"). Level 4 (integrated bidimensional) explanations are scored as correct if the child contrasts the values on both dimensions in a quantitative manner (e.g., "This side because it has two more weights than the other side but is only one farther out," or, "This side because it is seven out and three up, so it is 10; the other side is four out and five up, which is only nine"). Each child is assigned a score based on the highest level at which he or she answers at least one of the two problems correctly.

BIRTHDAY PARTY

This task was first introduced into the literature by Borke (1971) in order to assess young children's ability to empathize with others. Marini (1992) revised the task in order to index children's ability to take account of quantitative factors in reasoning about social dilemmas. The current version is based on Marini's work. Children are told a story about two characters (David and Cathy) who are having birthday parties. Next, they are shown a cartoon picture depicting (in a "thought cloud" above their heads) what each child was hoping to receive as a present. Finally, they are shown the set of gifts that the child actually received and are asked, "Now, who do you think is happier, David or Cathy? Or are they both happy?" Children are asked to name one of the characters (or both) and to explain their response. The two quantitative dimensions are the number of presents each story child "wished for" and the number of presents each actually "received."

The four developmental levels for the test are as follows: At Level 1 (*predimensional*), children can focus on the overall size of the presents received. At Level 2 (*unidimensional*), children can focus on the precise number of presents received when the number of the presents wished for is held constant. At Level 3 (*bidimensional*), children can notice the second, less salient dimension, that is, the number of presents wished for when the number of presents received is held constant. Finally, at Level 4 (*integrated bidimensional*), children can quantify the difference between the number of presents wished for and the number of presents actually received and develop some systematic procedure for comparing the differences.

Administration

Children are shown pictures of Cathy and David and are told the story described above. No warm-up questions are given, for children are familiar with a birthday party scenario. Administration of the task begins with the predimensional problems (two problems per level) and continues until children fail to answer both problems at a level.

Test Items

Predimensional Level (Level 1)

1. Cathy wants 2 and gets 6; David wants 2 and gets 2.
2. Cathy wants 3 and gets 4; David wants 3 and gets 7.

Unidimensional Level (Level 2)

1. Cathy wants 7 and gets 3; David wants 7 and gets 4.
2. Cathy wants 8 and gets 6; David wants 8 and gets 7.

Bidimensional Level (Level 3)

1. Cathy wants 6 and gets 4; David wants 7 and gets 4.
2. Cathy wants 4 and gets 5; David wants 5 and gets 5.

Integrated Bidimensional Level (Level 4)

1. Cathy wants 6 and gets 7; David wants 4 and gets 6.
2. Cathy wants 5 and gets 7; David wants 3 and gets 4.

Vectorial Level (Level 5)—If Necessary

1. Cathy wants 3 and gets 6; David wants 4 and gets 8.
2. Cathy wants 4 and gets 2; David wants 6 and gets 3.

Scoring

As in the Balance Beam task, children's response to each problem is scored as correct or incorrect on the basis of their explanations as well as their answers. Level 1 (predimensional) explanations are ones that mention only some sort of global quantitative assessment (e.g., "Because he has lots," or, "Because she has more"). Level 2 (unidimensional) explanations are ones that make mention of the number of presents received or show some sign of computing it (e.g., "David, because he got 4 and she got 3"). Level 3 (bidimensional) explanations are ones that include a quantitative reference to both task dimensions (e.g., "They both got 5, but Cathy wanted only 4, so she is happier," or, "They both got 5, but David got exactly 5, so he is happier"). Level 4 (integrated bidimensional) explanations are ones that draw a quantitative contrast between the amount wanted and that received by the two characters (e.g., "David has 2 more than he wanted, but Cathy got only 1 more than she wanted, so he is happier"). Each child is assigned a score based on the highest level at which he or she answers at least one of the two problems correctly.

DISTRIBUTIVE JUSTICE

This task was first introduced into the literature by Damon (1973) as a test of children's conception of distributive justice. It was then modified somewhat by DeMersseman (1976) and again by Marini (1992). The current version was developed for use in the present project in order to assess children's understanding of the way in which quantitative variables can affect social judgments and rewards. At the beginning of the task, children are asked to pretend that they are a father who wants to give a 5-dollar bill to one of his daughters as a reward for how well she has done on a school spelling quiz. For each presentation, children are shown how many words each of the two story children spelled correctly (indexed by the number of "stars" each received) and how many the father *expected* them to spell correctly. The two quantitative dimensions in this task are thus the "number of correctly spelled words" and the "number of words the father expected to be correct."

The four developmental levels are as follows: At Level 1 (*predimen-*

sional), children can focus on the overall size of the correctly spelled words: when one story child clearly spells many more words than the other, they give that child the reward. At Level 2 (*unidimensional*), children can focus on the precise number of words each story child spelled correctly when the number of words expected is held constant and give the one who spelled more correctly the reward. At Level 3 (*bidimensional*), children can notice the second, less salient dimension, that is, the number of words each was expected to spell correctly; when the number of words spelled correctly is equal, they can "decenter" and base their distribution on the number that was expected. Finally, at Level 4 (*integrated bidimensional*), children can compute the difference between the number of words expected to be correct and the number of words actually spelled correctly for each story child and develop some systematic procedure for allocating rewards.

Administration

Children are shown pictures of the father and his daughters and are told the story described above (the same scenario is given to boys and girls). No warm-up questions are given; previous studies have found that children are familiar with the idea of giving a reward on the basis of the higher achievement. Administration of the task begins with the predimensional problems (two problems per level) and continues until children fail to answer both problems at a level.

Test Items

Predimensional Level (Level 1)

1. Maria expected 4 right and got 3; Anna expected 4 right and got 7.
2. Maria expected 3 right and got 5; Anna expected 3 right and got 1.

Unidimensional Level (Level 2)

1. Maria expected 6 right and got 3; Anna expected 6 right and got 4.
2. Maria expected 5 right and got 7; Anna expected 5 right and got 6.

Bidimensional Level (Level 3)

1. Maria expected 5 right and got 4; Anna expected 6 right and got 4.
2. Maria expected 4 right and got 6; Anna expected 5 right and got 6.

Integrated Bidimensional Level (Level 4)

1. Maria expected 4 right and got 6; Anna expected 6 right and got 8.
2. Maria expected 5 right and got 7; Anna expected 3 right and got 4.

Vectorial Level (Level 5)—If Necessary*

1. Maria expected 3 right and got 6; Anna expected 4 right and got 8.
2. Maria expected 4 right and got 2; Anna expected 6 right and got 3.

Scoring

As in the Balance Beam task, children's response to each problem is scored as correct or incorrect on the basis of their explanations as well as their answers. At Level 1 (predimensional), children's responses are scored correct if they mention some global quantitative assessment (e.g., "Anna should get more because she got more stars," or, "Anna should get more because she studied harder"). At Level 2 (unidimensional), enumeration must be visible or mentioned in order to be scored as correct (e.g., "Maria should get more because she got one more right," or, "Because Maria got three right and Anna got four right, Anna should get more"). At Level 3 (bidimensional), the father's differential expectations must be mentioned because the girls' achievement is identical (e.g., "They both got four right, but the dad only expected Anna to get four correct, and he expected Maria to get five correct, so maybe she should get a bit less"). Finally, at Level 4 (integrated bidimensional), a comparison of the differences between what the father expected each girl to get and what each actually received must be mentioned in quantitative terms (e.g., "Maria got two more than her dad expected, but Anna only got one more"). Each child is assigned a score based on the highest level at which the child answered at least one of the two problems correctly.

MONEY KNOWLEDGE

The present task is based on work by Case and Sandieson (1987) and Griffin et al. (1992); it is designed to test children's understanding of the monetary values associated with North American coins and folding money and the way in which situations involving payment of money work. The four levels determined for this task are as follows: At Level 1 (*predimensional*), children can count by rote and quantify globally. However, they are not able to connect numbers and quantities; therefore, they cannot distinguish different denominations of money in any meaningful way. At Level 2 (*unidimensional*), children have some awareness of denominations and can work with one of them at a time, making comparisons of magnitude or figuring out simple problems involving how much change they should receive. At Level 3 (*bidimensional*), children can work simultaneously with two different scales or denominations, instead of just one, for both the foregoing problems. Finally, at Level 4 (*integrated bidimensional*), children can work with two different scales or denominations and convert from one to another.

Administration

Children are asked a series of questions beginning with predimensional problems. Administration continues until children fail to answer more than half the problems at a level.

Test Items

Predimensional Level (Level 1)

1a.* "Which is worth more, a dollar or a penny?"
1b.* "Which is worth less, a dollar or a penny?"
2a.* "Does a car cost a lot or a little?"
2b.* "Does a piece of gum cost a little or a lot?"
3. "I'm going to give you 1 penny [do so], and then I'm going to give you 3 more [do so]. How many pennies do you have altogether?"
4. "Here's one bunch of pennies [show 2 pennies], and here's another bunch [show 8 pennies]. Which bunch is worth more?"
5. "Here's one set of dollars [show 5 $1.00 bills], and here's another set [show 2 $1.00 bills]. Which is worth more?"

Unidimensional Level (Level 2)

1. "Now I'm going to show you some more money. [Show $5.00, $1.00, $2.00.] Which is worth the most?"
2. "If I give you this [show $5.00 bill] and this [show 2 $1.00 bills], how much money did I give you altogether?"
3. "Suppose you go to a store to buy a candy and you want to buy this candy. [Show index card with real piece of candy taped to it.] This candy costs 5 cents, but you look in your pocket, and you only have 4 cents. How much more money do you need to buy the candy?"

4.* "This time you want to buy this candy. This candy costs 7 cents, and you give 10 cents. How much do you get in change?"

5a. "[Show a dime and a nickel.] Which is worth more?"

5b. "[Show a $5.00 bill and 2 $1.00 bills.] Which is worth more?"

Bidimensional Level (Level 3)

1. "If I give you a dime, and then I give you 6 more [show no objects for this item], how much have I given you altogether?"

2. "[Show a $5.00 bill with 1 cent and a $1.00 bill with approximately 20 cents.] Which is worth more?"

3. "Suppose you want to buy this bike. The price tag shows $45.00. [Show bike picture.] You count your money, and you have 3 $20.00 bills. How much money do you get in change?"

4a.* "Which is closer to 8 cents, a nickel or a dime?"

4b.* "Which is closer to 19 cents, a quarter or a dime?"

Integrated Bidimensional Level (Level 4)

1. "If I give you 2 quarters, and then I give you 4 quarters, how much is it worth altogether?/How many cents have I given you?"

2a. "[Show visual array.] Which is closer to $25.35, $20.00 or $30.00?"

2b. "[Show visual array.] Which is closer to $46.45, $46.00 or $47.00?"

3a. "[Show visual array.] Which is closer to $40.00, $29.95 or $61.05?"

3b. "[Show visual array.] Which is closer to $15.00, $9.95 or $19.95?"

4a. "[Show 2 groups of coins.] Suppose you have a quarter and a dime and I have 4 dimes. Who has more money, you [child] or me [tester]?"

4b. "[Show 2 groups of coins.] Suppose you have 3 quarters and I have 5 dimes and 2 nickels. Who has more money, you [child] or me [tester]?"

5. "Your hot lunch cost $3.45, and you gave a $20.00 bill and 2 quarters. How much change should you receive?"

Vectorial Level (Level 5)—If Necessary*

1. "Suppose you had a quarter and a penny and someone gave you a dime and 8 pennies. How much would you have altogether?/How many cents would you have altogether?"

2. "Suppose you had 13 cents and someone gave you a quarter, a dime, and 4 pennies. How much would you have altogether?/How many cents would you have altogether?"

3. "Suppose you had 62 cents and you gave away a quarter and 2 pennies. How much would you have left?"

4. "Suppose you had 2 dimes, 2 nickels, and 6 pennies and you gave away 18 cents. How much would you have left?"

5. "Suppose you bought a book that cost $6.73 and you gave a $20.00 bill and 3 pennies. How much change should you receive?"

Scoring

Children's response to each problem is scored as correct or incorrect according to the predetermined acceptable response. Each child is assigned an average performance score.

TIME TELLING

This task is based on the work by Case, Sandieson, and Dennis (1986) and Griffin et al. (1992); it is designed to assess children's knowledge about time and their skill in reading time from a clock. The two quantitative dimensions are hours and minutes. The four levels determined for the task are as follows: At Level 1 (*predimensional*), children have a global understanding of the units in which time is expressed. They know that an hour is a long time and that a minute is a short time. At Level 2 (*unidimensional*), children can work with a time scale and can add or subtract hours to or from a given time. They also have a global awareness of time at the hour and half hour. At Level 3 (*bidimensional*), children can work simultaneously with two time scales, such as hours and minutes. Finally, at Level 4 (*integrated bidimensional*), children can convert from one time scale to another or answer questions requiring an understanding of the full time system.

Administration

Children are asked a series of questions beginning with predimensional problems. Administration continues until children fail to answer more than half the problems at a level.

Test Items

Predimensional Level (Level 1)

1.* "Suppose your parent tells you that you can play with your favorite toy for 1 minute. Is that a long time or a short time?"

2. "Now I'm going to draw 2 lines. You watch me. [Make 2 lines of equal length, one slow and the other fast.] Which one took a long time to make?"

3. "Which is longer, an hour or a minute?"

4. "Can you tell me something that happens early in the morning at your house?"

5. "This clock says 2 o'clock. See the hour hand here? Now I'm going to change it. [Demonstrate in front of child.] Now it says 5 o'clock. [Change again to 3:00, in full view of child.] Can you tell me what time this is?"

Unidimensional Level (Level 2)

1a. "Suppose I tell you I'll come to your house at 6 o'clock. I get there at 5 o'clock. Am I early or late?"

1b.* "Suppose I tell you I'll come to your house at 3 o'clock. I get there at 4 o'clock. Am I early or late?"

2a. "[Show child preset clock reading 4:00.] What time is this?"

2b.* "[Show child preset clock reading 4:30.] What time is this?"

3a. "[Show child preset clock reading 9:00.] What time is this?"

3b.* "[Show child preset clock reading 9:30.] What time is this?"

4a. "If it's 6:00 now [display visual], how long until 7:00?"

4b. "If it's 2:00 now [display visual], how long until 3:00?"

Bidimensional Level (Level 3)

1. "Suppose I wait in line for 30 minutes, and then I wait for another 30 minutes. How many minutes have I waited altogether?"

2a. "Which is longer, 1 hour and 50 minutes or 2 hours and 1 minute?"

2b. "Which is longer, 2 hours and 5 minutes or 1 hour and 45 minutes?"

3. "[Show child preset clock reading 2:15.] What time is this?"

4. "[Show child preset clock reading 4:10.] What time is this?"

5. "If it's 3:40 now [show], how long until 4:00?"

6. "If it's 6:10 now [show], how long until 7:00?"

Integrated Bidimensional Level (Level 4)

1. "If it is 7:20 now, how long until 9:45?"

2. "If it is 10:50 now, how long until 11:25?"

3. "[Show child picture of analog clock reading 1:08.] What time is this?"

4. "[Show child picture of analog clock reading 2:58.] What time is this?"

5. "It took John 90 minutes to go to school from home. It took him only an hour and a half to come home from school. Can you explain why?"

6a. "Which is longer, 2 hours or 90 minutes?"

6b. "Which is longer, 70 minutes or 1 hour and 5 minutes?"

7. "If you leave on a trip at 8:40 and the trip takes 30 minutes, what time will you arrive?"

Vectorial Level (Level 5)—If Necessary*

1. "If it is 2:50 now, how long until 4:35?"

2. "If it is 11:35 now, how long until 1:25?"

3. "If one job takes 3 hours and 45 minutes and another takes 1 hour and 35 minutes, how long will it take to finish them both?"

4. "If the lunch period begins at 12:20 and lasts for 45 minutes, what time will my watch show when it ends?"

5. "A train left Concord at 2:06 and arrived in Vicksburg at 7:27. How long was the trip?"

6. "A group of friends is going to the beach. The trip takes 1 hour each way, and they want to spend 6 hours at the beach. What time will they get home if they leave at 9:00?"

Scoring

Children's responses to each problem are scored as correct or incorrect according to the predetermined acceptable response. Each child is assigned an average performance score.

NUMBER KNOWLEDGE

This task is designed to assess children's understandings of the system of whole numbers. It utilizes items from previous studies on this topic by Baroody et al. (1985), Case and Griffin (1990), Case and Sandieson (1987, 1988), Case and Sowder (1990), and Siegler and Robinson (1982) as well as several new items developed for the present project.

The four developmental levels that have been established for the test are as follows: At Level 1 (*predimensional*), children are expected to count by rote and to quantify globally but not to connect number and quantity. At Level 2 (*unidimensional*), children are expected to have constructed a mental counting line that integrates their understanding of numbers and quantities. At Level 3 (*bidimensional*), children are expected to be able to work simultaneously with two mental counting lines. This means that they can keep track of "ones" and "tens" while adding or subtracting and understand the relation between them. It also means that they can use one counting line to compute the distance between two points on another counting line, thus constructing the notion of a mathematical "difference." At Level 4 (*integrated bidimensional*), children can extend their understanding of tens and ones to the full number system. They can also integrate "carrying" or "borrowing" with their mental addition and subtraction and can understand the way in which one difference and another can be related.

Administration

Children are given a warm-up question first; they are asked to count from 1 to 10. Following this question, they are asked a series of questions beginning with predimensional problems. Administration continues until children fail to answer more than half the problems at a level.

Test Items

Predimensional Level (Level 1)

1. "I'm going to show you some counting chips. [Show mixed array of 3 red and 4 blue chips.] Count the blue chips, and tell me how many there are."
2. "Here are some circles and triangles. [Show mixed array of 7 circles and 8 triangles.] Count just the triangles, and tell me how many there are."
3. "I'm going to give you 1 candy, and then I'm going to give you 2 more. [Do so.] How many do you have altogether?"
4. "I'm going to show you two piles of counting chips. [Show stacks of 5 red and 2 blue.] Which pile has more?"
5.† "Would you rather have 5 candies or 2 candies? Why?"

Unidimensional Level (Level 2)

1.‡ "If you had 4 chocolates and someone gave you 3 more, how many chocolates would you have altogether?"
2a. "What number comes right after 7?"
2b. "What number comes 2 numbers after 7?"
3a. "Which is bigger, 5 or 4?"
3b. "Which is bigger, 7 or 9?"
3c. "Which is smaller, 8 or 6?"
3d. "Which is smaller, 5 or 7?"
4a. "[Present visual array of triangle with numbers 5, 6, 2.] Which number is closer to 5? [Point to 5.] Is it 6 or 2? [Point at each number in turn.]"

4b. "[Present visual array of triangle with numbers 7, 4, 9.] Which number is closer to 7, 4 or 9? [Point at each number in turn.]"

5.*† "How much is 2 plus 4?"

6.*† "How much is 8 take away 6?"

7.*† "[Show visual array with numbers 8, 5, 2, and 6, and ask child to point to and name each numeral.] When you are counting, which of these numbers do you say first? When you are counting, which of these numbers do you say last?"

8a.*† "[Show visual array with numbers 6, 4, 2, and 9; then ask:] When you are counting backward, which of these numbers do you say first?"

8b.*† "[Show visual array with numbers 6, 4, 2, and 9; then ask:] When you are counting backward, which of these numbers do you say last?"

Bidimensional Level (Level 3)

1.*†‡ "How much is 12 plus 54?"

2.*†‡ "How much is 47 take away 21?"

3a. "Which is bigger, 69 or 71?"

3b. "Which is bigger, 32 or 28?"

4a. "Which is smaller, 27 or 32?"

4b. "Which is smaller, 51 or 39?"

5a. "[Present visual array of triangle with numbers 21, 25, 18.] Which number is closer to 21? Is it 25 or 18?"

5b. "[Present visual array of triangle with numbers 28, 31, 24.] Which number is closer to 28? Is it 31 or 24?"

6.*† "What number comes 5 numbers after 49?"

7.*† "What number comes 4 numbers before 60?"

8a.*† "How many numbers are there in between 2 and 6?"

8b.*† "How many numbers are there in between 7 and 9?"

8c.*† "How many numbers are there in between 3 and 9?"

9a.*† "Do you know what 2-digit numbers are? [If not, explain.] What is the biggest 2-digit number?"

9b.*† "What is the smallest 2-digit number?"

10a.*† "When you are counting backward, which number do you say first, 49 or 66?"

10b.*† "When you are counting backward, which number do you say last, 81 or 69?"

Integrated Bidimensional Level (Level 4)†

1. "What number comes 10 numbers after 99?"

2. "What number comes 9 numbers after 999?"

3a. "Which difference is bigger, the difference between 9 and 6 or the difference between 8 and 3?"

3b. "Which difference is bigger, the difference between 6 and 2 or the difference between 8 and 5?"

4a. "Which difference is smaller, the difference between 96 and 92 or the difference between 25 and 11?"

4b. "Which difference is smaller, the difference between 48 and 36 or the difference between 84 and 73?"

5a.‡ "How much is 13 plus 39? [Show card.]"

6.‡ "How much is 36 take away 18? [Show card.]"

7a. "I asked you about 2-digit numbers earlier. This time, I want to ask you about 5-digit numbers. What's the biggest 5-digit number?"

7b. "What's the smallest 5-digit number?"

8.‡ "How much is 301 take away 7?"

9. "It took John 90 minutes to go to school from home. It took him only an hour and a half to come home from school. Can you explain why?"

10a. "Which is closer to $25.35, $20.00 or $30.00?"

10b. "Which is closer to $46.45, $46.00 or $47.00?"

10c. "Which is closer to $40.00, $29.95 or $68.05?"

10d. "Which is closer to $15.00, $9.95 or $19.95?"

Vectorial Level (Level 5)—If Necessary†

1a. How much is 42 times 3?

1b. How much is 52 times 4?

2a. Which is closer to 0: -2.8 or 3.2?

2b. Which is closer to 0: 1.9 or -2.1?

3a. Which is closer to 1: -0.2 or 1.8?

3b. Which is closer to 1: -1.4 or 3.7?

4a. Which is closer to 0: $-\frac{3}{4}$ or 0.25?

4b. Which is closer to 0: $\frac{1}{2}$ or -0.25?

5a. How much is 126 divided by 6?

5b. How much is 248 divided by 4?

6a. How much is $\frac{3}{5}$ divided by 3?

6b. How much is 3 times $\frac{2}{3}$?

Scoring

Children's responses to each problem are scored as correct or incorrect according to the predetermined acceptable response. Each child is assigned an average performance score.

ADMINISTERING AND SCORING
OF THE NARRATIVE TESTS

STORYTELLING

In recent years, cognitive scientists have become interested in story structure (Mandler, 1982; Rumelhart, 1975) and the way in which children's understanding of this structure changes with age (Stein & Glenn, 1979). The particular test that we used in this study was developed by McKeough to document changes in children's understanding between the ages of 4 and 10 years (Case & McKeough, 1990; McKeough, 1992a; McKeough et al., 1994). Children are given prompts asking them to tell two stories, one about two prespecified characters (a little child and an old horse) and one about a child of their own age who has a problem. The objective is to assess how well children are able to elaborate and integrate a series of story events with motivations and internal states of the story characters.

The four levels of plot structure are as follows: At Level 1 (*preintentional*), stories describe a connected event sequence but contain no central problem or dilemma. As a result, such stories often appear to adults as being mere accounts of "familiar scripts" (e.g., eating dinner) or of "stories without a point." At Level 2 (*uni-intentional*), the first genuine plots emerge. They are organized around a problem or dilemma and describe a series of connected events that are directed to resolving the dilemma. The attempts may or may not be successful, but by the end of the story the listener normally feels some sense of closure. At Level 3 (*bi-intentional*), children's stories still center on a dilemma, but they additionally contain a "chain" of two or more event sequences eventually leading to its resolution. Finally, at Level 4 (*integrated bi-intentional*), story plots involve multiple attempts at resolution that are integrated into a nested series, with the result that the overall story assumes a more coherent form than a simple "chain."

THE DEVELOPMENT OF CHILDREN'S THOUGHT

Administration

Children are told that they will be asked to tell stories, given an "idea" to start out with, and asked to make up the rest on their own. Children are first asked, "Tell me a story about a little child and a kind old horse." They are then asked, "Tell a story about a child your age that has a problem (you know, something they want to make better) and what they do to solve it." Administration ends when there is a clear indication of the end of the story. The prompt, "Is that the end?" may be given if the child seems uncertain.

Scoring

In evaluating stories, raters must ask the following questions: (1) Does the story describe a series of connected events? (If no, score 0; if yes, advance.) (2) Does the story describe a central problem or dilemma? (If no, score 1; if yes, advance.) (3) Does the story describe a chain of 2 or more attempts to deal with this dilemma? (If no, score 2; otherwise advance.) Finally, (4) Does the story nest one attempt to deal with this dilemma within another, in such a fashion that the story assumes an overall coherence that is tighter than a simple "chain of events"? (If no, score 3; otherwise, score 4.) Operational definitions are provided for all the terms in these questions; thus, for example, an event chain is defined as a sequence of events that can be connected by the term *and next* and that can be reordered without affecting the plot.

MOTHER'S MOTIVES

This task was originally designed to assess children's understanding of the motives that might influence a mother's performance of four standard parenting functions (Goldberg-Reitman, 1992). In the present version, children are shown a three-panel cartoon, in which (1) two sisters are playing in the water at the beach, (2) the older sister dunks the younger sister's head under water, and (3) the younger sister coughs and cries for help. The children are then asked (1) what the girls' mother would do and why, (2) what the girls' mother might be thinking and why, and (3) what the mother might be feeling and why. The four levels of understanding for this task are as follows: At Level 1 (*preintentional*), children give an account based exclusively on a character's action. At Level 2 (*uni-intentional*), children can understand a character's inner state as a motive for action. At Level 3 (*bi-intentional*), children begin to focus on the characters' inner states and mention their feelings, moral judgments, and thoughts. Finally, at Level 4 (*integrated bi-intentional*), children can balance potentially conflicting inner states against one another.

Administration

Children are shown a cartoon picture and are given the story scenario and questions described above. Administration ends after all questions are asked.

Scoring

Children's responses are scored on the basis of the complexity of their understanding of the others' motives that are involved. At Level 1 (preintentional), responses predict what the mother will do in a reasonable fashion (e.g., "She will grab her little girl up from the water"); however, even when a thought or a feeling is explicitly called for, all they do is retell some part of the story (e.g., Experimenter: "What's she thinking?" Subject: "The sister dunked her head?" E: "Why's she thinking that?" S: "Cause the sister dunked her head"). At Level 2 (uni-intentional), children's responses include some mention of the mother's inner state. This state may be a thought that she might have about consequences (e.g., "The little girl might drown," or, "Sharks might eat her"), a feeling (e.g., "She's worried about her daughter"), or a social judgment (e.g., "That's bad to do").

At Level 3 (bi-intentional), responses to one of the experimenter's questions include more than one of the elements required at the uni-intentional level. For example, in response to the question about what the mother is thinking, a child might say, "The big girl was naughty [mother's social judgment] because the little girl could drown [mother's thought about consequence of event]." The response may also describe feelings or consequences for more than a single character (e.g., "She is angry at the big girl and worried about the little girl"). At Level 4 (integrated bi-intentional), two or more internal states are mentioned and tied together into a coherent whole. Questions about action are often answered probabilistically, in terms of the child's analysis of the mother's motives (e.g., "She may get her out of the water, or she might punish the sister, or maybe throw a life raft out there"). Responses may also refer to a consequence associated with feelings and judgments (e.g., "She thought she was going to drown, and that made her mad at her sister because she did a bad thing"). Since the questions are relatively open ended, children are assigned to the highest level that they achieve in any response.

EMPATHIC COGNITION

In research on empathy, children are often shown a simple cartoon sequence that tells a story and asked a question about how the main character in the story feels (Feshbach & Roe, 1968; Hughes et al., 1981). Recent work has attempted to make this sort of assessment more realistic by presenting children with videotaped vignettes rather than cartoons (Rukavina, 1985). The present measure was designed for young children by Bruchkowsky (1992). Its distinctive feature is that a child actress is used to portray the main character. The videotape lasts for 1 min and depicts a 10-year-old girl playing with her dog in a park. In the first scene, the young girl is clearly having fun, throwing the dog a ball and telling her mother that she considers her pet to be her "best friend." At the end of the scene, however, the dog chases the ball out into the street. A loud screech of tires is heard, and the camera cuts to the next scene, where the girl is sobbing on her mother's shoulder and saying, "It's hard to believe that Harry [the dog] is dead," "I will miss him so much," etc. After the film is over, the child is asked how he or she thinks the child in the videotape felt and why.

At all levels, children can identify the girl's feeling state (sad). The four levels of explanation for this sadness are as follows: At Level 1 (*preintentional*), children give an account based exclusively on the action depicted in the video. At Level 2 (*uni-intentional*), children refer to the girl's thought as about the future or her feelings for her dog. At Level 3 (*bi-intentional*), children mention two aspects of the girl's inner state and relate them, at least tentatively. Finally, at Level 4 (*integrated bi-intentional*), children mention two thoughts or feelings and relate them both to each other and to the events in the film in a coherent fashion.

Administration

Children are seated facing the video and told that they will be asked a few questions after they have seen it. Following the showing of the video, they are given a brief moment to compose themselves and then asked, "How does the girl in the video feel?" For each emotion word contained in the children's responses, they are asked, "What happened in the video that made the girl feel this way?" and, "Why did that make her feel that way?" If only a single emotion is mentioned, they are also asked whether the girl felt anything else; if a second emotion word is provided, the same two questions are repeated. Administration ends after all questions are asked.

Scoring

Children's responses are scored on the basis of the levels of empathic cognition. At Level 1 (preintentional), responses refer only to the single most salient feeling state of the character (e.g., "She is sad"). When children are asked why the character is sad, the response remains focused on the events that are depicted or implied (e.g., "The car hit him," or, "The doggie got killed"). At Level 2 (uni-intentional), the feeling state and the action are spontaneously linked in one sentence (e.g., "She's sad because a car hit her dog"). An internal state is also mentioned when the child is asked why this will make her sad (e.g., "Because she'll miss him"). For the purposes of scoring, thoughts about the future are considered to be an internal state (e.g., "Because she'll never be able to play with Harry again").

At Level 3 (bi-intentional), mention of two internal states is made in response to the initial question about how the girl felt (e.g., "To begin with she was really happy, but then at the end she was very sad"). Mention of two internal states is made in response to the question as to why the girl was feeling that way (e.g., "She loved him a lot, so she'll really miss him"). Responses may also refer to emotions not depicted or mentioned in the video and relate them to the most salient event (e.g., "The girl is angry at the driver [of the car] for hitting the dog"). At Level 4 (integrated bi-intentional), responses contain mention of two internal states and connect them directly, both to each other and to the events in the film (e.g., "She is happy at the beginning because she is playing with her favorite dog. Then when her dog is killed at the end she is very sad because now her best friend is gone"). Since the questions are relatively open ended, children are assigned to the highest level that they achieve in any response.

DEFINITION OF FEELINGS

This task was designed by Griffin (1992) to assess children's ability to define emotion words in an internal (intentional) fashion. In the current version, children are asked to define the following emotion words: *happy*, *proud*, and *embarrassed*. The four levels of intentional reasoning are as follows: At Level 1 (*preintentional*), children define emotion words exclusively on the basis of events or external situations. At Level 2 (*uni-intentional*), children make some mention of an inner state, be it a thought, a feeling, a desire, or a judgment. At Level 3 (*bi-intentional*), children mention two such components of the inner state. Finally, at Level 4 (*integrated bi-intentional*), children mention multiple internal states and relate them to each other in a coherent fashion.

Administration

A hand puppet is introduced to children as a child of their age who wants to become a real child. The children are told that the puppet wants to learn the meaning of words to be a real child and that their job is to help the puppet learn these meanings because "you're a real kid, and you know." For each of the three emotion words, children are asked first to define the word and then to think of a situation in which they felt such an emotion. Administration ends after all six questions have been answered.

Scoring

Children's responses are scored on the basis of the complexity of the definitions that they provide. At Level 1 (preintentional), responses refer primarily to behaviors (e.g., being happy is "playing" or "having an ice cream"). At Level 2 (uni-intentional), reference is made to behaviors in relation to internal states. The internal state may be a motive (e.g., being happy means, "You want a toy, and you get it"), a judgment (e.g., "When your mom buys you something and it's nice"), or a feeling (e.g., "You're happy when you get to play"). At Level 3 (bi-intentional), the response can refer to a behavioral event and contain both a motive and a judgment (e.g., for happy, "When you want to play baseball, and then your mom lets you play, so you feel good"). It may also refer to a two-part behavioral event that involves two distinct feelings (e.g., "When you're sad and somebody gives you a hug, then you feel happy again"). At Level 4 (integrated bi-intentional), responses include multiple references to feelings, motives, thoughts, and/or judgments that are integrated into a unified whole (e.g., for embarrassed, "Kelly is my friend. One day somebody said to her, 'Jason loves Kelly,' and everybody started cracking up, and so Kelly was really embarrassed"). Since the questions are relatively open ended, children are assigned to the highest level that they achieve in any response.

PSYCHOLOGICAL VERBS

This task was originally designed by Astington (1985) to assess children's understanding of verbs of intention such as *to plan, to want,* and *to intend.* For the present study, we modified the task so that children are described in situations in which increasingly complex intentions are described. The four levels determined for the task are as follows: At Level 1 (*preintentional*), children can identify situations in which actions take place. At Level 2 (*uni-intentional*), children can identify situations in which someone's intention to carry out an action is described. At Level 3 (*bi-intentional*), children can identify situations in which someone's intention as well as feelings are described. Finally, at Level 4 (*integrated bi-intentional*), children can integrate intention and feelings and use them to describe various situations.

Administration

Children are presented with a series of cartoons, each of which contains four pictures of children in different actions. They are then read a brief story describing one of the four pictures and asked to identify the one that best matches the story read to them. The situation described often involves some sort of numerical content. However, that content is not relevant to the particular questions asked. Once children select a picture, they are asked to explain their choice. Six short stories with cartoons are presented in increasing order of difficulty (two stories at each of the first three levels). Administration ends when all pictures are shown and all questions answered.

Scoring

Children's answers as well as explanations are scored. At Level 1 (preintentional), children are merely required to select from among four cartoons one that shows a character performing an action; for example, on one item, children are asked to select a cartoon that shows "Betty climbing the stairs to play with her four sisters" from the following four cartoons: (1) Betty climbing a set of stairs; (2) a set of stairs without Betty; (3) Betty going up a walk toward a house; and (4) a house. At Level 2 (uni-intentional), children are asked to select a picture showing a cartoon character who has the intention to perform an action that could be inferred from the context; the distractor cartoons in each case include a picture of the character already performing the action. For example, on one item, children are asked to select the picture showing that "Julie is planning to play on the monkey bars with her five friends." One of the four pictures (the correct answer) depicts Julie looking at her five friends, who are playing on the monkey bars; the other three show Julie already playing on the monkey bars with her five friends (this is the "distractor" for pre-intentional children), Julie looking at her five friends as they play jump rope, and Julie playing jump rope with her five friends.

At Level 3 (bi-intentional), children are asked to select a picture showing a character with an intention that can be inferred from the context and a feeling state that can be inferred from the character's facial expression. The distractors in this case include a character already performing the action and a character who is about to perform the action but has the wrong facial expression. For example, on one item, children are asked to select the picture showing that "Angela is planning to play jump rope with her four friends because she wants to get happy again." One of the pictures (the correct answer) shows a little girl with a sad expression on her face and four children playing jump rope in the background. The others show a little girl already playing jump rope with four friends, a little girl with a happy expression on her face and four children playing jump rope in the background, and a little girl with a sad expression on her face.

In order to be scored as functioning at a particular level, children must make an appropriate choice and give an appropriate explanation. If the child's explanation is appropriate, the answer is still scored as correct even if the choice is different from what we expected. To distinguish Level 4 (integrated bi-intentional) from Level 3, children are asked to explain why some children find Level 3 problems difficult. Level 4 responses make references to the way in which intentions and feelings are depicted in each cartoon (e.g., "She's frowning a lot here and here, so other kids think this one or maybe that one, but in this one she's planning and this one she's frowning more"). Each child is assigned a score based on the highest level at which the child answered at least one of the two items correctly or awarded a score of 4 if his or her rationale meets the Level 4 criterion.

AFFECTIVE CHANGE

This is a task that was designed for the present project to assess children's understanding of the role of expectation and intention in mediating affective change. Children are shown two sequences of cartoon pictures and told a story for each. The story describes a character who has certain expectations that are foiled or met, with a resultant change in affect. The four levels determined for the task are as follows: At Level 1 (*preintentional*), children's reasoning with regard to affective change is based solely on the actions depicted in the cartoon. At Level 2 (*uni-intentional*), children recognize a character's motivation in relation to the action in each event, but no clear link is made to account for the character's affective change. At Level 3 (*bi-intentional*), children can identify and relate to more than one motivation of the character that changes over time. Finally, at Level 4 (*integrated bi-intentional*), children can identify affective change in an integrated fashion.

Administration

Children are presented with two sets of cartoons, each of which is accompanied by a script. One of these scripts is as follows: "Here's Joey. His three friends called him up to play four-square. You need four people to play four-square. He was very excited to play. When he got to the playground, his three friends decided they would rather go to the movies and left. Now there were no other kids on the playground. Joey went home with a frown on his face." Following this presentation, children are asked to explain the character's actions and feelings. The specific questions for the example presented above are, (1) "Why does Joey go home with a frown?" (2) "Why does this [child's first answer] make him go home with a frown?" and, (3) "Does he feel anything else?" (if the answer to question 2 referred to a feeling), or, "Is there anything else?" (if question 2 was answered with reference to an event). A parallel set of questions is asked for the other story, with the specific details altered. Administration ends after all questions are answered.

Scoring

Children's answers as well as explanations are scored. At Level 1 (preintentional), responses provide an action-based account of the character's feelings or refer to a feeling but do not connect the two in any clear fashion (e.g., "Because they wouldn't play with him," or, "Because he's sad"). At Level 2 (uni-intentional), responses connect an internal state (desire, judgment, etc.) with an event in the story; the connection may be spontaneous or in response to one of the questions (e.g., "Because he wanted to play, but he couldn't"). At Level 3 (bi-intentional), responses relate two characters' states to the events in the story (e.g., "Because he was sad that his friends left and they wanted to do something else," or, "They changed their minds and left him, so he felt sad"). At Level 4 (integrated bi-intentional), responses refer to multiple intentional states that can potentially be balanced against one another; they also tend to refer to the themes of the stories as a whole rather than to pictures or events in isolation (e.g., "He was sad because he wanted to play, but they decided they'd rather see the movie").

ADMINISTRATION AND SCORING
OF THE SPATIAL TASKS

SERIATION

This task was designed on the basis of Piaget's seriation task and used in our study as a measure of central spatial structures. Children are required to reconstruct a series of patterns with sticks. At Level 1 (*preaxial*), children are able to make judgments about length in terms of long versus short as well as near versus far. At Level 2 (*uniaxial*), children are able to make judgments about length relative to a mental reference axis. At Level 3 (*biaxial*), children are able to make judgments about two sets of lengths, each relative to a different mental reference line. At Level 4 (*integrated biaxial*), children are able to make length judgments in terms of four quadrants that are formed by taking two orthogonal mental reference axes (i.e., horizontal and vertical) and relating them to each other in a coherent fashion.

Administration

Children are given an 11 × 17-inch sheet of paper and sticks and told that they will be asked to reproduce a pattern of sticks that will be shown to them. Children are shown a series of patterns, each of which shows sticks glued onto a sheet of paperboard. Before children begin to reproduce a pattern, the stimulus design on the paperboard is removed. Each pattern constructed by the children is photographed for subsequent scoring. Administration begins with the preaxial level items and continues until all items are given.

Scoring

Each pattern constructed by children is scored as passing or failing to pass the requirements of a level. At the preaxial level, children are considered as passing if the sticks are placed in a vertical order with a downward slope along the top, even if the bottoms do not form a straight line. At the uniaxial level, children are considered as passing if the sticks are placed in order of decreasing size from left to right, with the bottoms aligned in a linear fashion. At the biaxial level, children are considered as passing if their pattern indicates a straight center line (as a reference line to arrange the tops and bottoms of the sticks). At the integrated biaxial level, children are considered as passing if their pattern indicates correct upward and downward slopes along the top and bottom of the design, a straight center line, as well as uniform spacing. Each child is assigned a score based on the highest level passed.

CHECKERS

This task was designed on the basis of prior work by Olson (1970) as well as by Halford and McDonald (1977). In our version, children are asked to reconstruct a series of patterns with checkers glued onto a piece of cardboard with a grid. At Level 1 (*preaxial*), children are able to reconstruct a series of "next to" relations along a straight line. At Level 2 (*uniaxial*), children are able to reconstruct not only "next to" relations but also a "farther from/nearer than" spatial relation relative to a reference axis. At Level 3 (*biaxial*), children can divide the overall plane into two sections, each containing the same spatial relations as at the uniaxial level. At Level 4 (*integrated biaxial*), children are able to understand spatial relations in terms of a Cartesian plane, which requires simultaneous attention to two orthogonal (i.e., horizontal and vertical) axes.

Administration

Children are given a 9 × 9-square grid and 30 checkers. They are shown each pattern of checkers and asked to reproduce the pattern after the stimulus design is removed. Children's constructions are recorded on the scoring sheet. Administration begins with the preaxial level items and continues until all items are given.

Scoring

Each pattern constructed by the children is scored as passing or failing the requirements of a level. At the preaxial level, children are considered as passing if checkers form a straight line from one end of the checkerboard to the other end in the direction shown in the stimulus pattern (i.e., horizontal or vertical). Matching the exact column or row in the display (e.g., fourth vs. third) is not required, but maintaining the checkers in the same row from one edge to the other is required. At the uni-, bi-, as well as integrated biaxial levels, children must reproduce the exact pattern in order to score a pass. Each child is assigned a score based on the highest level passed.

MAP DRAWING

This task was designed on the basis of a classroom drawing task designed by Liben and Down (1989). Children are asked to draw a map of a model of a classroom. At Level 1 (*preaxial*), children can "fill" a sheet of paper with objects in the model without coherent spatial organization. At Level 2 (*uniaxial*), children understand spatial relations in one plane by relating each object to a mental reference axis. At Level 3 (*biaxial*), children can represent the relative positions of objects in the two major planes (i.e., front wall and floor), although they are unable to relate two planes in a coherent way. At Level 4 (*integrated biaxial*), children can represent spatial relations within and between two major planes as well as two side planes accurately.

Administration

The experimenter shows children a hand-drawn map of their own classroom, explaining that she pretended that she was up in an airplane looking down into the classroom when she drew it. She then identifies four or five objects in the map (e.g., "See? Here is your teacher's desk, and these are the tables where the children sit, and here is the chalkboard"). She concludes by reminding the child that this is not a regular picture; it is a map. Next, she introduces the child to a scale model of a traditional classroom (the model is 21 inches × 17.5 inches × 11.5 inches), saying, "Here is a little classroom just like a classroom in the school where I work. I would like you to draw a map of this classroom. You can pretend that you are up in an airplane and looking down into the classroom if you like."

Scoring

Children's drawings are evaluated using Berg's (1991) scoring criteria. Preaxial drawings tend to show a "bird's eye" (from the top) or a "painter's" view (from the side). In either case, relative positions of objects are not correctly depicted. Uniaxial drawings use a reference line (floor or front wall) to align the objects but do not reference any object jointly with regard to two orthogonal walls. Biaxial drawings show objects on the floor and the wall. They may use one panel to represent the plane formed by the main floor plan of the classroom and another panel to represent the plane formed by the front wall. Alternatively, they may draw the objects on the floor from above, using the "rows and columns" layout of the desks in the main floor section, but with some considerable drift and no accurate representation of objects on the diagonal. Integrated biaxial drawings depict all the objects in the model classroom from above, including ones that are placed diagonally, as though they were conjointly referenced on a Cartesian grid. Each child is assigned a level score, depending on the pattern that he or she generates.

MAP FOLLOWING

This task is newly developed by our research team and intended to assess children's understanding of spatial relations in a familiar school yard as represented on a two-dimensional plane as a map. At Level 1 (*preaxial*), children can relate landmarks on a map to those in a school yard and walk along a path, as long as the path is along the edge of the yard from one landmark to another that is adjacent to it. At Level 2 (*uniaxial*), children can follow a map and walk along a path in reference to a single axis. At Level 3 (*biaxial*), children can follow a map and walk along a path in reference to two orthogonal axes in immediate succession (this might be termed the orthogonal "tacking" strategy. At Level 4 (*integrated biaxial*), children walk along the complex path exactly as indicated in the diagram. They touch each diagonal object only at the point indicated, not at the end.

Administration

Children are taken outside to the sandbox area of their school playground. They are shown a previously prepared small map of this area mounted on a piece of thick cardboard. The objects whose position the map indicates are pointed out to them. They are then asked to follow a simple route from their existing position, going along the edge of the playground to an object indicated on a map (Route 1). Next, another map is given to them that indicates a more lengthy and irregular trip (Route 2). The actual paths that children take are recorded on the scoring sheet. Administration begins with Route 1 ends with Route 2. No time limit is imposed.

Scoring

Children's actual paths are evaluated using the following criteria. Children at the preaxial level are successful in navigating the straight path (Route 1) but are unable to follow Route 2. Children at the uniaxial level are successful in following Route 2 to the extent that they can scrutinize its overall contour, encoding it as going "up and away" from the baseline of the playground, then "over" for a while, then back down toward the baseline. They are also able to construct a physical path that actually follows this route by winding through the indicated set of objects in the way that a ship might pass between the port and starboard buoys in a channel, going "forward" and "over" as required.

At the biaxial level, children can hold an original course parallel to the vertical side of the map (i.e., one edge of the playground) until they touch the first object indicated on the map; they can then alter their course with a right-angled turn and set out on a course parallel to the second (orthogonal) boundary of the playground until they reach the second indicated object, and so on, until arriving at the final point on the map. At the integrated biaxial level, not only can children alter course and "tack" from one object to the next (alternating between two reference axes, as it were), but they can also hit the precise point indicated on each object, even if the object is located diagonally to their charted path of movement and thus has to be conjointly referenced to the two right-angled axes. Each child is assigned a level score based on his or her performance on the two Map Following items.

STILL LIFE DRAWING

This task was originally suggested to us by Ellen Winner. Children are presented with a display consisting of a coffee cup standing on a table, with a toothbrush upside down inside it and a tube of toothpaste lying in front of and next to it. The composition that children use allows us to determine children's levels of spatial understanding. At Level 1 (*preaxial*), children can fill up a page with objects from the display without organizing them relative to one another. At Level 2 (*uniaxial*), children can represent the relative position of objects in one plane by relating each object to a mental reference axis. At Level 3 (*biaxial*), children can use a second mental reference axis and place objects within the plane created by the two axes. At Level 4 (*integrated biaxial*), children can represent spatial relations within two major planes and coordinate the two planes in an integrated fashion.

Administration

Children are shown a display consisting of a table, a coffee cup, a toothbrush, and a tube of toothpaste. They are then provided with a set of colored pencils and a blank sheet of paper and asked to draw what they see. No time limit is imposed. Children's drawings are collected for scoring.

Scoring

The scoring criteria were developed by Charles Bleiker. Preaxial drawings should indicate the general shape of the most salient part of each object and the adjacency relations that obtain among them. Thus, for example, these drawings should depict the cup as a circle (for the opening) and the handle as a sort of U shape and place the second shape so that it is close to (ideally, touching) the second. Uniaxial drawings should indicate children's view of objects either from the top or from the side relative to an explicit or implicit reference axis that this viewpoint permits. Biaxial drawings should depict the projection of each object onto two different planes. The cup should now be rendered, as before, as a rectangle (its side view), but it should now have a circle (its top view) indicated at the top of the rectangle as well. This form of drawing is sometimes referred to as "characteristic view rendering." Integrated biaxial drawings should indicate a coordination of two separate planes, showing a classic perspective rendering. Objects are represented in a coherent fashion, with minimal distortion, from a viewpoint that contains information from both object planes. Prototypical drawings at each level were shown in Figure 24 above. Each child is assigned a level score based on his or her drawing and the prototype to which it bears the closest resemblance. Half scores are awarded if a drawing shares features of two successive prototypes.

PICTURE DRAWING

This task was taken directly from Dennis's (1992) study. It is designed to assess children's understanding of front-back and side-side relations in a drawing. The particular scene that the children are asked to draw is one in which a mother and a father are holding hands in a park with their baby in front of them and a tree far off behind. At Level 1 (*preaxial*), children can fill up a page with objects without any implied ground line. At Level 2 (*uniaxial*), children can represent space in relation to a single ground line. At Level 3 (*biaxial*), children can represent objects using an implied ground line for the foreground and another for the background. At Level 4 (*inte-*

grated *biaxial*), children can represent the foreground and the background as well as the unifying middle ground in between.

Administration

Children are provided with a sheet of 8.5 × 11-inch paper and a set of 13 colored pencils. They are then asked to draw the scene described above. The directions are read to children as often as they request or the interviewer feels necessary. No time limit is imposed. Children's drawings are collected for scoring.

Scoring

The scoring criteria were also adapted from Dennis's (1992) study. To be scored as preaxial, children must draw the requested figures. These figures, however, do not have to depict the spatial relation described in the story. Uniaxial drawings must show objects along a ground line, either explicit (a line drawn) or implicit (the bottom of the paper). Biaxial drawings show front-back relations by using two reference axes. Integrated biaxial drawings must create a Cartesian or an artist's perspective; that is, a middle ground is established that is used to connect the foreground and background. Prototypical drawings at each level were shown in Figures 17 and 26. Each child is assigned a level score based on his or her drawing and its resemblance to the prototype. Half scores may be awarded if a drawing possesses features of two adjacent prototypes.

HANDWRITING

Handwriting is one of the "classic" tasks used to assess children's spatial understanding. For our purpose, we selected a word, *Gargoyle,* that includes lowercase letters whose ascenders project above the x-height (e.g., *l*) and whose descenders project below the baseline (e.g., *g*) so that children's understanding of spatial relations among the various shapes of letters can be assessed. At Level 1 (*preaxial*), children should be able to reproduce letter-like figures without reference to a straight line. At Level 2 (*uniaxial*), children should be able to construct printed letters and place them with respect to a mental reference line. At Level 3 (*biaxial*), children should be able to use two mental reference lines to coordinate printed letters, but not in cursive. At Level 4 (*integrated biaxial*), children should be able to write in a cursive script that shows a coordination of two mental reference lines.

Administration

Children are told that the interviewer has a little dog at home named Gargoyle. They are then shown a card with this name printed on it and asked to copy it on a blank sheet of white paper. No time limit is imposed. Children's productions are collected for scoring.

Scoring

Scoring criteria were established for this study prior to data collection. Preaxial handwriting should represent the general configuration of most of the letters, but the letters need not be aligned in reference to the horizontal edges of the paper. Uniaxial handwriting should reproduce the letters along a single implied axis in such a way that a straight line could be drawn through all the letters. Biaxial handwriting should reproduce the lowercase letters along one implied line and the capital and other "large" letters (e.g., *l*) along a second one. Integrated biaxial handwriting should reproduce the name in cursive and succeed in drawing the diagonal lines connecting letters in an appropriate fashion. Children are assigned level scores.

APPENDIX D

SAMPLE LESSON FROM THE RIGHTSTART PROGRAM

Explicit objective.—For the numbers 1–5 (or 1–10), children will know that each number maps onto an object when counting and that each number maps onto a set. Children will gain beginning experience of the "take-away" operation and the predictability of results.

Implicit objective.—More capable children will have a chance to compare quantities, to use the generative rule (number + 1 = next number in series), and to make dimensional assessments.

Materials needed.—Counting chips (five colors); plastic jar (bank); cloth; mask.

ACTIVITY 1

Specific Objective

Child can count a set of objects and state numerical value of set correctly.

Procedure

Drop the counting chips on the table in a heap, and then place plastic jar in the center. Ask the first child to get 1 red chip and place it in the jar. Ask the second child to get 2 blue chips and place them in the jar, counting them out loud as they are dropped in. Ask the third child to get 3 white chips and place them in the jar, etc., until the fifth child gets 5 of a different color (e.g., yellow). Everyone has to watch to make sure that each child puts the right color and the right number in and does not make any mistakes.

When all the chips are in, hold up the jar and ask the children, "Which color has the most? Are there more red chips or more yellow chips?" Let the children answer, and then say, "Let's dump them out and count them to find out." Dump the chips out, and have the children count the red chips and the yellow chips to see which ones have the most. (*Note:* Pick an extreme contrast for this task.) Repeat with different quantities of chips (up to 10), allowing the more capable children to count the larger sets.

ACTIVITY 2: SUPERBOY/SUPERGIRL GAME

Specific Objective

Can count a set of objects and compute quantity. Beginning experience with "take-away" operation.

Procedure

Give the following instructions: "Now we're going to play the Superboy game. One person [instructor chooses and gives mask] will be Superboy/Supergirl. We're going to pretend these chips are money and this jar is a bank. [Give each child 5 chips, making sure that each child's chips are a different color.] Everyone count your money to see how much you have—remember how much money you have and what color your money is. Now each of you count your money into the bank. Does everyone remember their color and number? [Confirm that they do; if not, empty the bank, and count again.] Now, Superboy/Supergirl is going to come and borrow someone's chip, and we have to figure out whose chip he/she borrowed. [All close their eyes. Superboy/Supergirl removes *one* chip.] Now, did he/she borrow one of yours, or yours, or yours? How can we figure this out? Let's take all of the chips out of the bank [empty the bank], and everyone count their chips to see if they are all there."

Have the children count, determine which set is missing one, and predict what color chip Superboy/Supergirl must have borrowed. When a prediction is made, Superboy/Supergirl must return the borrowed chip so that the prediction can be tested. Repeat, giving each child a turn playing Superboy/Supergirl.

Variations

Repeat with different quantities of money put into the bank (e.g., from 6 to 10 chips each). When children are comfortable with this level of play, repeat with increasing quantities of money (2 to 4 chips) borrowed from the bank. These variations can be introduced at selected points in the training sequence (e.g., when children are comfortable counting sets of 6 or more), interspersed with other activities specified in later lessons.

REINFORCEMENT ACTIVITY: FIVE LITTLE CHILDREN LINE-UP GAME

Specific Objective

Provide daily experience with "take-away" operation.

Procedure

Tell the children, "When I tap you on the shoulder, it's your turn to leave the group to line up at the door to go back to your classroom. But first, let's see how many children are in this group. [Let the children count to determine quantity.] OK, let's sing our song. Five little children doing their work. [Tap one child on the shoulder and let him/her leave the group.] One lines up, and then there are ———. [Let the children compute or predict quantity.] Four little children doing their work. [Tap another child on the shoulder.] Another lines up, and then there are ———." Continue until all the children are lined up.

PROCEDURES AND PARAMETERS
FOR FITTING THE GROWTH OF WORKING MEMORY
WITH A SET OF LOGISTIC EQUATIONS

Figure E1 presents some empirical data on the growth of working memory, on two measures that are related to those used in the present study and that have been developed within the general program of research that gave rise to it. One is the Counting Span test (Case, Kurland, & Daneman, 1979; Case, Kurland & Goldberg, 1982). The other is the Spatial Span test (Crammond, 1992). As may be seen, the pattern of growth is logistic and could be reasonably fit by a family of equations with the same general formula as was used in the text.

The particular parameters that have been used are ones that are based on the assumption that performance on a working memory test does not give a direct measure of capacity but is more tightly constrained by capacity than is performance on other measures. Thus, working memory growth is a good variable to use as an estimate of capacity growth. In keeping with this assumption, I have used a standard logistic equation to fit the data in the figure, with the value of K (the carrying capacity) assumed to be equivalent to this hypothetical "basic" capacity and thus set equal to the variable K_t.

The curve that is illustrated in the figure has an initial value (I) of .05, a growth rate (GR) of 6%, and a carrying capacity (K_t) that grows from 1

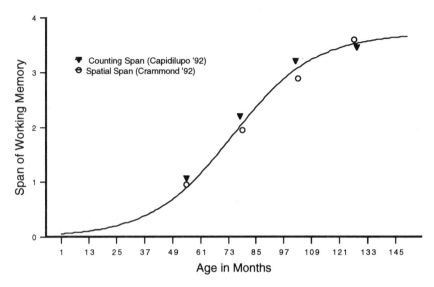

Fig. E1.—Theoretical growth curve fit to empirical data for the growth of children's working memory.

to 3.7, with a monthly growth rate of 4.5%. It is these values for K_t that are used in the text.

Note that adult span on working measures is often around 4.2 units, and this value can be used instead of 3.7 without altering the form of the graphs in the main text or the conclusions that are reached from them.

REFERENCES

Accredolo, L. (1979). Laboratory versus home: The effect of environment on the infant's choice of spatial reference system. *Developmental Psychology, 4,* 666–667.

Adams, M. J. (1990). *Beginning to read: Thinking and learning about print.* Cambridge, MA: MIT Press.

Anderson, N., & Cuneo, D. O. (1978). The height + width rule in children's judgments about quantity. *Journal of Experimental Psychology: General, 107,* 335–378.

Astington, J. W. (1985). *Children's understanding of promising.* Unpublished doctoral dissertation, Ontario Institute for Studies in Education, University of Toronto.

Astington, J. W. (1994). *The child's discovery of mind.* New York: Cambridge University Press.

Astington, J. W., Harris, P. L., & Olson, D. R. (Eds.). (1989). *Developing theories of mind.* New York: Cambridge University Press.

Baddeley, A. D., & Hitch, G. J. (1974). Working memory. In G. Bower (Ed.), *The psychology of learning and motivation: Advances in research and theory* (Vol. **8**). New York: Academic.

Baldwin, J. M. (1968). *The development of the child and of the race.* New York: Augustus M. Kelly. (Original work published 1894)

Baroody, A. J., Ganon, K., Berent, R., & Ginsburg, H. (1985). The development of basic mathematical abilities. *Acta Paedogogica, 1,* 133–150.

Bentley, A. M., Kvalsig, J., & Miller, R. (1990). The cognitive consequences of poverty: A neo-Piagetian study with Zulu children. *Applied Cognitive Psychology, 4,* 451–459.

Berg, R. (1991). Procedures for assessing figural complexity from drawings. In R. Case (Ed.), *The role of central conceptual structures in the development of children's numerical, literary, and spatial thought* (Year 1 Report to the Spencer Foundation). Stanford, CA: School of Education, Stanford University.

Bickhard, M. H. (1994). Staircase? How can we tell? *American Journal of Psychology,* **106,** 577–633.

Biemiller, A. F. (1966). *The effect of varying exposure to a novel object on manipulation by human infants.* Unpublished master's thesis, Cornell University.

Biemiller, A. F. (1993). Lake Wobegon revisited. *Educational Researcher,* **22**(9), 7–12.

Biggs, J., & Collis, K. (1982). *Evaluating the quality of learning: The SOLO taxonomy.* New York: Academic.

Bleiker, C. (1995). *Central conceptual structures in the development of children's drawings.* Unpublished Ph.D. dissertation, Stanford University.

Borke, H. (1971). Interpersonal perception of young children: Egocentrism or empathy? *Developmental Psychology, 5,* 663–669.

Borke, H. (1973). The development of empathy in Chinese and American children between 3 and 6 years of age: A cross-cultural study. *Developmental Psychology,* **9,** 102–108.

Bradley, L., & Bryant, P. (1985). *Rhyme and reason in reading and spelling* (International Academy for Research in Learning Disabilities Monograph, No. 1). Ann Arbor, MI.

Briars, D. J., & Larkin, J. H. (1984). An integrated model of skill in solving elementary word problems. *Cognition and Instruction,* **1,** 245–296.

Bruchkowsky, M. (1992). The development of empathic cognition in middle and early childhood. In R. Case (Ed.), *The mind's staircase: Exploring the conceptual underpinnings of children's thought and knowledge.* Hillsdale, NJ: Erlbaum.

Bruner, J. S. (1964). The course of cognitive growth. *American Psychologist,* **19,** 1–15.

Bruner, J. S. (1966). On cognitive growth. In J. S. Bruner, R. R. Oliver, & P. M. Greenfield (Eds.), *Studies in cognitive growth.* New York: Wiley.

Bruner, J. S. (1986). *Actual minds, possible worlds.* Cambridge, MA: Harvard University Press.

Bruner, J. S., Oliver, R. R., & Greenfield, P. M. (1966). *Studies in cognitive growth.* New York: Wiley.

Campbell, R. L., & Bickhard, M. H. (1992). Types of constraints on development: An interactivist approach. *Developmental Review,* **12,** 311–338.

Capodilupo, A. M. (1990). *Cognitive development in music: A neo-structural investigation of normally achieving and reading disabled children.* Unpublished doctoral dissertation, Ontario Institute for Studies in Education, University of Toronto.

Capodilupo, A. M. (1992). A neo-structural analysis of children's response to instruction in the sight-reading of musical notation. In R. Case (Ed.), *The mind's staircase: Exploring the conceptual underpinnings of children's thought and knowledge.* Hillsdale, NJ: Erlbaum.

Caraher, T. D., Caraher, D., & Schlieman, A. (1985). Mathematics in the streets and in the schools. *British Journal of Developmental Psychology,* **3,** 21–29.

Carey, S. (1985). *Conceptual change in childhood.* Cambridge, MA: MIT Press.

Carey, S. (1988). Reorganization of knowledge in the course of acquisition. In S. Strauss (Ed.), *Ontogeny, phylogeny, and historical development.* New York: Ablex.

Carpenter, T. P., Hiebert, J., & Moser, J. M. (1981). Problem structure and first-grade children's initial solution processes for simple addition and subtraction problems. *Journal for Research in Mathematics Education,* **12,** 27–39.

Carpenter, T. P., Moser, J. P., & Romberg, T. A. (1982). *Addition and subtraction: A cognitive perspective.* Hillsdale, NJ: Erlbaum.

Case, R. (1972). Validation of a neo-Piagetian capacity construct. *Journal of Experimental Child Psychology,* **14,** 287–302.

Case, R. (1975). Social class differences in intellectual development: A neo-Piagetian investigation. *Canadian Journal of Behavioral Science,* **7,** 78–95.

Case, R. (1977). Responsiveness to conservation training as a function of induced subjective uncertainty, M-space, and cognitive style. *Canadian Journal of Behavioural Science,* **9,** 12–25.

Case, R. (1978). Intellectual development from birth to adulthood: A neo-Piagetian investigation. In R. S. Siegler (Ed.), *Children's thinking: What develops?* Hillsdale, NJ: Erlbaum.

Case, R. (1985). *Intellectual development: Birth to adulthood.* New York: Academic.

Case, R. (Ed.). (1992a). *The mind's staircase: Exploring the conceptual underpinnings of children's thought and knowledge.* Hillsdale, NJ: Erlbaum.

Case, R. (1992b). The role of the frontal lobes in the regulation of cognitive development. *Brain and Cognition,* **20,** 51–73.

Case, R. (1993, April). *From situated activity to generalizable structures: Children's construction of the concept of number.* Paper presented at the meeting of the American Educational Research Association, San Francisco.

Case, R. (1995). Capacity based explanations of working memory growth: A brief history and a reevaluation. In F. M. Weinert & W. Schneider (Eds.), *Memory performance and competencies: Issues in growth and development.* Hillsdale, NJ: Erlbaum.

Case, R. (in press). Stages in the formation of an adult social identity. In S. Stryker & E. T. Higgins (Eds.), *Self, affect and society.* New York: Guilford.

Case, R., & Griffin, S. (1990). Child cognitive development: The role of central conceptual structures in the development of scientific and social thought. In C. A. Hauert (Ed.), *Developmental Psychology: Cognitive, perceptuo-motor, and neuropsychological perspectives.* Amsterdam: Elsevier Science.

Case, R., & Khanna, F. (1981). The missing links: Stages in children's progression from sensorimotor to logical thought. In K. W. Fischer (Ed.), *Cognitive development* (New Directions for Child Development, No. 12). San Francisco: Jossey-Bass.

Case, R., Krohn, C., & Bushey, B. (1992, April). *The acquisition of fractional number knowledge: A developmental analysis.* Paper presented at the meeting of the American Educational Research Association, San Francisco.

Case, R., Kurland, D. M., & Daneman, M. (1979, April). *Operational efficiency and the growth of working memory.* Paper presented at the meeting of the Society for Research in Child Development, San Francisco.

Case, R., Kurland, M., & Goldberg, J. (1982). Operational efficiency and the growth of short-term memory. *Journal of Experimental Child Psychology, 33,* 386–404.

Case, R., Marini, Z., McKeough, A., Dennis, S., & Goldberg, J. (1986). Horizontal structure in middle childhood: The emergence of dimensional operations. In I. Levine (Ed.), *Stage and structure: Re-opening the debate.* Norwood, NJ: Ablex.

Case, R., & McKeough, A. (1990). Schooling and the development of central conceptual structures: An example from the domain of children's narrative. *International Journal of Educational Psychology, 8,* 835–855.

Case, R., Okamoto, Y., Henderson, B., & McKeough, A. (1993). Consistency and inconsistency in cognitive development: Evidence for the presence of central conceptual structures. In R. Case & W. Edelstein (Eds.), *The new structuralism in cognitive development: Theory and research on individual pathways.* Basel: Karger.

Case, R., & Sandieson, R. (1987, March). *The influence of children's conceptual knowledge on their procedural knowledge, and vice versa.* Paper presented at the meeting of the American Educational Research Association, Washington, DC.

Case, R., & Sandieson, R. (1988). A developmental approach to the identification and teaching of central conceptual structures in middle school science and mathematics. In M. Behr & J. Hiebert (Eds.), *Research agenda in mathematics education: Number concepts and operations in the middle grades.* Hillsdale, NJ: Erlbaum.

Case, R., & Sandieson, R. (1992). Testing for the presence of a central numerical structure: Use of the transfer paradigm. In R. Case (Ed.), *The mind's staircase: Exploring the conceptual underpinnings of children's thought and knowledge.* Hillsdale, NJ: Erlbaum.

Case, R., Sandieson, R., & Dennis, S. (1986). Two cognitive developmental approaches to the design of remedial instruction. *Cognitive Development, 1,* 293–333.

Case, R., & Sowder, J. (1990). The development of computational estimation: A neo-Piagetian analysis. *Cognition and Instruction, 7,* 79–104.

Cellerier, G. (1972). Information processing tendencies in recent experiments in cognitive learning: Theoretical implications. In S. Farnham Diggory (Ed.), *Information processing in children.* New York: Academic.

Chapman, M. (1988). *Constructive evolution: Origins and development of Piaget's thought.* New York: Cambridge University Press.

Chi, M. T. H. (1976). Short-term memory limitations in children: Capacity or processing deficits? *Memory and Cognition*, **23**, 266–281.

Chi, M. T. H. (1988). Children's lack of access and knowledge reorganization: An example from the concept of animism. In M. Perlmutter & F. E. Weinert (Eds.), *Memory development: Universal changes and individual differences*. Hillsdale, NJ: Erlbaum.

Chi, M. T. H., & Rees, E. (1983). A learning framework for development. *Contributions to Human Development*, **9**, 71–107.

Chomsky, N. (1957). *Syntactic structures*. The Hague: Mouton.

Clogg, C. C. (1977). *Unrestricted and restricted maximum likelihood latent structure analysis: A manual for users* (Working Paper No. 1977-09). University Park: Pennsylvania State University, Population Issues Research Office.

Cole, M. (1990, May). *Cultural psychology: Some general principles and a concrete example*. Paper presented at the Second International Congress of Activity Theory, Lahti, Finland.

Cole, M., Gay, J., Glick, J. A., & Sharp, D. (1971). *The cultural context of learning and thinking*. New York: Basic.

Confrey, J. (1994). Splitting, similarity and rate of change: A new approach to multiplicative and exponential functions. In G. Herel & J. Confrey (Eds.), *The development of multiplicative reasoning in the learning of mathematics*. Albany: State University of New York Press.

Crammond, J. (1992). Analyzing the basic developmental processes of children with different types of learning disability. In R. Case (Ed.), *The mind's staircase: Exploring the conceptual underpinnings of children's thought and knowledge*. Hillsdale, NJ: Erlbaum.

Damon, W. (1973). *The child's conception of justice as related to logical thought*. Unpublished doctoral dissertation, University of California, Berkeley.

Damon, W. (1977). *The social world of the child*. San Francisco: Jossey-Bass.

Das, J. P., Kirby, J., & Jarmon, R. F. (1975). Simultaneous and successive syntheses: An alternative model for cognitive abilities. *Psychological Bulletin*, **82**, 87–103.

Dasen, P. R. (1972). Cross-cultural Piagetian research: A summary. *Journal of Cross-Cultural Psychology*, **6**, 156–172.

Davidov, V. V. (1982). The psychological characteristics of the formation of elementary mathematical operations in children. In T. P. Carpenter, J. P. Moser, & T. A. Romberg (Eds.), *Addition and subtraction: A cognitive perspective*. Hillsdale, NJ: Erlbaum.

Dellarosa, D. (1986). A computer simulation of children's arithmetic word-problem solving. *Behaviour Research Methods, Instruments and Computers*, **18**, 47–154.

DeLoache, J. S. (1989). The development of representation in young children. In H. W. Reese (Ed.), *Advances in Child Development and Behavior, 22*. New York: Academic.

DeMersseman, S. L. (1976). *A developmental investigation of children's moral reasoning and behavior in hypothetical and practical situations*. Unpublished doctoral dissertation, University of California, Berkeley.

Demetriou, A., Efklides, A., & Platsidou, M. (1993). The architecture and dynamics of developing mind: Experiential structuralism as a frame for unifying cognitive developmental theories. *Monographs of the Society for Research in Child Development*, **58**(5–6, Serial No. 234).

Demetriou, A., Platsidou, M., Efklides, A., Kazi, S., Syrmali, K., & Kiosseoglou, G. (1995). *Self-image and cognitive development: Structure, functions, and development of self-representation and self-evaluation from childhood to adolescence*. Unpublished manuscript, Aristotelian University of Thessaloniki.

Demetriou, A., Shayer, M., & Pervez, M. (1988). The structure and scaling of concrete operational thought: Three studies in four countries. *Genetic, Social, and General Psychology Monographs*, **114**, 307–376.

Dennis, S. (1992). Stage and structure in the development of children's spatial representations. In R. Case (Ed.), *The mind's staircase: Exploring the conceptual underpinnings of children's thought and knowledge.* Hillsdale, NJ: Erlbaum.

DeRibaupierre, A. (1993). Structural invariants and individual differences: On the difficulty of dissociating developmental and differential processes. In R. Case & W. Edelstein (Eds.), *The new structuralism in cognitive development: Theory and research on individual pathways.* Basel: Karger.

DeRibaupierre, A., & Pascual-Leone, J. (1979). Formal operations and M-power: A neo-Piagetian investigation. In D. Kuhn (Ed.), *Intellectual development beyond childhood* (New Directions in Child Development, No. 5). San Francisco: Jossey-Bass.

DeRibaupierre, A., Rieben, L., & Lautrey, J. (1991). Developmental change and individual differences: A longitudinal study using Piagetian tasks. *Genetic, Social, and General Psychology Monographs,* **117**, 285–311.

DeVos, G. A. (1973). *Socialization for achievement: Essays on the cultural psychology of the Japanese.* Berkeley: University of California Press.

Fan, N., Mueller, J. H., & Marinni, A. E. (in press). Solving difference problems: Wording primes coordination. *Cognition and Instruction.*

Feshbach, N. D., & Roe, K. (1968). Empathy in six- and seven-year-olds. *Child Development,* **39**, 133–145.

Fiati, T. A. (1992). Cross cultural variation in the structure of children's thought. In R. Case (Ed.), *The mind's staircase: Exploring the conceptual underpinnings of children's thought and knowledge.* Hillsdale, NJ: Erlbaum.

Fischer, K. W. (1980). A theory of cognitive development: The control and construction of hierarchies of skills. *Psychological Review,* **87**, 477–531.

Fischer, K. W., Hand, H. H., Watson, M. W., Van Parys, M., & Tucker, J. L. (1984). Putting the child into socialization: The development of social categories in preschool children. In L. Katz (Ed.), *Current Topics in Early Childhood Education, 5.* Norwood, NJ: Ablex.

Fischer, K. W., Knight, C. C., & Van Parys, M. (1993). Analyzing diversity in developmental pathways. In R. Case & W. Edelstein (Eds.), *The new structuralism in cognitive development: Theory and research on individual pathways.* Basel: Karger.

Flavell, J. H. (1978). Comments. In R. S. Siegler (Ed.), *Children's thinking: What develops?* Hillsdale, NJ: Erlbaum.

Flavell, J. H., Omanson, R. C., & Latham, C. (1978). Solving spatial perspective taking problems by rule versus computation: A developmental study. *Developmental Psychology,* **12**, 462-473.

Flavell, J. H., Shipstead, S. G., & Grofit, K. (1978). Young children's knowledge about visual perception: Hiding objects from others. *Child Development,* **49**, 1208–1211.

Fletcher, C. K. (1985). Understanding and solving word arithmetic problems: A computer simulation. *Behaviour Research Methods Instruments and Computers,* **17**, 464–571 Fodor, J. (1982). *The modularity of mind.* Cambridge, MA: MIT Press.

Fodor, J. (1982). *The modularity of mind.* Cambridge, MA: MIT Press.

Frake, C. O. (1985). Cognitive maps of time and tide among medieval seafarers. *Man,* **20**, 254–270.

Freeman, N. H. (1972). Process and product in children's drawing. *Perception,* **1**, 21–33.

Freeman, N. H. (1980). *Strategies of representation in young children.* London: Academic.

Furman, I. (1981). *The development of problem-solving strategies: A neo-Piagetian analysis of children's performance in a balance beam task.* Unpublished doctoral dissertation, University of California, Berkeley.

Gagne, R. M. (1968). Contributions of learning to human development. *Psychological Review,* **75**, 177–191.

Gardner, H. (1983). *Frames of mind.* New York: Basic.

Gardner, H. (1991). *The unschooled mind.* New York: Basic.

Gaudia, G. (1972). Race, social class, and age of achievement of conservation of Piaget's tasks. *Developmental Psychology,* **6,** 158–165.

Gelman, R. (1978). Counting in the preschooler: What does and what does not develop? In R. S. Siegler (Ed.), *Children's thinking: What develops?* Hillsdale, NJ: Erlbaum.

Gelman, R., & Greeno, J. G. (1989). On the nature of competence: Principles for understanding in a domain. In L. B. Resnick (Ed.), *Knowing and learning: Issues for a cognitive science of instruction.* Hillsdale, NJ: Erlbaum.

Globerson, T. (1983). Mental capacity and developmental functioning: Developmental and social class differences. *Developmental Psychology,* **19,** 225–250.

Goldberg-Reitman, J. R. (1992). Children's conception of their mother's role: A neo-structural analysis. In R. Case (Ed.), *The mind's staircase: Exploring the conceptual underpinnings of children's thought and knowledge.* Hillsdale, NJ: Erlbaum.

Goldman-Rakic, P. (1989a, August). *Cellular and circuit basis of working memory in prefrontal cortex of nonhuman primates.* Paper prepared for a conference on the prefrontal cortex sponsored by the Netherlands Institute for Brain Research, Amsterdam.

Goldman-Rakic, P. (1989b, June). *Working memory and the frontal lobes.* Paper presented at the Toronto General Hospital.

Gombrich, E. H. (1960). *Art and illusion.* New York: Pantheon.

Goodenough, F. L. (1926). *Measurement of intelligence by drawings.* Chicago: World Book Co.

Goodman, L. A. (1974). The analysis of systems of qualitative variables when some of them are unobservable: 1. A modified latent structure approach. *American Journal of Sociology,* **79,** 1179–1259.

Goodman, L. A. (1975). A new model for scaling response patterns: An application of the quasi-independence concept. *Journal of the American Statistical Association,* **70,** 755–768.

Green, B. F. (1952). Latent structure analysis and its relation to factor analysis. *Journal of the American Statistical Association,* **47,** 71–76.

Greeno, J. G. (1991). Number sense as situated knowing in a conceptual domain. *Journal for Research in Mathematics Education,* **22**(31), 170–218.

Greeno, J. G., & Resnick, L. (1993). *Conceptual growth of number and quantity.* Unpublished manuscript, Stanford University.

Griffin, S. A. (1992). Young children's understanding of their inner world: A neo-Piagetian analysis of the development of intrapersonal intelligence. In R. Case (Ed.), *The mind's staircase: Exploring the conceptual underpinnings of children's thought and knowledge.* Hillsdale, NJ: Erlbaum.

Griffin, S. A. (1994, July). *Working memory capacity and the acquisition of mathematical knowledge: Implications for learning and development.* Paper presented at the meeting of the International Society for the Study of Behavioral Development, Amsterdam.

Griffin, S. A. (1995). A cognitive-developmental analysis of pride, shame, and embarrassment in middle childhood. In K. Fischer & J. Tagney (Eds.), *The self-conscious emotions.* New York: Guilford.

Griffin, S. A. (in preparation). *Teaching number sense to children at risk for school failure: Effects of a 3-year intervention study.* Clark University.

Griffin, S. A., Case, R., & Capodilupo, S. (1995). Teaching for understanding: The importance of central conceptual structures in the elementary school mathematics curriculum. In A. McKeough, J. Lupart, & A. Marini (Eds.), *Teaching for transfer: Fostering generalization in learning.* Hillsdale, NJ: Erlbaum.

Griffin, S. A., Case, R., & Sandieson, R. (1992). Synchrony and asynchrony in the acquisition of children's everyday mathematical knowledge. In R. Case (Ed.), *The mind's staircase: Exploring the conceptual underpinnings of children's thought and knowledge.* Hillsdale, NJ: Erlbaum.

Griffin, S. A., Case, R., & Siegler, R. S. (1994). Rightstart: Providing the central conceptual prerequisites for first formal learning of arithmetic to students at risk for school failure. In K. McGilly (Ed.), *Classroom lessons: Integrating cognitive theory and classroom practice*. Cambridge, MA: MIT Press/Bradford.

Gustafsson, J.-E. (1988). Broad and narrow abilities in research on learning and instruction. In R. J. Sternberg (Ed.), *Advances in the psychology of intelligence* (Vol. 4). Hillsdale, NJ: Erlbaum.

Hagen, M. I. (1986). *Varieties of realism: Geometries of representational art*. New York: Cambridge University Press.

Halford, G. S. (1982). *The development of thought*. Hillsdale, NJ: Erlbaum.

Halford, G. S. (1993a). Central conceptual structures: Achievements and challenges. *Human Development, 36,* 300–308.

Halford, G. S. (1993b). *Children's understanding: The development of mental models*. Hillsdale, NJ: Erlbaum.

Halford, G. S., Mayberry, M. T., Hare, O. & Grant, P. (1994). The development of memory and processing capacity. *Child Development, 65,* 1330–1348.

Halford, G. S., & McDonald, C. (1977). Children's pattern construction as a function of age and complexity. *Child Development, 48,* 1096–1100.

Hamilton, V. L., Blumenfeld, P. C., Akoh, H., & Miura, K. (1989). Citizenship and scholarship in Japanese and American fifth grades. *American Educational Research Journal, 26,* 44–72.

Heath, S. B. (1984). *Ways with words: Language, life and work in communities and classrooms*. Cambridge: Cambridge University Press.

Hebb, D. O. (1949). *The organization of behavior*. New York: Wiley.

Hencke, R., & Fischer, K. W. (1993). Are there general structures in cognitive development? *Contemporary Psychology, 38,* 901–902.

Hess, R. D., McDevitt, T. M., & Chang, C.-M. (1987). Cultural variations in family beliefs about children's performance in mathematics: Comparisons among People's Republic of China, Chinese-Americans and Caucasian-American families. *Journal of Educational Psychology, 79,* 179–188.

Hoyrup, J. (1994). Varieties of mathematical discourse in premodern sociocultural contexts: Mesopotamia, Greece, and the Latin Middle Ages. In J. Hoyrup (Ed.), *Measure, number, and weight*. Albany: State University of New York Press.

Hughes, R., Tingle, B. A., & Swain, D. B. (1981). Development of empathic understanding in children. *Child Development, 52,* 122–128.

Inhelder, B., & Piaget, J. (1958). *The growth of logical thinking from childhood to adolescence*. New York: Basic.

Inhelder, B., & Piaget, J. (1964). *The early growth of logic in the child*. London: Routledge & Kegan Paul.

Inhelder, B., Sinclair, H., & Bovet, M. (1974). *Learning and the development of cognition*. Paris: Presses Universitaires de France.

Johnson, N. E. (1993). Case's neo-Piagetian theory: A work in progress. *Contemporary Psychology, 38,* 902–903.

Kaiser, H. (1960). The application of electronic computers to factor analysis. *Educational and Psychological Measurement, 29,* 141–151.

Kaufman, A. S., & Kaufman, N. L. (1983). *K-ABC: Kaufman Assessment Battery for Children*. Circle Pines, MN: American Guidance Service.

Keating, D. P. (in press). Habits of mind for a learning society: Educating for human development. In D. R. Olson & N. Torrance (Eds.), *Handbook for education and human development: New models of learning, teaching and schooling*. Oxford: Blackwell.

Keil, F. C. (1986). On the structure-dependent nature of stages of cognitive development. In I. Levin (Ed.), *Stage and structure: Reopening the debate.* Norwood, NJ: Ablex.

Kellogg, R. (1969). *Analyzing children's art.* Palo Alto, CA: National.

Kintsch, W., & Greeno, J. G. (1985). Understanding and solving word arithmetic problems. *Psychological Review*, **92**, 109–129.

Laurendeau, M., & Pinard, A. (1970). *Development of the concept of space in the child.* New York: International Universities Press.

Lautrey, J. (1993). Structure and variability: A plea for a pluralistic approach to cognitive development. In R. Case & W. Edelstein (Eds.), *The new structuralism in cognitive development: Theory and research on individual pathways.* Basel: Karger.

Lautrey, J., DeRibaupierre, A., & Rieben, L. (1985). Intra-individual variability in the development of concrete operations: Relations between logical and infra-logical operations. *Genetic, Social, and General Psychology Monographs*, **111**, 167–192.

Lave, J., & Wenger, E. (1991). *Situated learning: Legitimate peripheral participation.* Cambridge: Cambridge University Press.

Lesser, G. S., Fifer, G., & Clark, D. H. (1965). Mental abilities of children from different social class and cultural groups. *Monographs of the Society for Research in Child Development*, 30(4, Serial No. 102).

Lewis, M. D. (1994). Reconciling stage and specificity in neo-Piagetian theory: Self-organizing conceptual structures. *Human Development*, **37**, 143–169.

Lewis, M. D. (1995). Cognition-emotion feedback and the self-organization of developmental paths. *Human Development*, **38**, 71–102.

Liben, L. S., & Down, R. M. (1989). Understanding maps as symbols: The development of map concepts in children. In H. W. Reese (Ed.), *Advances in Child Development and Behavior, 22.* New York: Academic.

Luquet, G. H. (1927). *Le dessin enfantin* [Children's drawing]. Paris: Alcan.

Luria, A. R. (1966). *Higher cortical functions in man.* New York: Basic.

Mandler, J. M. (1982). Recent research on story grammars. In J. I. Lany & W. Kintsch (Eds.), *Language and comprehension.* Amsterdam: North-Holland.

Marini, Z. A. (1992). Synchrony and asynchrony in the development of children's scientific reasoning. In R. Case (Ed.), *The mind's staircase: Exploring the conceptual underpinnings of children's thought and knowledge.* Hillsdale, NJ: Erlbaum.

Marini, Z. A., & Case, R. (1993). The development of abstract reasoning about the physical and social world. *Child Development*, **65**, 147–159.

Markman, E. M. (1984). The acquisition and organization of categories by children. In C. Sophian (Ed.). *The origins of cognitive skills.* Hillsdale, NJ: Erlbaum.

Mayer, R. (1985). Mathematical ability. In R. J. Sternberg (Ed.), *Human abilities.* New York: Freeman.

McClelland, J. L., Rumelhart, D. E., & Hinton, G. E. (1987). The appeal of parallel distributed processing. In D. E. Rumelhart & J. L. McClelland (Eds.), *Parallel distributed processing: Explorations in the microstructure of cognition* (Vol. 1). Cambridge, MA: MIT Press.

McKeough, A. (1992a). A neo-Piagetian analysis of narrative and its development. In R. Case (Ed.), *The mind's staircase: Exploring the conceptual underpinnings of children's thought and knowledge.* Hillsdale, NJ: Erlbaum.

McKeough, A. (1992b). Testing for the presence of a central conceptual structure: Use of the transfer paradigm. In R. Case (Ed.), *The mind's staircase: Exploring the conceptual underpinnings of children's thought and knowledge.* Hillsdale, NJ: Erlbaum.

McKeough, A., Yates, T., & Marini, A. E. (1994). Intentional reasoning: A developmental study of behaviorally aggressive and normal boys. *Development and Psychopathology*, **6**, 285–304.

Miller, M. S., & Pascual-Leone, J. (1981, April). *Disconfirming Jensen experimentally: Intellectual versus executive-structural deficiency in underperforming low SES children*. Paper presented at the meeting of the Society for Research in Child Development, Boston.

Miller, R., Pascual-Leone, J., Campbell, C., & Juckes, T. (1990). *Learning and development: A neo-Piagetian cross-cultural analysis*. Durban, South Africa: University of Natal.

Miura, I. T. (1987). Mathematics achievement as a function of language. *Journal of Educational Psychology*, **79**, 79–82.

Miura, I. T., & Okamoto, Y. (1989). Comparisons of American and Japanese first graders' cognitive representation of number and understanding of place value. *Journal of Educational Psychology*, **81**, 109–113.

Mood, D., & Johnson, J. (1973). *Young children's awareness of the moods of others: Empathy or cognitive awareness?* (Technical Report No. 4). Centre for the Study of Cognitive Processes, Wayne State University.

Mordkowitz, E. R., & Ginsburg, H. P. (1987). Early academic socialization of successful Asian American college students. *Quarterly Newsletter of the Laboratory for Comparative Human Cognition*, **9**, 85–91.

Morra, S., Moizo, C., & Scopesi, A. M. (1988). Working memory (or the M-operator) and the planning of children's drawing. *Journal of Experimental Child Psychology*, **46**, 41–73.

Nelson, K. (1978). How children represent their knowledge of the world in and out of language: A preliminary report. In R. S. Siegler (Ed.), *Children's thinking: What develops?* Hillsdale, NJ: Erlbaum.

Nesher, P., Greeno, J. G., & Riley, M. S. (1982). The development of semantic categories for addition and subtraction. *Educational Studies in Mathematics*, **13**, 373–394.

Noelting, G. (1982). *Le developpement cognitif et le mecanisms de l'equilibration* [Cognitive development and the mechanisms of equilibration]. Chicoutimi, Quebec: Gaetan Morin.

Okamoto, Y. (1992). *A developmental analysis of children's processes for solving word problems*. Unpublished doctoral dissertation, Stanford University.

Okamoto, Y. (1994, April). *Computer simulations of children's developmental understanding of quantitative relations in text*. Paper presented at the meeting of the American Educational Research Association, New Orleans.

Okamoto, Y. (in press). Modeling children's understandings of quantitative relations in texts: A developmental perspective. *Cognition and Instruction*.

Olson, D. R. (1970). *Cognitive development: The child's acquisition of diagonality*. New York: Academic.

Olson, D. R. (1977). From utterance to test. *Harvard Educational Review*, **47**, 257–281.

Olson, D. R. (1994). *The world on paper: The conceptual and cognitive implications of writing and reading*. New York: Cambridge University Press.

Olson, D. R., & Bialystok, E. (1983). *Spatial cognition: The structure and development of mental representations of spatial relations*. Hillsdale, NJ: Erlbaum.

Pascual-Leone, J. (1969). *Cognitive development and cognitive style*. Unpublished doctoral dissertation, University of Geneva.

Pascual-Leone, J. (1970). A mathematical model for the transition rule in Piaget's development stages. *Acta Psychologica*, **32**, 301–345.

Pascual-Leone, J. (1974, August). *A neo-Piagetian process-structural model of Witkin's psychological differentiation*. Paper presented at the Second International conference of the Association for Cross-Cultural psychology, Kingston, Ontario.

Pascual-Leone, J. (1988). Organismic processes for neo-Piagetian theories: A dialectical causal account of cognitive development. In A. Demetriou (Ed.), *The neo-Piagetian theories of cognitive development: Toward an integration*. Amsterdam: Elsevier North-Holland.

Pascual-Leone, J. (1994). An experimentalist's understanding of children. *Human Development*, **37**, 370–385.

Pascual-Leone, J., & Smith, J. (1969). The encoding and decoding of symbols by children: A new experimental paradigm and a neo-Piagetian model. *Journal of Experimental Child Psychology*, **8**, 328–355.

Piaget, J. (1952). *The child's conception of number.* New York: Norton.

Piaget, J. (1960). *The psychology of intelligence.* Totowa, NJ: Littlefield, Adams.

Piaget, J. (1964). Development and learning. In R. E. Ripple & V. N. Rockcastle (Eds.), *Piaget rediscovered.* Ithaca, NY: Cornell University School of Education.

Piaget, J. (1970). Piaget's theory. In P. H. Mussen (Ed.), *Carmichael's handbook of child development.* New York: Wiley.

Piaget, J. (1972). Intellectual evolution from adolescence to adulthood. *Human Development*, **15**, 1–12.

Piaget, J., & Inhelder, R. (1956). *The child's conception of space.* London: Routledge & Kegan Paul. (Original work published in French in 1948)

Piaget, J., Inhelder, B., & Szeminska, A. (1960). *The child's conception of geometry.* New York: Basic.

Propp, V. (1968). *The morphology of the folktale.* Austin: University of Texas Press. (Original work published 1922)

Reid, D. (1992). Horizontal and vertical structure: Stages and substages in children's motor development. In R. Case (Ed.), *The mind's staircase: Exploring the conceptual underpinnings of children's thought and knowledge.* Hillsdale, NJ: Erlbaum.

Resnick, L. B. (1983). A developmental theory of number understanding. In H. P. Ginsburg (Ed.), *The development of mathematical thinking.* New York: Academic.

Resnick, L. B. (1989). Developing mathematical knowledge. *American Psychologist*, **44**, 162–169.

Reuchlin, M., & Bacher, F. (1989). *Les differences individuelles dan le developpement cognitif.* Paris: Presses Universitaires de France.

Riley, M. S., & Greeno, J. G. (1988). Developmental analysis of understanding language about quantities and of solving problems. *Cognition and Instruction*, **5**(1), 49–101.

Riley, M. S., Greeno, J. G., & Heller, J. I. (1983). Development of children's problem-solving ability in arithmetic. In H. P. Ginsburg (Ed.), *The development of mathematical thinking.* New York: Academic.

Rohlen, T. P. (1985). Order in Japanese society: Attachment, authority, and routine. *Journal of Japanese Studies*, **15**, 15–40.

Rohlen, T. P. (1995). Differences that make a difference: Explaining Japan's success. *Educational Policy*, **9**, 103–128.

Rukavina, I. (1985). *The development of cognitive and affective aspects of empathy.* Unpublished master's thesis, University of Toronto, Ontario Institute for Studies in Education.

Rumelhart, D. (1975). Notes on a schema. In D. G. Bobrow & A. Collis (Eds.), *Representation and understanding: Studies in cognitive science.* New York: Academic.

Rushton, J. P., Brainerd, C. J., & Pressley, M. (1983). Behavioral development and construct validity: The principle of aggregation. *Psychological Bulletin*, **94**, 18–38.

Saxe, G. B. (1988). The mathematics of child street vendors. *Child Development*, **59**, 1415–1425.

Scribner, S., & Cole, M. (1980). *Consequences of literacy.* Cambridge, MA: Harvard University Press.

Serafine, M. L. (1988). *Music as cognition: The development of thought in sound.* New York: Columbia University Press.

Siegler, R. S. (1976). Three aspects of cognitive development. *Cognitive Psychology*, **4**, 481–520.

Siegler, R. S. (1978). The origins of scientific reasoning. In R. S. Siegler (Ed.), *Children's thinking: What develops?* Hillsdale, NJ: Erlbaum.

Siegler, R. S. (1981). Developmental sequences within and between concepts. *Monographs of the Society for Research in Child Development,* **46**(2, Serial No. 189).

Siegler, R. S. (1986). A panoramic view of cognitive development. *Contemporary Psychology,* **31,** 329–331.

Siegler, R. S. (1990). In counting, young children's procedures precede principles. *Educational Psychology Review,* **3,** 127–135.

Siegler, R. S. (1995). Children's thinking: How does change occur? In W. Schneider & F. Weinert (Eds.), *Memory performance and competencies: Issues in growth and development.* Hillsdale, NJ: Erlbaum.

Siegler, R. S., & Robinson, M. (1982). The development of numerical understanding. In H. W. Reese & L. P. Lipsitt (Eds.), *Advances in Child Development and Behavior, 16.* New York: Academic.

Siegler, R. S., & Shrager, J. (1984). Strategy choices in addition and subtraction problems: How do children know what to do? In C. Sophian (Ed.), *The origins of cognitive skills.* Hillsdale, NJ: Erlbaum.

Simon, D. P., & Simon, H. A. (1978). Individual differences in solving physics problems. In R. S. Siegler (Ed.), *Children's thinking: What develops?* Hillsdale, NJ: Erlbaum.

Simon, H. A. (1972). Complexity and the representation of patterned sequences of symbols. *Psychological Review,* **79,** 369–382.

Snow, R. E., Kyllonen, P. C., & Marshalek, B. (1984). The topography of ability and learning correlations. In R. Sternberg (Ed.), *Advances in the psychology of intelligence.* Hillsdale, NJ: Erlbaum.

Spelke, E. S. (1988). Where perceiving ends and thinking begins: The apprehension of objects in infancy. In A. Yonas (Ed.), *Perceptual Development in Infancy* (Minnesota Symposia in Child Psychology). Hillsdale, NJ: Erlbaum.

Starkey, P. (1992). The early development of numerical reasoning. *Cognition,* **43,** 93–126.

Stein, N. L., & Glenn, C. G. (1979). An analysis of story comprehension in elementary school children. In R. Friedle (Ed.), *Discourse processing: Multidisciplinary perspectives.* Norwood, NJ: Ablex.

Stevenson, H. W., Lee, S.-Y., & Stigler, J. W. (1986). Mathematics achievement of Chinese, Japanese and American children. *Science,* **231,** 593–699.

Stevenson, H. W., & Stigler, J. W. (1992). *The learning gap.* New York: Summit.

Stigler, J. W., Lee, S.-Y., Lucker, W., & Stevenson, H. W. (1982). Curriculum and achievement in mathematics: A study of elementary school children in Japan, Taiwan and the United States. *Journal of Educational Psychology,* **74,** 315–322.

Stuss, D. T., & Benson, D. F. (1986). *The frontal lobes.* New York: Oxford University Press.

Thatcher, R. W. (1992). Cyclical cortical reorganization during early childhood. *Brain and Cognition,* **20,** 24–50.

Thelan, E., & Ulrich, B. D. (1991). Hidden skills: A dynamic systems analysis of treadmill stepping during the first year. *Monographs of the Society for Research in Child Development,* **56**(1, Serial No. 223).

Tobin, J. J., Wu, D. Y. H., & Davidson, D. H. (1989). *Preschool in three cultures.* New Haven, CT: Yale University Press.

Van Geert, P. (1991). A dynamic systems model of cognitive and language growth. *Psychological Review,* **98,** 3–53.

Van Geert, P. (1994). *Dynamic systems of development: Change between complexity and chaos.* Hemel Hempstead: Harvester Wheatsheaf.

Vygotsky, L. S. (1962). *Thought and language* (E. Hanfmann & G. Vaker, Trans.). Cambridge, MA: MIT Press. (Original work published 1934)

Wilkening, F. (1981). Integrating velocity, time, and distance information: A developmental study. *Cognitive Psychology*, **13**, 231–247.

Winner, E. (1989). How can Chinese children draw so well? *Journal of Aesthetic Education*, **23**, 41–65.

Witelson, S. (1983). Bumps on the brain: Right-left anatomic asymmetry as a key to functional lateralization. In S. J. Segalowitz (Ed.), *Language functions and brain organization*. London: Academic.

Yakovlev, P. I., & Lecours, A. R. (1967). The myelogenetic cycles of regional maturation of the brain. In A. Minkowski (Ed.), *Regional development of the brain in early life*. Oxford: Blackwell Scientific.

Yoshida, H. (1991). *Kodomo-wa kazu-wo donoyoni rikai shite irunoka* [Children's understanding of number]. Tokyo: Shinsho-sha.

ACKNOWLEDGMENTS

The general program of research reported in this *Monograph* took 6 years to complete and could not have been undertaken without assistance from many quarters.

Financial support for the project was provided by the Spencer Foundation through a grant to Robbie Case and a doctoral fellowship to Yukari Okamoto. The work reported in Chapter IV was supported by the James T. McDonnell Foundation through grants to Sharon Griffin and to Robbie Case. The work reported in Chapter VII received support from the Canadian Institute for Advanced Research. We are pleased to acknowledge the financial assistance provided by these organizations and the encouragement provided by their presidents: Larry Cremin, John Breur, and Fraser Mustard.

James Greeno and Edward Haertel served as consultants and co-supervisors of the work that is reported in Chapter II. Paul Van Geert and Kurt Fischer served as reviewers of the work that is reported in Chapter VII. Dan Keating and Bob Siegler served as reviewers of the entire manuscript. The intellectual contributions that these individuals made were substantial, and it is both a pleasure and an honor to acknowledge them.

Help in our studies of children's spatial development was provided by Sonja Dennis and Lynn Liben, who supplied us with the entire corpus of their data on children's drawing and classroom maps, respectively. Further help was provided by Ellen Winner, who advised us on the design of new spatial measures that would yield interesting cross-cultural data. Finally, assistance in gathering cross-cultural data on these and other measures was provided by Professor Tu Mei Ru and her colleagues in Nanjing and by Drs. Namiki and Oshima in Tokyo.

Graduate students at the University of Toronto who worked on the project included Sandra Capodilupo and Rosanne Menna. Graduate students at Stanford University who worked on the project included Deborah Barany, Rick Berg, Beverley Bushey, Nancy Beth Garrett, Amy Neel Gordon, Barbara Katzenberg, Carolyn Krohn, Beatrice Lauman, Richard

Mander, Cristina Tsai, Wang Lianquin, and Zhou Xin. Graduate students who worked on the project at Clark University included Jane Bannister, Margaret Carpenter, Susan Gardner, and Melanie Orphant. Without the intellectual and practical assistance that these individuals provided, the project could never have been undertaken, let alone completed.

Finally, administrative and secretarial support at Stanford was provided by Elayne Weissler Martello, Wilma Strenck, and Andrea Evans; additional clerical assistance was provided by Stephanie Yee. In Toronto, secretarial support was provided by Cynthia Slipp, Barbara Mainguy, and Christina Lopez. At Clark, administrative and secretarial support was provided by Mary O'Connor. To all these individuals, and to the many others who provided us with material or emotional support, we extend our heartfelt thanks.

COMMENTARY

A GRAND THEORY OF DEVELOPMENT

Robert S. Siegler

The stated goals of this *Monograph* are quite modest: to refine the construct of central conceptual structures (CCSs), to provide stronger empirical support for their importance, and to broaden the range of such structures that have been analyzed in detail. The unstated underlying goal, however, is much bolder: to provide a grand unifying theory of cognitive development. At a time when many developmentalists lament the absence of credible theories that identify structural commonalities among diverse aspects of children's thinking, Case, Okamoto, and their colleagues have attempted to provide just such a theory.

The effort to identify structures that underlie children's thinking is not new, of course; Case and other neo-Piagetian scholars have been pursuing it for more than 20 years. What is new is the type of unification being attempted. Cognitive theories can be divided into three main types: ones that posit one, several, or many basic units. For example, psychometric theories of intelligence were distinguished by whether they posited one underlying dimension (e.g., Spearman's *g*), several underlying dimensions (e.g., Thurstone's seven primary mental factors), or many underlying dimensions (e.g., Guilford's 120 factors). Similarly, theories of cognitive development can be distinguished by whether they focus on a single basic locus of development (e.g., Piaget's logical structures), several basic loci (e.g., Wellman & Gelman's, 1992, foundational theories of core domains), or many loci (e.g., Klahr's, 1992, production systems). Until his 1992 book, Case's theory was of the first type. Starting then, and continuing in this *Monograph*, it has become primarily a theory of the second type. Like Thurstone, Gardner, and a number of other theorists who posit several types of intelligence, Case also posits an overarching intellectual core that helps create each of the particular CCSs and that lends some similarity in age-typical reasoning across them. He also explicitly recognizes the role of associative knowledge of particular tasks in building up any given CCS. His theory's primary focus, however, is on the intermediate-level CCSs themselves.

In this *Monograph*, the focus is on the development of three such structures—those for number, narrative, and space—between the ages of 4 and 10. In each case, development is viewed as progressing from a predimensional level at around age 4, to a dimensional level at age 6, a bidimensional level at age 8, and an integrated bidimensional level at age 10. The conceptual structures are hypothesized to serve several functions. They are the center of children's thinking about a given domain, thus generating the types of broad, but not system-wide, unities documented in this *Monograph*. They also provide a base for future development; the more mature forms of each conceptual structure are extensions of the less mature forms in that domain. Finally, they reflect the maturational level of the system as a whole and thus constrain the thinking that is possible about any given topic.

Unique Contributions

The most obvious contribution of this *Monograph* is the very large amount of new empirical data, tasks, and areas studied. Case's work has always been notable for the range of tasks and domains to which he has applied his framework. The present *Monograph* continues this tradition. The strategy of studying very large numbers of tasks that have certain conceptual underpinnings in common allows him to identify surprising commonalities in performance. For example, the Case, Stephenson, Bleiker, and Okamoto analysis of the CCS for space leads them to posit common features in children's reasoning about seriation, their memory for arrangements of checkers, their ability to follow maps, and their drawing of still lifes. Substantial research literatures exist about each of these skills; the unique contribution of Case et al.'s research is to identify commonalities in performance across them.

Similar statements could have been made about Case (1985) or Case (1992). Several other features of the present *Monograph* represent clear advances over the earlier work, however. One is the use of more sophisticated analytic techniques than in previous studies. The use of complex correlational techniques, such as factor analysis and latent class analysis, is one useful innovation. These techniques provide quantitative indices of the unities in reasoning on the tasks hypothesized to map onto a given CCS.

Another innovation is the use of formal models to express theoretical ideas and to demonstrate how the proposed account could generate the types of changes that are seen in children's thinking. One example is the computer simulations used to model how children with varying levels of understanding of the numerical CCS would perform on arithmetic word problems. Another is the logistic growth function modeling of the relation between more specific and more general understanding. These formal models are especially interesting because they make clear implications of Case's overall theory that are difficult to infer from verbal descriptions of the theory.

Another important feature of this *Monograph* is Griffin and Case's use of training experiments to demonstrate the causal importance of CCSs. Previous training studies by Case and Sandieson (1992) and McKeough (1992) yielded evidence pointing in the same direction, but the experiments reported here are larger and better controlled. In two truly heroic experiments, Griffin and Case provided 17 small groups of children with 40 training sessions each in the quantitative CCS or a control procedure. The children were from low-income backgrounds; theoretically they were old enough to have learned the CCS, but they had not. The training was very effective. It led to gains not only on the tasks that were taught but also on a large number of tasks that were not taught but that were hypothesized to tap the same CCS. These transfer tasks were impressively diverse; they included problems involving balance scales, distributive justice, money, and number conservation. Math achievement tests and teacher ratings obtained a year later indicated that the benefits were long term, that they enabled children not only to gain knowledge but also to learn more effectively afterward. A traditional math readiness curriculum produced some gains, but not nearly as great as those produced by the program designed to help children construct the central conceptual structure.

The training studies also are noteworthy for raising a particularly interesting question. The children who participated in them were 5-year-olds from low-income backgrounds. Griffin and Case predicted that these children would benefit from the instruction because they were performing below their biologically dictated maximum level. As predicted, the children did benefit. However, this does not mean that children from higher-SES backgrounds who were younger but had comparable knowledge would not have benefited as much or more. If, as Griffin and Case hypothesized, the limiting factor is biological capacity, the children from higher-SES backgrounds would not be expected to learn as much from the curricula. On the other hand, as a rule of thumb, children who have progressed more rapidly in a domain in the past also are more skilled at acquiring new knowledge in it. Given that the higher-SES children reached the same level of reasoning at a younger age, this view would predict that they would benefit at least as much from the curriculum as lower-SES children with similar numerical knowledge.

Previous evidence reported by Case's research group suggests that, at minimum, younger children from higher-SES backgrounds would also derive substantial benefits from the curriculum. In Case's (1992) book, McKeough (1992) described a training regimen aimed at inculcating the narrative CCS in children from middle-class backgrounds. The ages of these children placed them in the heart of the predimensional period (mean chronological age = 4.10 years). McKeough's results showed a similar pattern of learning and transfer of the CCS to that shown by the older, low-SES children in the Griffin and Case study. Presenting the same curriculum to children from low- and middle-income backgrounds, with similar knowledge but different ages, could prove especially helpful for understand the relation between biological maturation and ability to acquire more advanced understanding of a CCS.

A final noteworthy strength of the *Monograph* is that it presents intriguing ideas. One of these is that the sources of social class differences in intellectual performance are not the same as the sources of national differences in intellectual performance. Case posits that social class differences reflect differing amounts of exposure to a wide range of particular experiences subsumed by each structure. Specifically, children from low-SES backgrounds are posited to have less exposure to a wide range of activities that contribute to the creation of the quantitative, narrative, and spatial CCSs. This leads to their performance being uniformly lower on the measures of these structures than that of children from middle- and upper-middle-SES backgrounds.

In contrast, national differences in intellectual performance are ascribed to differences in relative emphasis on particular skills within the cultures. For example, the emphasis in Chinese and Japanese culture on drawing skills is said to result in children in those cultures employing advanced drawing techniques, relative to age peers in Canada and the United States. However, the structural commonalities among all the children's drawing are used to argue that the cultural emphasis affects only those skills that are specifically taught. I only partially agree with this interpretation of the national and social class differences (for reasons discussed later), but I find intriguing even the parts with which I disagree.

Another intriguing idea, one that is at the heart of the basic account of development within the *Monograph*, is that of the hierarchical learning loop. Case and Okamoto propose that higher-level knowledge and lower-level knowledge exercise a mutually regulating influence. Experiences that lead to lower-level knowledge (e.g., knowledge of how to draw clothing) also lead to growth of more general knowledge (e.g., the spatial conceptual structure). Conversely, the more general knowledge regulates how quickly the more specific knowledge structures can grow.

These ideas are formalized as logistic growth function models. Within such models, the growth curve is determined by the starting point, the rate of growth for each subsequent unit of time, and the distance between the current level and the asymptote (with growth slowing as the current level approaches the asymptote). The logistic growth equations also provide a straightforward way of modeling how variations in instruction and other relevant features of the external environment contribute to variations in growth rates. The linked growth curves that Case presents allow modeling of simultaneous, and mutually regulating, contributions to development of internal and external sources of change. Adding to the generality of the account, the same model can be applied to different levels of the cognitive hierarchy. Thus, it can be applied to the relation between particular understandings relevant to a given CCS and the CCS as a whole and also to the relation between understandings of particular CCSs and the cognitive system as a whole.

Limitations

Formulating a general theory of development is an immensely challenging undertaking. Any effort to do so will inevitably be limited in a variety of ways. Three limits of the present *Monograph* are lack of explicit principles for determining the level implied by a given type of reasoning, arbitrary criteria for determining how well theoretical predictions must be met to constitute support for the theory, and seeming inconsistencies between the model as verbally stated and as realized in the formal model.

Lack of Explicit Principles for Assigning Tasks to Levels

One long-standing issue regarding neo-Piagetian theories concerns the failure to specify the principles by which types of reasoning are assigned to levels. To the extent that assignment of tasks to levels of reasoning seems arbitrary, ad hoc, or based on the investigators' general knowledge of children's thinking rather than on the particular theory, the support offered by the data for the theory is reduced.

Such problems arise in the present *Monograph* as well as in previous neo-Piagetian work. Consider tasks used to assess the integrated bidimensional level of understanding of the numerical CCS. Two items are used to measure understanding of other numerical systems. One involves knowing that 90 min is the same as 1.5 hours, the other that $25.35 is closer to $30.00 than to $20.00. But does the ability to answer such questions correctly reflect general quantitative reasoning capabilities? It might just reflect when certain knowledge and procedures are taught in school. Similarly, does being able to calculate mentally that $25 - 14$ is greater than $99 - 92$ reflect a particular conceptual structure or a combination of facility at mental arithmetic and working memory capability? After all, problems of the same form but with smaller numbers are used to assess reasoning at an earlier level. The same argument applies to the counting problems—does it really require a different structure to count from 99 to 108 than it does to count from 49 to 54, or are numbers below 100 just practiced more heavily in early elementary school classrooms? Missing minuend problems of the form ? − 4 = 3 are also used to assess integrated bidimensional reasoning, which is said to emerge around age 10. Yet, in previous research, Groen and Poll (1973) found that 7-year-olds could solve missing addend problems of almost identical form: 4 + ? = 7. What in the theory predicts that missing subtrahend problems should be so much harder than missing addend problems?

The effect of the lack of clearly stated rules for assigning tasks to difficulty levels is exacerbated by the limited range of data obtained on each task. In all cases, the data involve simply whether the child answered correctly. Such data provide only weak evidence regarding whether the child solved the task as posited by the theory. Other types of data—data on particular errors, on patterns of solution times, and on eye movements, for example—could provide more direct evidence regarding the reasoning underlying both successes and failures.

Case, Okamoto, and their collaborators acknowledge the uncertainty surrounding the assignment of particular tasks to particular levels of reasoning. Their position is that, even if some of the assignments are inaccurate, the large volume of tasks that produce the expected results argues for the overall validity of the classifications. This argument is somewhat persuasive.

Perhaps more compelling evidence for their position, however, comes from the transfer results of the Griffin and Case training studies. The fact that teaching a type of reasoning produces transfer to theoretically related tasks constitutes higher-quality evidence that children use the reasoning in solving the transfer tasks than does the fact that untrained children pass the tasks at the same age. Data from the training studies could be put to additional use by analyzing differences in transfer among tasks believed to tap the same theoretical structure. For example, children trained on the quantitative numerical structure showed considerably more transfer to the Balance Beam and Birthday Party tasks than did children given the reading readiness curriculum. However, the training did not lead to more transfer to the number conservation or Time Telling tests. Examining differences in transfer to tasks believed to tap the same CCS could help in refining analyses of how and when the CCSs affect children's reasoning.

What Counts as a Successful Prediction?

Another, somewhat related problem is uncertainty over how well data must fit theoretical predictions in order to count as support for the theory.

271

To illustrate, in the test of number conservation (Table 2), 50% or more correct answers at the age at which success on a given task was predicted was taken as support of the prediction. By this criterion, 13 of the 15 tasks said to tap bidimensional and integrated bidimensional reasoning were passed at the predicted age. In many studies inspired by Piaget's work, however, a criterion of 75% or more correct responses is used. By this criterion, only 4 of the 15 tasks were passed at the predicted age. The point is not that one criterion is inherently better than the other. Rather, the point is that the choice of one over the other seems arbitrary and that the exact criterion chosen greatly affects the degree to which the data can be viewed as supporting the theory.

The same problem arises in evaluating the correlations among performance on tasks hypothesized to tap the same CCS. For example, in Table 9, the median correlation among tasks measuring the narrative CCS is $r = .31$. In the same table, the median correlation among tasks measuring the numerical CCS is $r = .45$. In Table 20, the median correlation for tasks hypothesized to measure the spatial CCS is $r = .40$. These correlations are not negligible; indeed, most are statistically significant. Still, they also seem weaker than would be expected were the same CCS playing a dominant role in determining children's success on the tasks. For a randomly chosen pair of tasks used to measure a given CCS, knowing a child's score on one task reduces uncertainty about the child's score on the other task by no more than 20%. From my perspective, these data provide some support for the underlying theory, but far from unambiguous support.

Fit between the Formal Model and the Verbal Theory

One of the most intriguing parts of the *Monograph* is the logistic growth function modeling. Case's exposition provides an exceptionally clear introduction to such models, and it allows him to express his own ideas about the trajectory of cognitive growth elegantly.

My understanding of the implications of the mathematical equations, however, did not always match my understanding of the verbal text. Within the hierarchical, growing capacity models that Case espouses, learning at the more specific level feeds up the hierarchy to the more general level of understanding, which in turn regulates the rates at which the more specific understandings can grow.

One of the sources of appeal of Case's use of such models is that it appears to capture within a single depiction three hierarchical levels: specific tasks within a given conceptual structure, the several conceptual structures, and the cognitive system as a whole. Experience at lower levels contributes to the higher-level understandings, and the higher-level understandings, in turn, contribute to the more specific reasoning. This mutually regulative process produces commonalities in reasoning within and among the CCSs at any given time.

The equations would seem to imply positive transfer from one CCS to another. If children acquire more advanced understanding of a given CCS, it would feed upward to the systemic level, which would raise both the rate of learning of the other CCSs and the level that could ultimately be reached (by raising the asymptotic value). Yet Griffin and Case take the lack of transfer across CCSs, both immediately and when measured a year later, as support for the modularity of the CCSs as well as for the general theory. This view of the CCSs as modular seems inconsistent with the interactive nature of the logistic growth models.

Another major function served by the logistic growth model is to allow a straightforward account of why social class differences show a different pattern than national differences. When there are across-the-board differences in amount of experience with each specific task, the model produces across-the-board differences in performance, like those observed between children from middle-income and those from lower-income backgrounds. In contrast, when the model is given more experience on some tasks and less on others, it produces learning like that of children from different nations—that is, higher on some tasks, lower on others. In the abstract, all this seems fine.

The account also makes sense when applied to some of the particular results being explained. It seems reasonable that the detailed and repeated instruction in drawing received by Chinese and Japanese children would result in their drawing better but not necessarily in their developing a better understanding of space (although, even there, the hierarchical learning loop would seem to imply some positive transfer). It also seems reasonable that low-SES children would generally receive less experience with numbers, which would result in the observed pattern of lower performance on all the numerical tasks.

In other instances, however, the account seems more problematic. Is it true that low-SES children have less experience with space than do children from middle- and upper-middle-class backgrounds? I know of no evidence one way or the other, but intuitively it seems unlikely. Indeed, an argument could be made that, because such children are more often left unsupervised, they would explore their neighborhoods and other areas more extensively on their own, which would result in greater spatial knowledge. Without concrete evidence that children from low-income backgrounds have fewer experiences involving space, this account seems less than convincing.

The application of the account to the narrative CCS arouses similar concerns. Is it true that children from low-income backgrounds have less experience with narratives than do children from higher-income backgrounds? Again, I know of no strong evidence one way or the other, but, given the importance of storytelling and narrative in many low-income families and in groups of low-income children interacting among themselves, the account does not seem intuitively compelling.

These reactions, however, are exactly the kind that formal models should provoke. The logistic growth equations provided Case with a means of exploring how the patterns of development that he observed might arise. Regardless of whether the particular accounts are correct, they at least identify mechanisms that could produce the observed patterns. The models also invite others to conduct additional research to see whether the assumptions underlying the equations are realistic. Even if the particular accounts prove unrealistic, they will motivate efforts to generate more convincing explanations. In short, the models raise the ante for what counts as good science in this area.

Future Directions

In commenting on the research of investigators as insightful and energetic as Case and his colleagues, there is a constant temptation to suggest that they should pursue the issues central to one's own interests. I cannot resist this temptation.

What I would like them to do is to focus more directly on the process of change. The training studies conducted by Griffin and Case would seem to offer an especially interesting database for beginning this effort. At present, we know that the children learned a lot about numbers during their 40 training sessions, that they transferred their learning to novel tasks, and that they learned and transferred more than children in the control groups.

But how exactly did this learning take place? Was there a particular point in each child's learning when the child understood the numerical CCS, or did its construction occur only gradually? If there was a particular time of discovery, what led up to the discovery, what was the experience of discovery like, and how was it generalized beyond its initial context? If construction of the CCS occurred gradually, was there a consistent sequence to the construction? How did learning of individuals within each small group influence the learning of other children in it? What pretest variables, if any, predicted which children would make the most progress during training? How closely tied was degree of learning of the trained tasks to degree of generalization to the new tasks? And could the logistic growth equations be used to model learning at this molecular level as well as at the molar levels where they have been applied previously?

Case et al. could reasonably argue that they have done enough, that making this much progress toward a grand theory of cognitive development is an ample achievement, and that they should be given a little time to rest and enjoy what they have accomplished. So, OK, take the weekend off. But after that, there's a lot more work to be done. To make its maximum contribution, a grand theory must be shown to be consistent with development at the molecular level of detailed analyses of particular changes as well as at the level of overarching patterns. Ideally, it should help us better understand those particular changes as well.

Recent studies that have examined particular changes at a microgenetic level have converged on several conclusions (Kuhn, 1995; Siegler & Crowley, 1991). Individual children often think about a given phenomenon in multiple ways. They apply new ways of thinking inconsistently, even when they have previously applied the new way of thinking successfully on the identical problem. Discovery of new ways of thinking is a frequent rather than a rare event and is usually constrained by understanding of the goals that successful strategies must meet. The theory described in this *Monograph* will have made a major contribution even if it never tells us anything about these phenomena. I suspect, however, that applying the theory to understanding these and other issues regarding how change occurs may lead to even deeper insights about development than those already generated.

References

Case, R. (1985). *Intellectual development: A systematic reinterpretation.* New York: Academic.

Case, R. (Ed.). (1992). *The mind's staircase: Exploring the conceptual underpinnings of children's thought and knowledge.* Hillsdale, NJ: Erlbaum.

Case, R., & Sandieson, R. (1992). Testing for the presence of a central quantitative structure: Use of the transfer paradigm. In R. Case (Ed.), *The mind's staircase: Exploring the conceptual underpinnings of children's thought and knowledge.* Hillsdale, NJ: Erlbaum.

Groen, G. J., & Poll, M. (1973). Subtraction and the solution of open sentence problems. *Journal of Experimental Child Psychology,* **16,** 292–302.

Klahr, D. (1992). Information processing approaches to cognitive development. In M. H. Bornstein & M. E. Lamb (Eds.), *Developmental psychology: An advanced textbook* (3d ed.). Hillsdale, NJ: Erlbaum.

Kuhn, D. (1995). Microgenetic study of change: What has it told us? *Psychological Science,* **3,** 133–139.

McKeough, A. (1992). Testing for the presence of a central social structure: Use of the transfer paradigm. In R. Case (Ed.), *The mind's staircase: Exploring the conceptual underpinnings of children's thought and knowledge.* Hillsdale, NJ: Erlbaum.

Siegler, R. S., & Crowley, K. (1991). The microgenetic method: A direct means for studying cognitive development. *American Psychologist,* **46,** 606–620.

Wellman, H. M., & Gelman, S. A. (1992). Cognitive development: Foundational theories of core domains. In M. R. Rosenzweig & L. W. Porter (Eds.), *Annual review of psychology* (Vol. **43**). Palo Alto, CA: Annual Reviews.

COMMENTARY

CENTRAL CONCEPTUAL STRUCTURES:
SEEKING DEVELOPMENTAL INTEGRATION

Daniel P. Keating

The work reported by Case, Okamoto, and their colleagues in this *Monograph* is ambitious in several respects. At the most obvious level, the sheer amount of empirical evidence and the diversity of methods through which that evidence was gained are impressive and commendable.

The goals of the work, however, are equally ambitious. The first is to stake a controversial claim: that students of cognitive development have prematurely jettisoned Piaget's theoretical approach, in particular, its focus on central cognitive structures. In moving beyond the notion of centrality toward modularity, specificity, and relativity as the keys to understanding, the field has lost sight, in Case's view, of a compelling and unifying feature of cognitive development.

As if resurrecting Piaget's theory were not enough, the second goal is even bolder. It is no less than the construction of a unifying theory of cognitive development, one that incorporates the broad structures of development; the specificity of achievements within those broad structures; cultural, class, and individual differences in development; and the neurological substrates of these patterns. In this *Monograph*, Case and his colleagues present new evidence on each of these claims, with the exception of the last (for which prior evidence is cited). It is an impressive contribution, one that advances the science of cognitive development in many key respects.

Piaget Revisited

Not least among the *Monograph*'s accomplishments is reacquainting the field with Piaget's core theoretical concerns. These have become distorted

276

over time as merely the positions against which more "progressive" theories reacted. From Case's perspective, the particular distortion that is most troublesome is the tendency to view cognitive development as fundamentally local and specific, such that any semblance of general structural change is epiphenomenal and secondary. Rescuing the notion of centralized cognitive change from this pervasive zeitgeist is a key thrust of this *Monograph*.

This is not an easy task. The collapse of the Piagetian hegemony, at least in North America and England, can be attributed in part to the grand inclusiveness of the theory. The core of cognitive development in the traditional Piagetian formulation was the shift in core logical operations. Formulated in this way, the claim was an easy target for experimental work that rapidly generated exceptions to the rule. The tide quickly shifted toward views that emphasized specificity over generality. Case and Okamoto provide a balanced and helpful interpretation of this history and of the neo-Piagetian response that sought to balance this theoretical move against centrality by locating it not in logical structures but in processing capacity limitations.

The current effort extends that initial neo-Piagetian reply, but in a more integrative fashion. Rather than merely shifting the grounds for preserving a role for central cognitive change from logical operativity to processing capacity, the model reported in the present *Monograph* seeks to incorporate as well the seemingly "antigeneralist" perspectives of neonativist modularity and sociohistoric relativity.

In so doing, it revisits one of the most creative tensions in Piaget's own work, that between open systems and closed structures (Keating, 1990). The aspect of closed structures—the four broad stages of cognitive development, driven by a fixed sequence of increasingly complex logical operations—is the one more easily operationalized and therefore tested experimentally. It is this aspect of the theoretical model that failed to live up to its claims and that led to the history of theoretical moves well documented in this *Monograph*.

Less frequently noted in contemporary discussion of Piaget's work is the degree to which these closed structures were arrived at through the functioning of quite open systems. Constructivism as a general concept has of course survived, but interest in the full functional model of equilibration as an ongoing tension between accommodation and assimilation, operating in a rich contextual environment, has dropped off in tandem with the reaction against the structural component.

In many respects, Case's current model can be seen as revisiting this precise tension in Piaget's work. It does so, however, with a different mindset and a widely expanded set of tools. The structures to be delineated are not strictly logical or syntactic but instead are conceptual and semantic. By this single move, Case has opened up the structures to a wide range of

277

influences that are important to modularists and relativists alike. In addition, the structures are now multidimensional (related to however many central conceptual structures might exist—more on this below) rather than unidimensional (i.e., toward the fixed end point of formal operational logic).

In many ways, this tension between closed structures and open systems is even greater for Case's theory. With an ultimately fixed logical end point, Piaget's open-systems functions had little chance of floating away from their structural anchor. In contrast, by allowing permeable structures, Case is forced to be more specific about the constraints—biological, cultural, onto-genetic—that yield the coherence expected by the theory. The weight of evidence for coherence within particular central conceptual structures must then serve as the anchor, replacing the core logical structures posited by Piaget.

How well does it work? From this reworking of the classic positions, there is a very high yield of new insights and solid evidence to support them. As with any grand project, however, there are many new questions raised and some old questions not fully resolved. A sampling of each demonstrates both the scope and some limitations of the model in its present form.

Generality and Specificity: The Evidence

In previous work reviewed in this *Monograph,* Case and his colleagues have put forth a substantial body of evidence in support of the more general claim of coordinated cognitive development. In the evolution of his theoretical model, Case has gradually moved toward greater domain specificity while retaining core notions of centrality and generality. The key idea of central conceptual structures, the focus of this *Monograph,* is an attempt to integrate these tendencies.

Given this, evidence of broad coordination is no longer sufficient. (Nor was it sufficient for the earlier versions, according to Case's critics, whose concerns are addressed in this version.) Among the tests to which the new theory is put are the use of a broader range of tasks; the convergence within central conceptual structures (CCSs) and the discriminability between different CCSs; and the cross-cultural replicability of CCS growth patterns.

Overall, the evidence is quite supportive of the broad theoretical claims. The progress from predimensional, to unidimensional, to bidimensional, to integrated bidimensional emerges empirically across an impressive array of tasks and CCSs. The breadth of the tasks affords correlational analyses of consistency, and these fare quite well in general. The cultural contrasts in which features unrelated to CCSs show substantial variation, but with little effect on the CCS growth patterns, are a novel and particularly valuable contribution to the argument.

Thus, a number of key limitations of the empirical evidence that have been noted by prior critics are successfully addressed, either through new kinds of evidence or by theoretical reformulation. Several concerns remain, however.

The first of these is how clearly the consistency of performance reflects CCSs as opposed to task structures. The enormous effort involved in constructing tasks with the requisite dimensionalities is to be admired, but in the absence of formal transformation rules, to move from a conceptual domain to its accompanying task analyses, the possibility of criterion-guided task design remains. Devising tasks that (1) are feasible for the relevant age groups and (2) can be analyzed dimensionally is challenging. To the extent that task designs can be reciprocally influenced by dimensionality analyses *and* age-related performance criteria, their accuracy as CCS diagnostics is somewhat compromised.

The degree to which this is seen as a problem can be mitigated by the empirical consistency of the cross-task correlations within a CCS and associated lower correlations between CCSs. In other words, although it might be possible for task design to be guided by concerns other than pure dimensionality analysis, such influences ought to apply across the board rather than respecting CCS boundaries. This would tend to muddle the correlational pattern. As predicted by the theory, clear correlational patterns would serve to undermine the "contamination" criticism.

This evidence, as shown, for example, in Tables 9 and 10 of the *Monograph*, is substantial but not overwhelmingly persuasive. The mean intradomain correlations for numerical and narrative tasks are substantial, but the interdomain correlations are nontrivial as well. This is perhaps to be expected because the dimensionality shifts are occurring at roughly the same time, but this begs the question of how much convergence and how much discriminability is "enough." Post hoc accounts of deviations from the expected pattern—such as children's treatment of distributive justice as a social compensation rather than a distributional problem—are a bit disquieting, especially when they lead to a reform of the battery so as to retain for future versions those tasks that do appropriately "hang together."

This is another potential source of tension between criterion-driven and theory-driven task construction. To the extent that task design is criterion driven, the use of the tasks for theory testing is potentially confounding. Related to this is the extensive use of "proportion passing" as a key statistic. Such an analytic strategy yields more coherent outcomes, but defining cutoff points necessarily entails a truncation of the naturally occurring variance.

On the other hand, there are a number of reeds in this complex argument, and Case and Okamoto make the sensible case that it is the interlocking pattern of results that is persuasive rather than any single set of analyses. One analytic approach that might persuasively address some of these concerns is a normative longitudinal design. The use of group averages always tends to emphasize central tendencies, whereas the use of individual growth curves would be far less subject to the types of measurement issues raised above. Such growth curves would also be a more appropriate basis for comparison to dynamic systems modeling because it is the within-individual growth curves that are the focus of the theory rather than age-group performance.

What Is Central?

One of the more striking findings in the *Monograph* is the strength of the social class differences, especially in light of the relatively minor effects associated with cultural differences. The observed cultural differences tend to be associated with more specific, explicitly trained accomplishments, whereas more pervasive patterns of CCS differences are revealed in the social class gradients.

One potential explanation explored in the *Monograph* is that there is a more pervasive unavailability of the relevant experiential entries that form a part of the hierarchical feedback loop proposed by CCS theory. Whereas, in isolation, specific enhancements would not be likely to drive the general system very far—thus the absence of major cultural differences—the broader lack of relevant experiences—such as play with numerically based board games—might have a generally deleterious effect.

Although the dynamic modeling demonstrations enhance the plausibility of this account, there are several features that raise significant questions. One is the assumption about broad unavailability of relevant experiences. This claim is reasonably obvious in the case of number, where a wide variety of number-related activities tend to be common in the middle-class "home curriculum" but rarer in economically stressed households. For narrative structures, however, the picture is less obvious. Indeed, the widespread assumption—whose empirical status would require examination—of a more orally based, narrative culture among many lower-SES groups would tend to argue against the claim of pervasive unavailability.

The empirical observation of small cultural and large social class differences and the initial explanation of them raise some challenging questions for the theory. A central one is, How central is central? Although the breadth of domains explored in this *Monograph* is one of its main strengths, there remain some concerns regarding the selection of domains as central and the characterization of what is central about them.

The list of provisional CCSs extends and refines Gardner's (1983) list of "multiple intelligences." Although the sociohistoric perspective is recognized in the development of this list, there is a sense that the derived list is somehow more fundamental or basic to cognitive development. An interesting counter to this would be to explore CCSs that are key to survival in nonmodern societies. For example, the unidimensional ceiling on a numerical CCS in Fiati's (1992) study of an isolated premodern subsistence farming community in Africa would be interesting to contrast with the dimensionalities present in that group's perceptual differentiation of the physical environment. The contrast might be interesting on two levels: (1) the relative levels of sophistication for a skill of great as opposed to one of little value and (2) the relative difficulty of dimensionalizing a thoroughly contextualized cognitive space.

Closer to home, this second point deserves comment as well. One of the strengths of Case's approach is to apply a common task analysis strategy to a wide variety of domains, so as to examine in a comparative fashion the operation of CCSs. To achieve this, however, requires that any given domain needs to be framed in terms of its underlying "dimensions." An interesting question arises as to whether the dimensionalizing of narratives into motivational and goal structures captures what is central about a narrative mode of thought. This is not to suggest that such coordination of dimensions is neither possible nor informative about some key aspects of those cognitive structures. Rather, it is to wonder whether highly contextualized domains—such as functioning in a social domain—are as fully captured in a dimensional analysis as more paradigmatic domains like number (Bruner, 1986).

More broadly, the concern might be stated in terms of how new conceptual entries might be evaluated. Must CCSs be amenable to dimensionalization in order to qualify as central? Are there other types of potential CCSs that might be formulated but that might have a different structure? If, to be regarded as central, conceptual structures need to pass through the lens of dimensionality, do we risk losing important and otherwise central features of cognitive activity, particularly those with a more highly contextualized core?

Modeling Development Dynamically

One of the most attractive features of the current formulation of Case's theory is that it represents a serious attempt to achieve a new level of integration in cognitive developmental theory. In so doing, it goes a substantial way toward meeting the criticisms of earlier versions of the theory, especially those that focused on the relative impenetrability of the core structures to the dynamics of individual ontogeny (Lewis, 1994).

The attempt to explore this developmental integration of core changes and diversity is necessarily more exploratory than confirmatory in the early stages; the translation into specific models offers a rich new language with which to compare and contrast alternative views. The overview of logistic growth models is itself a model of clarity and a substantial intellectual contribution in its own right.

The introduction of this methodology, in a *Monograph* with such a wide range of other methods so usefully employed, represents a major accomplishment as a model of how to approach a complex research question. The insights gleaned from those multiple methods dramatically raise the stakes for the kinds of questions that are worth asking and the kinds of answers that count in advancing our understanding.

Work in any arena of scientific discourse that simultaneously refines the core questions, develops new methods for asking those questions, and generates important new empirical insights through the application of those methods represents a signal contribution. The work by Case, Okamoto, and their colleagues reported in this *Monograph* is destined to be viewed as such a contribution.

References

Bruner, J. S. (1986). *Actual minds, possible worlds.* Cambridge, MA: Harvard University Press.

Fiati, T. A. (1992). Cross-cultural variation in the structure of children's thought. In R. Case (Ed.), *The mind's staircase: Exploring the conceptual underpinnings of children's thought and knowledge.* Hillsdale, NJ: Erlbaum.

Gardner, H. (1983). *Frames of mind: The theory of multiple intelligences.* New York: Basic.

Keating, D. P. (1990). Structuralism, deconstruction, reconstruction: The limits of reasoning. In W. F. Overton (Ed.), *Reasoning, necessity, and logic: Developmental perspectives.* Hillsdale, NJ: Erlbaum.

Lewis, M. D. (1994). Recycling stage and specificity in neo-Piagetian theory: Self-organizing conceptual structures. *Human Development, 37,* 143–169.

MODELING THE PROCESS OF CONCEPTUAL CHANGE
IN A CONTINUOUSLY EVOLVING HIERARCHICAL SYSTEM

Robbie Case

It is an honor to have one's work examined so carefully, so insightfully, and in such a balanced fashion by two such distinguished colleagues. Commentaries of this sort afford a unique opportunity for seeing one's own theoretical system from the perspective of others and evaluating its strengths and weaknesses in that light. By and large, I find myself in agreement with most of the points that the commentators have raised regarding the empirical work that we report in this *Monograph*. There are a few aspects of the theory on which that work is based, however, that I would like to clarify.

The Nature of Central Conceptual Structures and
the Experience on Which Their Growth Is Dependent

Closed versus Open Conceptual Systems

As Keating points out, there is a tension in much of Piaget's work between the view of human thought as dynamic and open, thus assuming different forms in different times and places, and the view of human thought as predetermined and closed, thus assuming forms that are timeless and universal. As Keating also points out, the same tension may be seen in our work. The first point that I wish to clarify has to do with the locus of this tension in our system.

Like Piaget, we see the general sequence of levels through which children progress as being relatively fixed and universal (although the way in which we conceive of these levels and the constraints to which they are subject is somewhat different). Also, like Piaget, we see the general categories of intellectual structure that children construct as being relatively fixed across time and place. In contrast to Piaget, however, we do not see the structures themselves as being closed systems. To the contrary, we see them as open systems: ones that have taken a long time to reach their current point of development and that may well continue to evolve in the future.

For the structures that are acquired between the ages of 8 and 10 years, I believe that this point is made clear in the main body of the *Monograph*. The base-ten system for representing numbers is an inheritance from the Hindu Arabic tradition. The Cartesian system for representing three-dimensional space on paper is a legacy of the Western European tradition. Clearly, both structures are cultural creations, as are the partial understandings that children construct of these structures between the ages of 8 and 10. We hold the same to be true of all other central conceptual structures that children construct during the same age range, including those for representing music, social interaction, and motor activity.

The situation is less clear with regard to the structures that are acquired at the age of 6. As we indicate in Chapter VI, something analogous to a mental counting line is observed in all cultures and may have been present since prehistoric times. In addition, the mental number line represents an aspect of reality that is universal and that our evolutionary history has clearly prepared us to apprehend in the manner that we do. That having been said, however, the fact remains that the mental counting line that the 6-year-olds in our studies constructed had a number of components that are unique to our culture and era. Not all cultures have counting words for numbers higher than 3 or 4, yet these numbers and the words that are used for representing them were essential elements of the mental counting structure that our children constructed (see row *b*, Fig. 16, Chap. IV). Not all cultures give the numbers from 1 to 6 the canonical visual representations that ours does, yet these representations also form an integral part of the mental counting structure that our children constructed (row *d*, Fig. 16). Not all cultures count using their fingers; some use other body parts (Saxe, 1981). Yet digital representations and movements also constituted essential components of the counting structure that our children assembled. Finally, not all cultures label the relations between the numbers in the explicit manner that we do (i.e., *next, up, down*, etc.). Yet these labels were also essential elements of the mental number line that our children constructed and that our model attempted to capture (row *b*, Fig. 16).

Because it includes so many elements that are cultural constructions, the overall mental number line that children construct must clearly be classified as an open and dynamically evolving entity, not as a closed one. At the same time, as has already been mentioned, the structure also has certain features that are likely to be universal. The result is that the tension to which Keating refers is present in our system within each structure itself, rather than being distributed between the form of the structure and its functioning, as it is in Piaget's system.

Socially Structured Activity versus "Raw Experience"

The former point may appear to be a rather abstract—if not an abstruse—one. It attains a concrete relevance, however, when it comes to specifying the sort of experience that is necessary for acquiring the central conceptual structures that we have analyzed. Both commentators raise questions about our suggestion that children from different social classes may have differential access to the experience that is necessary for acquiring central conceptual structures. As Siegler points out, exposure to space is by no means an upper-class prerogative. As Keating points out, low-SES children often grow up in environments that are rich in oral narrative. Yet in both cases we assume that high-SES children are somehow privileged in the experience to which they are exposed. Why?

The reason is that we construe the structures in the culturally bound fashion that I have just described. I would agree with both critics that children from low-SES families often have equivalent exposure to space and narrative.[1] To this I would add that they also often have equivalent exposure to numbers. In our view, however, these equivalent experiences do not offer equivalent opportunities for constructing the central conceptual structures that we have described because the structures are not universal schemas for "mirroring" the spatial, numerical, or narrative world. They are culturally constructed systems for *analyzing* these aspects of the world and as such are dependent on experience with a strong cultural component.

Let me take a particular example. Adding two small quantities to find a total, making change with money, and telling the time on an analog timepiece are not just tasks that we created for the present research program, so as to assess children's ability to use a universal mental structure. Rather, they are the sorts of socially constructed activities to which our culture attaches considerable value and for which the mental number line is used in our daily cultural life. It is these sorts of activities, then, that we believe children must participate in if they are to develop their first mental counting structure; and it is to these sorts of activities that we think children of different SES groups are likely to have differential exposure.

A similar point may be made with regard to the central conceptual structures for space. Different social classes no doubt do get equal opportu-

---

[1] Note, however, Heath's (1990) caution about extending that analysis to children whose parents have migrated to an inner-city environment from a culture with stronger social cohesion and narrative roots.

nities to move through three-dimensional space and to solve the problems that this movement poses. However, the structure that we have proposed is one that was designed for *analyzing* space in a particular fashion and for depicting it on a two-dimensional surface. It is a creation of our culture, not just of our nervous systems. Once again, then, the activities that are most relevant to the emergence of this structure are the sort that we used to diagnose the presence of the structure in the first place: activities such as drawing and interpreting pictures, drawing and interpreting maps, arranging figures in neat rows and columns on a page, and engaging in grid-based games such as chess and checkers. It is to these sorts of activities—all of which are social constructions—that we claim different social classes have differential exposure.

The case of narrative is perhaps the most interesting. Like the act of finding one's way through space, the act of relating a sequence of social events to another person is very likely a cultural universal (Heath, 1983). The themes that narratives express may also be universal, or at least have a universal quality (Propp, 1922/1968). Once again, however, the particular structure that we have illustrated in Figure 5 (Chap. I) is one for *analyzing* social interaction in a particular fashion, not simply for encoding universal aspects of this interaction, and conveying them in language. It is a cultural rather than a biological creation.

What aspects of this structure are likely to vary most strongly from one culture to the next or from one era to the next within our own culture? We see the heavy emphasis on internal states, and the language and conventions that are used to refer to these states, as falling into this general category. Even at the 6-year-old level, the structure that we have analyzed already places a heavy emphasis on the inner thoughts, feelings, and desires of the protagonists, rather than on their authority, their status, or the various social influences to which they may be subject. This form of intentional analysis did not play a major role in Western literature in the Homeric era (Dodds, 1968), but it has come to play an increasingly important role in our own era, both in our literature and in our everyday life.

What sorts of activities might contribute to the development of this form of analysis? We cannot be certain, of course, but we see the sort of narrative exchange that takes place between adults and children in nursery schools or in middle-class homes at bedtime as being likely candidates. Such exchanges begin in a simple enough fashion. The adult and the child typically witness some sequence of events together, in either a fictional or a real-life context. What they do next is reconstruct these events and talk about them. It is at this point that the particular emphasis of our own culture and era becomes apparent, for adults will often ask children questions about what the various participants in the events must have been feeling, what they must have wanted, or what they must have been thinking, at particular points in time, even though they already know the answers. They will also share their own thoughts, desires, and feelings with the child in an open fashion. Once again, then, the sort of semistructured exchanges that we developed in the Mother's Motives task, the Empathy task, and the Definition of Feelings task are not just ones that we see as useful for diagnosing the presence of a universal story-line structure. Rather, they are ones that we see as crucial for acquiring the mental story-line structure in the first place. It is this sort of culturally structured activity, once again, to which we claim children from different social classes are likely to have differential exposure.

Nature of the Psychological Architecture within Which the Construction of Central Conceptual Structures Takes Place

Single- versus Multiple-Level Models

As Siegler points out, classic theories of intelligence tended to be of three types: those that postulated some very general sort of ability (e.g., Spearman's g), those that postulated a small set of "group factors" (e.g., verbal, spatial, and numerical ability), and those that postulated a large number of abilities that were of quite a specific sort. In fact, many of the debates on intelligence in the first half of the century had to do with which of these characterizations was most appropriate.

The way in which those debates have developed in the last twenty years offers an interesting object lesson for students of cognitive growth. With the invention of hierarchical factor analysis, it was shown that the presence of intellectual abilities of all three sorts can actually be discerned in the same correlation matrix (Gustaffson, 1984). By conducting a second-order factor analysis of specific factors, investigators were able to regenerate the "group factors" preferred by middle-level theorists; by conducting a third-order factor analysis on the latter factors, they were able to regenerate the general factor favored by general theorists. Faced with this technical demonstration, many theorists began to advocate a multilevel model (Caroll 1976; Snow, Kyellonen, & Marshalek, 1984).

Our belief is that theories of cognitive development need to move in a similar direction. Moreover, we see the work reported in the present *Monograph* as a step in that direction. It is true, as Siegler points out, that for the past several years we have primarily been concerned with clarifying the "middle-level" conceptual structures that children construct. However, this is not because we have given up our commitment to the notion that there are system-wide processes and constraints that shape children's cognitive development. Nor is it because we have given up our belief that task-specific representations, goals, and strategies are extremely important. Rather, it is because we see the middle-level structures and processes as a bridge between the other two and the key to understanding the operation of the overall system. The second point of clarification I would like to make, then, is this: at least in our eyes, the general theory that underpins our work is not a middle-level one. Rather, it is an interactive, multilevel one.

Two- versus Three-Level Learning Loops

If the system that we propose has three levels, why do the dynamic models presented in Chapter VII deal with only two of them? Why do they attempt to capture only the sort of reciprocal influence that exists between understanding that is task or context specific and understanding that applies across the full range of tasks in a domain? Why do they not deal with reciprocal influence between understanding that is domain general and understanding that is completely general, that is, that applies across the entire cognitive system? Siegler has raised this question in his Commentary, and he is right to do so.

Our answer is simple. As yet, we have not found a satisfactory way to conceptualize understanding that applies to the full range of domains that a child encounters. Indeed, we suspect that there may not *be* much understanding of this sort at this age, except possibly understanding of the self (Demetriou et al., 1995). This is not to say that there are no system-wide constructs in our theory whatever. (Neo-Piagetian theory is well known for its focus on system-wide capacity factors, and these factors play a vital role in the dynamic models that are presented in Chapter VII.) It is merely to say that we have been unable, as yet, to isolate a conceptual structure that is system-wide in its influence and that would be affected by domain-specific understandings in the fashion that Siegler suggests.

At such a time as we have a clearer sense of what such a structure might look like, we will model its operation in the same fashion that we have modeled the operation of intermediate structures. In the meantime, however, we would note that—in analyzing the performance of low-SES children—we actually did present a three-level as well as a two-level model. In the two-level model (Fig. 36a, Chap. VII), the benefits from task-specific experience were confined to the central conceptual structure. In the three-level model (Fig. 36b), the benefits at this level were fed further up the hierarchy, where they produced an increase in the functional capacity that was available. Although it is hard to be sure, the second model appears to provide a slightly better fit to the data from very low-SES populations than the first one.

Specific versus Intermediate Learning

Siegler ends his Commentary by pointing out that recent "microgenetic" analyses of development have yielded important new details on the process by which cognitive change takes place. He commends this methodology to us, as a way of linking our general model with behavioral data of a more microscopic sort. Indeed, if I understand him correctly, he believes that our general theory will not really stand on firm ground until it has been verified by means of microgenetic methods. I am in complete agreement that microgenetic studies generate interesting data. I also agree that the results from microanalytic studies must ultimately be integrated with those from macroanalytic studies. I would like to reemphasize, however, that the primary developmental change with which the present sequence of studies is concerned is one that takes place at an intermediate level of generality, in dynamic interaction with changes of a more specific and more general sort.

There are several potential problems, it seems to me, with studying changes of this middle-level sort in a microgenetic manner. The most obvious problem is that the structural changes in which we are interested are ones that take place *across* contexts, not within them. It is for this reason that we utilized latent structure analyses and transfer studies to demonstrate the existence of these structures in the first place: both these techniques allowed us to examine the relations *among* tasks, not just *within* them. If one were to enrich these studies with studies of a more microanalytic nature, one would somehow have to yoke several different microgenetic investigations together. Even then, it is not clear that one would be successful, for a second problem is that the changes for which one would be looking might not have any common visible component. Yet it is changes that do have a common visible component that are best suited to microgenetic study because their ontogenesis can be clarified by a detailed review of videotapes.

As if these two problems were not enough, there is a third problem, one that stems from the hypothesized interaction between middle-level changes and changes of a more general nature. These latter changes, which in the present model are conceived as involving the loosening of a general capacity constraint, are ones that take place over a much longer time scale than can be investigated within the context of a single microgenetic study. In a microgenetic investigation that we conducted some years ago (Case, 1977), we attempted to deal with this problem by compressing changes that normally take place over a long period into a tighter time frame. First, we selected children whose information-processing capacity was a bit lower than that normally associated with the type of learning in which we were interested. Then we increased the number of learning trials that these children received by a factor of three to four. What we discovered, however, was that the cognitive changes that we had witnessed in children with slightly higher capacities (who were typically a bit older) never took place in the children with lower capacities—even when the original knowledge level of the two groups was controlled and the experience received by the group with lower capacities was augmented in this fashion. Thus, no cognitive change ever took place in the lower group for us to study.

Whether such a finding would be replicated with the more powerful instructional treatments that we have developed in the present program of research I cannot say. Siegler commends such a study to us, and I agree with him that it would be interesting. In the absence of any work of this sort, however, my point is this. The methods that Siegler has developed in his microgenetic studies are designed to provide a detailed view of the sort of change that takes places over a short period of time on a specific task or set of tasks, by children who have already acquired the general developmental capacity that is necessary to make this change. It is not at all clear, however, that such methods can be easily adapted to the problem of studying the gradual emergence of intermediate-level structures, especially ones whose development is fed by a broad range of specific situations, on the one hand, and by a slowly changing systemic capacity, on the other. At the very least, it seems to me, one must acknowledge that the problems that remain to be solved before such studies can be conducted are not trivial. One "weekend off" is thus unlikely to be enough time to solve them.

Goals and Structure of the Present Theoretical Enterprise

Grand Theories versus Hierarchically Nested Theories

Both Siegler and Keating point out that the research reported in this *Monograph* is part of a larger project: one whose goal is the creation of a new theory of cognitive development. Interestingly, they both use similar terms to characterize this more general endeavor, namely, the creation of a "grand theory" (Siegler) or a "grand inclusive theory" (Keating). Unfortunately, such terms have a rather checkered intellectual history. They have virtually never been used by those who are engaged in creating general systems. Rather, they have been used by those who are critical of this sort of enterprise. The argument in which they have been embedded normally goes something like this:

> Early in the twentieth century, psychology was little more than a branch of philosophy. People thought that the enterprise could be conducted from one's armchair and that the goal was to explain the entire corpus of human behavior within some sort of broad overarching system. This was the age of "grand theory." Nowadays, we realize that what psychology needs is different. If it is to become a science, psychology needs to develop more local models: models that capture the fine structure of

important empirical phenomena and generate detailed predictions about them.

In recent years, the phrase "grand theory" has lost some of its negative connotations. Indeed, as Quentin Skinner (1988) has pointed out, there has been a resurgence of grand theory in the social sciences. It is precisely because of this resurgence, however, that I would like to make a final point, namely, that our enterprise is different from that of developing a grand theory in several respects: (1) The range of behavior that we take as our purview is a good deal more limited. (2) The linkage between our theory and empirical research is a good deal tighter. (3) Finally, and most important, the structure by which we achieve this linkage is a hierarchical or "nested" one.

This latter point deserves elaboration. In a local model, constructs are very tightly tied to a particular context, and predictions can be made in a fairly straightforward fashion because of this linkage. The problem arises when it comes to generalizing to a new context. Since there is no general theory, such generalization must be made with great caution and on a case-by-case basis. In a general theory of the "grand" variety, by contrast, generalization is not a problem. Rather, the problem is that empirical data can be dealt with only in a very global manner. As a consequence, detailed empirical predictions are rarely possible.

There is a third kind of enterprise, however, one that is intermediate between these two. In such an enterprise, the general theory is linked to intermediate theories that cover the major known instantiations of the general theory. These intermediate theories are in turn linked to models of a more specific sort, which capture the essential features of the most common situations or contexts to which the intermediate models are relevant. This is the sort of hierarchical theoretical structure that one often finds in physics (Lakatos, 1970), and it is the sort to which we aspire in the present program of research. Under ideal circumstances, we would like to have a general theory that deals with the overall architecture of the cognitive system, the way in which central conceptual structures figure in that architecture, and the way in which they develop. We would also like to have a set of intermediate-level theories, in which particular central conceptual structures are described in detail and the developmental changes in those structures are modeled. Finally, we would like to have a wide variety of more specific models in which a detailed analysis is made of the particular contexts and tasks that children encounter in their everyday life and the way in which central conceptual structures are accessed and applied in those tasks and contexts.

Although our present theory is very much a "work in progress," it already has this hierarchically nested structure. Moreover, this fact has certain interesting methodological and analytic consequences.

Problems of Proof in a Hierarchically Nested System

One of the most important consequences has to do with the way in which we find it necessary to proceed when an empirical prediction about a specific task is not confirmed. As Siegler notes, the majority of our specific task predictions were, in fact, confirmed. Contrary to appearance, however, when specific predictions were *not* confirmed, our procedure was not simply to rule in favor of the majority. The criterion that we adopted was to see whether a straightforward and testable explanation could be found for the anomaly in question at the level of our task-specific model. As long as this criterion could be met (as it was in all cases in the present research), we deemed it safe to proceed without altering our intermediate or general theories. Had this criterion not been met, however, we would have felt obliged to move up a level in the hierarchy and search for a modification at an intermediate or higher level.

The parallel between this sort of approach to experimentation and the hierarchical learning loop that we proposed for children is worth highlighting. In hierarchical learning, insights at the specific level are passed up to an intermediate level, but they have only a small effect unless they are joined by other insights of a specific nature. In testing a hierarchically nested theory, predictive problems of a specific sort invite some sort of modification at an intermediate level, but only if they are joined by other specific problems that cannot be dealt with at a local level. In both sorts of system, then, change at a specific level is often "fed up" the hierarchy rather gradually and has a really strongly transforming effect only when it is fed by many sources. I believe this to be a general principle, which applies to any conceptual system that is hierarchical and in a state of dynamic equilibrium.

Problems of Definition in a Hierarchically Nested System

There is a second consequence of the fact that our general theoretical structure is a hierarchically nested one. As Keating and Siegler both note, we do not offer a general set of definitions or rules that would allow someone to assign any existing cognitive task to a unique developmental stage in our system. Nor do we offer a general set of procedures that would allow someone to design a *new* cognitive task that can be so assigned. One of the main reasons for this is that our system is a hierarchically nested one. In the context of such a system, the general definitions or procedures that can be provided must of necessity be very abstract ones, which can be instantiated only with aid of a domain-specific model. In turn, the domain-specific models must be quite general ones, which can be instantiated only with the aid of models that are task or context specific. Although such a multilevel system can be developed in a principled and rigorous fashion, it does not permit the same sort of simple, rule-based approach to the problem of task classification as do single-level (or "grand") systems.

An example may help clarify this point. The new form of thought that emerges at the age of 6 might be characterized in our system—in general terms—as thought that involves the integration of two first-order symbol systems into a second-order system. One could perhaps add that the new system typically has its own notational system, its own history of cultural evolution, its own core structural unit, and its own set of external dimensions to which it applies. Regardless of how extensively one were to elaborate such a definition, however, or how much one were to clarify it, one would still not be able to use it to assign different cognitive tasks to one of these two developmental levels (first-order symbolic systems vs. second-order symbolic systems) in a reliable fashion. To achieve this sort of reliability, one would next have to consider a specific content domain (e.g., number) and provide a detailed specification of the core structure that children construct in this domain, as they make the transition to the new stage or level of thought. This was one of our main goals in the present program of research. The semantic properties of the 6-year-old number structure were specified in Chapter I (see Fig. 2), and the operational properties were specified in Chapter II (Study 2).

Although both these models were quite detailed, they could still not be applied to the problem of task classification in a completely reliable fashion. Before this final step could be taken, a more detailed set of models had to be constructed: one that specified the most important features of the problems for which the structures are relevant and the contexts in which they are applied. For the mental counting structure, this task was accomplished with the computer simulation model that was described in Chapter II. With this model in hand, we were able to classify all existing word problems with regard to their developmental level and a variety of novel problems as well. A similar set of procedures—not implemented in a running computer problem—were developed for classifying numerical problems of the sort described in Chapter III and creating new problems of the same general sort.[2]

As the foregoing example will, I hope, make clear, the problem with our system is not that it cannot provide objective definitions, rules, or procedures for assigning cognitive tasks to developmental levels. Rather, it is that

[2] These procedures are available on request.

one has to arrive at these rules or procedures in the hierarchical fashion just indicated and that the procedures themselves thus have a considerable degree of context specificity.

Note that, in the context of Piaget's system, the situation was quite different. Although Piaget acknowledged that domain- and task-specific factors had some effect, he also tended to see the influence of such factors as relatively minor, compared to factors of a general, formal nature. This made the problem of task classification a good deal less severe within the context of his system. Tasks that required formal operations, for example, could be distinguished from tasks that were concrete because their abstract nature was transparent. If a task's status on this dimension was not clear, one could analyze it in more detail, testing for the presence of the other defining properties of formal thought (e.g., "systematic consideration of all possible alternatives" and/or "application of an operation on an operation").

Of course, there were problems with Piaget's use of symbolic logic to characterize the structures of formal thought, and there were tasks that inhabited a "gray region" somewhere between formal and concrete thought. While these problems were not trivial, by and large the main difficulty with his system was not one of classifying novel or existing tasks. Rather, it was that, when tasks *were* classified in this fashion, the actual age norms often deviated from the developmental expectations quite widely.

The problem with the present system is different. It is that one can never make a prediction about a specific task solely on the basis of the general structural theory: in addition, one must always develop an intermediate model and a specific model that are relevant to the task in question and that will highlight the variables that are the most crucial ones and the experiential and/or endogenous factors that will moderate children's response to them (for an elaboration of this point, see Pascual-Leone, 1994).

Siegler and Keating both praise the increased precision with which we have been able to tie our theoretical modeling to the gathering of empirical data. They also both note the limitation that we have not been able to provide a set of general procedures for assigning tasks to developmental levels. The point with which I would like to conclude is simply this: these two features of our approach are opposite sides of the same coin. In effect, both are the result of our attempt to create a hierarchically nested theoretical system whose structure and dynamics mirror the structure and dynamics of children's cognitive systems, not just their general form or logic. In the long run, I believe, the construction of such theoretical systems will prove to be well worth the effort that they require, the complexity that they entail, and the occasional uncertainty that they generate. Indeed, I would venture the prediction that these features will eventually be judged as advantages of such systems, not disadvantages.

To summarize, the sort of general system that we have been developing is a multileveled one, with a hierarchically nested structure. Under optimal conditions, such systems can preserve and balance the benefits of completely local or completely general systems, while adding a potential new set of benefits of their own. One of these new benefits is the opportunity that is afforded for tuning the overall conceptual structure of a system to newly emerging aspects of empirical reality, in an open and dynamic yet principled fashion. Another potential benefit is that of generating principles and definitions that have broad general applicability but also the flexibility to be applied to local exemplars in a contextually sensitive fashion. I see both of these as features that have characterized those scientific systems in other disciplines that have endured the longest and ones that are well worth working toward in our own.

References

Caroll, J. B. (1976). Psychometric tests as cognitive tasks: A new "structure of intellect." In L. B. Resnick (Ed.), *The nature of intelligence.* Hillsdale, NJ: Erlbaum.

Case, R. (1977). Responsiveness to conservation training as a function of induced subjective uncertainty, M-space, and cognitive style. *Canadian Journal of Behavioural Science,* **9,** 12–25.

Demetriou, A., Platsidou, M., Efklides, A., Kazi, S., Syrmali, K., & Kiosseoglou, G. (1995). *Self-image and cognitive development: Structure, functions, and development of self-representation and self-evaluation from childhood to adolescence.* Unpublished manuscript, Aristotelian University of Thessaloniki.

Dodds, E. R. (1968). *The Greeks and the irrational.* Berkeley: University of California Press.

Gustaffson, J. E. (1984). A unifying model for the structure of intellectual abilities. *Intelligence,* **8,** 179–203.

Heath, S. B. (1983). *Ways with words: Language, life and work in communities and classrooms.* New York: Cambridge University Press.

Heath, S. B. (1990). The children of Trackton's children: Spoken and written language in social change. In J. S. Stigler, R. A. Schweder, & G. S. Herdt (Eds.), *Cultural psychology: The Chicago Symposia on Human Development.* New York: Cambridge University Press.

Lakatos, I. (1970). Falsification and the methodology of scientific research programmes. In I. Lakatos & A. Musgrave (Eds.), *Criticism and the growth of knowledge.* New York: Cambridge University Press.

Pascual-Leone, J. (1994). An experimentalist's understanding of children. *Human Development,* **37,** 370–384.

Propp, V. (1968). *The morphology of the folktale.* Austin: University of Texas Press. (Original work published 1922)

Saxe, G. B. (1981). Body parts as numerals: A developmental analysis of numeration among the Oksapmin in Papua New Guinea. *Child Development,* **52,** 306–316.

Skinner, Q. (1988). *The return of grand theory in the social sciences.* New York: Cambridge University Press.

Snow, R. E., Kyellonen, P. C., & Marshalek, B. (1984). The topography of ability and learning correlations. In R. Sternberg (Ed.), *Advances in the psychology of intelligence.* Hillsdale, NJ: Erlbaum.

CONTRIBUTORS

Robbie Case (Ph.D. 1971, University of Toronto) is professor of child development at the Institute of Child Study, University of Toronto, and a fellow of the Canadian Institute for Advanced Research. He is also professor of education (on leave) at Stanford University, where much of the present research was conducted. His current research focuses on children's understanding of rational numbers, SES gradients in school achievement, and dynamic models of cognitive and social growth.

Yukari Okamoto (Ph.D. 1992, Stanford University) is an assistant professor of education at the University of California, Santa Barbara, and the recipient of a Spencer Postdoctoral Fellowship from the National Academy of Education. Her current research focuses on children's quantitative reasoning and its development, simulation models of children's problem solving, and international comparisons of educational achievement.

Sharon Griffin (Ph.D. 1986, University of Toronto) is an assistant professor of education at Clark University. Together with Michael Mascolo, she is the editor of *What Develops in Emotional Development.* She is also the senior author of *Number Worlds,* an innovative program in elementary mathematics education. Her current research focuses on cognitive development, emotional development, and mathematics education for children at risk.

Anne McKeough (Ph.D. 1986, University of Toronto) is an associate professor of educational psychology at the University of Calgary. Together with Judy Lupart, she is the editor of *Toward the Practice of Theory-based Instruction, Teaching for Transfer,* and *Schools in Transition.* Her current research centers on the development of children's narrative in different social contexts.

Charles Bleiker (Ph.D. 1995, Stanford University) is an assistant professor of education at the University of New Mexico at Albuquerque. His research centers on the development of children's art, the role of cognition in aesthetic judgments, and the influence of art and aesthetics in children's early learning.

Barbara Henderson (B.A. 1984, Haverford College) is a doctoral student in the School of Education at Stanford University and a lecturer in child development at St. Mary's College of California. Her current research centers on children's writing and classroom processes that foster its development.

Kimberly Marra Stephenson (B.A. 1991, University of California, Los Angeles) is a doctoral student in the School of Education, Stanford University, and a primary teacher in the Palo Alto Unified School District. Her research interests include language, literacy, and culture.

Robert S. Siegler (Ph.D. 1974, State University of New York at Stony Brook) is a professor of psychology at Carnegie Mellon University. His research focuses on a variety of aspects of cognitive development, especially the acquisition of mathematical and scientific reasoning.

Daniel P. Keating (Ph.D. 1974, Johns Hopkins University) is professor of applied psychology in the Centre for Applied Cognitive Science at the Ontario Institute for Studies in Education in Toronto. He is also a fellow of the Canadian Institute for Advanced Research (CIAR) and director of the CIAR Program in Human Development.

STATEMENT OF EDITORIAL POLICY

The *Monographs* series is intended as an outlet for major reports of developmental research that generate authoritative new findings and use these to foster a fresh and/or better-integrated perspective on some conceptually significant issue or controversy. Submissions from programmatic research projects are particularly welcome; these may consist of individually or group-authored reports of findings from some single large-scale investigation or of a sequence of experiments centering on some particular question. Multiauthored sets of independent studies that center on the same underlying question can also be appropriate; a critical requirement in such instances is that the various authors address common issues and that the contribution arising from the set as a whole be both unique and substantial. In essence, irrespective of how it may be framed, any work that contributes significant data and/or extends developmental thinking will be taken under editorial consideration.

Submissions should contain a minimum of 80 manuscript pages (including tables and references); the upper limit of 150–175 pages is much more flexible (please submit four copies; a copy of every submission and associated correspondence is deposited eventually in the archives of the SRCD). Neither membership in the Society for Research in Child Development nor affiliation with the academic discipline of psychology are relevant; the significance of the work in extending developmental theory and in contributing new empirical information is by far the most crucial consideration. Because the aim of the series is not only to advance knowledge on specialized topics but also to enhance cross-fertilization among disciplines or subfields, it is important that the links between the specific issues under study and larger questions relating to developmental processes emerge as clearly to the general reader as to specialists on the given topic.

Potential authors who may be unsure whether the manuscript they are planning would make an appropriate submission are invited to draft an outline of what they propose and send it to the Editor for assessment. This mechanism, as well as a more detailed description of all editorial policies, evaluation processes, and format requirements, is given in the "Guidelines for the Preparation of *Monographs* Submissions," which can be obtained by writing to the Editor, Rachel K. Clifton, Department of Psychology, University of Massachusetts, Amherst, MA 01003.